NEW NETHERLANDS CIVIL CODE PATRIMONIAL LAW

(PROPERTY, OBLIGATIONS AND SPECIAL CONTRACTS)

NOUVEAU CODE CIVIL NÉERLANDAIS LE DROIT PATRIMONIAL

(LES BIENS, LES OBLIGATIONS ET LES CONTRATS PARTICULIERS)

NIEUW NEDERLANDS BURGERLIJK WETBOEK HET VERMOGENSRECHT

(ZAKENRECHT, VERBINTENISSENRECHT EN BIJZONDERE OVEREENKOMSTEN)

NEW NETHERLANDS CIVIL CODE PATRIMONIAL LAW

(PROPERTY, OBLIGATIONS AND SPECIAL CONTRACTS)

NOUVEAU CODE CIVIL NÉERLANDAIS LE DROIT PATRIMONIAL

(LES BIENS, LES OBLIGATIONS ET LES CONTRATS PARTICULIERS)

NIEUW NEDERLANDS BURGERLIJK WETBOEK HET VERMOGENSRECHT

(ZAKENRECHT, VERBINTENISSENRECHT EN BIJZONDERE OVEREENKOMSTEN)

translated by
traduit par
vertaald door

P.P.C. HAANAPPEL
McGill University

EJAN MACKAAY
Université de Montréal

under the auspices of
sous les auspices du
onder de auspicieën van

the Ministry of Justice of The Netherlands
ministère de la Justice des Pays-Bas
het Ministerie van Justitie van Nederland

at the/au

Quebec Centre of Private and Comparative Law
Centre de recherche en droit privé et comparé du Québec

KLUWER LAW AND TAXATION PUBLISHERS

Deventer ● Boston

Kluwer Law and Taxation Publishers
P.O. Box 23 Tel.: 31-5700-47261
7400 GA Deventer Telex: 49295
The Netherlands Fax: 31-5700-22244

Library of Congress Cataloging-in-Publication Data

Netherlands.
[Nieuw Burgerlijk Wetboek. Polyglot. Selections]
New Netherlands civil code: patrimonial law (property, obligations and special contracts) / translated by P.P.C. Haanappel, Ejan Mackaay = Nouveau code civil Néerlandais: le droit patrimonial (les biens, les obligations et contrats particuliers) / traduit par P.P.C. Haanappel, Ejan Mackaay.
p. cm.
English, Dutch and French.
Includes index.
ISBN 9065444823
1. Civil law--Netherlands. I. Haanappel, Peter P.C., 1949- .
II. Mackaay, Ejan. III. Title.
KKM494.31838.Z9 1990
346.492′002632--dc20
[344.9206002632] 90-4959
CIP

Cover design: Eset

ISBN 90 6544 482 3

Voorafgaande opmerkingen

De artikelen van het nieuw Nederlands Burgerlijk Wetboek zijn doorlopend genummerd voor ieder Boek afzonderlijk, maar niet van Boek tot Boek. Bij het citeren van artikelen moet daarom zowel het Boek- als het artikelnummer worden aangegeven, bijvoorbeeld 3:23 of 6:185.

De nummers die tussen haakjes zijn geplaatst na het artikel nummer verwijzen naar de voorlopige nummering die in de wetsontwerpen is gebruikt en die men ook terugvindt in de doctrine op de ontwerpen.

Preliminary Remarks

The articles of the new Dutch Civil Code are numbered consecutively within each Book, but not from one Book to the next. In citing an article, one should specify both the Book and the article number, for instance 3:23 or 6:185.

The numbers in parentheses following the article numbers refer to the provisional numbering system adopted at the drafting stage and followed in Dutch scholarly writings on the drafts.

Remarques préliminaires

Les articles du nouveau Code civil néerlandais sont numérotés consécutivement à l'intérieur du même Livre, mais non d'un Livre à l'autre. En citant un article, il convient d'indiquer le numéro du Livre aussi bien que celui de l'article, par exemple 3:23 ou 6:185.

Les chiffres entre parenthèses qui suivent les numéros des articles du Code renvoient à la numérotation provisoire adoptée dans les projets de loi et employée également dans la doctrine néerlandaise portant sur les projets.

INHOUDSOPGAVE
TABLE OF CONTENTS
TABLE DES MATIÈRES

Inhoudsopgave

PREFACE

This book contains the translation into English and French of those parts of the New Dutch Civil Code dealing with patrimonial law, to wit Books 3,5, 6 and 7, which are scheduled to come into force as a whole on 1 January 1992. These parts cover the core of the new Dutch patrimonial law (general principles, property, obligations, the contracts of sale, mandate, deposit and suretyship), leaving out only the Law of Successions (Book 4), the Law of Transport (Book 8) and a number of nominate contracts in Book 7.

The book is addressed to the legal community in the Netherlands as well as elsewhere. For Dutch lawyers it may be helpful to have the text of the new code available in two of the major languages of the European Community. The translation gives lawyers elsewhere access to the legislative innovations the Dutch have introduced into their entirely revised Code. It is hoped that the availability of the English and French translations side by side allows the non Dutch reader to have a finer grasp of the original Dutch version that either would provide by itself.

The idea of the translation was born at about the time of the publication, in the Canadian Province of Quebec, of the Civil Code Revision Office's Report on the Civil Code of Quebec (Éditeur officiel du Québec, 1978). This Report contained, in English and French - the official legislative languages of the Province of Quebec - a complete draft text for a New Quebec Civil Code. The parallelism between the recodification processes in The Netherlands and in Quebec was obvious to the two undersigned, both of whom received their first legal education in The Netherlands and are, at present, professors of law at Quebec Law Faculties. Both the Civil Code of The Netherlands of 1838 and the Civil Code of Lower Canada (Quebec) of 1866 are based upon the Code civil des français of 1804. Both recodifications are, in part, inspired by a desire to modernize the law and to codify existing jurisprudential rules. The present translation was undertaken as a means to draw closer comparisons between the recodifications in the two countries.

Besides the similarities, there are also substantial differences between the two Codes, as they are now being readied. Whereas the Quebec recodification, as to style, remains, like the 1804 and 1866 Codes, in the tradition of the 'popular Code', the Dutch recodification has taken the road of the more 'learned Code'. As a result, the new Code, in the original Dutch as well as in the English and French translations, is no easy reading. The terminology adopted in the English and French translation of the New Dutch Civil Code relies heavily upon the French Code of 1804 and upon the Quebec Code of 1866, and the 1977 Quebec Draft Civil Code, as well as the various Quebec Bills and Draft Bills which have been published subsequently in the course of the recodification process. It has been particularly helpful for the translators to have all the Quebec documents available in official English and French versions. As to the English language terminology of the translation, it should be added that a deliberate attempt has been made to use English civilian (as opposed to common law) terminology, as contained in the aforementioned bilingual texts and supplemented by English language civilian sources in the American State of Louisiana, in Scotland and in South Africa.

The translation was carried out in several steps. An initial translation of the Dutch texts would be prepared by the two undersigned, Haanappel into English, Mackaay into French. These translations would then be compared, corrected, where necessary, and harmonised, where possible, during regular meetings between the two translators. The translated texts would be revised by the linguistic advisers, each of them having the English as well as the French text to work with. The corrections suggested by the linguistic advisers would be reviewed in meetings between them and the translator involved. The corrected translations were reviewed globally, English and French simultaneously, in a few intensive meetings between Dr A.S. Hartkamp and both translators. Professor P.-A. Crépeau has undertaken a final reading of the English and French texts.

Preface

This translation has benefited measurably from the assistance of microcomputers. On the substantive side, these have improved the translating as well as the reviewing process by making it possible systematically to check the occurrence of words and expressions in any of the three languages involved. The three languages were integrated on microcomputer and the final trilingual version was directly produced from microcomputer onto laser printer.

Institutionally, this translation was made possible by a grant from the Ministry of Justice of The Netherlands, and by the availability of the resources of the Quebec Centre of Private and Comparative Law, of McGill University in Montreal. A project of this kind, stretching across national boundaries and over a ten year time span, is not a common pursuit and the translators wish to record their gratefulness to three persons in particular whose breadth of vision has made it possible for the project to take off and to be completed. Professor P.-A. Crépeau, O.C., Q.C., F.R.S.C., Director of the Quebec Centre of Private and Comparative Law, believed in the project from the outset; Prof. J.G. Sauveplanne, chairman of the Netherlands chapter of the Association Henri Capitant, established the contacts between the Ministry of Justice in The Hague and the Quebec group; Dr A.S. Hartkamp, formerly Counsel at the Legislative Section (New Civil Code) of the Ministry of Justice in The Hague, and at present Advocate-General at the Netherlands Supreme Court (Hoge Raad der Nederlanden), has been the project's advocate in The Hague and has seen the translation through its several stages.

Neither of the translators having English or French as his mother tongue, the translation in both languages required revision by native speakers of these languages. The revision of the English was carried out by Maître Cally Jordan and Maître George Petsikas, both graduates of McGill University, and now in private law practice; the French translation was revised by Professor Jean-Claude Gémar, of the Department of Linguistics and Philology at the Université de Montréal. Ms Winnifred Donders, graduate of the University of Amsterdam and of the University of Paris I (Panthéon-Sorbonne), has made an essential contribution to the creation of the subject indices in the three languages.

The ultimate responsibility for the quality of the translation rests, of course, with the undersigned only.

P.P.C. Haanappel
Professor of Law
McGill University

Ejan Mackaay
Professor of Law
Université de Montréal

Spring 1990

PRÉFACE

Le présent livre comporte les traductions anglaise et française des parties du Code civil néerlandais portant sur le droit patrimonial, à savoir les Livres 3, 5, 6 et 7, qui devront être mises en vigueur en bloc au 1er janvier 1992. Ces parties forment le noyau du nouveau droit patrimonial néerlandais (principes généraux, biens, obligations, les contrats nommés de la vente, du mandat, du dépôt et du cautionnement), laissant de côté seulement le droit des successions (Livre 4), le droit des transports (Livre 8) et un certain nombre de contrats nommés au Livre 7.

Ce livre s'adresse à la communauté juridique, aux Pays-Bas aussi bien qu'ailleurs. Pour les juristes néerlandais, il peut être commode d'avoir à leur disposition le texte du nouveau code dans deux des langues principales des Communautés européennes. La traduction fournit aux juristes d'ailleurs un accès aux innovations législatives que les Néerlandais ont introduites dans leur code intégralement révisé. La présentation côte à côte des traductions anglaise et française devrait permettre au lecteur non néerlandophone de mieux saisir les nuances de la version originale néerlandaise que l'une ou l'autre seule ne le pourrait.

L'idée de la traduction est née à l'époque de la parution, dans la province du Québec, au Canada, du Rapport sur le Code civil préparé par l'Office de révision du Code civil (Éditeur officiel du Québec, 1978). Le Rapport proposa, en anglais et en français - les deux langues de la législation de la province - un projet complet de nouveau Code civil du Québec. Les parallèles entre les processus de recodification engagés aux Pays-Bas et au Québec étaient évidents aux deux soussignés, tous deux étant de formation juridique initiale néerlandaise et maintenant professeurs dans des facultés de droit au Québec. Le Code civil des Pays-Bas de 1838 aussi bien que celui du Bas-Canada (Québec) de 1866 ont eu pour modèle le Code civil des français de 1804. Les deux recodifications ont été entreprises entre autres dans un souci de moderniser le droit et de codifier les règles jurisprudentielles existantes. La traduction présentée ici fut envisagée à l'origine comme un moyen de faire des comparaisons plus poussées entre les recodifications dans les deux pays.

À côté des similitudes, il y a aussi des différences entre les deux Codes tels qu'ils se présentent actuellement. La recodification au Québec, à l'instar des codes de 1804 et de 1866, demeure, en son style, dans la tradition du «code populaire». La recodification néerlandaise, au contraire, s'est engagée sur la voie du «code savant». Aussi le nouveau code, tant en sa version originale néerlandaise que dans les traductions anglaise et française, n'est-il pas d'une lecture facile. La terminologie adoptée dans les traductions anglaise et française du nouveau Code civil néerlandais puise abondamment au Code français de 1804 et au Code québécois de 1866, de même qu'au Projet de Code civil de 1977 et aux projets et avant-projets de loi qui ont été rendus publics postérieurement, dans le cadre du processus de recodification. Les traducteurs ont trouvé particulièrement commode d'avoir eu à leur disposition les documents québécois dans leurs versions anglaise et française officielles. En ce qui concerne la traduction anglaise, il convient de souligner l'effort conscient d'adopter le vocabulaire anglais de droit civil (par opposition à l'anglais de common law) que l'on trouve dans ces textes bilingues, complété par des sources de droit civil en langue anglaise provenant de l'État de Louisiane (États-Unis), de l'Écosse et de l'Afrique du Sud.

Le processus de la traduction comportait plusieurs étapes. Une première traduction fut préparée par les deux soussignés, Haanappel vers l'anglais, Mackaay vers le français. Au cours réunions régulières, ces traductions furent comparées, corrigées, là où c'était nécessaire, harmonisées, là où c'était possible. Les textes traduits furent ensuite révisés par des conseillers linguistiques, chacun d'eux ayant à sa disposition le texte anglais aussi bien que le texte français. Les corrections proposées par les conseillers linguistiques ont été ensuite revues au cours de réunions avec le traducteur concerné. Les traductions ainsi corrigées furent revues globalement, en anglais et en français simultanément, pendant quelques sessions intensives réunissant M. A.S. Hartkamp et les deux traducteurs. M. le professeur P.-A. Crépeau a fait la lecture finale de l'anglais et du français.

La traduction a profité du concours appréciable de la micro-informatique. Sur le fond, les micro-ordinateurs ont amélioré le processus de traduction et de révision en rendant possible des recherches systématiques de l'occurrence de termes dans l'une quelconque des trois langues du projet. Les trois versions ont été intégrées sur micro-informatique et la version trilingue finale a été produite directement à partir de micro-ordinateurs sur l'imprimante au laser.

Sur le plan institutionnel, le projet a été rendu possible grâce à une subvention du ministère de la Justice des Pays-Bas et aux ressources du Centre de recherche en droit privé et comparé du Québec, rattaché à l'Université McGill à Montréal. Un projet de ce type, qui s'étend au delà des frontières nationales et sur une période de dix ans, n'est pas chose commune et les traducteurs tiennent à remercier trois personnes en particulier dont la vision a permis de faire décoller le projet et de le mener à bonne fin. M. le professeur P.-A. Crépeau, o.c., c.r., de la société royale du Canada, directeur du Centre de recherche en droit privé et comparé du Québec, a cru au projet dès le départ; M. le professeur J.G. Sauveplanne, président de la section néerlandaise de l'Association Henri Capitant, a établi les contacts nécessaires entre le ministère de la Justice à La Haye et le groupe québécois; M. A.S. Hartkamp, jusqu'à récemment juriste conseil à la section de la législation (nouveau Code civil) du ministère de la Justice à La Haye et actuellement avocat-général près la Cour de cassation des Pays-Bas (Hoge Raad der Nederlanden), s'est fait l'interlocuteur du projet à La Haye et a suivi la traduction dans ses versions successives.

Ni l'un ni l'autre traducteur n'ayant l'anglais ou le français comme langue maternelle, il était impératif de faire procéder à une révision de la traduction par des personnes de langue anglaise et de langue française. La révision de l'anglais a été l'oeuvre de Mes Cally Jordan et George Petsikas, tous deux diplômés de la Faculté de droit de l'Université McGill et actuellement en pratique privée; la traduction française a été révisée par M. le professeur Jean-Claude Gémar, du Département de linguistique et philologie de l'Université de Montréal. Mme Winnifred Donders, diplômée de l'Université d'Amsterdam et de l'Université de Paris I (Panthéon-Sorbonne), a joué un rôle essentiel dans la création des index analytiques dans les trois langues.

Il va sans dire que les soussignés sont seuls responsables de la qualité de la traduction.

P.P.C. Haanappel
professeur de droit à
McGill University

Ejan Mackaay
professeur de droit à
l'Université de Montréal

Printemps 1990

CIVIL CODE REVISION IN THE NETHERLANDS 1947-1992

Dr Arthur S. Hartkamp[1]

1. THE REVISION PROGRAMME

1. The publication of this book marks a decisive point in the recodification effort in the Netherlands which has been under way since 1947. The first two books of the New Civil Code came into force in 1970 (the Law of Persons and Family Law), and in 1976 (Law of Legal Persons). Because the Dutch Government has now decided that the core of the new Code (Books 3, 5, 6 and part of 7), containing the law of property and the law of obligations, will enter into force by January 1st, 1992, the revision programme has nearly reached its goal: to replace the 150 year old existing Civil and Commercial Codes by one "consolidated" new Code comprising civil law, commercial law, consumer law, much of the private law legislation which was enacted outside the Codes, and codifying the results of an increasingly important body of judge-made law (jurisprudence).

2. The old Civil Code dates back to 1838. It is the third Civil Code in force in the Netherlands. The first came into being in 1809, by order of King Louis Napoléon, brother of the Emperor. It had much in common with the French Code Napoléon, although not to such an extent as generally thought. In 1811, after the incorporation of the Netherlands into the French Empire, it was replaced by the Code Napoléon itself. Immediately after the liberation from French rule in 1813, attempts were made to draft a national Code, which were finally crowned with success in 1838. Apart from a number of more or less important subjects in the law of persons and family law (notably the law of matrimonial property), the law of successions and the law of property, this Code was largely, often *verbatim*, based upon the Code Napoléon.

This does not hold true, however, for its system. Since the Dutch Civil Code returned to the requirement of delivery for the transfer of ownership as known in Roman and ancient Dutch law, a clear distinction was made between the law of property and the law of obligations; consequently they were set out in the 2nd and 3rd Books respectively. The law of successions was also included in the 2nd Book. In addition, the 1838 Civil Code contained a 4th Book with provisions on the law of evidence and the law of prescription. The system bears a striking resemblance to that of the Institutes of Gaius and Justinian, and also to the *Inleidinge tot de Hollandsche Rechts-geleerdheid* (Introduction to the Dutch Jurisprudence) of 1631, by the famous Dutch lawyer Hugo de Groot (Grotius).[2] There are still other departures from the French system, e.g., a title with general provisions on the law of obligations.

3. The Dutch Commercial Code, too, dates back to 1838; its only predecessor was the French *Code de Commerce* (1811-1838). The distinction between civil and commercial law did not exist in the Dutch united provinces before the French revolution: Hugo de

---

1 Advocate-General at the *Hoge Raad* (Supreme Court) of the Netherlands; former member of the Civil Code Revision Office of the Ministry of Justice of the Netherlands; member of the Governing Council of UNIDROIT; member of the Royal Netherlands Academy of Sciences.

2 Hugo de Groot, *Inleidinge tot de Hollandsche Rechts-geleerdheid*, re-edited by F. Dovring, H.F.W.D. Fischer and E.M. Meijers, Leyden University Press, 1965 (2nd ed.).

Groot, in his *Inleidinge*, deals with both branches of law. The same is true of other classical Dutch authors and even for the draft of the Civil Code made by the Dutch jurist Johannes van der Linden in 1807. Bringing together, in the New Civil Code, civil and commercial law is also the logical outcome of a development which started in 1838. In fact, article 1 of the Dutch Commercial Code provides that, apart from explicit derogations, the Civil Code applies to all subjects dealt with in the Commercial Code. Also, in 1838, the special courts of commerce, introduced in the Napoleonic era, were abolished. Subsequently, the law of bankruptcy was taken out of the Commercial Code and put into a special statute, no longer restricted to merchants (1893). Finally, in 1934, almost all remaining differences between merchants and non-merchants were banned from private law. Under these circumstances it is no longer appropriate to arrange civil law and commercial law in separate Codes. In the new Code, commercial law is incorporated in Books 2 (Legal Persons), 7 (Special Contracts) and 8 (Law of Transport).

4. Both the old Civil and the old Commercial Code can be considered as outdated on many points. However, this does not apply to a number of socially weighty subjects, with respect to which radical changes were made both in the Codes themselves and in separate statutes: e.g., with regard to juvenile law, lease and hire (residential and agricultural), leasing, the labour contract, hire-purchase, industrial and intellectual property, company law, and so forth. Unfortunately, however, the Dutch legislators failed to adapt the law of property and the law of obligations to modern standards. This omission is quite understandable, where one realizes that - not to speak of social pressure - changes can be brought about much more easily in more or less independent parts of the law than in such general and interdependent parts as the law of property and the law of obligations. Here a partial revision is often not possible without necessarily touching upon so many other subjects that it either does not arrive at any changes at all, or at least not at all the changes required.

The gap in the development of private law resulting from this situation was subsequently filled, for the greater part, by judge-made law. Undoubtedly, the most spectacular example hereof is the law of unlawful acts (torts) which is almost completely a creation of the courts. In other fields as well, the courts have bridged the gap between the Code and the rapid social developments of the present century. As much as this development can be welcomed in itself, it also proved to have a fatal influence on the legislators' unenthusiastic partial changes and their advocates.

A bifurcated approach to civil law revision was the result. On the one hand, voices grew ever louder from those who preferred to entrust the development of the law to the subtly differentiating and more concrete approach of the courts; this approach, however, produces an increasingly opaque law. On the other hand, there were those who proposed legislative changes, hoping that they would produce more transparent rules. Partial revisions, however, became increasingly difficult: an innovation would not only have to fit into the Civil Code, but also into the much more complicated network of judge-made law, into which almost every provision of the Civil Code separately and the Code as a whole are interwoven. All this led to a situation in which the private law was unsurveyably laid down in partially obsolete Codes, many special statutes and a great number of judicial decisions: a situation basically different from the intention of the Constitution which provides (since 1789) that private law (including commercial law and the law of civil procedure) shall be laid down by the legislators in general Codes, subject to their power to regulate specific subjects in separate enactments.

5. In the end, the advocates of recodification carried the day in the Netherlands. In 1947, Professor E.M. Meijers of the University of Leyden, who had insisted upon the need for recodification for a long time, was entrusted with the mandate to draft a new Civil Code. This Code would consist of 9 Books:

I. Law of Persons and Family Law (including the law of matrimonial property);

II. Legal Persons (general part, associations, corporations with limited liability, foundations);
III. Patrimonial Law in General, i.e., provisions applicable to all subsequent books;
IV. Law of Successions;
V. Property and Real Rights;
VI. General Part of the Law of Obligations;
VII. Special Contracts;
VIII. Law of Transport;
(IX. Law of Products of the Mind).

This system was maintained until today with the exception of Book 9, abandoned for reasons to be discussed in Section II. That section discusses the system of the new Code in its present form.

6. Professor Meijers began his work by consulting a great number of experts on many problems which were to be settled in the new Civil Code. It was decided that 52 of the most important subjects, especially those which had some political implications, should be submitted to Parliament with a view to obtaining its binding advice as to the policies to be followed. This first phase of the work need not be discussed here; three articles by Dainow were devoted to it (see Select Bibliography, on p. XLIII).

Although Meijers would have preferred to publish the draft as a whole, the Preliminary Title and Books 1-4 together with the Explanatory Commentary ("Toelichting") were published separately in 1954. This happened upon the insistence of Minister of Justice Donker, a convinced advocate of recodification, who feared that interest in the undertaking would disappear if the first results were unduly long in forthcoming. A few months later, Meijers died. It was decided that the work would be continued by a "triumvirate", consisting of J. Drion, F.J. de Jong, and J. Eggens who was later replaced by G. de Grooth. The work on most of the other books could be continued on the basis of the more or less elaborate preliminary drafts of texts and commentaries which Meijers had already prepared.

7. The triumvirate published the draft of Book 5 in 1955, and the draft of Book 6 in 1961. As to Book 7, special contracts, a different procedure was adopted. Because of the range of subjects and the specialized knowledge required for a number of the subjects to be dealt with in this Book, the Minister of Justice decided to divide the material among a number of jurists, who separately undertook to draft text and commentary of one or more of the some 20 titles. One member of the triumvirate was commissioned to co-ordinate these drafts and to determine their final formulation. The draft was presented to the Minister in 1972. Book 8 on transport law was entrusted to a specialist in the field of maritime law, H. Schadee. Its first part, containing general provisions on the contract of transport, maritime law and the law of inland waterway navigation, was published in 1972; its second part, transport by road, in 1976.

Deliberations in Parliament of the drafts (each book is submitted and discussed as a separate bill) started in 1954, when the drafts of Books 1-4 were tabled in the Dutch Lower House; Book 5 followed two years later. The draft of Book 6 was presented in 1964. The first book was enacted in 1959, the second in 1960, the fourth in 1969. Books 3, 5, 6 and 8 (first part) followed in 1979-1980. Unfortunately, practice has shown that much time passes between the moment that an act is adopted and that it is put into force. Putting into force is prepared by another act, called the "Invoeringswet" (an *Act to Put into Force*), which contains (1) transitional law, (2) necessary adaptations of other Codes and statutes, (3) changes which are made in the act already passed.

8. An important question is whether it is possible and desirable to put into operation certain books separately from others. The question was answered in the affirmative for Books 1 and 2, which were brought into force in 1970 and 1976 respectively.

Books 3, 5 and 6, however, are so closely interrelated that it was considered necessary to put them into force together. To that end, a complex legislative operation was required, which contained not only the elements of the "Invoeringswet" mentioned above, but also some new acts called for by the New Code (e.g., an act on public registers for registered immoveable property); moreover, it was felt indispensable to rewrite an entire book of the Code of Civil Procedure (law of seizure), and to enact four titles of Book 7 on Special Contracts, among which the important contract of sale (see nos. 15 and 31). This huge complex of legislation, divided into approximately 15 separate but interrelated acts, passed Parliament between 1986 and 1990. On January 1st of 1992, the new rules will come into force.

Book 8 will also come into force soon. Book 4 and the remaining contracts of Book 7 will become operative later in the 90s, in the order in which Parliament will see it fit to adopt them.

9. As a conclusion to this first section, it may be said that the work has taken considerably more time than envisaged at the outset, but fortunately the fear that this would cause the interest in the work to vanish, both on the part of the politicians and on the part of legal science and practice, has not materialized. Right from the beginning, the influence of the drafts and explanatory commentaries on Dutch legal practice has been considerable. The drafts have exerted their influence on the legislators, who in some instances introduced parts of them as separate enactments, and who, when drafting private law legislation, followed the terminology and system of the Draft Code as much as possible. The drafts have also influenced judge-made law: in many cases the Dutch *Hoge Raad* (Supreme Court) has interpreted rules in the present Code and Statutes so as to conform to the new solutions adopted in the Draft Code or in the explanatory commentaries ("anticipatory interpretation"). This attitude of the courts in its turn compelled legal practice to orient itself step by step towards the new law. In this effort, it was assisted by legal science: textbooks already treated their subject matter on the basis of the system of the new Code and paid due attention to its contents. Thus, the coming into existence of the new Civil Code of the Netherlands may well be called a common effort of the Dutch legal community as a whole.

II. THE SYSTEM OF THE NEW CODE

10. *Book 1: Law of Persons and Family Law.* As mentioned before, Books 1 and 2 were already brought into force in 1970 and 1976. *Book 1* contains the law of persons and family law, including marriage, matrimonial property, divorce and adoption. Interestingly enough, the law of divorce was again modernized separately in 1971. This indicates that the creation of a new Code does not bar further development of the law through legislation. On the contrary, it is much easier to adapt a modern and systematic body of law than an aged codification buried under judge-made law. Since 1971, so many other important innovations have been brought about or are envisaged in this branch of the law that, according to some Dutch lawyers, the year 1970 merely marked the beginning of the real revision of the law of persons and family law in the Netherlands.

Book 2 contains the *Law of Legal Persons*: associations, company law, foundations. The book begins with a number of general provisions applying to all legal persons.

11. *Book 3: Patrimonial Law in General.* The most drastic change compared with the system of the present Civil Code - in fact also with the system of any other codification in civil law countries - is contained in Book 3, "Patrimonial law in general". Its principle is twofold.

To begin with, some issues which traditionally were treated partially in the law of contracts and partially in the law of successions, are now provided for in Book 3; these subjects relate to patrimonial law as a whole. In the first place, this applies to the concept of a juridical act: general requirements for its validity (consent, capacity); protection of persons who in good faith rely on the appearance of a valid consent; conditions and terms; the effects of a juridical act which is contrary to law, *boni mores* or public order; conversion and partial nullity; defects of consent; fraud of creditors; some forms of legal relief, ratification and confirmation. Secondly, the law of procuration, which at present forms an incoherent and confusing part of the contract of mandate, is provided for in Book 3 (with the exception of some specific rules on the authority to act on behalf of a legal person).

Furthermore, corporeal and incorporeal things are considered as being equivalent; consequently, rules which are related to both categories are brought together in one and the same book. Thus, a great number of subjects which were traditionally - since Roman Law - treated as part of the law of property, have been transferred to Book 3, such as the provisions on transfer of corporeal and incorporeal things; possession; "*gemeenschap*" (community); those rights *in rem* which can have as their object both corporeal and incorporeal things, i.e., usufruct, pledge and hypothec; privileges, and the right of retention; finally, general definitions of "property" and "things", fruits, components of things, dismembered rights, and so forth, as well as related general regulations, notably the provisions regarding the public registers for registered immoveable property.

In this context, two new subjects dealt with in Book 3 should be mentioned. First, a title (Title 6) will be devoted to fiduciary administration ("*bewind*"). It should be borne in mind that the concept of trust is unknown to Dutch law. In practice various forms of *fiducia cum amico* exist, which to some extent pursue the same ends. However, since the *fiducia* does not fit into the civil law concept of ownership, it is not contained in the new Civil Code. Instead, ample possibilities for fiduciary administration are created. However, this title is omitted from the present translation, since it will only become operative together with Book 4 on Successions.

The other new subject deals with a number of general provisions on rights of action (Title 11). They concern, *inter alia*, the power to obtain judgment against a person who is obliged to fulfil a duty on behalf of the plaintiff; rules regarding specific performance; the rule that a judgment can replace the deed for the juridical act which the defendant was obliged to perform; and, finally, the prescription of rights of action.

12. *Book 4: Law of Successions*. In the French Civil Code, the law of successions is considered as a mode of acquiring property and is therefore included in its third book. This system was followed in the old Dutch Civil Code (art. 639), which was one of the reasons for putting it in the second Book (Law of things, including property). The new Dutch Civil Code abandons this idea, because it is one-sided. Not only does property pass to the heirs, but the same is true of other rights *in rem*, possession, rights *in personam*, industrial and intellectual property, as well as obligations. The law of successions concerns the patrimony of the deceased as a whole. Therefore it is the subject of a separate book (Book 4), situated between Patrimonial Law in General and the books containing the various kinds of patrimonial rights. These rights are arranged according to their object: the rights in corporeal things, the rights *in personam*, and - according to the original intention of Professor Meijers - the rights in the products of the mind (traditionally called the rights of industrial and intellectual property).

13. *Book 5: Real Rights*. The first of these categories is laid down in Book 5: the rights in corporeal things or "rights *in rem*". This book includes moveable and immoveable things, servitudes imposed by law, conventional servitudes, and some other rights *in rem* unknown to the French Code civil, but derived from ancient Dutch law. As previously indicated, some rights *in rem* have been transferred to Book 3, since they are not restricted

to corporeal things. These rights are designated as "dismembered rights"; of this *genus*, the rights *in rem* of Book 5 constitute a *species*.

14. *Book 6: General Part of the Law of Obligations*. The law of obligations is contained in Books 6, 7 and the greater part of Book 8. Book 6 contains the "general part" of the law of obligations. It consists of 5 titles. The first title, "Obligations in General", contains provisions applying to all obligations regardless of their source. Many of these provisions are new, such as the general provisions on natural obligations, the greater part of those on joint obligations and plurality of creditors, a separate chapter on default of the creditor, and chapters on performance and the effects of non-performance of obligations. There is also a chapter on reparation of damage, which applies to both contractual and extra-contractual liability, with the consequence that a number of legal effects of contractual non-performance and of unlawful acts could be harmonized. Moreover, there is a chapter devoted to the obligation to pay a sum of money, in which attention is paid to the rule of nominalism, payment by postal money transfer ("*giro*"), legal interest for default in the payment of a sum of money, and debts in foreign currency.

Title 2, the "Transfer of claims and debts and renunciation of claims", also contains many innovations, such as those with regard to subrogation, the consequences of the transfer of claims, and the taking over of debts and contracts. The third title is entirely devoted to unlawful acts (torts); some of its noteworthy innovations are discussed below. Title 4 contains provisions on obligations arising from sources other than unlawful act or contract, namely, *negotiorum gestio* (management of the affairs of another), *solutio indebiti* (undue payment), and the general action for unjustified enrichment.

Finally, title 5 is devoted to the general provisions on the law of contract. Among the many new rules are those on standard terms; on the extent to which a party is bound by general conditions (fixed by the other party and usually deposited at some place open to the public) of which he did not know the contents at the time the contract was entered into; on judicial control of unreasonable general conditions; on formation of contracts; on effects against third parties of covenants concerning registered property; on good faith; and on frustration of contract in the event of unforeseen circumstances.

Although it has been rightly pointed out that more than half of Book 6 deals with questions on which the old Code was silent, its size is not much larger than that of the four titles which it is to replace. The number of articles is even smaller. In spite of its great flexibility, characteristic of this part of the law, the old law of obligations undoubtedly belonged to the most obsolete parts of Dutch codified law.

15. *Book 7: Special Contracts*. The special contracts are arranged in three successive groups: (1) contracts which lead to the transfer of a thing (sale, exchange, loan for consumption, gifts) or which grant the use of a thing (lease and hire, loan for use); (2) contracts concerning activities undertaken by one party on behalf of another (mandate, the publishing contract, deposit, the labour contract, the collective labour contract, the contract of enterprise, partnership); (3) other contracts (suretyship, contract of settlement ("*vaststellingsovereenkomst*"), bills of exchange and cheques, and aleatory contracts including insurance). In accordance with Meijers' intention to bring private law as a whole into one Code, some contracts which are now classified in separate statutes (e.g., lease of land, the collective labour contract) will be placed in Book 7. Besides, part of the Commercial Code will be transferred to Book 7 (see no. 3). Finally, Book 7 contains some new contracts, viz. the publishing contract and the contract of settlement, of which "transaction" in the old Code only forms a species. Only four titles will enter into force together with Books 3, 5 and 6: sale (including exchange), mandate, deposit and suretyship. These contracts therefore form part of this translation.

16. *Book 8: Law of Transport*. This book not only sets forth the law of transport by sea and inland waterway, as presently contained in the Code of Commerce, but also the law of transport by road and by air. Noteworthy innovations are, among others, a title

with general provisions on transportation contracts, including a section on the contract of travel, and a section on the moving contract.

17. *Law of Industrial and Intellectual Property.* Originally, it was intended to devote the last book of the new Code (Book 9) to the third category of patrimonial rights: "the rights in the *products of the mind*". The statutes containing these rights (at that time: patents, trade marks, copyright, trade name) were to be split up. The provisions of a private law character would be included in Book 9, whereas those of an administrative, procedural and penal character were to be placed elsewhere.

Since then, the situation with regard to these rights has drastically changed. A unification of patent law is under preparation and has already partially been achieved in Europe. With respect to the law of trade marks, a uniform law has been passed and put into force in the Benelux: the same occurred with the new law of designs and models.

It goes without saying that it is impossible to split up such uniform acts, as it was initially planned for the national statutes. It would not be elegant, however, to transfer these acts as a whole to Book 9 of the Civil Code, since they contain more than private law alone. Moreover, this would have the practical disadvantage that one and the same article would carry a different number in Book 9 and in the uniform acts. More importantly, these acts, which contain their own provisions for transfer, pledge, etc. would badly fit into the system of the new Code. The once envisaged simplification and the better connection with the codified civil law would not be attained. For these reasons it is unlikely that Book 9 will come out according to the original plan made for it. Since it would not be very appropriate to limit Book 9 to a rudimentary form, in which only the law of copyright and trade name is incorporated, the fate of this book seems sealed. An official decision, however, has yet to be taken.

18. *Preliminary title.* Another part of the Code, as originally planned but afterwards abandoned, is the Preliminary title. Its nine articles were divided into two groups. The first one settled the order of importance of the various sources of law: statutory law, custom, equity. For instance, it laid down the rule that a suppletive provision of law can be set aside by custom or equity, whereas a mandatory provision cannot. These rules have been harshly criticized and have been deleted, which leaves the issue to the courts.

The second group concerned subjective rights, especially the doctrine of abuse of rights. These provisions have been transferred to the first title of Book 3. Consequently, the preliminary title has been deleted as a whole.

19. *Conclusion.* It will be clear from the preceding remarks that the new Dutch Civil Code is organized according to a rather strict pattern of general rules preceding more detailed rules, sometimes in various layers. This is especially notable in contractual matters, where the relevant rules are not only found in the applicable chapters of Books 7 and 8 (if any), but in addition thereto in Book 3 (e.g., the will and its defects), Book 6, Title 1 (law of obligations in general) and Title 5 (law of contracts in general). In the law of property there may be two or three layers (Books 3 and 5), and the same holds true for the law of successions (Books 3 and 4), etc. In this respect the Code resembles to a certain extent the German *Bürgerliches Gesetzbuch* (B.G.B.), although with an important difference: in the B.G.B. the general part covers the entire Code, whereas in the new Dutch Code the general part only relates to patrimonial law.

There is, however, another systematic feature of the new Code to be noted. In many instances there are provisions, often at the end of a section or chapter, which instruct the courts, if possible, to apply by way of analogy the preceding rules to cases not directly governed by them. For instance, the provisions on contracts in general are declared applicable to other multilateral juridical acts of a patrimonial nature, such as the ones creating a servitude or partitioning a succession (art. 216 of Book 6). Sometimes, this even purports to extend the scope of application outside the law of property or obligations (art. 59 of Book 3 on juridical acts). At first sight, this feature seems to be diametrically opposed to the one previously discussed, but in reality it fulfils a comparable function: provisions of this kind amount, as it were, to a tentative general part in instances where a proper one is not possible or feasible (Comp. art. 7 of the Swiss Civil Code, art. 1324 of the Italian Civil Code, and art. 876 of the Austrian Civil Code).

III. THE CONTENTS OF THE NEW CODE

20. The mandate which Professor Meijers accepted in 1947, was brief: "To draft a new Civil Code". This wording allowed the greatest possible latitude to modify the law in force and to bring the Civil Code up to date. On the one hand, it is clear that it was not intended that the new Civil Code would fundamentally change the existing law as developed by legislation and jurisprudence. On the other, the work must not be misunderstood as a mere restatement of the law with the aim to remove superfluous and obsolete provisions, and to codify judge-made law and special statutes. The previous sections have shown that Meijers decidedly did not approach his task in such a limited way. By means of some examples it will be shown that the law itself has undergone many important and interesting innovations. The examples will be restricted to patrimonial law and will focus on the law of obligations. For obvious reasons the references have to be brief.

21. In *Book 3*, the first notable innovation is the protection of the person who acquires an immoveable thing from a seller who is not entitled to alienate the thing. If the impediment lies in a fact which could have been registered in the public registers for immoveables, the acquirer receives full title if the registration was not made, provided that he did not know the impediment. The same protection is granted to an acquirer who relies on an inaccurate registration which the owner failed to correct although he could reasonably have done so (Articles 24 and 26 of Book 3). Moreover, although the rule has been retained that the transfer of a thing requires a valid title, the lack of a title cannot be invoked against a third person acquiring the thing in good faith (Article 88 of Book 3).

As to the acquisition of moveable things, the rule that "possession vaut titre", taken over in the Dutch Civil Code from the French Civil Code, has been interpreted by the Dutch Supreme Court in the sense that a person acquiring the thing in good faith and by onerous title from another person who is not the owner, acquires full title. This rule has been retained in article 86 of Book 3, but has been modified in several ways. Among other things, the rule has been extended to the acquisition of lost things, as well as to the acquisition of stolen things, provided that the acquirer is a consumer who acquires the thing in the ordinary course of the seller's business.

A juridical act requires a relevant will and the declaration thereof. However, if there is a discrepancy between the will and the declaration of which the other party could not be aware, the act is valid. If a declaration, either explicit or implicit, creates the appearance of the existence or of the non-existence of a juridical relationship, a third person in good faith may rely on that appearance if he acts upon it (Articles 33, 35 and 36 of Book 3).

To the traditional defects of consent (threat, fraud, error) a fourth one, "abuse of circumstances", has been added. It does not require financial loss. A number of relevant circumstances are enumerated in Article 44, para. 4, of Book 3: a situation of necessity, dependency, wantonness, abnormal mental condition, or lack of experience. These examples make it clear that the circumstances of which advantage has been taken, not only include economic or factual necessity, but also a particular state of mind of the victim.

The new Title 3.6 on fiduciary administration ("bewind"), which will replace the *fiducia cum amico*, was mentioned in no. 11. In fact, Article 84, para. 3, of Book 3 prohibits any fiduciary title. This affects also the *fiducia cum creditore* (transfer by way of security), which Dutch jurisprudence developed following the lead of German law. It has been replaced by a right of non-possessory pledge, which is governed by the general law of pledge (Articles 237 and 239 of Book 3). There are, however, some exceptions which show that it is a weaker right than a possessory pledge. If the debtor is not the owner of the thing or if the thing is already encumbered with dismembered rights, the creditor allowing the thing to remain in the hands of the debtor will not obtain a valid right of pledge, until the thing enters into his possession, provided that he relies in good faith on the debtor's power to dispose of it at that time (Article 238 of Book 3).

22. The *law of successions* (*Book 4*) has been the subject of intense debate for many years. The general tendency is to strengthen the position of the surviving spouse at the expense of the children and in spite of their legitimate portion. In the old Dutch Civil Code the spouse is an heir together with the children, but (s)he has no legitimate portion. It proves to be extremely difficult to find a suitable compromise between this rule and the views of the advocates of the surviving spouse, many of whom go so far as to plead that the spouse be declared sole heir and, moreover, be entitled to claim the entire inheritance if this would be necessary for his (her) sustenance. In 1981, the Dutch Government proposed - on the basis of a compromise between the Minister of Justice and the Justice Committee of Parliament - that the surviving spouse will have a usufruct by operation of the law, which includes - in principle - the power to dispose of property, and which prevails over the children's legitimate portion. Moreover, this portion will be transformed from a property right into a pecuniary claim. If the testator in his last will excludes the rights of the surviving spouse, the latter may nevertheless claim a usufruct of the succession insofar as such right is necessary in order to safeguard his (her) sustenance. It has not proved possible, however, to decide upon this issue together with Books 3, 5 and 6, so that Book 4 will come into force at a later stage.

23. The *law of property* (in the restricted sense discussed in no. 13) will also be modernized. To be noted are, among others, a regulation of the subject of lost objects (Title 5.2), a provision granting the State the ownership of the territorial sea (Article 25 of Book 5), and several enlargements of the concept of servitudes (Title 5.6).

24. One of the most important elements of *Book 6* (*General part of the law of obligations*) is the role of good faith in juridical relationships. In Article 2 of Book 6 it is expressly stated that good faith (which in the law of obligations will be renamed "reasonableness and equity") cannot only supplement obligations arising from contract or from other sources, but can also extinguish them or exclude their application. The article provides that "creditor and debtor must, as between themselves, act in accordance with the requirements of reasonableness and equity", and para. 2 adds that "A rule binding upon them by virtue of the law, usage or a juridical act does not apply to the extent that, in the given circumstances, this would be unacceptable according to criteria of reasonableness and equity". This provision is to apply to all obligations, whereas the old Civil Code (Article 1374 para. 3, same wording in Article 1134 para. 3 French C.C.) restricts the operation of good faith to obligations arising from contract. Moreover, it attributes to it only the first of the two functions mentioned above, whereas the new Article 2 of Book 6, para. 2, acknowledges a "restrictive" function as well. In this, the new Code follows jurisprudence which has adopted the principle of good faith in this restrictive sense primarily (but not exclusively) in cases where the creditor, by his own acts or omissions, forfeits his claim against the debtor.

The effect of good faith in the law of contracts is dealt with in several articles of the section on the legal effects of contracts. Article 248 of Book 6 applies the principles, as expressed in Article 2 of Book 6, to contracts; and according to Article 216 of Book 6, these rules are applicable *per analogiam* to all other multilateral juridical acts of a patrimonial nature (see no. 19 above).

The same is true of article 258 of Book 6 which elaborates upon the subject with a view to "imprévision" (unforeseen circumstances). The first sentence reads: "Upon the demand of one of the parties, the judge may modify the effects of the contract, or he may set it aside in whole or in part on the basis of unforeseen circumstances which are of such a nature that the cocontracting party, according to criteria of reasonableness and equity, may not expect that the contract be maintained in an unmodified form". Similar provisions have been drafted in other fields, e.g., legacies and servitudes. It must be noted that the expression "unforeseen circumstances" should not be taken in its literal sense. The test does not relate to what parties have foreseen or could foresee, but asks whether the *contract* makes sufficient provision for the supervening event.

25. The law of natural obligations is set forth in Articles 3-5 of Book 6. Solidary obligations (Articles 6 *et seq.*) will become much more important in the future, since the section will apply to all cases where persons are liable to repair the same damage (see Article 102 of Book 6).

Rights of suspension are granted not only in all instances of counter-obligations arising from contract, but also in other cases where the suspension of performance is justified having regard to the relationship between the debts (Article 52-56 and 262-264 of Book 6). The position of the creditor entitled to suspend the restitution of a thing belonging to the other party (right of retention) is considerably strengthened, whether in or outside the case of bankruptcy (Articles 290-295 of Book 6).

A new section is devoted to the default of the creditor (Articles 58-73 of Book 6). The effects of non-performance of obligations are set forth in Articles 74-94 of Book 6. The debtor is not only liable in case of fault but also if the non-performance may be imputed to him according to common opinion. The law adds a liability without fault for persons and things used in the performance of an obligation. The obligation to pay damages arises immediately once proper performance has become impossible. In other cases, except where the contract fixes a time for performance, the debtor must be put into default to perform, whether he performed in the wrong way or did not perform at all. The same requirements apply to the right to set aside a contract (Article 265 of Book 6).

A debtor in default is in principle entitled to purge his default, provided that he offers to pay compensation for costs incurred and for damage. He is also entitled to summon the creditor to choose between his rights (to performance, damages, setting aside, etc.); if the creditor does not comply with the request within a reasonable period, he merely retains his right to claim damages.

A stipulated penalty may be reduced by the court if equity clearly so demands, but not below the amount of legal damages. On the other hand, if the penalty is meant to replace legal damages, the court nevertheless has the power to award supplementary damages if equity so demands (Article 94 of Book 6).

26. The section on reparation of damage (Articles 95-110 of Book 6) applies to both contractual and extra-contractual liability. It contains several new rules, among others on the causal connection between the event on which liability is based and the damage (Article 98: to put it shortly, the only criterion is reasonableness), on immaterial damage and on liability in case of the death of the victim (Articles 106 and 108, both rather restrictive).

The section closes with two interesting Articles. Article 109 grants the courts the power to reduce an obligation to pay damages on the ground that paying full compensation "would lead to clearly unacceptable results." Among the factors to be taken into consideration are the nature of the liability (e.g., risk vs. fault), the relationship between the parties, and their respective financial positions. There is no power to reduce damages if the debtor's liability is or should have been covered by insurance. Article 110 allows the Government to limit certain forms of liability by Regulation, in order to ensure that such liability can be covered by insurance.

27. The section on "obligations to pay a sum of money" (Articles 111-126) deals with the payment by postal transfer ("giro") (Article 114; comp. Article 46), legal interest for default in the payment of a sum of money, and debts in foreign currency. Title 6.2

(Articles 142-161), called "Transfer of claims and debts and renunciation of claims", contains innovations in the field of subrogation, the effects of the transfer of claims, and the taking over of debts and contracts.

28. The *law of unlawful acts* (torts), at present governed by a number of provisions taken from the French *Code civil* and elaborated upon by the judiciary, will be set forth in Title 6.3 of the new Civil Code (Articles 162 *et seq.*). In accordance with legal developments in many other countries, the most important alterations in this area consist of a shift from liability based on fault to liability based on risk. The latter was not unknown in the old Dutch law, but was restricted to vicarious liability for damage caused by employees, by the collapse of buildings, by vessels and (with some important restrictions) by automobiles. Furthermore, there were cases where a presumption of fault could be rebutted by the defendant; thus parents were liable for unlawful acts committed by their minor children, unless they proved that the omission to take such measures for the prevention of the loss to third persons as could reasonably have been required of them, could not be imputed to them. But unlike in French and Belgian law, the Dutch courts have not deduced strict liability (nor a presumption of fault) from Article 1403 para. 1 (the counterpart of Article 1384 para. 1 French C.C.).

Against this position the new Dutch Civil Code provides for strict liability for things (Articles 173-183). In principle, Article 173 will cover all things, whether "dangerous" or not, but subject to the restriction borrowed from Belgian law that the damage be caused by a defect inherent in the thing. Since this restriction would not be appropriate for dangerous substances (where the danger is among the characteristics of the thing), the provision will be coupled by a special rule on those substances. Moreover, there are articles on animals and buildings which in one way or another extend the liability resulting from the article on things in general. The section does not cover automobiles, vessels and aircraft. Provisions on those forms of liability will be incorporated into Book 8 (law of transport). The rules of Articles 185-193 on product liability conform to the relevant EEC Directive on the subject matter.

The person liable is the possessor of the thing. The rationale is very practical: this person can be easily traced by the victim, and it will normally be him who takes out insurance for damage caused by the thing. There are exceptions, however, the most important one being nearly as important as the main rule itself. If things or substances are employed in carrying out a business or profession, liability rests upon the person carrying out that business or profession (Article 181). If, for instance, an explosion in a factory wounds a third person, the victim will often not be able to prove which thing or substance lays at the root of the damage. It falls to the person running the factory to take out insurance for his activities as a whole, regardless of who is the possessor of the things and substances he employs, and regardless of whether the damage was caused by a thing or by an employee working in the factory.

On the same grounds, the new Code extends the liability of the employer for his employees (Article 170); and it introduces a new case of strict liability for independent contractors, provided that they are employed in the business of the employer (Article 171).

As to the liability for a person's own actions, the new Dutch Code retains as its main rule the requirement of fault (Article 162, para. 3). But there are important exceptions: a mental or bodily defect will no longer impede the attribution of an unlawful act to the wrongdoer (Article 165; Comp. Art. 489 para. 2 French C.C.). On the other hand, children until fourteen year of age have been entirely exempted from liability for unlawful acts (Article 164). In return, the parents will be liable for these children regardless of any fault on their part (Article 169).

This is merely a general outline of the new law of unlawful acts, which is quite extensive and rich in details. In conclusion, one may mention the power of the government to fix amounts by Regulation which liability (especially that based on risk) is not to exceed (see no. 26 *in fine*), and the power of the courts to refuse to grant an injunction for an unlawful activity (e.g., a factory causing hindrance) on the ground that it serves important societal interests (Article 168).

29. Under the old Code, Dutch law did not allow an action for unjustified enrichment. Such has been the decision of the Dutch Supreme Court, contrary to its counterparts in France and Belgium. Catching up with these countries and with more recent codifications elsewhere (notably, Germany, Switzerland, Italy), Article 212 of Book 6 lays down the general rule: "A person who has been unjustifiably enriched at the expense of another must, to the extent that this is reasonable, make reparation for the damage suffered by that other person up to the amount of his enrichment." The restriction "to the extent that this is reasonable" purports to exclude, *inter alia*, the restitution of an enrichment imposed upon a person without his consent.

30. The fifth and last title of Book 6 is concerned with contracts in general. The most interesting feature is a new section on general conditions, a subject on which the old Code was silent. The section (Articles 231-247) centres around the provision that general conditions (all clauses regularly employed by one of the parties) of an unreasonably onerous nature may be annulled (Article 233). This provision is followed by a list of some thirty clauses which are either deemed or presumed to meet that test, but only in contracts concluded with consumers (Articles 236-238). Finally, there is the power of consumer and business organizations to apply for an injunction against unreasonable clauses whether listed or not (Articles 240-243).

The notion of "standard terms" is to be distinguished from general conditions: the former is a set of provisions applying *ipso iure* to a contract of a certain type. Standard terms will be drafted by commissions appointed by the Minister of Justice and require the approval of the Government (Article 214). A special statute will provide that the commissions will consist mainly of members proposed by interested business circles and - if consumer interests are concerned - by consumer organizations.

There is a section on the formation of contracts, partly derived from the Uniform Law on Formation of Contracts for the International Sale of Goods, adopted at the Hague in 1964. However, it also contains a provision on error (Article 228), to a considerable extent inspired by the common law notion of misrepresentation.

The rules on good faith and *imprévision* (unforeseen circumstances), contained in section 3 on the legal effects of contracts, have already been discussed in no. 24 above. Moreover, the section deals with the legal effects of contracts as to third persons, e.g., persons acquiring a thing with a right or an obligation qualitatively attached to it. As to the doctrine of stipulations for the benefit of a third person, there is a new provision stating that if an employer is exonerated from liability for the unlawful conduct of his employee, the latter can avail himself of the same defence against a person seeking compensation from him (Article 257).

Finally, Articles 265-279 of section 4 are concerned with the setting aside of bilateral contracts for non-performance. Setting aside is possible in case of non-performance, irrespective of whether the debtor is liable in damages or whether the non-performance is due to superior force; it may be effected - either totally or partially - by a mere notice in writing, and will lack retroactive effect.

31. It is not within the scope of this introduction to discuss the contents of the special contracts contained in Book 7 (see the enumeration in no. 15 above). As mentioned before, four titles of this Book are to be enacted and brought into force simultaneously with Books 3, 5 and 6, on account of their close relationship with subject matters set forth in those Books. The other titles will follow in the course of this decade. This poses an important problem as to the extent to which *consumer law* is to be embodied in the new Civil Code, e.g., in the law of sale, the contract of work, the contract of services, insurance, suretyship or the contract of travel.

In principle, there is a tradition in the Netherlands to incorporate into the Civil and Commercial Codes new rules on the protection of socially and economically weaker parties: the labour contract (1907), hire-purchase (1936), trade agents (1977) and residential leases (several protective statutes were combined in 1979). The lease of land and the collective labour contract, presently governed by separate statutes, will be inserted into the new Book 7. It is consistent with this approach to deal with private law aspects of consumer protection in the same way. Major examples are the new section in Book 6 on general conditions (see no. 30 above) and the title on the contract of sale (7.1).

The draft bill of this title was based mainly on the 1964 Hague Uniform Law on Contracts for the International Sale of Goods. This concept has been retained, but a number of articles on consumer sales has been added to the draft as submitted to Parliament. The same pattern has been followed in the other titles mentioned above. A key question in this respect is the amount of mandatory law needed in these fields, which are of course considered against the background of the section on general conditions in Book 6. The experience so far indicates that the rules controlling general conditions do not render mandatory law superfluous as a supplementary means of protecting the weaker party to the contract.

IV. CONCLUSION

32. It is clear from the preceding survey that the new Civil Code offers a great number of new rules, designed to meet the needs of modern society in the Netherlands. As to the direction of the innovations, some general tendencies may be observed. There is a remarkable increase in provisions protecting persons, either acting in good faith upon the appearance of a relevant will, or acquiring in good faith a thing from a non-owner. The notion of reasonableness and equity, as well as other "open-ended concepts", like unjust enrichment, play a prominent part in the law of obligations and beyond. The protection of weaker persons (minors, employees, consumers, victims of unlawful acts) has been extended. The general interest has been recognized as a relevant factor within private law (see, for instance, Articles 12 and 14 of Book 3 and Articles 168 and 259 of Book 6). There are a great many improvements of a more "technical" nature, not even mentioned before, which can also be combined to show a general tendency; e.g., the provisions hampering the legal effects of nullity and reducing the instances of such uncontrollable a phenomenon as retroactive effect.

33. The sources of these innovations are manifold and cannot be traced here. However, it is appropriate in this context to mention the extensive studies in comparative law undertaken by the drafters, as a mere glance into the Commentary on Book 6 and its hundreds of footnotes will reveal. Just one figure may illustrate this fact: pages 372-413 of the Commentary on Book 6 (in the English translation, published in 1977. See Select Bibliography hereafter), being exactly half of the explanatory Commentary of title 6.3 (law of unlawful acts), contain 220 footnotes; 120 of these include references to statutory law, court decisions and literature of the following countries: Austria, Belgium, England, France, Germany, Greece, Hungary, Italy, Portugal, Switzerland, the Scandinavian countries, Canada, the USA, South Africa and Japan. There are also references to the history of law, to both domestic and foreign writers, and to legislation.

The importance of the inspiration derived from these comparative studies can hardly be overestimated. It has been said that, as a result, Dutch private law will no longer belong to the group of French inspired systems of law, but rather to the Germanic group. There may be some truth in this as far as the systematic approach, the abstract language, and a number of rather technical details are concerned. However, in regard to the important innovations, some of which were mentioned before, foreign influences are much more balanced. The most important example of French-Belgian inspiration is, it is submitted, the shift to liability without fault in the law of unlawful acts; influence from the common law may be seen, e.g., in the articles on error, undue influence, anticipatory breach of contract, and liability for independent contractors; German influence is visible in the new section on general conditions and in the rules on the role of good faith (reasonableness and equity) in contract law. Moreover, the new Code is indebted to uniform law, especially to the Hague and Vienna Uniform Sales Acts of 1964 and 1980, which exerted their influence not only in the law of sale proper, but also in the sections on non-performance and on the formation of contracts in the general law of obligations (Book 6). It is submitted that there is merit in the observation by Kötz and Zweigert :

> "It is very doubtful whether the new Civil Code still really belongs to the French tradition. As evidenced by the accompanying materials, it rests everywhere upon thorough comparative considerations, and it may be that it has found its own style, based upon a continental European *ius commune*".[3]

[3] "Ob das neue Burgerlijk Wetboek wirklich noch der französischen Tradition zugerechnet werden kann ist sehr zweifelhaft. Jedenfalls beruht es - wie aus den Gesetzesbegründungen zu entnehmen ist - überall auf gründlichen rechtsvergleichenden Ueberlegungen, und es mag sein, dass es zu einem eigenen, auf kontinental-europäischem ius commune beruhenden Stil gefunden hat".(*Einführung in die Rechtsvergleichung auf dem Gebiete des Privatrechts I*, 1984, p. 119). See also the English translation: Konrad Zweigert et Hein Kötz, *Introduction to comparative law*, Oxford: Clarendon Press, 1987, Second revised ed., Vol. I, p. 105.

LA RÉVISION DU CODE CIVIL AUX PAYS-BAS 1947-1992

Arthur S. Hartkamp[1]

I. LE PROGRAMME DE LA RÉVISION

1. La publication du présent livre marque un point tournant dans le processus de la recodification aux Pays-Bas commencé en 1947. Les deux premiers Livres du nouveau Code civil sont déjà en vigueur: le Livre premier (*Des personnes et de la famille*) depuis 1970, le Livre deuxième (*Des personnes morales*) depuis 1976. Le gouvernement des Pays-Bas s'est maintenant engagé à mettre en vigueur le noyau du nouveau Code au premier janvier 1992. Ce noyau comprend les Livres troisième, cinquième et sixième, ainsi qu'une partie du Livre septième, englobant le droit des biens et des obligations. Avec la mise en vigueur de ces Livres, le programme de révision du Code civil s'approche de son but, soit remplacer le Code actuel qui a plus de 150 ans par un nouveau Code «consolidé» dans lequel sont réunis le droit civil, le droit commercial, le droit de la consommation et une grande partie de la législation de droit privé hors du Code ainsi que des dispositions codifiant un corps de plus en plus important de règles élaborées par la jurisprudence.

2. Le Code civil actuel des Pays-Bas date de 1838. Il est le troisième Code civil en vigueur au pays. Le premier Code civil a été mis en vigueur en 1809, pendant le règne de Louis Napoléon, frère de l'Empereur. Ce Code avait beaucoup de points communs avec le Code Napoléon, moins cependant qu'on ne le prétend généralement. En 1811, lors de l'intégration des Pays-Bas à l'empire français, ce Code fut remplacé par le Code Napoléon lui-même. Dès après la libération de la domination française, en 1813, des efforts furent entrepris visant à rédiger un Code authentiquement néerlandais. Ces efforts furent couronnés de succès en 1838. Sauf pour un certain nombre de sujets d'importance variable dans le droit des personnes et de la famille (en particulier en ce qui touche les conventions matrimoniales), le droit des successions et le droit des biens, ce Code s'inspirait abondamment, souvent jusque dans les termes, du Code Napoléon.

Cette ressemblance de forme ne s'étendait pas toutefois au système du Code. Le Code civil néerlandais retournait au droit romain et à l'ancien droit néerlandais en exigeant la délivrance comme condition du transfert de la propriété. Le Code opérait en conséquence une distinction nette entre le droit des biens et le droit des obligations, exposés aux Livres deuxième et troisième respectivement. Le droit des successions fut placé dans le Livre deuxième. Un quatrième Livre, en outre, regroupait les dispositions relatives à la preuve et à la prescription. Ce système ressemble de manière saisissante à celui des Instituts de Gaius et de Justinien, ainsi qu'à celui proposé par Grotius dans son *Inleidinge tot de Hollandsche Rechts-geleerdheid* (Introduction à la jurisprudence hollandaise)[2] de 1631. D'autres ruptures avec le système du Code Napoléon se trouvent entre autres dans les dispositions générales du droit des obligations.

---

[1] Avocat général près le *Hoge Raad* (Cour de cassation) des Pays-Bas; ancien juriste conseil, membre de la Section de Révision du Code civil du ministère de la Justice des Pays-Bas; membre du Conseil de direction d'Unidroit; membre de l'Académie royale néerlandaise des sciences.

[2] Hugo de Groot, *Inleidinge tot de Hollandsche Rechts-geleerdheid*, ré-édité par les soins de F. Dovring, H.F.W.D. Fischer et E.M. Meijers, aux Presses universitaires de Leyde, 1965 (2e éd.)

3. Le Code de commerce néerlandais date, lui aussi, de 1838; son seul prédécesseur est le Code de commerce français qui a été en vigueur au pays de 1811 jusqu'à 1838. La distinction entre le droit civil et le droit commercial n'existait pas dans les provinces unies des Pays-Bas avant la Révolution française. Dans son *Inleidinge*, Grotius traite des deux branches du droit ensemble; il en est de même des autres auteurs de l'ancien droit néerlandais et même du projet de Code civil préparé en 1807 par les soins du juriste néerlandais Johannes van der Linden. La réunification du droit civil et du droit commercial est l'aboutissement d'un processus commencé en 1838. L'article premier du Code de commerce néerlandais dispose que, sauf dérogation expresse, le Code civil s'applique à toutes matières réglées dans le Code de commerce. En outre, les tribunaux de commerce, créés aux Pays-Bas au cours de l'époque napoléonienne, furent abolis en 1838. Le droit de la faillite a été enlevé au Code de commerce et placé, en 1893, dans une loi particulière dont l'application n'était plus restreinte aux seuls commerçants. Enfin en 1934 presque toutes les différences qui restaient entre commerçants et non-commerçants furent supprimées. Dans ces circonstances, la disposition du droit civil et du droit commercial dans des codes distincts n'était plus justifiable. Aussi, le droit commercial se retrouve-t-il au Livre deuxième (*Des personnes morales*), au Livre septième (*Des Contrats particuliers*) et au Livre huitième (*Du droit des transports*).

4. Le Code civil aussi bien que le Code de commerce actuels doivent être considérés comme dépassés sur de nombreux points. Cette observation ne vaut pas pour toute une gamme de matières d'intérêt social immédiat, pour lesquelles des réformes ont été instituées aussi bien à l'intérieur des Codes que dans des lois particulières. Que l'on songe au droit des jeunes, aux baux résidentiel et agricole, au contrat de travail, au contrat de crédit-bail, à la propriété industrielle et intellectuelle, au droit des sociétés et autres. Mais le législateur néerlandais n'a malheureusement pas adapté le droit des biens et le droit des obligations à l'âge moderne. L'omission s'explique par la facilité relative - sans compter la pression sociale en ce sens - de réformer des secteurs plus ou moins indépendants du droit au regard de la tâche complexe de réviser l'ensemble de règles générales et aux multiples interrelations que forment le droit des biens et le droit des obligations. Une révision même partielle de celles-ci est rarement possible sans toucher à une multitude d'autres sujets, ce qui fait que la révision risque de s'enliser ou d'apporter une partie seulement des réformes nécessaires.

Le retard en résultant dans le développement du droit privé a été comblé pour une bonne partie par la jurisprudence. Le droit des actes illicites constitue l'exemple le plus spectaculaire d'une création presque intégralement jurisprudentielle. Dans d'autres domaines également, les tribunaux ont su bâtir des ponts entre le Code et la société en évolution rapide au cours du XXe siècle. Autant on peut se féliciter de cette initiative des tribunaux, autant il faut regretter son effet démobilisant sur les timides efforts de réforme partielle et leurs défenseurs.

Il en est résulté une bifurcation des approches préconisées à l'égard de la modernisation du droit civil. D'un côté, il y avait ceux qui préconisaient la voie des distinctions subtiles élaborées cas par cas par les tribunaux; cette approche donne toutefois lieu à un droit de plus en plus opaque. De l'autre côté, il y avait ceux qui préconisaient des réformes législatives, en raison de l'espoir qu'elles comportent d'aboutir à des ensembles de règles plus transparents; mais cette approche se heurte à la difficulté pratique, de plus en plus contraignante, d'insérer harmonieusement les règles ainsi réformées dans le système, dont la complexité ne cesse de croître, du Code et de la jurisprudence afférente. Devant les difficultés pratiques de toute réforme, on s'est retrouvé au milieu du XXe siècle avec un droit privé d'une incontrôlable opacité, dont le contenu était éparpillé dans des Codes pour partie dépassés, dans une panoplie de lois particulières et dans une multitude de décisions de justice. On était bien loin de l'intention exprimée dans la Constitution depuis 1789 de formuler le droit privé (le droit commercial et le droit judiciaire y compris) dans des Codes généraux, des sujets spécifiques étant relégués aux lois particulières.

5. Les tenants de la recodification l'ont finalement emporté aux Pays-Bas. En 1947, le professeur E.M. Meijers, de l'Université de Leyde, qui avait longtemps insisté sur la nécessité de la recodification, s'est vu confier le mandat de rédiger un nouveau Code civil. Le Code devait comporter neuf livres:

I. Des personnes et de la famille (les régimes matrimoniaux y compris);
II. Des personnes morales (partie générale, les associations, les sociétés à responsabilité limitée, les fondations);
III. Du droit patrimonial en général (comportant des dispositions applicables à l'ensemble des livres suivants);
IV. Des successions;
V. De la propriété et des droits réels;
VI. Partie générale du droit des obligations;
VII. Des contrats particuliers;
VIII. Du droit des transports;
(IX. Des droits sur les produits de l'esprit.)

Ce plan a été maintenu jusqu'à nos jours, sauf pour ce qui est du Livre neuvième, abandonné pour des raisons qui seront exposées à la section II. Examinons brièvement l'historique de la réforme, avant d'aborder à la section II l'examen systématique du nouveau Code en sa forme actuelle.

6. Le professeur Meijers a commencé par une vaste consultation d'experts pour déterminer les points devant être réglés dans le nouveau Code civil. Cette consultation l'amena à dresser une liste de 52 sujets de grande importance pratique et politique sur lesquels il voulait solliciter le point de vue du parlement quant aux orientations à suivre. Cette phase de la réforme a été décrite en détail dans trois articles de J. Dainow[3] et ne sera pas reprise ici.

Bien que Meijers eût préféré publier le projet de Code civil comme un tout, le Titre préliminaire et une première version des Livres 1 à 4, accompagnés d'un commentaire (*Toelichting*), furent publiés en 1954. La publication avait lieu sur les instances du ministre de la Justice, M. Donker, ardent défenseur de la recodification, qui craignait que l'élan fût perdu si les premiers résultats se faisaient trop attendre. Quelques mois après la publication, Meijers décéda. La décision fut alors prise de confier la continuation de son travail à un comité composé de trois personnes, MM. J. Drion, F.J. de Jong et J. Eggens, ce dernier étant remplacé plus tard par G. de Grooth. Ce comité continua le travail sur la base des versions préliminaires, à divers degrés d'avancement, des textes et des commentaires que Meijers avait déjà préparés.

7. Le comité publia un projet de Livre cinquième en 1955 et un projet de Livre sixième en 1961. Pour le Livre septième, traitant des contrats particuliers, une méthode de travail différente fut adoptée. En raison de la diversité de sujets et des vastes connaissances requises pour les matières des vingt titres de ce Livre, le ministre décida de découper la matière et de confier à différents juristes le mandat de rédiger un ou plusieurs titres. L'un des membres du comité de trois avait pour mandat d'harmoniser les différents titres et de préparer un projet final. Ce projet fut présenté au ministre de la Justice en 1972. Le livre huitième, portant sur le droit des transports, fut confié en entier à un spécialiste de droit maritime, M. H. Schadee. Une première partie, comportant les règles générales du contrat de transport, le droit maritime et le droit de la navigation intérieure, fut publiée en 1972; une deuxième partie, traitant du transport par route, le fut en 1976.

Chaque Livre fut proposé au Parlement sous la forme d'un projet de loi distinct. Les délibérations du parlement sur ces projets a commencé en 1954, avec l'introduction des projets correspondant aux quatre premiers Livres. Le projet de Livre cinquième suivit deux

3 Voir la bibliographie sommaire ci-après.

ans après et celui du Livre sixième, en 1964. Le Livre premier fut voté en 1959, le Livre deuxième en 1960, le Livre quatrième en 1969. Les Livres troisième, cinquième, sixième et huitième (première partie) suivirent en 1979-1980. L'expérience a démontré qu'un délai considérable s'écoule entre l'adoption de ces lois et leur mise en vigueur. La raison en est que la mise en vigueur requiert une loi spéciale de mise en application, qui comporte le droit transitoire, les adaptations nécessaires aux autres Codes et lois ainsi que les modifications au texte déjà adopté.

8. Une question importante est celle de savoir s'il est possible et désirable de mettre en vigueur certains Livres séparément des autres. Dans le cas des deux premiers Livres du nouveau Code néerlandais, la question a reçu une réponse affirmative: le Livre premier a été mis en vigueur en 1970, le Livre deuxième, en 1976.

Cette solution n'a pas été retenue dans le cas des Livres 3, 5 et 6. Les rapports entre ces Livres sont si étroits qu'il fallait procéder à la mise en vigueur en bloc. Dans le cas de ces trois Livres, la mise en vigueur est une opération complexe, puisqu'elle comporte non seulement les éléments déjà évoqués de la loi de mise en application mais aussi des lois nouvelles auxquelles renvoient des dispositions du nouveau Code (par exemple une loi sur les registres publics pour l'inscription des biens immatriculés). Il a paru nécessaire, en outre, de réviser un Livre entier du Code de procédure civile (celui qui traite des saisies) et de rédiger quatre titres du Livre septième sur les contrats particuliers, comportant notamment l'important contrat de vente[4]. Cet ensemble complexe de 15 lois reliées fut voté au Parlement néerlandais entre 1986 et 1990; il entrera en vigueur au 1er janvier 1992. Le Livre huitième entrera, lui aussi, en vigueur sous peu. Quant au Livre quatrième et aux autres contrats particuliers prévus au Livre septième, ils entreront en vigueur au cours des années 1990, dans l'ordre où il plaira au Parlement de les adopter.

9. La conclusion s'impose que l'élaboration du nouveau Code civil néerlandais a pris bien plus longtemps que prévu à l'origine. Heureusement, la crainte de voir fléchir l'intérêt pour la réforme dans les milieux politiques et dans ceux de la doctrine et de la pratique du droit ne s'est pas vérifiée. Dès le départ du processus de réforme, les projets de texte du Code et des commentaires ont exercé une influence considérable sur la pratique du droit aux Pays-Bas. Ils ont de même influencé le législateur qui en a adopté des parties sous forme de lois particulières et qui, dans la mesure du possible, a suivi dans la législation ordinaire la terminologie et le système du nouveau Code. Ils ont en outre influencé la jurisprudence: dans de nombreux cas, le *Hoge Raad* (Cour de cassation) des Pays-Bas a interprété le Code actuel et la législation de manière à les rendre conformes aux solutions retenues dans le projet de Code ou dans les commentaires. Cette pratique a été baptisée «l'interprétation par anticipation». L'attitude du plus haut tribunal et des autres tribunaux à sa suite ont contraint la pratique du droit à s'aligner progressivement sur le nouveau droit. Ce mouvement a été secondé par la doctrine: les auteurs ont traité leurs matières en suivant le système du nouveau Code et en tenant compte de son contenu. La naissance du nouveau Code néerlandais résulte d'un véritable effort conjoint de tous les groupes composant la communauté juridique des Pays-Bas.

II. LE SYSTÈME DU NOUVEAU CODE

10. *Livre premier: Des personnes et de la famille.* Comme il a été mentionné, les Livres premier et deuxième sont en vigueur depuis 1970 et 1976 respectivement. Le Livre premier comporte le droit des personnes et le droit de la famille, y compris le mariage, les régimes matrimoniaux, le divorce et l'adoption. Il est intéressant de noter que le droit

4 Voir les paragraphes 15 et 31.

relatif au divorce a été modernisé séparément en 1971. Cela démontre que la création d'un nouveau Code n'empêche pas la réforme du droit par la législation ordinaire. Au contraire, il est plus facile d'adapter un corps moderne et systématisé de règles de droit qu'une codification vieillie ensevelie sous la jurisprudence. Depuis 1971, tant d'autres innovations ont été adoptées ou sont en passe de l'être que, pour certains juristes néerlandais, l'an 1970 n'a marqué que le commencement de la véritable révision du droit des personnes et de la famille aux Pays-Bas.

Le Livre deuxième comporte le droit des personnes morales: les associations, les sociétés commerciales, les fondations. Le Livre commence par l'énonciation d'un ensemble de dispositions générales s'appliquant à toutes les personnes morales.

11. *Livre troisième. Du droit patrimonial en général.* Le Livre troisième marque le changement le plus radical par rapport au système du Code civil actuel, et même par rapport à l'ensemble des codifications dans les pays de tradition civiliste. Ce livre se fonde sur un double principe.

D'abord, on a regroupé dans ce Livre des questions que l'on trouvait auparavant tantôt dans le droit des contrats, tantôt dans le droit des successions, mais qui s'appliquent, à la vérité, à l'ensemble du droit patrimonial. Cela vaut en premier lieu pour le concept de l'acte juridique: les conditions générales de sa validité (consentement, capacité); la protection des personnes se fiant de bonne foi à l'apparence d'un consentement valide; les actes à terme ou sous condition; les effets d'un acte juridique contraire à la loi, aux bonnes moeurs ou à l'ordre public; la conversion et la nullité partielle; les vices de consentement; les actes en fraude des droits des créanciers; la ratification et la confirmation. En deuxième lieu, la procuration, qui forme dans le droit actuel une partie confuse des règles concernant le mandat, a trouvé ici une expression unifiée (à l'exception de quelques règles spécifiques concernant la faculté d'agir au nom d'une personne morale).

Le deuxième principe pose que l'on doit traiter de façon équivalente les choses corporelles et incorporelles et que, partant, les règles applicables aux deux catégories à la fois doivent être regroupées dans le même Livre. Ainsi, ont été placées au Livre troisième un grand nombre de matières traitées depuis le droit romain comme partie du droit des biens: le transfert des choses corporelles et incorporelles; la possession; la communauté; les droits réels pouvant porter des choses corporelles aussi bien qu'incorporelles, à savoir l'usufruit, le gage et l'hypothèque; les privilèges et le droit de rétention; enfin, les définitions générales des biens et des choses, des fruits, des composantes de choses, des droits démembrés et autres, de même que les régimes généraux afférents comme celui des registres publics pour les biens immobiliers immatriculés.

Il convient de faire deux autres observations. En premier lieu, un titre entier, le Titre sixième - *De l'administration du bien d'autrui*, sera consacré à l'administration fiduciaire. Il faut se rappeler que l'institution du *trust* est inconnue en droit néerlandais. En pratique, plusieurs formes de *fiducia cum amico* visant le même but ont été élaborées. Mais la fiducie n'étant pas compatible avec la conception civiliste de la propriété, elle a été supprimée dans le nouveau Code. À sa place ont été créées d'amples possibilités d'administration fiduciaire. Le titre en question entrera en vigueur en même temps que le droit des successions et a pour cette raison été omis de la présente traduction.

Une autre nouveauté du Livre troisième est un ensemble de dispositions générales relatives aux actions en justice. Elles touchent entre autres la faculté de demander un jugement à l'encontre d'une personne tenue d'accomplir une obligation au profit du demandeur; des règles concernant l'exécution en nature; la règle voulant que le jugement puisse tenir lieu de l'acte auquel le défendeur était tenu de prêter son concours; la prescription des actions.

12. *Livre quatrième. Du droit des successions.* Dans le Code civil français, le droit des successions est traité comme un mode d'acquisition de la propriété et est placé pour cette raison dans le Livre troisième. Ce point de vue a également été adopté dans l'ancien Code civil néerlandais (art. 639), ce qui explique sa place au Livre deuxième portant sur le

droit des biens. Le nouveau Code civil néerlandais abandonne cette conception considérée comme incomplète. La succession concerne certes les choses, mais aussi les autres droits réels, la possession, les droits personnels les droits de propriété intellectuelle ou industrielle de même que les obligations. Le droit des successions touche le patrimoine du défunt dans son ensemble. Pour cette raison, il doit faire l'objet d'un Livre distinct (le Livre quatrième) se situant entre le droit patrimonial en général (Livre troisième) et les Livres portant sur les diverses espèces de droits subjectifs patrimoniaux. Ces droits sont arrangés suivant leur objet: les droits sur les choses corporelles, les droits personnels et - d'après la conception initiale de Meijers - les droits sur les produits de l'esprit (traditionnellement appelés droits de propriété intellectuelle ou industrielle).

13. *Livre cinquième. Des droits réels.* La première de ces catégories fait l'objet du Livre cinquième: les droits sur les choses corporelles et les droits in rem. Ce Livre traite des choses mobilières et immobilières, des servitudes imposées par la loi ou créées par convention et d'autres droits *in rem* provenant de l'ancien droit néerlandais qui sont inconnus dans le Code civil français. Comme il a été mentionné plus haut, certains droits *in rem* qui ne portent pas exclusivement sur des choses corporelles ont été transférés au Livre troisième. Ils portent le nom «droits démembrés»; les droits *in rem* du Livre cinquième en sont des espèces.

14. *Livre sixième. Le droit des obligations (partie générale).* Le droit des obligations fait l'objet des Livres sixième, septième et (en grande partie) huitième. Le Livre sixième en contient la «partie générale». Il comporte cinq titres. Le premier, «Des obligations en général», s'applique à toute obligation, quelle qu'en soit la source. Bon nombre de ces dispositions sont neuves, comme les règles générales portant sur les obligations naturelles, la plupart des dispositions relatives aux obligations solidaires et à la pluralité des créanciers, le chapitre distinct sur le défaut du créancier et les chapitres sur l'exécution des obligations et sur les effets du manquement à leur exécution. Il convient de relever également le chapitre portant sur la réparation du dommage, qui s'applique à la responsabilité contractuelle aussi bien qu'extra-contractuelle et qui a permis d'harmoniser bon nombre des effets de l'inexécution - dans le domaine contractuel - et de l'acte illicite - dans le domaine extra-contractuel. Ce titre comporte en outre un chapitre consacré à l'obligation de payer une somme d'argent, réaffirmant le principe du nominalisme, réglant le transfert en monnaie scripturale (*giro*), prévoyant le taux d'intérêt légal pour le défaut de payer une somme d'argent et aménageant le régime des dettes libellées en monnaie étrangère.

Le titre deuxième, *De la transmission des créances et des dettes et de l'abandon des créances*, comporte également de nombreuses innovations, notamment en matière de subrogation, des effets du transfert des créances et de la reprise de dettes et de contrats. Le titre troisième porte exclusivement sur l'acte illicite; les innovations remarquables qu'il comporte feront l'objet d'une discussion ci-après. Le titre quatrième énonce les règles relatives aux obligations de source autre que l'acte illicite ou le contrat, à savoir la gestion d'affaire, le paiement de l'indu et l'action générale en enrichissement injustifié.

Le titre cinquième, enfin, est consacré aux principes généraux des contrats. Parmi les nombreuses dispositions nouvelles de ce titre, il convient de mentionner les dispositions relatives aux matières suivantes: les conditions générales, prévoyant dans quelle mesure une partie contractante est liée par les conditions générales - formulées par l'autre partie et habituellement déposées à un endroit accessible au public - dont elle ne connaissait pas le contenu au moment de conclure le contrat; le contrôle judiciaire des conditions générales déraisonnables; la formation des contrats; les effets à l'égard de tiers de stipulations portant sur des biens immatriculés; la bonne foi; l'inexécution du contrat à la suite de circonstances imprévues.

Bien que plus de la moitié du Livre sixième traite de questions sur lesquelles l'ancien Code est silencieux, sa taille est à peine plus importante que les quatre titres qu'il est appelé à remplacer. Le nombre d'articles est même plus réduit. Malgré la grande souplesse du droit des obligations, cette branche du droit était sans doute parmi les parties les plus désuètes du droit codifié néerlandais.

15. *Livre septième. Des contrats particuliers.* Les contrats nommés sont regroupés en trois ensembles: (1) les contrats emportant transfert d'une chose (vente, échange, prêt de consommation, donation) ou en concédant l'usage (louage de choses, prêt à usage); (2) les contrats relatifs aux activités entreprises par une personne pour le compte d'une autre (mandat, contrat d'édition, dépôt, contrat de travail, convention collective de travail, contrat d'entreprise, société civile); (3) autres contrats (cautionnement, transaction (*vaststellingsovereenkomst*), effets de commerce, contrats aléatoires, dont l'assurance). Conformément à l'intention de Meijers de réunir en un seul Code l'ensemble du droit privé, plus contrats faisant actuellement l'objet d'une législation particulière (bail rural, convention collective de travail) trouveront leur place au Livre septième. En outre, une partie du Code de commerce sera transférée au Livre septième[5]. En dernier lieu, on trouvera au Livre septième plusieurs «nouveaux» contrats, à savoir le contrat d'édition et le contrat de transaction, dont l'ancien Code ne traite qu'un cas particulier.

Quatre titres seulement entreront en vigueur en même temps que les Livres 3, 5 et 6, à savoir ceux portant sur la vente et l'échange, sur le mandat, sur le dépôt et sur le cautionnement. Ces contrats font pour cette raison partie de la présente traduction.

16. *Livre huitième. Le droit des transports.* Ce Livre énonce non seulement le droit maritime et le droit de la navigation intérieure qui se trouvent dans le Code de commerce actuel, mais aussi le droit du transport routier et aérien. Il convient de mentionner des innovations au chapitre des dispositions générales du contrat de transport, y compris le contrat de voyage et le contrat de déménagement.

17. *Le droit de la propriété intellectuelle et industrielle.* À l'origine il était prévu de consacrer un livre entier du nouveau Code (le Livre neuvième) à la troisième catégorie de droits subjectifs patrimoniaux: les droits sur les *produits de l'esprit.* Les lois régissant ces matières - à l'époque, le brevet d'invention, la marque de commerce, le droit d'auteur, le nom commercial - devraient être divisées. Les dispositions à caractère civil devraient trouver une place au Livre neuvième du Code civil, celles qui avaient un caractère administratif, pénal ou de procédure, ailleurs.

Depuis lors, la situation de ces droits a considérablement évolué. L'unification du droit des brevets en Europe est en préparation et a été réalisée pour partie. Pour ce qui concerne les marques de commerce, une loi uniforme a été votée et mise en application dans les pays du Benelux; il en est de même pour les dessins industriels et les modèles.

Il ne peut évidemment être question de découper ces lois uniformes, comme il était prévu à l'origine pour les lois nationales. Il ne serait pas non plus élégant d'intégrer ces lois au Livre neuvième, puisqu'elles comportent plus que du droit privé seulement. Cela entraînerait le désavantage supplémentaire que les articles ne porteraient pas le même numéro au Livre neuvième du Code et dans la loi uniforme. En outre, ces lois comportent leurs propres dispositions relatives au transfert, à la mise en gage et autres questions semblables, qui sont difficilement compatibles avec le système du nouveau Code. La simplification envisagée de ces droits et leur intégration avec l'ensemble du droit civil codifié paraissaient donc hors de portée. Pour cette raison, il est peu probable que le Livre neuvième sera rédigé tel qu'il fut envisagé à l'origine. Comme il serait, en outre, peu approprié de proposer un Livre neuvième tronqué, limité aux seuls droit d'auteur et droit du nom commercial, le sort de ce Livre paraît réglé. Une décision officielle n'a cependant pas été prise.

18. *Le titre préliminaire.* Une autre partie du Code prévue à l'origine mais abandonnée par la suite est le titre préliminaire. Les neuf articles prévus à ce titre étaient

---

5 Voir le paragraphe 3.

repartis en deux groupes. Les articles du premier groupe réglaient l'ordre de priorité qu'il faut accorder aux différentes sources du droit: loi, coutume, équité. Il était prévu, par exemple, que le droit supplétif, mais non le droit impératif, pouvait être écarté par la coutume ou l'équité. Ces dispositions, sévèrement critiquées, ont été supprimée, ce qui relègue le problème aux tribunaux.

Le deuxième groupe de dispositions du titre préliminaire concernait les droits subjectifs, en particulier la doctrine de l'abus de ces droits. Ces dispositions ont été transférées au titre premier du Livre troisième. En conséquence, le titre préliminaire a été supprimé en entier.

19. *Conclusion.* Le survol du nouveau Code civil néerlandais démontre sa structure générale, rigoureusement suivie, parfois à plusieurs niveaux, de règles générales précédant des règles plus détaillées. Cette structure est particulièrement évidente en matière contractuelle, où les règles se trouvent non seulement dans les chapitres pertinents des Livres septième et huitième, mais aussi dans le Livre troisième - par exemple les actes de volonté et leurs défauts - et dans le Livre sixième, titre premier (*Des obligations en général*) et titre cinquième (*Des contrats en général*). De même, le droit des biens comporte des dispositions à deux ou trois niveaux au sein des Livres troisième et cinquième, et il en est également ainsi pour le droit des successions aux Livres troisième et quatrième. Le nouveau Code civil néerlandais ressemble en cela au *Bürgerliches Gesetzbuch (BGB*, le Code civil allemand), bien qu'avec la nuance essentielle que la partie générale du BGB s'adresse à l'ensemble du Code, alors que la partie générale du nouveau Code néerlandais porte sur le droit patrimonial seulement.

Une autre caractéristique du système du Code néerlandais mérite d'être soulignée. C'est que l'on trouve, à la fin de nombreux chapitres ou sections, une disposition enjoignant les tribunaux à appliquer, si possible, les règles qui précèdent aux cas non spécifiquement régis par elles. Les règles du contrat en général sont ainsi déclarées applicables aux autres actes juridiques multilatéraux à caractère patrimonial, tels ceux par lesquels est établie une servitude ou est opérée la répartition d'une succession (article 216 du Livre sixième). Parfois, l'extension envisagée dépasse les limites du droit des biens et des obligations, comme c'est le cas de l'article 59 du Livre troisième en matière d'actes juridiques. Au premier abord, ces dispositions paraissent contredire la structure générale évoquée en début de paragraphe; en réalité, elles remplissent une fonction comparable, celle d'esquisser une partie générale dans les cas où il n'est pas possible ou à-propos de la formuler proprement. En cela, le nouveau Code néerlandais suit l'exemple de l'article 7 du Code civil suisse, de l'article 1324 du Code civil italien et de l'article 876 du Code civil autrichien.

III. LE CONTENU DU NOUVEAU CODE

20. Le mandat conféré au professeur Meijers en 1947 était bref: «Rédiger un nouveau Code civil». Cette formule devait permettre la plus grande latitude possible de modifier le droit en vigueur et de mettre à jour le Code. Il est évident cependant que le nouveau Code civil ne devait pas modifier fondamentalement le droit existant tel qu'il a été formé par la législation et la jurisprudence. En revanche, la révision ne devait être entendue comme une simple refonte visant à supprimer les dispositions superflues ou désuètes et à codifier le droit créé par la jurisprudence et par des lois particulières. Les sections précédentes ont bien montré que Meijers ne concevait pas les composantes d'un nouveau Code de façon si limitée. Il demeure à démontrer à l'aide de quelques exemples que le contenu aussi a fait l'objet d'innovations importantes et intéressantes. L'exposé se limitera au droit patrimonial, en particulier au droit des obligations, et devra, pour des raisons évidentes, être relativement bref.

21. Dans le *Livre troisième*, la première innovation à signaler est la protection accordée aux articles 24 et 26 à celui qui a acquis un immeuble d'un vendeur n'ayant pas le pouvoir de l'aliéner. Si le vice est constitué d'un fait susceptible d'inscription sur les registres des immeubles, mais que l'inscription n'ait pas été effectuée, l'acquéreur obtient plein titre, à la condition qu'il ne connaissait pas le vice. Cette protection est également accordée à l'acquéreur qui s'est fié à une inscription inexacte que le propriétaire n'a pas corrigée alors qu'il pouvait le faire. En outre, même si l'on a maintenu le principe voulant que le transfert d'une chose requiert un titre valide, l'absence de titre ne peut être opposée au tiers acquéreur de bonne foi (article 88).

S'agissant de l'acquisition de meubles, la règle «en fait de meubles, possession vaut titre», reprise dans le Code civil néerlandais à l'instar du Code français, a été interprétée par la plus haute instance judiciaire des Pays-Bas dans le sens que, en acquérant, de bonne foi et à titre onéreux, une chose d'une personne qui n'en est pas propriétaire, on en obtient plein titre. La règle a été reprise à l'article 86 du Livre troisième, mais sous réserve de plusieurs modifications significatives. Elle s'applique aux choses perdues aussi bien qu'aux choses volées, à la condition, quant à ces dernières, que l'acquéreur soit un consommateur qui les a acquises dans le cours du commerce ordinaire du vendeur.

L'acte juridique requiert la présence d'une volonté et son expression. S'il y a écart entre la volonté et l'expression sans que l'autre partie puisse s'en rendre compte, l'acte est valide. Si l'expression, explicite ou non, crée l'apparence de l'existence - ou de l'absence - d'un rapport juridique, le tiers qui de bonne foi agit en se fiant à cette apparence est protégé[6].

Aux vices de consentement classiques, soit la crainte, le dol, l'erreur, un quatrième a été ajouté, «l'abus tiré des circonstances». Pour que se produise ce vice, la perte financière n'est pas nécessaire; les circonstances pouvant donner lieu à ce vice sont énumérées - non limitativement - au quatrième paragraphe de l'article 44 du Livre troisième: la nécessité, la dépendance, la légèreté, l'état mental anormal, l'inexpérience. Ces exemples démontrent que les circonstances visées dont on a tiré profit englobent non seulement les cas de nécessité économique ou de fait, mais aussi l'état mental de la victime.

Le nouveau titre sixième du Livre troisième, portant sur l'administration du bien d'autrui, en remplacement de l'institution de la *fiducia cum amico*, a été mentionné au paragraphe 11. En fait l'article 84 interdit, en son troisième paragraphe, tout titre de fiducie. Cette interdiction touche aussi la *fiducia cum creditore* (transfert à titre de sûreté), élaborée par la jurisprudence néerlandaise suivant le modèle du droit allemand. Cette forme de fiducie a été remplacée par le gage sans dépossession, prévu aux articles 237 et 239 du Livre troisième et régi par les principes généraux du gage. Cette institution présente cependant quelques traits montrant qu'il s'agit d'un droit plus faible que le gage avec dépossession. Si le débiteur n'est pas propriétaire de la chose mise en gage ou si celle-ci est déjà grevée de droits démembrés, le créancier qui permet qu'elle demeure en la possession du débiteur n'acquiert un droit valide de gage qu'au moment où il en obtient lui-même la possession, pourvu cependant qu'il se fie de bonne foi au pouvoir du débiteur à ce moment-là[7].

22. Le *droit des successions (Livre quatrième)* a fait l'objet de débats intenses depuis des années. La tendance générale est de renforcer la position du conjoint survivant au détriment des enfants et en dépit de leur portion légitime. L'ancien Code prévoit que le conjoint est héritier au même titre que les enfants, mais sans portion légitime. Il se révèle extrêmement délicat de trouver un compromis entre la règle de l'ancien Code et la position des défenseurs du conjoint survivant, dont bon nombre soutiennent même que le conjoint survivant soit institué seul héritier et puisse réclamer l'ensemble de la succession si cela est nécessaire pour son entretien. En 1981, le gouvernement néerlandais a proposé, sur la foi

6 Art. 33, 35 et 36 du Livre sixième.
7 Art. 283 du Livre sixième.

d'un compromis entre le ministre de la Justice et la Commission juridique du Parlement, d'accorder de plein droit au conjoint survivant un usufruit sur la succession qui comporte - en principe - le pouvoir de disposer et qui a préséance sur la portion légitime des enfants. En outre, cette portion devrait être transformée d'un droit de propriété en une créance pécuniaire. Si le testateur, dans sa dernière volonté, exclut les droits du conjoint survivant, ce dernier peut néanmoins réclamer l'usufruit de la succession dans la mesure où cela est nécessaire pour son entretien. Il s'est révélé impossible d'entériner cette solution en même temps que les Livres qui font l'objet de la présente traduction, et le Livre quatrième entrera donc en vigueur à une date ultérieure.

23. Les dispositions relatives aux *biens réels* (au sens restreint adopté au paragraphe 13) seront également modernisées. Il convient de mentionner à cet égard, au Livre cinquième, les règles relatives aux biens perdus, au titre deuxième, une disposition accordant à l'État la propriété de la mer territoriale, à l'article 25, et plusieurs extensions du concept de servitudes, au titre sixième.

24. L'un des traits les plus importants du *Livre sixième* (*Partie générale du droit des obligations*) concerne le rôle de la bonne foi dans les rapports juridiques. Dès l'article 2 du Livre sixième est énoncé le principe que la bonne foi, renommée «les critères de raison et d'équité» dans le droit des obligations, est susceptible non seulement de suppléer aux obligations résultant du contrat ou d'autres sources, mais aussi de les éteindre ou d'en exclure l'application. L'article porte, en son premier paragraphe, que «le créancier et le débiteur sont tenus de se comporter l'un envers l'autre suivant les exigences de raison et d'équité» et le paragraphe 2 y ajoute que «la règle à laquelle leur rapport est soumis en vertu de la loi, de l'usage ou d'un acte juridique ne s'applique pas dans la mesure où, en la circonstance, cela serait inacceptable d'après des critères de raison et d'équité». Cette disposition est appelée à régir toute obligation, alors que dans l'ancien Code, à l'article 1374, paragraphe 3, qui suit en cela l'article 1134, du Code civil français, la portée de la bonne foi est restreinte aux obligations résultant du contrat. La disposition de l'ancien Code ne confère à la bonne foi que la première fonction, «extensive», et la non la fonction «restrictive» que prévoit en outre le nouveau Code. Le nouveau Code suit ici la jurisprudence, qui a adopté le principe de la bonne foi en ce sens restrictif principalement - mais non exclusivement - pour les cas du créancier qui, par son propre acte ou omission, ne peut plus, de bonne foi, faire valoir sa créance contre le débiteur.

L'effet de la bonne foi dans les contrats fait l'objet de plusieurs articles dans la section traitant des effets juridiques des contrats. Le principe de l'article 2 du Livre sixième est particularisé pour les contrats à l'article 248 et est déclaré applicable par analogie à tout autre acte juridique multilatéral à caractère patrimonial à l'article 216[8].

Le principe de la bonne foi se trouve également en matière d'imprévision, à l'article 258 du Livre sixième. La première phrase de cet article se lit ainsi: «Le juge peut, à la demande de l'une des parties, modifier les effets du contrat ou le résoudre ou résilier en tout ou en partie en raison de circonstances imprévues d'une nature telle que, d'après des critères de raison et d'équité, l'autre partie ne peut s'attendre au maintien intégral du contrat». Des dispositions analogues ont été formulées en matière de legs et de servitudes. Il convient de noter que le terme «circonstances imprévues» ne doit pas s'entendre littéralement. Le critère n'est pas ce que les parties ont prévu ou pouvaient prévoir, mais la question de savoir si le contrat comporte des précisions suffisantes visant à régler des éventualités ultérieures.

25. Le droit des obligations naturelles est énoncé aux articles 3 à 5 du Livre sixième.

[8] Voir aussi le paragraphe 19 ci-dessus.

Les obligations solidaires, prévues aux articles 6 et suivants, auront une importance accrue à l'avenir, puisque la section en question s'appliquera à tous les cas où plusieurs personnes sont tenues de réparer le même dommage[9].

Les droits de suspension sont reconnus non seulement dans tous les cas d'obligations réciproques résultant d'un contrat mais également dans tout autre cas où la suspension de la prestation se justifie en considération du rapport entre les obligations[10]. La position du créancier qui a droit de suspendre la remise du bien appartenant à son cocontractant (droit de rétention) est considérablement renforcée, dans les situations de faillite comme dans les autres cas[11].

Une section nouvelle est consacrée au défaut du créancier[12].

Les effets de l'inexécution des obligations sont réglés aux articles 74 à 94 du Livre sixième. Le débiteur est responsable non seulement de sa faute, mais aussi de circonstances qui lui incombent «suivant l'opinion généralement admise»[13]. Le droit impose une responsabilité sans égard à la faute pour les personnes et les choses employées dans l'exécution de l'obligation. L'obligation de payer des dommages-intérêts naît dès lors que l'exécution conforme de l'obligation se révèle impossible. Dans les autres cas[14], le débiteur doit être mis en demeure d'exécuter, qu'il ait mal exécuté ou n'ait pas exécuté du tout[15]. La mise en demeure est également une condition de l'exercice de la faculté de résolution ou de résiliation, prévue à l'article 265 du Livre sixième.

Le débiteur en demeure a en principe la faculté de la purger, pourvu qu'il offre de payer les dommages-intérêts et les frais courus[16]. Il peut en outre sommer le créancier d'indiquer lequel de ses droits (à l'exécution, à la réparation du dommage, à la résiliation) il entend exercer; le créancier qui ne répond pas en temps opportun à cette sommation ne conserve que le droit de demander réparation du dommage.

Une peine stipulée peut être réduite par le tribunal si l'équité l'exige, mais ne peut l'être en deça des dommages-intérêts prévus par la loi. Si la peine a été stipulée en remplacement des dommages-intérêts prévus par la loi, le tribunal a néanmoins le pouvoir d'accorder des dommages supplémentaires si l'équité l'exige[17].

26. La section concernant la réparation du dommage, soit les articles 95 à 110 du Livre sixième, s'applique à la responsabilité contractuelle et extra-contractuelle également. Elle comporte plusieurs règles nouvelles, dont celle, prévue à l'article 98, qui porte sur la nature du lien causal entre l'événement qui est source de la responsabilité et le dommage, ainsi que celles des articles 106 et 108, toutes les deux plutôt restrictives, sur le dommage moral (immatériel) et sur la responsabilité dans le cas du décès de la victime.

La section se termine par deux articles intéressants. L'article 109 accorde aux tribunaux le pouvoir de réduire une obligation de payer des dommages au motif qu'«une réparation intégrale entraînerait des conséquences manifestement inacceptables». Parmi les facteurs devant être pris en considération sont la nature de la responsabilité (par exemple, pour faute ou pour risque), le rapport entre parties et leurs situations financières respectives. Ce pouvoir de réduction n'existe pas si la responsabilité du débiteur faisait l'objet d'une assurance ou devait l'être.

L'article 110 autorise le gouvernement à limiter certaines formes de responsabilité par décret, en vue de rendre possible leur assurance.

---

9 Voir aussi l'article 102 du Livre sixième.

10 Voir articles 52 à 56 et 262 à 264 du Livre sixième.

11 Voir article 290 à 295 du Livre sixième.

12 Article 58 à 73 du Livre sixième.

13 Article 75 du Livre sixième.

14 Sauf les hypothèses de la demeure sans mise en demeure, prévues à l'article 83 du Livre sixième.

15 Voir l'article 82 du Livre sixième.

16 Article 86 du Livre sizième.

17 Article 94 du Livre sixième.

27. La section onzième, *Des obligations portant sur le paiement d'une somme d'argent*[18], traite des virements scripturaux (*giro*)[19], de l'intérêt légal en cas de défaut de payer une somme d'argent et des dettes libellées en monnaie étrangère.

Le deuxième titre du Livre sixième, *De la transmission des créances et des dettes et de la renonciation aux créances*, comporte des innovations en matière de subrogation, des effets de la transmission de créances et de la reprise de dettes et de contrats.

28. Le *droit de la responsabilité civile extracontractuelle* (l'acte illicite) fait l'objet du titre troisième du Livre sixième[20]. Actuellement ce droit est contenu dans quelques dispositions empruntées au Code civil français, qui ont fait l'objet de vastes développements jurisprudentiels. Conformément aux développements dans de nombreux pays, les modifications proposées en cette matière dans le nouveau Code civil néerlandais consistent à remplacer, dans de nombreux cas, la responsabilité basée sur la faute par celle qui est basée sur le risque. Celle-ci n'était pas inconnue dans le droit antérieur, mais se limitait aux cas de la responsabilité résultant des actes de préposés, de la ruine des bâtiments ou encore de l'usage de navires ou d'automobiles (avec des restrictions importantes). Il y avait en outre des cas de présomption réfragable de faute; les parents étaient ainsi responsables des actes commis par leurs enfants mineurs, à moins qu'ils n'établissent qu'on ne pouvait leur imputer l'omission de prendre, en vue de prévenir les pertes occasionnées aux tiers, les mesures de précaution normalement requises en la circonstance. Contrairement à la jurisprudence française et belge, les tribunaux néerlandais n'ont pas lu en l'article 1403, paragraphe premier, qui est l'équivalent de l'article 1384, paragraphe premier, une responsabilité sans égard à la faute ni une présomption de faute.

Par opposition au droit antérieur, le nouveau Code prévoit, aux articles 173 à 183, la responsabilité sans égard à la faute pour les choses. En principe, cette règle s'applique à toutes les choses, qu'elles soient «dangereuses» ou non, sous réserve de la restriction, empruntée au droit belge, que le dommage soit causé par un vice inhérent de la chose. Étant donné que cette restriction ne conviendrait aux substances dangereuses - celles où le danger fait partie des caractéristiques de la chose - une règle spéciale concernant ces substance sera ajoutée à la règle générale. Il y a en outre des articles concernant les animaux et les bâtiments qui particularisent pour ces choses la règle générale. La section ne traite pas de véhicules automobiles, de navires ou d'aéronefs. La responsabilité pour ces choses sera réglée au Livre huitième (Droit des transports). Les dispositions en matière de responsabilité du fait des produits, aux articles 185 à 193, se conforment à la directive adoptée sur le sujet par le Conseil des Communautés européennes.

La personne responsable est le possesseur de la chose. La raison est pratique: il peut être facilement retracé par la personne ayant subi le préjudice et ce sera normalement lui qui souscrit une assurance pour le dommage causé par la chose. Cette règle souffre cependant des exceptions, dont la principale est presque aussi importante que la règle elle-même. Si les choses sont employées dans le cadre d'une entreprise ou activité professionnelle, l'article 181 porte que la responsabilité incombe à la personne engagée dans cette entreprise ou activité professionnelle. Si, par exemple, l'explosion dans une usine cause une blessure à un tiers, celui-ci sera souvent incapable d'établir quelle chose ou substance a causé le dommage. Il incombe alors à la direction de l'entreprise de souscrire une assurance pour l'ensemble de ses activités, sans égard à la propriété des choses ou substances employées et à la question de savoir si le dommage est causé par la chose elle-même ou par un employé oeuvrant à l'usine.

Pour les mêmes raisons, le nouveau Code, à l'article 170, élargit la responsabilité du commettant pour les actes des préposés et introduit, à l'article 171, un nouveau cas de responsabilité du maître de l'ouvrage, sans égard à la faute, pour les faits d'entrepreneurs indépendants, aux services desquels il a eu recours dans le cadre de son entreprise.

---

[18] Articles 111 à 126 du Livre sixième.

[19] Article 114, à comparer avec l'article 46 du Livre sixième.

[20] Articles 162 et suivants.

S'agissant de la responsabilité pour ses propres actes, le nouveau Code civil néerlandais, en son article 162, paragraphe 3, conserve le principe de la faute. Il y a cependant des exceptions importantes: l'incapacité mentale ou physique n'empêchera plus désormais l'imputation de la responsabilité pour un acte illicite[21]; en revanche, les enfants ayant moins de 14 ans ont été entièrement exemptés de cette responsabilité[22], mais leurs parents le seront pour eux sans égard à leur propre faute[23].

Ce qui précède ne constitue qu'un aperçu du nouveau régime très vaste et riche en détails de la responsabilité délictuelle. Il convient de mentionner en terminant le pouvoir accordé au gouvernement de fixer par décret le plafond de la responsabilité (notamment pour risque)[24] et le pouvoir, accordé aux tribunaux à l'article 168 du Livre sixième, de refuser de prononcer une injonction interdisant un acte illicite, par exemple interdisant les troubles créés par une usine, en raison des «intérêts pressants de la société».

29. Le droit néerlandais actuel n'admet pas l'action pour enrichissement injustifié. Telle a été la position adoptée par la juridiction suprême du pays, contrairement à ses homologues en France et en Belgique. En vue de se mettre au pas avec ces pays et avec des codifications plus récentes ailleurs, en Allemagne, en Suisse et en Italie notamment, une nouvelle règle générale est prévue à l'article 212 du Livre sixième: «Celui qui a été enrichi injustement aux dépens d'autrui doit, dans la mesure où cela est convenable, réparer le dommage de celui-ci jusqu'à concurrence de son enrichissement». La précision «dans la mesure où cela est convenable» vise à exclure entre autres le cas de la restitution d'un enrichissement imposé à une personne sans son consentement.

30. Le cinquième et dernier titre du Livre sixième porte sur les contrats en général. La nouveauté la plus intéressante est la section traitant des conditions générales[25], sujet sur lequel l'ancien Code demeure silencieux. Les conditions générales sont des clauses régulièrement employées par l'une des parties à un contrat. La disposition centrale de la nouvelle section, l'article 233, prévoit que les conditions anormalement onéreuses sont annulables. Suivent, aux articles 236 à 238, une trentaine de clauses qui, employées dans des contrats conclus avec des consommateurs, sont réputées ou présumées avoir ce caractère. La section prévoit en outre, aux articles 240 à 243, la faculté pour des organisations représentant des consommateurs ou des milieux des affaires de demander une décision de la cour pour s'opposer à une clause anormalement onéreuse.

Le Code établit une distinction entre les conditions générales (*algemene voorwaarden*) et le règlement-cadre (*standaardregeling*). Le règlement-cadre comporte un ensemble de dispositions qui s'appliquent de plein droit à un contrat d'un certain type, sauf dérogation par les parties dans les cas où elle est permise. L'article 214 prévoit que les règlements-cadre seront rédigés par des commissions nommées par le ministre de la Justice et qu'ils seront sujets à l'approbation du gouvernment. Une loi particulière déterminera la composition des commissions; les membres seront choisis principalement dans les milieux des affaires et des consommateurs concernés.

S'agissant de la formation des contrats, le titre cinquième s'inspire en partie des principes de la Convention de La Haye de 1964, portant loi uniforme sur la formation des contrats de vente internationale des objets mobiliers corporels. La disposition sur l'erreur, à l'article 228, est cependant inspirée du concept de *misrepresentation* de la common law.

Les règles au sujet de la bonne foi et de l'imprévision, qui paraissent à la troisième section, ont déjà été évoquées au paragraphe 24. Cette section traite en outre des effets des contrats à l'égard de tiers, par exemple des personnes qui acquièrent une chose à laquelle

---

21 Article 165 du Livre sixième, qui doit être mis en rapport avec l'article 489, paragraphe 2, du Code civil français.

22 Article 164 du Livre sixième.

23 Article 169 du Livre sixième.

24 Voir le paragraphe 26.

25 Articles 231 à 247 du Livre sixième.

un droit ou une obligation est attaché. Pour ce qui touche le sujet relié de la stipulation pour autrui, il y a une nouvelle disposition, à l'article 257, prévoyant que lorsque l'employeur est exempt de la responsabilité pour les actes illicites de son employé, ce dernier peut se prévaloir de la même exemption à l'encontre du tiers qui le poursuit en réparation du dommage.

Il convient de mentionner, en dernier lieu, les dispositions des articles 265 à 279 en matière de résilitation des contrats synallagmatiques pour cause d'inexécution. La résiliation est possible sans égard à la question de savoir si le débiteur est tenu à la réparation du dommage ou non, l'inexécution dans ce dernier cas étant due à la force majeure. La résiliation, qu'elle soit partielle ou totale, est effectuée par simple avis écrit et ne rétroagit pas.

31. Il n'est pas possible, dans le cadre de cette introduction, de traiter en détail des différents contrats nommés du Livre septième[26]. Quatre titres seulement de ce Livre seront mis en vigueur en même temps que les Livres troisième, cinquième et sixième, en raison de leur rapport intime avec les matières traitées dans ces trois livres. Les autres titres suivront au cours de la décennie. Cette mise en vigueur par étapes pose un problème important pour ce qui touche l'intégration du droit de la consommation au nouveau Code civil, dans la mesure où des dispositions de ce droit se trouvent entre autres dans les articles sur la vente, sur le contrat de services et d'entreprise, sur le contrat d'assurance, sur le cautionnement et sur le contrat de voyage.

Il existe aux Pays-Bas une tradition d'intégrer au Code civil et au Code commercial les dispositions des lois portant protection de parties faibles sur le plan social ou économique. Cela a été fait pour le contrat de travail, en 1907, pour la vente à tempérament, en 1936, pour les agents commerciaux, en 1977, et pour un ensemble de dispositions en matière de baux résidentiels, en 1979. Le bail rural et la convention collective de travail, dont le régime est actuellement établi par des lois particulières, seront insérés au Livre septième du nouveau Code civil. Il cadre bien avec cette politique d'intégrer au Code civil les aspects privés de la protection du consommateur. On en trouve des exemples au Livre sixième, au chapitre des conditions générales[27], ainsi qu'au titre premier du Livre septième, qui traite de la vente.

Le projet de ce titre s'inspirait principalement de Convention de La Haye de 1964, portant loi uniforme sur la vente internationale des objets mobiliers corporels. Ce cadre a été maintenu mais, dans le projet soumis au Parlement, ont été ajoutées un certain nombre de dispositions en matière de vente aux consommateurs. La même approche a été adoptée dans les autres titres évoqués ci-dessus. La question centrale, du point de vue de la politique législative, concerne le nombre de dispositions impératives nécessaires pour le droit de la consommation, qui s'inscrit tout de même dans le cadre général de la section du Livre sixième portant sur des conditions générales. L'expérience, à ce jour, indique que les règles en matière de conditions générales ne permettent pas de faire l'économie de règles impératives visant à protéger la partie la plus faible au contrat.

IV. CONCLUSION

32. Le survol précédent nous a permis de mettre en évidence le nombre important de règles nouvelles dans le nouveau Code civil, qui ont pour but de répondre aux besoins d'une société moderne. Quelques tendances générales peuvent être discernées dans ces innovations. Il convient de mentionner les dispositions tendant à protéger des personnes qui ont, de bonne foi, agi sur une apparence de volonté chez un autre ou qui ont, de bonne foi, acquis un bien d'une personne qui n'en est pas propriétaire. Le critère de la raison et

[26] Voir l'énumération au paragraphe 15.
[27] Voir le paragraphe 30.

de l'équité et d'autres concepts à contenu ouvert jouent un rôle de premier plan dans le droit des obligations. La protection des parties faibles - mineurs, employés, consommateurs, victimes d'actes illicites - a été étendue. L'intérêt public a été reconnu comme élément pertinent au sein même du droit privé[28]. Une dernière tendance générale peut être observée dans l'effet cumulatif d'un certain nombre de modifications techniques en matière de nullité: elles ont pour effet de restreindre les suites de la nullité et en particulier de circonscrire les cas du problème si délicat de sa force rétroactive.

33. Les sources de ces innovations sont multiples et ne peuvent être retracées ici. Il convient cependant de noter l'important effort de droit comparé fourni par les rédacteurs du nouveau Code. Un simple coup d'oeil sur les centaines de renvois dans le commentaire accompagnant le Livre sixième suffit pour s'en convaincre. Qu'il nous soit permis de mentionner une seule statistique. Dans la traduction anglaise du Livre sixième en 1977[29], la moitié du commentaire sur le titre troisième du Livre sixième, portant sur l'acte illicite, aux pages 372 à 413, comporte 220 notes. Sur ces 220 notes, 120 comportent des renvois à la législation, la jurisprudence et la doctrine des pays suivants: l'Allemagne, la Belgique, la France, la Grèce, l'Italie, la Suisse, la Hongrie, la Grande-Bretagne, les pays scandinaves, l'Autriche, le Portugal, le Canada, les États-Unis, l'Afrique du Sud et le Japon. Il y a en outre des renvois à l'histoire du droit, lue autant à travers les auteurs, nationaux et étrangers, qu'à travers la législation.

L'apport des sources comparatives au nouveau droit civil néerlandais ne peut guère être surestimé. Pour certains, il en résulte une mutation profonde qui fait que le droit néerlandais n'appartiendra plus à la famille civiliste française, mais plutôt au groupe germanique. Il y a sans doute une part de vérité dans cette observation, pour ce qui concerne l'approche systémique, la langue abstraite et le nombre de détails techniques. Mais l'examen des innovations dont il a été fait état plus haut aboutit à une image plus nuancée, laissant place à des influences multiples. La plus importante innovation d'inspiration franco-belge est le changement dans le droit de la responsabilité civile vers une responsabilité sans égard à la faute. L'influence de la *common law* est manifeste par la réception de doctrines concernant l'erreur, la *undue influence*, l'*anticipatory breach* et la responsabilité des entrepreneurs indépendants. Quant à l'influence allemande, elle se manifeste dans les règles concernant les conditions générales et dans les règles sur la bonne foi (le critère de la raison et de l'équité) en matière contractuelle. Le nouveau Code civil doit en outre beaucoup aux lois uniformes, en particulier aux Conventions de La Haye (1964) et de Vienne (1980) en matière de vente internationale, dont l'influence s'est fait sentir non seulement dans le droit de la vente proprement dit, mais aussi dans les sections traitant de la formation et de l'inexécution des contrats dans le droit général des obligations au Livre sixième.

Kötz et Zweigert ont sans doute vu juste lorsqu'ils affirment:

> «Le nouveau *Burgerlijk Wetboek* doit-il toujours être compté comme appartenant à la tradition française? La réponse paraît douteuse. Il se fonde en tout cas, faut-il conclure à la lecture du commentaire législatif, partout sur de solides considérations comparatives; peut-être a-t-il forgé un style propre qui repose sur le *ius commune* du continent européen»[30].

---

28 Voir par exemple les articles 12 et 14 du Livre troisième et les articles 168 et 259 du Livre sixième.

29 Voir la bibliographie sommaire. Traduction d'une version antérieure, sans rapport avec la présente.

30 «Ob das neue Burgerlijk Wetboek wirklich noch der französischen Tradition zugerechnet werden kann ist sehr zweifelhaft. Jedenfalls beruht es - wie aus den Gesetzesbegründungen zu entnehmen ist - überall auf gründlichen rechtsvergleichenden Ueberlegungen, und es mag sein, dass es einem eigenen, auf kontinental-europäischem ius commune beruhenden Stil gefunden hat..» Kötz et Zweigert, *Einführung in die Rechtsvergleichung auf dem Gebiete des Privatrechts*, t. I, 1984, p. 119; traduction anglaise: Konrad Zweigert et Hein Kötz, *Introduction to comparative law*, Oxford: Clarendon Press, 1987, Second revised ed., Vol. I, p. 105.

SELECT BIBLIOGRAPHY
of the literature on the new Dutch Civil Code

BIBLIOGRAPHIE SOMMAIRE
de la doctrine sur le nouveau Code civil néerlandais

Appendix to the preceding article by / Annexe à l'article précédent de
Arthur S. Hartkamp

A. IN LANGUAGES OTHER THAN DUTCH/ EN LANGUES AUTRES QUE LE NÉERLANDAIS

E.M. Meijers, *La réforme du Code Civil néerlandais*, Verzamelde Privaatrechtelijke Opstellen (V.P.O.) I (1954) p. 150-173.

E.M. Meijers, *Case Law and Codified Systems of Private Law*, V.P.O. I p. 181-193.

E.M. Meijers, *La révision du Code Civil néerlandais*, V.P.O. I p. 194-204.

J. Dainow, *Civil Code Revision in the Netherlands: The Fifty Questions*, 5 Am. J. Comp. L. (1956) p. 595-610.

J. Dainow, *Civil Code Revision in the Netherlands: General Problems*, 17 Louisiana Law Review (1957) p. 273-293.

J. Dainow, *Civil Code Revision in the Netherlands: Some New Developments in Obligations and Property*, in XXth Century Comparative and Conflicts Law (Legal Essays in honour of Hessel E. Yntema) (1961), p. 172-189.

A. von Overbeck, Zeitschrift für Rechtsvergleichung 3 (1962), p. 190 e.v. (on Book 6 / sur le Livre sixième)

F.H. Lawson, 12 Int. and Comp. Law Quarterly (1963) p. 1071-1072. (on Book 6 / sur le Livre sixième)

Unofficial Translation of Book 6 of the Draft of a New Netherlands Civil Code, 17 Netherlands International Law Review (1970) p. 225-274, with an Introduction by H. Drion, and Notes on some general problems of terminology by F.H. Lawson.

L.F. Ganshof et Ch.J.J.M. Petit, *Nouveau Code Civil Néerlandais: Livre I. Droit des Personnes et de la Famille* (1972).

Arthur Hartkamp, *Civil Code Revision in the Netherlands: A Survey of its System and Contents, and its Influence on Dutch Legal Practice,* Louisiana Law Review 1975 (Special Issue) p. 1059-1090.

The Netherlands Civil Code. Book 6, The Law of Obligations, Draft Text and Commentary (1977) (This Book includes the Unofficial Translation and the articles of H. Drion and F.H. Lawson, mentioned above).

Fokkema/Chorus/Hondius/Lisser, *Introduction to Dutch Law for Foreign Lawyers* (1978) p. 11, 35-37, 40-41. Second edition in preparation, including chapters on the New Civil Code.

W. Snijders, *Vers un nouveau Code Civil néerlandais. État des Travaux*, Revue de Droit International et de Droit Comparé 56 (1979), p. 223-231.

Jürgen Basedow, *Grundfragen der Vertragsrechtreform. Niederländische Erfahrungen*, Zeitschrift für vergleichende Rechtswissenschaft 79 (1980) p. 132-148.

T.B. Smith, *The influence abroad of the modern Dutch movement for Code Revision*, WPNR 5503 (1980).

Arthur Hartkamp, *Responsabilité délictuelle sans faute*, in / dans: Actes du Congrès «Codification: Valeurs et Langage», tenu à Montréal, Conseil de la Langue française, 1981, p. 625-646.

Arthur Hartkamp, *Vers un nouveau Code Civil Néerlandais*, Revue internationale de droit comparé (1982), p. 319 ff.

E.H. Hondius, *Recodification of the Law in the Netherlands*, Neth. Int. Law Review 1982, p. 348 ff.

E.H. Hondius, *Neukodifikation des niederländischen Zivilrechts*, Versicherungsrecht (25 Karlsruher Forum, Jubiläumsausgabe 1983), p. 41 ff.

A.R. Bloembergen, *Schadenersatz im neuen niederländischen Zivilgesetzbuch*, Versicherungsrecht, op.cit., p. 4 ff.

Johannes Gerhart Jonas, *Die verschuldensunabhängige ausservertragliche Haftung für Sachen im Entwurf zum Nieuw Burgerlijk Wetboek der Niederlande.* Ein Beitrag zur Reform des deutschen Gefährdungshaftungsrechts (München, 1987).

B. IN DUTCH/ EN LANGUE NÉERLANDAISE

For all literature in the Dutch language see the bibliographies in / Pour toute la littérature en langue néerlandaise, voir les bibliographies dans

C.J. van Zeben & G.J.L. Seesink, *Nederlandse Wetgeving, Nieuw Burgerlijk Wetboek.*

and in / et dans

A.S. Hartkamp, *Compendium van het vermogensrecht volgens het nieuwe Burgerlijk Wetboek*, 3rd ed. / 3e éd. 1988, no. / no3a *et passim.*

The draft bills and all the official documents are published in / Les projets de loi et tous les documents officiels sont publiés dans

C.J. van Zeben (et al.), *Parlementaire Geschiedenis van het nieuwe Burgerlijk Wetboek*,

of which the following volumes have appeared / dont les volumes suivants ont été publiés:

Algemeen Deel. Voorgeschiedenis en algemene Inleiding (1961);
Boek 1 (without date/ sans date);
Boek 1, Invoeringswet (1969);
Boek 2 (without date/ sans date);
Boek 2, Invoeringswet (1977);
Boek 3 (1981);
Boek 5 (1981);
Boek 6 (1981);
Boeken 3,5 en 6, Invoeringswet (several volumes/ plusieurs tomes) (from July 1990/ à partir du mois de juillet 1990).

BOEK 3
ALGEMEEN GEDEELTE VAN HET VERBINTENISSENRECHT

BOOK 3
PATRIMONIAL LAW IN GENERAL

LIVRE TROISIÈME
DU DROIT PATRIMONIAL EN GÉNÉRAL

TITEL 1 ALGEMENE BEPALINGEN

TITLE 1 GENERAL PROVISIONS

TITRE PREMIER DISPOSITIONS GÉNÉRALES

AFDELING 1 Begripsbepalingen

Section 1 Definitions

Section première Définitions

Art. 1. (3.1.1.0) Goederen zijn alle zaken en alle vermogensrechten.

Property[1] is comprised of all things and of all patrimonial rights.

Les biens comprennent toutes les choses et tous les droits patrimoniaux.

Art. 2. (3.1.1.1) Zaken zijn de voor menselijke beheersing vatbare stoffelijke objecten.

Things are corporeal objects susceptible of human control.

Les choses sont les objets matériels susceptibles de maîtrise par l'homme.

Art. 3. (3.1.1.2) - 1. Onroerend zijn de grond, de nog niet gewonnen delfstoffen, de met de grond verenigde beplantingen, alsmede de gebouwen en werken die duurzaam met de grond zijn verenigd, hetzij rechtstreeks, hetzij door vereniging met andere gebouwen of werken.
- 2. Roerend zijn alle zaken die niet onroerend zijn.

1. The following are immoveable: land, unextracted minerals, plants attached to land, buildings and works durably united with land, either directly or through incorporation with other buildings or works.
2. All things which are not immoveable, are moveable.

1. Sont immeubles les fonds de terre, les minéraux non encore extraits, les plantations unies à la terre, ainsi que les constructions et ouvrages unis au fonds de façon durable soit directement, soit par incorporation à d'autres constructions ou ouvrages.
2. Sont meubles toutes les choses qui ne sont pas immeubles.

Art. 4. (3.1.1.3) - 1. Al hetgeen volgens verkeersopvatting onderdeel van een zaak uitmaakt, is bestanddeel van die zaak.
- 2. Een zaak die met een hoofdzaak zodanig verbonden wordt dat zij daarvan niet kan worden afgescheiden zonder dat beschadiging van betekenis wordt toegebracht aan een der zaken, wordt bestanddeel van de hoofdzaak.

1. A component part of a thing is anything which, according to common opinion, forms part of that thing.

1. Tout ce qui, d'après l'opinion généralement admise, fait partie d'une chose est composante de cette chose.

---

1 The term "property" includes both the Dutch singular ("goed") and the Dutch plural ("goederen").

2. A thing which is attached to a principal thing in such a manner that it cannot be separated therefrom without substantial damage being done to either, becomes a component part of that thing.

2. Une chose qui se rattache à une chose principale de telle façon qu'elle ne puisse en être séparée sans que l'une ou l'autre subisse un dommage substantiel devient composante de la chose principale.

Art. 5. (3.1.1.3a) Inboedel is het geheel van tot huisraad en tot stoffering en meubilering van een woning dienende roerende zaken, met uitzondering van boekerijen en verzamelingen van voorwerpen van kunst, wetenschap of geschiedkundige aard.

Household effects are all moveable things which serve as household objects, decoration or furniture in a dwelling, except collections of books or of art, and objects of a scientific or historical nature.

Le mobilier comprend l'ensemble des meubles meublants destinés à l'ameublement et à l'ornement d'un logement, à l'exception des bibliothèques et des collections d'objets d'art, de science ou de nature historique.

Art. 6. (3.1.1.5) Rechten die, hetzij afzonderlijk hetzij tezamen met een ander recht, overdraagbaar zijn, of er toe strekken de rechthebbende stoffelijk voordeel te verschaffen, ofwel verkregen zijn in ruil voor verstrekt of in het vooruitzicht gesteld stoffelijk voordeel, zijn vermogensrechten.

Patrimonial rights are those which, either separately or together with another right, are transferable; rights which are intended to procure a material benefit to their holder; or rights which have been acquired in exchange for actual or expected material benefit.

Sont patrimoniaux les droits qui sont transférables séparément ou conjointement avec un autre droit, ceux qui visent à procurer à leur titulaire un avantage matériel ou encore ceux qui ont été acquis en contrepartie d'un avantage matériel qui a déjà été fourni ou qu'on fait miroiter.

Art. 7. (3.1.1.6) Een afhankelijk recht is een recht dat aan een ander recht zodanig verbonden is, dat het niet zonder dat andere recht kan bestaan.

A dependent right[1] is one which is related to another right in such a fashion that it cannot exist independently thereof.

Est dépendant[2] le droit qui se rattache à un autre droit d'une manière telle qu'il ne peut exister sans lui.

Art. 8. (3.1.1.7) Een beperkt recht is een recht dat is afgeleid uit een meer omvattend recht, hetwelk met het beperkte recht is bezwaard.

A dismembered right is one which is derived from a more comprehensive right, the latter being encumbered with the dismembered right.

Est démembré le droit qui est tiré d'un droit plus étendu, lequel est grevé du droit démembré.

Art. 9. (3.1.1.9) - 1. Natuurlijke vruchten zijn zaken die volgens verkeersopvatting als vruchten van andere zaken worden aangemerkt.
- 2. Burgerlijke vruchten zijn rechten die volgens verkeersopvatting als vruchten van goederen worden aangemerkt.

---

[1] Examples are the rights of hypothec, pledge, servitude and suretyship. See also the related but more encompassing term "nevenrecht" (accessory right) in article 142 of Book 6.

[2] Par ex. l'hypothèque, le gage, le cautionnement, la servitude. Voir aussi, à l'art. 142 du Livre sixième, le terme «droit accessoire» (*nevenrecht*), qui englobe en outre certains droits non patrimoniaux.

- 3. De afzonderlijke termijnen van een lijfrente gelden als vruchten van het recht op de lijfrente.
- 4. Een natuurlijke vrucht wordt een zelfstandige zaak door haar afscheiding, een burgerlijke vrucht een zelfstandig recht door haar opeisbaar worden.

1. Natural fruits are things which, according to common opinion, are considered to be fruits of other things.

2. Civil fruits are rights which, according to common opinion, are considered to be fruits of property.
3. The individual arrears of life-rents are deemed to be fruits of the right to the life-rent.
4. A natural fruit which is separated from a thing becomes an independent thing; a civil fruit becomes an independent right by becoming exigible.

1. Sont fruits naturels les choses qui, d'après l'opinion généralement admise, sont considérées comme les fruits d'une autre chose.
2. Sont fruits civils les droits qui, d'après l'opinion généralement admise, sont considérés comme les fruits de biens.
3. Les versements périodiques d'une rente viagère sont réputés fruits de la rente viagère.
4. Le fruit naturel devient une chose autonome lorsqu'il est séparé de la chose dont il provient; le fruit civil devient un droit autonome lorsqu'il devient exigible.

Art. 10. (3.1.1.10) Registergoederen zijn goederen voor welker overdracht of vestiging inschrijving in daartoe bestemde openbare registers noodzakelijk is.

Registered property is property the transfer or creation of which requires entry in the public registers, provided for that purpose.

Sont biens immatriculés ceux pour le transfert ou la constitution desquels est nécessaire une inscription dans les registres publics prévus à cette fin.

Art. 11. (3.1.1.12) Goede trouw van een persoon, vereist voor enig rechtsgevolg, ontbreekt niet alleen, indien hij de feiten of het recht, waarop zijn goede trouw betrekking moet hebben, kende, maar ook indien hij ze in de gegeven omstandigheden behoorde te kennen. Onmogelijkheid van onderzoek belet niet dat degene die goede reden tot twijfel had, aangemerkt wordt als iemand die de feiten of het recht behoorde te kennen.

Where good faith of a person is required to produce a juridical effect, such person is not acting in good faith if he knew the facts or the law to which his good faith must relate or if, in the given circumstances, he should know them. Impossibility to inquire does not prevent the person, who had good reasons to be in doubt, from being considered as someone who should know the facts or the law.

Dans les cas où la bonne foi d'une personne est requise pour que se produise un effet juridique, elle fait défaut non seulement si la personne connaissait les faits ou le droit sur lesquels doit porter sa bonne foi, mais encore si, dans les circonstances, elle aurait dû les connaître. L'impossibilité de vérifier n'empêche pas que celui qui avait de bonnes raisons de douter soit assimilé à une personne devant connaître les faits ou le droit.

Art. 12. (3.1.1.13) Bij de vaststelling van wat redelijkheid en billijkheid eisen, moet rekening worden gehouden met algemeen erkende rechtsbeginselen, met de in Nederland levende rechtsovertuigingen en met de maatschappelijke en persoonlijke belangen, die bij het gegeven geval zijn betrokken.

In determining what reasonableness and equity require, reference must be made to generally accepted principles of law, to current juridical views in the Netherlands, and to the particular societal and private interests involved.

En déterminant ce que demandent la raison et l'équité, on doit tenir compte des principes de droit généralement reconnus, des conceptions du droit qui ont cours aux Pays-Bas, ainsi que des intérêts sociaux et personnels en cause.

Art. 13. (3.1.1.14) - 1. Degene aan wie een bevoegdheid toekomt, kan haar niet inroepen, voor zover hij haar misbruikt.
- 2. Een bevoegdheid kan onder meer worden misbruikt door haar uit te oefenen met geen ander doel dan een ander te schaden of met een ander doel dan waarvoor zij is verleend of in geval men, in aanmerking nemende de onevenredigheid tussen het belang bij de uitoefening en het belang dat daardoor wordt geschaad, naar redelijkheid niet tot die uitoefening had kunnen komen.
- 3. Uit de aard van een bevoegdheid kan voortvloeien dat zij niet kan worden misbruikt.

1. The holder of a right[1] may not exercise it to the extent that it is abused.

2. Instances of abuse of right are the exercise of a right with the sole intention of harming another or for a purpose other than that for which it was granted; or the exercise of a right where its holder could not reasonably have decided to exercise it, given the disproportion between the interest to exercise the right and the harm caused thereby.

3. The nature of the right can be such that it cannot be abused.

1. Le titulaire ne peut se prévaloir d'un pouvoir[2] qui lui appartient dans la mesure où l'exercice de ce pouvoir constitue un abus.

2. Un pouvoir peut être abusé, entre autres, du fait qu'on l'exerce dans le seul but de nuire à autrui ou dans un but différent de celui pour lequel il est accordé, ou encore lorsque, devant la disproportion entre l'intérêt favorisé par son exercice et l'intérêt qui s'en trouve lésé, le titulaire n'aurait pu normalement arriver à la décision de l'exercer.

3. Un pouvoir peut être tel que, de par sa nature, il est insusceptible d'abus.

Art. 14. (3.1.1.15) Een bevoegdheid die iemand krachtens het burgerlijk recht toekomt, mag niet worden uitgeoefend in strijd met geschreven of ongeschreven regels van publiekrecht.

A right which a person has pursuant to private law, may not be exercised contrary to the written or unwritten rules of public law.

Un pouvoir qui revient à quelqu'un en vertu du droit privé ne peut être exercé à l'encontre des règles écrites ou non écrites du droit public.

Art. 15. (3.1.1.16) De artikelen 11-14 vinden buiten het vermogensrecht toepassing, voor zover de aard van de rechtsbetrekking zich daartegen niet verzet.

---

1 Depending on the context, the word "bevoegdheid" has been translated either as "right" or as "power". To have "bevoegdheid" has sometimes been translated as "to be entitled to", "to be empowered to" or "to be authorized to".

2 Le terme néerlandais employé est «*bevoegdheid*», plutôt que le terme habituel plus spécifique «*recht*», qui se traduit par droit. La traduction par le terme «pouvoir» (substantif aussi bien que verbe) (de droit privé) veut exprimer ce caractère plus général.

Articles 11 - 14 apply to areas other than patrimonial law to the extent that this is not incompatible with the nature of the juridical relationship involved.

Les articles 11 à 14 s'appliquent en dehors du droit patrimonial, dans la mesure où la nature du rapport juridique ne s'y oppose pas.

AFDELING 2 Inschrijvingen betreffende registergoederen

Section 2 Entries regarding registered property

Section deuxième Des inscriptions relatives aux biens immatriculés

Art. 16. (3.1.2.1) - 1. Er worden openbare registers gehouden, waarin feiten die voor de rechtstoestand van registergoederen van belang zijn, worden ingeschreven.
- 2. Welke deze openbare registers zijn, waar en op welke wijze een inschrijving in de registers kan worden verkregen, welke stukken daartoe aan de bewaarder moeten worden aangeboden, wat deze stukken moeten inhouden, hoe de registers worden ingericht, hoe de inschrijvingen daarin geschieden, en hoe de registers kunnen worden geraadpleegd, wordt geregeld bij de wet.

1. Entries concerning the juridical status of registered property are made in public registers, kept for that purpose.
2. The law provides which public registers will be kept, the manner and place of making an entry, the kind and content of the documents to be filed with the registrar, the organization of the registers, the manner of registration and the consultation procedure.

1. Sont tenus des registres publics dans lesquels sont inscrits des faits relatifs à la situation juridique des biens immatriculés.
2. La loi prévoit quels registres publics tenir, les conditions d'inscription, le type de documents à déposer auprès du conservateur et leur contenu, l'organisation ainsi que le mode d'inscription et de consultation des registres.

Art. 17. (3.1.2.2) - 1. Behalve die feiten waarvan inschrijving krachtens andere wetsbepalingen mogelijk is, kunnen in deze registers de volgende feiten worden ingeschreven:

a. rechtshandelingen die een verandering in de rechtstoestand van registergoederen brengen of in enig ander opzicht voor die rechtstoestand van belang zijn;

b. erfopvolgingen die registergoederen betreffen, daaronder begrepen de opvolging door de Staat krachtens artikel 879, tweede lid, en de inbezitstelling krachtens artikel 1175 van het vierde Boek;

c. vervulling van de voorwaarde, gesteld in een ingeschreven voorwaardelijke rechtshandeling, en de verschijning van een onzeker tijdstip, aangeduid in de aan een ingeschreven rechtshandeling verbonden tijdsbepaling, alsmede de dood van een vruchtgebruiker van een registergoed;

d. reglementen en andere regelingen die tussen medegerechtigden in registergoederen zijn vastgesteld;

e. rechterlijke uitspraken die de rechtstoestand van registergoederen of de bevoegdheid daarover te beschikken betreffen, mits zij uitvoerbaar bij voorraad zijn of een verklaring van de griffier wordt overgelegd, dat daartegen geen gewoon rechtsmiddel meer openstaat of dat hem drie maanden na de uitspraak niet van het instellen van een gewoon

rechtsmiddel is gebleken, benevens de tegen de bovenbedoelde uitspraken ingestelde rechtsmiddelen;

f. instelling van rechtsvorderingen en indiening van verzoekschriften ter verkrijging van een rechterlijke uitspraak die de rechtstoestand van een registergoed betreft;

g. executoriale en conservatoire beslagen op registergoederen;

h. naamsveranderingen die tot registergoederen gerechtigde personen betreffen;

i. verjaring die leidt tot verkrijging van een registergoed of tenietgaan van een beperkt recht dat een registergoed is;

j. overheidsbeschikkingen en uitspraken, waarbij een krachtens een bijzondere wetsbepaling ingeschreven overheidsbeschikking wordt vernietigd, ingetrokken of gewijzigd.

- 2. Huur- en pachtovereenkomsten en andere feiten die alleen persoonlijke rechten geven of opheffen, kunnen slechts worden ingeschreven, indien een bijzondere wetsbepaling dit toestaat.

1. In addition to facts which may be registered under other statutory provisions, the following facts may be entered in public registers:

a. juridical acts which modify the juridical status of registered property or which in any other way affect it;

b. successions involving registered property, including the succession by the State pursuant to article 879, paragraph 2, and the taking of possession pursuant to article 1175 of Book 4;

c. the fulfillment of a condition in a registered conditional juridical act, the arrival of an undetermined date, indicated in a term contained in a registered juridical act, and the death of a usufructuary of registered property;

d. regulations and other rules which have been established between joint title-holders in registered property;

e. judgments affecting the juridical status of registered property or the power to dispose of such property, provided that such judgments are provisionally enforceable, or provided that a declaration of the clerk of the court that there remains no ordinary means of appeal is presented, or that three months have expired since the date of the judgment and no ordinary means of appeal has come to his attention; and appeals lodged against the aforementioned judgments;

1. Outre les faits dont l'inscription est possible en vertu d'autres dispositions de la loi, peuvent être inscrits les faits suivants:

a. Les actes juridiques qui modifient la situation juridique de biens immatriculés ou qui intéressent cette situation de quelque autre manière;

b. Les successions touchant des biens immatriculés, y compris la succession par l'État conformément à l'article 879, deuxième paragraphe, et l'envoi en possession conformément à l'article 1175 du Livre quatrième;

c. L'accomplissement d'une condition énoncée dans un acte juridique conditionnel immatriculé, l'arrivée d'une date indéterminée visée à l'acte juridique à terme qui est immatriculé, ainsi que la mort de l'usufruitier d'un bien immatriculé;

d. Les règlements et autres règles établis entre cotitulaires de droits sur des biens immatriculés;

e. Les jugements touchant la situation juridique de biens immatriculés ou le pouvoir d'en disposer, pourvu qu'ils soient susceptibles d'exécution provisoire ou que soit déposée une déclaration du greffier portant qu'aucune voie de recours n'est plus ouverte contre eux ou que, trois mois après jugement, il n'a connaissance d'aucune voie de recours contre eux; les voies de recours formées contre les jugements visés plus haut;

f. the institution of actions and the submission of petitions to obtain a judicial decision concerning the juridical status of registered property;
g. executory and conservatory seizures of registered property;
h. name changes involving persons entitled to registered property;
i. prescription resulting in the acquisition of registered property or the extinction of a dismembered right which itself qualifies as registered property;
j. decisions of a public authority and judgments which annul, repeal or modify such a decision that has been registered pursuant to a specific statutory provision.

2. Leases[1] and other facts which create or extinguish merely personal rights cannot be registered in the absence of a specific statutory provision permitting it.

f. L'exercice d'actions et la présentation de requêtes en vue d'obtenir un jugement sur la situation juridique du bien immatriculé;
g. Les saisies-exécution et les saisies conservatoires frappant des biens immatriculés;
h. Les changements de nom de titulaires de droits sur des biens immatriculés;
i. La prescription donnant lieu à l'acquisition d'un bien immatriculé ou à l'extinction d'un droit démembré qui est lui-même un bien immatriculé;
j. Les décisions d'une autorité administrative et les jugements portant annulation, retrait ou modification d'une décision de ce type, qui a été inscrite en application d'une disposition particulière de la loi.

2. Les baux[2] et autres faits qui ne créent ou n'éteignent que des droits personnels peuvent être inscrits seulement si une disposition particulière de la loi l'autorise.

Art. 18. (3.1.2.2a) Worden de bewaarder der registers stukken ter inschrijving aangeboden, dan verstrekt hij de aanbieder een bewijs van ontvangst, vermeldende de aard dier stukken alsmede dag, uur en minuut van de aanbieding.

Where documents are filed with the registrar for entry in the registers, he issues a receipt to the person filing them, indicating the nature of the documents as well as the day, hour and minute of the filing.

Lorsque des documents sont présentés au conservateur des registres pour inscription, celui-ci remet à la personne qui les présente un récépissé en indiquant la nature, ainsi que le jour, l'heure et la minute de la présentation.

Art. 19. (3.1.2.3) - 1. Bestaat bij de bewaarder der registers tegen een inschrijving geen bezwaar, dan geschiedt deze terstond na de aanbieding.
- 2. Als tijdstip van inschrijving geldt het tijdstip van aanbieding van de voor de inschrijving vereiste stukken.
- 3. Op verlangen van de aanbieder tekent de bewaarder de verrichte inschrijving op het ontvangstbewijs aan.
- 4. Indien de bewaarder vermoedt dat de in de aangeboden stukken vermelde kenmerken niet overeenstemmen met die welke met betrekking tot het registergoed behoren te worden vermeld, of dat de in te schrijven rechtshandeling door een onbevoegde is verricht of onverenigbaar is met een andere rechtshandeling, ter inschrijving waarvan hem de nodige stukken zijn aangeboden, is hij bevoegd de aanbieder en andere belanghebbenden daarop opmerkzaam te maken.

---

1 The Dutch text makes a distinction between contracts of 'huur' and of 'pacht'. The latter term only relates to leases of land (farm leases). The former covers all other forms of lease and hire.

2 Le néerlandais emploie des termes distincts pour le bail à ferme (*pacht*) et les autres types de bail (*huur*).

1. An entry in the registers is made immediately upon filing, unless the registrar objects.
2. The entry is deemed to have taken place at the time of filing of the documents required for registration.
3. Upon the demand of the person filing, the registrar notes on the receipt the entry which has been made.
4. If the registrar suspects that the characteristics mentioned in the filed documents do not correspond to those which ought to appear for the registered property in question, or if he suspects that the juridical act to be registered has been performed by a person lacking the power of disposition or is incompatible with another juridical act, for the registration of which the necessary documents have been filed with him, he may bring this to the attention of the person filing the documents and to other interested parties.

1. Lorsque le conservateur ne voit pas d'empêchement à l'inscription, celle-ci a lieu immédiatement après la présentation.
2. L'inscription est réputée avoir lieu au moment de la présentation des documents requis pour l'inscription.
3. Sur demande de la personne qui présente les documents, le conservateur note sur le récépissé l'inscription effectuée.
4. Si le conservateur soupçonne que les caractéristiques mentionnées dans les documents déposés ne correspondent pas à celles qui doivent être mentionnées pour le bien immatriculé en question, il peut attirer sur ce point l'attention de celui qui présente les documents et des autres personnes intéressées; il en va de même s'il soupçonne que l'acte juridique devant être inscrit a été accompli par une personne ne pouvant disposer du bien, ou est incompatible avec un autre acte juridique pour l'inscription duquel les documents nécessaires lui ont déjà été présentés.

Art. 20. (3.1.2.4) - 1. De bewaarder der registers weigert een inschrijving te doen, wanneer de voor een inschrijving nodige stukken niet worden aangeboden, wanneer de aangeboden stukken niet aan de wettelijke eisen voldoen of wanneer een ander wettelijk vereiste voor inschrijving niet is vervuld. Hij boekt de aanbieding in het register van voorlopige aantekeningen met vermelding van de gerezen bezwaren.
- 2. Wanneer de weigering ten onrechte is geschied, beveelt de president van de rechtbank, rechtdoende in kort geding, op vordering van de belanghebbende de bewaarder de inschrijving alsnog te verrichten, zulks onverminderd de bevoegdheid van de gewone rechter. De president kan de oproeping van door hem aan te wijzen andere belanghebbenden gelasten. Het bevel van de president is van rechtswege uitvoerbaar bij voorraad.
- 3. Wordt de geweigerde inschrijving alsnog bevolen, dan verricht de bewaarder haar terstond nadat de eiser haar opnieuw heeft verzocht.
- 4. Indien de belanghebbende binnen veertien dagen na de oorspronkelijke aanbieding aan de bewaarder een dagvaarding in kort geding ter verkrijging van het in lid 2 bedoelde bevel heeft doen uitbrengen en de aanvankelijk geweigerde inschrijving alsnog is verricht op een hernieuwde aanbieding van dezelfde stukken, gedaan binnen zeven dagen na een in eerste aanleg gegeven bevel, wordt de inschrijving geacht te zijn geschied op het tijdstip waarop de oorspronkelijke aanbieding plaatsvond. Hetzelfde geldt, indien de bewaarder op een hernieuwde aanbieding alsnog overgaat tot inschrijving binnen veertien dagen hetzij na de oorspronkelijke aanbieding, hetzij na een hem tijdig uitgebrachte dagvaarding hangende het geding in eerste aanleg.
- 5. Een feit waarvan slechts blijkt uit een overeenkomstig lid 1, tweede zin, geboekt stuk wordt geacht niet door raadpleging van de registers kenbaar te zijn, tenzij het krachtens het vorige lid geacht moet worden reeds ten tijde van de raadpleging ingeschreven te zijn geweest.

- 6. Een voorlopige aantekening wordt door de bewaarder doorgehaald, zodra hem is gebleken dat de voorwaarden voor toepassing van het vierde lid niet meer kunnen worden vervuld, of de inschrijving met inachtneming van het tijdstip van oorspronkelijke aanbieding alsnog heeft plaatsgevonden.

1. Where the documents required for an entry are not filed, or where the filed documents do not conform to statutory requirements, or where another statutory requirement for registration has not been fulfilled, the registrar shall refuse to make the entry. He enters the filing of the documents in a register of provisional notations, along with a statement of his objections.
2. Where the refusal is not justifiable, the president of the district court, acting summarily, upon the demand of the interested party, orders the registrar to make the entry without prejudice to the jurisdiction of the ordinarily competent judge. The president may order that other interested parties, designated by him, be summoned. The order of the president is, of right, provisionally enforceable.
3. The registrar shall make the refused entry forthwith, upon the renewed request of the plaintiff who has obtained such an order.
4. If, within fourteen days from the original filing of the documents, the interested party has issued a summons for a summary proceeding to obtain the order referred to in paragraph 2, and if the originally refused entry has as yet been made upon a renewed filing of the same documents within seven days from an order given in first instance, the entry is deemed to have taken place at the time of the original filing. The same applies if, upon a renewed filing, the registrar as yet proceeds to the registration within fourteen days, either from the original filing or from a summons which has been issued to him timely pending the dispute in first instance.

1. Le conservateur refuse de faire une inscription lorsque les documents nécessaires ne sont pas présentés ou que les documents présentés ne sont pas conformes aux exigences de la loi, ou encore qu'une autre condition légale d'inscription n'est pas remplie. Il porte la présentation dans le registre des notes provisoires avec mention des objections soulevées.

2. Lorsque le refus est mal fondé, le président du tribunal de première instance, statuant en référé, sur demande de la partie intéressée, ordonne au conservateur d'effectuer l'inscription, sans préjudice de la compétence de la juridiction ordinaire. Le président peut ordonner la convocation d'autres intéressés qu'il désigne. L'ordonnance du président est, de plein droit, exécutoire par provision.

3. Sur nouvelle requête fondée sur l'ordonnance, le conservateur effectue immédiatement l'inscription refusée.

4. L'inscription est censée avoir eu lieu au moment de la présentation initiale, si l'intéressé a fait délivrer au conservateur, dans les quatorze jours suivant cette présentation, une assignation en référé en vue d'obtenir l'ordonnance visée au paragraphe 2, et que l'inscription refusée initialement a été effectuée sur présentation renouvelée des mêmes documents, dans les sept jours suivant l'ordonnance en première instance. Il en est de même si le conservateur, sur une demande renouvelée, accepte d'effectuer l'inscription dans les quatorze jours de la présentation initiale ou d'une assignation qui lui a été délivrée en temps utile, pendant le litige en première instance.

5. A fact, the existence of which only appears from a provisional notation in the sense of the second sentence of paragraph 1, is deemed not to be knowable by consultation of the registers, unless, pursuant to the preceeding paragraph, it is deemed already to have been registered at the time of consultation.
6. The registrar cancels a provisional notation as soon as it is apparent that the conditions for application of paragraph 4 can no longer be complied with, or as soon as the registration has as yet taken place, taking into account the time of the original filing of the documents.

5. Le fait dont l'existence n'est constatée que par une pièce inscrite conformément au premier paragraphe, deuxième phrase, est réputé être de ceux dont on ne peut prendre connaissance par la consultation des registres, à moins que, par l'effet du paragraphe précédent, il soit censé avoir été déjà inscrit lors de la consultation.

6. Le conservateur radie la note provisoire dès qu'il a acquis la conviction que les conditions requises pour l'application du paragraphe 4 ne peuvent plus être remplies ou que l'inscription a eu lieu dans le respect du moment de la présentation initiale.

Art. 21. (3.1.2.4a) - 1. De rangorde van inschrijvingen die op een zelfde registergoed betrekking hebben, wordt bepaald door de volgorde der tijdstippen van inschrijving, tenzij uit de wet een andere rangorde voortvloeit.
- 2. Vinden twee inschrijvingen op één zelfde tijdstip plaats en zouden deze leiden tot onderling onverenigbare rechten van verschillende personen op dat goed, dan wordt de rangorde bepaald:
a. ingeval de ter inschrijving aangeboden akten op verschillende dagen zijn opgemaakt: door de volgorde van die dagen;
b. ingeval beide akten op dezelfde dag zijn opgemaakt en het notariële akten, daaronder begrepen notariële verklaringen, betreft: door de volgorde van de tijdstippen waarop ieder van die akten of verklaringen is opgemaakt.

1. The rank of entries pertaining to the same registered property is determined by the order in which they have been registered, unless a different order results from the law.
2. Where two entries are made at the same time and where they would lead to mutually incompatible rights of different persons to the same property, the rank shall be determined:
a. in the event that the deeds presented for registration have been executed on different days, by the order of those days;
b. in the event that both deeds, being notarial deeds and including notarial declarations, have been executed on the same day, by the order of the times of execution of those deeds or declarations.

1. Le rang des inscriptions se rapportant au même bien immatriculé est déterminé par l'ordre dans lequel elles ont été effectuées, à moins qu'un ordre différent ne découle de la loi.
2. Lorsque deux inscriptions ont lieu au même moment et que des personnes différentes obtiendraient de ce fait des droits incompatibles sur ce bien, le rang est déterminé:
a. Lorsque les actes présentés pour inscription ont été passés à des jours différents: par l'ordre de ces jours;
b. Lorsque les deux actes, tous deux actes notariés ou déclarations notariées, ont été rédigés le même jour: par l'ordre des moments où chacun des actes ou déclarations a été rédigé.

Art. 22. (3.1.2.5) Wanneer een feit in de registers is ingeschreven, kan daarna de geldigheid van de inschrijving niet meer worden betwist op grond

dat de formaliteiten die voor de inschrijving worden vereist, niet zijn in acht genomen.

Once a fact has been entered in the registers, the validity of the registration cannot subsequently be contested on the grounds that the formalities required for the registration have not been observed.

Lorsqu'un fait a été inscrit dans les registres, on ne peut plus contester la validité de l'inscription sur la base de l'inobservation des formalités requises pour l'inscription.

Art. 23. (3.1.2.6) Het beroep van een verkrijger van een registergoed op goede trouw wordt niet aanvaard, wanneer dit beroep insluit een beroep op onbekendheid met feiten die door raadpleging van de registers zouden zijn gekend.

An acquirer of registered property may not plead good faith if, in doing so, he would invoke his ignorance of facts which would have been known to him by consultation of the registers.

L'acquéreur d'un bien immatriculé n'est pas admis à invoquer sa bonne foi si, pour le faire, il doit se prévaloir de son ignorance de faits qu'il aurait pu connaître en consultant les registres.

Art. 24. (3.1.2.7) - 1. Indien op het tijdstip waarop een rechtshandeling tot verkrijging van een recht op een registergoed onder bijzondere titel in de registers wordt ingeschreven, een eveneens voor inschrijving in de registers vatbaar feit niet met betrekking tot dat registergoed ingeschreven was, kan dit feit aan de verkrijger niet worden tegengeworpen, tenzij hij het kende.
- 2. Het eerste lid is niet van toepassing ten aanzien van:
a. feiten die naar hun aard vatbaar zijn voor inschrijving in een register van de burgerlijke stand, een huwelijksgoederenregister of een boedelregister, ook indien het feit in een gegeven geval daarin niet kan worden ingeschreven, omdat daarop de Nederlandse wet niet van toepassing is;
b. in het curateleregister ingeschreven ondercuratelestelling en opheffing van curatele;
c. in het faillissementsregister en in het surséanceregister ingeschreven rechterlijke uitspraken;
d. aanvaarding en verwerping van een nalatenschap;
e. verjaring.
- 3. Het eerste lid is evenmin van toepassing ten aanzien van erfopvolgingen en uiterste wilsbeschikkingen die op het tijdstip van de inschrijving van de rechtshandeling nog niet ingeschreven waren, doch daarna, mits binnen drie maanden na de dood van de erflater, alsnog in de registers zijn ingeschreven.

1. If at the time of registration of a juridical act to acquire a right to registered property by particular title, a fact which is also susceptible of entry in the registers was not entered in reference to that registered property, this fact cannot be opposed to the acquirer, unless he knew it.
2. The first paragraph does not apply to:

1. Si, lors de l'inscription d'un acte juridique ayant pour objet l'acquisition à titre particulier d'un droit sur un bien immatriculé, les registres ne font pas état, relativement à ce bien, d'un fait également susceptible d'inscription dans les registres, ce fait ne peut être opposé à l'acquéreur, à moins qu'il n'en ait eu connaissance.
2. Le premier paragraphe ne s'applique pas:

a. facts which according to their nature are susceptible of entry in a register of civil status, a matrimonial property register or a successions register, even if the fact cannot be registered in a given instance because the law of the Netherlands does not apply to it;
b. placement under and termination of curatorship, entered in the register of curatorship;
c. judgments entered in the bankruptcy register or in the register of receivership;
d. acceptance and rejection of a succession;
e. prescription.

3. Furthermore, the first paragraph does not apply to successions and testamentary dispositions which were not registered at the moment of the registration of the juridical act, but which were thereafter entered in the registers within three months of the death of the *de cujus*.

a. Aux faits qui, d'après leur nature, sont susceptibles d'inscription dans un registre de l'état civil, dans un registre des conventions matrimoniales ou dans un registre des successions, même si, dans un cas particulier, le fait ne peut y être inscrit parce que la loi néerlandaise ne s'applique pas à lui;
b. À la mise en curatelle[1] et à sa levée, inscrites dans le registre des curatelles;
c. Aux jugements inscrits dans les registres des faillites et des sursis de paiement;
d. À l'acceptation d'une succession et à sa renonciation;
e. À la prescription;

3. Le premier paragraphe ne s'applique pas non plus aux successions et aux dispositions de dernière volonté non encore inscrites au moment de l'inscription de l'acte juridique, mais qui le sont dans les trois mois suivant le décès du défunt.

Art. 25. (3.1.2.8) Indien op het tijdstip waarop een rechtshandeling ter verkrijging van een recht op een registergoed onder bijzondere titel wordt ingeschreven, een feit met betrekking tot dat registergoed in de registers was ingeschreven krachtens een authentieke akte waarin het feit door een ambtenaar met kracht van authenticiteit werd vastgesteld, kan de onjuistheid van dit feit aan de verkrijger niet worden tegengeworpen, tenzij hij deze onjuistheid kende of door raadpleging van de registers de mogelijkheid daarvan had kunnen kennen.

If, at the time of registration of a juridical act to acquire a right to registered property by particular title, a fact pertaining to that registered property was entered in the registers pursuant to an authentic deed in which this fact was authenticated by a civil servant, the inaccuracy of this fact cannot be invoked against the acquirer, unless he knew it or could have known of the possibility thereof by consulting the registers.

Si, lors de l'inscription d'un acte juridique ayant pour objet l'acquisition à titre particulier d'un droit sur un bien immatriculé, un fait relatif à ce bien était inscrit dans les registres sur la foi d'un acte authentique par lequel un fonctionnaire a établi ce fait avec force authentique, l'acquéreur ne peut se voir opposer l'inexactitude de ce fait, à moins qu'il n'en ait eu connaissance ou qu'il n'ait pu, par la consultation des registres, en connaître la possibilité.

Art. 26. (3.1.2.8a) Indien op het tijdstip waarop een rechtshandeling ter verkrijging van een recht op een registergoed onder bijzondere titel wordt

1 En droit néerlandais, la curatelle s'applique aux majeurs (art. 378 du Livre premier du Code civil), la tutelle ne s'applique qu'aux mineurs, alors qu'en droit français, les deux institutions peuvent s'appliquer aux majeurs, étant des régimes de protection différente. Dans la traduction, le seul terme «curatelle» a été retenu pour tout régime s'appliquant aux majeurs.

ingeschreven, met betrekking tot dat registergoed een onjuist feit in de registers ingeschreven was, kan de onjuistheid van dit feit door hem die redelijkerwijze voor overeenstemming van de registers met de werkelijkheid had kunnen zorgdragen, aan de verkrijger niet worden tegengeworpen, tenzij deze de onjuistheid kende of door raadpleging van de registers de mogelijkheid daarvan had kunnen kennen.

If, at the time of registration of a juridical act to acquire a right to registered property by particular title, an inaccurate fact pertaining to that registered property was entered in the registers, the inaccuracy of this fact cannot be invoked against the acquirer by a person who could reasonably have ensured the conformity of the registers with the reality, unless the acquirer knew the inaccuracy or could have known of the possibility thereof by consulting the registers.

Si, lors de l'inscription d'un acte juridique ayant pour objet l'acquisition à titre particulier d'un droit sur un bien immatriculé, un fait inexact relatif à ce bien était inscrit dans les registres, l'acquéreur ne peut se voir opposer l'inexactitude de ce fait par celui qui aurait normalement pu assurer la conformité des registres à la réalité, à moins qu'il n'ait eu connaissance de cette inexactitude ou qu'il n'ait pu, par la consultation des registres, en connaître la possibilité.

Art. 27. (3.1.2.9) - 1. Hij die beweert enig recht op een registergoed te hebben, kan alle belanghebbenden bij openbare oproeping, en daarnaast hen die als rechthebbende of beslaglegger op dat goed ingeschreven staan, ieder bij name dagvaarden om te horen verklaren dat hem het recht waarop hij aanspraak maakt, toekomt. Alvorens een zodanige eis toe te wijzen, kan de rechter de maatregelen bevelen en de bewijsopdrachten doen, welke hij in het belang van mogelijke niet-verschenen rechthebbenden nuttig oordeelt. Artikel 79, eerste lid, van het Wetboek van Burgerlijke Rechtsvordering is niet van toepassing. Een krachtens dit artikel verkregen verklaring wordt niet in de registers ingeschreven, voordat het vonnis in kracht van gewijsde is gegaan.

- 2. Tegen het vonnis is geen verzet toegelaten. Hoger beroep en cassatie staan volgens de gewone regels open, behoudens de volgende uitzonderingen. Artikel 335 van het Wetboek van Burgerlijke Rechtsvordering is niet van toepassing. De dagvaarding waarbij het rechtsmiddel wordt ingesteld, moet op straffe van niet-ontvankelijkheid binnen acht dagen worden ingeschreven in het register, bedoeld in artikel 433 van het Wetboek van Burgerlijke Rechtsvordering. De termijn voor hoger beroep begint voor niet-verschenen belanghebbenden te lopen vanaf de betekening van de uitspraak aan hen bij name, voor zover zij ingeschreven waren, of bij openbaar exploit, zo zij niet ingeschreven waren. Cassatie staat alleen open voor verschenen belanghebbenden.

- 3. De krachtens lid 1 ingeschreven verklaring wordt ten aanzien van niet-verschenen belanghebbenden die niet bij name zijn gedagvaard, vermoed juist te zijn, zolang het tegendeel niet bewezen is. Op de onjuistheid kan echter geen beroep worden gedaan ten nadele van hen die, daarmee onbekend, de verkrijger van het vonnis onder bijzondere titel zijn opgevolgd.

- 4. Een openbare oproeping als bedoeld in lid 1 geschiedt overeenkomstig artikel 4 onder 7º, tweede en derde lid van het Wetboek van Burgerlijke Rechtsvordering. Een openbaar exploit als bedoeld in lid 2 geschiedt op dezelfde wijze, tenzij de rechter nadere maatregelen voorschrijft als bedoeld in lid 1. De in lid 1 bedoelde maatregelen kunnen bestaan in het voorschrijven van al of niet herhaalde aankondigingen van

een door de rechter vast te stellen inhoud in één of meer binnen- of buitenlandse dagbladen.

1. A person who claims to have a right to registered property can summon all interested parties by public notice, and, in addition, can summon individually each registered title-holder or seizor of the property to the hearing which declares that he is entitled to the right to which he lays a claim. Before making such a declaration, the judge may take measures and require the submission of evidence which he deems useful in the interest of title-holders who may not have appeared. Article 79, paragraph 1 of the Code of Civil Procedure does not apply. A declaration obtained by virtue of this article is not entered in the registers until the judgment has become final.
2. Opposition to the judgment is not permitted. Save the following exceptions, appeal and cassation are possible according to the ordinary rules. Article 335 of the Code of Civil Procedure does not apply. The summons whereby appeal or cassation is lodged must, within eight days and on pain of disallowance, be entered in the register referred to in article 433 of the Code of Civil Procedure. For interested parties who have not appeared, the appeal period starts to run as of the day of personal service of the judgment on them to the extent that they were registered, or by public summons if they were not. Cassation is only open to interested parties who have appeared.
3. With regard to interested parties who have not appeared and have not been summoned individually, the declaration which has been registered pursuant to paragraph 1 is presumed accurate until proven to the contrary. Any inaccuracy, however, cannot be invoked to the detriment of those who, unaware thereof, have succeeded by particular title to the person obtaining the judgment.

1. Celui qui prétend avoir un droit sur un bien immatriculé peut assigner, par avis public, toutes les personnes intéressées et, en outre, nommément, ceux qui sont inscrits relativement à ce bien comme titulaire ou créancier saisissant, afin de l'entendre déclarer titulaire du droit auquel il prétend. Avant de faire droit à une telle demande, le juge peut ordonner les mesures et la production des preuves qu'il estime utiles dans l'intérêt de titulaires éventuels qui n'ont pas comparu. L'article 79, premier paragraphe, du Code de procédure civile ne s'applique pas. Une déclaration obtenue en vertu de cet article n'est pas inscrite dans les registres avant que le jugement n'ait acquis autorité de chose jugée.
2. L'opposition n'est pas ouverte contre le jugement. L'appel et le pourvoi en cassation sont ouverts suivant les règles ordinaires, sauf les exceptions suivantes. L'article 335 du Code de procédure civile ne s'applique pas. À peine d'irrecevabilité, l'assignation par laquelle le recours est formé doit, dans les huit jours, être inscrite sur le registre visé à l'article 433 du Code de procédure civile. Le délai d'appel court, pour les intéressés qui n'ont pas comparu, à compter de la signification du jugement qui leur est adressée nommément, dans la mesure où ils étaient inscrits, ou par exploit public, s'ils ne l'étaient pas. Le pourvoi en cassation n'est ouvert qu'aux intéressés qui ont comparu.

3. À l'égard des personnes intéressées qui n'ont pas comparu et qui n'ont pas été nommément assignées, la déclaration inscrite en vertu du paragraphe premier est présumée exacte tant que le contraire n'a pas été établi. On ne peut cependant en invoquer l'inexactitude au préjudice de ceux qui, ignorants de ce fait, sont devenus des ayants cause à titre particulier de celui qui a obtenu le jugement.

4. The public notice referred to in paragraph 1 is issued according to article 4 *sub* 7, paragraphs 2 and 3 of the Code of Civil Procedure. A public summons referred to in paragraph 2 is issued in the same manner, unless the judge takes measures pursuant to paragraph 1. The measures referred to in paragraph 1 may be the publication, repeatedly or not, of notices in one or more domestic or foreign newspapers, the content of which may be determined by the judge.

4. La convocation publique visée au paragraphe premier a lieu conformément à l'article 4, point 7o, paragraphes 2 et 3 du Code de procédure civile. L'exploit public visé au paragraphe 2 a lieu de la même façon, à moins que le juge n'ordonne des mesures précises, visées au paragraphe premier. Ces mesures peuvent consister en l'a publication d'annonces, dont le juge fixe le contenu, à publier une ou plusieurs fois dans un ou plusieurs journaux nationaux ou étrangers.

Art. 28. (3.1.2.10) - 1. Is een inschrijving waardeloos, dan zijn degenen te wier behoeve zij anders zou hebben gestrekt, verplicht van deze waardeloosheid aan hem die daarbij een onmiddellijk belang heeft, op diens verzoek een schriftelijke verklaring af te geven. De verklaringen vermelden de feiten waarop de waardeloosheid berust, tenzij de inschrijving een hypotheek of een beslag betreft.
- 2. Verklaringen als in lid 1 bedoeld kunnen in de registers worden ingeschreven. Indien de inschrijving een hypotheek of een beslag betreft, machtigen deze verklaringen na inschrijving gezamenlijk de bewaarder tot doorhaling daarvan.

1. Where a registration has no effect, those who would otherwise have benefitted from the registration must, upon the request of a person having a direct interest, provide a written declaration thereof. Unless the registration pertains to a hypothec or a seizure, such declarations must mention the reasons why the registration is without effect.
2. Declarations referred to in paragraph 1 may be entered in the registers. Where the registration pertains to a hypothec or a seizure, these declarations, once registered, jointly authorize the registrar to cancel it.

1. Lorsqu'une inscription est sans effet[1], ceux qui en auraient bénéficié sont obligés de délivrer, à sa requête, une déclaration écrite à celui qui y a un intérêt direct. Ces déclarations énoncent les faits dont résulte l'ineffectivité, à moins que l'inscription ne porte sur une hypothèque ou sur une saisie.

2. Les déclarations visées au paragraphe premier peuvent être inscrites dans les registres. Si l'inscription porte sur une hypothèque ou sur une saisie, les déclarations, mises ensemble, autorisent, une fois inscrites, le conservateur à la radier.

Art. 29. (3.1.2.10a) - 1. Worden de vereiste verklaringen niet afgegeven, dan verklaart de rechtbank de inschrijving waardeloos op vordering van de onmiddellijk belanghebbende. Wordt ter verkrijging van dit bevel iemand die in de registers staat ingeschreven gedagvaard, dan worden daarmee tevens gedagvaard al zijn rechtverkrijgenden die geen nieuwe inschrijving hebben genomen.
- 2. Alvorens een zodanige verklaring uit te spreken kan de rechter de maatregelen bevelen en de bewijsopdrachten doen, welke hij in het belang van mogelijk niet-verschenen rechthebbenden nuttig oordeelt.
- 3. Verzet, hoger beroep en cassatie moeten op straffe van niet-ontvankelijkheid binnen acht dagen na het instellen van het rechtsmiddel

[1] Le néerlandais emploie le terme «*waardeloos*» (sans valeur), terme inédit, qui se distingue de la nullité, de la caducité et de l'inopérabilité.

worden ingeschreven in de registers, bedoeld in de artikelen 85 en 433 van het Wetboek van Burgerlijke Rechtsvordering. Zo alle ingeschreven gedaagden zijn verschenen, is artikel 79, eerste lid, van dat wetboek niet van toepassing. Zo voor een ingeschreven gedaagde geen verzet, maar hoger beroep openstaat, geldt hetzelfde voor zijn rechtverkrijgenden die geen nieuwe inschrijving hebben genomen. In afwijking van artikel 81 van dat wetboek begint de termijn van verzet in elk geval te lopen vanaf de betekening van het vonnis aan de ingeschreven gedaagde, ook als de betekening niet aan hem in persoon geschiedt, zulks mede ten opzichte van zijn rechtverkrijgenden die geen nieuwe inschrijving hebben genomen, tenzij de rechter hiertoe nadere maatregelen heeft bevolen en aan dat bevel niet is voldaan. Cassatie staat alleen open voor verschenen belanghebbenden.

- 4. Het vonnis dat de verklaring bevat, kan niet worden ingeschreven, voordat het in kracht van gewijsde is gegaan. Indien de waardeloze inschrijving een hypotheek of beslag betreft, machtigt het vonnis na inschrijving de bewaarder tot doorhaling daarvan.

1. Where the required declarations have not been provided, the district court declares the registration to be without effect upon the demand of a directly interested party. Where, in order to obtain this court order, a person who is entered in the registers, is summoned, all his successors, who have not made a new registration, have thereby also been summoned.

2. Before making such a declaration, the judge may take measures and require the submission of evidence which he deems useful in the interest of title-holders who have not appeared.

3. On pain of disallowance and within eight days from the time that they are initiated, opposition, appeal and cassation must be entered in the registers referred to in articles 85 and 443 of the Code of Civil Procedure. Article 79, paragraph 1 of said Code does not apply where all registered defendants have appeared. Where appeal rather than opposition is available to a registered defendant, the same applies to his successors who have not made a new registration. Contrary to article 81 of said Code, in any case the opposition period starts to run as of service of the judgment on the registered defendant, even if service is not in person; such service also begins the opposition period with respect to the registered defendant's unregistered successors, unless the judge has ordered that further measures be taken with

1. Lorsque les déclarations requises ne sont pas délivrées, le tribunal de première instance, à la demande de la partie directement intéressée, déclare l'inscription sans effet. L'assignation, pour l'obtention de cette ordonnance, d'une personne inscrite aux registres vaut à l'égard de tous ses ayants cause qui n'ont pas fait effectuer une nouvelle inscription.

2. Avant de prononcer une telle déclaration, le juge peut ordonner les mesures et la production des preuves qu'il estime utiles dans l'intérêt de titulaires éventuels qui n'ont pas comparu.

3. L'opposition, l'appel et le pourvoi en cassation doivent, à peine d'irrecevabilité, être inscrits, dans les huit jours de leur formation, sur les registres visés aux articles 85 et 433 du Code de procédure civile. Lorsque tous les défendeurs inscrits ont comparu, l'article 79, premier paragraphe, dudit code ne s'applique pas. Lorsque un défendeur inscrit peut former non pas opposition, mais appel, il en est de même pour ses ayants cause qui n'ont pas fait effectuer une nouvelle inscription. Par dérogation à l'article 81 dudit code, le délai d'opposition court, en tout cas, à compter de la signification du jugement au défendeur inscrit, lors même que celle-ci ne lui a pas été faite en personne; il court également à l'égard de ses ayants cause qui n'ont pas fait effectuer une nouvelle inscription, à moins que le juge n'ait ordonné des mesures précises à ce sujet et que cette ordonnance

respect to the foregoing and such order has not been complied with. Cassation is only open to interested parties who have appeared.

4. The judgment containing the declaration cannot be registered until it is final. If the registration which had no effect pertains to a hypothec or a seizure, the judgment, once registered, authorizes the registrar to cancel it.

n'ait pas été suivie. Le pourvoi en cassation n'est ouvert qu'aux intéressés qui ont comparu.

4. Le jugement comportant la déclaration ne peut être inscrit avant d'avoir acquis force de chose jugée. Si l'inscription sans effet porte sur une hypothèque ou une saisie, le jugement, une fois inscrit, autorise le conservateur à les radier.

Art. 30. (3.1.2.11) - 1. De Staat is jegens belanghebbenden aansprakelijk voor de schade die zij lijden, doordat in strijd met de wet een inschrijving is geweigerd of geschied.

- 2. De Staat is eveneens aansprakelijk voor alle verdere vergissingen, verzuimen, vertragingen of andere onregelmatigheden van zijn ambtenaren, gepleegd bij het houden van de registers of bij het opmaken of afgeven van afschriften, uittreksels en getuigschriften.

- 3. De Staat is ook aansprakelijk, wanneer iemand ten gevolge van omstandigheden die naar redelijkheid en billijkheid niet voor zijn rekening komen, door toepassing van een der artikelen 24, 25 of 27 zijn recht verliest.

1. The State is liable to interested parties for damage suffered as a result of a registration which has been refused or made in violation of the law.

2. The State is also liable for all further errors, omissions, delays or other irregularities committed by its civil servants in keeping the registers or in drafting or issuing copies, extracts and certificates.

3. The State is also liable where a person loses a right by application of articles 24, 25 or 27 as a result of circumstances for which the latter cannot reasonably or equitably be accountable.

1. L'État est responsable à l'égard des intéressés du préjudice résultant d'une inscription refusée ou effectuée en violation de la loi.

2. L'État est de même responsable des erreurs, omissions, retards et de toutes autres irrégularités que ses fonctionnaires ont commis dans la tenue des registres ou encore dans la rédaction ou la délivrance de copies, d'extraits ou de certificats.

3. L'État est également responsable de la perte d'un droit que subit le titulaire par l'application des articles 24, 25 ou 27, à la suite de circonstances dont il ne serait raisonnable ni équitable qu'elles incombent à ce dernier.

Art. 31. (3.1.2.12) Waar een wetsbepaling die betrekking heeft op registergoederen, een notariële akte of een notariële verklaring voorschrijft, is een akte of verklaring van een Nederlandse notaris vereist.

A deed or declaration of a Dutch notary is required, where a statutory provision pertaining to registered property prescribes a notarial deed or notarial declaration.

Lorsqu'une disposition de la loi portant sur les biens immatriculés exige un acte ou une déclaration notariés, elle vise l'acte ou la déclaration d'un notaire néerlandais.

TITEL 2 RECHTSHANDELINGEN

TITLE 2 JURIDICAL ACTS

TITRE DES ACTES JURIDIQUES

Art. 32. (3.2.1) - 1. Iedere natuurlijke persoon is bekwaam tot het verrichten van rechtshandelingen, voor zover de wet niet anders bepaalt.
- 2. Een rechtshandeling van een onbekwame is vernietigbaar. Een eenzijdige rechtshandeling van een onbekwame, die niet tot een of meer bepaalde personen gericht was, is echter nietig.

1. Every natural person has the capacity to perform juridical acts to the extent that the law does not provide otherwise.
2. A juridical act of an incapable person may be annulled. A unilateral juridical act of an incapable person, however, is null where it is not addressed to one or more specifically determined persons.

1. Toute personne physique a la capacité d'accomplir des actes juridiques dans la mesure où la loi ne dispose pas autrement.
2. L'acte juridique de l'incapable est annulable. Est nul cependant l'acte juridique unilatéral de l'incapable, qui n'est pas adressé à une ou plusieurs personnes déterminées.

Art. 33. (3.2.2) Een rechtshandeling vereist een op een rechtsgevolg gerichte wil die zich door een verklaring heeft geopenbaard.

A juridical act requires an intention to produce juridical effects, which intention has manifested itself by a declaration.

L'acte juridique nécessite un acte de volonté qui est destiné à produire un effet de droit et qui s'est manifesté par une déclaration.

Art. 34. (3.2.2a) - 1. Heeft iemand wiens geestvermogens blijvend of tijdelijk zijn gestoord, iets verklaard, dan wordt een met de verklaring overeenstemmende wil geacht te ontbreken, indien de stoornis een redelijke waardering der bij de handeling betrokken belangen belette, of indien de verklaring onder invloed van die stoornis is gedaan. Een verklaring wordt vermoed onder invloed van de stoornis te zijn gedaan, indien de rechtshandeling voor de geestelijk gestoorde nadelig was, tenzij het nadeel op het tijdstip van de rechtshandeling redelijkerwijze niet was te voorzien.
- 2. Een zodanig ontbreken van wil maakt een rechtshandeling vernietigbaar. Een eenzijdige rechtshandeling die niet tot een of meer bepaalde personen gericht was, wordt door het ontbreken van wil echter nietig.

1. Where a person whose mental faculties are permanently or temporarily impaired makes a declaration, the intention corresponding to that declaration is deemed to be lacking if the impairment prevented a reasonable appraisal of the interests involved or if the declaration was made under influence of that disturbance. Unless the prejudice

1. Lorsqu'une personne fait une déclaration alors que ses facultés mentales sont dérangées de façon permanente ou temporaire, la volonté conforme à cette déclaration est réputée absente si le dérangement empêche une appréciation raisonnable des intérêts en présence ou s'il a influencé la déclaration. Le dérangement est présumé avoir influencé la déclaration si

was not reasonably foreseeable at the time of the juridical act, a declaration is presumed to have been made under the influence of the disturbance, if the juridical act was prejudicial to the mentally disturbed person.
2. A juridical act without such intention may be annulled. However, the absence of intention renders a unilateral juridical act null where it is not addressed to one or more specifically determined persons.

l'acte juridique porte préjudice à la personne dérangée, à moins que le préjudice n'ait pas été raisonnablement prévisible au moment de l'acte.

2. Une telle absence de volonté rend annulable l'acte juridique. L'absence de volonté rend cependant nul l'acte juridique unilatéral qui n'est pas adressé à une ou plusieurs personnes déterminées.

Art. 35. (3.2.3) Tegen hem die eens anders verklaring of gedraging, overeenkomstig de zin die hij daaraan onder de gegeven omstandigheden redelijkerwijze mocht toekennen, heeft opgevat als een door die ander tot hem gerichte verklaring van een bepaalde strekking, kan geen beroep worden gedaan op het ontbreken van een met deze verklaring overeenstemmende wil.

The absence of intention in a declaration cannot be invoked against a person who has interpreted another's declaration or conduct, in conformity with the sense which he could reasonably attribute to it in the circumstances, as a declaration of a particular tenor made to him by that other person.

Lorsqu'une personne fait une déclaration ou adopte un comportement non conformes à sa volonté, le défaut de volonté ne peut être opposé à celui qui a compris cette déclaration ou ce comportement, d'après le sens qu'il pouvait raisonnablement leur donner dans les circonstances, comme constituant une déclaration de portée déterminée à son adresse.

Art. 36. (3.2.3a) Tegen hem die als derde op grond van een verklaring of gedraging, overeenkomstig de zin die hij daaraan onder de gegeven omstandigheden redelijkerwijze mocht toekennen, het ontstaan, bestaan of tenietgaan van een bepaalde rechtsbetrekking heeft aangenomen en in redelijk vertrouwen op de juistheid van die veronderstelling heeft gehandeld, kan door degene om wiens verklaring of gedraging het gaat, met betrekking tot deze handeling op de onjuistheid van die veronderstelling geen beroep worden gedaan.

A third person who under the circumstances reasonably bases an assumption as to the creation, existence or extinction of a juridical relationship on a declaration or conduct of another, and has acted reasonably on the basis of the accuracy of that assumption, cannot have invoked against him the inaccuracy of that assumption by the other person.

Le tiers qui, sur la foi d'une déclaration ou d'un comportement et d'après le sens qu'il pouvait raisonnablement leur donner dans les circonstances, a cru à la création, à l'existence ou à l'extinction d'un rapport juridique et a agi en se fiant raisonnablement à l'exactitude de cette croyance ne peut se voir opposer au sujet de cet acte, par l'auteur de la déclaration ou du comportement concernés, l'inexactitude de cette croyance.

Art. 37. (3.2.4) - 1. Tenzij anders is bepaald, kunnen verklaringen, met inbegrip van mededelingen, in iedere vorm geschieden, en kunnen zij in een of meer gedragingen besloten liggen.
- 2. Indien bepaald is dat een verklaring schriftelijk moet worden gedaan, kan zij, voor zover uit de strekking van die bepaling niet anders volgt, ook bij exploit geschieden.

- 3. Een tot een bepaalde persoon gerichte verklaring moet, om haar werking te hebben, die persoon hebben bereikt. Nochtans heeft ook een verklaring die hem tot wie zij was gericht, niet of niet tijdig heeft bereikt, haar werking, indien dit niet of niet tijdig bereiken het gevolg is van zijn eigen handeling, van de handeling van personen voor wie hij aansprakelijk is, of van andere omstandigheden die zijn persoon betreffen en rechtvaardigen dat hij het nadeel draagt.
- 4. Wanneer een door de afzender daartoe aangewezen persoon of middel een tot een ander gerichte verklaring onjuist heeft overgebracht, geldt het ter kennis van de ontvanger gekomene als de verklaring van de afzender, tenzij de gevolgde wijze van overbrenging door de ontvanger was bepaald.
- 5. Intrekking van een tot een bepaalde persoon gerichte verklaring moet, om haar werking te hebben, die persoon eerder dan of gelijktijdig met de ingetrokken verklaring bereiken.

1. Unless otherwise provided, declarations, including communications, can be made in any form; declarations may be inferred from conduct.
2. A declaration which must be made in writing can also be made by summons, to the extent that the necessary implication of the provision in question does not produce a different result.
3. A declaration made to a specifically determined person, in order to be effective, must have reached that person. Nevertheless, even a declaration which has not reached the person to whom it was made, or has not reached him in time, does have effect if this situation results from his own act, from the act of persons for whom he is responsible, or from other circumstances which are personal to him and justify that he suffer the consequences.
4. Unless the recipient has determined the means of communication, in the event that the declaration has been inaccurately communicated to the recipient by the person or means of communication designated by the sender, the declaration as received is deemed to be the declaration of the sender.
5. In order to be effective notice of withdrawal of a declaration made to a specified person must have reached that person before or at the same time as the withdrawn declaration.

1. Sauf disposition contraire, les déclarations, y compris les communications, peuvent être faites sous toute forme; elles peuvent aussi s'inférer d'une conduite.
2. S'il est disposé qu'une déclaration doit être faite par écrit, elle peut l'être par exploit, dans la mesure où il n'en découle pas autrement de la nature de la disposition en question.
3. Une déclaration adressée à une personne déterminée ne produit effet que si elle lui est parvenue. Toutefois, même la déclaration qui ne parvient pas à son destinataire ou qui lui parvient en retard produit effet si cette situation résulte du fait de ce dernier ou de personnes dont il est responsable ou encore d'autres circonstances qui le concernent et qui justifient qu'il en subisse le préjudice.
4. Lorsque la personne ou le moyen choisi par l'expéditeur pour communiquer une déclaration destinée à un tiers la transmet incorrectement, la déclaration de l'expéditeur est réputée être ce qui a été porté à la connaissance du destinataire, sauf si ce dernier a fixé le mode de communication adopté.
5. Le retrait d'une déclaration adressée à une personne déterminée ne produit effet que s'il parvient à cette personne avant la déclaration retirée ou en même temps que celle-ci.

Art. 38. (3.2.5) - 1. Tenzij uit de wet of uit de aard van de rechtshandeling anders voortvloeit, kan een rechtshandeling onder een tijdsbepaling of een voorwaarde worden verricht.
- 2. De vervulling van een voorwaarde heeft geen terugwerkende kracht.

1. Unless the law or the nature of a juridical act pruduces a different result, a juridical act can be performed subject to a term or condition.
2. The fulfilment of a condition does not produce retroactive effect.

1. Un acte juridique peut être assorti d'un terme ou d'une condition, à moins qu'il n'en résulte autrement de la loi ou de la nature de l'acte.
2. L'accomplissement de la condition n'a pas d'effet rétroactif.

Art. 39. (3.2.6) Tenzij uit de wet anders voortvloeit, zijn rechtshandelingen die niet in de voorgeschreven vorm zijn verricht, nietig.

Unless the law produces a different result, juridical acts which have not been performed in the prescribed form are null.

À moins qu'il n'en résulte autrement de la loi, est nul l'acte juridique qui n'a pas été accompli en la forme prescrite.

Art. 40. (3.2.7) - 1. Een rechtshandeling die door inhoud of strekking in strijd is met de goede zeden of de openbare orde, is nietig.
- 2. Strijd met een dwingende wetsbepaling leidt tot nietigheid van de rechtshandeling, doch, indien de bepaling uitsluitend strekt ter bescherming van één der partijen bij een meerzijdige rechtshandeling, slechts tot vernietigbaarheid, een en ander voor zover niet uit de strekking van de bepaling anders voortvloeit.
- 3. Het vorige lid heeft geen betrekking op wetsbepalingen die niet de strekking hebben de geldigheid van daarmede strijdige rechtshandelingen aan te tasten.

1. A juridical act which by its content or necessary implication is contrary to good morals or public order is null.
2. Violation of an imperative statutory provision entails nullity of the juridical act; if, however, the provision is intended solely for the protection of one of the parties to a multilateral juridical act, the act may only be annulled; in both cases this applies to the extent that the necessary implication of the provision does not produce a different result.
3. Statutory provisions which do not purport to invalidate juridical acts contrary to them, are not affected by the preceding paragraph.

1. Est nul l'acte juridique qui par son contenu ou sa portée est contraire aux bonnes moeurs ou à l'ordre public.
2. Est nul l'acte juridique contraire à une disposition impérative de la loi; toutefois, il est seulement annulable si la disposition impérative vise exclusivement la protection de l'une des parties à un acte juridique multilatéral; il en est ainsi, dans l'un et l'autre cas, dans la mesure où il n'en résulte pas autrement de la nature de la disposition.
3. Le paragraphe précédent ne vise pas les dispositions de la loi dont l'objet n'est pas de rendre invalides les actes juridiques qui leur sont contraires.

Art. 41. (3.2.7a) Betreft een grond van nietigheid slechts een deel van een rechtshandeling, dan blijft deze voor het overige in stand, voor zover dit, gelet op inhoud en strekking van de handeling, niet in onverbrekelijk verband met het nietige deel staat.

The nullity of part of a juridical act does not affect the rest of the act, to the extent that, taking into consideration the content and necessary implication of the act, the parts are so inextricably related so as not to be severable.

Lorsqu'une cause de nullité touche seulement une partie d'un acte juridique, il demeure valide dans ses autres parties, dans la mesure où, d'après le contenu et la portée de l'acte, elles ne présentent pas un rapport indissociable avec la partie nulle.

Art. 42. (3.2.8) Beantwoordt de strekking van een nietige rechtshandeling in een zodanige mate aan die van een andere, als geldig aan te merken rechtshandeling, dat aangenomen moet worden dat die andere rechtshandeling zou zijn verricht, indien van de eerstgenoemde wegens haar ongeldigheid was afgezien, dan komt haar de werking van die andere rechtshandeling toe, tenzij dit onredelijk zou zijn jegens een belanghebbende die niet tot de rechtshandeling als partij heeft medegewerkt.

Where the necessary implication of a null juridical act corresponds to such a degree to that of another juridical act, which is to be considered as valid, so as to imply that the latter juridical act would have been performed had the former been abandoned because of its invalidity, then the former shall be given the effect of the latter juridical act, unless this would be unreasonable to an interested person not party to the act.

L'acte juridique nul reçoit l'effet d'un autre acte considéré comme valide lorsque la portée de l'acte nul correspond à tel point à celle de l'autre qu'il faut présumer que celui-ci eût été accompli si l'on avait renoncé à l'acte nul à cause de son invalidité; cette solution n'est pas retenue lorsqu'elle se révèle injuste à l'égard d'un intéressé non partie à cet acte juridique.

Art. 43. (3.2.9) - 1. Rechtshandelingen die, hetzij rechtstreeks, hetzij door tussenkomende personen, strekken tot verkrijging door:

a. rechters, leden van het openbaar ministerie, gerechtsauditeurs, griffiers, advocaten, procureurs, deurwaarders en notarissen van goederen waarover een geding aanhangig is voor het gerecht, onder welks rechtsgebied zij hun bediening uitoefenen;

b. ambtenaren, van goederen die door hen of te hunnen overstaan worden verkocht, of

c. personen met openbaar gezag bekleed, van goederen die toebehoren aan het Rijk, provincies, gemeenten of andere openbare instellingen en aan hun beheer zijn toevertrouwd,

zijn nietig en verplichten de verkrijgers tot schadevergoeding.

- 2. Lid 1 onder a heeft geen betrekking op uiterste wilsbeschikkingen, door een erflater ten voordele van zijn wettelijke erfgenamen gemaakt, noch op rechtshandelingen krachtens welke deze erfgenamen goederen der nalatenschap verkrijgen.

- 3. In het geval bedoeld in het eerste lid onder c is de rechtshandeling geldig, indien zij met Onze goedkeuring is geschied of het een verkoop in het openbaar betreft. Indien de rechtshandeling strekt tot verkrijging door een lid van de gemeenteraad, onderscheidenlijk de burgemeester komt de in de vorige zin bedoelde bevoegdheid tot goedkeuring toe aan gedeputeerde staten, onderscheidenlijk de Commissaris van de Koningin.

1. The following juridical acts which, either directly or through intervening persons, are intended as a means of acquiring property, are null and oblige acquirers to pay damages:

1. Sont nuls et, pour les acquéreurs, source d'une obligation d'indemnisation les actes juridiques qui visent, directement ou par personnes interposées, l'acquisition:

a. acts pertaining to the acquisition, by judges, members of the office of the public prosecutor, assistant judges, clerks, advocates, solicitors, bailiffs and notaries, of property in respect of which procedures are pending before the court in whose jurisdiction they exercise their profession;
b. acts pertaining to the acquisition, by civil servants, of property which is sold by them or before them; or
c. acts pertaining to the acquisition, by persons holding public office, of property which belongs to the State, Provinces, Communes or other public bodies and of which the management has been entrusted to them.

2. Paragraph 1 *sub* a does neither apply to testamentary provisions made by a testator in favour of his legal heirs nor to juridical acts pursuant to which these heirs acquire property of the succession.

3. In the case referred to in paragraph 1 *sub* c, the juridical act is valid if it has been done with Our[1] approval or if it is a public sale. The power of approval referred to in the preceding sentence is exercised by Provincial Executives,[2] where the act pertains to the acquisition by a member of the Council of a Commune, and by Provincial Commissioners of the Queen where it pertains to the acquisition by a burgomaster.

a. Par les juges, les membres du ministère public, les assesseurs, les greffiers, les avocats, les procureurs, les huissiers et les notaires, de biens faisant l'objet d'un litige devant le tribunal dans le ressort duquel ils exercent leurs fonctions;
b. Par les fonctionnaires, de biens dont la vente a lieu par eux ou devant eux;
c. Par les personnes investies de pouvoirs publics, de biens appartenant à l'État, aux provinces, aux communes ou à d'autres organismes publics et qui sont confiés à leur gestion.

2. Le paragraphe 1er, point a., ne porte pas sur les dispositions de dernière volonté du défunt au profit de ses héritiers légaux, ni sur les actes juridiques par lesquels ces derniers acquièrent les biens de la succession.

3. Dans le cas visé au paragraphe 1er, point c., l'acte juridique est valable s'il a lieu avec Notre[3] approbation ou s'il s'agit d'une vente publique. Lorsque l'acte juridique visé à la phrase précédente porte sur l'acquisition d'un bien par un membre du conseil communal, le pouvoir d'approbation prévu à la phrase précédente appartient au Conseil exécutif des États provinciaux[4]; s'il s'agit d'une acquisition par le maire, ce pouvoir appartient au Commissaire de la Reine pour la province.

Art. 44. (3.2.10) - 1. Een rechtshandeling is vernietigbaar, wanneer zij door bedreiging, door bedrog of door misbruik van omstandigheden is tot stand gekomen.
- 2. Bedreiging is aanwezig, wanneer iemand een ander tot het verrichten van een bepaalde rechtshandeling beweegt door onrechtmatig deze of een derde met enig nadeel in persoon of goed te bedreigen. De bedreiging moet zodanig zijn, dat een redelijk oordelend mens daardoor kan worden beïnvloed.
- 3. Bedrog is aanwezig, wanneer iemand een ander tot het verrichten van een bepaalde rechtshandeling beweegt door enige opzettelijk daartoe gedane onjuiste mededeling, door het opzettelijk daartoe verzwijgen van enig feit

1 "Our" refers to the Crown.
2 Official Dutch title: Gedeputeerde Staten.
3 «Notre», «Nous» se rapportent à la Couronne. La loi néerlandaise est rédigée comme s'il s'agissait d'une proclamation du souverain.
4 Gedeputeerde Staten. Ce terme désigne la branche exécutive de l'autorité provinciale.

dat de verzwijger verplicht was mede te delen, of door een andere kunstgreep. Aanprijzingen in algemene bewoordingen, ook al zijn ze onwaar, leveren op zichzelf geen bedrog op.
- 4. Misbruik van omstandigheden is aanwezig, wanneer iemand die weet of moet begrijpen dat een ander door bijzondere omstandigheden, zoals noodtoestand, afhankelijkheid, lichtzinnigheid, abnormale geestestoestand of onervarenheid, bewogen wordt tot het verrichten van een rechtshandeling, het tot stand komen van die rechtshandeling bevordert, ofschoon hetgeen hij weet of moet begrijpen hem daarvan zou behoren te weerhouden.
- 5. Indien een verklaring is tot stand gekomen door bedreiging, bedrog of misbruik van omstandigheden van de zijde van iemand die geen partij bij de rechtshandeling is, kan op dit gebrek geen beroep worden gedaan jegens een wederpartij die geen reden had het bestaan ervan te veronderstellen.

1. A juridical act may be annulled when it has been entered into as a result of threat, fraud or abuse of circumstances.
2. A person who induces another to execute a certain juridical act by unlawfully threatening him or a third party with harm to his person or property, makes a threat. The threat must be such that a reasonable person would be influenced by it.
3. A person who induces another to execute a certain juridical act by intentionally providing him with inaccurate information, by intentionally concealing any fact he was obliged to communicate, or by any other artifice, commits fraud. Representations in general terms, even if they are untrue, do not as such constitute fraud.
4. A person who knows or should know that another is being induced to execute a juridical act as a result of special circumstances - such as state of necessity, dependency, wantonness, abnormal mental condition or inexperience - and who promotes the creation of that juridical act, although what he knows or ought to know should prevent him therefrom, commits an abuse of circumstances.
5. If a declaration has been made as a result of threat, fraud or abuse of circumstances on the part of a person who is not party to the juridical act, this defect cannot be invoked against a party to the juridical act who had no reason to assume its existence.

1. Est annulable l'acte juridique formé à la suite d'une menace, d'un dol ou d'un abus tiré des circonstances.
2. Il y a menace lorsqu'une personne en amène une autre à passer un acte juridique en inspirant illicitement à celle-ci ou à un tiers la crainte d'un préjudice personnel ou matériel. La menace doit être de nature à influencer une personne douée d'un jugement normal.
3. Il y a dol, lorsqu'une personne, au moyen de fausses informations fournies dans cette intention, du silence gardé intentionnellement sur un fait qu'elle était obligée de communiquer ou de toute autre manoeuvre, en amène une autre à passer un acte juridique. Vanter quelque chose en termes généraux, même faussement, n'est pas en soi constitutif de dol.
4. Une personne abuse des circonstances lorsqu'elle encourage la passation d'un acte juridique par une autre, tout en sachant ou devant comprendre, ce qui eût dû l'en retenir, que cette dernière y a été induite par des circonstances particulières, telles que la nécessité, la dépendance, la légèreté, l'état mental anormal, l'inexpérience.
5. Si le dol, la menace ou l'abus des circonstances ayant provoqué une déclaration sont le fait d'une personne non partie à l'acte juridique, ce vice ne peut être opposé à la partie à l'acte qui n'avait aucune raison d'en présumer l'existence.

Art. 45. (3.2.11) - 1. Indien een schuldenaar bij het verrichten van een onverplichte rechtshandeling wist of behoorde te weten dat daarvan

benadeling van een of meer schuldeisers in hun verhaalsmogelijkheden het gevolg zou zijn, is de rechtshandeling vernietigbaar en kan de vernietigingsgrond worden ingeroepen door iedere door de rechtshandeling in zijn verhaalsmogelijkheden benadeelde schuldeiser, onverschillig of zijn vordering vóór of na de handeling is ontstaan.
- 2. Een rechtshandeling anders dan om niet, die hetzij meerzijdig is, hetzij eenzijdig en tot een of meer bepaalde personen gericht, kan wegens benadeling slechts worden vernietigd, indien ook degenen met of jegens wie de schuldenaar de rechtshandeling verrichtte, wisten of behoorden te weten dat daarvan benadeling van een of meer schuldeisers het gevolg zou zijn.
- 3. Wordt een rechtshandeling om niet wegens benadeling vernietigd, dan heeft de vernietiging ten aanzien van de bevoordeelde die wist noch behoorde te weten dat van de rechtshandeling benadeling van een of meer schuldeisers het gevolg zou zijn, geen werking, voor zover hij aantoont dat hij ten tijde van de verklaring of het instellen van de vordering tot vernietiging niet ten gevolge van de rechtshandeling gebaat was.
- 4. Een schuldeiser die wegens benadeling tegen een rechtshandeling opkomt, vernietigt deze slechts te zijnen behoeve en niet verder dan nodig is ter opheffing van de door hem ondervonden benadeling.
- 5. Rechten, door derden te goeder trouw anders dan om niet verkregen op goederen die het voorwerp waren van de vernietigde rechtshandeling, worden geëerbiedigd. Ten aanzien van de derde te goeder trouw die om niet heeft verkregen, heeft de vernietiging geen werking voor zover hij aantoont dat hij op het ogenblik dat het goed van hem wordt opgeëist, niet ten gevolge van de rechtshandeling gebaat is.

1. If a debtor, in the performance of a juridical act to which he is not obligated, knew or ought to have known that his act would adversely affect the recourses of one or several of his creditors against his patrimony, the act may be annulled; any creditor whose recourses have been adversely affected by the juridical act may invoke this ground for annulment, irrespective of whether his claim has arisen before or after the act.
2. Acts by gratuitous title excepted, a juridical act, either multilateral or unilateral and directed at one or more specifically determined persons, can only be annulled because of prejudice to a creditor, if those persons with whom or in respect of whom the debtor performed the juridical act knew or ought to have known that prejudice to one or more creditors would result from it.
3. Where a juridical act by gratuitous title is annulled because of prejudice, the annulment has no effect against a beneficiary who neither knew nor ought to have known that prejudice to one or more creditors would be the result of the

1. Si le débiteur accomplit un acte juridique auquel il n'était pas tenu, sachant ou devant savoir qu'il en résulterait une diminution des possibilités de recouvrement pour un ou plusieurs des créanciers, l'acte est annulable et la cause d'annulation peut être invoquée par tout créancier qui subit de ce fait un préjudice, que sa créance soit antérieure ou postérieure à l'acte.

2. On ne peut annuler pour ce motif un acte juridique autre qu'à titre gratuit, qui est soit multilatéral soit unilatéral et adressé à des personnes déterminées, que si ceux avec qui ou à l'égard de qui le débiteur l'a accompli savaient ou devaient savoir qu'il en résulterait un préjudice pour un ou plusieurs créanciers.

3. Lorsqu'on annule un acte juridique à titre gratuit pour cause de préjudice, cette annulation est sans effet à l'égard du bénéficiaire qui ne savait, ni ne devait savoir qu'il en résulterait un préjudice pour un ou plusieurs créanciers, dans la mesure où il

juridical act, but only to the extent that this beneficiary shows that, at the time of the declaration or the institution of the action to annul, he did not derive profit from the juridical act.

4. A creditor attacking a juridical act as being prejudicial to him, only annuls the act in his own favour and no further than necessary to remove the prejudice which he has experienced.

5. Rights which third parties in good faith have acquired, other than by gratuitous title, in property which was the object of the annulled juridical act shall be respected. With respect to a third party in good faith who has acquired property by gratuitous title, the annulment shall have no effect to the extent that he shows that at the time the property is claimed from him he does not derive profit from the juridical act.

justifie que, au moment de la déclaration d'annulation ou de l'exercice de l'action en annulation, il ne tirait pas de profit de cet acte.

4. Lorsque le créancier attaque un acte juridique qui lui est préjudiciable, il ne l'annule qu'à son égard et dans la seule mesure nécessaire pour supprimer le préjudice qu'il a subi.

5. Sont respectés les droits acquis, autrement qu'à titre gratuit, par des tiers de bonne foi sur des biens qui faisaient l'objet de l'acte juridique annulé. L'annulation ne produit aucun effet à l'égard du tiers acquéreur de bonne foi à titre gratuit dans la mesure où il justifie que, au moment où le bien lui est réclamé, il ne tire pas de profit de l'acte juridique.

Art. 46. (3.2.11a) - 1. Indien de rechtshandeling waardoor een of meer schuldeisers zijn benadeeld, is verricht binnen één jaar voor het inroepen van de vernietigingsgrond en de schuldenaar zich niet reeds voor de aanvang van die termijn tot die rechtshandeling had verplicht, wordt vermoed dat men aan beide zijden wist of behoorde te weten dat een zodanige benadeling het gevolg van de rechtshandeling zou zijn:

1°. bij overeenkomsten, waarbij de waarde der verbintenis aan de zijde van de schuldenaar aanmerkelijk die der verbintenis aan de andere zijde overtreft;

2°. bij rechtshandelingen ter voldoening van of zekerheidstelling voor een niet opeisbare schuld;

3°. bij rechtshandelingen, door de schuldenaar die een natuurlijk persoon is, verricht met of jegens:

a. zijn echtgenoot, zijn pleegkind of een bloed- of aanverwant tot in de derde graad;

b. een rechtspersoon waarin hij, zijn echtgenoot, zijn pleegkind of een bloed- of aanverwant tot in de derde graad bestuurder of commissaris is, dan wel waarin deze personen, afzonderlijk of tezamen, als aandeelhouder rechtstreeks of middellijk voor ten minste de helft van het geplaatste kapitaal deelnemen;

4°. bij rechtshandelingen, door de schuldenaar die rechtspersoon is, verricht met of jegens een natuurlijk persoon:

a. die bestuurder of commissaris van de rechtspersoon is, dan wel met of jegens diens echtgenoot, pleegkind of bloed- of aanverwant tot in de derde graad;

b. die al dan niet tezamen met zijn echtgenoot, zijn pleegkinderen en zijn bloed- of aanverwanten tot in de derde graad, als aandeelhouder rechtstreeks of middellijk voor ten minste de helft van het geplaatste kapitaal deelneemt;

c. wiens echtgenoot, pleegkinderen of bloed- of aanverwanten tot in de derde graad, afzonderlijk of tezamen, als aandeelhouder rechtstreeks

of middellijk voor tenminste de helft van het geplaatste kapitaal deelnemen;

5°. bij rechtshandelingen, door de schuldenaar die rechtspersoon is, verricht met of jegens een andere rechtspersoon, indien

a. een van deze rechtspersonen bestuurder is van de andere;

b. een bestuurder, natuurlijk persoon, van een van deze rechtspersonen, of diens echtgenoot, pleegkind of bloed- of aanverwant tot in de derde graad, bestuurder is van de andere;

c. een bestuurder, natuurlijk persoon, of een commissaris van een van deze rechtspersonen, of diens echtgenoot, pleegkind of bloed- of aanverwant tot in de derde graad, afzonderlijk of tezamen, als aandeelhouder rechtstreeks of middellijk voor ten minste de helft van het geplaatste kapitaal deelneemt in de andere;

d. in beide rechtspersonen voor ten minste de helft van het geplaatste kapitaal rechtstreeks of middellijk wordt deelgenomen door dezelfde rechtspersoon, dan wel dezelfde natuurlijke persoon, al dan niet tezamen met zijn echtgenoot, zijn pleegkinderen en zijn bloed- of aanverwanten tot in de derde graad;

6°. bij rechtshandelingen, door de schuldenaar die rechtspersoon is, verricht met of jegens een groepsmaatschappij.

- 2. Met een echtgenoot wordt een andere levensgezel gelijkgesteld.

- 3. Onder pleegkind wordt verstaan hij die duurzaam als eigen kind is verzorgd en opgevoed.

- 4. Onder bestuurder, commissaris of aandeelhouder wordt mede verstaan hij die minder dan een jaar vóór de rechtshandeling bestuurder, commissaris of aandeelhouder is geweest.

- 5. Indien de bestuurder van een rechtspersoon-bestuurder zelf een rechtspersoon is, wordt deze rechtspersoon met de rechtspersoon-bestuurder gelijkgesteld.

1. If the juridical act which has adversely affected one or several creditors has been performed within the year preceding the time the ground for annulment was invoked, and if the debtor had not bound himself to that juridical act prior to such period, there is a presumption that, on both sides, one knew or ought to have known that prejudice to a creditor or creditors would be the result of the juridical act:

1° in contracts whereby the value of the obligation on the debtor's side considerably exceeds that of the obligation on the other side;

2° in juridical acts to pay or to guarantee a debt which is not exigible;

3° in juridical acts performed by a debtor, who is a natural person, with or with respect to:

1. Si un acte juridique portant préjudice à un ou plusieurs créanciers a été accompli dans l'année précédant le moment où la cause d'annulation a été invoquée et que le débiteur ne s'y était pas déjà engagé avant le début de ce délai, il est présumé que les deux parties savaient ou devaient savoir qu'un tel préjudice résulterait de l'acte:

1° S'agissant de contrats, si la valeur de l'obligation du côté du débiteur dépasse nettement celle de l'obligation de l'autre;

2° Si l'acte juridique vise le paiement d'une dette non exigible ou la constitution de sûreté pour une telle dette;

3° Si l'acte juridique a été accompli par une personne physique débitrice:

a. his spouse, his foster child or a relative by blood or marriage up to the third degree;
b. a legal person in which he, his spouse, foster child or relative by blood or marriage up to the third degree is an officer or director, or a legal person in which the aforementioned persons, either separately or jointly, hold as shareholders, directly or indirectly, at least one half of the issued stock;

4° in juridical acts performed by a debtor, who is a legal person, with or with respect to a natural person:

a. who is an officer or director of that legal person, or with or with respect to his spouse, foster child or relative by blood or marriage up to the third degree;
b. who, whether or not together with his spouse, foster children or relatives by blood or marriage up to the third degree, holds as shareholder, directly or indirectly, at least one half of the issued stock;
c. whose spouse, foster children or relatives by blood or marriage up to the third degree hold as shareholders, separately or jointly, directly or indirectly, at least one half of the issued stock;

5° in juridical acts performed by a debtor, who is a legal person, with or with respect to another legal person, if
a. one of these legal persons is an officer of the other;
b. an officer of one of these legal persons, himself a natural person, his spouse, foster child or relative by blood or marriage up to the third degree is an officer of the other legal person;

a. Avec son conjoint, son pupille ou avec un parent ou allié jusqu'au troisième degré, ou à leur égard;
b. Avec une personne morale dont le débiteur, son conjoint, son pupille ou l'un de ses parents ou alliés jusqu'au troisième degré est dirigeant ou administrateur ou dont ces personnes, individuellement ou conjointement, contrôlent, à titre d'actionnaires, directement ou indirectement, au moins la moitié du capital souscrit, ou à l'égard de ces personnes;
4° Si l'acte juridique a été accompli par une personne morale débitrice avec une personne naturelle ou à l'égard de cette dernière:
a. Si la personne physique est son dirigeant ou administrateur, ou avec le conjoint, le pupille ou l'un des parents ou alliés jusqu'au troisième degré d'une telle personne ou à leur égard;
b. Si la personne physique, seule ou avec ses conjoint, pupilles, parents et alliés jusqu'au troisième degré, contrôle à titre d'actionnaire, directement ou indirectement, au moins la moitié du capital souscrit;
c. Si les conjoint, pupilles, parents et alliés jusqu'au troisième degré de la personne physique contrôlent, individuellement ou conjointement, à titre d'actionnaires, directement ou indirectement, au moins la moitié du capital souscrit;
5° S'il agit d'actes juridiques accomplis par une personne morale débitrice avec une autre personne morale ou à l'égard de cette dernière:
a. L'une de ces personnes morales étant dirigeant de l'autre;
b. Un dirigeant, personne physique, de l'une de ces personnes morales ou son conjoint, pupille, parent ou allié jusqu'au troisième degré étant dirigeant de l'autre;

c. an officer, who is a natural person, or a director of one of these legal persons, or his spouse, foster child or relative by blood or marriage up to the third degree, separately or jointly, hold as shareholders, directly or indirectly, at least one half of the issued stock of the other legal person;

d. the same legal person or the same natural person, whether or not together with his spouse, foster children and relatives by blood or marriage up to the third degree holds, directly or indirectly, at least one half of the issued stock in both legal persons;

6° in juridical acts performed by a debtor, who is a legal person, with or with respect to a group company.

2. A spouse includes any other partner in life.

3. A foster child is a person who has been durably looked after and educated as an own child.

4. An officer, director or shareholder includes a person who had that capacity less than a year prior to the juridical act.

5. A legal person includes a legal person-officer, if the officer of a legal person-officer is itself a legal person.

c. Un dirigeant, personne physique, ou un administrateur de l'une de ces personnes morales ou son conjoint, pupille, parent ou allié jusqu'au troisième degré, individuellement ou conjointement, contrôlant à titre d'actionnaires, directement ou indirectement, au moins la moitié du capital souscrit de l'autre personne morale;

d. Les deux personnes morales étant contrôlées pour au moins la moitié du capital souscrit par la même personne morale ou encore par la même personne physique ou ses conjoint, pupilles, parents ou alliés jusqu'au troisième degré;

6° Si l'acte juridique a été accompli par une personne morale débitrice avec une société faisant partie du même groupe ou à l'égard de celui-ci;

2. Est assimilé au conjoint tout autre compagnon de vie.

3. Par pupille on entend l'enfant qui a été traité et élevé de façon durable comme l'enfant propre des parents.

4. Les termes dirigeant, administrateur et actionnaire englobent les personnes qui ont eu l'une de ces qualités dans l'année précédant l'acte juridique.

5. Si le dirigeant d'une personne morale dirigeante est lui-même une personne morale, celle-ci est assimilée à la personne morale dirigeante.

Art. 47. (3.2.11b) In geval van benadeling door een rechtshandeling om niet, die de schuldenaar heeft verricht binnen één jaar vóór het inroepen van de vernietigingsgrond, wordt vermoed dat hij wist of behoorde te weten dat benadeling van een of meer schuldeisers het gevolg van de rechtshandeling zou zijn.

In the event of prejudice caused by a juridical act by gratuitous title which the debtor has performed within the year preceding the time the ground for annulment was invoked, there is a presumption that he knew or ought to have known that prejudice to one or several creditors would be the result of the juridical act.

Le débiteur qui a accompli un acte juridique à titre gratuit dans l'année précédant le moment où la cause d'annulation a été invoquée est présumé avoir su ou dû savoir qu'il en résulterait un préjudice pour un ou plusieurs créanciers.

Art. 48. (3.2.11c) Onder schuldenaar in de zin van de drie vorige artikelen is begrepen hij op wiens goed voor de schuld van een ander verhaal kan worden genomen.

For the purposes of the three preceding articles, a debtor includes a person against whose property recourse can be taken for the debt of another.

Aux fins des trois articles précédents, le terme débiteur s'entend également de celui dont le bien est sujet au recouvrement pour la dette d'une autre personne.

Art. 49. (3.2.13) Een vernietigbare rechtshandeling wordt vernietigd hetzij door een buitengerechtelijke verklaring, hetzij door een rechterlijke uitspraak.

Where a juridical act is subject to annulment, it can be annulled either by extrajudicial declaration or by judgment.

L'acte juridique annulable est annulé par déclaration extrajudiciaire ou par jugement.

Art. 50. (3.2.14) - 1. Een buitengerechtelijke verklaring die een rechtshandeling vernietigt, wordt door hem in wiens belang de vernietigingsgrond bestaat, gericht tot hen die partij bij de rechtshandeling zijn.
- 2. Een buitengerechtelijke verklaring kan een rechtshandeling met betrekking tot een registergoed die heeft geleid tot een inschrijving in de openbare registers of tot een tot levering van een registergoed, bestemde akte, slechts vernietigen indien alle partijen in de vernietiging berusten.

1. An extrajudicial declaration annulling a juridical act is addressed by the person in whose interest the ground for annulment has been given, to those who are parties to the juridical act.
2. An extrajudicial declaration cannot annul a juridical act pertaining to registered property which has led to an entry in the public registers or to a deed intended to deliver registered property, unless all parties agree to the annulment.

1. Celui en faveur de qui existe la cause d'annulation adresse la déclaration extrajudiciaire annulant un acte juridique aux personnes qui étaient parties à l'acte.

2. Une déclaration extrajudiciaire ne peut, si ce n'est avec l'acquiescement de toutes les parties, annuler un acte juridique portant sur un bien immatriculé, qui a donné lieu à une inscription dans les registres ou à un acte passé aux fins de délivrance.

Art. 51. (3.2.15) - 1. Een rechterlijke uitspraak vernietigt een rechtshandeling, doordat zij een beroep in rechte op een vernietigingsgrond aanvaardt.
- 2. Een rechtsvordering tot vernietiging van een rechtshandeling wordt ingesteld tegen hen die partij bij de rechtshandeling zijn.
- 3. Een beroep in rechte op een vernietigingsgrond kan te allen tijde worden gedaan ter afwering van een op de rechtshandeling steunende vordering of andere rechtsmaatregel. Hij die dit beroep doet, is verplicht om zo spoedig mogelijk daarvan mededeling te doen aan de partijen bij de rechtshandeling die niet in het geding zijn verschenen.

1. A judgment annuls a juridical act by accepting a ground for annulment which has been judicially invoked.
2. An action to annul a juridical act is instituted against the persons who are parties to the juridical act.

1. Un jugement annule l'acte juridique en accueillant le moyen qui invoque la cause d'annulation.
2. L'action en annulation d'un acte juridique est intentée contre ceux qui sont parties à l'acte.

3. A ground for annulment may always be invoked judicially as a defence against a claim or other legal measure based upon the juridical act. The person who does so must, as soon as possible, notify the parties to the juridical act who have not appeared in the case.

3. Une cause d'annulation d'un acte juridique peut à tout moment être invoquée en justice pour repousser une action ou autre mesure de droit fondée sur cet acte. Celui qui l'invoque est tenu d'en aviser dès que possible les parties à l'acte qui n'ont pas comparu.

Art. 52. (3.2.17) - 1. Rechtsvorderingen tot vernietiging van een rechtshandeling verjaren:
a. in geval van onbekwaamheid: drie jaren nadat de onbekwaamheid is geëindigd, of, indien de onbekwame een wettelijke vertegenwoordiger heeft, drie jaren nadat de handeling ter kennis van de wettelijke vertegenwoordiger is gekomen;
b. in geval van bedreiging of misbruik van omstandigheden: drie jaren nadat deze invloed heeft opgehouden te werken;
c. in geval van bedrog, dwaling of benadeling: drie jaren nadat het bedrog, de dwaling of de benadeling is ontdekt;
d. in geval van een andere vernietigingsgrond: drie jaren nadat de bevoegdheid om deze vernietigingsgrond in te roepen, aan degene aan wie deze bevoegdheid toekomt, ten dienste is komen te staan.
- 2. Na de verjaring van de rechtsvordering tot vernietiging van de rechtshandeling kan deze niet meer op dezelfde vernietigingsgrond door een buitengerechtelijke verklaring worden vernietigd.

1. Actions to annul a juridical act are prescribed:
a. in the event of incapacity, by three years from the termination of the incapacity or, if the incapable person has a legal representative, by three years from the time the act has come to the attention of the legal representative;
b. in the event of threat or abuse of circumstances, by three years from the time this influence has ceased to operate;
c. in the event of fraud, error or prejudice to creditors, by three years from their discovery;
d. in the event of other grounds for annulment, by three years from the time the right to invoke this ground for annulment has become available to the person possessing the right.
2. Once prescription of the action to annul a juridical act has been completed, the act can no longer be annulled upon the same ground by an extrajudicial declaration.

1. L'action en nullité d'un acte juridique se prescrit:
a. Dans le cas d'incapacité: par trois ans à compter du moment où l'incapacité a pris fin ou, si l'incapable a un représentant légal, par trois ans à compter du moment où ce dernier a eu connaissance de l'acte;
b. Dans le cas de menace ou d'abus tiré des circonstances: par trois ans après la cessation de cette influence;
c. Dans le cas de dol, d'erreur ou de préjudice causé aux créanciers: par trois ans après leur découverte;
d. Dans le cas des autres causes d'annulation: par trois ans à compter du moment où le titulaire de l'action en annulation est en droit de l'exercer.
2. Après la prescription de l'action en annulation d'un acte juridique, l'annulation de cet acte ne peut plus être provoquée pour la même cause par déclaration extrajudiciaire.

Art. 53. (3.2.17b) - 1. De vernietiging werkt terug tot het tijdstip waarop de rechtshandeling is verricht.

- 2. Indien de reeds ingetreden gevolgen van een rechtshandeling bezwaarlijk ongedaan gemaakt kunnen worden, kan de rechter desgevraagd aan een vernietiging geheel of ten dele haar werking ontzeggen. Hij kan aan een partij die daardoor onbillijk wordt bevoordeeld, de verplichting opleggen tot een uitkering in geld aan de partij die benadeeld wordt.

1. Annulment has retroactive effect to the time the juridical act was executed.
2. The judge may, if so demanded, refuse to give effect to an annulment in whole or in part, if the juridical act has already produced effects which can only be undone with difficulty. He may order that a party who is prejudiced by his decision be compensated by a party who unjustly benefits from it.

1. L'annulation rétroagit jusqu'au moment de la passation de l'acte.
2. Si les effets déjà intervenus d'un acte juridique peuvent difficilement être anéantis[1], le juge peut, sur demande, priver l'annulation d'effet en tout ou partie. Il peut obliger la partie qui profite injustement de cette décision à payer une indemnité à celui qui de ce fait subit un préjudice.

Art. 54. (3.2.17c) - 1. De bevoegdheid om ter vernietiging van een meerzijdige rechtshandeling een beroep te doen op misbruik van omstandigheden vervalt, wanneer de wederpartij tijdig een wijziging van de gevolgen van de rechtshandeling voorstelt, die het nadeel op afdoende wijze opheft.
- 2. Bovendien kan de rechter op verlangen van een der partijen, in plaats van een vernietiging wegens misbruik van omstandigheden uit te spreken, ter opheffing van dit nadeel de gevolgen van de rechtshandeling wijzigen.

1. The power to invoke abuse of circumstances in order to annul a multilateral juridical act lapses when the other party timely proposes a modification to the effects of the juridical act which adequately removes the prejudice.
2. Furthermore, instead of pronouncing the annulment for abuse of circumstances, the judge may, upon the demand of one of the parties, modify the effects of the juridical act to remove this prejudice.

1. La faculté d'invoquer un abus des circonstances afin d'annuler un acte juridique multilatéral s'éteint lorsque l'autre partie propose en temps utile une modification des effets de l'acte, mettant fin au préjudice de façon adéquate.

2. Le juge, en outre, à la demande de l'une des parties, peut, au lieu de prononcer l'annulation de l'acte juridique sur la base d'un abus des circonstances, en modifier les effets afin de supprimer le préjudice.

Art. 55. (3.2.18) - 1. De bevoegdheid om ter vernietiging van een rechtshandeling een beroep op een vernietigingsgrond te doen vervalt, wanneer hij aan wie deze bevoegdheid toekomt, de rechtshandeling heeft bevestigd, nadat de verjaringstermijn ter zake van de rechtsvordering tot vernietiging op die grond een aanvang heeft genomen.
- 2. Eveneens vervalt de bevoegdheid om een beroep op een vernietigingsgrond te doen, wanneer een onmiddellijk belanghebbende na de aanvang van de verjaringstermijn aan hem aan wie deze bevoegdheid toekomt een redelijke termijn heeft gesteld om te kiezen tussen bevestiging en vernietiging en deze binnen deze termijn geen keuze heeft gedaan.

---

[1] Ce terme nouveau (ongedaanmaken) est également employé aux articles 311 du Livre troisième et 24, 25, 210 et 211 du Livre sixième, lorsqu'il s'agit de défaire les prestations déjà effectuées dans l'exécution d'un contrat nul. Le terme «remise en état» correspond au terme néerlandais différent «*herstel in de oude toestand*».

1. The power to invoke a ground for annulment in order to annul a juridical act lapses when the person in possession of this right confirms the juridical act after the prescription period for the action to annul upon that ground has started to run.
2. The power to invoke a ground for annulment also lapses when, after the commencement of the prescription period, a directly interested person has given notice to the person who possesses the right to annul, requiring him to choose between a confirmation and an annulment, within a reasonable period, and this person has made no choice within that period.

1. Celui qui a la faculté d'invoquer une cause d'annulation afin d'annuler un acte juridique en est déchu lorsqu'il confirme l'acte après que le délai de prescription de l'action en annulation pour cette cause a commencé à courir.

2. Celui qui a la faculté d'invoquer une cause d'annulation afin d'annuler un acte juridique en est également déchu lorsque, après que le délai de prescription a commencé à courir, une personne directement intéressée lui a imparti un délai raisonnable pour choisir entre la confirmation et l'annulation et qu'il n'a fait pas son choix dans le temps imparti.

Art. 56. (3.2.18b) Voor de toepassing van de artikelen 50-55 gelden mede als partij:
a. in geval van eenzijdige tot een of meer bepaalde personen gerichte rechtshandeling: die personen;
b. in geval van andere eenzijdige rechtshandelingen: zij die onmiddellijk belanghebbenden zijn bij de instandhouding van die handeling.

In applying articles 50 - 55, a party includes
a. in the case of a unilateral juridical act directed at one or more specifically determined persons: those persons;
b. in the case of other unilateral juridical acts: those who have a direct interest in maintaining the act.

Aux fins des articles 50 à 55 sont assimilées aux parties à un acte:
a. S'agissant d'un acte juridique unilatéral adressé à une ou plusieurs personnes déterminées: ces personnes;
b. S'agissant des autres actes juridiques unilatéraux: ceux qui sont directement intéressés au maintien de l'acte.

Art. 57. (3.2.19) Behoeft een rechtshandeling om het beoogde gevolg te hebben goedkeuring, machtiging, vergunning of enige andere vorm van toestemming van een overheidsorgaan of van een andere persoon, die geen partij bij de rechtshandeling is, dan kan iedere onmiddellijk belanghebbende aan hen die partij bij de rechtshandeling zijn geweest, aanzeggen dat, indien niet binnen een redelijke, bij die aanzegging gestelde termijn die toestemming wordt verkregen, de handeling te zijnen aanzien zonder gevolg zal blijven.

Where a juridical act, in order to produce its intended effect, needs the approval, authorization, licensing or any other form of consent of a public authority or another person who is not a party to the juridical act, every directly interested person can give notice to those who have been party to the juridical act, that the act shall have no effect in his respect, unless the consent is obtained within a reasonable period indicated in the notice.

Lorsqu'un acte juridique requiert, pour produire effet, l'approbation, l'autorisation, la permission ou une autre forme de consentement de l'autorité publique ou d'une personne autre qui n'est pas partie à l'acte, toute personne directement intéressée peut donner avis aux parties à cet acte que, si le consentement requis n'est pas obtenu dans le délai raisonnable fixé dans cet avis, l'acte restera sans effet à son égard.

Art. 58. (3.2.20) - 1. Wanneer eerst na het verrichten van een rechtshandeling een voor haar geldigheid gesteld wettelijk vereiste wordt vervuld, maar alle onmiddellijk belanghebbenden die zich op dit gebrek hadden kunnen beroepen, in de tussen de handeling en de vervulling van het vereiste liggende tijdsruimte de handeling als geldig hebben aangemerkt, is daarmede de rechtshandeling bekrachtigd.
- 2. Het vorige lid is niet van toepassing op het geval dat een rechtshandeling nietig is als gevolg van handelingsonbekwaamheid van degene die haar heeft verricht en deze vervolgens handelingsbekwaam wordt.
- 3. Inmiddels verkregen rechten van derden behoeven aan bekrachtiging niet in de weg te staan, mits zij worden geëerbiedigd.

1. Where a legal condition for the validity of a juridical act is fulfilled only after its execution, but all directly interested parties who could have invoked this defect have regarded the act as valid during the period between the act and the fulfillment of the legal condition, the juridical act will thereby have been regularized.
2. The preceding paragraph does not apply to a juridical act which is null due to the incapacity of the person who has performed the act in the event that this person is subsequently capacitated.
3. Rights which have been acquired by third parties in the interim need not be a bar to regularization, provided that these rights are respected.

1. Un acte juridique dont une condition légale de validité est remplie seulement après la formation de l'acte est régularisé lorsque toutes les personnes directement intéressées qui auraient pu invoquer ce vice ont considéré l'acte comme valide dans l'intervalle de temps séparant le moment de la formation et celui où la condition est remplie.
2. Le paragraphe précédent ne s'applique pas à un acte juridique nul pour cause de l'incapacité de celui qui l'a accompli, lorsque ce dernier acquiert ensuite la capacité.
3. Pourvu qu'ils soient respectés, les droits acquis dans l'intervalle par des tiers ne s'opposent pas à la régularisation.

Art. 59. (3.2.21) Buiten het vermogensrecht vinden de bepalingen van deze titel overeenkomstige toepassing, voor zover de aard van de rechtshandeling of van de rechtsbetrekking zich daartegen niet verzet.

The provisions of this title apply *mutatis mutandis* to areas of the law other than patrimonial law to the extent that they are not incompatible with the nature of the juridical act or relationship.

Les dispositions du présent titre s'appliquent par analogie dans les domaines autres que le droit patrimonial dans la mesure où la nature de l'acte ou du rapport juridique ne s'y oppose pas.

TITEL 3 VOLMACHT

TITLE 3 PROCURATION

TITRE TROISIÈME DE LA PROCURATION

Art. 60. (3.3.1) - 1. Volmacht is de bevoegdheid die een volmachtgever verleent aan een ander, de gevolmachtigde, om in zijn naam rechtshandelingen te verrichten.

- 2. Waar in deze titel van rechtshandeling wordt gesproken, is daaronder het in ontvangst nemen van een verklaring begrepen.

1. Procuration is the power which a person, called a principal,[1] grants to another, the procurator, to perform juridical acts in his name.
2. For the purposes of this title a juridical act includes the acceptance of a declaration.

1. La procuration est le pouvoir qu'une personne, l'auteur, accorde à une autre, le procureur, d'accomplir des actes juridiques en son nom.
2. Aux fins du présent titre la réception d'une déclaration est considérée comme un acte juridique.

Art. 61. (3.3.2) - 1. Een volmacht kan uitdrukkelijk of stilzwijgend worden verleend.
- 2. Is een rechtshandeling in naam van een ander verricht, dan kan tegen de wederpartij, indien zij op grond van een verklaring of gedraging van die ander heeft aangenomen en onder de gegeven omstandigheden redelijkerwijze mocht aannemen dat een toereikende volmacht was verleend, op de onjuistheid van deze veronderstelling geen beroep worden gedaan.
- 3. Indien een volgens wet of gebruik openbaar gemaakte volmacht beperkingen bevat, die zo ongebruikelijk zijn dat de wederpartij ze daarin niet behoefde te verwachten, kunnen deze haar niet worden tegengeworpen, tenzij zij ze kende.

1. Procuration can be granted expressly or tacitly.
2. Where a juridical act has been performed in the name of another person, the other party who, on the basis of a declaration or conduct of that other person, has presumed and in the given circumstances could reasonably presume the existence of a sufficient procuration, may not have invoked against him the inaccuracy of this presumption.
3. If a procuration, which has been made public pursuant to law or usage, contains restrictions which are so unusual that the other party should not have anticipated their existence, they cannot be invoked against such party, unless he had actual knowledge of them.

1. La procuration peut être accordée de façon expresse ou tacite.
2. Lorsqu'un acte juridique est accompli au nom d'une autre personne, l'autre partie qui, sur la foi d'une déclaration ou de la conduite de cette autre personne, a cru et pouvait dans les circonstances raisonnablement croire à l'existence d'une procuration suffisante ne peut se voir opposer l'inexactitude de cette croyance.
3. Si une procuration, publiée de la manière prévue par la loi ou par l'usage, comporte des restrictions si inusitées que l'autre partie ne devait pas s'attendre à les y trouver, ces restrictions ne lui sont pas opposables, à moins qu'elle n'en ait eu connaissance.

Art. 62. (3.3.3) - 1. Een algemene volmacht strekt zich slechts uit tot daden van beschikking, indien schriftelijk en ondubbelzinnig is bepaald dat zij zich ook tot die daden uitstrekt. Onder algemene volmacht wordt verstaan de volmacht die alle zaken van de volmachtgever en alle rechtshandelingen omvat, met uitzondering van hetgeen ondubbelzinnig is uitgesloten.
- 2. Een bijzondere volmacht die in algemene bewoordingen is verleend, strekt zich slechts uit tot daden van beschikking, indien dit ondubbelzinnig is bepaald. Niettemin strekt een volmacht die voor een bepaald doel is

[1] "Principal" is a term with common law connotations. No suitable English civilian term, however, is available.

verleend, zich uit tot alle daden van beheer en van beschikking die dienstig kunnen zijn tot het bereiken van dit doel.

1. A general procuration does not extend to acts of disposition, unless this has been unequivocally provided in writing. A general procuration is the procuration which applies to all affairs of the principal and to all juridical acts, with the exception of that which has been unequivocally excluded.
2. A special procuration which has been granted in general terms does not extend to acts of disposition, unless this has been unequivocally provided. Nevertheless, a procuration granted for a specific purpose extends to all acts of management and disposition which can serve to attain this purpose.

1. La procuration générale ne s'étend aux actes de disposition que s'il est ainsi stipulé par écrit et sans équivoque. Par procuration générale, on entend celle qui porte sur toutes les affaires appartenant à l'auteur et sur tous les actes juridiques, sous réserve de ce qui est exclu sans équivoque.

2. La procuration spéciale exprimée en termes généraux ne s'étend aux actes de disposition que s'il est ainsi stipulé sans équivoque. Toutefois, la procuration accordée dans un but spécifique s'étend à tout acte d'administration ou de disposition pouvant servir à l'atteindre.

Art. 63. (3.3.4) - 1. De omstandigheid dat iemand onbekwaam is tot het verrichten van rechtshandelingen voor zichzelf, maakt hem niet onbekwaam tot het optreden als gevolmachtigde.
- 2. Wanneer een volmacht door een onbekwaam persoon is verleend, is een krachtens die volmacht door de gevolmachtigde verrichte rechtshandeling op gelijke wijze geldig, nietig of vernietigbaar, als wanneer zij door de onbekwame zelf zou zijn verricht.

1. The fact that a person is incapable of performing juridical acts for himself does not make him incapable of acting as a procurator.
2. A juridical act performed by a procurator pursuant to a procuration granted by an incapable is valid, null or annulable just as it would have been, had it been performed by the incapable person himself.

1. L'incapacité d'une personne d'accomplir des actes juridiques ne l'empêche pas d'agir comme procureur.

2. L'acte juridique accompli par un procureur en vertu d'une procuration accordée par un incapable est valide, nul ou annulable de la même façon que l'aurait été l'acte accompli par l'incapable lui-même.

Art. 64. (3.3.5) Tenzij anders is bepaald, is een gevolmachtigde slechts in de navolgende gevallen bevoegd de hem verleende volmacht aan een ander te verlenen:
- **a. voor zover de bevoegdheid hiertoe uit de aard der te verrichten rechtshandelingen noodzakelijk voortvloeit of in overeenstemming is met het gebruik;**
- **b. voor zover de verlening van de volmacht aan een andere persoon in het belang van de volmachtgever noodzakelijk is en deze zelf niet in staat is een voorziening te treffen;**
- **c. voor zover de volmacht goederen betreft, die gelegen zijn buiten het land waarin de gevolmachtigde zijn woonplaats heeft.**

Unless otherwise provided, a procurator may grant his procuration to another person only in the following cases:

Sauf stipulation contraire, le procureur ne peut accorder à un tiers la procuration qu'il a lui-même reçue que dans les cas suivants:

a. to the extent that the power to delegate flows necessarily from the nature of the juridical acts to be performed or is in conformity with usage;
b. to the extent that the delegation of the procuration is necessary in the interest of the principal who is unable to act himself;
c. to the extent that the procuration concerns property which is situated outside the country in which the procurator has his domicile.

a. Dans la mesure où le pouvoir de ce faire découle nécessairement de la nature des actes juridiques à accomplir ou est conforme à l'usage;
b. Dans la mesure où cette transmission est nécessaire dans l'intérêt de l'auteur qui n'est pas en état de prendre lui-même des mesures;
c. Dans la mesure où la procuration porte sur des biens situés en dehors du pays où le procureur a son domicile.

Art. 65. (3.3.5a) Is een volmacht aan twee of meer personen tezamen verleend, dan is ieder van hen bevoegd zelfstandig te handelen, tenzij anders is bepaald.

Where a procuration has been granted to two or more persons together, each of them is empowered to act independently, unless it has been provided otherwise.

Lorsque la procuration est accordée à plusieurs personnes conjointement, chacune d'elles peut agir de façon indépendante, à moins qu'il ne soit stipulé autrement.

Art. 66. (3.3.6) - 1. Een door de gevolmachtigde binnen de grenzen van zijn bevoegdheid in naam van de volmachtgever verrichte rechtshandeling treft in haar gevolgen de volmachtgever.
- 2. Voor zover het al of niet aanwezig zijn van een wil of van wilsgebreken, alsmede bekendheid of onbekendheid met feiten van belang zijn voor de geldigheid of de gevolgen van een rechtshandeling, komen ter beoordeling daarvan de volmachtgever of de gevolmachtigde of beiden in aanmerking, al naar gelang het aandeel dat ieder van hen heeft gehad in de totstandkoming van de rechtshandeling en in de bepaling van haar inhoud.

1. A principal is bound by the juridical act which has been performed in his name by the procurator acting within the limits of his power.
2. To the extent that the existence of intent, of defects of consent or of the awareness of certain facts, or the absence of these factors are relevant to the validity or to the effects of a juridical act, consideration is given to those factors as they relate to the principal, the procurator, or both, according to the part which each of them has played in the formation of the juridical act and in the determination of its content.

1. L'auteur d'une procuration est lié par l'acte juridique accompli en son nom par le procureur dans les limites de son pouvoir.

2. Dans la mesure où la présence ou l'absence de volonté ou de vices de consentement ou la connaissance ou l'ignorance de faits déterminent la validité ou les effets d'un acte juridique, sont prises en considération celles de l'auteur de la procuration, celles du procureur, ou celles de l'un et de l'autre, selon la part de chacun dans la formation de l'acte et la détermination de son contenu.

Art. 67. (3.3.7) - 1. Hij die een overeenkomst aangaat in naam van een nader te noemen volmachtgever, moet diens naam noemen binnen de door de wet, de overeenkomst of het gebruik bepaalde termijn of, bij gebreke hiervan, binnen een redelijke termijn.

- 2. Wanneer hij de naam van de volmachtgever niet tijdig noemt, wordt hij geacht de overeenkomst voor zichzelf te hebben aangegaan, tenzij uit de overeenkomst anders voortvloeit.

1. A person who enters into a contract in the name of a principal yet to be named must disclose the principal's name within the period provided for by law, contract or usage or, in the absence thereof, within a reasonable period.
2. When he does not disclose the name of the principal in a timely fashion, he is deemed to have entered into the contract for himself, unless the contract produces a different result.

1. Celui qui conclut un contrat au nom d'une personne dont l'identité reste à révéler doit dévoiler cette identité dans le délai fixé par la loi, par le contrat ou par l'usage ou, à défaut, dans un délai raisonnable.

2. Faute d'avoir respecté ce délai, il est réputé avoir conclu le contrat pour lui-même, à moins qu'il n'en découle autrement de la nature du contrat.

Art. 68. (3.3.7a) Tenzij anders is bepaald, kan een gevolmachtigde slechts dan als wederpartij van de volmachtgever optreden, wanneer de inhoud van de te verrichten rechtshandeling zo nauwkeurig vaststaat, dat strijd tussen beider belangen uitgesloten is.

Unless otherwise provided, a procurator may only enter into a juridical act with his principal where the content of the juridical act to be performed is so precisely determined that conflict between their interests is excluded.

À moins de stipulation contraire, le procureur peut conclure un acte juridique avec l'auteur de la procuration seulement lorsque le contenu de cet acte est établi de façon si précise qu'un conflit de leurs intérêts est exclu.

Art. 69. (3.3.8) - 1. Wanneer iemand zonder daartoe bevoegd te zijn als gevolmachtigde in naam van een ander heeft gehandeld, kan laatstgenoemde de rechtshandeling bekrachtigen en haar daardoor hetzelfde gevolg verschaffen, als zou zijn ingetreden wanneer zij krachtens een volmacht was verricht.
- 2. Is voor het verlenen van een volmacht tot de rechtshandeling een bepaalde vorm vereist, dan geldt voor de bekrachtiging hetzelfde vereiste.
- 3. Een bekrachtiging heeft geen gevolg, indien op het tijdstip waarop zij geschiedt, de wederpartij reeds heeft te kennen gegeven dat zij de handeling wegens het ontbreken van een volmacht als ongeldig beschouwt, tenzij de wederpartij op het tijdstip dat zij handelde heeft begrepen of onder de gegeven omstandigheden redelijkerwijs heeft moeten begrijpen dat geen toereikende volmacht was verleend.
- 4. Een onmiddellijk belanghebbende kan degene in wiens naam gehandeld is, een redelijke termijn voor de bekrachtiging stellen. Hij behoeft niet met een gedeeltelijke of voorwaardelijke bekrachtiging genoegen te nemen.
- 5. Rechten door de volmachtgever vóór de bekrachtiging aan derden verleend, blijven gehandhaafd.

1. A juridical act entered into by a person acting, without the right to do so, as procurator in the name of another, may be ratified by the latter and the juridical act will then have the same effect as if it had been performed pursuant to a procuration.

1. Lorsqu'une personne, sans en avoir le pouvoir, a agi comme procureur au nom d'une autre, celle-ci peut ratifier l'acte juridique, lui conférant ainsi l'effet qu'il aurait produit s'il avait été accompli en vertu d'une procuration.

2. Where a particular formality is required for the granting of a procuration to perform a juridical act, the same formality shall apply to the ratification.

3. Ratification has no effect, if at the time it is done, the third party has already let it be known that he considers the act to be invalid for want of procuration, unless this third party understood or under the circumstances ought to have understood, at the time of his acting, that no sufficient procuration had been granted.

4. A directly interested person can determine a reasonable period for ratification by the person in whose name the act has been performed. He does not have to accept a partial or conditional ratification.

5. Rights granted by the principal to third persons before the ratification, are respected.

2. Lorsque la procuration relative à l'accomplissement d'un acte juridique requiert une forme particulière, la ratification est soumise à la même forme.

3. La ratification est sans effet si l'autre partie à l'acte juridique a déjà fait savoir, au moment de la ratification, qu'elle considère cet acte comme invalide en raison de l'absence de procuration, à moins que, au moment où elle a agi, elle ait compris ou, dans les circonstances, ait normalement dû comprendre qu'une procuration suffisante n'avait pas été accordée.

4. Toute personne directement intéressée peut impartir à celui au nom de qui l'acte juridique a été accompli un délai raisonnable de ratification. Elle n'est pas tenue de se contenter d'une ratification partielle ou conditionnelle.

5. Les droits que l'auteur de la procuration a concédés à des tiers avant la ratification sont maintenus.

Art. 70. (3.3.9) Hij die als gevolmachtigde handelt, staat jegens de wederpartij in voor het bestaan en de omvang van de volmacht, tenzij de wederpartij weet of behoort te begrijpen dat een toereikende volmacht ontbreekt of de gevolmachtigde de inhoud van de volmacht volledig aan de wederpartij heeft medegedeeld.

He who acts as procurator warrants to the other party the existence and the extent of the procuration, unless the other party knows or ought to know that a sufficient procuration is lacking, or unless the procurator has fully communicated the content of the procuration to the other party.

Celui qui agit comme procureur garantit à l'autre partie l'existence et l'étendue de sa procuration, sauf si celle-ci sait ou doit comprendre qu'une procuration suffisante fait défaut, ou si le procureur lui a communiqué intégralement le contenu de la procuration.

Art. 71. (3.3.10) - 1. Verklaringen, door een gevolmachtigde afgelegd, kunnen door de wederpartij als ongeldig van de hand worden gewezen, indien zij de gevolmachtigde terstond om bewijs van de volmacht heeft gevraagd en haar niet onverwijld hetzij een geschrift waaruit de volmacht volgt is overgelegd, hetzij de volmacht door de volmachtgever is bevestigd. - 2. Bewijs van volmacht kan niet worden verlangd, indien de volmacht door de volmachtgever ter kennis van de wederpartij was gebracht, indien zij op een door wet of gebruik bepaalde wijze was bekendgemaakt, of indien zij voortvloeit uit een aanstelling waarmede de wederpartij bekend is.

1. A party may refuse to accept a declaration made by a procurator, if he has forthwith asked the procurator for proof of the procuration and he does not receive without delay proof in writing of

1. Une partie à qui le procureur fait des déclarations peut les rejeter si, après avoir demandé sur le champ une preuve de la procuration, un écrit à cet effet ne lui est pas remis sans tarder et la procuration ne lui est

the procuration nor confirmation thereof by the principal.
2. Proof of procuration cannot be required if the principal has informed the other party of the procuration, if it has been made public in a manner determined by law or usage, or if it results from an appointment known to the other party.

pas non plus confirmée sans délai par l'auteur.
2. On ne peut exiger la preuve d'une procuration, si l'auteur l'a portée à la connaissance de l'autre partie, si elle a été publiée de la manière prévue par la loi ou l'usage ou si elle découle d'une nomination dont l'autre partie a connaissance.

Art. 72. (3.3.11) Een volmacht eindigt:
a. door de dood, de ondercuratelestelling of het faillissement van de volmachtgever;
b. door de dood, de ondercuratelestelling of het faillissement van de gevolmachtigde, tenzij anders is bepaald;
c. door herroeping door de volmachtgever;
d. door opzegging door de gevolmachtigde.

Procuration is terminated:
a. upon the death, by the placement under curatorship, or by the bankruptcy of the principal;
b. upon the death, by the placement under curatorship, or by the bankruptcy of the procurator, unless otherwise provided;
c. by revocation by the principal;
d. by renunciation by the procurator.

La procuration finit:
a. Par le décès, la mise en curatelle ou la faillite de l'auteur;
b. Par le décès, la mise en curatelle ou la faillite du procureur, sauf stipulation contraire;
c. Par la révocation par l'auteur;
d. Par la renonciation du procureur.

Art. 73. (3.3.12) - 1. Niettegenstaande de dood of de ondercuratelestelling van de volmachtgever blijft de gevolmachtigde bevoegd de rechtshandelingen te verrichten, die nodig zijn voor het beheer van een onderneming.
- 2. Niettegenstaande de dood of de ondercuratelestelling van de volmachtgever blijft de gevolmachtigde bevoegd rechtshandelingen te verrichten, die niet zonder nadeel kunnen worden uitgesteld. Hetzelfde geldt indien de gevolmachtigde de volmacht heeft opgezegd.
- 3. De in de vorige leden vermelde bevoegdheid eindigt een jaar na het overlijden, de ondercuratelestelling of de opzegging.

1. Notwithstanding the death or the placement under curatorship of the principal, the procurator remains empowered to perform juridical acts which are necessary for the management of a business.
2. Notwithstanding the death or the placement under curatorship of the principal, the procurator remains empowered to perform juridical acts which cannot be postponed without causing prejudice. The same applies if the procurator has renounced the procuration.

1. Nonobstant le décès ou la mise en curatelle de l'auteur, le procureur conserve le pouvoir d'accomplir les actes juridiques nécessaires à l'administration d'une entreprise.
2. Nonobstant le décès ou la mise en curatelle de l'auteur, le procureur conserve le pouvoir d'accomplir les actes juridiques qui ne peuvent être différés sans préjudice. Il en est de même si le procureur a renoncé à la procuration.

3. The power referred to in the preceding paragraphs ceases one year after the death, the placement under curatorship or the renunciation.

3. Le pouvoir dont il est fait état aux paragraphes précédents disparaît un an après le décès, la mise en curatelle ou la renonciation.

Art. 74. (3.3.13) - 1. Voor zover een volmacht strekt tot het verrichten van een rechtshandeling in het belang van de gevolmachtigde of van een derde, kan worden bepaald dat zij onherroepelijk is, of dat zij niet eindigt door de dood of ondercuratelestelling van de volmachtgever. Eerstgenoemde bepaling sluit, tenzij anders blijkt, de tweede in.
- 2. Bevat de volmacht een bepaling als in het vorige lid bedoeld, dan mag de wederpartij aannemen dat het aldaar voor de geldigheid van die bepaling gestelde vereiste vervuld is, tenzij het tegendeel voor haar duidelijk kenbaar is.
- 3. Tenzij anders is bepaald, kan de gevolmachtigde een overeenkomstig het eerste lid onherroepelijk verleende volmacht ook buiten de in artikel 64 genoemde gevallen aan een ander verlenen.
- 4. De rechtbank kan op verzoek van de volmachtgever, of van een erfgenaam of de curator van de volmachtgever, een bepaling als in het eerste lid bedoeld wegens gewichtige redenen wijzigen of buiten werking stellen.

1. To the extent that the object of the procuration is the performance of a juridical act which is in the interest of the procurator or a third person, it may be provided that the procuration shall be irrevocable or that it will not terminate upon the death or by the placement under curatorship of the principal. The former provision includes the latter, unless a different intention is evident.
2. Where the procuration contains a provision referred to in the preceding paragraph, the other party may assume that the requirements for the validity of that provision have been fulfilled, unless the contrary must be obvious to him.
3. Unless otherwise provided, the procurator may grant to another an irrevocable procuration which has been granted to him pursuant to the first paragraph, even outside the cases referred to in article 64.
4. The district court, upon the request of the principal, an heir or the curator of the principal may, for serious reasons, modify or render inoperative a provision as referred to in the first paragraph.

1. Dans la mesure où la procuration a pour objet l'accomplissement d'un acte juridique dans l'intérêt du procureur ou d'un tiers, il peut être stipulé qu'elle est irrévocable ou encore que le décès ou la mise en curatelle de l'auteur n'y met pas fin. La première stipulation inclut la deuxième, à moins qu'il n'y apparaisse autrement.
2. Lorsque la procuration contient une stipulation visée au paragraphe précédent, l'autre partie peut présumer remplie la condition de validité qui y est prévue, à moins que le contraire ne doive lui être apparent.
3. Sauf disposition contraire, le procureur peut, même en dehors des cas prévus à l'article 64, accorder à un tiers la procuration irrévocable qu'il a reçue conformément au paragraphe premier.
4. À la requête de l'auteur de la procuration, d'un héritier ou du curateur de l'auteur, le tribunal de première instance peut, pour des motifs graves, modifier ou rendre inopérante une stipulation visée au paragraphe premier.

Art. 75. (3.3.14) - 1. Na het einde van de volmacht moet de gevolmachtigde desgevorderd geschriften waaruit de volmacht blijkt, teruggeven of toestaan dat de volmachtgever daarop aantekent dat de volmacht is geëindigd. In geval van een bij notariële akte verleende

volmacht tekent de notaris die de minuut onder zijn berusting heeft, op verzoek van de volmachtgever het einde van de volmacht daarop aan.
- 2. Wanneer te vrezen is dat een gevolmachtigde van een volmacht ondanks haar einde gebruik zal maken, kan de volmachtgever zich wenden tot de president van de rechtbank met verzoek de wijze van bekendmaking van het einde van de volmacht te bepalen, die ten gevolge zal hebben dat het tegen een ieder kan worden ingeroepen. Tegen een toewijzende beschikking krachtens dit lid is geen hogere voorziening toegelaten.

1. After termination of the procuration the procurator, upon demand, must either give back the documents which are evidence of the procuration or allow the principal to note on them that the procuration has been terminated. Where a procuration is granted by notarial deed, the notary who is in possession of the *minute* notes, upon the request of the principal, the termination of the procuration on that *minute*.
2. A principal who has reason to believe that a procurator will make use of a procuration despite its termination, may request that the president of the district court determine the manner of publication of the termination of the procuration; this termination is opposable to all upon publication. No appeal lies from a judgment granting a request pursuant to this paragraph.

1. À l'expiration de la procuration, le procureur remet, sur demande, les écrits qui en font preuve ou permet à l'auteur d'y noter qu'elle a pris fin. Dans le cas d'une procuration par acte notarié, le notaire en possession de la minute, à la requête de l'auteur, note sur celle-ci l'expiration de la procuration.

2. Lorsqu'il faut craindre que le procureur ne se serve d'une procuration quoi qu'elle ait pris fin, l'auteur peut demander au président du tribunal de première instance de déterminer la manière de publier la cessation de la procuration, rendant cette cessation opposable à tous. La décision accueillant la demande est insusceptible d'appel.

Art. 76. (3.3.16) - 1. Een oorzaak die de volmacht heeft doen eindigen, kan tegenover een wederpartij die noch van het einde van de volmacht, noch van die oorzaak kennis droeg, slechts worden ingeroepen:
a. indien het einde van de volmacht of de oorzaak die haar heeft doen eindigen aan de wederpartij was medegedeeld of was bekend gemaakt op een wijze die krachtens wet of verkeersopvattingen meebrengt dat de volmachtgever het einde van de volmacht aan de wederpartij kan tegenwerpen;
b. indien de dood van de volmachtgever van algemene bekendheid was;
c. indien de aanstelling of tewerkstelling, waaruit de volmacht voortvloeide, op een voor derden kenbare wijze was beëindigd;
d. indien de wederpartij van de volmacht op geen andere wijze had kennis gekregen dan door een verklaring van de gevolmachtigde.
- 2. In de gevallen van het vorige lid is de gevolmachtigde die voortgaat op naam van de volmachtgever te handelen, tot schadevergoeding gehouden jegens de wederpartij die van het einde van de volmacht geen kennis droeg. Hij is niet aansprakelijk indien hij wist noch behoorde te weten dat de volmacht was geëindigd.

1. An event which has terminated the procuration may only be invoked against the other party who had no knowledge of the termination of the procuration nor of the event in the following circumstances:

1. La cause d'expiration de la procuration ne peut être opposée à l'autre partie qui n'avait connaissance ni de la fin, ni de la cause, que dans les cas suivants:

a. if the termination of the procuration or the event which has terminated it has been communicated to the other party or has been made public in a manner which, by virtue of law or common opinion, justifies that the principal can set up the termination of the procuration against the other party;
b. if the death of the principal was generally known;
c. if the appointment or employment that gave rise to the procuration has been terminated in a fashion apparent to third persons;
d. if the other party has obtained knowledge of the procuration solely by means of a declaration by the procurator.

2. A procurator who continues to act in the name of the principal in the circumstances described in the preceding paragraph is liable to pay damages to the other party who did not know of the termination of the procuration. The procurator is not liable if he did not know nor ought to have known that the procuration had been terminated.

a. Si la fin de la procuration ou la cause d'expiration a été communiquée à l'autre partie, ou si elle a été publiée d'une manière suffisante pour qu'en vertu de la loi ou de l'opinion généralement admise, on puisse le lui opposer;
b. Si le décès de l'auteur était de notoriété publique;
c. Si a pris fin de façon apparente pour les tiers la nomination ou la fonction dont résultait la procuration;
d. Si l'autre partie n'avait eu connaissance de la procuration par aucune autre voie qu'une déclaration du procureur.

2. Dans les cas visés au paragraphe précédent, le procureur qui continue d'agir au nom de l'auteur doit des dommages-intérêts à l'autre partie si celle-ci ignorait que la procuration avait pris fin. Il n'en est pas tenu s'il n'avait ni ne devait avoir connaissance de l'expiration de la procuration.

Art. 77. (3.3.16a) Wordt ondanks de dood van de volmachtgever krachtens de volmacht een geldige rechtshandeling verricht, dan worden de erfgenamen van de volmachtgever en de wederpartij gebonden alsof de handeling bij het leven van de volmachtgever was verricht.

A valid juridical act, performed pursuant to the procuration and despite the death of the principal, binds the heirs of the principal and the other party as if the act had been performed during the lifetime of the principal.

L'acte juridique valide accompli en vertu d'une procuration malgré le décès de l'auteur lie les héritiers et celui qui y est partie, comme si l'acte avait été accompli du vivant de l'auteur.

Art. 78. (3.3.16b) Wanneer iemand optreedt als vertegenwoordiger uit anderen hoofde dan volmacht, zijn de artikelen 63 lid 1, 66 lid 1, 67, 69, 70, 71 en 75 lid 2 van overeenkomstige toepassing, voor zover uit de wet niet anders voortvloeit.

Where a person acts as a representative otherwise than pursuant to a procuration, paragraph 1 of article 63, paragraph 1 of article 66, articles 67, 69, 70 and 71, and article 75, paragraph 2 apply *mutatis mutandis* to the extent that the law does not produce a different result.

Les articles 63, paragraphe premier, 66, paragraphe premier, 67, 69, 70, 71 et 75, deuxième paragraphe, s'appliquent par analogie à celui qui agit comme représentant en vertu d'un titre autre que la procuration, dans la mesure où il n'en résulte pas autrement de la loi.

Art. 79. (3.3.16c) Buiten het vermogensrecht vinden de bepalingen van deze titel overeenkomstige toepassing, voor zover de aard van de rechtshandeling of van de rechtsbetrekking zich daartegen niet verzet.

The provisions of this title apply *mutatis mutandis* to areas of the law other than patrimonial law to the extent that they are not incompatible with the nature of the juridical act or relationship.

Les dispositions du présent titre s'appliquent par analogie au droit autre que patrimonial, dans la mesure où la nature de l'acte ou du rapport juridique ne s'y oppose pas.

TITEL 4 VERKRIJGING EN VERLIES VAN GOEDEREN

TITLE 4 ACQUISITION AND LOSS OF PROPERTY

TITRE QUATRIÈME DE L'ACQUISITION ET DE LA PERTE DES BIENS

AFDELING 1 Algemene bepalingen

Section 1 General provisions

Section première Dispositions générales

Art. 80. (3.4.1.1) - 1. Men kan goederen onder algemene en onder bijzondere titel verkrijgen.
- 2. Men verkrijgt goederen onder algemene titel door erfopvolging, door boedelmenging en door opvolging in het vermogen van een rechtspersoon die heeft opgehouden te bestaan.
- 3. Men verkrijgt goederen onder bijzondere titel door overdracht, door verjaring en door onteigening, en voorts op de overige in de wet voor iedere soort aangegeven wijzen van rechtsverkrijging.
- 4. Men verliest goederen op de voor iedere soort in de wet aangegeven wijzen.

1. Property is acquired by general and by particular title.
2. Property is acquired by general title through inheritance, fusion of patrimonies[1] or succession to the patrimony of a legal person which has ceased to exist.
3. Property is acquired by particular title by transfer, prescription, expropriation and in any other manner of acquisition of rights provided by law according to their kind.
4. Property is lost in the ways provided by law according to their kind.

1. Les biens s'acquièrent à titre universel et à titre particulier.
2. L'acquisition de biens à titre universel a lieu par succession, par confusion des patrimoines[2] et par la succession au patrimoine d'une personne morale qui a cessé d'exister.
3. L'acquisition de biens à titre particulier a lieu par transfert, par prescription et par expropriation et en outre par les autres modes d'acquisition prévus par la loi selon leur nature.
4. La perte des biens a lieu suivant les modes prévus par la loi selon leur nature.

[1] Fusion of patrimonies only occurs by marriage.

[2] En droit néerlandais, la confusion des patrimoines ne se réalise que par le mariage.

Art. 81. (3.4.1.2) - 1. Hij aan wie een zelfstandig en overdraagbaar recht toekomt, kan binnen de grenzen van dat recht de in de wet genoemde beperkte rechten vestigen. Hij kan ook zijn recht onder voorbehoud van een zodanig beperkt recht overdragen, mits hij de voorschriften zowel voor overdracht van een zodanig goed, als voor vestiging van een zodanig beperkt recht in acht neemt.

- 2. Beperkte rechten gaan teniet door:

a. het tenietgaan van het recht waaruit het beperkte recht is afgeleid;

b. verloop van de tijd waarvoor, of de vervulling van de ontbindende voorwaarde waaronder het beperkte recht is gevestigd;

c. afstand;

d. opzegging, indien de bevoegdheid daartoe bij de wet of bij de vestiging van het recht aan de hoofdgerechtigde, aan de beperkt gerechtigde of aan beiden is toegekend;

e. vermenging;

en voorts op de overige in de wet voor iedere soort aangegeven wijzen van tenietgaan.

- 3. Afstand en vermenging werken niet ten nadele van hen die op het tenietgaande beperkte recht op hun beurt een beperkt recht hebben. Vermenging werkt evenmin ten voordele van hen die op het bezwaarde goed een beperkt recht hebben en het tenietgaande recht moesten eerbiedigen.

1. A person who is entitled to an independent and transferable right, may, within the limits of that right, establish the dismembered rights recognized by law. He may also transfer his right subject to such a dismembered right, provided that he respect the rules pertaining to both the transfer of such property and the establishment of such a dismembered right.

2. Dismembered rights are extinguished by:

a. the extinction of the right from which the dismembered right is derived;

b. the lapse of the time for which, or the fulfillment of the resolutory condition under which the dismembered right has been established;

c. abandonment;[1]

d. renunciation, if the power to renounce has been granted by law or upon the establishment of the right, to the holder of the principal right, the holder of the dismembered right or to both;

e. confusion;[3]

1. Le titulaire d'un droit autonome et transmissible peut, dans les limites de ce droit, le démembrer de la manière prévue par la loi. Il peut également transférer son droit, sous réserve d'un tel droit démembré, pourvu qu'il respecte les prescriptions relatives au transfert d'un tel bien, ainsi que celles relatives à l'établissement d'un tel droit démembré.

2. Un droit démembré s'éteint:

a. Par l'extinction du droit dont il est tiré;

b. Par l'expiration du temps pour lequel il a été établi ou par l'accomplissement de la condition résolutoire sous laquelle il l'a été;

c. Par l'abandon[2];

d. Par la renonciation, si cette faculté a été accordée, par la loi ou lors de constitution du droit, au titulaire du droit principal ou au titulaire du droit démembré ou aux deux;

e. Par la confusion;

---

1 In the New Dutch Civil Code abandonment is a bilateral juridical act. See art. III: 98.

2 Selon le nouveau Code civil néerlandais, l'abandon d'un droit démembré (*afstand*) exige le concours de deux parties: il s'agit d'un acte bilatéral (Voir l'article 98 du Livre troisième).

3 Confusion of the qualities of debtor and creditor.

and in any other manner of extinction provided by law according to their kind.
3. Abandonment and confusion do not operate to the detriment of those who in their turn have a dismembered right in the dismembered right which is extinguished. Likewise confusion does not operate in favour of those who have a dismembered right in the encumbered property and were obliged to respect the right which is extinguished.

et en outre par les autres modes d'extinction prévus par la loi selon la nature des droits.
3. L'abandon et la confusion ne nuisent pas à ceux qui, pour leur part, ont un droit démembré sur le droit démembré qui s'éteint. De même, la confusion ne profite pas à ceux qui ont un droit démembré sur le bien grevé et qui devaient respecter le droit qui s'éteint.

Art. 82. (3.4.1.2a) Afhankelijke rechten volgen het recht waaraan zij verbonden zijn.

Dependent rights follow the right to which they are connected.

Les droits dépendants suivent celui auquel ils se rattachent.

AFDELING 2 Overdracht van goederen en afstand van beperkte rechten

Section 2 Transfer of property and abandonment of dismembered rights

Section deuxième Du transfert des biens et de l'abandon des droits démembrés

Art. 83. (3.4.2.1) - 1. Eigendom, beperkte rechten en vorderingsrechten zijn overdraagbaar, tenzij de wet of de aard van het recht zich tegen een overdracht verzet.
- 2. De overdraagbaarheid van vorderingsrechten kan ook door een beding tussen schuldeiser en schuldenaar worden uitgesloten.
- 3. Alle andere rechten zijn slechts overdraagbaar, wanneer de wet dit bepaalt.

1. Ownership, dismembered rights and debts[1] are transferable, unless this is precluded by law or by the nature of the right.
2. Transferability of debts can also be excluded by agreement between creditor and debtor.
3. Other rights are not transferable except if so provided by law.

1. La propriété, les droits démembrés et les créances[2] sont transmissibles, à moins que la loi ou la nature du droit ne s'y oppose.
2. La transmissibilité des créances peut aussi être exclue par stipulation entre créancier et débiteur.
3. Les autres droits ne sont transmissibles que si la loi le prévoit.

---

1 For the Dutch term "vorderingsrecht", the term "debt" in English seems preferable to the gallicism "creance" ("*créance*" in French). The Dutch and French terms express the idea on the active side of having the right to claim, whereas the English expresses the idea on the passive side of having to pay, to perform. As a consequence, both "schuld" (expressing the passive side in Dutch) and "schuldvordering" have normally been translated by "debt". The more general Dutch term "vordering" has frequently been translated by the noun "claim".

2 Les termes néerlandais «*vorderingsrecht*», «*schuldvordering*», «*vordering*» et «*inschuld*» sont traduits indifféremment par créance.

Art. 84. (3.4.2.2) - 1. Voor overdracht van een goed wordt vereist een levering krachtens geldige titel, verricht door hem die bevoegd is over het goed te beschikken.
- 2. Bij de titel moet het goed met voldoende bepaaldheid omschreven zijn.
- 3. Een rechtshandeling die ten doel heeft een goed over te dragen tot zekerheid of die de strekking mist het goed na de overdracht in het vermogen van de verkrijger te doen vallen, is geen geldige titel van overdracht van dat goed.
- 4. Wordt ter uitvoering van een voorwaardelijke verbintenis geleverd, dan wordt slechts een recht verkregen, dat aan dezelfde voorwaarde als die verbintenis is onderworpen.

1. Transfer of property requires delivery pursuant to a valid title by the person who has the right to dispose of the property.
2. The title must describe the property in a sufficiently precise manner.
3. A juridical act which is intended to transfer property for purposes of security or which does not have the purpose of bringing the property into the patrimony of the acquirer, after transfer, does not constitute valid title for transfer of that property.
4. Where delivery is made in the performance of a conditional obligation, the right so acquired is subject to the same condition as the obligation.

1. Le transfert des biens requiert la délivrance en vertu d'un titre valable, effectuée par celui qui a le droit de disposer du bien.
2. Le titre doit décrire le bien avec suffisamment de précision.
3. Ne constitue pas un titre valable de transfert l'acte juridique qui vise à transférer le bien aux fins de sûreté ou qui n'a pas pour objet de le faire tomber dans le patrimoine de l'acquéreur après le transfert.
4. La délivrance effectuée en exécution d'une obligation conditionnelle transfère un droit soumis à la même condition.

Art. 85. (3.4.2.2a) - 1. Een verbintenis strekkende tot overdracht van een goed voor een bepaalde tijd, wordt aangemerkt als een verbintenis tot vestiging van een vruchtgebruik op het goed voor de gestelde tijd.
- 2. Een verbintenis strekkende tot overdracht van een goed onder opschortende tijdsbepaling, wordt aangemerkt als een verbintenis tot onmiddellijke overdracht van het goed met gelijktijdige vestiging van een vruchtgebruik van de vervreemder op het goed voor de gestelde tijd.

1. An obligation which is intended to transfer property for a certain specific period is deemed to be an obligation to establish a usufruct upon the property during that specific period.
2. An obligation which is intended to transfer property under a suspensive term is deemed to be an obligation to transfer the property immediately, and establishes simultaneously a usufruct upon the property in favour of the alienator during the relevant period.

1. L'obligation ayant pour objet de transférer un bien pour un temps déterminé est réputée obligation de constituer un usufruit sur ce bien pour le temps fixé.
2. L'obligation ayant pour objet le transfert d'un bien sous un terme suspensif est réputée obligation de transférer immédiatement le bien avec constitution simultanée d'usufruit en faveur de l'aliénateur durant le temps fixé.

Art. 86. (3.4.2.3a) - 1. Ondanks onbevoegdheid van de vervreemder is een overdracht overeenkomstig artikel 90, 91 of 93 van een roerende zaak, niet-

registergoed, of een recht aan toonder of order geldig, indien de overdracht anders dan om niet geschiedt en de verkrijger te goeder trouw is.

- 2. Rust op een in het vorige lid genoemd goed dat overeenkomstig artikel 90, 91 of 93 anders dan om niet wordt overgedragen, een beperkt recht dat de verkrijger op dit tijdstip kent noch behoort te kennen, dan vervalt dit recht, in het geval van overdracht overeenkomstig artikel 91 onder dezelfde opschortende voorwaarde als waaronder geleverd is.

- 3. Niettemin kan de eigenaar van een roerende zaak, die het bezit daarvan door diefstal heeft verloren, deze gedurende drie jaren, te rekenen van de dag van de diefstal af, als zijn eigendom opeisen, tenzij:

a. de zaak door een natuurlijke persoon die niet in de uitoefening van een beroep of bedrijf handelde, is verkregen van een vervreemder die van het verhandelen aan het publiek van soortgelijke zaken anders dan als veilinghouder zijn bedrijf maakt in een daartoe bestemde bedrijfsruimte, zijnde een gebouwde onroerende zaak of een gedeelte daarvan met de bij het een en ander behorende grond, en in de normale uitoefening van dat bedrijf handelde; of

b. het geld dan wel toonder- of orderpapier betreft.

- 4. Op de in het vorige lid bedoelde termijn zijn de artikelen 316, 318 en 319 betreffende de stuiting van de verjaring van een rechtsvordering van overeenkomstige toepassing.

1. Although an alienator lacks the right to dispose of the property, a transfer pursuant to articles 90, 91 or 93 of a moveable thing, unregistered property, or a right payable to bearer or order is valid, if the transfer is not by gratuitous title and if the acquirer is in good faith.

2. Where property mentioned in paragraph 1 and having been transferred, otherwise than by gratuitous title and according to articles 90, 91 or 93, is encumbered with a dismembered right which the acquirer does not know nor ought to have known at the time of the transfer, this right is extinguished; in the case of a transfer according to article 91, the extinction is subject to the same suspensive condition as the delivery.

3. Nevertheless, the owner of a moveable thing, who has lost its possession through theft, may revendicate it during a period of three years from the day of theft, unless

a. the thing has been acquired by a natural person, not acting in the exercise of a profession or business, from an alienator whose business it is to deal with the public in similar

1. Le fait que l'aliénateur n'ait pas le droit de disposer d'un bien n'invalide pas le transfert, effectué conformément aux articles 90, 91 ou 93, d'une chose mobilière non immatriculée ou d'un droit au porteur ou à ordre[1] si le transfert a lieu autrement qu'à titre gratuit, l'acquéreur étant de bonne foi.

2. Lorsque le bien visé au paragraphe précédent qui, conformément aux articles 90, 91 ou 93, est transféré autrement qu'à titre gratuit est grevé d'un droit démembré que l'acquéreur ne connaît ni ne devait connaître au moment du transfert, ce droit s'éteint, cette extinction étant soumise, dans le cas d'un transfert effectué conformément à l'article 91, à la même condition suspensive que le transfert.

3. Le propriétaire d'une chose mobilière, qui en a perdu la possession par suite d'un vol, peut néanmoins la revendiquer comme étant sa propriété pendant une période de trois ans à compter du vol, à moins:

a. Que l'acquéreur, personne physique agissant autrement que dans l'exercice d'une activité professionnelle ou d'une entreprise, a acquis la chose d'un aliénateur faisant commerce de choses

[1] Le néerlandais emploie ici le terme «*droit* au porteur ou à ordre» (*recht aan toonder of order*), néologisme désignant le droit faisant l'objet d'un titre au porteur ou à ordre. Au paragraphe 3, alinéa b, on rencontre cependant le terme habituel «*titres* au porteur ou à ordre» (*toonder- of orderpapier*).

things, otherwise than at a public sale, on business premises destined for that purpose, being an immoveable structure or part thereof with the land belonging thereto, and provided that the alienator be in the ordinary exercise of his business; or

b. money or documents payable to bearer or order are involved.

4. Articles 316, 318 and 319 regarding the interruption of the prescription of a right of action apply *mutatis mutandis* to the period referred to in the preceding paragraph.

semblables avec le public, autrement qu'en qualité d'encanteur, dans un espace commercial destiné à cette fin, cet espace constituant une chose immobilière construite, ou partie d'icelle, avec le fonds attenant, et qui a agi dans l'exercice ordinaire de ce commerce;

b. Qu'il s'agisse d'argent ou de titres au porteur ou à ordre;

4. Les articles 316, 318 et 319 relatifs à l'interruption de la prescription de l'action en justice s'appliquent par analogie au délai visé au paragraphe précédent.

Art. 87. (3.4.2.3aa) - 1. Een verkrijger die binnen drie jaren na zijn verkrijging gevraagd wordt wie het goed aan hem vervreemdde, dient onverwijld de gegevens te verschaffen, die nodig zijn om deze terug te vinden of die hij ten tijde van zijn verkrijging daartoe voldoende mocht achten. Indien hij niet aan deze verplichting voldoet, kan hij de bescherming die het vorige artikel aan een verkrijger te goeder trouw biedt, niet inroepen.
- 2. Het vorige lid is niet van toepassing ten aanzien van geld.

1. An acquirer, who is asked within three years from his acquisition to identify the alienator, must, without delay, provide all information which is necessary to trace that person or which he could have considered as being sufficient for that purpose at the time of his acquisition. If he does not comply with this obligation, he may not invoke the protection which the preceding article affords to an acquirer in good faith.

2. The preceding paragraph does not apply to money.

1. L'acquéreur auquel on demande, dans les trois ans de l'acquisition du bien, d'en identifier l'aliénateur est tenu de fournir sans délai les renseignements nécessaires pour retrouver ce dernier ou ceux qu'il pouvait juger suffisants pour ce faire lors de l'acquisition. À défaut de remplir cette obligation, il ne peut se prévaloir de la protection que l'article précédent accorde à l'acquéreur de bonne foi.

2. Le paragraphe précédent ne s'applique pas aux sommes d'argent.

Art. 88. (3.4.2.3b) Ondanks onbevoegdheid van de vervreemder is een overdracht van een registergoed, van een recht op naam, of van een ander goed waarop artikel 86 niet van toepassing is, geldig, indien de verkrijger te goeder trouw is en de onbevoegdheid voortvloeit uit de ongeldigheid van een vroegere overdracht, die niet het gevolg was van onbevoegdheid van de toenmalige vervreemder.

Although an alienator lacks the right to dispose of property, the transfer of registered property, a nominative right or other property to which article 86 does not apply, is valid if the acquirer is in good faith and if the lack of the right to dispose results from the invalidity of a

Le fait que l'aliénateur n'ait pas le pouvoir de disposer du bien n'invalide pas le transfert d'un bien immatriculé, d'un droit nominatif[1] ou de tout autre bien non soumis à l'article 86, si l'acquéreur est de bonne foi et si le défaut de pouvoir en disposer résulte de l'invalidité d'un transfert précédent, dont

[1] Le nouveau Code oppose ce type de droit à ceux faisant l'objet d'un titre à ordre ou au porteur.

previous transfer, which itself did not result from the lack of the right to dispose of the alienator at the time.

la cause ne soit pas due au même défaut chez l'aliénateur d'alors.

Art. 89. (3.4.2.4) - 1. De voor overdracht van onroerende zaken vereiste levering geschiedt door een daartoe bestemde, tussen partijen opgemaakte notariële akte, gevolgd door de inschrijving daarvan in de daartoe bestemde openbare registers. Zowel de verkrijger als de vervreemder kan de akte doen inschrijven.
- 2. De tot levering bestemde akte moet nauwkeurig de titel van overdracht vermelden; bijkomstige bedingen die niet de overdracht betreffen, kunnen in de akte worden weggelaten.
- 3. Treedt bij een akte van levering iemand als gevolmachtigde van een der partijen op, dan moet in de akte de volmacht nauwkeurig worden vermeld.
- 4. Het in dit artikel bepaalde vindt overeenkomstige toepassing op de levering, vereist voor de overdracht van andere registergoederen.

1. Delivery required for the transfer of immoveable things is made by notarial deed intended for that purpose and drawn up between the parties, followed by its entry in the public registers provided for that purpose. Either the acquirer or the alienator may have the deed registered.
2. The deed intended for delivery must clearly specify the title of transfer; accessory stipulations which do not concern the transfer may be omitted in the deed.
3. Where in a deed of delivery a person acts as procurator of one of the parties, the procuration must be clearly specified in the deed.
4. The provisions of this article apply *mutatis mutandis* to the delivery required for the transfer of other registered property.

1. La délivrance requise pour le transfert des choses immobilières s'opère par la passation d'un acte notarié à cet effet entre les parties, suivi de son inscription sur les registres publics prévus à cette fin. Tant l'acquéreur que l'aliénateur peut faire inscrire l'acte.
2. L'acte devant servir à la délivrance doit indiquer de façon précise le titre de transfert; les stipulations accessoires qui ne touchent pas le transfert peuvent être omises.
3. Lorsque l'une des parties est représentée par procureur à l'acte de délivrance, la procuration doit y être mentionnée de façon précise.
4. Les dispositions du présent article s'appliquent par analogie à la délivrance requise pour le transfert d'autres biens immatriculés.

Art. 90. (3.4.2.5) 1. De levering vereist voor de overdracht van roerende zaken, niet-registergoederen, die in de macht van de vervreemder zijn, geschiedt door aan de verkrijger het bezit der zaak te verschaffen.
- 2. Blijft de zaak na de levering in handen van de vervreemder, dan werkt de levering tegenover een derde die een ouder recht op de zaak heeft, eerst vanaf het tijdstip dat de zaak in handen van de verkrijger is gekomen, tenzij de oudere gerechtigde met vervreemding heeft ingestemd.

1. Delivery required for the transfer of moveable things which are unregistered property and which are under the control of the alienator is made by giving possession of the thing to the acquirer.

1. La délivrance requise pour le transfert des choses mobilières non immatriculées qui sont sous la puissance de l'aliénateur s'opère par la mise en possession de l'acquéreur.

2. Delivery of a thing which remains in the hands of the alienator has no effect with respect to a third person who has a prior right to the thing, until the time when the thing has come into the hands of the acquirer, unless the third person has consented to the alienation.

2. Lorsque la chose demeure entre les mains de l'aliénateur après la délivrance, celle-ci ne produit effet à l'égard du tiers qui a sur elle un droit antérieur qu'à compter du moment où elle est passée aux mains de l'acquéreur, à moins que le tiers n'ait accepté l'aliénation.

Art. 91. (3.4.2.5a) De levering van in het vorige artikel bedoelde zaken ter uitvoering van een verbintenis tot overdracht onder opschortende voorwaarde, geschiedt door aan de verkrijger de macht over de zaak te verschaffen.

The delivery of things referred to in the preceding article in the performance of an obligation to transfer under suspensive condition is accomplished by giving the acquirer control over the thing.

La délivrance des choses visées à l'article précédent en exécution d'une obligation de transférer sous condition suspensive s'effectue lorsqu'elles sont mises sous la puissance de l'acquéreur.

Art. 92. (3.4.2.5b) - 1. Heeft een overeenkomst de strekking dat de een zich de eigendom van een zaak die in de macht van de ander wordt gebracht, voorbehoudt totdat een door de ander verschuldigde prestatie is voldaan, dan wordt hij vermoed zich te verbinden tot overdracht van de zaak aan de ander onder opschortende voorwaarde van voldoening van die prestatie.
- 2. Een eigendomsvoorbehoud kan slechts geldig worden bedongen ter zake van vorderingen betreffende de tegenprestatie voor door de vervreemder aan de verkrijger krachtens overeenkomst geleverde of te leveren zaken of krachtens een zodanige overeenkomst tevens ten behoeve van de verkrijger verrichte of te verrichten werkzaamheden, alsmede ter zake van de vorderingen wegens tekortschieten in de nakoming van zodanige overeenkomsten. Voor zover een voorwaarde op deze grond nietig is, wordt zij voor ongeschreven gehouden.
- 3. Een voorwaarde als in lid 1 bedoeld wordt voor vervuld gehouden, wanneer de vervreemder op enige andere wijze dan door voldoening van de tegenprestatie wordt bevredigd, wanneer de verkrijger van zijn verplichting daartoe wordt bevrijd uit hoofde van artikel 60 van Boek 6, of wanneer de verjaring van de rechtsvordering ter zake van de tegenprestatie is voltooid. Behoudens afwijkend beding, geldt hetzelfde bij afstand van het recht op de tegenprestatie.

1. Where a contract is intended to reserve to one party the ownership of a thing which is placed under the control of the other party, until a prestation owed by the latter has been performed, the former is presumed to obligate himself to the transfer of the thing to the latter under a suspensive condition of performance of that prestation.[1]

1. Celui qui, par contrat, se réserve la propriété d'une chose qui est mise sous la puissance d'une autre partie jusqu'à l'exécution par celle-ci d'une prestation est présumé s'engager à lui transférer la chose sous la condition suspensive de cette exécution.

[1] "Prestation" is a civilian term in Scotland and in Québec. It means that which the debtor of an obligation is required to give, to do or not to do. See also the *Private Law Dictionary and Bilingual Lexicon*, Montreal: Quebec Research Centre of Private and Comparative Law, 1988.

2. Reservation of title may only be validly stipulated with respect to claims concerning the counterprestation for things delivered or to be delivered by the alienator to the acquirer pursuant to a contract, or for work performed or to be performed pursuant to such a contract for the benefit of the acquirer, as well as with respect to claims for failure to perform such contracts. To the extent that a condition is null upon this ground, it is held to be unwritten.
3. A condition referred to in paragraph 1 is deemed to be fulfilled, when the alienator receives satisfaction otherwise than by performance of the counterprestation; when the acquirer is relieved of his obligation to perform pursuant to article 60 of Book 6; when the prescription of the right of action in respect of the counterprestation has been completed. In the absence of a stipulation to the contrary, the same applies in the event of abandonment of the right to the counterprestation.

2. La réserve de propriété ne peut être stipulée validement que pour garantir les créances se rapportant à la contre-prestation de choses que l'aliénateur a livrées ou doit livrer à l'acquéreur en vertu du contrat, ou de travaux entrepris ou à entreprendre pour l'acquéreur aux termes d'un tel contrat, ou encore les créances résultant d'un manquement dans l'exécution de tels contrats. Dans la mesure où une condition est nulle pour cette cause, elle est tenue pour non écrite.
3. La condition visée au paragraphe premier est réputée accomplie lorsque l'aliénateur reçoit satisfaction autrement que par l'exécution de la contre-prestation, lorsque l'acquéreur est libéré de son obligation en vertu de l'article 60 du Livre sixième ou que l'action relative à la contrepartie est prescrite. Sauf stipulation contraire, il en est de même au cas d'abandon du droit à la contre-prestation.

Art. 93. (3.4.2.6) De levering, vereist voor de overdracht van een recht aan toonder waarvan het toonderpapier in de macht van de vervreemder is, geschiedt door de levering van dit papier op de wijze en met de gevolgen als aangegeven in de artikelen 90, 91 en 92. Voor overdracht van een recht aan order, waarvan het orderpapier in de macht van de vervreemder is, geldt hetzelfde, met dien verstande dat voor de levering tevens endossement vereist is.

Delivery required for the transfer of a right payable to bearer, the instrument of which is under the control of the alienator, is made by delivery of the document in the manner and with the effects as specified in articles 90, 91, and 92. The same applies to the transfer of a right payable to order which is under the control of the alienator, provided that the document is also endorsed.

La délivrance requise pour le transfert d'un droit au porteur dont le titre est sous la puissance de l'aliénateur s'effectue par la délivrance de ce titre de la manière et avec les effets prévus aux articles 90, 91 et 92. Il en va de même du transfert d'un droit à ordre, dont le titre est sous la puissance de l'aliénateur, étant entendu que la délivrance requiert en outre l'endossement.

Art. 94. (3.4.2.7) - 1. Buiten de in het vorige artikel geregelde gevallen worden tegen een of meer bepaalde personen uit te oefenen rechten geleverd door een daartoe bestemde akte, en mededeling daarvan aan die personen door de vervreemder of verkrijger.
- 2. De levering van een tegen een bepaalde, doch op de dag waarop de akte wordt opgemaakt onbekende persoon uit te oefenen recht dat op die dag aan de vervreemder toebehoort, werkt terug tot die dag, indien de mededeling met bekwame spoed wordt gedaan, nadat die persoon bekend is geworden.

- 3. De personen tegen wie het recht moet worden uitgeoefend, kunnen verlangen dat hun een door de vervreemder gewaarmerkt uittreksel van de akte en haar titel wordt ter hand gesteld. Bedingen die voor deze personen van geen belang zijn, behoeven daarin niet te worden opgenomen. Is van een titel geen akte opgemaakt, dan moet hun de inhoud, voor zover voor hen van belang, schriftelijk worden medegedeeld.

1. In cases other than those provided for in the preceding article, rights to be exercised against one or more specifically determined persons are delivered by means of a deed intended for that purpose and notice thereof given by the alienator or acquirer to those persons.
2. Delivery of a right to be exercised against a specifically determined person, unknown on the day when the deed is drawn up, is retroactive to that day, provided that the right belongs to the alienator on that day and notification is made expeditiously once that person has been ascertained.
3. Persons against whom the right is to be exercised can demand that they be given an extract, certified by the alienator, of the deed and the title upon which it is based. Stipulations which are of no importance to these persons need not be included in the extract. If no deed has been drawn up of a title, the content of the title must be communicated to them in writing to the extent that it is of importance to them.

1. Hors les cas prévus à l'article précédent, la délivrance requise pour le transfert de droits qui s'exercent à l'égard de personnes déterminées s'effectue par un acte à cet effet et par la notification de ces personnes par l'aliénateur ou par l'acquéreur.
2. La délivrance d'un droit qui s'exerce à l'égard d'une personne déterminée, mais inconnue au jour de la rédaction de l'acte, rétroagit à ce jour, pourvu que le droit appartienne à l'aliénateur au jour en question et que la notification requise soit faite promptement dès que l'identité de cette personne est connue.
3. Les personnes à l'égard desquelles le droit doit être exercé peuvent demander que leur soit remis un extrait, certifié par l'aliénateur, de l'acte et du titre sur lequel celui-ci est fondé. Les stipulations qui ne présentent pas d'intérêt pour ces personnes peuvent être omises. Si le titre n'a pas été consigné dans un acte, son contenu doit, dans la mesure où il les intéresse, leur être communiqué par écrit.

Art. 95. (3.4.2.7a) Buiten de in de artikelen 89-94 geregelde gevallen en behoudens het in de artikelen 96 en 98 bepaalde, worden goederen geleverd door een daartoe bestemde akte.

In cases other than those provided for in articles 89 - 94 and without prejudice to articles 96 and 98, property is delivered by a deed intended for that purpose.

En dehors des cas prévus aux articles 89 à 94 et sous réserve des dispositions des articles 96 et 98, la délivrance d'un bien s'opère par un acte dressé à cet effet.

Art. 96. (3.4.2.7b) De levering van een aandeel in een goed geschiedt op overeenkomstige wijze en met overeenkomstige gevolgen als is bepaald met betrekking tot levering van dat goed.

Delivery of a share in property is made analogously to delivery of that property and has analogous effects.

La délivrance d'une part dans un bien s'opère de manière et avec des effets analogues à ce qui est prévu pour celle du bien lui-même.

Art. 97. (3.4.2.10) - 1. Toekomstige goederen kunnen bij voorbaat worden geleverd, tenzij het verboden is deze tot onderwerp van een overeenkomst te maken of het registergoederen zijn.

- 2. Een levering bij voorbaat van een toekomstig goed werkt niet tegen iemand die het goed ingevolge een eerdere levering bij voorbaat heeft verkregen. Betreft het een roerende zaak, dan werkt zij jegens deze vanaf het tijdstip dat de zaak in handen van de verkrijger is gekomen.

1. With the exception of registered property and property which cannot be the subject matter of a contract, future property may be delivered in advance.
2. Delivery in advance of future property has no effect against a person who has acquired the property in advance as a result of an earlier delivery. In the case of a moveable thing, the delivery has effect against this person from the time the thing has come into the hands of the acquirer.

1. La délivrance de biens futurs peut avoir lieu par anticipation, à moins que ceux-ci ne puissent faire l'objet d'un contrat ou qu'ils ne soient des biens immatriculés.
2. La délivrance anticipée d'un bien futur ne produit aucun effet à l'encontre de celui qui l'a acquis par une délivrance anticipée antérieure. Lorsqu'il s'agit d'une chose mobilière, elle produit effet à l'égard de celui-ci à compter du moment où la chose est venue entre les mains de l'acquéreur.

Art. 98. (3.4.2.11) Tenzij de wet anders bepaalt, vindt al hetgeen in deze afdeling omtrent de overdracht van een goed is bepaald, overeenkomstige toepassing op de vestiging, de overdracht en de afstand van een beperkt recht op een zodanig goed.

Unless otherwise provided by law, this section on the transfer of property applies *mutatis mutandis* to the establishment, transfer and abandonment of a dismembered right on such property.

À moins de disposition contraire de la loi, tout ce qui est prévu dans la présente section au sujet du transfert d'un bien s'applique de manière analogue à la constitution, au transfert et à l'abandon d'un droit démembré sur ce bien.

AFDELING 3 Verkrijging en verlies door verjaring

Section 3 Acquisition and loss by prescription

Section troisième De l'acquisition et de la perte par prescription

Art. 99. (3.4.3.1) Rechten op roerende zaken die niet-registergoederen zijn, en rechten aan toonder of order worden door een bezitter te goeder trouw verkregen door een onafgebroken bezit van drie jaren, andere goederen door een onafgebroken bezit van tien jaren.

Rights in moveable things which are not registered property and rights under documents payable to bearer and order are acquired by a possessor in good faith by uninterrupted possession for three years; other property is acquired by uninterrupted possession for ten years.

Les droits sur des choses mobilières non immatriculées et les droits au porteur ou à ordre se prescrivent en faveur du possesseur de bonne foi par une possession non interrompue de trois ans; les autres biens se prescrivent par une possession non interrompue de dix ans.

Art. 100. (3.4.3.2) Hij die een nalatenschap in bezit heeft genomen, kan die nalatenschap en de daartoe behorende goederen niet eerder door verjaring ten nadele van de rechthebbende verkrijgen dan nadat diens vordering tot opeising van die nalatenschap is verjaard.

A person who has taken possession of a succession cannot acquire that succession by prescription nor the property belonging to it to the detriment of the title-holder until after the latter's action to claim that succession has been prescribed.

Celui qui a pris possession d'une succession ne peut prescrire celle-ci ni les biens qui la composent au détriment du titulaire avant que ne soit prescrite l'action qu'a ce dernier en vue de la réclamer.

Art. 101. (3.4.3.3) Een verjaring begint te lopen met de aanvang van de dag na het begin van het bezit.

Prescription begins to run with the commencement of the day following the beginning of the possession.

La prescription court à compter du lendemain du jour où a commencé la possession.

Art. 102. (3.4.3.4) - 1. Hij die een ander onder algemene titel in het bezit opvolgt, zet een lopende verjaring voort.
- 2. Hetzelfde doet de bezitter te goeder trouw die het bezit van een ander anders dan onder algemene titel heeft verkregen.

1. A person who succeeds to the possession of another by general title continues an already running prescription.
2. The same applies to the possessor in good faith who has acquired possession from another person otherwise than by general title.

1. La prescription continue à courir au profit de celui qui, à titre universel, succède à une personne dans la possession d'un bien.
2. Il en est de même du possesseur de bonne foi qui, autrement qu'à titre universel, a acquis d'une autre personne la possession d'un bien.

Art. 103. (3.4.3.4a) Onvrijwillig bezitsverlies onderbreekt de loop der verjaring niet, mits het bezit binnen het jaar wordt terugverkregen of een binnen het jaar ingestelde rechtsvordering tot terugverkrijging van het bezit leidt.

Involuntary loss of property does not interrupt prescription, provided that possession is recovered within a year or an action instituted within a year leads to such recovery.

La dépossession involontaire n'interrompt pas la prescription, pourvu que la remise en possession s'effectue dans le délai d'un an ou qu'elle résulte d'une action intentée dans le même délai.

Art. 104. (3.4.3.5) - 1. Wanneer de verjaring van de rechtsvordering strekkende tot beëindiging van het bezit wordt gestuit of verlengd, wordt daarmede de verkrijgende verjaring dienovereenkomstig gestuit of verlengd.
- 2. In dit en de beide volgende artikelen wordt onder verjaring van een rechtsvordering de verjaring van de bevoegdheid tot tenuitvoerlegging van de uitspraak waarbij de eis is toegewezen, begrepen.

1. Interruption or extension of prescription of the right of action to terminate possession interrupts or

1. Lorsque la prescription d'une action visant à faire cesser la possession est interrompue ou prolongée[1], la prescription

1 Le nouveau Code civil remplace ici le concept «suspendre» (et «suspension») du droit actuel. Voir aussi les art. 320 et 321 du Livre troisième.

extends acquisitive prescription accordingly.
2. In this and the two following articles prescription of the right of action includes prescription of the right to execute the judgment maintaining the action.

acquisitive est de la même manière interrompue ou prolongée.
2. Pour l'application du présent article et des deux articles suivants, la prescription d'une action comprend celle du droit d'exécuter le jugement accueillant la demande.

Art. 105. (3.4.3.8) - 1. Hij die een goed bezit op het tijdstip waarop de verjaring van de rechtsvordering strekkende tot beëindiging van het bezit wordt voltooid, verkrijgt dat goed, ook al was zijn bezit niet te goeder trouw.
- 2. Heeft iemand vóór dat tijdstip het bezit onvrijwillig verloren, maar het na dat tijdstip, mits binnen het jaar na het bezitsverlies of uit hoofde van een binnen dat jaar ingestelde rechtsvordering, terugverkregen, dan wordt hij als de bezitter op het in het vorige lid aangegeven tijdstip aangemerkt.

1. A person who possesses property at the time of the completion of the prescription of the right of action to terminate possession, acquires the property even if his possession was not in good faith.
2. Provided that a person who has involuntarily lost possession before the completion of the prescription of the right of action to terminate possession, has recovered it within the year following the loss of possession or by virtue of an action instituted within that year, he is deemed to be the possessor at the time indicated in the preceding paragraph.

1. Celui qui possède un bien au moment où se prescrit l'action visant à faire cesser la possession acquiert ce bien, lors même que sa possession n'était pas de bonne foi.
2. Est réputé possesseur au moment visé au paragraphe précédent, celui qui, ayant involontairement perdu la possession avant ce moment, l'a repris dans l'année qui a suivi la dépossession ou en vertu d'une action exercée dans le même délai.

Art. 106. (3.4.3.8a) Wanneer de verjaring van de rechtsvordering van een beperkt gerechtigde tegen de hoofdgerechtigde tot opheffing van een met het beperkte recht strijdige toestand wordt voltooid, gaat het beperkte recht teniet, voor zover de uitoefening daarvan door die toestand is belet.

To the extent that the exercise of a dismembered right is prevented by a situation incompatible with the right, that right is extinguished by the prescription of the right of action of the holder of the dismembered right against the holder of the principal right to terminate that situation.

Dans la mesure où il est impossible d'exercer un droit démembré à cause d'une situation incompatible avec le contenu de ce droit, la prescription de l'action du titulaire du droit démembré à l'encontre du titulaire du droit principal visant à faire cesser cette situation éteint également le droit démembré.

TITEL 5 BEZIT EN HOUDERSCHAP

TITLE 5 POSSESSION AND DETENTION

TITRE CINQUIÈME DE LA POSSESSION ET DE LA DÉTENTION

Art. 107. (3.5.1) - 1. Bezit is het houden van een goed voor zichzelf.
- 2. Bezit is onmiddellijk, wanneer iemand bezit zonder dat een ander het goed voor hem houdt.
- 3. Bezit is middellijk, wanneer iemand bezit door middel van een ander die het goed voor hem houdt.
- 4. Houderschap is op overeenkomstige wijze onmiddellijk of middellijk.

1. Possession is the fact of detaining property for oneself.
2. A person who possesses property which is not detained for him by another has immediate possession.
3. A person who possesses property which is detained for him by another has mediate possesion.
4. *Mutatis mutandis* detention is mediate or immediate.

1. La possession est le fait de détenir un bien pour soi-même.
2. La possession est immédiate lorsqu'une personne possède le bien sans qu'une autre le détienne pour elle.
3. La possession est médiate lorsqu'une personne possède le bien par l'intermédiaire d'une autre qui le détient pour elle.
4. La détention est, de manière analogue, immédiate ou médiate.

Art. 108. (3.5.2) Of iemand een goed houdt en of hij dit voor zichzelf of voor een ander doet, wordt naar verkeersopvatting beoordeeld, met inachtneming van de navolgende regels en overigens op grond van uiterlijke feiten.

Whether somebody detains property and whether he does so for himself or for another, is determined according to common opinion, taking into account the following rules and, otherwise, the facts as they appear.

Pour juger si une personne détient un bien et si elle le détient pour elle-même ou pour une autre, on se réfère à l'opinion généralement admise, en observant les règles qui suivent et, pour le reste, en se fiant aux faits apparents.

Art. 109. (3.5.3) Wie een goed houdt, wordt vermoed dit voor zichzelf te houden.

A person is presumed to detain property for himself.

On est présumé détenir un bien pour soi-même.

Art. 110. (3.5.4) Bestaat tussen twee personen een rechtsverhouding die de strekking heeft dat hetgeen de ene op bepaalde wijze zal verkrijgen, door hem voor de ander zal worden gehouden, dan houdt de ene het ter uitvoering van die rechtsverhouding door hem verkregene voor de ander.

Where there exists a juridical relationship between two persons to the effect that what one of them will acquire in a specified manner will be detained by him

Lorsqu'il existe entre deux personnes un rapport juridique portant que l'une détiendra pour l'autre ce qu'elle acquerra d'une façon spécifique, la première détient pour la

for the other, the former detains for the latter what has been acquired by him in the performance of the juridical relationship.

seconde ce qu'elle acquiert en donnant suite à ce rapport.

Art. 111. (3.5.5) Wanneer men heeft aangevangen krachtens een rechtsverhouding voor een ander te houden, gaat men daarmede onder dezelfde titel voort, zolang niet blijkt dat hierin verandering is gebracht, hetzij ten gevolge van een handeling van hem voor wie men houdt, hetzij ten gevolge van een tegenspraak van diens recht.

A person who has begun detention for another pursuant to a juridical relationship continues to do so under the same title, so long as no change is apparent in his title which results either from an act by the person for whom he holds or from the latter's right having been contested.

Celui qui a commencé à détenir pour autrui en vertu d'un rapport juridique continue au même titre tant qu'il n'apparaît pas qu'il y a eu changement de titre à la suite d'un acte de celui pour qui il détient, ou à la suite d'une contestation du droit de celui-ci.

Art. 112. (3.5.6) Bezit wordt verkregen door inbezitneming, door overdracht of door opvolging onder algemene titel.

Possession is acquired by taking possession, by transfer or by succession by general title.

La possession s'acquiert par occupation, par transfert ou par succession à titre universel.

Art. 113. (3.5.7) - 1. Men neemt een goed in bezit door zich daarover de feitelijke macht te verschaffen.
- 2. Wanneer een goed in het bezit van een ander is, zijn enkele op zichzelf staande machtsuitoefeningen voor een inbezitneming onvoldoende.

1. A person takes possession of property by acquiring actual control of it.
2. Where property is in the possession of another, isolated acts of control are insufficient for taking possession.

1. On prend possession d'un bien en s'en assurant le contrôle matériel.
2. Lorsqu'un bien se trouve en la possession d'autrui, des actes de contrôle isolés ne suffisent pas pour constituer une prise de possession.

Art. 114. (3.5.8) Een bezitter draagt zijn bezit over door de verkrijger in staat te stellen die macht uit te oefenen, die hij zelf over het goed kon uitoefenen.

A possessor transfers his possession by enabling the acquirer to exercise such control over the property as he himself was able to exercise over it.

Le possesseur transfère la possession en permettant à l'acquéreur d'exercer sur le bien le contrôle qu'il pouvait lui-même exercer.

Art. 115. (3.5.9) Voor de overdracht van het bezit is een tweezijdige verklaring zonder feitelijke handeling voldoende:
a. wanneer de vervreemder de zaak bezit en hij haar krachtens een bij de levering gemaakt beding voortaan voor de verkrijger houdt;
b. wanneer de verkrijger houder van de zaak voor de vervreemder was;
c. wanneer een derde voor de vervreemder de zaak hield, en haar na de overdracht voor de ontvanger houdt. In dit geval gaat het bezit niet

over voordat de derde de overdracht heeft erkend, dan wel de vervreemder of de verkrijger de overdracht aan hem heeft medegedeeld.

A bilateral declaration without material acts is sufficient for the transfer of possession:
a. where the alienator possesses the thing and henceforth detains it for the acquirer by virtue of a stipulation made at the time of delivery;
b. where the acquirer was detentor of the thing for the alienator;
c. where a third party detained the thing for the alienator and detains it for the recipient after the transfer. In this event possession does not pass until the third party has acknowledged the transfer or has been notified of it by the alienator or acquirer.

La possession peut être transférée par une déclaration bilatérale sans acte matériel:
a. Lorsque l'aliénateur possède la chose et que, en vertu d'une stipulation lors de la délivrance, il la détient désormais pour l'acquéreur;
b. Lorsque l'acquéreur détenait la chose pour l'aliénateur;
c. Lorsqu'un tiers détenait la chose pour l'aliénateur et que, après le transfert, il la détient pour le destinataire. Dans ce cas, la possession n'est transférée que lorsque le tiers a reconnu le transfert ou que l'aliénateur ou l'acquéreur le lui a communiqué.

Art. 116. (3.5.10) Hij die onder een algemene titel een ander opvolgt, volgt daarmede die ander op in diens bezit en houderschap, met alle hoedanigheden en gebreken daarvan.

The possession and detention of the successor by general title is of the same quality and subject to the same defects as that of his predecessor.

Le successeur à titre universel succède à son auteur dans la possession et la détention des biens, avec tous les défauts et qualités de celles-ci.

Art. 117. (3.5.11) - 1. Een bezitter van een goed verliest het bezit, wanneer hij het goed kennelijk prijsgeeft, of wanneer een ander het bezit van het goed verkrijgt.
- 2. Zolang niet een der in het vorige lid genoemde gronden van bezitsverlies zich heeft voorgedaan, duurt een aangevangen bezit voort.

1. A possessor of property loses possession when it is evident that he abandons the property or when another acquires possession of it.
2. Possession which has begun continues until one of the grounds of loss of possession mentioned in the preceding paragraph has occurred.

1. Le possesseur d'un bien en perd la possession lorsque il l'abandonne manifestement ou qu'un tiers en acquiert la possession.
2. La possession une fois commencée continue tant que n'est pas survenue l'une des causes de perte de possession visées au paragraphe précédent.

Art. 118. (3.5.12) - 1. Een bezitter is te goeder trouw, wanneer hij zich als rechthebbende beschouwt en zich ook redelijkerwijze als zodanig mocht beschouwen.
- 2. Is een bezitter eenmaal te goeder trouw, dan wordt hij geacht dit te blijven.
- 3. Goede trouw wordt vermoed aanwezig te zijn; het ontbreken van goede trouw moet worden bewezen.

1. A possessor who believes himself to be the title-holder and is reasonably justified in that belief, is a possessor in good faith.
2. Once a possessor is in good faith, he is considered to remain so.
3. Good faith is presumed; absence of good faith must be proven.

1. Est possesseur de bonne foi celui qui se considère comme titulaire d'un droit et pouvait raisonnablement se considérer comme tel.
2. Dès lors que le possesseur est de bonne foi, il est censé le demeurer.
3. La bonne foi se présume; l'absence de bonne foi doit être prouvée.

Art. 119. (3.5.13) - 1. De bezitter van een goed wordt vermoed rechthebbende te zijn.
- 2. Ten aanzien van registergoederen wijkt dit vermoeden, wanneer komt vast te staan dat de wederpartij of diens rechtsvoorganger te eniger tijd rechthebbende was en dat de bezitter zich niet kan beroepen op verkrijging nadien onder bijzondere titel waarvoor inschrijving in de registers vereist is.

1. The possessor of property is presumed to be the title-holder.
2. This presumption is set aside in respect of registered property, where it is established that another party or his predecessor was title-holder at any time and the possessor cannot invoke subsequent acquisition by particular title requiring entry in the registers.

1. Le possesseur d'un bien est présumé en être le titulaire.
2. À l'égard des biens immatriculés, cette présomption est écartée lorsqu'il est établi que l'autre partie ou son auteur en a été le titulaire à un quelconque moment et que le possesseur ne peut se prévaloir d'une acquisition subséquente à titre particulier pour laquelle l'inscription sur les registres est requise.

Art. 120. (3.5.14) - 1. Aan een bezitter te goeder trouw behoren de afgescheiden natuurlijke en de opeisbaar geworden burgerlijke vruchten toe.
- 2. De rechthebbende op een goed, die dit opeist van een bezitter te goede trouw of die het van deze heeft terugontvangen, is verplicht de ten behoeve van het goed gemaakte kosten alsmede de schade waarvoor de bezitter op grond van het in titel 3 van Boek 6 bepaalde uit hoofde van zijn bezit jegens derden aansprakelijk mocht zijn, aan deze te vergoeden, voor zover de bezitter niet door de vruchten van het goed en de overige voordelen die hij ter zake heeft genoten, voor het een en ander is schadeloos gesteld. De rechter kan de verschuldigde vergoeding beperken, indien volledige vergoeding zou leiden tot onbillijke bevoordeling van de bezitter jegens de rechthebbende.
- 3. Zolang een bezitter te goeder trouw de hem verschuldigde vergoeding niet heeft ontvangen, is hij bevoegd de afgifte van het goed op te schorten.
- 4. Het in dit artikel bepaalde is ook van toepassing op hem die meent en mocht menen dat hij het bezit rechtmatig heeft verkregen, ook al weet hij dat de handelingen die voor de levering van het recht nodig zijn, niet hebben plaatsgevonden.

1. Separated natural fruits and civil fruits which have become exigible belong to the possessor in good faith.

1. Les fruits naturels après séparation et les fruits civils devenus exigibles appartiennent au possesseur de bonne foi.

2. The title-holder of property who claims it from a possessor in good faith or has recovered it from him is obliged to reimburse him for the costs expended on the property, as well as for the damages for which, by virtue of the rules of title 3 of Book 6, the possessor might be liable toward third persons by reason of his possession; this obligation ceases to the extent that the possessor has been indemnified by the fruits of the property and the other benefits which he has drawn from it. The judge may reduce the reimbursement due if full reimbursement would result in an inequitable advantage of the possessor over the title-holder.

3. As long as a possessor in good faith has not received the reimbursement due to him, he has the right to suspend restitution of the property.

4. The provisions of this article also apply to a person who believes and could believe that he has lawfully acquired possession, although he knows that the acts necessary for delivery of the right have not taken place.

2. Le titulaire d'un bien qui le revendique au possesseur de bonne foi, ou qui se l'est fait restituer par celui-ci, est tenu de lui rembourser les frais engagés pour le bien; il doit également lui verser les dommages-intérêts auxquels le possesseur pourrait, en raison de sa possession, être tenu envers des tiers en vertu des dispositions du titre troisième du Livre sixième; cette obligation disparaît dans la mesure où le possesseur a été indemnisé par les fruits du bien et par les autres avantages dont il a bénéficié. Si le remboursement intégral entraîne pour le possesseur un avantage qui serait inéquitable à l'égard du titulaire, le juge peut le réduire.

3. Tant que le possesseur de bonne foi n'a pas reçu le remboursement dû, il a le droit de suspendre la restitution du bien.

4. Les dispositions du présent article s'appliquent également à celui qui croit et pouvait croire avoir acquis la possession légalement, quoi qu'il sache que les actes requis pour la délivrance du droit n'ont pas eu lieu.

Art. 121. (3.5.15) - 1. Een bezitter die niet te goeder trouw is, is jegens de rechthebbende behalve tot afgifte van het goed ook verplicht tot het afgeven van de afgescheiden natuurlijke en de opeisbaar geworden burgerlijke vruchten, onverminderd zijn aansprakelijkheid op grond van het in titel 3 van Boek 6 bepaalde voor door de rechthebbende geleden schade.
- 2. Hij heeft tegen de rechthebbende alleen een vordering tot vergoeding van de kosten die hij ten behoeve van het goed of tot winning van de vruchten heeft gemaakt, voor zover hij deze vergoeding van de rechthebbende kan vorderen op grond van het bepaalde omtrent ongerechtvaardigde verrijking.
- 3. Het in dit artikel bepaalde is ook op de bezitter te goeder trouw van toepassing vanaf het tijdstip waarop de rechthebbende zijn recht tegen hem heeft ingeroepen.

1. Without prejudice to his liability by virtue of the rules of title 3 of Book 6 for the damage suffered by the title-holder and in addition to the restitution of the property, a possessor who is not in good faith is obliged to restore to the title-holder the separated natural fruits and the civil fruits which have become exigible.

2. He may claim against the title-holder reimbursement of the costs which he has expended on the property or which he has made to produce the fruits only to the extent that his claim can be based on the rules regarding unjust enrichment.

1. Outre la remise du bien, le possesseur qui n'est pas de bonne foi est tenu envers le titulaire du bien de remettre les fruits naturels qui ont été séparés et les fruits civils devenus exigibles, sans préjudice de sa responsabilité, en vertu des dispositions du titre troisième du Livre sixième, du dommage subi par le titulaire.

2. Il a contre le titulaire du bien une action en remboursement des frais qu'il a engagés pour le bien ou en vue de produire les fruits, dans la seule mesure où il peut le lui demander en vertu des dispositions relatives à l'enrichissement injustifié.

3. The provisions of this article also apply to the possessor in good faith from the moment the title-holder invokes his right against him.

3. Le présent article s'applique également au possesseur de bonne foi dès que le titulaire du bien a invoqué son droit contre lui.

Art. 122. (3.5.15a) Indien de rechthebbende ter bevrijding van de door hem ingevolge de beide vorige artikelen verschuldigde vergoedingen op zijn kosten het goed aan de bezitter wil overdragen, is de bezitter gehouden hieraan mede te werken.

If the title-holder, at his own expense, wants to transfer the property to the possessor in order to free himself from the reimbursements due by virtue of the two preceding articles, the possessor must cooperate in the transfer.

Si le titulaire du bien, pour acquitter les remboursements qu'il doit en vertu des deux articles précédents, veut transférer, à ses frais, le bien au possesseur, celui-ci est tenu d'y prêter son concours.

Art. 123. (3.5.15b) Heeft de bezitter van een zaak daaraan veranderingen of toevoegingen aangebracht, dan is hij bevoegd om, in plaats van de hem op grond van de artikelen 120 en 121 daarvoor toekomende vergoeding te vorderen, deze veranderingen of toevoegingen weg te nemen, mits hij de zaak in de oude toestand terugbrengt.

Where the possessor of a thing has made changes or additions to it, he has the right to remove them instead of claiming the reimbursement to which he is entitled by virtue of articles 120 and 121, provided that he restores the thing to its original condition.

Lorsque le possesseur d'une chose a apporté à celle-ci des modifications ou des additions, il peut les enlever plutôt que d'exiger les remboursements qui lui reviennent aux termes des articles 120 et 121, pourvu qu'il remette la chose dans son état antérieur.

Art. 124. (3.5.16) Wanneer iemand een goed voor een ander houdt en dit door een derde als rechthebbende van hem wordt opgeëist, vindt hetgeen in de voorgaande vier artikelen omtrent de bezitter is bepaald, te zijnen aanzien toepassing met inachtneming van de rechtsverhouding waarin hij tot die ander stond.

In the event that a third person claims property as title-holder from somebody who detains it for another person, the four preceding articles apply to the detentor, due regard being had to the juridical relationship between him and the other person.

Les dispositions relatives au possesseur contenues dans les quatre articles précédents s'appliquent à celui qui détient pour une autre personne un bien qu'un tiers lui réclame en tant que titulaire, compte tenu du rapport juridique entre le détenteur et cette autre personne.

Art. 125. (3.5.17) - 1. Hij die het bezit van een goed heeft verkregen, kan op grond van een daarna ingetreden bezitsverlies of bezitsstoornis tegen derden dezelfde rechtsvorderingen instellen tot terugverkrijging van het goed en tot opheffing van de stoornis, die de rechthebbende op het goed toekomen. Nochtans moeten deze rechtsvorderingen binnen het jaar na het verlies of de stoornis worden ingesteld.

- 2. De vordering wordt afgewezen, indien de gedaagde een beter recht dan de eiser heeft tot het houden van het goed of de storende handelingen krachtens een beter recht heeft verricht, tenzij de gedaagde met geweld of

op heimelijke wijze aan de eiser het bezit heeft ontnomen of diens bezit heeft gestoord.
- 3. Het in dit artikel bepaalde laat voor de bezitter, ook nadat het in het eerste lid bedoelde jaar is verstreken, en voor de houder onverlet de mogelijkheid een vordering op grond van onrechtmatige daad in te stellen, indien daartoe gronden zijn.

1. He who has acquired possession of property can, on the basis of a subsequent loss of or disturbance in the possession, institute the same actions against third persons to recover the property and to remove the disturbance as the title-holder of the property. Nevertheless, these actions must be instituted within the year following the loss or disturbance.
2. The action is rejected if the defendant has a better right than the plaintiff to the detention of the property or if he has performed the disturbing acts pursuant to a better right, unless the defendant has taken possession from the plaintiff or has disturbed his possession in a violent or surreptitious manner.
3. Nothing in this article deprives the possessor, even after the expiry of the year referred to in the first paragraph, or the detentor of the possibility, should there be grounds, to institute an action on the basis of an unlawful act.

1. Celui qui a acquis la possession d'un bien dispose contre les tiers, au cas de perte ou de trouble subséquents dans sa possession, des mêmes actions que le titulaire pour recouvrer le bien ou faire cesser le trouble. Néanmoins, ces actions doivent être intentées dans le délai d'un an à compter de la perte ou du trouble.
2. L'action est rejetée si le défendeur a un meilleur droit à détenir le bien que le demandeur ou qu'il a troublé ce dernier dans sa possession en vertu d'un meilleur titre, à moins que le défendeur, de façon violente ou clandestine, n'ait enlevé la possession du bien au demandeur ou ne l'ait troublé dans sa possession.
3. Le présent article ne porte pas atteinte au droit du possesseur, même après l'expiration de la période d'un an visée au premier paragraphe, ou à celui du détenteur, d'intenter une action en responsabilité civile, s'il y a cause.

TITEL 6 BEWIND

TITLE 6 ADMINISTRATION OF THE PROPERTY OF ANOTHER

TITRE SIXIÈME DE L'ADMINISTRATION DU BIEN D'AUTRUI

Art. 126-165. Gereserveerd.

Reserved.

Réservés.

TITEL 7 GEMEENSCHAP

TITLE 7 COMMUNITY

TITRE SEPTIÈME DE LA COMMUNAUTÉ

AFDELING 1 Algemene bepalingen

Section 1 General provisions

Section première Dispositions générales

Art. 166. (3.7.1.1) - 1. Gemeenschap is aanwezig, wanneer een of meer goederen toebehoren aan twee of meer deelgenoten gezamenlijk.
- 2. De aandelen van de deelgenoten zijn gelijk, tenzij uit hun rechtsverhouding anders voortvloeit.
- 3. Op de rechtsbetrekkingen tussen de deelgenoten is artikel 2 van Boek 6 van overeenkomstige toepassing.

1. Community exists when property belongs to two or more partners jointly.

2. The shares of partners are equal, unless their juridical relationship produces a different result.
3. Article 2 of Book 6 applies *mutatis mutandis* to the juridical relations between partners.

1. Il y a communauté lorsque des biens appartiennent conjointement à plusieurs partenaires.
2. Les parts sont égales entre les partenaires, à moins qu'il n'en résulte autrement de leur rapport juridique.
3. L'article 2 du Livre sixième s'applique par analogie aux rapports juridiques entre les partenaires.

Art. 167. (3.7.1.1a) Goederen die geacht moeten worden in de plaats van een gemeenschappelijk goed te treden behoren tot de gemeenschap.

Property which is deemed to take the place of common property belongs to the community.

Fait partie de la communauté le bien qui est réputé se substituer à un bien commun.

Art. 168. (3.7.1.2) - 1. De deelgenoten kunnen het genot, het gebruik en het beheer van gemeenschappelijke goederen bij overeenkomst regelen.
- 2. Voor zover een overeenkomst ontbreekt, kan de kantonrechter op verzoek van de meest gerede partij een zodanige regeling treffen, zo nodig met onderbewindstelling van de goederen. Hij houdt daarbij naar billijkheid rekening zowel met de belangen van partijen als met het algemeen belang.
- 3. Een bestaande regeling kan op verzoek van de meest gerede partij door de kantonrechter wegens onvoorziene omstandigheden gewijzigd of buiten werking gesteld worden.
- 4. Een regeling is ook bindend voor de rechtverkrijgenden van een deelgenoot.
- 5. Op een overeenkomstig lid 2 ingesteld bewind zijn, voor zover de kantonrechter niet anders heeft bepaald, de artikelen 433 lid 1, 435, 436 leden 1-3, 437, 438 lid 1, 439, 441 lid 1, eerste zin, en 442-448 van Boek 1 van toepassing. Het kan door een gezamenlijk besluit van de deelgenoten of op verzoek van een hunner door de kantonrechter worden opgeheven.

1. Partners may make rules by contract for the enjoyment, use and management of common property.
2. To the extent that there is no contract, the judge of the subdistrict court may issue such rules at the request of any interested party and, if necessary, he may put the property under administration. In doing so he must take into account, in an equitable fashion, both the interests of the parties and the general interest.
3. At the request of any interested party, existing rules may be modified or rendered inoperative by the judge of the subdistrict court upon the ground of unforeseen circumstances.
4. The rules referred to above also bind the successors of a partner.
5. To the extent that the judge of the subdistrict court has not provided otherwise, articles 433 paragraph 1, 435, 436 paragraphs 1 - 3, 437, 438 paragraph 1, 439, 444 paragraph 1, first sentence and 442 - 448 of Book 1 apply to administration instituted according to paragraph 2 of this article. Such administration may be terminated by a joint decision of the partners or by the judge of the subdistrict court at the request of one of them.

1. Les partenaires peuvent établir par contrat des règles relatives à la jouissance, à l'usage et à la gestion des biens communs.
2. Dans la mesure où le contrat fait défaut, le juge d'instance peut, sur la requête de la partie la plus diligente, établir des règles, assorties, si nécessaire, d'un régime d'administration des biens. Il tient compte, en toute équité, de l'intérêt des parties aussi bien que de l'intérêt général.
3. À la requête de la partie la plus diligente, le juge d'instance peut, en raison de circonstances imprévues, modifier ou rendre inopérantes les règles établies.
4. Ces règles lient également les ayants cause d'un partenaire.
5. S'appliquent au régime d'administration institué conformément au paragraphe 2, dans la mesure où le juge d'instance n'a pas disposé autrement, le paragraphe premier de l'article 433, l'article 435, les paragraphes 1er à 3 de l'article 436, l'article 437, le paragraphe premier de l'article 438, l'article 439, la première phrase du paragraphe premier de l'article 441 et les articles 442 à 448 du Livre premier. Le régime prend fin par décision conjointe des partenaires ou par celle du juge d'instance sur la requête de l'un d'entre eux.

Art. 169. (3.7.1.3) Tenzij een regeling anders bepaalt, is iedere deelgenoot bevoegd tot het gebruik van een gemeenschappelijk goed, mits dit gebruik met het recht van de overige deelgenoten te verenigen is.

Unless the rules provide otherwise, any one partner is entitled to use common property, provided that this is compatible with the right of the other partners.

À moins que les règles ne disposent autrement, chaque partenaire peut faire usage du bien commun, pourvu que cet usage soit compatible avec le droit des autres partenaires.

Art. 170. (3.7.1.3a) - 1. Handelingen dienende tot gewoon onderhoud of tot behoud van een gemeenschappelijk goed, en in het algemeen handelingen die geen uitstel kunnen lijden, kunnen door ieder der deelgenoten zo nodig zelfstandig worden verricht. Ieder van hen is bevoegd ten behoeve van de gemeenschap verjaring te stuiten.
- 2. Voor het overige geschiedt het beheer door de deelgenoten tezamen, tenzij een regeling anders bepaalt. Onder beheer zijn begrepen alle handelingen die voor de normale exploitatie van het goed dienstig kunnen zijn, alsook het aannemen van aan de gemeenschap verschuldigde prestaties.
- 3. Tot andere handelingen betreffende een gemeenschappelijk goed dan in de vorige leden vermeld, zijn uitsluitend de deelgenoten tezamen bevoegd.

1. Acts for the purpose of ordinary maintenance or preservation of common property and, generally, acts which cannot be postponed may be performed by any one of the partners, if necessary independently of the others. Any one partner has the right to interrupt prescription for the benefit of the community.
2. In all other cases the partners manage the property together, unless the rules provide otherwise. Management includes all acts which may serve the normal exploitation of the property as well as the acceptance of prestations owed to the community.
3. Except for those acts referred to in the preceding paragraphs, only the partners acting together have the power to perform acts concerning common property.

1. Chacun des partenaires peut, de façon autonome si nécessaire, faire les actes relatifs à l'entretien ordinaire ou à la conservation du bien commun et, d'une manière générale, ceux qui n'admettent aucun retard. Chacun d'eux a le pouvoir d'interrompre la prescription au profit de la communauté.

2. Pour les actes autres, la gestion est commune, à moins que les règles n'y pourvoient autrement. Par gestion, on entend tous les actes relatifs à l'exploitation normale du bien, ainsi que l'acceptation des prestations dues à la communauté.

3. À l'exception de ceux visés aux paragraphes précédents, tous les actes concernant les biens communs doivent être accomplis par les partenaires agissant conjointement.

Art. 171. (3.7.1.3b) Tenzij een regeling anders bepaalt, is iedere deelgenoot bevoegd tot het instellen van rechtsvorderingen en het indienen van verzoekschriften ter verkrijging van een rechterlijke uitspraak ten behoeve van de gemeenschap. Een regeling die het beheer toekent aan een of meer der deelgenoten, sluit, tenzij zij anders bepaalt, deze bevoegdheid voor de anderen uit.

Unless the rules provide otherwise, any one partner has the right to institute actions and to submit petitions to obtain a judicial decision for the benefit of the community. Rules delegating management to one or more partners deprive the other partners of this right, unless otherwise provided.

À moins que les règles ne disposent autrement, chaque partenaire a le droit d'intenter toute action en justice et de présenter toute requête pour obtenir une décision judiciaire au bénéfice de la communauté. La règle qui confie la gestion à un ou plusieurs partenaires retire ce pouvoir aux autres, à moins qu'elle ne dispose autrement.

Art. 172. (3.7.1.4) Tenzij een regeling anders bepaalt, delen de deelgenoten naar evenredigheid van hun aandelen in de vruchten en andere voordelen die het gemeenschappelijke goed oplevert, en moeten zij in dezelfde evenredigheid bijdragen tot de uitgaven die voortvloeien uit handelingen welke bevoegdelijk ten behoeve van de gemeenschap zijn verricht.

Unless the rules provide otherwise, the partners participate in the fruits and other benefits which common property yields in proportion to their shares; they must contribute, in the same proportion, to the expenses which result from acts duly performed in the interest of the community.

À moins que les règles ne disposent autrement, les partenaires recueillent les fruits et autres avantages provenant du bien commun proportionnellement à leurs parts; ils contribuent dans la même proportion aux dépenses résultant d'actes valablement accomplis dans l'intérêt de la communauté.

Art. 173. (3.7.1.5) Ieder der deelgenoten kan van degene onder hen die voor de overigen beheer heeft gevoerd, jaarlijks en in ieder geval bij het einde van het beheer rekening en verantwoording vorderen.

Annually, and in any event upon the termination of the management, each of the partners may claim the rendering of accounts from the partner who has carried out the management for the others.

Chacun des partenaires peut demander, chaque année et, de toute façon, à la fin de la gestion, des comptes à celui d'entre eux qui a géré pour les autres.

Art. 174. (3.7.1.7) - 1. De rechter die ter zake van een vordering tot verdeling bevoegd zou zijn of voor wie een zodanige vordering reeds aanhangig is kan een deelgenoot op diens verzoek ten behoeve van de voldoening van een voor rekening van de gemeenschap komende schuld of om andere gewichtige redenen machtigen tot het te gelde maken van een gemeenschappelijk goed. Indien een deelgenoot voor wie een te verkopen goed een bijzondere waarde heeft, bereid is het goed tegen vergoeding van de geschatte waarde over te nemen, kan de voormelde rechter deze overneming bevelen.
- 2. De in lid 1 bedoelde rechter kan een deelgenoot op diens verzoek machtigen een gemeenschappelijk goed te bezwaren met een recht van pand of hypotheek tot zekerheid voor de voldoening van een voor rekening van de gemeenschap komende schuld die reeds bestaat of waarvan het aangaan geboden is voor het behoud van een goed der gemeenschap.

1. The judge who would have jurisdiction in an action for partition, or the judge who has already been seized of such an action may authorize a partner, at his request, to realize common property in order to pay a debt for which the community is answerable or for other serious reasons. If a partner for whom such property has a particular value wishes to acquire it upon payment of its estimated value, the aforementioned judge may order that this be done.
2. The judge referred to in paragraph 1 may authorize a partner, at his request, to encumber common property with a right of pledge or hypothec as security for the payment of a debt for which the community is answerable, whether that debt already exists or must as yet be contracted for the preservation of community property.

1. Le juge qui aurait compétence à connaître d'une action en partage ou qui est déjà saisi d'une telle action peut autoriser un partenaire, sur sa requête, à réaliser un bien commun pour le paiement d'une dette incombant à la communauté, ou pour d'autres motifs sérieux. Si l'un des partenaires, pour qui ce bien a une valeur particulière, est prêt à l'acquérir moyennant paiement de la valeur estimée, le juge précité peut ordonner cette transmission.

2. Le juge visé au paragraphe premier peut autoriser un partenaire, sur sa requête, à grever un bien commun d'un droit de gage ou d'hypothèque en garantie d'une dette déjà existante ou devant être contractée pour la conservation d'un bien commun et qui incombe à la communauté.

Art. 175. (3.7.1.8) - 1. Tenzij uit de rechtsverhouding tussen de deelgenoten anders voortvloeit, kan ieder van hen over zijn aandeel in een gemeenschappelijk goed beschikken.
- 2. Indien uit de rechtsverhouding tussen de deelgenoten voortvloeit dat zij niet, tenzij met aller toestemming, bevoegd zijn over hun aandeel te

beschikken, zijn de leden 3 en 4 van artikel 168 van overeenkomstige toepassing.
- 3. De schuldeisers van een deelgenoot kunnen zijn aandeel in een gemeenschappelijk goed uitwinnen. Na de uitwinning van een aandeel kunnen beperkingen van de bevoegdheid om over de aandelen te beschikken niet worden ingeroepen tussen de verkrijger van dat aandeel en de overige deelgenoten.

1. Any one partner may dispose of his share in common property, unless the juridical relationship between the partners produces a different result.
2. If, as a result of their juridical relationship, the partners do not have the power to dispose of their share except with the consent of all of them, paragraphs 3 and 4 of article 168 apply *mutatis mutandis*.
3. Creditors may seize and execute against the share of a partner in common property. After seizure and execution against a share, limitations on the power to dispose of the shares cannot be invoked between the acquirer of such a share and the remaining partners.

1. À moins qu'il n'en résulte autrement du rapport juridique entre les partenaires, chacun d'eux peut disposer de sa part dans un bien commun.
2. S'il résulte du rapport juridique entre partenaires qu'ils ne peuvent, sauf du consentement de tous, disposer de leur part, les paragraphes 3 et 4 de l'article 168 s'appliquent par analogie.
3. Les créanciers d'un partenaire peuvent saisir et exécuter la part de celui-ci dans un bien commun. Après saisie et exécution de cette part, les restrictions au pouvoir de disposer des parts ne peuvent être invoquées dans les rapports entre l'acquéreur et les autres partenaires.

Art. 176. (3.7.1.8a) - 1. De verkrijger van een aandeel of een beperkt recht daarop moet van de verkrijging onverwijld mededeling doen aan de overige deelgenoten of aan degene die door de deelgenoten of de rechter met het beheer over het goed is belast.
- 2. Een overgedragen aandeel wordt verkregen onder de last aan de gemeenschap te vergoeden hetgeen de vervreemder haar schuldig was. Vervreemder en verkrijger zijn hoofdelijk voor deze vergoeding aansprakelijk. De verkrijger kan zich aan deze verplichting onttrekken door zijn aandeel op zijn kosten aan de overige deelgenoten over te dragen; dezen zijn verplicht aan een zodanige overdracht mede te werken.
- 3. De vorige leden zijn niet van toepassing bij uitwinning van de gezamenlijke aandelen in een gemeenschappelijk goed.

1. The acquirer of a partnership share or of a dismembered right pertaining to it must, without delay, notify the remaining partners or the person appointed manager of the property by the partners or by the judge, of the acquisition.
2. A share which has been transferred is acquired subject to the obligation to compensate the community for what the alienator owed to it. The alienator and the acquirer are solidarily liable for this compensation. The acquirer may avoid this obligation by transferring the share, at his own expense, to the remaining partners who are obliged to cooperate in such a transfer.

1. L'acquéreur d'une part ou d'un droit démembré sur une part doit, sans tarder, dénoncer l'acquisition aux autres partenaires ou à celui que les partenaires ou le juge ont chargé de la gestion du bien.
2. La part transférée est acquise à charge d'indemniser la communauté de ce que lui devait l'aliénateur. L'aliénateur et l'acquéreur sont solidairement responsables de cette indemnisation. L'acquéreur peut se soustraire à cette responsabilité en transférant, à ses frais, sa part aux autres partenaires; ceux-ci sont tenus de prêter leur concours à ce transfert.

3. The preceding paragraphs do not apply to seizure and execution against the totality of shares in common property.

3. Les paragraphes précédents ne s'appliquent pas à la saisie-exécution de l'ensemble des parts d'un bien commun.

Art. 177. (3.7.1.8b) - 1. Wordt een gemeenschappelijk goed verdeeld of overgedragen, terwijl op het aandeel van een deelgenoot een beperkt recht rust, dan komt dat recht te rusten op het goed voor zover dit door die deelgenoot wordt verkregen, en wordt het goed voor het overige van dat recht bevrijd, onverminderd hetgeen de beperkt gerechtigde of de deelgenoot op wiens aandeel zijn recht rust, krachtens hun onderlinge verhouding van de ander wegens een door deze aldus ontvangen overwaarde heeft te vorderen.
- 2. Een verdeling, alsmede een overdracht waartoe de deelgenoten zich na bezwaring met het beperkte recht hebben verplicht, behoeft de medewerking van de beperkt gerechtigde.
- 3. Een bij toedeling van het goed aan de in het eerste lid genoemde deelgenoot bedongen recht van pand of hypotheek tot waarborg van hetgeen hij aan een of meer der deelgenoten ten gevolge van de verdeling schuldig is of mocht worden, heeft, mits het gelijktijdig met de levering van het hem toegedeelde daarop wordt gevestigd, voorrang boven een beperkt recht dat een deelgenoot tevoren op zijn aandeel had gevestigd.

1. Where common property is partitioned or transferred, while the share of a partner is encumbered with a dismembered right, that right will encumber the property to the extent that it is acquired by that partner; for the remainder the property is freed from it. This rule, however, is without prejudice to what the holder of the dismembered right or the partner whose share is encumbered with that right can claim from one another, pursuant to their mutual relationship, for excess value received.
2. A partition as well as a transfer to which the partners have bound themselves after encumbrance with a dismembered right, requires the cooperation of the holder of the dismembered right.
3. A right of pledge or hypothec, stipulated on the occasion of the attribution of the property to the partner referred to in the first paragraph, as guarantee for what he owes or might owe to one or more partners as a result of the partition, has preference over a dismembered right which a partner had previously established on his share, provided that it is established on what has been attributed to him at the same time as the delivery thereof.

1. Lorsqu'un bien commun fait l'objet d'un partage ou d'un transfert alors que la part d'un partenaire se trouve grevée d'un droit démembré, ce droit grève le bien dans la mesure où ce partenaire l'acquiert et s'éteint pour le surplus, sans préjudice de ce que le titulaire du droit démembré ou le partenaire dont la part est grevée de ce droit peut, en vertu de leur rapport réciproque, réclamer à l'autre en raison d'une plus-value que celui-ci aurait ainsi acquise.

2. Le partage, de même que le transfert auquel les partenaires se sont engagés après que le droit démembré est venu grever le bien exige, le concours du titulaire de ce droit.

3. Le droit de gage ou d'hypothèque, stipulé lors de l'attribution du bien au partenaire visé au paragraphe premier en garantie de ce qu'il doit ou pourra devoir à d'autres partenaires à la suite du partage, prend rang avant le droit démembré qu'un partenaire aurait établi antérieurement sur sa part, pourvu que ce droit soit établi sur ce qui lui est attribué au moment même où il en prend délivrance.

Art. 178. (3.7.1.9) - 1. Ieder der deelgenoten, alsmede hij die een beperkt recht op een aandeel heeft, kan te allen tijde verdeling van een gemeenschappelijk goed vorderen, tenzij uit de aard van de gemeenschap of uit het in de volgende leden bepaalde anders voortvloeit.
- 2. Op verlangen van een deelgenoot kan de rechter voor wie een vordering tot verdeling aanhangig is, bepalen dat alle of sommige opeisbare schulden die voor rekening van de gemeenschap komen, moeten worden voldaan alvorens tot de verdeling wordt overgegaan.
- 3. Indien de door een onmiddellijke verdeling getroffen belangen van een of meer deelgenoten aanmerkelijk groter zijn dan de belangen die door de verdeling worden gediend, kan de rechter voor wie een vordering tot verdeling aanhangig is, op verlangen van een deelgenoot een of meermalen, telkens voor ten hoogste drie jaren, een vordering tot verdeling uitsluiten.
- 4. Indien geen vordering tot verdeling aanhangig is, kan een beslissing als bedoeld in de leden 2 en 3 op verzoek van ieder van de deelgenoten worden gegeven door de rechter die ter zake van de vordering tot verdeling bevoegd zou zijn.
- 5. Zij die bevoegd zijn verdeling te vorderen, kunnen hun bevoegdheid daartoe een of meer malen bij overeenkomst, telkens voor ten hoogste vijf jaren, uitsluiten. De leden 3 en 4 van artikel 168 zijn op een zodanige overeenkomst van overeenkomstige toepassing.

1. Any one partner, as well as the holder of a dismembered right upon a partnership share, may at any time demand partition of common property, unless the nature of the community or the provisions of the following paragraphs produce a different result.
2. Upon the demand of a partner, the judge seized of an action for partition may determine that all or certain exigible debts for which the community is answerable, must be paid before proceeding to the partition.
3. If the interests of one or more partners which are harmed by an immediate partition are considerably greater than the interests served by the partition, the judge seized of an action for partition may, upon the demand of such a partner, exclude proceedings, once or repeatedly, for a maximum of three years on each occasion.
4. If no action for partition has been brought, a decision pursuant to paragraphs 2 and 3 may be rendered at the request of any of the partners by the judge who would have jurisdiction in an action for partition.

1. Chacun des partenaires, de même que celui qui a un droit démembré sur une part, peut demander en tout temps le partage du bien commun, à moins qu'il n'en résulte autrement de la nature de la communauté ou des dispositions des paragraphes suivants.

2. À la demande d'un partenaire, le juge saisi d'une action en partage peut décider que toutes les dettes exigibles qui incombent à la communauté, ou certaines d'entre elles, doivent être payées avant qu'il ne soit procédé au partage.
3. Si les intérêts d'un ou de plusieurs partenaires lésés par un partage immédiat dépassent considérablement les intérêts favorisés, le juge saisi d'une action en partage peut, à la demande d'un partenaire, exclure l'action une ou plusieurs fois, pour une période ne pouvant chaque fois excéder trois ans.

4. Si aucune action en partage n'est pendante, une décision comme celles que prévoient les paragraphes 2 et 3 peut être rendue, sur la requête de chacun des partenaires, par le juge qui aurait compétence de connaître d'une action en partage.

5. Those who have the right to demand partition can exclude their power to do so by contract, once or repeatedly, for a maximum of five years on each occasion. Paragraphs 3 and 4 of article 168 apply to such a contract *mutatis mutandis*.

5. Ceux qui ont la faculté de demander le partage peuvent exclure cette faculté par contrat une ou plusieurs fois, dans chaque cas pour au plus cinq ans. Les paragraphes 3 et 4 de l'article 168 s'appliquent par analogie à un tel contrat.

Art. 179. (3.7.1.9a) - 1. Indien verdeling van een gemeenschappelijk goed wordt gevorderd, kan ieder der deelgenoten verlangen dat alle tot de gemeenschap behorende goederen en de voor rekening van de gemeenschap komende schulden in de verdeling worden begrepen, tenzij er gewichtige redenen zijn voor een gedeeltelijke verdeling. Van de verdeling worden die goederen uitgezonderd, die wegens een der in artikel 178 genoemde gronden onverdeeld moeten blijven.
- 2. De omstandigheid dat bij een verdeling een of meer goederen zijn overgeslagen, heeft alleen ten gevolge dat daarvan een nadere verdeling kan worden gevorderd.
- 3. Op de toedeling van een schuld is afdeling 3 van titel 2 van Boek 6 van toepassing.

1. If partition of common property is demanded, any one of the partners may demand that all property belonging to the community and all debts for which the community is answerable be included in the partition, unless there are serious reasons for a partial partition. Property which must remain undivided for one of the reasons mentioned in article 178 is excluded from the partition.
2. The omission of certain property in a partition only has the effect that a supplementary partition thereof can be demanded.
3. Section 3 of title 2 of Book 6 applies to the attribution of a debt.

1. Si le partage d'un bien commun est demandé, chacun des partenaires peut exiger que tous les biens appartenant à la communauté et toutes les dettes incombant à celle-ci en fassent l'objet, à moins qu'il n'existe des motifs sérieux pour un partage partiel. Sont exclus du partage les biens qui doivent rester indivis pour un des motifs mentionnés à l'article 178.

2. Le fait que des biens aient été omis d'un partage n'a pour effet que de permettre une demande en partage supplémentaire.

3. La section troisième du titre deuxième du Livre sixième s'applique à l'attribution d'une dette.

Art. 180. (3.7.1.9b) - 1. Een schuldeiser die een opeisbare vordering op een deelgenoot heeft, kan verdeling van de gemeenschap vorderen, doch niet verder dan nodig is voor het verhaal van zijn vordering. Artikel 178 lid 3 is van toepassing.
- 2. Heeft een schuldeiser een bevel tot verdeling van de gemeenschap verkregen dan behoeft de verdeling zijn medewerking.

1. A creditor who has an exigible claim against a partner may demand partition of the community, but not beyond what is necessary for the recovery of his claim. Article 178, paragraph 3 applies.

2. Where a creditor has obtained an order for partition of the community, such partition requires his cooperation.

1. Le créancier qui a une créance exigible à l'encontre d'un partenaire peut demander le partage de la communauté, mais non au delà de ce qui est nécessaire pour le recouvrement de cette créance. Le paragraphe 3 de l'article 178 s'applique.
2. Lorsque le créancier a obtenu un ordre de partage de la communauté, le partage exige son concours.

Art. 181. (3.7.1.10) - 1. Voor het geval dat deelgenoten of zij wier medewerking vereist is, niet medewerken tot een verdeling nadat deze bij rechterlijke uitspraak is bevolen, benoemt de rechter die in eerste aanleg van de vordering tot verdeling heeft kennis genomen, indien deze benoeming niet reeds bij die uitspraak heeft plaatsgehad, op verzoek van de meest gerede partij een onzijdig persoon die hen bij de verdeling vertegenwoordigt en daarbij hun belangen naar eigen beste inzicht behartigt. Hebben degenen die niet medewerken tegenstrijdige belangen, dan wordt voor ieder van hen een onzijdig persoon benoemd.
- 2. Een onzijdig persoon is verplicht hetgeen aan de door hem vertegenwoordigde persoon ingevolge de verdeling toekomt, voor deze in ontvangst te nemen en daarover tot de afgifte aan de rechthebbende op de voet van artikel 410 van Boek 1 het bewind te voeren.
- 3. De beloning die de onzijdige persoon ten laste van de rechthebbende toekomt, wordt op zijn verzoek vastgesteld door de rechter die hem benoemde.

1. Where partners or persons whose cooperation is required do not cooperate in a partition after it has been ordered by judgment, the judge who, in first instance, has heard the action for partition, appoints a neutral person at the request of any interested party, if such appointment had not already been made in the judgment; the neutral person represents the parties in the partition and looks after their interests to the best of his ability. Where those who do not cooperate have conflicting interests, a neutral person is appointed for each of them.
2. A neutral person must take delivery of that which, as a result of the partition, accrues to the person whom he represents, and he must administer it, on the basis of article 410 of Book 1, until its remittance to the title-holder.
3. The remuneration due to the neutral person by the title-holder is determined, at the request of the neutral person, by the judge who appointed him.

1. Lorsque des partenaires ou ceux dont le concours est requis ne collaborent pas au partage ordonné par jugement, le juge qui a connu en première instance de l'action en partage, sur la requête de la partie la plus diligente, nomme une personne neutre, si la nomination n'a pas déjà été faite par ce jugement; celle-ci les représente lors du partage et agit dans leurs intérêts selon son meilleur jugement. Si ceux qui ne collaborent pas ont des intérêts opposés, une personne neutre est nommée pour chacun d'entre eux.
2. La personne neutre est tenue de prendre livraison de ce qui revient au représenté à la suite du partage et de l'administrer conformément à l'article 410 du Livre premier jusqu'à sa remise au titulaire.
3. Sur la requête de la personne neutre, le juge qui l'a nommée fixe la rémunération qui lui revient et dont la charge incombe au titulaire.

Art. 182. (3.7.1.11) Als een verdeling wordt aangemerkt iedere rechtshandeling waartoe alle deelgenoten, hetzij in persoon, hetzij vertegenwoordigd, medewerken en krachtens welke een of meer van hen een of meer goederen der gemeenschap met uitsluiting van de overige deelgenoten verkrijgen. De handeling is niet een verdeling, indien zij strekt tot nakoming van een voor rekening van de gemeenschap komende schuld aan een of meer deelgenoten, die niet voortspruit uit een rechtshandeling als bedoeld in de vorige zin.

A juridical act is deemed to be a partition if all partners participate therein either personally or by a representative and if, pursuant to the act, one or several of them acquire property belonging to the community to the exclusion of the remaining partners. The act is not a partititon if it is intended as payment to one or more partners of a debt for which the community is answerable and which does not result from a juridical act as referred to in the preceding sentence.

Est réputé acte de partage tout acte juridique auquel collaborent tous les partenaires, personnellement ou par représentant, et en vertu duquel un ou plusieurs d'entre eux acquièrent des biens de la communauté à l'exclusion des autres. Tel acte ne constitue pas un partage s'il sert au paiement à des partenaires d'une dette qui incombe à la communauté et ne résulte pas d'un acte juridique visé à la phrase précédente.

Art. 183. (3.7.1.12) - 1. De verdeling kan geschieden op de wijze en in de vorm die partijen goeddunkt, mits de deelgenoten en zij wier medewerking vereist is, allen het vrije beheer over hun goederen hebben en in persoon of bij een door hen aangewezen vertegenwoordiger medewerken, dan wel in geval van bewind over hun recht, worden vertegenwoordigd door de bewindvoerder, voorzien van de daartoe vereiste toestemming of machtiging.
- 2. In andere gevallen moet, tenzij de rechter anders bepaalt, de verdeling geschieden bij notariële akte en worden goedgekeurd door de kantonrechter die bevoegd is de wettelijke vertegenwoordiger van degene die het vrije beheer over zijn goederen mist, tot beschikkingshandelingen te machtigen.
- 3. Indien een der partijen minderjarig is of onder curatele staat, moeten de toeziende voogd en de toeziende curator bij de verdeling tegenwoordig zijn.

1. Partition may take place in the manner and form agreeable to the parties, provided that the partners and those whose cooperation is required are free to manage their property, and that they cooperate either personally or through a designated representative; in the event that their rights are under administration, they must be represented by the administrator invested with the required consent or authorization.
2. In other cases, unless the judge determines otherwise, the partition must be made by notarial deed and must be approved by the judge of the subdistrict court who has jurisdiction to authorize the legal representative of the person, who lacks the freedom to manage his own property, to perform acts of disposition.
3. If one of the parties is a minor or is under curatorship, the subrogate guardian or the subrogate curator must be present at the partition.

1. Le partage peut avoir lieu de la façon et dans la forme que les parties jugent utiles, pourvu que les partenaires et ceux dont le concours est exigé aient tous la libre gestion de leurs biens et collaborent personnellement ou par un représentant qu'ils ont désigné; si leurs droits sont soumis à un régime d'administration, ils doivent être représentés par l'administrateur, muni du consentement ou de l'autorisation requis.

2. Dans les autres cas, à moins que le juge ne dispose autrement, le partage doit avoir lieu par acte notarié et être approuvé par le juge d'instance, qui a compétence pour autoriser à accomplir des actes de disposition le représentant légal de celui qui n'a pas la libre gestion de ses biens.

3. Si l'une des parties est mineure ou a été mise en curatelle, le partage doit avoir lieu en présence du subrogé tuteur ou du subrogé curateur.

Art. 184. (3.7.1.13) - 1. Ieder der deelgenoten kan bij een verdeling verlangen dat op het aandeel van een andere deelgenoot wordt toegerekend hetgeen deze aan de gemeenschap schuldig is. De toerekening geschiedt ongeacht de gegoedheid van de schuldenaar. Is het een schuld onder tijdsbepaling, dan wordt zij voor haar contante waarde op het tijdstip der verdeling toegerekend.
- 2. Het vorige lid is niet van toepassing op schulden onder een opschortende voorwaarde die nog niet vervuld is.

1. In a partition, any one of the partners may demand that what another partner owes to the community be imputed to his share. Imputation takes place irrespective of the solvency of the debtor. If a debt is subject to a term, its cash value at the time of partition is its imputed value.
2. The preceding paragraph does not apply to debts under a suspensive condition which has not yet been fulfilled.

1. Chacun des partenaires peut exiger, lors du partage, que soit imputé à la part d'un autre partenaire ce que celui-ci doit à la communauté. L'imputation a lieu sans égard à la solvabilité du débiteur. La dette à terme est imputée à sa valeur au comptant au moment du partage.
2. Le paragraphe précédent ne s'applique pas aux dettes contractées sous une condition suspensive non encore accomplie.

Art. 185. (3.7.1.14) - 1. Voor zover de deelgenoten en zij wier medewerking vereist is, over een verdeling niet tot overeenstemming kunnen komen, gelast op vordering van de meest gerede partij de rechter de wijze van verdeling of stelt hij zelf de verdeling vast, rekening houdende naar billijkheid zowel met de belangen van partijen als met het algemeen belang.
- 2. Als wijzen van verdeling komen daarbij in aanmerking:
a. toedeling van een gedeelte van het goed aan ieder der deelgenoten;
b. overbedeling van een of meer deelgenoten tegen vergoeding van de overwaarde;
c. verdeling van de netto-opbrengst van het goed of een gedeelte daarvan, nadat dit op een door de rechter bepaalde wijze zal zijn verkocht.
- 3. Zo nodig kan de rechter bepalen dat degene die overbedeeld wordt, de overwaarde geheel of ten dele in termijnen mag voldoen. Hij kan daaraan de voorwaarde verbinden dat zekerheid tot een door hem bepaald bedrag en van een door hem bepaalde aard wordt gesteld.

1. To the extent that the partners and those whose cooperation is required cannot reach agreement on a partition, the judge, upon the demand of any interested party, orders the manner of partition or decides upon the partition himself, taking into account, in an equitable fashion, both the interests of the parties and the general interest.
2. The following manners of partition may be adopted:
a. attribution of part of the property to each of the partners;
b. over-attribution to one or more partners against compensation for the excess value;

1. Dans la mesure où les partenaires et ceux dont le concours est exigé ne peuvent se mettre d'accord sur le partage, le juge, à la demande de la partie la plus diligente, fixe le mode de partage ou établit lui-même le partage, en tenant compte, en toute équité, tant des intérêts des parties que de l'intérêt général.
2. Conviennent comme modes de partage:
a. L'attribution d'une part du bien à chacun des partenaires;
b. La surattribution à un ou plusieurs partenaires contre paiement d'une soulte;

c. partition of the net proceeds of the property or part thereof after its sale in the manner determined by the judge.

3. If necessary, the judge may determine that the person who has been over-attributed may pay the excess value wholly or partially in instalments. He may attach the condition thereto that security be furnished, the type and amount of which he determines.

c. Le partage du produit net de la totalité ou d'une partie du bien, lorsqu'il aura été vendu de la façon déterminée par le juge.

3. Le juge peut déterminer, si nécessaire, que le bénéficiaire d'une surattribution peut acquitter la soulte, en tout ou partie, par versements périodiques. Il peut y attacher la condition que sera constituée sûreté d'une nature et pour une somme qu'il détermine.

Art. 186. (3.7.1.14a) - 1. Voor de overgang van het aan ieder der deelgenoten toegedeelde is een levering vereist op dezelfde wijze als voor overdracht is voorgeschreven.
- 2. Hetgeen een deelgenoot verkrijgt, houdt hij onder dezelfde titel als waaronder de deelgenoten dit tezamen vóór de verdeling hielden.

1. In order to transmit to each partner that what has been attributed to him, delivery is required in the same manner as presribed for transfer.

2. A partner detains the property which he acquires under the same title as the partners detained it jointly before the partition.

1. La transmission de ce qui est attribué à chacun des partenaires exige une délivrance de la même manière qu'il est prévu pour le transfert.

2. Le partenaire détient ce qu'il acquiert, au même titre que les partenaires conjointement avant le partage.

Art. 187. (3.7.1.15) - 1. De papieren en bewijzen van eigendom, tot de toegedeelde goederen behorende, worden overgegeven aan hem, aan wie de goederen zijn toegedeeld.
- 2. Algemene boedelpapieren en stukken als bedoeld in lid 1, die betrekking hebben op aan meer deelgenoten toegedeelde goederen, verblijven bij hem die de meerderheid der betrokken deelgenoten daartoe heeft benoemd, onder verplichting aan de overige deelgenoten inzage, en zo iemand dit verlangt, afschriften of uittreksels op diens kosten af te geven.
- 3. Bij gebreke van een meerderheid als bedoeld in het vorige lid geschiedt de daar bedoelde benoeming op verlangen van een deelgenoot door de rechter die de verdeling vaststelt, of in andere gevallen op verzoek van een deelgenoot door de kantonrechter. Tegen een beslissing krachtens dit lid is geen hogere voorziening toegelaten.

1. Documents and ownership titles pertaining to the attributed property shall be remitted to the person to whom the property has been attributed.

2. General property documents and documents referred to in paragraph 1, which pertain to property that has been attributed to several partners, are kept by the person who has been appointed for that purpose by the majority of the partners involved. He must allow the other partners to inspect the documents

1. Les documents et titres de propriété se rapportant aux biens attribués sont remis à celui à qui ces biens ont été attribués.

2. Des documents généraux afférents à la masse et les pièces visées au paragraphe premier, qui se rapportent aux biens attribués à plusieurs partenaires, demeurent à celui que la majorité des partenaires concernés a nommé à cette fin, à charge pour lui d'en permettre la consultation aux autres et, si quelqu'un le demande, de lui en

and, if any one of them so demands, he must provide him, at his expense, with copies and extracts.

livrer, aux frais de celui-ci, des copies ou des extraits.

3. Where the majority as referred to in the preceding paragraph cannot be attained, the relevant appointment is made, upon the demand of a partner, by the judge who decides upon the partition, and in all other cases by the judge of the subdistrict court at the request of a partner. No appeal lies from a decision pursuant to this paragraph.

3. À défaut d'une majorité comme celle que vise le paragraphe précédent, la nomination qu'il prévoit est faite, à la demande d'un partenaire, par le juge établissant le partage ou, dans les autres cas, sur la requête d'un partenaire, par le juge d'instance. La décision prise conformément au présent paragraphe est insusceptible d'appel.

Art. 188. (3.7.1.16) - 1. Tenzij anders is overeengekomen, zijn deelgenoten verplicht in evenredigheid van hun aandelen elkander de schade te vergoeden die het gevolg is van een uitwinning of stoornis, voortgekomen uit een vóór de verdeling ontstane oorzaak, alsmede, wanneer een vordering voor het volle bedrag is toegedeeld, de schade die voortvloeit uit onvoldoende gegoedheid van de schuldenaar op het ogenblik van de verdeling.

- 2. Wordt een deelgenoot door zijn eigen schuld uitgewonnen of gestoord, dan zijn de overige deelgenoten niet verplicht tot vergoeding van zijn schade.

- 3. Een verplichting tot vergoeding van schade die voortvloeit uit onvoldoende gegoedheid van de schuldenaar vervalt door verloop van drie jaren na de verdeling en na het opeisbaar worden van de toegedeelde vordering.

- 4. Indien verhaal op een deelgenoot voor zijn aandeel in een krachtens het eerste lid verschuldigde schadevergoeding onmogelijk blijkt, wordt het aandeel van ieder der andere deelgenoten naar evenredigheid verhoogd.

1. Unless otherwise agreed, partners are obliged to compensate each other in proportion to their shares for damage that results from an eviction or disturbance, the cause of which originated before the partition, as well as for damage which, when a claim has been attributed for the full amount, results from insufficient solvency of the debtor at the time of the partition.

2. Where a partner is evicted or disturbed by his own fault, the remaining partners are not obliged to compensate him for the damage suffered.

3. An obligation to compensate for damage resulting from insufficient solvency of the debtor ceases by the lapse of three years after the partition and the exigibility of the attributed claim.

4. If recourse against a partner for his share in compensation pursuant to the first paragraph proves to be impossible, the share of each of the other partners is increased proportionally.

1. Sauf stipulation contraire, les partenaires sont tenus les uns envers les autres, proportionnellement à leurs parts, de réparer le préjudice qui résulte d'une éviction ou d'un trouble dont la source est antérieure au partage; il en est de même du préjudice qui résulte de la solvabilité insuffisante du débiteur au moment du partage, lorsqu'il s'agit d'une créance qui a été attribuée pour le plein montant.

2. Si un partenaire est évincé ou troublé par sa propre faute, les autres ne sont pas tenus de réparer le préjudice qu'il en subit.

3. L'obligation de réparer le préjudice résultant de la solvabilité insuffisante du débiteur s'éteint par trois ans après le partage et après que la créance attribuée est devenue exigible.

4. S'il se révèle impossible de recouvrer la part des dommages-intérêts que doit un partenaire en vertu du paragraphe premier, la part de chacun des autres est augmentée proportionnellement.

AFDELING 2 Enige bijzondere gemeenschappen

Section 2
Some special communities

Section deuxième
Quelques communautés particulières

Art. 189. (3.7.2.0) - 1. De bepalingen van deze titel gelden niet voor een huwelijksgemeenschap, maatschap, vennootschap of rederij, zolang zij niet ontbonden zijn, noch voor de gemeenschap van een in appartementsrechten gesplitst gebouw, zolang de splitsing niet is opgeheven.
- 2. Voor de gemeenschap van een nalatenschap, voor een ontbonden huwelijksgemeenschap, maatschap, vennootschap of rederij en voor de gemeenschap van een gebouw waarvan de splitsing in appartementsrechten is opgeheven, gelden de volgende bepalingen van deze afdeling, alsmede die van de eerste afdeling, voor zover daarvan in deze afdeling niet wordt afgeweken.

1. The provisions of this title do not apply to a marital community, a partnership, a commercial partnership or a shipping partnership,[1] as long as they have not been dissolved; they do not apply either to the community of a building divided into apartment rights, as long as the division has not been terminated.
2. The following provisions of this section as well as the provisions of the first section, to the extent that this section does not deviate from them, apply to the community of a succession, to a dissolved marital community, partnership, commercial partnership or shipping partnership, and to the community of a building the division of which into apartment rights has been terminated.

1. Les dispositions du présent titre ne s'appliquent pas à la communauté entre époux, à la société civile, commerciale ou d'armement, tant qu'elles ne sont pas dissoutes, ni à la communauté d'un immeuble divisé par appartements, tant qu'il n'a pas été mis fin à la division.

2. S'appliquent à la communauté d'une succession, à la communauté entre époux ou la société civile, commerciale ou d'armement dissoutes, à la communauté d'un immeuble après qu'a été mis fin à la division par appartements les dispositions suivantes de la présente section, ainsi que celles de la section première, dans la mesure où il n'y est pas dérogé dans la présente section.

Art. 190. (3.7.2.1) - 1. Een deelgenoot kan niet beschikken over zijn aandeel in een tot de gemeenschap behorend goed afzonderlijk, en zijn schuldeisers kunnen een zodanig aandeel niet uitwinnen, zonder toestemming van de overige deelgenoten.
- 2. Nochtans kan een deelgenoot op een zodanig aandeel ook zonder toestemming van de andere deelgenoten een recht van pand of hypotheek vestigen. Zolang het goed tot de gemeenschap behoort, kan de pand- of hypotheekhouder niet tot verkoop overgaan, tenzij de overige deelgenoten hierin toestemmen.

1 "Vennootschap" and "rederij" have been translated as "commercial partnership" and as "shipping partnership" respectively. The use of the term "partnership" seems preferable to the term "company", since the "vennootschap" and the "rederij" do not have legal personality, contrary to the "naamloze vennootschap" ("company limited by shares") and the "besloten vennootschap" ("private company with limited liability") of Book 2 of the New Civil Code (cf. English translation of Book 2 by Warendorf and Thomas, Deventer: Kluwer, February 1988).

1. A partner may not separately dispose of his share in property belonging to the community, and his creditors may not seize and execute against such as share, without the consent of the other partners.
2. Nevertheless, a partner can establish a right of pledge or of hypothec upon such a share, even without the consent of the other partners. Unless the other partners consent, the pledgee and the hypothecary creditor may not proceed to the sale of the property as long as it belongs to the community.

1. Le partenaire ne peut disposer de sa part dans un bien appartenant à la communauté séparément, ni ses créanciers, saisir et exécuter une telle part, sans le consentement des autres partenaires.
2. Néanmoins, le partenaire peut établir sur une telle part, même sans le consentement des autres partenaires, un droit de gage ou d'hypothèque. Tant que le bien fait partie de la communauté, le créancier gagiste ou hypothécaire ne peut procéder à la vente, à moins que les autres partenaires n'y consentent.

Art. 191. (3.7.2.2) - 1. Tenzij uit de rechtsverhouding tussen de deelgenoten anders voortvloeit, kan ieder der deelgenoten over zijn aandeel in de gehele gemeenschap beschikken en kunnen zijn schuldeisers een zodanig aandeel uitwinnen.
- 2. Indien uit de rechtsverhouding tussen de deelgenoten voortvloeit dat zij niet, tenzij met aller toestemming bevoegd zijn over hun aandeel te beschikken, zijn de leden 3 en 4 van artikel 168 van overeenkomstige toepassing.

1. Unless their juridical relationship produces a different result, any one of the partners may dispose of his share in the totality of the community, and his creditors can seize and execute against such a share.
2. If, as a result of their juridical relationship, the partners do not have the power to dispose of their share, except with their unanimous consent, paragraphs 3 and 4 of article 168 apply *mutatis mutandis*.

1. À moins qu'il n'en résulte autrement du rapport juridique entre partenaires, chacun d'eux peut disposer de sa part dans la communauté entière et les créanciers peuvent saisir et exécuter une telle part.
2. S'il résulte du rapport juridique entre partenaires qu'ils ne peuvent, sauf du consentement de tous, disposer de leur part, les paragraphes 3 et 4 de l'article 168 s'appliquent par analogie.

Art. 192. (3.7.2.2a) Tot de gemeenschap behorende schulden kunnen op de goederen van de gemeenschap worden verhaald.

Recourse can be taken against property of the community for debts belonging to it.

Le recouvrement des dettes faisant partie d'une communauté peut être poursuivi sur les biens de celle-ci.

Art. 193. (3.7.2.2b) Een schuldeiser wiens vordering op de goederen van de gemeenschap kan worden verhaald, is bevoegd zich tegen verdeling van de gemeenschap te verzetten. Een verdeling die na dit verzet is tot stand gekomen, is vernietigbaar met dien verstande dat de vernietigingsgrond slechts kan worden ingeroepen door de schuldeiser die zich verzette en dat hij de verdeling slechts te zijnen behoeve kan vernietigen en niet verder dan nodig is tot opheffing van de door hem ondervonden benadeling.

Where a creditor may take recourse for his claim against property of the community, he has the right to object to its partition. A partition accomplished after such an objection may be annulled; in this case the ground for annulment may only be invoked by a creditor who raised an objection, and he can only annul the partition in his own favour and no further than necessary to remove the prejudice which he has suffered.

Le créancier dont la créance peut être recouvrée sur les biens de la communauté peut s'opposer au partage de celle-ci. Le partage effectué après une telle opposition est annulable, étant entendu que seul le créancier opposant peut invoquer la cause d'annulation, qu'il ne peut annuler le partage qu'à son égard et dans la seule mesure nécessaire pour supprimer le préjudice qu'il a subi.

Art. 194. (3.7.2.3) - 1. Ieder der deelgenoten kan vorderen dat een verdeling aanvangt met een boedelbeschrijving.
- 2. Een deelgenoot die opzettelijk tot de gemeenschap behorende goederen verzwijgt, zoek maakt of verborgen houdt, verbeurt zijn aandeel in die goederen aan de andere deelgenoten.

1. Any one of the partners may demand that a partition commence with the making of an inventory.
2. A partner who intentionally suppresses the existence of property belonging to the community, who causes it to be lost or who hides it, forfeits his share in that property to the other partners.

1. Chacun des partenaires peut demander que le partage commence par un inventaire.
2. Le partenaire qui délibérément tait des biens appartenant à la communauté, les égare ou les cache perd sa part dans ces biens au profit des autres partenaires.

AFDELING 3 Nietige en vernietigbare verdelingen

Section 3 Null partitions and partitions subject to annulment

Section troisième Des partages nuls et annulables

Art. 195. (3.7.3.1) - 1. Een verdeling waaraan niet alle deelgenoten en alle andere personen wier medewerking vereist was, hebben deelgenomen, is nietig, tenzij zij is geschied bij een notariële akte, in welk geval zij slechts kan worden vernietigd op vordering van degene die niet aan de verdeling heeft deelgenomen. Deze rechtsvordering verjaart door verloop van één jaar nadat de verdeling te zijner kennis gekomen is.
- 2. Heeft aan een verdeling iemand deelgenomen die niet tot de gemeenschap gerechtigd was, of is een deelgenoot bij de verdeling opgekomen voor een groter aandeel dan hem toekwam, dan kan het ten onrechte uitgekeerde ten behoeve van de gemeenschap worden teruggevorderd; voor het overige blijft de verdeling van kracht.

1. A partition in which all the partners and all other persons whose cooperation was required have not participated, is null, unless it has been done by notarial deed, in which event it can be annulled only upon the demand of the person who has not participated in the partition. This

1. Est nul le partage auquel n'ont pas participé tous les partenaires et toutes les personnes autres dont le concours était requis, à moins qu'il n'ait été fait par acte notarié; dans ce cas, il ne peut être annulé qu'à la demande de celui qui n'a pas participé au partage. Cette action se prescrit

right of action is prescribed one year after such a person has become aware of the partition.

par un an à compter du moment où il a eu connaissance du partage.

2. Where a person who was not entitled to the community has participated in a partition or where, in a partition, a partner has obtained a larger share than he was entitled to, the amount which has been wrongly paid can be reclaimed for the benefit of the community; otherwise the partition remains valid.

2. Lorsqu'a participé au partage une personne qui n'avait aucun titre à faire valoir dans la communauté, ou qu'un partenaire a obtenu, lors du partage, une part plus grande qu'il ne lui revenait, ce qui a été payé à tort peut être répété au profit de la communauté; le partage demeure valide pour le surplus.

Art. 196. (3.7.3.2) - 1. Behalve op de algemene voor vernietiging van rechtshandelingen geldende gronden is een verdeling ook vernietigbaar, wanneer een deelgenoot omtrent de waarde van een of meer der te verdelen goederen en schulden heeft gedwaald en daardoor voor meer dan een vierde gedeelte is benadeeld.
- 2. Wanneer een benadeling voor meer dan een vierde is bewezen, wordt de benadeelde vermoed omtrent de waarde van een of meer der te verdelen goederen en schulden te hebben gedwaald.
- 3. Om te beoordelen of benadeling heeft plaatsgehad, worden de goederen en schulden der gemeenschap geschat naar hun waarde op het tijdstip van de verdeling. Goederen en schulden die onverdeeld zijn gelaten worden niet meegerekend.
- 4. Een verdeling is niet op grond van dwaling omtrent de waarde van een of meer der te verdelen goederen en schulden vernietigbaar, indien de benadeelde de toedeling te zijnen bate of schade heeft aanvaard.

1. In addition to the general grounds for annulment of juridical acts, a partition may also be annulled when a partner has erred with respect to the value of property or debts to be divided and has thereby suffered lesion[1] for more than one quarter of that value.

1. Outre les causes générales d'annulation des actes juridiques, le partage peut également être annulé lorsqu'un partenaire a commis une erreur sur la valeur d'un ou de plusieurs biens ou dettes à partager et qu'il est de ce fait lésé pour plus du quart.

2. Where lesion exceeding one quarter has been proven, there is a presumption that the victim has erred with respect to the value of the property or debts to be partitioned.

2. Lorsqu'une lésion de plus du quart est établie, la partie lésée est présumée avoir commis une erreur sur la valeur d'un ou de plusieurs biens ou dettes à partager.

3. In order to determine whether lesion has taken place, the property and debts of the community are evaluated as at the time of the partition. Property and debts which have been left undivided are not included.

3. Afin de déterminer s'il y a eu lésion, les biens et les dettes de la communauté sont évalués au moment du partage. Les biens et les dettes indivis ne sont pas comptés.

4. A partition cannot be annulled on grounds of error with respect to the value of property or debts to be divided if the victim has accepted the attribution at his risk and peril.

4. Le partage ne peut être annulé pour cause d'erreur sur la valeur d'un ou de plusieurs biens ou dettes à partager si la personne lésée en a accepté l'attribution à ses risques et périls.

[1] Whereas in title 2 of Book 3 "benadeling" has been translated as "prejudice", it seems proper to translate it as "lesion" in this context of error as to economic value, a defect of consent which in civil law has traditionally been called "lesion".

Art. 197. (3.7.3.3) De bevoegdheid tot vernietiging van een verdeling uit hoofde van benadeling vervalt, wanneer de andere deelgenoten aan de benadeelde hetzij in geld, hetzij in natura opleggen hetgeen aan diens aandeel ontbrak.

The right to annul a partition because of lesion lapses upon the other partners compensating the victim either in money or in kind for what was lacking in his share.

Le pouvoir d'annuler le partage pour cause de lésion s'éteint lorsque les autres partenaires paient en supplément à la personne lésée, en argent ou en nature, ce qui manquait à sa part.

Art. 198. (3.7.3.3a) Wordt een beroep in rechte op vernietigbaarheid van een verdeling gedaan, dan kan de rechter, onverminderd het in de artikelen 53 en 54 bepaalde, op verlangen van een der partijen de verdeling wijzigen, in plaats van de vernietiging uit te spreken.

In proceedings to annul a partition the judge may, without prejudice to articles 53 and 54, and upon the demand of one of the partners, modify the partition instead of pronouncing its annulment.

Lorsqu'est invoquée en justice l'annulabilité du partage, le juge peut, à la demande de l'une des parties et sans préjudice des dispositions 53 et 54, modifier le partage au lieu d'en prononcer l'annulation.

Art. 199. (3.7.3.3b) Op een verdeling zijn de artikelen 228-230 van Boek 6 niet van toepassing.

Articles 228 - 230 of Book 6 do not apply to a partition.

Les articles 228 à 230 du Livre sixième ne s'appliquent pas au partage.

Art. 200. (3.7.3.4) Een rechtsvordering tot vernietiging van een verdeling vervalt door verloop van drie jaren na de verdeling.

The right of action to annul a partition ceases by the lapse of three years after the partition.

L'action en annulation de partage s'éteint dans le délai de trois ans à compter du partage.

TITEL 8 VRUCHTGEBRUIK

TITLE 8 USUFRUCT

TITRE HUITIÈME DE L'USUFRUIT

Art. 201. (3.8.1) Vruchtgebruik geeft het recht om goederen die aan een ander toebehoren, te gebruiken en daarvan de vruchten te genieten.

Usufruct gives a right to use property belonging to another and to enjoy the fruits thereof.

L'usufruit donne le droit de se servir de biens appartenant à un autre et de jouir des fruits de ces biens.

Art. 202. (3.8.2) Vruchtgebruik ontstaat door vestiging of door verjaring.

Usufruct is created by establishment or by prescription.

L'usufruit naît par établissement ou par prescription.

Art. 203. (3.8.3) - 1. Vruchtgebruik kan worden gevestigd ten behoeve van één persoon, ofwel ten behoeve van twee of meer personen hetzij gezamenlijk hetzij bij opvolging. In het laatste geval moeten ook de later geroepenen op het ogenblik van de vestiging bestaan.
- 2. Vruchtgebruik kan niet worden gevestigd voor langer dan het leven van de vruchtgebruiker. Vruchtgebruik ten behoeve van twee of meer personen wast bij het einde van het recht van een hunner bij dat van de anderen aan, bij ieder in evenredigheid van zijn aandeel, en eindigt eerst door het tenietgaan van het recht van de laatst overgeblevene, tenzij anders is bepaald.
- 3. Is de vruchtgebruiker een rechtspersoon, dan eindigt het vruchtgebruik door ontbinding van de rechtspersoon, en in ieder geval na verloop van dertig jaren na de dag van vestiging.

1. Usufruct can be established in favour of one person or of two or more persons, either jointly or consecutively. In the latter case, persons who will be called to the usufruct consecutively must exist at the time of its establishment.
2. Usufruct cannot be established for a period longer than the lifetime of the usufructuary. A usufruct in favour of two or more persons accrues to each remaining usufructuary, proportionately to his share, upon the termination of the right of one of them; unless otherwise provided, it is not terminated until the extinction of the right of the last remaining usufructuary.
3. Where the usufructuary is a legal person, the usufruct is terminated by the dissolution of the legal person and, in any event, by the lapse of thirty years from the day of its establishment.

1. L'usufruit peut être établi au profit d'une personne ou de plusieurs personnes, conjointement ou consécutivement. Dans ce dernier cas, ceux qui seront appelés plus tard doivent exister au moment de l'établissement.
2. L'usufruit ne peut être établi pour une durée plus longue que la vie de l'usufruitier. Lorsque l'usufruit est établi au profit de plusieurs personnes et que prend fin le droit de l'un d'entre eux, le droit des autres s'accroît d'autant, proportionnellement à la part de chacun; l'usufruit ne prend fin que par l'extinction du droit du dernier usufruitier, à moins qu'il n'ait été disposé autrement.
3. Lorsque l'usufruitier est une personne morale, l'usufruit s'éteint par la dissolution de celle-ci et, dans tous les cas, par l'écoulement de trente ans à compter du jour de l'établissement.

Art. 204. (3.8.3a) - 1. Bij een uiterste wilsbeschikking kan bewind worden ingesteld over een daarbij gelegateerd vruchtgebruik of over de goederen waarop het rust. In geval van vruchtgebruik krachtens een andere titel dan legaat, kan dit bij notariële akte geschieden.
- 2. Op het bewind zijn de artikelen 433 lid 1, 435, 436 leden 1-3, 437, 438 lid 1, 439, 441 leden 1 en 4, 442-448 en 449 lid 2 van Boek 1 van toepassing met dien verstande dat de vruchtgebruiker en de hoofdgerechtigde beiden als rechthebbende gelden, voor zover uit hun rechtsverhouding niet anders voortvloeit.

1. A usufruct bequeathed by legacy or the property subject to it may be put under administration by the will bequeathing such legacy. Where the usufruct is established pursuant to a title other than a legacy, such administration may be instituted by a notarial deed.

1. Peut être institué, par disposition de dernière volonté, un régime d'administration sur un usufruit qui y est légué ou sur les biens qui en sont grevés. Dans le cas d'un usufruit établi par un titre autre que le legs, l'institution peut avoir lieu par acte notarié.

2. Articles 433, paragraph 1, 435, 436, paragraphs 1-3, 437, 438, paragraph 1, 439, 441, paragraphs 1 and 4, 442 - 448 and 449, paragraph 2 of Book 1 apply to this administration, in which case both the usufructuary and the holder of the principal right are considered as title-holders to the extent that their juridical relationship does not produce a different result.

2. S'appliquent au régime d'administration le paragraphe premier de l'article 433, l'article 435, les paragraphes 1er à 3 de l'article 436, l'article 437, le paragraphe premier de l'article 438, l'article 439, les paragraphes 1er et 4 de l'article 441, les articles 442 à 448 et le paragraphe 2 de l'article 449 du Livre premier, étant entendu que l'usufruitier et le titulaire principal sont tous les deux censés être titulaires dans la mesure où il n'en résulte pas autrement de leur rapport juridique.

Art. 205. (3.8.4) - 1. Tenzij een bewind reeds tot een voldoende boedelbeschrijving heeft geleid of daartoe verplicht, moet de vruchtgebruiker in tegenwoordigheid of na behoorlijke oproeping van de hoofdgerechtigde een notariële beschrijving van de goederen opmaken. De beschrijving kan ondershands worden opgemaakt, indien de hoofdgerechtigde tegenwoordig is en hoofdgerechtigde en vruchtgebruiker een regeling hebben getroffen omtrent haar bewaring.
- 2. Zowel de vruchtgebruiker als de hoofdgerechtigde hebben het recht om in de beschrijving alle bijzonderheden te doen opnemen, die dienstig zijn om de toestand waarin de aan het vruchtgebruik onderworpen zaken zich bevinden, te doen kennen.
- 3. De hoofdgerechtigde is bevoegd de levering en afgifte van de aan het vruchtgebruik onderworpen goederen op te schorten, indien de vruchtgebruiker niet terzelfder tijd zijn verplichting tot beschrijving nakomt.
- 4. De vruchtgebruiker moet jaarlijks aan de hoofdgerechtigde een ondertekende nauwkeurige opgave zenden van de goederen die niet meer aanwezig zijn, van de goederen die daarvoor in de plaats zijn gekomen, en van de voordelen die de goederen hebben opgeleverd en die geen vruchten zijn.
- 5. De vruchtgebruiker kan van de verplichtingen die ingevolge de voorgaande leden op hem rusten, niet worden vrijgesteld.
- 6. Tenzij anders is bepaald, komen de kosten van de beschrijving en van de in lid 4 bedoelde jaarlijkse opgave ten laste van de vruchtgebruiker.

1. Unless a sufficient inventory must be or has already been drawn up for a usufruct which is under administration, the usufructuary must make a notarial inventory of the property in the presence of, or after proper convocation of, the holder of the principal right. The inventory may be made by deed under private writing if the holder of the principal right is present, and if he and the usufructuary have made arrangements for the safekeeping of the inventory.

1. À moins qu'un régime d'administration n'ait déjà donné lieu à un inventaire suffisant ou n'y oblige, l'usufruitier doit faire, en présence du titulaire principal ou après avoir dûment convoqué celui-ci, un inventaire notarié des biens. L'inventaire peut être fait sous seing privé si le titulaire principal est présent et que l'usufruitier et lui ont réglé la façon de conserver le document d'inventaire.

2. The usufructuary as well as the holder of the principal right have the right to have included in the inventory all

2. L'usufruitier, comme le titulaire principal, peut faire inscrire dans l'inventaire tous les détails utiles à l'établissement de

particulars which are useful to identify the condition of the things subject to the usufruct.

l'état dans lequel se trouvent les biens soumis à l'usufruit.

3. The holder of the principal right has the right to suspend the delivery and the remittance of the property subject to the usufruct if the usufructuary does not simultaneously perform his obligation to make an inventory.

3. Le titulaire principal peut suspendre la délivrance et la remise des biens soumis à l'usufruit, si l'usufruitier ne remplit pas simultanément son obligation de faire l'inventaire.

4. The usufructuary must send annually to the holder of the principal right a detailed, signed statement of property which is no longer there, of property which has taken its place, and of the benefits which the property has yielded and which are not fruits.

4. L'usufruitier envoie chaque année au titulaire principal une déclaration détaillée et signée des biens qui ne sont plus là, de ceux qui s'y sont substitués et des avantages qu'ils ont produits et qui ne sont pas des fruits.

5. The usufructuary may not be exempted from the obligations imposed upon him pursuant to the preceding paragraphs.

5. L'usufruitier ne peut être dispensé des obligations qui lui incombent en vertu des paragraphes précédents.

6. Unless otherwise provided, the usufructuary bears the expenses of the inventory and of the annual statement referred to in paragraph 4.

6. Sauf disposition contraire, les frais de l'inventaire et de la déclaration annuelle visée au paragraphe 4 sont à la charge de l'usufruitier.

Art. 206. (3.8.5.) - 1. De vruchtgebruiker moet voor de nakoming van zijn verplichtingen jegens de hoofdgerechtigde zekerheid stellen, tenzij hij hiervan is vrijgesteld of de belangen van de hoofdgerechtigde reeds voldoende zijn beveiligd door de instelling van een bewind.
- 2. Is de vruchtgebruiker van het stellen van zekerheid vrijgesteld, dan kan de hoofdgerechtigde jaarlijks verlangen dat hem de aan het vruchtgebruik onderworpen zaken worden getoond. Ten aanzien van waardepapieren en gelden kan, behoudens bijzondere omstandigheden, met overlegging van een verklaring van een geregistreerde krediet-instelling worden volstaan.

1. The usufructuary must furnish security for the performance of his obligations toward the holder of the principal right, unless he has been exempted from doing so or the interests of the holder of the principal right have already been sufficiently secured by the institution of administration.

1. L'usufruitier doit fournir au titulaire principal sûreté pour l'exécution de ses obligations à l'égard de ce dernier, à moins qu'il n'en soit dispensé ou que les intérêts du titulaire principal ne soient déjà suffisamment sauvegardés par l'établissement d'un régime d'administration.

2. Where the usufructuary has been exempted from furnishing security, the holder of the principal right may annually require that the things subject to the usufruct be shown to him. With respect to money and commercial paper the production of a statement of a registered credit institution suffices except in special circumstances.

2. Lorsque l'usufruitier a été dispensé de fournir sûreté, le titulaire principal peut demander chaque année que lui soient présentées les choses soumises à l'usufruit. Pour les effets de commerce et l'argent, il suffit de remettre une déclaration provenant d'une institution de crédit enregistrée, sauf circonstances particulières.

Art. 207. (3.8.6) - 1. Een vruchtgebruiker mag de aan het vruchtgebruik onderworpen goederen gebruiken of verbruiken overeenkomstig de bij de vestiging van het vruchtgebruik gestelde regels of, bij gebreke van zodanige regels, met inachtneming van de aard van de goederen en de ten aanzien van het gebruik of verbruik bestaande plaatselijke gewoonten.
- 2. Een vruchtgebruiker is voorts bevoegd tot alle handelingen die tot een goed beheer van de aan het vruchtgebruik onderworpen goederen dienstig kunnen zijn. Tot alle overige handelingen ten aanzien van die goederen zijn de hoofdgerechtigde en de vruchtgebruiker slechts tezamen bevoegd.
- 3. Jegens de hoofdgerechtigde is de vruchtgebruiker verplicht ten aanzien van de aan het vruchtgebruik onderworpen goederen en het beheer daarover de zorg van een goed vruchtgebruiker in acht te nemen.

1. The usufructuary may use or consume property subject to the usufruct according to the rules made at the time of establishment of the usufruct or, in their absence, with due regard to the nature of the property and local usage governing use or consumption.
2. Furthermore, a usufructuary is entitled to perform all acts which may serve the good management of the property subject to the usufruct. All other acts pertaining to the property can only be performed by the holder of the principal right and the usufructuary jointly.
3. The usufructuary is obligated toward the holder of the principal right to exercise the care of a good usufructuary with respect to the property subject to the usufruct and its management.

1. L'usufruitier peut se servir des biens soumis à l'usufruit ou les consommer, conformément aux règles fixées lors de l'établissement de l'usufruit ou, à défaut, eu égard à la nature des biens et aux coutumes locales relatives à l'usage ou la consommation.
2. L'usufruitier a, en outre, le pouvoir de faire tous les actes qui peuvent être utiles à la bonne gestion des biens soumis à l'usufruit. Tous les autres actes relatifs à ce bien ne peuvent être accomplis que par le titulaire principal et l'usufruitier conjointement.
3. L'usufruitier est tenu, à l'égard du titulaire principal, d'observer, relativement aux biens soumis à l'usufruit et à leur gestion, les soins d'un bon usufruitier.

Art. 208. (3.8.6a) - 1. Van zaken die aan het vruchtgebruik zijn onderworpen, mag de vruchtgebruiker de bestemming die deze bij de aanvang van het vruchtgebruik hadden, niet veranderen zonder toestemming van de hoofdgerechtigde of machtiging van de kantonrechter.
- 2. Tenzij in de akte van vestiging anders is bepaald, is de vruchtgebruiker van een zaak, zowel tijdens de duur van zijn recht als bij het einde daarvan, bevoegd om aan de zaak aangebrachte veranderingen en toevoegingen weg te nemen, mits hij de zaak in de oude toestand terugbrengt.

1. The usufructuary may not change the destination which the things subject to the usufruct had at the beginning of the usufruct, without the consent of the holder of the principal right or the authorization of the judge of the subdistrict court.

1. L'usufruitier ne peut, sans le consentement du titulaire principal ou l'autorisation du juge d'instance, changer la destination qu'avaient lors de l'établissement de l'usufruit les choses qui y sont soumises.

2. Unless otherwise provided in the deed of establishment, the usufructuary of a thing is entitled, both for the duration of his right and upon its termination, to remove changes and additions made to the thing, provided that he restores it to its original condition.

2. À moins de disposition contraire dans l'acte d'établissement, l'usufruitier d'une chose peut, aussi bien pendant la durée de l'usufruit qu'à la fin, enlever les modifications et ajouts qu'il a faits à la chose, pourvu qu'il remette celle-ci en l'état primitif.

Art. 209. (3.8.7) - 1. De vruchtgebruiker is verplicht het voorwerp van zijn vruchtgebruik ten behoeve van de hoofdgerechtigde te verzekeren tegen die gevaren, waartegen het gebruikelijk is een verzekering te sluiten. In ieder geval is de vruchtgebruiker, indien een gebouw aan zijn vruchtgebruik is onderworpen, verplicht dit tegen brand te verzekeren.
- 2. Voor zover de vruchtgebruiker aan de in het eerste lid omschreven verplichtingen niet voldoet, is de hoofdgerechtigde bevoegd zelf een verzekering te nemen en is de vruchtgebruiker verplicht hem de kosten daarvan te vergoeden.

1. The usufructuary must insure the object of his usufruct in favour of the holder of the principal right for risks it is customary to insure. In all cases where a building is subject to usufruct, the usufructuary must insure it against fire.

2. To the extent that the usufructuary does not fulfil the obligations described in the first paragraph, the holder of the principal right is entitled to take out insurance for which the usufructuary must reimburse him.

1. L'usufruitier est tenu d'assurer l'objet de l'usufruit au bénéfice du titulaire principal contre les risques pour lesquels il est d'usage de souscrire une assurance. Dans tous les cas où l'usufruit porte sur un édifice, l'usufruitier est tenu de l'assurer contre l'incendie.

2. Dans la mesure où l'usufruitier ne remplit pas les obligations énoncées au paragraphe premier, le titulaire principal peut lui-même souscrire une assurance dont l'usufruitier est tenu de lui rembourser les frais.

Art. 210. (3.8.8) - 1. Tenzij bij de vestiging anders is bepaald, is de vruchtgebruiker bevoegd in en buiten rechte nakoming te eisen van aan het vruchtgebruik onderworpen vorderingen en tot het in ontvangst nemen van betalingen.
- 2. Tenzij bij de vestiging anders is bepaald, is hij tot ontbinding en opzegging van overeenkomsten slechts bevoegd, wanneer dit tot een goed beheer dienstig kan zijn.
- 3. De hoofdgerechtigde is slechts bevoegd de in de vorige leden genoemde bevoegdheden uit te oefenen, indien hij daartoe toestemming van de vruchtgebruiker of machtiging van de kantonrechter heeft gekregen. Tegen de machtiging van de kantonrechter krachtens dit lid is geen hogere voorziening toegelaten.

1. Unless otherwise provided at the time of establishment, the usufructuary is entitled to demand, judicially and extra-judicially, the performance of claims subject to the usufruct and to accept payments.

1. À moins qu'il n'ait été disposé autrement lors de l'établissement, l'usufruitier peut demander, en justice et par acte civil, l'exécution des créances soumises à l'usufruit et percevoir les paiements.

2. Unless otherwise provided at the time of establishment, the usufructuary is only entitled to set aside contracts to the extent that this may serve good management.
3. The holder of the principal right is not entitled to exercise the powers referred to in the preceding paragraphs, unless he has obtained consent to do so from the usufructuary or authorization from the judge of the subdistrict court. No appeal lies from the authorization of the judge of the subdistrict court pursuant to this paragraph.

2. À moins qu'il n'ait été disposé autrement lors de l'établissement, l'usufruitier peut résilier les contrats seulement lorsque cela peut être utile à une bonne gestion.
3. Le titulaire principal ne peut exercer les pouvoirs énoncés aux paragraphes précédents que s'il a obtenu le consentement de l'usufruitier ou l'autorisation du juge d'instance. La décision du juge d'instance en vertu du présent paragraphe est insusceptible d'appel.

Art. 211. (3.8.9) - 1. Ook wanneer bij de beschrijving of in een jaarlijkse opgave een of meer goederen die aan het vruchtgebruik onderworpen zijn, slechts naar hun soort zijn aangeduid, behoudt de hoofdgerechtigde daarop zijn recht.
- 2. De vruchtgebruiker is verplicht zodanige goederen afgescheiden van zijn overig vermogen te houden.

1. The holder of the principal right retains his right to property subject to the usufruct even though it has only been indicated in the inventory or in an annual statement according to its kind.
2. The usufructuary must keep such property separate from his remaining patrimony.

1. Lors même que des biens soumis à l'usufruit n'ont été indiqués que par leur espèce dans l'inventaire ou dans une déclaration annuelle, le titulaire principal conserve son droit sur eux.
2. L'usufruitier est tenu de garder de tels biens séparés du reste de son patrimoine.

Art. 212. (3.8.10) - 1. Voor zover de aan een vruchtgebruik onderworpen goederen bestemd zijn om vervreemd te worden, is de vruchtgebruiker tot vervreemding overeenkomstig hun bestemming bevoegd.
- 2. Bij de vestiging van het vruchtgebruik kan aan de vruchtgebruiker de bevoegdheid worden gegeven ook over andere dan de in het vorige lid genoemde goederen te beschikken. Ten aanzien van deze goederen vinden de artikelen 208, 210 lid 2 en 217 lid 2, en 3, tweede zin, en lid 4, geen toepassing.
- 3. In andere gevallen mag een vruchtgebruiker slechts vervreemden of bezwaren met toestemming van de hoofdgerechtigde of machtiging van de kantonrechter. De machtiging wordt alleen gegeven, wanneer het belang van de vruchtgebruiker of de hoofdgerechtigde door de vervreemding of bezwaring wordt gediend en het belang van de ander daardoor niet wordt geschaad.

1. To the extent that property subject to a usufruct is intended to be alienated, the usufructuary is entitled to alienate it in conformity with its destination.

1. Dans la mesure où les biens soumis à l'usufruit sont destinés à être aliénés, l'usufruitier peut les aliéner conformément à leur destination.

2. At the time of establishment of the usufruct, the usufructuary may also be given the power to dispose of property other than that mentioned in the preceding paragraph. Articles 208, 210, paragraph 2 and 217 paragraphs 2 and 3, second sentence and paragraph 4 do not apply to such property.
3. In other cases a usufructuary may not alienate or encumber property without the consent of the holder of the principal right or the authorization of the judge of the subdistrict court. Authorization is not granted, unless it is in the interest of the usufructuary or the holder of the principal right and does not prejudice the interest of the other.

2. Lors de l'établissement, l'usufruitier peut obtenir le pouvoir de disposer de biens autres que ceux visés au paragraphe précédent. L'article 208, le paragraphe 2 de l'article 210 et les paragraphes 2, 3, deuxième phrase, et 4 de l'article 217 ne s'appliquent pas à ces biens.

3. Dans les autres cas, l'usufruitier ne peut aliéner ou grever un bien qu'avec le consentement du titulaire principal ou l'autorisation du juge d'instance. L'autorisation est donnée seulement lorsque l'aliénation ou la constitution de charge peut servir les intérêts de l'usufruitier ou du titulaire principal et ne nuit pas aux intérêts de l'autre.

Art. 213. (3.8.11) - 1. Hetgeen in de plaats van aan vruchtgebruik onderworpen goederen treedt doordat daarover bevoegdelijk wordt beschikt, behoort aan de hoofdgerechtigde toe en is eveneens aan het vruchtgebruik onderworpen. Hetzelfde is het geval met hetgeen door inning van aan vruchtgebruik onderworpen vorderingen wordt ontvangen, en met vorderingen tot vergoeding die in de plaats van aan vruchtgebruik onderworpen goederen treden, waaronder begrepen vorderingen ter zake van waardevermindering van die goederen.
- 2. Ook zijn aan het vruchtgebruik onderworpen de voordelen die een goed tijdens het vruchtgebruik oplevert en die geen vruchten zijn.

1. Property taking the place of property subject to the usufruct and duly disposed of, belongs to the holder of the principal right and is also subject to the usufruct. The same applies to what is received from the collection of debts subject to the usufruct and to claims for compensation which take the place of property subject to the usufruct, including claims resulting from depreciation of that property.
2. The benefits which property yields during the usufruct, and which are not fruits are also subject to the usufruct.

1. Le bien qui, à la suite d'un acte de disposition régulier, se substitue à celui qui était soumis à l'usufruit appartient au titulaire principal et est également soumis à l'usufruit. Il en est de même de ce qui est perçu en recouvrement des créances soumises à l'usufruit et des créances en indemnisation qui se substituent aux biens soumis à l'usufruit, y compris celles qui en compensent la dépréciation.
2. Les avantages produits par un bien pendant qu'il est soumis à l'usufruit et qui ne sont pas des fruits sont également soumis à cet usufruit.

Art. 214. (3.8.12) - 1. Tenzij bij de vestiging anders is bepaald, moeten gelden die tot het vruchtgebruik behoren, in overleg met de hoofdgerechtigde vruchtdragend belegd of in het belang van de overige aan het vruchtgebruik onderworpen goederen besteed worden.
- 2. In geval van geschil omtrent hetgeen ten aanzien van de in het eerste lid bedoelde gelden dient te geschieden, beslist daaromtrent de persoon die bij de vestiging van het vruchtgebruik daartoe is aangewezen, of bij gebreke van een zodanige aanwijzing, de kantonrechter. Tegen een beschikking van de kantonrechter krachtens dit lid is geen hogere voorziening toegelaten.

1. Unless otherwise provided at the time of establishment, money subject to the usufruct must, in consultation with the holder of the principal right, be invested fructiferously or be expended in the interest of the other property subject to the usufruct.
2. In the event of disagreement as to what is to be done with the money referred to in the first paragraph, the person who has been designated for that purpose at the time of establishment of the usufruct decides the issue or, in the absence of such designation, the judge of the subdistrict court. No appeal lies from a decision of the subdistrict court judge pursuant to this paragraph.

1. À moins qu'il n'ait été disposé autrement lors de l'établissement, les sommes d'argent soumises à l'usufruit doivent être placées de manière rentable, en consultation avec le titulaire principal, ou déboursées dans l'intérêt des autres biens soumis à l'usufruit.
2. En cas de désaccord sur ce qu'il convient de faire des sommes d'argent visées au paragraphe premier, la décision appartient à celui qui est désigné à cette fin lors de l'établissement ou, à défaut d'une telle désignation, au juge d'instance. La décision du juge d'instance en vertu du présent paragraphe est insusceptible d'appel.

Art. 215. (3.8.13) - 1. Komt de vruchtgebruiker de bevoegdheid tot gehele of gedeeltelijke vervreemding of vertering van aan het vruchtgebruik onderworpen goederen toe, dan kan de hoofdgerechtigde bij het einde van het vruchtgebruik afgifte vorderen van de in vruchtgebruik gegeven goederen of hetgeen daarvoor in de plaats getreden is, voor zover de vruchtgebruiker of zijn rechtverkrijgenden niet bewijzen dat die goederen verteerd of door toeval tenietgegaan zijn.
- 2. Bij de vestiging van het vruchtgebruik kunnen een of meer personen worden aangewezen, wier toestemming voor de vervreemding en voor de vertering nodig is. Staat het vruchtgebruik onder bewind, dan zijn de vervreemding en de vertering van de medewerking van de bewindvoerder afhankelijk.
- 3. Komt de vruchtgebruiker de bevoegdheid tot vervreemding of vertering toe, dan mag hij de goederen ook voor gebruikelijke kleine geschenken bestemmen.

1. Where the usufructuary is entitled to alienate or spend,[1] wholly or partially, the property subject to the usufruct, the holder of the principal right can, upon the termination of the usufruct, claim the remittance of the property given in usufruct or that which has taken its place, to the extent that the usufructuary or his successors do not establish that the property has been spent or has perished by fortuitous event.

1. Lorsque l'usufruitier a le pouvoir d'aliéner et de dépenser[2], en tout ou en partie, les biens soumis à l'usufruit, le titulaire principal peut, à la fin de l'usufruit, demander la remise des biens ou de ce qui leur a été substitué, dans la mesure où l'usufruitier ou ses ayants cause ne justifient pas que ces biens ont été dépensés ou ont péri par cas fortuit.

---

1 This institution resembles the *fideicommissum de residuo*. The term "to spend" ("verteren") must be distinguished from "to consume" ("verbruiken") in article 207 of Book 3. "To spend" here means that the usufructuary may touch capital without incurring the obligation to replace it at a later time.

2 Cette institution s'approche du *Fideicommissum de residuo*. L'usufruitier a le droit d'entamer le capital sans avoir l'obligation de le remplacer ultérieurement. Le terme «dépenser» (*verteren*) doit être distingué de «consommer» (*verbruiken*) à l'article 207 du Livre troisième.

2. At the time of establishment of the usufruct, one or more persons, whose consent is necessary for alienating and spending the property, may be designated. Where the usufruct is under administration, alienation and spending require the cooperation of the administrator.
3. Where the usufructuary is entitled to alienate or spend, he may also make small customary gifts of the property.

2. Il peut être désigné, lors de l'établissement, des personnes dont le consentement est nécessaire pour aliéner ou dépenser un bien soumis à l'usufruit. Lorsque l'usufruit est soumis à un régime d'administration, l'aliénation et la dépense requièrent le concours de l'administrateur.

3. Lorsque l'usufruitier a le pouvoir d'aliéner et de dépenser les biens, il peut également les donner dans les limites de cadeaux d'usage.

Art. 216. (3.8.14) De vruchtgebruiker komen alle vruchten toe, die tijdens het vruchtgebruik afgescheiden of opeisbaar worden. Bij de vestiging van het vruchtgebruik kan nader worden bepaald wat met betrekking tot het vruchtgebruik als vrucht moet worden beschouwd.

The usufructuary is entitled to all fruits which become separated or exigible during the usufruct. At the time of establishment of the usufruct, it may be specified what, in relation to the usufruct, must be considered as fruits.

Tous les fruits séparés ou devenus exigibles au cours de l'usufruit reviennent à l'usufruitier. Lors de l'établissement, il peut être précisé ce qui, en rapport avec l'usufruit, doit être considéré comme fruit.

Art. 217. (3.8.16) - 1. De vruchtgebruiker is bevoegd de aan het vruchtgebruik onderworpen zaken te verhuren of te verpachten, voor zover bij de vestiging van het vruchtgebruik niet anders is bepaald.
- 2. Indien bij de vestiging van het vruchtgebruik een onroerende zaak niet verhuurd of verpacht was, kan de vruchtgebruiker niet verhuren of verpachten zonder toestemming van de hoofdgerechtigde of machtiging van de kantonrechter, tenzij de bevoegdheid daartoe hem bij de vestiging van het vruchtgebruik is toegekend.
- 3. Na het einde van het vruchtgebruik is de hoofdgerechtigde verplicht een bevoegdelijk aangegane huur of verpachting gestand te doen. Hij kan nochtans gestanddoening weigeren, voor zover zonder zijn toestemming hetzij de overeengekomen tijdsduur van de huur langer is dan met het plaatselijk gebruik overeenstemt of bedrijfsruimte in de zin van artikel 1624 lid 2 is verhuurd voor een langere tijd dan vijf jaren, hetzij de verpachting is geschied voor een langere duur dan twaalf jaren voor hoeven en zes jaren voor los land, hetzij de verhuring of verpachting is geschied op ongewone, voor hem bezwarende voorwaarden.
- 4. De hoofdgerechtigde verliest de bevoegdheid gestanddoening te weigeren, wanneer de huurder of pachter hem een redelijke termijn heeft gesteld om zich omtrent de gestanddoening te verklaren en hij zich niet binnen deze termijn heeft uitgesproken.
- 5. Indien de hoofdgerechtigde volgens de vorige leden niet verplicht is tot gestanddoening van een door de vruchtgebruiker aangegane verhuring van woonruimte waarin de huurder bij het eindigen van het vruchtgebruik zijn hoofdverblijf heeft en waarop de artikelen 1623a-1623f van toepassing zijn, moet hij de huurovereenkomst niettemin met de huurder voortzetten met dien verstande dat artikel 1623k, tweede lid, van overeenkomstige toepassing is.

1. To the extent not otherwise provided at the time of establishment of the usufruct, the usufructuary has the right to lease the things subject to the usufruct.
2. Unless the power to lease had been given to the usufructuary at the time of establishment of the usufruct, he may only lease an immoveable thing, which was not leased at the time of establishment of the usufruct, with the consent of the holder of the principal right or the authorization of the judge of the subdistrict court.
3. Upon the termination of the usufruct, the holder of the principal right must respect a lease which has been duly entered into. Nevertheless, he can refuse to do so to the extent that, without his consent, the agreed duration of the lease exceeds that which is in accordance with local usage; where commercial space in the sense of article 1624, paragraph 2 has been leased for a period exceeding five years; where the lease has been made for a period exceeding twelve years for farmsteads or six years for agricultural land; or where the lease contains unusual conditions which are onerous for the holder of the principal right.
4. The holder of the principal right loses the right to refuse to respect a lease where the lessee has given him a reasonable period to declare himself on the maintenance of the lease and where he has not done so within this period.
5. If, pursuant to the preceding paragraphs, the holder of the principal right is not obliged to respect the lease of a dwelling, entered into by the usufructuary, and if upon the termination of the usufruct the lessee has his principal place of residence in this dwelling to which articles 1623a - 1623f apply, he must nevertheless continue the contract of lease and hire with the lessee, in which case article 1623k, paragraph 2 applies *mutatis mutandis*.

1. L'usufruitier peut donner à bail les choses soumises à l'usufruit, dans la mesure où il n'a pas été disposé autrement lors de l'établissement de l'usufruit.
2. Si une chose immobilière ne faisait pas l'objet d'un bail lors de l'établissement de l'usufruit, l'usufruitier ne peut la donner à bail sans le consentement du titulaire principal ou l'autorisation du juge d'instance, à moins que ce pouvoir ne lui ait été accordé lors de l'établissement.
3. Le titulaire principal est tenu, après la fin de l'usufruit, de respecter le bail conclu régulièrement. Toutefois, il peut s'y refuser dans la mesure où, sans son consentement, la durée convenue du bail dépasse ce que prévoit l'usage local; il en est de même lorsque un espace commercial au sens de l'article 1624, paragraphe 2 a été donné à bail pour plus de cinq ans ou lorsque le bail portant sur une ferme a été conclu pour plus de douze ans ou le bail portant sur des terres agricoles pour plus de six ans, ou encore lorsque le bail a été conclu à des conditions inhabituelles qui sont onéreuses pour le titulaire principal.
4. Le titulaire principal ne peut plus refuser de respecter le bail, lorsque le preneur[1] lui a fixé un délai raisonnable pour déclarer s'il entend respecter le bail et qu'il ne s'est pas prononcé dans ce délai.
5. Le titulaire principal qui, conformément aux paragraphes précédents, n'est pas tenu de respecter le bail d'espace d'habitation conclu par l'usufruitier, dans lequel le locataire, au moment de la fin de l'usufruit, a sa résidence principale et auquel s'appliquent les articles 1623a à 1623f, doit néanmoins continuer le bail avec ce dernier, étant entendu que le paragraphe 2 de l'article 1623k s'applique par analogie.

Art. 218. (3.8.17) Tot het instellen van rechtsvorderingen en het indienen van verzoekschriften ter verkrijging van een rechterlijke uitspraak die zowel het recht van de vruchtgebruiker als dat van de hoofdgerechtigde

[1] Le terme «preneur» est employé lorsque le texte néerlandais vise indistinctement les baux résidentiels et commerciaux d'une part, et les baux ruraux, de l'autre. Lorsque seuls les baux résidentiels et commerciaux sont visés, on emploie le terme «locataire».

betreft, is ieder van hen bevoegd, mits hij zorg draagt dat de ander tijdig in het geding wordt geroepen.

Both the usufructuary and the holder of the principal right are entitled to institute actions and to submit petitions to obtain a judicial decision concerning their respective rights, provided that each ensures that the other is timely joined in the proceedings.

L'usufruitier comme le titulaire principal peuvent intenter des actions ou présenter des requêtes visant à obtenir une décision judiciaire concernant les droits de chacun d'eux à la fois, pourvu qu'il s'assure que l'autre soit mis en cause en temps utile.

Art. 219. (3.8.17a) Buiten de gevallen, geregeld in de artikelen 88 en 197 van Boek 2, blijft de uitoefening van stemrecht, verbonden aan een goed dat aan vruchtgebruik is onderworpen, de hoofdgerechtigde toekomen, tenzij bij de vestiging van het vruchtgebruik anders is bepaald.

Except for the cases governed by articles 88 and 197 of Book 2, and unless otherwise provided at the time of establishment of the usufruct, the exercise of the right to vote attached to property subject to usufruct remains with the holder of the principal right.

Hormis les cas prévus aux articles 88 et 197 du Livre deuxième, l'exercice du droit de vote attaché à un bien soumis à l'usufruit demeure réservé au titulaire principal, à moins qu'il n'ait été disposé autrement lors de l'établissement de l'usufruit.

Art. 220. (3.8.18) - 1. Gewone lasten en herstellingen worden door de vruchtgebruiker gedragen en verricht. De vruchtgebruiker is verplicht, wanneer buitengewone herstellingen nodig zijn, aan de hoofdgerechtigde van deze noodzakelijkheid kennis te geven en hem gelegenheid te verschaffen tot het doen van deze herstellingen. De hoofdgerechtigde is niet tot het doen van enige herstelling verplicht.
- 2. Nochtans is een hoofdgerechtigde, aan wie tengevolge van een beperking in het genot van de vruchtgebruiker een deel van de vruchten toekomt, verplicht naar evenredigheid bij te dragen in de lasten en kosten, die volgens het voorgaande lid ten laste van de vruchtgebruiker komen.

1. Ordinary charges are borne and ordinary repairs are performed by the usufructuary. When extraordinary repairs are necessary, the usufructuary must advise the holder of the principal right and give him the opportunity to make these repairs. The holder of the principal right is not obliged to make any repairs.
2. Nevertheless, the holder of the principal right who, as a result of a limitation upon the enjoyment of the usufructuary, is entitled to a share of the fruits, must contribute proportionally to the charges and expenses which, according to the preceding paragraph, are at the charge of the usufructuary.

1. L'usufruitier assume les charges et les réparations ordinaires. Lorsque des réparations extraordinaires sont nécessaires, l'usufruitier est tenu d'en aviser le titulaire principal et de lui laisser la possibilité de les effectuer. Le titulaire principal n'est tenu à aucune réparation.

2. Toutefois, le titulaire principal à qui revient une partie des fruits en raison d'une restriction apportée à la jouissance de l'usufruitier, est tenu de contribuer proportionnellement aux charges et frais qui incombent à l'usufruitier en vertu du paragraphe précédent.

Art. 221. (3.8.19) - 1. Indien de vruchtgebruiker in ernstige mate tekortschiet in de nakoming van zijn verplichtingen, kan de rechtbank op

vordering van de hoofdgerechtigde aan deze het beheer toekennen of het vruchtgebruik onder bewind stellen.
- 2. De rechtbank kan hangende het geding het vruchtgebruik bij voorraad onder bewind stellen.
- 3. De rechtbank kan voor het bewind of beheer zodanige voorschriften geven als zij dienstig acht. Op het bewind zijn, voor zover deze voorschriften niet anders bepalen, de artikelen 433 lid 1, 435, 436 leden 1-3, 437, 438 lid 1, 439, 441 leden 1 en 4 en 442-449 van Boek 1 van toepassing met dien verstande dat de vruchtgebruiker en de hoofdgerechtigde beiden als rechthebbende gelden, voor zover uit hun rechtsverhouding niet anders voortvloeit.

1. If the usufructuary seriously fails in the performance of his obligations the district court may, upon the demand of the holder of the principal right, grant the management to the latter or put the usufruct under administration.
2. Pending the case, the district court may provisionally put the usufruct under administration.
3. The district court may give such instructions for the administration or management as it deems useful. To the extent that these instructions do not provide otherwise, articles 433, paragraph 1, 435, 436, paragraphs 1 - 3, 437, 438, paragraph 1, 439, 441, paragraphs 1 and 4, and 442 - 449 of Book 1 apply, in which case both the usufructuary and the holder of the principal right are considered as title-holders, to the extent that their juridical relationship does not produce a different result.

1. Si l'usufruitier manque sérieusement à ses obligations, le tribunal de première instance peut, à la demande du titulaire principal, accorder la gestion à celui-ci ou soumettre l'usufruit à un régime d'administration.
2. Pendant le litige, le tribunal peut soumettre l'usufruit à un régime d'administration par provision.
3. Le tribunal peut édicter pour l'administration ou la gestion les prescriptions qu'il juge utiles. S'appliquent au régime d'administration, dans la mesure où ces prescriptions ne disposent pas autrement, le paragraphe premier de l'article 433, l'article 435, les paragraphes 1er à 3 de l'article 436, l'article 437, le paragraphe premier de l'article 438, l'article 439, les paragraphes 1er et 4 de l'article 441, les articles 442 à 449 du Livre premier, étant entendu que l'usufruitier et le titulaire principal sont tous les deux censés être titulaires, dans la mesure où il n'en résulte pas autrement de leur rapport juridique.

Art. 222. (3.8.20) - 1. Wanneer een nalatenschap, onderneming of soortgelijke algemeenheid in vruchtgebruik is gegeven, kan de hoofdgerechtigde van de vruchtgebruiker verlangen dat de tot die algemeenheid behorende schulden uit de tot het vruchtgebruik behorende goederen worden voldaan of, voor zover de hoofdgerechtigde deze schulden uit eigen middelen heeft voldaan, dat hem het betaalde, vermeerderd met rente van de dag der betaling af, uit het vruchtgebruik wordt teruggegeven. Voldoet de vruchtgebruiker een schuld uit eigen vermogen, dan behoeft de hoofdgerechtigde hem het voorgeschotene eerst bij het einde van het vruchtgebruik terug te geven.
- 2. Het in het voorgaande lid bepaalde vindt overeenkomstige toepassing, wanneer het vruchtgebruik is gevestigd op bepaalde goederen en daarop buitengewone lasten drukken.

1. Where a succession, business or a similar universality has been given in usufruct, the holder of the principal right may require of the usufructuary that the debts belonging to the universality be paid from the property subject to the usufruct or, to the extent that the holder of the principal right has paid these debts himself, that he be reimbursed from the usufruct with accrued interest as of the day of payment. Where the usufructuary pays a debt from his own patrimony, the holder of the principal right does not have to reimburse the sum so advanced until the termination of the usufruct.
2. The provisions of the preceding paragraph apply *mutatis mutandis* where the usufruct has been established on property which is encumbered with extraordinary charges.

1. Lorsque l'usufruit porte sur une succession, sur une entreprise ou sur une universalité semblable, le titulaire principal peut demander à l'usufruitier d'acquitter les dettes faisant partie de cette universalité sur les biens soumis à l'usufruit; dans la mesure où le titulaire principal les a payées de ses propres deniers, il peut lui demander le remboursement sur les biens soumis à l'usufruit de ce qu'il a payé et des intérêts courus à compter du jour du paiement. Lorsque l'usufruitier acquitte une dette de ses propres deniers, le titulaire principal n'est tenu de lui rembourser la somme avancée qu'à la fin de l'usufruit.
2. Les dispositions du paragraphe précédent s'appliquent par analogie à l'usufruit établi sur des biens déterminés qui sont grevés de charges extraordinaires.

Art. 223. (3.8.20a) Een vruchtgebruiker kan zijn recht overdragen of bezwaren zonder dat daardoor de duur van het recht gewijzigd wordt. Naast de verkrijger is de oorspronkelijke vruchtgebruiker hoofdelijk voor alle uit het vruchtgebruik voortspruitende verplichtingen jegens de hoofdgerechtigde aansprakelijk. Is aan de oorspronkelijke vruchtgebruiker bij de vestiging van het vruchtgebruik een grotere bevoegdheid tot vervreemding, verbruik of vertering gegeven dan de wet aan de vruchtgebruiker toekent, dan komt die ruimere bevoegdheid niet aan de latere verkrijgers van het vruchtgebruik toe.

A usufructuary may transfer or encumber his right without thereby modifying the duration of the right. The acquirer and the original usufructuary are solidarily liable to the holder of the principal right for all obligations resulting from the usufruct. Where, at the time of establishment of the usufruct, the original usufructuary has been given more extensive power to alienate, consume or spend than that granted by law, subsequent acquirers of the usufruct are not entitled to do this.

L'usufruitier peut transférer ou grever son droit sans que la durée en soit modifiée. L'usufruitier originaire et l'acquéreur sont tenus solidairement à l'égard du titulaire principal des obligations découlant de l'usufruit. Lorsqu'il a été accordé à l'usufruitier originaire, lors de l'établissement, un pouvoir d'aliénation, de consommation ou de dépense, plus étendu que celui qu'accorde la loi, ce pouvoir plus étendu n'appartient pas aux acquéreurs subséquents.

Art. 224. (3.8.21a) Indien een vruchtgebruiker uit hoofde van de aan het vruchtgebruik verbonden lasten en verplichtingen op zijn kosten afstand van zijn recht wil doen, is de hoofdgerechtigde gehouden hieraan mede te werken.

If a usufructuary wants to abandon his right, at his own expense, because of the charges and obligations attached to the usufruct, the holder of the principal right must cooperate herein.

Si l'usufruitier veut, à ses frais, abandonner son droit en raison des charges et obligations afférentes à l'usufruit, le titulaire principal est tenu d'y prêter son concours.

Art. 225. (3.8.22) Na het eindigen van het vruchtgebruik rust op de vruchtgebruiker of zijn rechtverkrijgenden de verplichting de goederen ter beschikking van de hoofdgerechtigde te stellen.

Upon the termination of the usufruct, the usufructuary or his successors are under the obligation to put the property at the disposal of the holder of the principal right.

Après que l'usufruit a pris fin, l'usufruitier ou ses ayants cause ont l'obligation de mettre les biens à la disposition du titulaire principal.

Art. 226. (3.8.24) - 1. Op een recht van gebruik en een recht van bewoning vinden de regels betreffende vruchtgebruik overeenkomstige toepassing, behoudens de navolgende bepalingen.
- 2. Indien enkel het recht van gebruik is verleend, heeft de rechthebbende de bevoegdheid de aan zijn recht onderworpen zaken te gebruiken en er de vruchten van te genieten, die hij voor zich en zijn gezin behoeft.
- 3. Indien enkel het recht van bewoning is verleend, heeft de rechthebbende de bevoegdheid de aan zijn recht onderworpen woning met zijn gezin te bewonen.
- 4. Hij die een der in dit artikel omschreven rechten heeft, kan zijn recht niet vervreemden of bezwaren, noch de zaak door een ander laten gebruiken of de woning door een ander laten bewonen.

1. The rules regarding usufruct apply *mutatis mutandis* to the right of use and the right of habitation, except for the following provisions.
2. The holder of a mere right of use is entitled to use the things subject to his right and, to the extent of his needs and those of his family, to enjoy their fruits.
3. The holder of a mere right of habitation is entitled to inhabit, with his family, the dwelling subject to his right.
4. A person having one of the rights described in this article cannot alienate or encumber it; nor can he allow the thing to be used or the dwelling to be inhabited by another person.

1. Les dispositions relatives à l'usufruit s'appliquent par analogie aux droits d'usage et d'habitation, sous réserve de ce qui suit.
2. Si le seul droit d'usage a été accordé, le titulaire de ce droit peut se servir de la chose qui en fait l'objet et en percevoir les fruits jusqu'à concurrence de ses besoins et de ceux de sa famille.
3. Si le seul droit d'habitation a été accordé, le titulaire de ce droit peut habiter avec sa famille la demeure qui en fait l'objet.
4. Le titulaire de l'un des droits visés au présent article ne peut ni aliéner ou grever ce droit, ni permettre à un tiers d'utiliser la chose ou d'habiter la demeure.

TITEL 9 RECHTEN VAN PAND EN HYPOTHEEK

TITLE 9 RIGHTS OF PLEDGE AND HYPOTHEC

TITRE NEUVIÈME DES DROITS DE GAGE ET D'HYPOTHÈQUE

AFDELING 1 Algemene bepalingen

Section 1 General provisions

Section première Dispositions générales

Art. 227. (3.9.1.1) - 1. Het recht van pand en het recht van hypotheek zijn beperkte rechten, strekkende om op de daaraan onderworpen goederen een vordering tot voldoening van een geldsom bij voorrang boven andere schuldeisers te verhalen. Is het recht op een registergoed gevestigd, dan is het een recht van hypotheek; is het recht op een ander goed gevestigd, dan is het een recht van pand.
- 2. Een recht van pand of hypotheek op een zaak strekt zich uit over al hetgeen de eigendom van de zaak omvat.

1. The right of pledge and the right of hypothec are dismembered rights intended to provide recourse against the property subjected thereto for a claim for the payment of a sum of money, with preference over other creditors. Where such right has been established upon registered property, it is a hypothec; where it has been established upon other property, it is a pledge.
2. A right of pledge or hypothec upon a thing attaches to all that the ownership of the thing encompasses.

1. Le droit de gage et le droit d'hypothèque sont des droits démembrés permettant à un créancier, par préférence aux autres créanciers, de poursuivre sur les biens grevés le recouvrement d'une créance portant sur une somme d'argent. Etabli sur un bien immatriculé, ce droit est une hypothèque; établi sur tout autre bien, il est un gage.

2. Le droit de gage ou d'hypothèque sur une chose s'étend à tout ce que comprend la propriété de cette chose.

Art. 228. (3.9.1.2) Op alle goederen die voor overdracht vatbaar zijn, kan een recht van pand hetzij van hypotheek worden gevestigd.

A right of pledge or hypothec can be established on all property susceptible of transfer.

Tous les biens susceptibles de transfert peuvent faire l'objet d'un droit de gage ou d'hypothèque.

Art. 229. (3.9.1.3) - 1. Het recht van pand of hypotheek brengt van rechtswege mee een recht van pand op alle vorderingen tot vergoeding die in de plaats van het verbonden goed treden, waaronder begrepen vorderingen ter zake van waardevermindering van het goed.
- 2. Dit pandrecht gaat boven ieder op de vordering gevestigd ander pandrecht.

1. *De jure*, the right of pledge or hypothec entails a right of pledge upon all claims for compensation which take the place of the pledged or hypothecated property, including claims resulting from its depreciation.
2. This right of pledge has preference over any other right of pledge established on the claim.

1. Le droit de gage ou d'hypothèque emporte de plein droit un droit de gage sur toutes les créances en indemnisation qui se substituent au bien grevé, celles qui en compensent la dépréciation y comprises.

2. Ce droit de gage a préférence sur tout autre droit de gage établi sur cette créance.

Art. 230. (3.9.1.4) Een recht van pand of hypotheek is ondeelbaar, zelfs dan wanneer de verbintenis waarvoor het recht is gevestigd, twee of meer schuldeisers of schuldenaars heeft en de verbintenis tussen hen wordt verdeeld.

A right of pledge or hypothec is indivisible even when the obligation which it secures has two or more creditors or debtors and the obligation is divided between them.

Le droit de gage ou d'hypothèque est indivisible, lors même que l'obligation pour laquelle il a été établi comporte plusieurs créanciers ou débiteurs et qu'elle est divisée entre eux.

Art. 231. (3.9.1.5) - 1. Een recht van pand of hypotheek kan zowel voor een bestaande als voor een toekomstige vordering worden gevestigd. De vordering kan op naam, aan order of aan toonder luiden. Zij kan zowel een vordering op de pand- of hypotheekgever zelf als een vordering op een ander zijn.
- 2. De vordering waarvoor pand of hypotheek wordt gegeven, moet voldoende bepaalbaar zijn.

1. A right of pledge or hypothec can be established for an existing as well as a future claim. The claim can be nominative, payable to order or to bearer. It can be a claim against the grantor of the pledge or hypothec himself as well as a claim against another person.
2. The claim for which pledge or hypothec is given must be sufficiently determinable.

1. Le droit de gage ou d'hypothèque peut garantir une créance déjà existante autant qu'une créance future. La créance peut être nominative, à ordre ou au porteur. Elle peut être une créance contre le constituant de ce droit ou contre un tiers.

2. La créance pour laquelle le gage ou l'hypothèque est consenti doit être suffisamment déterminable.

Art. 232. Gereserveerd.

Reserved.

Réservé.

Art. 233. (3.9.1.6a) - 1. De pand- of hypotheekgever die niet tevens de schuldenaar is, is aansprakelijk voor waardevermindering van het goed, voor zover de waarborg van de schuldeiser daardoor in gevaar wordt gebracht en daarvan aan de pand- of hypotheekgever of aan een persoon waarvoor deze aansprakelijk is, een verwijt kan worden gemaakt.
- 2. Door hem ten behoeve van het goed anders dan tot onderhoud daarvan gemaakte kosten kan hij van de pand- of hypotheekhouder terugvorderen, doch slechts indien deze zich op het goed heeft verhaald en voor zover genoemde kosten tot een hogere opbrengst van het goed te diens bate hebben geleid.

1. The grantor of a pledge or hypothec, who is not himself the debtor, is liable for depreciation of the property to the extent that the security of the creditor is endangered by this depreciation and that he or a person for whom he is responsible can be blamed therefore.

2. The grantor referred to in the preceding paragraph can claim from the pledgee or hypothecary creditor expenses other than the costs of maintenance incurred in relation to the property, but only if the latter has taken recourse against the property and to the extent that these expenses have led to higher proceeds of the property in his favour.

1. Le constituant d'un droit de gage ou d'hypothèque, qui n'est pas en même temps débiteur, est responsable de la dépréciation du bien dans la mesure où la possibilité de recouvrement qu'a le créancier s'en trouve mise en péril et que reproche peut en être fait au constituant ou à une personne dont il est responsable.
2. Il peut répéter du créancier gagiste ou hypothécaire les frais engagés au profit du bien autrement que pour son entretien, mais seulement si celui-ci s'est payé sur le bien et dans la mesure où ces frais ont fait augmenter à son avantage la somme réalisée.

Art. 234. (3.9.1.6b) - 1. Indien voor een zelfde vordering zowel goederen van de schuldenaar als van een derde zijn verpand of verhypothekeerd, kan de derde, wanneer de schuldeiser tot executie overgaat, verlangen dat die van de schuldenaar mede in de verkoop worden begrepen en het eerst worden verkocht.
- 2. Zijn voor een zelfde vordering twee of meer goederen verpand of verhypothekeerd en rust op een daarvan een beperkt recht dat de schuldeiser bij de executie niet behoeft te eerbiedigen, dan heeft de beperkt gerechtigde een overeenkomstige bevoegdheid als in het eerste lid is vermeld.
- 3. Indien de schuldeiser weigert aan een op lid 1 of lid 2 gegrond verlangen te voldoen, kan de president van de rechtbank op verzoek van de meest gerede partij of, in geval van een hypotheek, van de notaris ten overstaan van wie de verkoop zal geschieden, op deze weigering beslissen. Het verzoek schorst de executie. Tegen een beschikking krachtens dit lid is geen hogere voorziening toegelaten.

1. If property of both the debtor and a third person has been pledged or hypothecated to secure one and the same debt, the third person can demand from the creditor who proceeds to execution that the property of the debtor be included in the sale as well and that it be sold first.
2. Where for one and the same debt two or more items of property have been pledged or hypothecated, one of which is encumbered with a dismembered right which the creditor does not have to respect in the execution, the holder of the dismembered right has *mutatis mutandis* the same right as the one referred to in the first paragraph.

1. Si les biens donnés en gage ou hypothéqués pour une seule créance appartiennent pour partie au débiteur et pour partie à un tiers, ce dernier peut demander au créancier qui procède à l'exécution que les biens du débiteur soient également compris dans la vente et soient vendus les premiers.
2. Lorsque plusieurs biens ont été donnés en gage ou hypothéqués pour une seule créance et que l'un d'entre eux est grevé d'un droit démembré que le créancier n'est pas tenu de respecter lors de l'exécution, le titulaire de ce droit a un pouvoir analogue à celui visé au premier paragraphe.

3. If the creditor refuses to comply with a demand based upon paragraphs 1 or 2, the president of the district court may rule upon this refusal, at the request of any interested party or, in the case of a hypothec, at the request of the notary before whom the sale will take place. The request suspends execution. No appeal lies from a decision pursuant to this paragraph.

3. Si le créancier refuse d'obtempérer à une demande fondée sur le paragraphe 1 ou 2, le président du tribunal de première instance peut, sur requête de la partie la plus diligente ou, dans le cas d'une hypothèque, du notaire devant qui doit avoir lieu la vente, statuer sur le refus. La requête suspend l'exécution. La décision prise en vertu du présent paragraphe est insusceptible d'appel.

Art. 235. (3.9.1.7) Elk beding waarbij de pand- of hypotheekhouder de bevoegdheid wordt gegeven zich het verbonden goed toe te eigenen, is nietig.

Any stipulation whereby the pledgee or the hypothecary creditor is given the power to appropriate the pledged or hypothecated property is null.

Est nulle toute stipulation accordant au créancier gagiste ou hypothécaire le droit de s'approprier le bien grevé.

AFDELING 2 Pandrecht

Section 2
The right of pledge

Section deuxième
Du droit de gage

Art. 236. (3.9.2.1) - 1. Pandrecht op een roerende zaak, op een recht aan toonder of order, of op het vruchtgebruik van een zodanige zaak of recht, wordt gevestigd door de zaak of het toonder- of orderpapier te brengen in de macht van de pandhouder of van een derde omtrent wie partijen zijn overeengekomen. De vestiging van een pandrecht op een recht aan order of op het vruchtgebruik daarvan vereist tevens endossement.
- 2. Op andere goederen wordt pandrecht gevestigd op overeenkomstige wijze als voor de levering van het te verpanden goed is bepaald.

1. The right of pledge on a moveable thing, on a right payable to bearer or order, or on the usufruct of such a thing or right, is established by bringing the thing or the document to bearer or order under the control of the pledgee or of a third person agreed upon by the parties. Furthermore, endorsement is required for the establishment of a right of pledge on a right payable to order or on the usufruct thereof.
2. The right of pledge on other property is established *mutatis mutandis* in the same fashion as that provided for the delivery of such property.

1. Le droit de gage sur une chose mobilière, sur un droit au porteur ou à ordre ou sur l'usufruit de telle chose ou de tel droit s'établit en plaçant la chose ou le titre au porteur ou à ordre en la puissance du créancier gagiste ou d'un tiers convenu entre les parties. L'établissement d'un droit de gage sur un droit à ordre ou sur l'usufruit d'un tel droit requiert, en outre, l'endossement.

2. Sur tous les autres biens, le droit de gage s'établit de manière analogue à ce qui est prévu pour leur délivrance.

Art. 237. (3.9.2.2) - 1. Pandrecht op een roerende zaak, op een recht aan toonder, of op het vruchtgebruik van een zodanige zaak of recht, kan ook worden gevestigd bij authentieke of geregistreerde onderhandse akte,

zonder dat de zaak of het toonderpapier wordt gebracht in de macht van de pandhouder of van een derde.
- 2. De pandgever is verplicht in de akte te verklaren dat hij tot het verpanden van het goed bevoegd is alsmede hetzij dat op het goed geen beperkte rechten rusten, hetzij welke rechten daarop rusten.
- 3. Wanneer de pandgever of de schuldenaar in zijn verplichtingen jegens de pandhouder tekortschiet of hem goede grond geeft te vrezen dat in die verplichtingen zal worden tekortgeschoten, is deze bevoegd te vorderen dat de zaak of het toonderpapier in zijn macht of in die van een derde wordt gebracht. Rusten op het goed meer pandrechten, dan kan iedere pandhouder jegens wie de pandgever of de schuldenaar tekortschiet, deze bevoegdheid uitoefenen, met dien verstande dat een andere dan de hoogst gerangschikte slechts afgifte kan vorderen aan een tussen de gezamenlijke pandhouders overeengekomen of door de rechter aan te wijzen pandhouder of derde.
- 4. Wanneer de pandgever of de schuldenaar in zijn verplichtingen jegens de pandhouder die een bij voorbaat gevestigd pandrecht op te velde staande vruchten of beplantingen heeft, tekortschiet, kan de kantonrechter de pandhouder op diens verzoek machtigen zelf de te velde staande vruchten of beplantingen in te oogsten. Is de pandgever eigenaar van de grond of ontleent hij zijn recht op de vruchten of beplantingen aan een beperkt recht op de grond, dan kan de beschikking waarbij het verzoek wordt toegewezen, worden ingeschreven in de openbare registers.
- 5. Tegen een beschikking krachtens het vorige lid is geen hogere voorziening toegelaten.

1. The right of pledge on a moveable thing, on a right payable to bearer, or on the usufruct of such a thing or right, can also be established by an authentic deed or a registered deed under private writing, without the thing or the document to bearer being brought under the control of the pledgee or of a third person.
2. The grantor of the pledge must declare in the deed that he is entitled to pledge the property, and furthermore that the property is not encumbered with dismembered rights or, if it is, by which rights it is encumbered.
3. Where the grantor of the pledge or the debtor fails to perform his obligations toward the pledgee, or gives him good reason to fear that there will be such a failure, the pledgee is entitled to demand that the thing or the document to bearer be brought under his control or that of a third person. Where there are several rights of pledge on the property, each pledgee toward whom the grantor or the debtor fails to perform his obligations can exercise this right, in which case the pledgee junior in rank can only demand

1. Le droit de gage sur une chose mobilière, sur un droit au porteur ou sur l'usufruit de telle chose ou de tel droit peut également être établi par acte authentique ou par acte sous seing privé enregistré, sans que la chose ou le titre au porteur soit placé en la puissance du créancier gagiste ou d'un tiers.

2. Le constituant est tenu de déclarer dans l'acte qu'il a le pouvoir de donner en gage le bien et, de plus, que celui-ci n'est grevé d'aucun droit démembré, ou, au contraire, de quels droits il est grevé.

3. Lorsque le constituant ou le débiteur manque à ses obligations à l'égard du créancier gagiste ou lui donne de justes motifs de craindre qu'il y manquera, celui-ci a le droit de demander que la chose ou le titre au porteur soient placés en sa puissance ou sous celle d'un tiers. Lorsque le bien est grevé de plusieurs droits de gage, tout créancier gagiste à l'égard duquel le constituant ou le débiteur manque à ses obligations peut exercer ce pouvoir; toutefois, celui qui n'est pas le premier en rang ne peut demander la remise qu'à un

delivery to a pledgee or third person agreed upon by the pledgees jointly, or to be appointed by the judge.

4. Where the grantor of the pledge or the debtor fails to perform his obligations toward a pledgee who has a right of pledge created in advance upon unplucked fruits or uncut plants, the judge of the subdistrict court may, at the request of the pledgee, authorize him to harvest these fruits or plants himself. Where the grantor of the pledge is owner of the land or derives his right to the fruits or plants from a dismembered right upon the land, the decision granting the request can be entered in the public registers.

5. No appeal lies from a decision pursuant to the preceding paragraph.

créancier gagiste ou à un tiers agréé par l'ensemble des créanciers gagistes ou devant être nommé par le juge.

4. Lorsque le constituant ou le débiteur manque à ses obligations à l'égard du créancier gagiste titulaire d'un droit de gage établi par anticipation sur des fruits ou plantations sur pied, le juge d'instance peut autoriser celui-ci, sur sa requête, à en faire la récolte. Lorsque le constituant est propriétaire du sol ou qu'il tire son droit sur les fruits ou plantations d'un droit démembré sur le sol, la décision accordant la requête peut être inscrite sur les registres publics.

5. La décision prise en vertu du paragraphe précédent est insusceptible d'appel.

Art. 238. (3.9.2.2a) - 1. Ondanks onbevoegdheid van de pandgever is de vestiging van een pandrecht op een roerende zaak, op een recht aan toonder of order of op het vruchtgebruik van een zodanige zaak of recht geldig, indien de pandhouder te goeder trouw is op het tijdstip waarop de zaak of het toonder- of geëndosseerde orderpapier in zijn macht of in die van een derde is gebracht.

- 2. Rust op een in lid 1 genoemd goed een beperkt recht dat de pandhouder op het in dat lid bedoelde tijdstip kent noch behoort te kennen, dan gaat het pandrecht in rang boven dit beperkte recht.

- 3. Wordt het pandrecht gevestigd op een roerende zaak waarvan de eigenaar het bezit door diefstal heeft verloren, of op een vruchtgebruik op een zodanige zaak, dan zijn lid 3, aanhef en onder b, en lid 4 van artikel 86 van overeenkomstige toepassing.

1. A right of pledge on a moveable thing, on a right payable to bearer or order, or on the usufruct of such a thing or right, established by a grantor who lacks the right to dispose of such a thing or right, is valid if the pledgee be in good faith at the time the thing, the document to bearer, or the endorsed document to order was brought under his control or that of a third person.

2. Where property referred to in paragraph 1 is encumbered with a dismembered right, knowledge of which the pledgee does not have nor ought to have at the time referred to in that paragraph, the right of pledge ranks before the dismembered right.

1. Le droit de gage établi sur une chose mobilière, sur un droit au porteur ou à ordre ou sur l'usufruit d'une telle chose ou d'un tel droit par un constituant qui n'avait pas le droit d'en disposer est valide si le créancier gagiste est de bonne foi au moment où la chose, le titre au porteur ou à ordre endossé a été placé en sa puissance ou celle d'un tiers.

2. Lorsqu'un bien visé au paragraphe premier est grevé d'un droit démembré dont le créancier gagiste n'a pas ni ne doit avoir connaissance au moment indiqué au paragraphe premier, le droit de gage prend rang avant le droit démembré.

3. Where the right of pledge is established on a moveable thing, the possession of which the owner has lost through theft, or where it is established on the usufruct of such a thing, paragraph 3, at its beginning and at *sub* b, and paragraph 4 of article 86 apply *mutatis mutandis*.

3. Lorsque le droit de gage est établi sur une chose mobilière dont le propriétaire a perdu la possession à la suite d'un vol, ou sur l'usufruit d'une telle chose, le paragraphe 3, en son début et au point b., et le paragraphe 4 de l'article 86 s'appliquent par analogie.

Art. 239. (3.9.2.3) - 1. Pandrecht op een tegen een of meer bepaalde personen uit te oefenen recht dat niet aan toonder of order luidt, of op het vruchtgebruik van een zodanig recht kan ook worden gevestigd bij authentieke of geregistreerde onderhandse akte, zonder mededeling daarvan aan die personen, mits dit recht op het tijdstip van de vestiging van het pandrecht reeds bestaat of rechtstreeks zal worden verkregen uit een dan reeds bestaande rechtsverhouding.
- 2. Het tweede lid van artikel 237 is van overeenkomstige toepassing.
- 3. Wanneer de pandgever of de schuldenaar in zijn verplichtingen jegens de pandhouder tekortschiet of hem goede grond geeft te vrezen dat in die verplichtingen zal worden tekortgeschoten, is deze bevoegd van de verpanding mededeling te doen aan de in het eerste lid genoemde personen. Pandhouder en pandgever kunnen overeenkomen dat deze bevoegdheid op een ander tijdstip ingaat.
- 4. Artikel 88 geldt slechts voor de pandhouder wiens recht overeenkomstig lid 1 is gevestigd, indien hij te goeder trouw is op het tijdstip van de in lid 3 bedoelde mededeling.

1. A right of pledge on a right which can be exercised against one or more specifically determined persons and which is not payable to bearer or order, or a right of pledge on the usufruct of such a right, can also be established by an authentic deed or a registered deed under private writing without notification thereof to those persons, provided that the right in question already exists at the time of the establishment of the right of pledge or will be directly acquired pursuant to a juridical relationship already existing at that time.
2. Paragraph 2 of article 237 applies *mutatis mutandis*.
3. Where the grantor of the pledge or the debtor fails to perform his obligations toward the pledgee or gives him good reason to fear that there will be such a failure, the pledgee is entitled to notify the persons referred to in the first paragraph of the pledging. The pledgee and the grantor of the pledge may agree that this right will become effective at some other point in time.

1. Le droit de gage sur un droit, autre qu'un droit au porteur ou à ordre, susceptible d'être exercé à l'encontre de personnes déterminées, ou sur l'usufruit d'un tel droit peut s'établir également par acte authentique ou par acte sous seing privé enregistré, sans avis à ces personnes, pourvu que ce droit existe déjà au moment de l'établissement du droit de gage ou qu'il soit par la suite acquis directement à partir d'un rapport juridique déjà existant au même moment.
2. Le deuxième paragraphe de l'article 237 s'applique par analogie.
3. Lorsque le constituant ou le débiteur manque à ses obligations à l'égard du créancier gagiste ou lui donne des motifs de craindre qu'il y manquera, celui-ci peut informer les personnes visées au premier paragraphe de la mise en gage. Le créancier gagiste et le constituant peuvent convenir que ce pouvoir ne prendra effet qu'à compter d'un autre moment.

4. Article 88 only applies to the pledgee whose right has been established according to paragraph 1, if he is in good faith at the time of the notification referred to in paragraph 3.

4. L'article 88 ne vaut qu'à l'égard du créancier gagiste dont le droit a été établi conformément au paragraphe premier, s'il est de bonne foi au moment de la communication visée au paragraphe 3.

Art. 240. (3.9.2.3a) Pandrecht op een aandeel in een goed wordt gevestigd op overeenkomstige wijze en met overeenkomstige gevolgen als voorgeschreven ten aanzien van de vestiging van pandrecht op dat goed.

A right of pledge on a share in property is established *mutatis mutandis* in the same fashion and with the same effects as those provided for the establishment of the right of pledge on that property.

Le droit de gage sur une part dans un bien s'établit de manière et avec des effets analogues à ce qui est prévu pour celui qui porte sur le bien lui-même.

Art. 241. (3.9.2.3b) De pandhouder is verplicht desgevorderd aan de pandgever een schriftelijke verklaring af te geven van de aard en, voor zover mogelijk, het bedrag van de vordering waarvoor het verpande tot zekerheid strekt.

The pledgee must give the grantor, upon demand, a written declaration of the nature and, to the extent possible, of the amount of the claim for which pledged property serves as security.

Le créancier gagiste est tenu, sur demande, de fournir au constituant une déclaration écrite de la nature et, dans la mesure du possible, du montant de la créance garantie par le gage.

Art. 242. (3.9.2.4) Een pandhouder is niet bevoegd het goed dat hij in pand heeft, te herverpanden, tenzij deze bevoegdheid hem ondubbelzinnig is toegekend.

A pledgee is not entitled to repledge the property pledged to him, unless this power has been unequivocally granted to him.

Le créancier gagiste n'a pas le pouvoir de gager à son tour le bien qu'il tient en gage à moins d'y avoir été autorisé de façon non équivoque.

Art. 243. (3.9.2.5) - 1. Hij die uit hoofde van een pandrecht een zaak onder zich heeft, moet als een goed pandhouder voor de zaak zorgdragen.
- 2. Door een pandhouder betaalde kosten tot behoud en tot onderhoud, met inbegrip van door hem betaalde aan het goed verbonden lasten, moeten hem door de pandgever worden terugbetaald; het pandrecht strekt mede tot zekerheid daarvoor. Andere door hem ten behoeve van het pand gemaakte kosten kan hij van de pandgever slechts terugvorderen, indien hij ze met diens toestemming heeft gemaakt, onverminderd diens aansprakelijkheid uit zaakwaarneming of ongerechtvaardigde verrijking.

1. A person who detains a thing pursuant to a right of pledge must take care of it as a good pledgee.
2. The grantor of the pledge must reimburse the pledgee for the expenses which the latter has paid for preservation and maintenance, including charges attached to the property that he has paid

1. Celui qui détient un bien en vertu d'un droit de gage doit y veiller en bon créancier gagiste.
2. Les frais engagés par le créancier gagiste pour la conservation et l'entretien, y compris le paiement des charges touchant le bien, doivent lui être remboursés par le constituant; le droit de gage garantit cette

for; the right of pledge also serves as security for the reimbursement. The pledgee cannot claim from the grantor other expenses which he has incurred for the benefit of the pledged property, unless he has made them with the consent of the grantor; the foregoing is without prejudice to the grantor's liability arising from management of the affairs of another or from unjustified enrichment.

dette également. Le créancier gagiste ne peut réclamer au constituant les autres frais encourus au profit du bien que s'il les a engagés avec le consentement de celui-ci, sans préjudice de la responsabilité de celui-ci en vertu de la gestion d'affaires ou de l'enrichissement sans cause.

Art. 244. (3.9.2.5a) Tenzij anders is bedongen, strekt een pandrecht tot zekerheid van een of meer bepaalde vorderingen tevens tot zekerheid voor drie jaren rente die over deze vorderingen krachtens overeenkomst of wet verschuldigd is.

Unless otherwise stipulated, a right of pledge securing one or more specifically determined claims also serves as security for three years interest owing on these claims by contract or by law.

À moins de stipulation contraire, le droit de gage garantissant des créances déterminées s'étend également à l'intérêt qui est dû sur celles-ci pour une période de trois ans en vertu d'un contrat ou de la loi.

Art. 245. (3.9.2.6) Tot het instellen van rechtsvorderingen tegen derden ter bescherming van het verpande goed is zowel de pandhouder als de pandgever bevoegd, mits hij zorg draagt dat de ander tijdig in het geding wordt geroepen.

The pledgee as well as the grantor are entitled to institute actions against third persons to protect the pledged property, provided that the one who does so ensures that the other is joined in the action in a timely manner.

Le créancier gagiste, comme le constituant, peut intenter des actions contre des tiers afin de protéger le gage, pourvu qu'il s'assure que l'autre soit mis en cause en temps utile.

Art. 246. (3.9.2.7) - 1. Rust het pandrecht op een vordering, dan is de pandhouder bevoegd in en buiten rechte nakoming daarvan te eisen en betalingen in ontvangst te nemen. Deze bevoegdheden blijven bij de pandgever, zolang het pandrecht niet aan de schuldenaar van de vordering is medegedeeld.

- 2. Degene aan wie de in lid 1 bedoelde bevoegdheden toekomen, is tevens bevoegd tot opzegging, wanneer de vordering niet opeisbaar is, maar door opzegging opeisbaar gemaakt kan worden. Hij is jegens de ander gehouden niet nodeloos van deze bevoegdheid gebruik te maken.

- 3. Rust op de vordering meer dan één pandrecht, dan komen de in de vorige leden aan de pandhouder toegekende bevoegdheden alleen aan de hoogst gerangschikte pandhouder toe.

- 4. Na mededeling van de verpanding aan de schuldenaar kan de pandgever deze bevoegdheden slechts uitoefenen, indien hij daartoe toestemming van de pandhouder of machtiging van de kantonrechter heeft gekregen.

- 5. Bij inning van een verpande vordering door de pandhouder of met machtiging van de kantonrechter door de pandgever komen de pandrechten waarmee de vordering bezwaard was, op het geïnde te rusten.

1. Where a debt has been pledged, the pledgee is entitled to demand its performance judicially and extra-judicially and to receive payment. These powers remain with the grantor of the pledge until notice of the right of pledge has been given to the debtor.
2. The person who has the powers referred to in paragraph 1, is also entitled to call the debt when the claim, although not exigible, can be made so. In respect of the other party he may not use this power needlessly.
3. Where more than one right of pledge encumbers a debt, the powers granted to the pledgee in the preceding paragraphs can only be exercised by the pledgee with the highest rank.
4. After notification of the pledging to the debtor, the grantor of the pledge cannot exercise these powers, unless he has received permission to do so from the pledgee or authorization from the judge of the subdistrict court.
5. Upon collection of a pledged debt by the pledgee or, with the authorization of the judge of the subdistrict court, by the grantor of the pledge, the rights of pledge encumbering the debt will become attached to the proceeds collected.

1. Lorsque le gage porte sur une créance, le créancier gagiste peut en demander l'exécution en justice et par acte civil et en percevoir paiement. Ces pouvoirs appartiennent au constituant tant que le débiteur n'a pas été informé de l'existence du droit de gage.
2. Le titulaire des pouvoirs visés au paragraphe premier peut aussi demander le remboursement de la dette, quoi qu'elle ne soit pas exigible mais le devienne par la demande. Il est tenu envers l'autre partie de ne pas se prévaloir inutilement de ce droit.
3. Lorsqu'une créance est grevée de plusieurs droits de gage, les pouvoirs accordés au créancier gagiste aux paragraphes précédents appartiennent seulement au premier en rang.
4. Après l'avis au débiteur de la mise en gage, le constituant ne peut exercer ces pouvoirs qu'avec le consentement du créancier gagiste ou avec l'autorisation du juge d'instance.
5. Lorsque le créancier gagiste ou, avec l'autorisation du juge d'instance, le constituant procède au recouvrement d'une créance mise en gage, les droits de gage viennent grever la somme réalisée.

Art. 247. (3.9.2.8) Buiten de gevallen, geregeld in de artikelen 89 en 198 van Boek 2, blijft de uitoefening van stemrecht, verbonden aan een goed waarop een pandrecht rust, de pandgever toekomen, tenzij anders is bedongen.

Except for the cases governed by articles 89 and 198 of Book 2, the exercise of the right to vote attached to property encumbered by a right of pledge remains with the grantor of the pledge, unless otherwise stipulated.

Hormis les cas prévus aux articles 89 et 198 du Livre deuxième, l'exercice du droit de vote attaché à un bien grevé d'un droit de gage demeure réservé au constituant, sauf stipulation contraire.

Art. 248. (3.9.2.9) - 1. Wanneer de schuldenaar in verzuim is met de voldoening van hetgeen waarvoor het pand tot waarborg strekt, is de pandhouder bevoegd het verpande goed te verkopen en het hem verschuldigde op de opbrengst te verhalen.
- 2. Partijen kunnen bedingen dat eerst tot verkoop kan worden overgegaan, nadat de rechter op vordering van de pandhouder heeft vastgesteld dat de schuldenaar in verzuim is.
- 3. Een lager gerangschikte pandhouder of beslaglegger kan het verpande goed slechts verkopen met handhaving van de hoger gerangschikte pandrechten.

1. Where the debtor is in default of paying that for which the pledge serves as security, the pledgee is entitled to sell the pledged property and to take recourse against the proceeds for what is owed to him.
2. The parties may stipulate that no sale will take place until after the judge, upon the demand of the pledgee, has determined that the debtor is in default.
3. A pledgee or seizor with a lower rank can only sell the pledged property subject to the higher ranking rights of pledge.

1. Lorsque le débiteur est en demeure de payer ce que garantit le gage, le créancier gagiste a le pouvoir de le vendre et de se payer sur le produit.
2. Les parties peuvent convenir qu'il sera procédé à la vente uniquement après que le juge aura constaté, à la demande du créancier gagiste, que le débiteur est en demeure.
3. Le créancier gagiste ou le saisissant de rang inférieur ne peut vendre le gage que sous réserve des droits de gage de rang plus élevé.

Art. 249. (3.9.2.10) - 1. Tenzij anders is bedongen, is een pandhouder die tot verkoop wil overgaan verplicht, voor zover hem dit redelijkerwijze mogelijk is, ten minste drie dagen tevoren de voorgenomen verkoop met vermelding van plaats en tijd op bij algemene maatregel van bestuur te bepalen wijze mede te delen aan de schuldenaar en de pandgever, alsmede aan hen die op het goed een beperkt recht hebben of daarop beslag hebben gelegd.
- 2. De aanzegging moet zo nauwkeurig mogelijk de som aangeven, waarvoor het pand kan worden gelost. Lossing kan tot op het tijdstip van de verkoop plaatsvinden, mits ook de reeds gemaakte kosten van executie worden voldaan.

1. Unless otherwise stipulated, in order to proceed to a sale, a pledgee must, to the extent that this is reasonably possible, give at least three days notice of the intended sale with mention of place and time to the debtor and the grantor of the pledge. The notice must also be given to seizors of the property and to holders of dismembered rights. The manner in which notice is given is provided for by regulation.
2. The notice must indicate, as accurately as possible, the sum for which the pledge may be redeemed. Redemption can take place up to the time of sale, provided that the costs of execution which have already been incurred are also paid.

1. Sauf stipulation contraire, le créancier gagiste qui veut procéder à la vente est tenu, dans la mesure où cela lui est raisonnablement possible, d'aviser, au moins trois jours à l'avance, de son intention de vendre et de l'endroit et du temps de la vente le débiteur et le constituant, ainsi que ceux qui ont un droit démembré sur le bien ou qui l'ont saisi. L'avis est donné de la façon prescrite par décret.
2. L'avis doit indiquer le plus précisément possible la somme permettant de libérer le gage. La libération peut intervenir à tout moment jusqu'à la vente, pourvu que soient également acquittés les frais d'exécution déjà engagés.

Art. 250. (3.9.2.11) - 1. De verkoop geschiedt in het openbaar naar de plaatselijke gewoonten en op de gebruikelijke voorwaarden.
- 2. Bestaat het pand uit goederen die op een markt of beurs verhandelbaar zijn, dan kan de verkoop geschieden op een markt door tussenkomst van een makelaar in het vak of ter beurze door die van een bevoegde tussenpersoon overeenkomstig de regels en gebruiken die aldaar voor een gewone verkoop gelden.
- 3. De pandhouder is bevoegd mede te bieden.

1. The sale takes place in public according to local customs and upon the usual conditions.
2. The sale of pledged property which can be traded in a market or at an exchange may take place in a market through the intervention of an appropriate broker or, at an exchange, through the intervention of a qualified intermediary, according to rules and usages in force for an ordinary sale at such market or exchange.
3. The pledgee has the right to bid.

1. La vente a lieu en public selon les coutumes locales et aux conditions habituelles.
2. La vente d'un gage négociable sur un marché ou à la bourse peut avoir lieu, sur le marché, par l'entremise d'un courtier en la matière ou, à la bourse, par celle d'un intermédiaire compétent, d'après les règles et usages qui y régissent les ventes ordinaires.
3. Le créancier gagiste peut participer aux enchères.

Art. 251. (3.9.2.12) - 1. Tenzij anders is bedongen, kan de president van de rechtbank op verzoek van de pandhouder of de pandgever bepalen dat het pand zal worden verkocht op een van het vorige artikel afwijkende wijze, of op verzoek van de pandhouder bepalen dat het pand voor een door de president van de rechtbank vast te stellen bedrag aan de pandhouder als koper zal verblijven.
- 2. Nadat de pandhouder bevoegd is geworden tot verkoop over te gaan, kunnen pandhouder en pandgever een van het vorige artikel afwijkende wijze van verkoop overeenkomen. Rust op het verpande goed een beperkt recht of een beslag, dan is daartoe tevens de medewerking van de beperkt gerechtigde of de beslaglegger vereist.

1. Unless otherwise stipulated, the president of the district court may determine, at the request of the pledgee or the grantor of the pledge, that the pledged property will be sold in a manner which deviates from the preceding article; at the request of the pledgee, the president of the district court may also determine that the pledged property will remain with the pledgee as buyer for an amount to be determined by him.
2. The pledgee who has become entitled to proceed to a sale may agree with the grantor to a manner of sale which deviates from the preceding article. Where the pledged property is encumbered with a dismembered right or is under seizure, the cooperation of the holder of the dismembered right or of the seizor is also required.

1. Sauf stipulation contraire, le président du tribunal de première instance peut déterminer, sur requête du créancier gagiste ou du constituant, que le gage sera vendu d'une manière qui déroge à celle prévue à l'article précédent; il peut également déterminer, sur la requête du créancier gagiste, que le bien soit laissé à ce dernier en tant qu'acheteur pour une somme fixée par lui.
2. Le créancier gagiste qui a acquis le pouvoir de procéder à la vente peut convenir avec le constituant d'une manière de vendre qui déroge à celle prévue à l'article précédent. Lorsque le gage fait l'objet d'un droit démembré ou d'une saisie, le concours du titulaire de ce droit ou du saisissant est également requis.

Art. 252. (3.9.2.13) Tenzij anders is bedongen, is de pandhouder verplicht, voor zover hem dit redelijkerwijze mogelijk is, uiterlijk op de dag volgende op die van de verkoop daarvan op bij algemene maatregel van bestuur te bepalen wijze kennis te geven aan de schuldenaar en de pandgever, alsmede aan hen die op het goed een beperkt recht hebben of daarop beslag hebben gelegd.

Unless otherwise stipulated and to the extent that this is reasonably possible, the pledgee must give notice of the sale to the debtor, the grantor of the pledge as well as to seizors of the property and to holders of dismembered rights; the notice must be given, at the latest, on the day following the sale. The manner in which it is given is provided for by regulation.

Sauf stipulation contraire, le créancier gagiste est tenu, dans la mesure où cela lui est raisonnablement possible, de faire part de la vente, au plus tard le lendemain du jour où elle a eu lieu, au débiteur, au constituant et à ceux qui ont un droit démembré sur le bien ou qui l'ont saisi; la notification se fait de la façon prescrite par décret.

Art. 253. (3.9.2.14) - 1. De pandhouder houdt, na voldoening van de kosten van executie, van de netto-opbrengst af het aan hem verschuldigde bedrag waarvoor hij pandrecht heeft. Het overschot wordt aan de pandgever uitgekeerd. Zijn er pandhouders of andere beperkt gerechtigden, wier recht op het goed door de executie is vervallen, of hebben schuldeisers op het goed of op de opbrengst beslag gelegd, dan handelt de pandhouder overeenkomstig het bepaalde in artikel 490b van het Wetboek van Burgerlijke Rechtsvordering.
- 2. De pandhouder kan de door hem aan de voormelde belanghebbenden uit te keren bedragen niet voldoen door verrekening, tenzij het een uitkering aan de pandgever betreft en deze uitkering niet plaats vindt gedurende diens faillissement of surséance of de vereffening van zijn nalatenschap.

1. After paying the costs of execution, the pledgee deducts from the net proceeds the amount which is owed to him and for which he has a right of pledge. The balance is paid to the grantor of the pledge. Where there are pledgees or other holders of dismembered rights whose right to the property has been extinguished by the execution, or where creditors have seized the property or the proceeds, the pledgee must act according to the provisions of article 490b of the Code of Civil Procedure.
2. The pledgee may not pay the amounts which he owes to the aforementioned persons by way of compensation,[1] unless it concerns a payment to the grantor of the pledge, which is not made during the latter's bankruptcy, receivership or the settlement of his succession.

1. Après acquittement des frais d'exécution, le créancier gagiste retient du produit net la somme qui lui est due et pour laquelle il avait le droit de gage. Le solde est remis au constituant. Lorsqu'il y a des créanciers gagistes ou d'autres titulaires de droits démembrés dont le droit sur le bien s'est éteint à la suite de l'exécution, ou lorsque des créanciers ont saisi le bien ou le produit de la vente, le créancier gagiste agit alors conformément à ce qui est disposé à l'article 490b du Code de procédure civile.

2. Le créancier gagiste ne peut acquitter par voie de de compensation les sommes qu'il doit aux intéressés, à moins qu'il ne s'agisse d'un paiement au constituant qui ne soit pas effectué au cours de la faillite ou du sursis de paiement de ce dernier ni durant la liquidation de sa succession.

Art. 254. (3.9.2.14a) - 1. Wanneer op roerende zaken die volgens verkeersopvatting bestemd zijn om een bepaalde onroerende zaak duurzaam te dienen en door hun vorm als zodanig zijn te herkennen, of op

1 "Compensation" ("verrekening") is used here as the English civil law equivalent of the common law term "set-off" (see *infra* section 12 of title 1 of Book 6). Elsewhere in this translation, "compensation" is also used in another sense, namely in the sense of reparation (of damage) ("(schade)vergoeding") (see *inter alia, infra* section 10 of title 1 of Book 6).

machinerieën of werktuigen die bestemd zijn om daarmede een bedrijf in een bepaalde hiertoe ingerichte fabriek of werkplaats uit te oefenen, overeenkomstig artikel 237 een pandrecht is gevestigd voor een vordering waarvoor ook hypotheek gevestigd is op die onroerende zaak, fabriek of werkplaats of op een daarop rustend beperkt recht, kan worden bedongen dat de schuldeiser bevoegd is de verpande en verhypothekeerde goederen tezamen volgens de voor hypotheek geldende regels te executeren.
- 2. Executeert de schuldeiser overeenkomstig het beding, dan zijn de artikelen 268-273 op het pandrecht van overeenkomstige toepassing en is de toepasselijkheid van de artikelen 248-253 uitgesloten.
- 3. Het beding kan, onder vermelding van de pandrechten waarop het betrekking heeft, worden ingeschreven in de registers waarin de hypotheek is ingeschreven.

1. Where a right of pledge has been established, pursuant to article 237, on moveable things which, according to common opinion, are destined to serve durably a specific immoveable thing and which by their form are recognizable as such, or where such a right has been established on machinery or tools destined to be used in carrying out a business in a specific factory or workshop set up for this purpose, and where this right of pledge has been established for a claim for which a hypothec has also been established upon that immoveable thing, factory or workshop or on a dismembered right encumbering them, it may be stipulated that the creditor be entitled to execute against the pledged and hypothecated property together according to the rules governing hypothec.
2. Where the creditor executes pursuant to such a stipulation, articles 268 - 273 apply *mutatis mutandis* to the right of pledge and the applicability of articles 248 - 253 of this section is excluded.
3. The stipulation can be entered in the registers in which the hypothec has been entered with mention of the rights of pledge to which it relates.

1. Lorsqu'un droit de gage est établi conformément à l'article 237 sur des choses mobilières qui, d'après l'opinion généralement admise, sont destinées à servir de façon durable un immeuble déterminé et que leur forme permet de reconnaître comme telles, ou lorsque ce droit est établi sur des machines ou outils destinés à être utilisés, en vue de l'exploitation d'un commerce, dans une usine ou un atelier déterminé et équipé à cette fin, et que ce droit de gage garantit une créance en outre garantie par une hypothèque grevant cet immeuble, usine ou atelier ou grevant un droit démembré portant sur ledit immeuble, usine ou atelier, il peut être stipulé que le créancier a le pouvoir de procéder à une seule exécution des biens gagés et hypothéqués conformément aux règles régissant l'hypothèque.

2. Sont appliqués par analogie à l'exécution qui a lieu en vertu d'une telle stipulation les articles 268 à 273 au droit de gage; les articles 248 à 253 de la présente section ne s'appliquent pas.
3. La stipulation peut être inscrite sur les registres où est inscrite l'hypothèque, avec la mention des droits de gage sur lesquels elle porte.

Art. 255. (3.9.2.15) - 1. Bestaat het pand uit geld dan is de pandhouder, zodra zijn vordering opeisbaar is geworden, zonder voorafgaande aanzegging bevoegd zich uit het pand te voldoen overeenkomstig artikel 253. Hij is daartoe verplicht, indien de pandgever zulks vordert en deze bevoegd is de vordering in de verpande valuta te voldoen.
- 2. Artikel 252 vindt overeenkomstige toepassing.

1. Where the pledge consists of money, the pledgee is entitled to take recourse against it according to article 253 without previous notification as soon as his debt has become exigible. He must do so if the grantor of the pledge so demands and if the latter has the right to pay the debt in the pledged currency.
2. Article 252 applies *mutatis mutandis.*

1. Lorsque le gage porte sur de l'argent, le créancier gagiste a le droit, dès que sa créance est devenue exigible et sans autre avis, de se payer sur le gage conformément à l'article 253. Il y est tenu si le constituant le demande et si celui-ci a le droit de se libérer dans la monnaie dans laquelle le gage a été établi.
2. L'article 252 s'applique par analogie.

Art. 256. (3.9.2.16) Wanneer een pandrecht is tenietgegaan, is de pandhouder verplicht te verrichten hetgeen zijnerzijds nodig is opdat de pandgever de hem toekomende feitelijke macht over het goed herkrijgt, en desverlangd aan de pandgever een schriftelijk bewijs te verstrekken dat het pandrecht geëindigd is. Is de vordering waarvoor het pandrecht tot zekerheid strekte met een beperkt recht bezwaard, dan rust een overeenkomstige verplichting op de beperkt gerechtigde.

After the extinction of the right of pledge, the pledgee must do all that is necessary for the grantor of the pledge to recover the factual control of the property to which the latter is entitled and, if so demanded, the pledgee must give written proof to the grantor that the right of pledge has been extinguished. Where the claim for which the right of pledge constituted security is encumbered with a dismembered right, this obligation rests *mutatis mutandis* upon the holder of the dismembered right.

Après l'extinction du droit de gage, le créancier gagiste est tenu de faire le nécessaire pour que le constituant recouvre sur le bien le contrôle matériel qui lui appartient et de fournir, sur demande, une preuve écrite établissant que le droit de gage s'est éteint. Lorsque la créance garantie par le gage est grevée d'un droit démembré, une obligation analogue incombe au titulaire de ce droit.

Art. 257. (3.9.2.17) Indien degene die uit hoofde van een pandrecht een zaak onder zich heeft, in ernstige mate in de zorg voor de zaak tekortschiet, kan de rechtbank op vordering van de pandgever of een pandhouder bevelen dat de zaak aan een van hen wordt afgegeven of in gerechtelijke bewaring van een derde wordt gesteld.

If the person who detains a thing by virtue of a right of pledge seriously fails in taking care of the thing, the district court may, upon the demand of the grantor of the pledge or of a pledgee, order that the thing be given to one of them or be placed in judicial deposit with a third person.

Si celui qui détient une chose en vertu d'un droit de gage manque gravement aux soins qu'il convient d'y apporter, le tribunal de première instance peut, à la demande du constituant ou du créancier gagiste, ordonner que la chose soit remise à l'un d'entre eux ou soit placée en dépôt judiciaire entre les mains d'un tiers.

Art. 258. (3.9.2.18) - 1. Wanneer een in pand gegeven goed als bedoeld in artikel 236 lid 1 in de macht van de pandgever komt, eindigt het pandrecht, tenzij het met toepassing van artikel 237 lid 1 werd gevestigd.
- 2. Afstand van een pandrecht kan geschieden bij enkele overeenkomst, mits van de toestemming van de pandhouder uit een schriftelijke verklaring blijkt.

1. Unless the right of pledge was established with application of article 237, paragraph 1, it is terminated when the pledged property referred to in article 236, paragraph 1 comes under the control of the grantor of the pledge.
2. A right of pledge can be abandoned by simple contract, provided that the consent of the pledgee is evidenced by a written declaration.

1. Le droit de gage s'éteint lorsque le bien donné en gage tel que visé à l'article 236, paragraphe 1er, tombe en la puissance du constituant, à moins que le droit n'ait été établi par application de l'article 237, paragraphe 1er.
2. L'abandon du droit de gage a lieu par simple convention, pourvu que le consentement du constituant apparaisse dans une déclaration écrite.

AFDELING 3 Pandrecht van certificaathouders

Section 3 The right of pledge of certificate holders

Section troisième Du droit de gage des détenteurs de certificats

Art. 259. (3.9.3.1) - 1. Wanneer iemand door het uitgeven van certificaten derden doet delen in de opbrengst van door hem op eigen naam verkregen aandelen of schuldvorderingen, hebben de certificaathouders een vordering tot uitkering van het hun toegezegde tegen de uitgever van de certificaten.
- 2. Zijn de oorspronkelijke aandelen of schuldvorderingen op naam gesteld en de certificaten uitgegeven met medewerking van de uitgever van de oorspronkelijke aandelen of schuldvorderingen, dan verkrijgen de certificaathouders tevens gezamenlijk een pandrecht op die aandelen of schuldvorderingen. Zijn de certificaten uitgegeven voor schuldvorderingen op naam zonder medewerking van de schuldenaar, dan verkrijgen de certificaathouders een zodanig pandrecht door mededeling van de uitgifte aan de schuldenaar. Zijn de certificaten uitgegeven voor aandelen of schuldvorderingen aan toonder, dan verkrijgen de certificaathouders een zodanig pandrecht, zonder dat het papier in de macht van de certificaathouders of een derde behoeft te worden gebracht.
- 3. Dit pandrecht geeft aan de certificaathouders alleen de bevoegdheid in geval van niet-uitbetaling van het hun verschuldigde met inachtneming van de volgende regels het pand geheel of gedeeltelijk te doen verkopen en zich uit de opbrengst te voldoen. Een certificaathouder die hiertoe wenst over te gaan, wendt zich tot de president van de rechtbank van de woonplaats van degene die de certificaten heeft uitgegeven met verzoek een bewindvoerder over het pand te benoemen, die voor de verkoop en de verdeling van de opbrengst zorg draagt. Indien niet alle certificaathouders met de verkoop instemmen, wordt slechts een deel van het pand dat overeenkomt met het recht van de andere certificaathouders verkocht; de rechten van deze laatsten gaan door de verdeling van de opbrengst onder hen teniet. De president kan op verlangen van elke certificaathouder of ambtshalve maatregelen bevelen in het belang van de certificaathouders die niet met de verkoop hebben ingestemd, en bepalen dat de verkoop door hem moet worden goedgekeurd, wil zij geldig zijn.

1. Where a person, by issuing certificates, causes third parties to share in the revenues of shares or debts which he has acquired in his own name, the certificate holders have a claim against the issuer of the certificates for payment of what has been promised to them.
2. Where the original shares or debts are nominative and if the certificates have been issued with the cooperation of the issuer of the original shares or debts, the certificate holders also acquire jointly a right of pledge on those shares or debts. Where certificates have been issued in respect of nominative debts without the cooperation of the debtor, the certificate holders acquire such a right of pledge by notification of the issuance to the debtor. Where the certificates have been issued in respect of shares or debts payable to bearer, the certificate holders acquire such a right of pledge without the document being brought under the control of the certificate holders or of a third person.
3. This right of pledge only gives the certificate holders the right to have the pledged property sold, in whole or in part, in the event of non-payment of what is due to them and the right to be paid by preference from the proceeds, subject to the observance of the following rules. A certificate holder who wishes to do so, applies to the president of the district court of the domicile of the issuer of the certificates with the request that an administrator be appointed to the pledged property, who attends to the sale and the distribution of the proceeds. If not all the certificate holders agree to the sale, only the part of the pledged property corresponding to the right of the remaining certificate holders is sold; the rights of these remaining certificate holders are extinguished by the partition of the proceeds between them. Upon the demand of any one certificate holder or *ex officio*, the president may order that measures be taken in the interest of certificate holders who have not consented to the sale and he may determine that the sale must be approved by him in order to be valid.

1. Lorsque une personne, par l'émission de certificats, fait participer des tiers aux revenus tirés d'actions ou de créances qu'elle a acquises en son propre nom, les détenteurs de certificats ont contre l'émetteur une action pour le versement de ce qui leur a été promis.
2. Lorsque les actions ou les créances initiales sont nominatives et que les certificats ont été émis avec le concours de l'émetteur des actions ou créances, les détenteurs des certificats acquièrent en outre conjointement sur celles-ci un droit de gage. Lorsque les certificats portent sur des créances nominatives et ont été émis sans le concours du débiteur, les détenteurs acquièrent un tel droit de gage par la notification de l'émission au débiteur. Lorsque les certificats émis portent sur des créances au porteur, les détenteurs acquièrent un tel droit de gage sans qu'il soit nécessaire de placer les titres en leur puissance ou en celle d'un tiers.

3. Ce droit de gage ne donne aux détenteurs de certificats que le droit, en cas de non-paiement de ce qui leur est dû et conformément aux règles suivantes, de le faire vendre en tout ou partie et de se faire payer par préférence sur le produit. Le détenteur de certificats qui désire y procéder adresse au président du tribunal de première instance du domicile de l'émetteur une requête que soit nommé un administrateur du gage, qui veille à la vente et à la distribution du produit. Si tous les détenteurs de certificats ne consentent pas à la vente, est vendue seulement la partie du gage correspondant aux droits des autres; les droits de ces derniers s'éteignent par le partage du produit entre eux. Le président peut, à la demande de tout détenteur de certificats ou d'office, ordonner des mesures dans l'intérêt des détenteurs de certificats qui n'ont pas consenti à la vente, et déterminer que la vente, pour être valide, requiert son approbation.

AFDELING 4 Recht van hypotheek

Section 4	*Section quatrième*
The right of hypothec	*Du droit d'hypothèque*

Art. 260. (3.9.4.2) - 1. Hypotheek wordt gevestigd door een tussen partijen opgemaakte notariële akte waarbij de hypotheekgever aan de hypotheekhouder hypotheek op een registergoed verleent, gevolgd door haar inschrijving in de daartoe bestemde openbare registers. De akte moet een aanduiding bevatten van de vordering waarvoor de hypotheek tot zekerheid strekt, of van de feiten aan de hand waarvan die vordering zal kunnen worden bepaald. Tevens moet het bedrag worden vermeld waarvoor de hypotheek wordt verleend of, wanneer dit bedrag nog niet vaststaat, het maximumbedrag dat uit hoofde van de hypotheek op het goed kan worden verhaald. De hypotheekhouder moet in de akte woonplaats kiezen in Nederland.
- 2. Tenzij anders is bedongen, komen de kosten van verlening en vestiging ten laste van de schuldenaar.
- 3. Bij de in het eerste lid bedoelde akte kan iemand slechts krachtens een bij authentieke akte verleende volmacht als gevolmachtigde voor de hypotheekgever optreden.
- 4. Voor het overige vinden de algemene voorschriften die voor vestiging van beperkte rechten op registergoederen gegeven zijn, ook op de vestiging van een hypotheek toepassing.

1. A hypothec is established by a notarial deed drawn up between the parties in which the grantor gives hypothec to the hypothecary creditor on registered property, followed by the entry of the deed in the public registers provided for that purpose. The deed must contain an indication of the claim for which the hypothec serves as security, or of the facts on the basis of which that claim can be determined. The amount for which the hypothec is granted must also be mentioned or, when this amount has not yet been determined, the maximum amount for which recourse may be taken against the property pursuant to the hypothec. In the deed the hypothecary creditor must elect domicile in the Netherlands.
2. Unless otherwise stipulated, the debtor bears the expenses of granting and establishing the hypothec.

1. L'hypothèque est constituée par acte notarié entre les parties, portant que le constituant la consent au créancier hypothécaire sur un bien immatriculé, et par l'inscription subséquente de l'acte sur les registres publics prévus à cette fin. L'acte doit indiquer la créance garantie par l'hypothèque ou les faits qui permettront de la déterminer. Doit également être mentionnée la somme pour laquelle l'hypothèque est consentie ou, lorsque cette somme n'est pas encore fixée, le maximum que l'hypothèque permet de recouvrer sur le bien hypothéqué. Le créancier hypothécaire doit, dans l'acte, élire domicile aux Pays-Bas.
2. Sauf stipulation contraire, les frais engagés pour consentir l'hypothèque et pour la constituer[1] sont à la charge du débiteur.

[1] Tout comme le transfert d'un bien, l'établissement d'un droit réel démembré requiert en droit néerlandais deux actes juridiques successifs. Cf. art. 84 et 98 du Livre troisième.

3. A person cannot act as procurator for the grantor of the hypothec in the deed referred to in the first paragraph, unless the procuration has been granted by an authentic deed.
4. In all other cases, the general rules governing the establishment of dismembered rights upon registered property also apply to the establishment of a hypothec.

3. Un procureur ne peut agir au nom du constituant lors de la passation de l'acte visé au paragraphe 1 que si la procuration lui a été accordée par acte authentique.

4. En dehors de ce qui est prévu aux paragraphes précédents, la constitution de l'hypothèque est soumise aux dispositions générales régissant l'établissement de droits démembrés sur des biens immatriculés.

Art. 261. (3.9.4.5) - 1. Is bij een koopovereenkomst hypotheek op het verkochte goed tot waarborg van onbetaalde kooppenningen bedongen en is dit beding in de leveringsakte vermeld, dan heeft deze hypotheek, mits de akte waarbij zij werd verleend tegelijk met de leveringsakte wordt ingeschreven, voorrang boven alle andere aan de koper ontleende rechten, ten aanzien waarvan tegelijk een inschrijving plaatsvond.
- 2. Lid 1 vindt overeenkomstige toepassing op een bij een verdeling bedongen hypotheek op een toegedeeld goed tot waarborg van hetgeen hij aan wie het goed is toegedeeld, aan de andere deelgenoten ten gevolge van de verdeling schuldig is of mocht worden.

1. A hypothec, stipulated in a contract of sale, upon the property sold to secure the unpaid purchase price and mentioned in the deed of delivery has, provided that the deed granting the hypothec has been registered at the same time as the deed of delivery, preference over all other rights derived from the buyer which have been registered at the same time.
2. Paragraph 1 applies *mutatis mutandis* to a hypothec which, on the occasion of a partition, has been stipulated upon attributed property to secure the amount which the person, to whom the property has been attributed, owes or may come to owe to the remaining partners as a consequence of the partition.

1. Lorsque, dans le cadre d'une vente et avec mention dans l'acte de délivrance, une hypothèque a été consentie sur le bien vendu, en garantie du paiement du prix, et que l'acte la constatant a été inscrit simultanément avec l'acte de délivrance, elle a préférence sur tous les autres droits tirés de l'acheteur dont l'inscription a eu lieu en même temps.
2. Le paragraphe premier s'applique par analogie à l'hypothèque consentie, lors du partage, sur un bien attribué en garantie d'une dette présente ou éventuelle résultant du partage, qui incombe à celui à qui le bien est attribué, au profit des autres partenaires.

Art. 262. (3.9.4.6) - 1. Bij een notariële akte die in de registers wordt ingeschreven, kan worden bepaald dat een hypotheek ten aanzien van een of meer hypotheken op hetzelfde goed een hogere rang heeft dan haar volgens het tijdstip van haar inschrijving toekomt, mits uit de akte blijkt dat de gerechtigden tot die andere hypotheek of hypotheken daarin toestemmen.
- 2. Met overeenkomstige toepassing van het eerste lid kan ook worden bepaald dat een hypotheek en een ander beperkt recht ten aanzien van elkaar worden geacht in andere volgorde te zijn ontstaan dan is geschied.

1. A notarial deed entered in the registers may stipulate that a hypothec will have a higher rank in respect of one

1. Il peut être stipulé par acte notarié inscrit sur les registres, qu'une hypothèque a, à l'égard d'autres hypothèques sur le

or more hypothecs upon the same property than would result from the time of its registration, provided that the deed show that the title-holders of the other hypothec or hypothecs consent to it.
2. Applying paragraph 1 *mutatis mutandis*, it may also be stipulated that a hypothec and another dismembered right are deemed to have been created in respect of each other in an order different from the one which actually occurred.

même bien, un rang plus élevé que celui que lui donne la date de son inscription, pourvu que l'acte fasse apparaître le consentement des titulaires de ces autres hypothèques.

2. Par application analogique du paragraphe premier, il peut être stipulé qu'une hypothèque et un autre droit démembré sont censés, l'un à l'égard de l'autre, être nés dans un ordre différent de celui qui s'est produit en réalité.

Art. 263. (3.9.4.7) - 1. Tenzij in de hypotheekakte anders is bepaald, strekt een hypotheek tot zekerheid van een of meer bepaalde vorderingen tevens tot zekerheid voor drie jaren rente die daarover krachtens de wet verschuldigd is.
- 2. Een beding dat een hypotheek tot zekerheid van een of meer bepaalde vorderingen tevens strekt tot zekerheid van rente over een langer tijdvak dan drie jaren zonder vermelding van een maximumbedrag, is nietig.

1. Unless the deed of hypothec stipulates otherwise, a hypothec securing one or more specifically determined claims also serves as security for three years interest owing on these claims by law.
2. A stipulation that a hypothec to secure one or more specifically determined claims also serves as security for interest for a period exceeding three years, without reference to a maximum amount, is null.

1. Sauf stipulation contraire, l'hypothèque qui garantit des créances déterminées garantit également l'intérêt couru sur celles-ci en vertu de la loi pendant une période de trois ans.
2. Est nulle la stipulation qu'une hypothèque qui garantit des créances déterminées en garantit également l'intérêt pendant une période dépassant trois ans, s'il n'est pas fait état d'une somme maximale.

Art. 264. (3.9.4.8) - 1. Indien de hypotheekakte een uitdrukkelijk beding bevat waarbij de hypotheekgever in zijn bevoegdheid is beperkt, hetzij om het bezwaarde goed buiten toestemming van de hypotheekhouder te verhuren of te verpachten, hetzij ten aanzien van de wijze waarop of van de tijd gedurende welke het goed zal kunnen worden verhuurd of verpacht, hetzij ten aanzien van de vooruitbetaling van huur- of pachtpenningen, hetzij om het recht op de huur- of pachtpenningen te vervreemden of te verpanden, kan dit beding niet alleen tegen latere verkrijgers van het bezwaarde goed, maar ook tegen de huurder of pachter en tegen degene aan wie het recht op de huur- of pachtpenningen werd vervreemd of verpand, worden ingeroepen, zulks zowel door de hypotheekhouder, als na de uitwinning van het bezwaarde goed door de koper, dit laatste echter alleen voor zover deze bevoegdheid op het tijdstip van de verkoop nog aan de hypotheekhouder toekwam en deze de uitoefening daarvan blijkens de verkoopvoorwaarden aan de koper overlaat.
- 2. De inroeping kan niet geschieden, voordat het in artikel 544 van het Wetboek van Burgerlijke Rechtsvordering bedoelde exploit van aanzegging of overneming is uitgebracht. De bepalingen betreffende vernietigbaarheid zijn van toepassing met dien verstande dat de termijn van artikel 52 lid 1 loopt vanaf de voormelde aanzegging of overneming en dat een in strijd met het beding gekomen rechtshandeling slechts wordt vernietigd ten behoeve

van degene die het inroept, en niet verder dan met diens recht in overeenstemming is.
- 3. Indien het beding is gemaakt met betrekking tot hoeven of los land, heeft het slechts werking voor zover het niet in strijd is met enig dwingend wettelijk voorschrift omtrent pacht. Zodanig beding heeft geen werking, voor zover de grondkamer bindend aan de pachtovereenkomst een daarmee strijdige inhoud heeft gegeven, dan wel het beding niet kon worden nageleefd, omdat de grondkamer een wijzigingsovereenkomst die aan het beding beantwoordde, heeft vernietigd. Een beding dat de hypotheekgever verplicht is hoeven voor kortere tijd dan twaalf jaren en los land voor kortere tijd dan zes jaren te verpachten, is nietig.
- 4. Indien het beding is gemaakt met betrekking tot huur van woonruimte of huur van bedrijfsruimte, heeft het slechts werking, voor zover het niet in strijd is met enig dwingend wettelijk voorschrift omtrent zodanige huur. Het beding dat de verhuur van woonruimte of bedrijfsruimte uitsluit, kan niet tegen de huurder worden ingeroepen, voor zover de woonruimte of bedrijfsruimte ten tijde van de vestiging van de hypotheek reeds was verhuurd en de nieuwe verhuring niet op ongewone, voor de hypotheekhouder meer bezwarende gronden heeft plaatsgevonden.
- 5. Voor zover een beroep op een beding tot gevolg zal hebben dat de huurder van woonruimte waarop de artikelen 1623a-1623f van toepassing zijn, moet ontruimen, kan het beding slechts worden ingeroepen nadat de president van de rechtbank daartoe op verzoek van de hypotheekhouder verlof heeft verleend. Het verlof is niet vereist ten aanzien van een huurovereenkomst met vernietiging waarvan de huurder schriftelijk heeft ingestemd of die is tot stand gekomen na de bekendmaking, bedoeld in artikel 516 van het Wetboek van Burgerlijke Rechtsvordering.
- 6. De president verleent het verlof, tenzij ook met instandhouding van de huurovereenkomst kennelijk een voldoende opbrengst zal worden verkregen om alle hypotheekhouders die het beding hebben gemaakt en dit jegens de huurder kunnen inroepen, te voldoen. Zo hij het verlof verleent, veroordeelt hij tevens de opgeroepen of verschenen huurders en onderhuurders tot ontruiming en stelt hij een termijn vast van ten hoogste één jaar na de betekening aan de huurder of onderhuurder van zijn beschikking, waarbinnen geen ontruiming mag plaatsvinden. Tegen een beschikking waarbij het verlof wordt verleend, staat geen hogere voorzieningen open.
- 7. Indien het recht van de huurder of pachter door vernietiging krachtens lid 2 verloren gaat, wordt aan hem uit de bij de executie verkregen netto-opbrengst van het goed met voorrang onmiddellijke na hen tegen wie hij zijn recht niet kon inroepen, een vergoeding uitgekeerd ten bedrage van de schade die hij als gevolg van de vernietiging lijdt. Is de koper bevoegd het beding in te roepen, dan wordt van hetgeen aan de schuldeisers met een lagere rang toekomt, een met de te verwachten schade overeenkomend bedrag gereserveerd, totdat vaststaat dat de koper van zijn bevoegdheid geen gebruik maakt.
- 8. Onder de huurder in de zin van dit artikel wordt begrepen degene die ingevolge artikel 1623g lid 1 of artikel 1623h lid 1 medehuurder is.

1. An express stipulation in the deed of hypothec may limit the grantor of the hypothec in his power: to lease the encumbered property without the consent of the hypothecary creditor; to determine the manner in which or the time during which the property can be leased; to determine the payment in advance of rent instalments; or to alienate or pledge the right to rent instalments Such stipulation may be invoked not only against subsequent acquirers of the encumbered property, but also against the lessee and the person who acquires the right to the rent instalments or has a right of pledge on them; the stipulation may be invoked by the hypothecary creditor, as well as by the buyer after the forced sale of the encumbered property, but only to the extent that this right still belonged to the hypothecary creditor at the time of the sale and that he has left the exercise thereof to the buyer, as evidenced by the conditions of sale.

2. The stipulation may not be invoked before the summons of notification or of take-over, referred to in article 544 of the Code of Civil Procedure, has been issued. The provisions regarding annulment apply, in which case the period of article 52, paragraph 1 runs from the aforementioned notification or take-over, and in which case a juridical act which has become contrary to the stipulation is only annulled in favour of the person invoking it and no further than the act is incompatible with his right.

3. Such a stipulation made in respect of farmsteads or agricultural land has no effect to the extent that it is contrary to any imperative statutory provision regarding farm leases. It has no effect to the extent that the land chamber has in a binding fashion given the contract of farm lease a content contrary to the stipulation or to the extent that the stipulation could not be complied with because of an annulment by the land chamber of a contract of modification corresponding to the stipulation. A stipulation obliging the grantor of the hypothec to lease farmsteads for a period of less than twelve years, or agricultural land for a period of less than six years is null.

1. On peut, dans un acte hypothécaire comportant une stipulation expresse à cet effet, limiter conventionnellement le pouvoir du constituant de donner à bail le bien grevé sans le consentement du créancier hypothécaire; de la même façon, on peut limiter le pouvoir du constituant de déterminer les conditions ou la durée de location du bien, ou le paiement anticipé du loyer, ou son pouvoir d'aliéner ou de mettre en gage le droit au loyer. Une telle stipulation est opposable non seulement aux acquéreurs subséquents du bien grevé, mais également au locataire et au bénéficiaire de l'aliénation ou de la mise en gage du droit au loyer, et ce par le créancier hypothécaire aussi bien que par l'acheteur du bien grevé après l'exécution forcée, mais par ce dernier seulement dans la mesure où ce pouvoir appartenait encore au créancier hypothécaire au moment de la vente et qu'il ressort des conditions de vente que celui-ci transmet l'exercice de ce pouvoir à l'acheteur.

2. La stipulation ne peut être invoquée avant la signification de l'exploit de notification ou de reprise visé à l'article 544 du Code de procédure civile. Les dispositions relatives à l'annulation s'appliquent, étant entendu que le terme visé au paragraphe premier de l'article 52 ne court qu'à compter de la notification ou de la reprise mentionnées et que l'acte juridique qui contrevient à la stipulation est annulé seulement à l'égard de celui qui l'invoque et pas plus que dans la mesure de l'incompatibilité entre cet acte et son droit.

3. Si la stipulation porte sur des fermes ou des terres agricoles, elle ne produit effet que dans la mesure où elle ne contrevient pas à une disposition impérative concernant le bail rural. Une telle stipulation n'a pas d'effet dans la mesure où la chambre agricole a donné impérativement au bail rural un contenu incompatible ou lorsque la stipulation ne pouvait être respectée, la chambre agricole ayant annulé le contrat de modification donnant suite à la stipulation. Est nulle la stipulation obligeant le constituant à donner à bail des fermes pour des périodes inférieures à 12 ans ou des terres agricoles pour des périodes inférieures à six ans.

4. Such a stipulation made in respect of the lease and hire of residential or commercial space has no effect to the extent that it is contrary to any imperative statutory provision regarding such lease and hire. A stipulation excluding lease and hire of residential or commercial space cannot be invoked against the lessee to the extent that the residential or commercial space was already leased at the time of the establishment of the hypothec and that the new lease has not been made upon unusual conditions more onerous to the hypothecary creditor.

5. To the extent that invoking the stipulation will result in the lessee of a dwelling, to whom articles 1623a - 1623f apply, having to vacate residential space, the stipulation cannot be invoked until the president of the district court has granted permission to do so at the request of the hypothecary creditor. Permission is not required with respect to a contract of lease and hire, the annulment of which the lessee has consented to in writing, or with respect to a contract of lease and hire which has been entered into after the publication referred to in article 516 of the Code of Civil Procedure.

6. The president grants permission, unless, even when maintaining the contract of lease and hire, it is obvious that sufficient proceeds will be obtained to satisfy all hypothecary creditors who have made the stipulation and can invoke it against the lessee. If the president grants permission, he also orders the lessees and sub-lessees who have been summoned or who have appeared, to vacate the premises in question and he fixes a period not exceeding one year from the notification of his decision to the lessee or sub-lessee, within which the vacating may not take place. No appeal lies from a decision granting this permission.

7. Where a lessee loses his right by annulment pursuant to paragraph 2, compensation is paid to him for the damage which he suffers as the consequence of the annulment out of the net proceeds of the property produced by the execution with preference immediately after the persons against whom he could not invoke his right.

4. Lorsque la stipulation porte sur le bail d'espace d'habitation ou d'espace commercial, elle ne produit effet que dans la mesure où elle n'est pas contraire à une disposition impérative de la loi portant sur un tel bail. La stipulation excluant la mise en location d'espace d'habitation ou d'espace commercial n'est pas opposable au locataire dans la mesure où l'espace d'habitation ou commercial était déjà loué au moment de la constitution d'hypothèque et où le nouveau bail n'a pas été conclu à des conditions inhabituelles et plus onéreuses pour le créancier hypothécaire.

5. Dans la mesure où la stipulation aura pour effet d'obliger le locataire d'espace d'habitation auquel s'appliquent les articles 1623a à 1623f à évacuer les lieux loués, elle ne peut être invoquée qu'avec la permission du président du tribunal de première instance, accordée sur la requête du créancier hypothécaire. La permission n'est pas requise dans le cas d'un bail annulé avec l'acquiescement du locataire ou conclu après la publication visée à l'article 516 du Code de procédure civile.

6. Le président accorde la permission, à moins qu'il ne soit manifeste que, même en maintenant le bail, on peut obtenir un produit suffisant pour satisfaire tous les créanciers hypothécaires qui ont fait la stipulation et peuvent l'invoquer contre le locataire. En accordant l'autorisation, il condamne à l'évacuation les locataires et sous-locataires qui ont été convoqués ou qui ont comparu et il fixe un délai d'au plus un an à compter de la signification au locataire ou sous-locataire à l'intérieur duquel l'évacuation ne peut avoir lieu. La décision accordant l'autorisation est insusceptible d'appel.

7. Lorsque le droit du preneur se perd par annulation conformément au paragraphe 2, il est versé à ce dernier, sur le produit net résultant de l'exécution du bien, une indemnité au montant du préjudice qu'il subit à la suite de l'annulation; cette indemnité prend rang immédiatement après ceux contre qui il ne pouvait invoquer son droit. Lorsque l'acheteur peut invoquer la

Where the buyer has the right to invoke the stipulation, an amount corresponding to the expected damage is set aside from what belongs to creditors with a lower rank until such time as it has been established that the buyer will not use his right.

8. A lessee in the sense of this article includes the person who is a co-lessee by virtue of article 1623g, paragraph 1 or article 1623h, paragraph 1.

stipulation, on réserve, sur ce qui revient aux créanciers de rang inférieur, une somme correspondant au préjudice qu'on peut prévoir, jusqu'à ce qu'il soit établi que l'acheteur ne se prévaudra pas de ce pouvoir.

8. Au sens du présent article, on entend également par locataire celui qui est colocataire par l'effet du paragraphe premier de l'article 1623g ou du paragraphe premier de l'article 1623h.

Art. 265. (3.9.4.8a) Indien de hypotheekakte een uitdrukkelijk beding bevat, volgens hetwelk de hypotheekgever de inrichting of gedaante van het bezwaarde goed niet of niet zonder toestemming van de hypotheekhouder mag veranderen, kan op dit beding geen beroep worden gedaan, wanneer tot de verandering machtiging is verleend aan de huurder door de kantonrechter op grond van de bepalingen betreffende huur van bedrijfsruimte of aan de pachter of verpachter door de grondkamer op grond van de bepalingen betreffende pacht.

An express stipulation in the deed of hypothec forbidding the grantor of the hypothec to change the structure or form of the encumbered property, or to change it without the consent of the hypothecary creditor, cannot be invoked where the judge of the subdistrict court has authorized the lessee to make the change on the basis of the provisions regarding lease and hire of commercial space, or where the land chamber has granted this authorization to the lessee or lessor on the basis of the provisions regarding farm leases.

On ne peut se prévaloir de la stipulation expressément inscrite dans l'acte hypothécaire et en vertu de laquelle le constituant ne peut, ou ne peut sans le consentement du créancier hypothécaire, modifier la structure ou la forme du bien grevé, lorsque le juge d'instance, se fondant sur les dispositions relatives au bail d'espace commercial, a autorisé le locataire à effectuer la modification ou que la chambre agricole, se fondant sur les dispositions relatives au bail rural, en a fait de même à l'égard du preneur ou du bailleur.

Art. 266. (3.9.4.8b) Is een zaak aan hypotheek onderworpen en heeft de hypotheekgever hieraan na de vestiging van de hypotheek veranderingen of toevoegingen aangebracht zonder dat hij verplicht was deze mede tot onderpand voor de vordering te doen strekken, dan is hij bevoegd deze veranderingen en toevoegingen weg te nemen, mits hij de zaak in de oude toestand terugbrengt en desverlangd voor de tijd dat dit nog niet is geschied, ter zake van de waardevermindering zekerheid stelt. Degene die gerechtigd is tot te velde staande vruchten of beplantingen, is bevoegd deze in te oogsten; kon dit voor de executie niet geschieden, dan zijn hij en de koper verplicht zich jegens elkaar te gedragen overeenkomstig de verplichtingen die afgaande en opkomende pachters op grond van de bepalingen betreffende pacht jegens elkaar hebben.

Where a thing is subjected to a hypothec and where the grantor of the hypothec has made changes or additions to it, after

Lorsque, après la constitution de l'hypothèque, le constituant a apporté des modifications ou des additions à la chose

its establishment, and where he was not under an obligation to make these changes or additions serve as additional security for the claim, he has the right to remove them, provided that he restore the thing to its original condition and that, until this has been done, he provide security for the depreciation upon demand. The person who is entitled to unplucked fruits or uncut plants has the right to harvest them; where this could not be done before the execution, the title-holder and the buyer are obliged to act toward each other according to the obligations which coming and going lessees have toward each other on the basis of the provisions regarding farm leases.

soumise à hypothèque[1] sans être tenu de les faire servir également de garantie pour la créance, il peut les enlever, pourvu qu'il remette la chose en l'état originaire et qu'il fournisse, sur demande, sûreté pour la dépréciation, tant que la remise en état n'a pas eu lieu. Le titulaire des fruits ou plantations sur pied a le droit de les récolter; lorsque cela n'a pu avoir lieu avant l'exécution forcée, l'acheteur et lui sont tenus de se comporter, l'un à l'égard de l'autre, conformément aux obligations qu'ont entre eux les anciens et nouveaux preneurs en vertu des dispositions relatives au bail rural.

Art. 267. (3.9.4.9) In de hypotheekakte kan worden bedongen dat de hypotheekhouder bevoegd is om het verhypothekeerde goed in beheer te nemen, indien de hypotheekgever in zijn verplichtingen jegens hem in ernstige mate te kort schiet en de president van de rechtbank hem machtiging verleent. Eveneens kan in de akte worden bedongen dat de hypotheekhouder bevoegd is de aan de hypotheek onderworpen zaak onder zich te nemen, indien zulks met het oog op de executie vereist is. Zonder uitdrukkelijke bedingen mist de hypotheekhouder deze bevoegdheden.

The deed of hypothec may stipulate that the hypothecary creditor be entitled to take over the management of the hypothecated property if the grantor of the hypothec seriously fails in the performance of his obligations toward him and if the president of the district court grants him authorization to do so. The deed may also stipulate that the hypothecary creditor be entitled to take the thing subjected to the hypothec under his control if this is required in view of the execution. The hypothecary creditor does not have these rights, unless they are expressly stipulated.

Il peut être stipulé dans l'acte hypothécaire que le créancier a le pouvoir, si le constituant manque gravement à ses obligations et que le président du tribunal de première instance l'autorise, d'assumer la gestion du bien hypothéqué. Il peut également y être stipulé que le créancier a le pouvoir de prendre la chose soumise à hypothèque en sa puissance si cela est requis en vue de l'exécution forcée. Le créancier hypothécaire n'a pas ces pouvoirs s'ils ne sont pas expressément stipulés.

Art. 268. (3.9.4.11) - 1. Indien de schuldenaar in verzuim is met de voldoening van hetgeen waarvoor de hypotheek tot waarborg strekt, is de hypotheekhouder bevoegd het verbonden goed in het openbaar ten overstaan van een bevoegde notaris te doen verkopen.
- 2. Op verzoek van de hypotheekhouder of de hypotheekgever kan de president van de rechtbank bepalen dat de verkoop ondershands zal geschieden bij een overeenkomst die hem bij het verzoek ter goedkeuring

[1] Le Code néerlandais emploie ici le terme «*onderworpen*», qui englobe l'hypothèque sur la chose (chose grevée) ainsi que l'hypothèque sur un droit démembré grevant la chose. La distinction est rendue en français par le terme «soumis à hypothèque».

wordt voorgelegd. Indien door de hypotheekgever of door een hypotheekhouder, beslaglegger of beperkt gerechtigde, die bij een hogere opbrengst van het goed belang heeft, voor de afloop van de behandeling van het verzoek aan de president een gunstiger aanbod wordt voorgelegd, kan deze bepalen dat de verkoop overeenkomstig dit aanbod zal geschieden.
- 3. Het in lid 2 bedoelde verzoek wordt ingediend binnen de in het Wetboek van Burgerlijke Rechtsvordering daarvoor bepaalde termijn. Tegen een beschikking krachtens lid 2 is geen hogere voorziening toegelaten.
- 4. Een executie als in de vorige leden bedoeld geschiedt met inachtneming van de daarvoor in het Wetboek van Burgerlijke Rechtsvordering voorgeschreven formaliteiten.
- 5. De hypotheekhouder kan niet op andere wijze zijn verhaal op het verbonden goed uitoefenen. Een daartoe strekkend beding is nietig.

1. If the debtor is in default of paying that for which the hypothec serves as security, the hypothecary creditor is entitled to have the encumbered property sold in public before a notary having authority to do so.
2. At the request of the hypothecary creditor or the grantor of the hypothec, the president of the district court may determine that there be a private sale by contract submitted to him for approval together with the request. If the grantor of the hypothec, a hypothecary creditor, seizor or holder of a dismembered right who has an interest in obtaining higher proceeds for the property, submits a more advantageous offer to the president before the end of the hearing of the request, the president may determine that the sale be made according to this offer.
3. The request referred to in paragraph 2 is submitted within the period provided for that purpose in the Code of Civil Procedure. No appeal lies from a decision pursuant to paragraph 2.
4. The execution referred to in the preceding paragraphs is carried out according to the formalities prescribed for that purpose in the Code of Civil Procedure.
5. The hypothecary creditor may not take recourse against the encumbered property in any other manner. Any stipulation to this effect is null.

1. Si le débiteur est en demeure de payer la dette hypothécaire, le créancier peut faire vendre publiquement le bien grevé devant un notaire ayant compétence pour ce faire.
2. Sur la requête du créancier hypothécaire ou du constituant, le président du tribunal de première instance peut déterminer qu'il y aura vente privée par un contrat qui lui est soumis pour approbation avec la requête. Si le constituant, un créancier hypothécaire, un saisissant ou le titulaire d'un droit démembré, qui est intéressé à un produit plus élevé soumet, avant la fin de l'instruction de la requête, au président du tribunal de première instance une offre plus avantageuse, celui-ci peut déterminer que la vente aura lieu conformément à cette offre.
3. La requête visée au paragraphe 2 doit être présentée dans le délai prévu au Code de procédure civile. La décision en vertu du paragraphe 2 est insusceptible d'appel.
4. L'exécution forcée visée aux paragraphes précédents a lieu en suivant les formalités prescrites à cette fin au Code de procédure civile.
5. Le créancier hypothécaire ne peut poursuivre d'aucune autre façon le recouvrement de sa créance sur le bien grevé. Toute stipulation à cet effet est nulle.

Art. 269. (3.9.4.14) Tot op het tijdstip van de toewijzing ter veiling of van de goedkeuring door de president van de onderhandse verkoop kan de verkoop worden voorkomen door voldoening van hetgeen waarvoor de hypotheek tot waarborg strekt, alsmede van de reeds gemaakte kosten van executie.

Until the adjudication at public auction or the approval by the president of the private sale, the sale may be prevented by paying that for which the hypothec serves as security and the costs of execution which have already been made.

Jusqu'à l'adjudication lors d'une vente aux enchères ou jusqu'à l'approbation par le président d'une vente privée, on peut éviter la vente en payant la dette hypothécaire ainsi que les dépenses d'exécution déjà engagées.

Art. 270. (3.9.4.16) - 1. De verkoper is gehouden de koopprijs te voldoen in handen van de notaris, te wiens overstaan de openbare verkoop heeft plaatsgevonden of door wie de akte van overdracht ingevolge de onderhandse verkoop is verleden. De kosten van de executie worden uit de koopprijs voldaan.

- 2. Wanneer geen hypotheken van een ander dan de verkoper zijn ingeschreven en geen schuldeiser op het goed of of op de koopprijs beslag heeft gelegd of zijn vordering ontleent aan artikel 264 lid 7, en evenmin door de executie een beperkt recht op het goed vervalt, draagt de notaris aan de verkoper uit de netto-opbrengst van het goed af hetgeen aan deze blijkens een door hem aan de notaris te verstrekken verklaring krachtens zijn door hypotheek verzekerde vordering of vorderingen toekomt; het overschot keert de notaris uit aan hem wiens goed is verkocht.

- 3. Zijn er meer hypotheekhouders of zijn er schuldeisers of beperkt gerechtigden als in het vorige lid bedoeld, dan stort de notaris de netto-opbrengst onverwijld bij een door hem aangewezen bewaarder die aan de eisen van artikel 445 van het Wetboek van Burgerlijke Rechtsvordering voldoet. Wanneer het goed door de eerste hypotheekhouder is verkocht en deze vóór of op de betaaldag aan de notaris een verklaring heeft overgelegd van hetgeen hem van de opbrengst toekomt krachtens de door de eerste hypotheek verzekerde vordering of andere vorderingen die eveneens door hypotheek zijn verzekerd en in rang onmiddellijk bij de eerste aansluiten, met vermelding van schuldeisers wier vordering boven de zijne rang neemt, blijft de storting nochtans achterwege voor hetgeen aan de verkoper blijkens deze verklaring toekomt, en keert de notaris dit aan deze uit. Deze verklaring moet zijn voorzien van een aantekening van de president van de rechtbank binnen welker rechtsgebied het verbonden goed zich geheel of grotendeels bevindt, inhoudende dat hij de verklaring heeft goedgekeurd, nadat hem summierlijk van de juistheid ervan is gebleken. Tegen de goedkeuring is geen hogere voorziening toegelaten.

- 4. Ingeval de notaris ernstige redenen heeft om te vermoeden dat de hem ingevolge de leden 2 of 3 verstrekte verklaring onjuist is, kan hij de uitkering aan de hypotheekhouder opschorten tot de in lid 3 aangewezen president op vordering van de meest gerede partij of op verlangen van de notaris omtrent de uitkering heeft beslist.

- 5. Wanneer de hypotheekhouders, de schuldeisers die op het goed of op de koopprijs beslag hebben gelegd of hun vordering ontlenen aan artikel 264 lid 7, de beperkt gerechtigden wier recht door de executie vervalt, alsmede degene wiens goed is verkocht het vóór de betaaldag omtrent de verdeling van de te storten som eens zijn geworden, blijft de storting achterwege en keert de notaris aan ieder het hem toekomende uit.

- 6. Voor zover de verplichtingen welke ingevolge dit artikel op de notaris rusten, niet worden nagekomen, is de Staat jegens belanghebbenden voor de daaruit voor hen voortvloeiende schade met de notaris hoofdelijk aansprakelijk.

- 7. Van het in dit artikel bepaalde kan in de verkoopvoorwaarden niet worden afgeweken.

1. The seller must pay the purchase price to the notary before whom the public auction has taken place or by whom the deed of transfer pursuant to the private sale has been drafted. The costs of execution are paid from the purchase price.

2. Where no hypothecs other than the seller's have been registered, and where no creditor has seized the property or purchase price, or derives his claim from article 264 paragraph 7, and where no dismembered right upon the property nor a right of a lessee has been extinguished by the execution, the notary pays to the seller, from the net proceeds of the property, all that is owed to the seller pursuant to his claim or claims secured by hypothec, and that appears in a declaration to be given by the seller to the notary; the notary pays the balance to the person whose property has been sold.

3. Where there are several hypothecary creditors or where there are creditors or holders of dismembered rights referred to in the preceding paragraph, the notary deposits the net proceeds without delay with a custodian whom he designates and who meets the requirements of article 445 of the Code of Civil Procedure. Nevertheless, the deposit is not made and the notary pays to the seller the amount owed to him as it appears from the declaration mentioned below where the seller is the first hypothecary creditor; this creditor must have submitted to the notary, before or on the day of payment, a declaration of the amount owed to him from the proceeds pursuant to the claim secured by the first hypothec or pursuant to other claims which have also been secured by hypothec immediately following the first one in rank, together with a list of creditors whose claims rank before his. This declaration must bear the endorsement of the president of the district court in whose jurisdiction the encumbered property is wholly or largely situated, stating that he has approved the declaration after a summary verification of its accuracy. No appeal lies from the approval.

1. Le vendeur est tenu de verser le prix de vente entre les mains du notaire devant qui la vente publique a eu lieu ou qui a reçu l'acte de transfert faisant suite à la vente privée. Les frais d'exécution sont acquittés sur le prix de vente.

2. Lorsqu'aucune hypothèque autre que celle du vendeur n'est inscrite, qu'aucun créancier n'a saisi le bien ou le prix de vente, ni ne tient sa créance du paragraphe 7 de l'article 264 et qu'aucun droit démembré grevant le bien ni aucun droit d'un preneur ne s'éteint par l'exécution forcée, le notaire remet au vendeur la part du produit net correspondant à la somme de ses créances hypothécaires d'après une déclaration que celui-ci lui fournit; le notaire remet le solde à celui dont le bien a été vendu.

3. Lorsqu'il y a plusieurs créanciers hypothécaires, ou bien des créanciers ou des titulaires de droits démembrés visés au paragraphe précédent, le notaire verse sans délai le produit net entre les mains d'un dépositaire par lui désigné qui satisfait aux exigences de l'article 445 du Code de procédure civile. Lorsque le bien a été vendu par le créancier hypothécaire de premier rang et que celui-ci remet au notaire, avant ou le jour même de paiement, une déclaration de ce qui lui revient en vertu de la créance hypothécaire de premier rang ou en vertu d'autres créances hypothécaires dont le rang suit immédiatement, en indiquant alors les créanciers dont les créances prennent rang avant la sienne, il n'y a pas lieu de verser la somme qui revient au vendeur d'après cette déclaration; le notaire la lui remet. La déclaration doit comporter une mention du président du tribunal de première instance dans le ressort duquel se trouve le bien grevé en entier ou en grande partie, indiquant qu'il l'a approuvée, après vérification sommaire de son exactitude. L'approbation est insusceptible d'appel.

4. If the notary has serious reasons to believe that the declaration given to him pursuant to paragraphs 2 or 3 is inaccurate, he may suspend payment to the hypothecary creditor until the president referred to in paragraph 3 has ruled on the payment upon the demand of any interested party or of the notary.

5. Where the hypothecary creditors, the creditors who have seized the property or the purchase price or who derive their claim from article 264 paragraph 7, the holders of dismembered rights whose rights are extinguished by the execution as well as the person whose property has been sold have agreed, before the day of payment, upon the distribution of the sum to be deposited, the deposit is not made and the notary pays to each what is owed to him.

6. To the extent that the notary breaches the obligations which rest upon him pursuant to this article, the State and the notary are solidarily liable to interested parties for the damage resulting therefrom.

7. The conditions of sale may not derogate from the provisions of this article.

4. Si le notaire a des motifs graves de soupçonner que la déclaration qui lui a été remise conformément aux paragraphes 2 ou 3 est inexacte, il peut suspendre le versement au créancier hypothécaire jusqu'à ce que, à la demande de la partie la plus diligente ou du notaire, le président visé au paragraphe 3 ait statué.

5. Lorsque, avant le jour du paiement, la distribution de la somme à verser fait l'objet d'un accord entre les créanciers hypothécaires, les créanciers qui ont saisi le bien ou le prix de vente, ou qui tiennent leur créance du paragraphe 7 de l'article 264, les titulaires de droits démembrés qui s'éteignent par l'exécution forcée, ainsi que celui dont le bien a été vendu, le versement n'a pas lieu et le notaire remet à chacun ce qui lui revient.

6. Dans la mesure où il y a inexécution des obligations incombant au notaire en vertu du présent article, l'État et le notaire sont solidairement responsables envers les personnes intéressées du préjudice en résultant.

7. On ne peut déroger, dans les conditions de vente, aux dispositions du présent article.

Art. 271. (3.9.4.17) - 1. Na de betaling van de koopprijs zijn alle in het vijfde lid van het vorige artikel genoemde belanghebbenden bevoegd een gerechtelijke rangregeling te verzoeken om tot verdeling van de opbrengst te komen overeenkomstig de formaliteiten die in het Wetboek van Burgerlijke Rechtsvordering zijn voorgeschreven.
- 2. Indien deze belanghebbenden met betrekking tot de verdeling alsnog tot overeenstemming komen en daarvan door een authentieke akte doen blijken aan de bewaarder bij wie de opbrengst is gestort, dan keert deze aan ieder het hem volgens deze akte toekomende uit.

1. After payment of the purchase price, all interested parties mentioned in the fifth paragraph of the preceding article are entitled to request a judicial ranking in order to proceed to the distribution of the proceeds according to the formalities prescribed in the Code of Civil Procedure.

2. If these interested parties as yet reach an agreement regarding the distribution and submit proof thereof in the form of an authentic deed to the custodian with whom the proceeds have been deposited, the latter pays to each what is owed to him according to the deed.

1. Après le paiement du prix de vente, tout intéressé mentionné au cinquième paragraphe de l'article précédent peut requérir une collocation judiciaire pour qu'il soit procédé à une distribution du produit suivant les formalités prescrites par le Code de procédure civile.

2. Si, après cette requête, les intéressés parviennent encore à une entente sur la répartition et en apportent la preuve par acte authentique au dépositaire entre les mains duquel a été versé le produit, celui-ci remet à chacun ce qui lui revient d'après l'acte.

Art. 272. (3.9.4.18) - 1. Een verkoper die van de notaris betaling heeft ontvangen, is verplicht desverlangd aan hem wiens goed is verkocht, en aan de schuldenaar binnen één maand na de betaling rekening en verantwoording te doen.
- 2. Een hypotheekhouder, een schuldeiser of een beperkt gerechtigde, die in de rangregeling is begrepen, kan binnen één maand na de sluiting daarvan gelijke rekening en verantwoording vragen, indien hij daarbij een rechtstreeks belang heeft.

1. A seller who has received payment from the notary must, upon demand, within one month from payment, render account to the person whose property has been sold and to the debtor.
2. A hypothecary creditor, an ordinary creditor or a holder of a dismembered right included in the ranking may, within one month from the termination thereof, also ask for the rendering of account, if he has an immediate interest in doing so.

1. Le vendeur qui a été payé par le notaire est tenu, sur demande, de rendre compte, dans le délai d'un mois, du paiement à celui dont le bien a été vendu et au débiteur.

2. Le créancier hypothécaire, le créancier chirographaire ou le titulaire d'un droit démembré compris dans la collocation, et dont l'intérêt est direct, peut de la même façon demander des comptes dans le délai d'un mois suivant l'établissement de cette collocation.

Art. 273. (3.9.4.19) - 1. Door de levering ingevolge een executoriale verkoop en de voldoening van de koopprijs gaan alle op het verkochte goed rustende hypotheken teniet en vervallen de ingeschreven beslagen, alsook de beperkte rechten die niet tegen de verkoper ingeroepen kunnen worden.
- 2. Wanneer de koper aan de president van de rechtbank binnen welker rechtsgebied het verbonden goed zich geheel of grotendeels bevindt, de bewijsstukken overlegt, dat de verkoop met inachtneming van de wettelijke voorschriften heeft plaatsgehad en dat de koopprijs in handen van de notaris is gestort, wordt hem van het tenietgaan en vervallen van de in het vorige lid bedoelde hypotheken, beperkte rechten en beslagen een verklaring verstrekt. Tegen de beschikking die een zodanige verklaring inhoudt, is geen hogere voorziening toegelaten.
- 3. De verklaring kan bij of na de levering in de registers worden ingeschreven. Zij machtigt dan de bewaarder der registers tot doorhaling van de inschrijvingen betreffende hypotheken en beslagen.

1. All hypothecs encumbering the property sold, the registered seizures and the dismembered rights which cannot be invoked against the seller, are extinguished by the delivery pursuant to a forced sale and the payment of the purchase price.
2. A declaration of the extinction of the hypothecs, dismembered rights and seizures referred to in the preceding paragraph is given to the buyer upon submission to the president of the district court in whose jurisdiction the property is wholly or largely situated of documentary

1. Toute hypothèque grevant le bien, de même que les saisies inscrites et les droits démembrés qui ne peuvent être invoqués contre le vendeur, s'éteignent par la délivrance qui suit la vente forcée et par le paiement du prix de vente.

2. L'acheteur qui remet au président du tribunal de première instance, dans le ressort duquel se trouve le bien grevé en entier ou en grande partie, les documents prouvant que la vente a eu lieu conformément aux prescriptions de la loi et que le prix de vente a été versé entre les mains du notaire se fait

evidence that the sale has taken place with due regard to the statutory rules and that the purchase price has been paid to the notary. No appeal lies from the decision containing such a declaration.
3. The declaration can be entered in the registers at the time of or after the delivery. It authorizes the registrar to cancel the entries regarding hypothecs and seizures.

remettre une déclaration constatant l'extinction des hypothèques, droits démembrés et saisies visés au paragraphe précédent. La décision comportant une telle déclaration est insusceptible d'appel.
3. La déclaration peut être inscrite sur les registres lors de la délivrance ou après celle-ci. Elle autorise le conservateur des registres à radier les inscriptions concernant les hypothèques et les saisies.

Art. 274. (3.9.4.20) - 1. Wanneer een hypotheek is tenietgegaan, is de schuldeiser verplicht aan de rechthebbende op het bezwaarde goed op diens verzoek en op diens kosten bij authentieke akte een verklaring af te geven, dat de hypotheek is vervallen. Is de vordering waarvoor de hypotheek tot zekerheid strekte met een beperkt recht bezwaard, dan rust een overeenkomstige verplichting op de beperkt gerechtigde.
- 2. Deze verklaringen kunnen in de registers worden ingeschreven. Zij machtigen dan tezamen de bewaarder tot doorhaling.
- 3. Worden de vereiste verklaringen niet afgegeven, dan is artikel 29 van overeenkomstige toepassing.
- 4. Is de hypotheek door vermenging tenietgegaan, dan wordt de bewaarder tot doorhaling gemachtigd door een daartoe strekkende verklaring, afgelegd bij authentieke akte door hem aan wie het goed toebehoort, tenzij op de vordering een beperkt recht rust.

1. Where a hypothec has been extinguished, the creditor must, at the request and at the expense of the title-holder to the encumbered property, issue him a declaration of this extinction in the form of an authentic deed. *Mutatis mutandis* the holder of a dismembered right has the same obligation where the claim secured by the hypothec is encumbered with a dismembered right.
2. These declarations can be entered in the registers. Together they authorize the registrar to cancellation.
3. Where the required declarations are not issued, article 29 applies *mutatis mutandis*.
4. Where the hypothec has been extinguished by confusion, the registrar is authorized to cancel it by a declaration to that effect made by authentic deed by the person to whom the property belongs, unless the claim is encumbered with a dismembered right.

1. Le créancier dont l'hypothèque est éteinte est tenu de remettre au titulaire du bien grevé, sur la requête et aux frais de ce dernier, une déclaration en forme authentique constatant l'extinction. Lorsque la créance hypothécaire est grevée d'un droit démembré, le titulaire de ce droit a une obligation analogue.
2. Ces déclarations peuvent être inscrites sur les registres. Ensemble, elles autorisent le conservateur à la radiation.
3. L'article 29 s'applique par analogie dans l'hypothèse où les déclarations requises ne sont pas délivrées.
4. Lorsque l'hypothèque est éteinte par la confusion, le conservateur est autorisé à la radier par une déclaration à cet effet, faite par acte authentique par celui à qui appartient le bien, à moins qu'un droit démembré ne grève la créance.

Art. 275. (3.9.4.20a) Een volmacht tot het afleggen van een verklaring als bedoeld in het vorige artikel moet schriftelijk zijn verleend.

A procuration to make a declaration referred to in the preceding article must be granted in writing.

La procuration permettant de faire une déclaration visée à l'article précédent doit être accordée par écrit.

TITEL 10 VERHAALSRECHT OP GOEDEREN

TITLE 10 THE RIGHT OF RECOURSE[1] AGAINST PROPERTY

TITRE DIXIÈME DU DROIT DE RECOUVREMENT SUR LES BIENS

AFDELING 1 Algemene bepalingen

Section 1 General provisions

Section première Dispositions générales

Art. 276. (3.10.1.1) Tenzij de wet of een overeenkomst anders bepaalt, kan een schuldeiser zijn vordering op alle goederen van zijn schuldenaar verhalen.

Unless otherwise provided by law or contract, a creditor can take recourse for his claim against all the property of his debtor.

Sauf disposition contraire de la loi ou du contrat, le créancier peut recouvrer sa créance sur tous les biens de son débiteur.

Art. 277. (3.10.1.2) - 1. Schuldeisers hebben onderling een gelijk recht om, na voldoening van de kosten van executie, uit de netto-opbrengst van de goederen van hun schuldenaar te worden voldaan naar evenredigheid van ieders vordering, behoudens de door de wet erkende redenen van voorrang. - 2. Bij overeenkomst van een schuldeiser met de schuldenaar kan worden bepaald dat zijn vordering jegens alle of bepaalde andere schuldeisers een lagere rang neemt dan de wet hem toekent.

1. Except for the causes of preference recognized by law, after payment of the costs of execution, creditors have, amongst themselves, an equal right to be paid from the net proceeds of the property of their debtor in proportion to their claims.
2. A contract between creditor and debtor may stipulate that the claim of the creditor take, in respect of all or certain other creditors, a rank lower than that granted to it by law.

1. Après acquittement des frais de l'exécution, les créanciers ont entre eux un droit égal à être payé sur le produit net des biens de leur débiteur en proportion de leurs créances, sauf les causes de préférence reconnues par la loi.

2. Par contrat entre le créancier et le son débiteur, il peut être disposé que la créance aura à l'égard de tous les autres créanciers ou de certains d'entre eux un rang inférieur à celui accordé par la loi.

[1] Essentially the "right of recourse" means the right of a creditor to seize and execute against the assets of his debtor. In civilian terminology it is often said that all the assets of a debtor form the "common pledge" of his creditors.

Art. 278. (3.10.1.3) - 1. Voorrang vloeit voort uit pand, hypotheek en voorrecht en uit de andere in de wet aangegeven gronden.
- 2. Voorrechten ontstaan alleen uit de wet. Zij rusten of op bepaalde goederen of op alle tot een vermogen behorende goederen.

1. Preference results from pledge, hypothec, privilege and other grounds provided for by law.
2. Privileges only arise from the law. They apply to specific property only or to all the property forming part of the patrimony.

1. La préférence résulte du gage, de l'hypothèque et du privilège, ainsi que d'autres causes prévues par la loi.
2. Les privilèges naissent de la loi seulement. Ils portent sur des biens déterminés ou sur tous les biens composant le patrimoine.

Art. 279. (3.10.1.3a) Pand en hypotheek gaan boven voorrecht, tenzij de wet anders bepaalt.

Unless otherwise provided for by law, pledge and hypothec rank before privileges.

Le gage et l'hypothèque prennent rang avant le privilège, à moins que la loi ne dispose autrement.

Art. 280. (3.10.1.3b) Voorrechten op bepaalde goederen hebben voorrang boven die welke op alle tot een vermogen behorende goederen rusten, tenzij de wet anders bepaalt.

Unless otherwise provided for by law, privileges upon specific property rank before those upon all the property forming part of the patrimony.

Les privilèges sur des biens déterminés prennent rang avant ceux qui grèvent tous les biens composant le patrimoine, à moins que la loi ne dispose autrement.

Art. 281. (3.10.1.3c) - 1. Onderscheiden voorrechten die op hetzelfde bepaalde goed rusten, hebben gelijke rang, tenzij de wet anders bepaalt.
- 2. De voorrechten op alle goederen worden uitgeoefend in de volgorde waarin de wet hen plaatst.

1. Unless otherwise provided for by law, different privileges upon one and the same property have equal rank.
2. Privileges upon all the property are exercised in the order in which the law ranks them.

1. Les privilèges grevant un même bien déterminé sont de rang égal, à moins que la loi ne dispose autrement.
2. Les privilèges sur l'ensemble des biens s'exercent dans l'ordre dans lequel les place la loi.

Art. 282. (3.10.1.3d) Indien door een executie een ander beperkt recht dan pand of hypotheek vervalt, omdat het niet kan worden ingeroepen tegen een pand- of hypotheekhouder of een beslaglegger op het goed, wordt aan de beperkt gerechtigde uit de netto-opbrengst van het goed, met voorrang onmiddellijk na de vorderingen van degenen tegen wie hij zijn recht niet kan inroepen, terzake van zijn schade een vergoeding uitgekeerd. De vergoeding wordt gesteld op het bedrag van de waarde die het vervallen recht, zo het bij de executie in stand zou zijn gebleven, ten tijde van de executie zou hebben gehad.

A holder of a dismembered right other than pledge or hypothec, whose right is extinguished by execution because it cannot be invoked against a pledgee, hypothecary creditor or seizor of the property, is compensated for his damage from the net proceeds of the property, by preference, immediately after the claims of those against whom he cannot invoke his right. The compensation is fixed at the amount of the value which the extinguished right would have had at the time of execution if, on that occasion, it had been maintained.

Si un droit démembré autre que le gage ou l'hypothèque, ne pouvant être invoqué ni contre le créancier gagiste ou hypothécaire ni contre le saisissant du bien, s'éteint par l'exécution forcée, il est versé au titulaire de ce droit, sur le produit net résultant de l'exécution du bien, une indemnité pour le préjudice qu'il subit; cette indemnité prend rang immédiatement après les créances de ceux contre qui il ne peut invoquer son droit. Elle est fixée au montant de la valeur qu'aurait eue le droit éteint au moment de l'exécution, s'il avait été maintenu lors de celle-ci.

AFDELING 2 Bevoorrechte vorderingen op bepaalde goederen

Section 2 Privileged claims on specific property

Section troisième Des créances privilégiées sur des biens déterminés

Art. 283. (3.10.3.2) Een voorrecht op een bepaald goed strekt zich mede uit over vorderingen tot vergoedingen die in de plaats van dat goed zijn getreden, waaronder begrepen vorderingen ter zake van waardevermindering van het goed.

A privilege upon specific property also extends to all claims for compensation which have taken the place of the property, including claims for its depreciation.

Le privilège sur un bien déterminé s'étend également aux créances en indemnisation qui se sont substituées à ce bien, celles qui en compensent la dépréciation y comprises.

Art. 284. (3.10.3.3) - 1. Een vordering tot voldoening van kosten, tot behoud van een goed gemaakt, is bevoorrecht op het goed dat aldus is behouden.
- 2. De schuldeiser kan de vordering op het goed verhalen, zonder dat hem rechten van derden op dit goed kunnen worden tegengeworpen, tenzij deze rechten na het maken van de kosten tot behoud zijn verkregen. Een na het maken van die kosten overeenkomstig artikel 237 gevestigd pandrecht kan slechts aan de schuldeiser worden tegengeworpen, indien de zaak of het toonderpapier in de macht van de pandhouder of een derde is gebracht. Een na het maken van die kosten overeenkomstig artikel 90 verkregen recht kan slechts aan de schuldeiser worden tegengeworpen, indien tevens aan de eisen van lid 2 van dat artikel is voldaan.
- 3. Het voorrecht heeft voorrang boven alle andere voorrechten, tenzij de vorderingen waaraan deze andere voorrechten zijn verbonden, na het maken van de kosten tot behoud zijn ontstaan.

1. A claim for recovery of costs incurred in preserving property creates a privilege upon the property so preserved.

1. La créance pour le recouvrement des frais engagés pour la conservation d'un bien donne un privilège sur le bien ainsi conservé.

2. The creditor can take recourse against the property for the claim without the rights of third persons to this property being invoked against him, unless those rights have been acquired after the costs of preservation have been incurred. A right of pledge established according to article 237, after these costs have been incurred, cannot be invoked against the creditor, unless the thing or the document payable to bearer has been brought under the control of the pledgee or of a third person. A right which has been acquired according to article 90, after these costs have been incurred, cannot be invoked against the creditor, unless the requirements of paragraph 2 of that article have also been fulfilled.

2. Le créancier peut recouvrer sa créance sur le bien sans qu'il puisse se voir opposer les droits qu'y détiennent des tiers, à moins que ces droits n'aient été acquis après qu'ont été engagés les frais de conservation. Le droit de gage établi conformément à l'article 237, après qu'ont été engagés les frais de conservation, peut être opposé au créancier seulement si la chose ou le titre au porteur a été mis en la puissance du gagiste ou d'un tiers. Le droit acquis conformément à l'article 90, après qu'ont été engagés ces frais, n'est opposable au créancier que si les conditions du paragraphe 2 de cet article sont également remplies.

3. The privilege ranks before all other privileges, unless the claims to which these other privileges are attached have arisen after the costs of preservation have been incurred.

3. Ce privilège prend rang avant tous les autres, à moins que les créances auxquelles s'attachent ces privilèges ne soient nées après qu'ont été engagés les frais de conservation.

Art. 285. (3.10.3.5) - 1. Hij die uit hoofde van een overeenkomst tot aanneming van werk een vordering wegens bearbeiding van een zaak heeft, is deswege op die zaak bevoorrecht, mits hij persoonlijk aan de uitvoering van in de uitoefening van zijn bedrijf aangenomen werk pleegt deel te nemen dan wel een vennootschap of een rechtspersoon is, waarvan een of meer beherende vennoten of bestuurders dit plegen te doen. Het voorrecht vervalt na verloop van twee jaren sedert het ontstaan van de vordering.
- 2. Het voorrecht heeft voorrang boven een overeenkomstig artikel 237 op de zaak gevestigd pandrecht, tenzij dit recht eerst na het ontstaan van de bevoorrechte vordering is gevestigd en de zaak in de macht van de pandhouder of een derde is gebracht.

1. The person who, pursuant to a contract of enterprise, has a claim for work done on a thing, has a privilege upon this thing, provided that he usually participate personally in the performance of the work contracted for, within the framework of his business, or that it be a partnership or legal person in which one or more managing partners or directors usually do so. The privilege is extinguished two years after the claim has arisen.

1. Celui qui, en vertu d'un contrat d'entreprise, a une créance résultant de travaux effectués sur une chose a un privilège sur celle-ci, pourvu qu'il ait l'habitude de participer personnellement à l'exécution des travaux auxquels il s'est engagé dans le cadre de son entreprise; lorsque le créancier est une société ou une personne morale, il a ce privilège pourvu qu'un ou plusieurs associés gérants ou dirigeants aient cette habitude. Le privilège s'éteint dans un délai de deux ans à compter de la naissance de la créance.

2. The privilege ranks before a right of pledge established upon the thing pursuant to article 237, unless this right has been established after the privileged

2. Le privilège prend rang avant le droit de gage établi sur la chose conformément à l'article 237, à moins que ce droit ne soit postérieur à la créance privilégiée et que la

claim has arisen and the thing has been brought under the control of the pledgee or of a third person.

chose n'ait été mise en la puissance du gagiste ou d'un tiers.

Art. 286. (3.10.3.6) - 1. De door een appartementseigenaar of een vruchtgebruiker van een appartementsrecht aan de gezamenlijke appartementseigenaars of de vereniging van eigenaars verschuldigde, in het lopende of het voorafgaande kalenderjaar opeisbaar geworden bijdragen zijn bevoorrecht op het appartementsrecht.
- 2. In geval van bearbeiding van een gebouw dat in appartementen is verdeeld, rust het voorrecht van artikel 285 op ieder appartement voor het bedrag, waarvoor de eigenaar van dat appartement aansprakelijk is.
- 3. Bij samenloop van het voorrecht van het eerste lid en dat van artikel 285 heeft het laatstgenoemde voorrang.

1. There is a privilege upon an apartment right for the contributions which the owner of an apartment or a usufructuary of an apartment right owes to the joint owners of the apartments or to the association of owners, and which have become exigible during the current or preceding calendar year.
2. In the event of work being done upon a building which has been divided into apartments, the privilege referred to in article 5 rests upon each apartment for the amount for which the owner of that apartment is responsible.
3. In the event of concurrence of the privileges of the first paragraph and of article 5, the latter prevails.

1. Donnent un privilège sur un droit d'appartement[1] les cotisations que le propriétaire de l'appartement ou l'usufruitier du droit sur l'appartement doit aux propriétaires d'appartements conjointement ou à l'association des propriétaires, et qui sont devenues exigibles au cours de l'année civile courante ou de la précédente.
2. Dans le cas de travaux effectués à un immeuble divisé par appartements, le privilège visé à l'article 5 porte sur chaque appartement pour la somme dont son propriétaire est responsable.
3. En cas de concurrence entre le privilège visé au paragraphe 1 et celui qui est visé à l'article 5, ce dernier a préséance.

Art. 287. (3.10.3.15) - 1. De vordering tot vergoeding van schade is bevoorrecht op de vordering die de schuldenaar uit hoofde van verzekering van zijn aansprakelijkheid op de verzekeraar mocht hebben, voor zover deze vordering de verplichting tot vergoeding van deze schade betreft.
- 2. De schuldeiser kan zijn vordering op de vordering waarop het voorrecht rust verhalen, zonder dat hem rechten van derden op deze laatste vordering kunnen worden tegengeworpen.

1. The claim for compensation of damage creates a privilege upon any claim which the debtor might have against the insurer pursuant to liability insurance, to the extent that this claim relates to the obligation to compensate the damage.
2. The creditor can take recourse for his claim against the claim on which the privilege rests, without the rights of third persons to this latter claim being invoked against him.

1. La créance en indemnisation d'un préjudice comporte un privilège sur la créance que pourrait avoir le débiteur contre l'assureur en vertu d'une assurance de responsabilité, dans la mesure où cette dernière créance touche l'obligation de réparer le préjudice.
2. Le créancier peut recouvrer sur cette créance ce qui lui est dû, sans que puissent lui être opposés les droits des tiers sur celle-ci.

---

1 Voir Livre V, titre 10.

AFDELING 3 Bevoorrechte vorderingen op alle goederen

Section 3
Privileged claims on all property

Section troisiième
Des créances privilégiées sur l'ensemble des biens

Art. 288. (3.10.4.1) De bevoorrechte vorderingen op alle goederen zijn de vorderingen ter zake van:

a. de kosten van de aanvraag tot faillietverklaring, doch alleen ter zake van het faillissement dat op de aanvraag is uitgesproken, alsmede van de kosten, door een schuldeiser gemaakt, ter verkrijging van vereffening buiten faillissement;

b. de kosten van lijkbezorging, voor zover zij in overeenstemming zijn met een stand en het fortuin van de overledene;

c. hetgeen een arbeider, een gewezen arbeider en hun nabestaanden ter zake van reeds vervallen termijnen van pensioen van de werkgever te vorderen hebben, voor zover de vordering niet ouder is dan een jaar;

d. hetgeen waarop een arbeider, niet zijnde een bestuurder van de rechtspersoon bij wie hij in dienst is, een gewezen arbeider en hun nabestaanden ter zake van in de toekomst tot uitkering komende termijnen van toegezegd pensioen jegens de werkgever recht hebben;

e. al hetgeen een arbeider over het lopende en het voorafgaande kalenderjaar in geld op grond van de arbeidsovereenkomst van zijn werkgever te vorderen heeft, alsmede de bedragen door de werkgever aan de arbeider in verband met de beëindiging van de dienstbetrekking verschuldigd uit hoofde van de bepalingen van het Burgerlijk Wetboek betreffende de arbeidsovereenkomst.

Privileges upon all property exist for claims in respect of:

a. the costs of the petition in bankruptcy, but only for a bankruptcy declared upon this demand, as well as the costs incurred by a creditor to obtain a settlement outside bankruptcy proceedings;

b. funeral expenses to the extent that they are in accordance with the status and fortune of the decesased;

c. the amount of the claim of an employee, former employee or his relatives against the employer for arrears of pension, to the extent that the claim is not older than one year;

d. the amount of the claim of an employee, other than a director of the legal person in whose service he is, a former employee or his relatives against the employer for instalments of promised pension to which they will be entitled in the future;

Les créances privilégiées sur l'ensemble des biens sont celles relatives:

a. Aux frais d'une demande de faillite, uniquement si la faillite est prononcée à la suite de cette demande, de même qu'aux frais engagés par le créancier en vue d'obtenir une liquidation en dehors de la faillite;

b. Aux frais funéraires, dans la mesure où ils sont conformes à la situation et à l'état de fortune du défunt;

c. À la somme que peuvent réclamer à l'employeur l'employé, l'ancien employé et leurs proches parents pour les versements échus de la pension de retraite de l'employé, dans la mesure où la créance ne date pas de plus d'un an;

d. À la somme à laquelle ont droit à l'égard de l'employeur l'employé qui n'est pas dirigeant de la personne morale qui l'emploie, l'ancien employé et leurs proches parents pour les versements à échoir d'une pension de retraite promise;

e. the full amount of the claim of an employee against his employer for money owed to him pursuant to the contract of employment for the current and preceding calendar year as well as the amounts which the employer owes to the employee pursuant to the cessation of employment according to the provisions of the Civil Code pertaining to the contract of employment.

e. À tout ce que peut réclamer en argent, relativement aux années civiles courante et précédente, l'employé en vertu de son contrat de travail, de même qu'aux sommes que lui doit l'employeur en vertu des dispositions du Code civil relatives au contrat de travail à la suite de la cessation de l'emploi.

Art. 289. (3.10.4.2) - 1. Eveneens bevoorrecht op alle goederen zijn de vorderingen die zijn ontstaan uit de oplegging van de in de artikeleln 49 en 50 van het Verdrag tot oprichting van de Europese Gemeenschap voor Kolen en Staal van 18 april 1951, (Trb. 1951, 82) bedoelde heffingen en verhogingen wegens vertraging in de betaling van deze vorderingen.
2. Dit voorrecht heeft dezelfde rang als het voorrecht terzake van de vordering wegens omzetbelasting.

1. Privileges upon all property also exist for claims which have arisen from the imposition of the charges and increases for delay in the payment of these claims, as referred to in articles 49 and 50 of the Treaty Establishing the European Coal and Steel Community of April 18, 1951 (Trb. 1951, 82)[1].
2. This privilege has the same rank as that in respect of the claim for sales tax.

1. Sont également privilégiées les créances nées de l'imposition des prélèvements visés aux articles 49 et 50 du Traité instituant la Communauté européenne du charbon et de l'acier du 18 avril 1951 (Trb. 1951, 82)[2], ainsi que les augmentations en raison de retard dans le paiement de ces créances.
2. Ce privilège a le même rang que celui qui se rattache à l'impôt sur le chiffre d'affaires.

AFDELING 4 Retentierecht

Section 4
The right of retention

Section quatrième
Du droit de rétention

Art. 290. (3.10.4A.1) Retentierecht is de bevoegdheid die in de bij de wet aangegeven gevallen aan een schuldeiser toekomt, om de nakoming van een verplichting tot afgifte van een zaak aan zijn schuldenaar op te schorten totdat de vordering wordt voldaan.

The right of retention is the power which a creditor has, in the cases provided for by law, to suspend the performance of an obligation to surrender a thing to his debtor until payment of the debt.

Le droit de rétention est le pouvoir appartenant au créancier, dans les cas prévus par la loi, de suspendre l'exécution de l'obligation de remettre une chose au débiteur jusqu'à ce que la créance soit payée.

1 Trb.: *Tractatenblad*, Treaty Series.
2 Trb.: *Tractatenblad*, le journal officiel des traités.

Art. 291. (3.10.4A.2) - 1. De schuldeiser kan het retentierecht mede inroepen tegen derden die een recht op de zaak hebben verkregen, nadat zijn vordering was ontstaan en de zaak in zijn macht was gekomen.
- 2. Hij kan het retentierecht ook inroepen tegen derden met een ouder recht, indien zijn vordering voortspruit uit een overeenkomst die de schuldenaar bevoegd was met betrekking tot de zaak aan te gaan, of hij geen reden had om aan de bevoegdheid van de schuldenaar te twijfelen.

1. The creditor can also invoke the right of retention against third persons having acquired a right to the thing after the creditor's claim has arisen and the thing has come under his control.
2. He can also invoke the right of retention against third persons with a prior right, if his claim results from a contract which the debtor had the power to enter into in respect of the thing, or if the creditor had no reason to doubt such power.

1. Le créancier peut également invoquer le droit de rétention à l'égard des tiers qui ont acquis un droit sur la chose après le moment où sa créance est née et où la chose est venue en sa puissance.
2. Il peut aussi invoquer son droit de rétention contre les tiers qui ont un droit antérieur, si sa créance résulte d'un contrat que le débiteur avait le pouvoir de conclure relativement à la chose ou s'il n'avait aucune raison de douter du pouvoir de ce dernier.

Art. 292. (3.10.4A.4) De schuldeiser kan zijn vordering op de zaak verhalen met voorrang boven allen tegen wie het retentierecht kan worden ingeroepen.

The creditor can take recourse for his claim against the thing with preference over all persons against whom the right of retention can be invoked.

Le créancier peut recouvrer sa créance sur la chose de préférence à tous ceux contre qui le droit de rétention peut être invoqué.

Art. 293. (3.10.4A.4a) Het retentierecht kan mede worden uitgeoefend voor de kosten die de schuldeiser heeft moeten maken ter zake van de zorg die hij krachtens de wet ten aanzien van de zaak in acht moet nemen.

The right of retention can also be exercised for the expenses which the creditor has had to incur for the care which, pursuant to law, he must exercise in respect of the thing.

Le droit de rétention peut également être exercé pour les frais que le créancier a dû engager pour les soins que la loi l'oblige à apporter à la chose.

Art. 294. (3.10.4A.5) Het retentierecht eindigt doordat de zaak in de macht komt van de schuldenaar of de rechthebbende, tenzij de schuldeiser haar weer uit hoofde van dezelfde rechtsverhouding onder zich krijgt.

The right of retention is terminated in the event that the thing comes under the control of the debtor or the title-holder, unless the creditor regains it pursuant to the same juridical relationship.

Le droit de rétention prend fin lorsque la chose vient en la puissance du débiteur ou du titulaire de cette chose, à moins qu'elle ne revienne au créancier en vertu du même rapport juridique.

Art. 295. (3.10.4A.5a) Raakt de zaak uit de macht van de schuldeiser, dan kan hij haar opeisen onder dezelfde voorwaarden als een eigenaar.

The creditor who loses control of the thing can reclaim it under the same conditions as an owner.

Le créancier qui perd la puissance sur la chose peut la réclamer aux mêmes conditions que le propriétaire.

TITEL 11 RECHTSVORDERINGEN

TITLE 11 RIGHTS OF ACTION

TITRE ONZIÈME DES ACTIONS EN JUSTICE

Art. 296. (3.11.1) - 1. Tenzij uit de wet, uit de aard der verplichting of uit een rechtshandeling anders volgt, wordt hij die jegens een ander verplicht is iets te geven, te doen of na te laten, daartoe door de rechter, op vordering van de gerechtigde, veroordeeld.
- 2. Hij die onder een voorwaarde of een tijdsbepaling tot iets is gehouden, kan onder die voorwaarde of tijdsbepaling worden veroordeeld.

1. Unless the law, the nature of the obligation[1] or a juridical act produce a different result, the person who is obliged to give, to do or not to do something vis-à-vis another is ordered to do so by the judge upon the demand of the person to whom the obligation is owed.
2. Where the obligation is subject to a condition or a term, the judge may order its performance subject to that condition or term.

1. Le juge, à la demande du créancier[2] de l'obligation[3], condamne celui qui est obligé envers un autre à donner, faire ou ne pas faire quelque chose à exécuter cette obligation, à moins qu'il n'en résulte autrement de la loi, de la nature de l'obligation ou d'un acte juridique.
2. Celui qui est obligé sous condition ou à terme peut être condamné sous la condition ou le terme prévu.

Art. 297. (3.11.2) Indien een prestatie door tenuitvoerlegging van een executoriale titel wordt afgedwongen, heeft dit dezelfde rechtsgevolgen als die van een vrijwillige nakoming van de uit die titel blijkende verplichting tot die prestatie.

If a prestation is enforced by the execution of an executory title, this has the same juridical effect as that of voluntary performance of the obligation as it appears from that title.

Si l'exécution d'une prestation est forcée au moyen d'un titre exécutoire, elle produit des effets juridiques identiques à ceux de l'exécution volontaire de l'obligation que sous-tend ce titre.

Art. 298. (3.11.2a) Vervolgen twee of meer schuldeisers ten aanzien van één goed met elkaar botsende rechten op levering, dan gaat in hun onderlinge verhouding het oudste recht op levering voor, tenzij uit de wet,

---

1 The word "obligation" ("verplichting") in this Title has a broader meaning than the same English term (but in Dutch: "verbintenis") in Book 6. In articles 307, 317 and 323, however, "obligation" is used in the narrower, technical sense of Book 6.

2 Le néerlandais emploie «*gerechtigde*» (titulaire). La traduction littérale semble prêter à confusion.

3 Le Code néerlandais emploie partout dans ce titre, sauf aux articles 307, 317 et 323, le terme *verplichting*, distinct de *verbintenis* qui correspond au sens habituel du terme français *obligation*. *Verplichting* est un terme plus vaste qui se traduirait littéralement par *devoir*. Ce terme n'a pas en français de connotation juridique précise, raison pour laquelle le terme *obligation* a été employé.

uit de aard van hun rechten, of uit de eisen van redelijkheid en billijkheid anders voortvloeit.

Unless the law, the nature of their rights or the requirements of reasonableness and equity produce a different result, where two or more creditors pursue conflicting rights to delivery in respect of one and the same property, the oldest right to delivery has preference in their mutual relationship.

Lorsque plusieurs créanciers poursuivent, sur le même bien, des droits à la délivrance incompatibles, le droit le plus ancien a préséance dans leurs rapports réciproques, à moins qu'il n'en résulte autrement de la loi, de la nature des droits ou des exigences de la raison et de l'équité.

Art. 299. (3.11.3) - 1. Wanneer iemand niet verricht waartoe hij is gehouden, kan de rechter hem jegens wie de verplichting bestaat, op diens vordering machtigen om zelf datgene te bewerken waartoe nakoming zou hebben geleid.
- 2. Op gelijke wijze kan hij jegens wie een ander tot een nalaten is gehouden, worden gemachtigd om hetgeen in strijd met die verplichting is verricht, teniet te doen.
- 3. De kosten die noodzakelijk zijn voor de uitvoering der machtiging, komen ten laste van hem die zijn verplichting niet is nagekomen. De uitspraak waarbij de machtiging wordt verleend, kan tevens de voldoening van deze kosten op vertoon van de daartoe nodige, in de uitspraak te vermelden bescheiden gelasten.

1. Where a person does not do what he is obliged to do, the judge may, upon demand, authorize the creditor of the obligation to effectuate himself that which would have resulted from the performance.
2. Likewise the creditor of an obligation not to do can be authorized to undo what has been done in breach of the obligation.
3. The expenses which are necessary for the execution as authorized are borne by the person who has failed to perform his obligation. The judgment granting the authorization may also order the payment of these expenses, upon presentation of the documents which it declares to be required for this purpose.

1. Lorsqu'une personne n'exécute pas ce à quoi elle est obligée, le juge peut autoriser le créancier qui le demande à effectuer lui-même ce qui aurait résulté de l'exécution.
2. Le créancier d'une obligation de ne pas faire peut, de la même façon, se faire autoriser à enlever ce qui a été fait en violation de cette obligation.
3. Les dépenses qui ont dû être engagées afin d'assurer l'exécution ainsi autorisée sont à la charge du débiteur en inexécution. Le jugement accordant l'autorisation peut également ordonner le paiement de ces dépenses, sur présentation des documents qu'il requiert à cette fin.

Art. 300. (3.11.4) - 1. Is iemand jegens een ander gehouden een rechtshandeling te verrichten, dan kan, tenzij de aard van de rechtshandeling zich hiertegen verzet, de rechter op vordering van de gerechtigde bepalen dat zijn uitspraak dezelfde kracht heeft als een in wettige vorm opgemaakte akte van degene die tot de rechtshandeling gehouden is, of dat een door hem aan te wijzen vertegenwoordiger de handeling zal verrichten. Wijst de rechter een vertegenwoordiger aan, dan kan hij bepalen dat de door deze te verrichten handeling zijn goedkeuring behoeft.

- 2. Is de gedaagde gehouden om tezamen met de eiser een akte op te maken, dan kan de rechter bepalen dat zijn uitspraak in de plaats van de akte of een deel daarvan zal treden.

1. Unless it is incompatible with the nature of the juridical act, where a person must perform a juridical act toward another the judge may, upon the demand of the creditor of the obligation, determine that his judgment shall have the same force as a deed drawn up, in the form provided for by law, by the person who must perform the juridical act; or he may determine that a representative to be appointed by him will perform the act. Where the judge appoints a representative, he may determine that the act to be performed by the latter needs his approval.

2. Where the defendant must draw up a deed together with the plaintiff, the judge may determine that his judgment shall take the place of the deed or part thereof.

1. Lorsqu'une personne est obligée à l'égard d'une autre à accomplir un acte juridique, le juge peut, à la demande du créancier et si la nature de l'acte ne s'y oppose pas, déclarer que son jugement produit un effet identique à celui d'un acte qu'aurait dressé celui qui y est obligé dans les formes prévues par la loi; il peut aussi ordonner qu'un représentant qu'il désigne l'accomplira. En désignant un représentant, le juge peut décider que l'acte accompli par celui-ci soit soumis à son approbation.

2. Lorsque le défendeur et le demandeur sont tenus d'établir conjointement un acte écrit, le juge peut déclarer que son jugement en tient lieu, en tout ou partie.

Art. 301. (3.11.4a) - 1. Een uitspraak waarvan de rechter heeft bepaald dat zij in de plaats treedt van een tot levering van een registergoed bestemde akte of van een deel van een zodanige akte, kan slechts in de openbare registers worden ingeschreven, indien zij is betekend aan degene die tot de levering werd veroordeeld, en

a. in kracht van gewijsde is gegaan, of

b. uitvoerbaar bij voorraad is en een termijn van veertien dagen of zoveel korter of langer als in de uitspraak is bepaald, sedert de betekening van de uitspraak is verstreken.

- 2. Verzet, hoger beroep en cassatie moeten op straffe van niet-ontvankelijkheid binnen acht dagen na het instellen van het rechtsmiddel worden ingeschreven in de registers, bedoeld in de artikelen 85 en 433 van het Wetboek van Burgerlijke Rechtsvordering. In afwijking van artikel 81 van dat wetboek begint de verzettermijn te lopen vanaf de betekening van het vonnis aan de veroordeelde, ook als de betekening niet aan hem in persoon geschiedt.

- 3. Indien de werking van een uitspraak als bedoeld in lid 1 door de rechter aan een voorwaarde is gebonden, weigert de bewaarder de inschrijving van die uitspraak, indien niet tevens een notariële verklaring of een authentiek afschrift daarvan wordt overgelegd, waaruit van de vervulling van de voorwaarde blijkt.

1. A judgment whereby the judge has determined that it takes the place of a deed or part thereof intended to deliver registered property, cannot be entered in the public registers, unless notice of it has been served upon the person ordered to deliver, and unless

a. the judgment has become final; or

1. Lorsque le juge a décidé que le jugement tient lieu de l'acte devant servir à la délivrance d'un bien immatriculé ou d'une partie de tel acte, ce jugement ne peut être inscrit dans les registres publics que s'il a été signifié à la personne condamnée à la délivrance et

a. Qu'il soit passé en force de chose jugée, ou

b. it is provisionally enforceable and a period of fourteen days or so much longer or shorter as determined in the judgment has passed since notice of the judgment was served.
2. On pain of disallowance, opposition, appeal and cassation must be entered in the registers referred to in articles 85 and 433 of the Code of Civil Procedure within eight days from the institution of the remedy. Contrary to article 81 of that Code, the period of opposition starts to run as of service of the judgment on the person ordered to deliver, even if service is not made to him in person.
3. If the judge has made the effect of a judgment, as referred to in paragraph 1, subject to a condition, the registrar shall refuse the registration of that judgment, unless a notarial declaration or authentic copy thereof is also submitted attesting to the fulfillment of the condition.

b. Qu'il soit susceptible d'exécution provisoire et que, depuis la signification, se soit écoulé un délai de quatorze jours ou tant de plus ou de moins que prévoit le jugement.
2. L'opposition, l'appel et le pourvoi en cassation doivent, à peine d'irrecevabilité, être inscrits, dans les huit jours après avoir été formés, sur les registres visés aux articles 85 et 433 du Code de procédure civile. Par dérogation à l'article 81 de ce Code, le délai d'opposition court à compter de la signification du jugement à la personne condamnée, même si la signification ne lui est pas faite à personne.
3. Si le juge a déterminé que le jugement, visé au paragraphe premier, ne prend effet qu'une fois accomplie une condition, le conservateur refuse l'inscription du jugement s'il ne lui est pas remis également une déclaration notariée ou une copie authentique d'une telle déclaration, constatant l'accomplissement de la condition.

Art. 302. (3.11.7) Op vordering van een bij een rechtsverhouding onmiddellijk betrokken persoon spreekt de rechter omtrent die rechtsverhouding een verklaring van recht uit.

The judge renders a declaratory judgment on a juridical relationship upon the demand of the person directly concerned.

À la demande d'une personne directement intéressée à un rapport juridique, le juge rend sur celui-ci un jugement déclaratoire.

Art. 303. (3.11.8) Zonder voldoende belang komt niemand een rechtsvordering toe.

A person has no right of action where he lacks sufficient interest.

Aucune action en justice n'appartient à celui qui n'y a pas un intérêt suffisant.

Art. 304. (3.11.9) Een rechtsvordering kan niet van het recht tot welks bescherming zij dient, worden gescheiden.

A right of action cannot be severed from the right it serves to protect.

L'action en justice ne peut être séparée du droit qu'elle sert à protéger.

Art. 305. (3.11.9a) De in de voorgaande artikelen van deze titel aan de rechter toegekende bevoegdheden komen mede aan scheidsmannen toe, tenzij partijen anders zijn overeengekomen.

Unless the parties have otherwise agreed, arbitrators exercise the same powers as the ones granted to the judge in the preceding articles of this title.

Les pouvoirs reconnus au juge aux articles précédents du présent titre reviennent également aux arbitres, à moins que les parties n'en aient autrement convenu.

Art. 306. (3.11.10) Indien de wet niet anders bepaalt, verjaart een rechtsvordering door verloop van twintig jaren.

Unless otherwise provided for by law, rights of action are prescribed by twenty years.

Si la loi ne dispose pas autrement, l'action en justice se prescrit par vingt ans.

Art. 307. (3.11.11) - 1. Een rechtsvordering tot nakoming van een verbintenis uit overeenkomst tot een geven of een doen verjaart door verloop van vijf jaren na de aanvang van de dag, volgende op die waarop de vordering opeisbaar is geworden.
- 2. In geval van een verbintenis tot nakoming na onbepaalde tijd loopt de in lid 1 bedoelde termijn pas van de aanvang van de dag, volgende op die waartegen de schuldeiser heeft medegedeeld tot opeising over te gaan, en verjaart de in lid 1 bedoelde rechtsvordering in elk geval door verloop van twintig jaren na de aanvang van de dag, volgende op die waartegen de opeising, zonodig na opzegging door de schuldeiser, op zijn vroegst mogelijk was.

1. A right of action to claim the performance of a contractual obligation to give or to do is prescribed by five years from the beginning of the day following the one on which the claim has become exigible.
2. For an obligation to perform at an indeterminate time, the period referred to in paragraph 1 does not begin to run until the day following the one by which the creditor has given notice of his intention to claim performance; and, in any case the right of action referred to in paragraph 1 is prescribed by twenty years from the beginning of the day following the one on which the claim would have become exigible at its earliest, if need be after notification to that effect by the creditor.

1. L'action en exécution d'une obligation contractuelle de donner ou de faire se prescrit par cinq ans à compter du lendemain du jour où la créance est devenue exigible.

2. Dans le cas d'une obligation dont la date d'exécution est indéterminée, le délai visé au paragraphe premier court seulement à compter du début du jour qui suit celui pour lequel le créancier a communiqué son intention de l'exiger; l'action visée au paragraphe premier se prescrit dans tous les cas par vingt ans à compter du début du jour suivant celui où l'exécution pouvait être exigée pour la première fois, le cas échéant après préavis du créancier.

Art. 308. (3.11.12) Rechtsvorderingen tot betaling van renten van geldsommen, lijfrenten, dividenden, huren, pachten en voorts alles wat bij het jaar of een kortere termijn moet worden betaald, verjaren door verloop van vijf jaren na de aanvang van de dag, volgende op die waarop de vordering opeisbaar is geworden.

Rights of action for the payment of interest on sums of money, of life rents, dividends, rents[1] and furthermore rights of action for all amounts payable annually or more frequently, are prescribed by five years from the beginning of the day following the one on which the claim has become exigible.

Les actions en paiement d'intérêts sur des sommes d'argent, de rentes viagères, de dividendes, de loyers et, en outre, de tout ce qui est payable annuellement ou par période plus courte se prescrivent par cinq ans à compter du lendemain du jour où la créance est devenue exigible.

1 The Dutch text makes a distinction between "huren" and "pachten": rents in general and rents for the lease of land. See also *supra* footnote at art. 17.

Art. 309. (3.11.12a) Een rechtsvordering uit onverschuldigde betaling verjaart door verloop van vijf jaren na de aanvang van de dag, volgende op die waarop de schuldeiser zowel met het bestaan van zijn vordering als met de persoon van de ontvanger is bekend geworden en in ieder geval twintig jaren nadat de vordering is ontstaan.

A right of action for recovery of things not due is prescribed by five years from the beginning of the day following the one on which the creditor has become aware of both the existence of his claim and the person of the *accipiens*, and, in any event, by twenty years from the day the claim has arisen.

L'action en répétition de l'indu se prescrit par cinq ans à compter du lendemain du jour où le créancier a eu connaissance tant de l'existence de sa créance que de la personne qui a reçu l'indu et, dans tous les cas, par vingt ans à compter de la naissance de la créance.

Art. 310. (3.11.13) Een rechtsvordering tot vergoeding van schade of tot betaling van een bedongen boete verjaart door verloop van vijf jaren na de aanvang van de dag, volgende op die waarop de benadeelde zowel met de schade of de opeisbaarheid van de boete als met de daarvoor aansprakelijke persoon bekend is geworden, en in ieder geval door verloop van twintig jaren na de gebeurtenis waardoor de schade is veroorzaakt of de boete opeisbaar is geworden.

A right of action to compensate for damage or to pay a stipulated penalty is prescribed by five years from the beginning of the day following the one on which the victim has become aware of both the damage or the exigibility of the penalty and the person responsible therefore, and, in any case, by twenty years following the event which has caused the damage or has made the penalty exigible.

L'action en réparation de dommages ou en paiement d'une peine stipulée se prescrit par cinq ans à compter du lendemain du jour où la victime a eu connaissance tant du préjudice ou de l'exigibilité de la peine que de la personne responsable et, dans tous les cas, par vingt ans à compter de l'événement qui a causé le préjudice ou rendu la peine exigible.

Art. 311. (3.11.13aa) - 1. Een rechtsvordering tot ontbinding van een overeenkomst op grond van een tekortkoming in de nakoming daarvan of tot herstel van een tekortkoming verjaart door verloop van vijf jaren na de aanvang van de dag, volgende op die waarop de schuldeiser met de tekortkoming bekend is geworden en in ieder geval twintig jaren nadat de tekortkoming is ontstaan.
- 2. Een rechtsvordering tot ongedaanmaking als bedoeld in artikel 271 van Boek 6 verjaart door verloop van vijf jaren na de aanvang van de dag, volgende op die waarop de overeenkomst is ontbonden.

1. A right of action to set aside a contract for failure to perform it or a right of action to correct such failure is prescribed by five years from the beginning of the day following the one on which the creditor has become aware of the failure and, in any case, by twenty years from the day the failure has occurred.

1. L'action en résiliation d'un contrat pour inexécution ou en correction d'un manquement dans l'exécution se prescrit par cinq ans à compter du lendemain du jour où le créancier a eu connaissance du manquement et, dans tous les cas, par vingt ans à compter de la survenance de l'inexécution.

2. A right of action to undo as referred to in article 271 of Book 6 is prescribed by five years from the beginning of the day following the one on which the contract has been set aside.

2. L'action en anéantissement visée à l'article 271 du Livre sixième se prescrit par cinq ans à compter du début du jour suivant celui de la résiliation du contrat.

Art. 312. (3.11.13ab) Rechtsvorderingen terzake van een tekortkoming in de nakoming, alsmede die tot betaling van wettelijke of bedongen rente en die tot afgifte van vruchten, verjaren, behoudens stuiting of verlenging, niet later dan de rechtsvordering tot nakoming van de hoofdverplichting of, zo de tekortkoming vatbaar is voor herstel, de rechtsvordering tot herstel van de tekortkoming.

Rights of action for failure in performance, for payment of legal or conventional interest or for the delivery of fruits are, save interruption or extension, prescribed no later than the right of action for the performance of the principal obligation, or, where the failure is susceptible of correction, no later than the right of action to claim correction of the failure.

Les actions au sujet d'un manquement dans l'exécution, de même que les actions en paiement d'intérêts légaux ou conventionnels ou en remise de fruits, se prescrivent, sauf interruption ou prolongation, pas plus tard que l'action en exécution de l'obligation principale ou, lorsque l'inexécution est susceptible de correction, que l'action en correction.

Art. 313. (3.11.15) Indien de wet niet anders bepaalt, begint de termijn van verjaring van een rechtsvordering tot nakoming van een verplichting om te geven of te doen met de aanvang van de dag, volgende op die waarop de onmiddellijke nakoming kan worden gevorderd.

Unless otherwise provided for by law, the prescription period of a right of action for the performance of an obligation to give or to do begins to run at the beginning of the day following the one on which the immediate performance can be claimed.

Si la loi ne dispose pas autrement, le délai de prescription d'une action en exécution d'une obligation de donner ou de faire court à compter du lendemain du jour où l'exécution immédiate peut être exigée.

Art. 314. (3.11.15a) - 1. De termijn van verjaring van een rechtsvordering tot opheffing van een onrechtmatige toestand begint met de aanvang van de dag, volgende op die waarop de onmiddellijke opheffing van die toestand gevorderd kan worden.

- 2. De termijn van verjaring van een rechtsvordering strekkende tot beëindiging van het bezit van een niet-rechthebbende begint met de aanvang van de dag, volgende op die waarop een niet-rechthebbende bezitter is geworden of de onmiddellijke opheffing gevorderd kon worden van de toestand waarvan diens bezit de voortzetting vormt.

1. The prescription period of a right of action to terminate an unlawful situation begins to run at the beginning of the day following the one on which the immediate termination of that situation can be claimed.

1. La prescription de l'action visant à faire cesser une situation illégale court à compter du lendemain du jour où l'on peut en demander la cessation immédiate.

2. The prescription period of a right of action to terminate the possession of a non-title-holder begins to run at the beginning of the day following the one on which the non-title-holder has become possessor or on which the immediate termination of the situation of which his possession forms the continuation could be claimed.

2. La prescription d'une action visant à faire cesser la possession d'un bien par celui qui n'en est pas le titulaire court à compter du début du jour suivant celui où la possession a commencé ou celui où l'on pouvait demander la cessation immédiate de la situation dont la possession constitue la suite.

Art. 315. (3.11.15b) De termijn van verjaring van een rechtsvordering tot opeising van een nalatenschap begint met de aanvang van de dag, volgende op die van het overlijden van de erflater.

The prescription period of a right of action to claim a succession begins to run at the beginning of the day following the one of the death of the *de cujus*.

La prescription de l'action en réclamation de succession court à compter du lendemain du jour du décès du défunt.

Art. 316. (3.11.16) - 1. De verjaring van een rechtsvordering wordt gestuit door het instellen van een eis, alsmede door iedere andere daad van rechtsvervolging van de zijde van de gerechtigde, die in de vereiste vorm geschiedt.
- 2. Leidt een ingestelde eis niet tot toewijzing, dan is de verjaring slechts gestuit, indien binnen zes maanden, nadat het geding door het in kracht van gewijsde gaan van een uitspraak of op andere wijze is geëindigd, een nieuwe eis wordt ingesteld en deze alsnog tot toewijzing leidt. Wordt een daad van rechtsvervolging ingetrokken, dan stuit zij de verjaring niet.
- 3. De verjaring van een rechtsvordering wordt ook gestuit door een handeling, strekkende tot verkrijging van een bindend advies, mits van die handeling met bekwame spoed mededeling wordt gedaan aan de wederpartij en zij tot verkrijging van een bindend advies leidt. Is dit laatste niet het geval, dan is het vorige lid van overeenkomstige toepassing.

1. Prescription of a right of action is interrupted by the institution of an action or by any other act of judicial recourse instituted in the required form by the person entitled to do so.
2. Where an action which has been instituted is not upheld, prescription is not interrupted, unless, within six months after the final judgment or other termination of the case, a new action is instituted and is as yet upheld. Where an act of judicial recourse is withdrawn, prescription is not interrupted.

1. La prescription d'une action est interrompue par l'intention d'une action en justice par le titulaire, ainsi que par tout autre recours en justice qu'il exerce dans la forme requise.
2. Lorsque l'action n'est pas accueillie, la prescription est interrompue seulement si, dans les six mois après que le litige a pris fin par un jugement qui a force de chose jugée ou autrement, une nouvelle action est intentée qui, elle, est accueillie. Lorsqu'un recours en justice est abandonné, il n'interrompt pas la prescription.

3. Prescription of a right of action is also interrupted by an act to obtain a binding opinion, provided that the other party is expeditiously notified of it and that a binding opinion actually results. Where this is not the case the preceding paragraph applies *mutatis mutandis*.

3. La prescription est également interrompue par un acte visant l'obtention d'un avis liant les parties[1], pourvu que l'autre partie en soit notifiée promptement et que l'avis soit effectivement donné. Dans le cas contraire, le paragraphe précédent s'applique par analogie.

Art. 317. (3.11.17) - 1. De verjaring van een rechtsvordering tot nakoming van een verbintenis wordt gestuit door een schriftelijke aanmaning of door een schriftelijke mededeling waarin de schuldeiser zich ondubbelzinnig zijn recht op nakoming voorbehoudt.
- 2. De verjaring van andere rechtsvorderingen wordt gestuit door een schriftelijke aanmaning, indien deze binnen zes maanden wordt gevolgd door een stuitingshandeling als in het vorige artikel omschreven.

1. Prescription of a right of action to claim performance of an obligation is interrupted by a written warning or by a written communication in which the creditor unequivocally reserves his right to performance.
2. Prescription of other rights of action is interrupted by a written warning followed within six months by an act of interruption as described in the preceding article.

1. La prescription de l'action en exécution d'une obligation est interrompue par une sommation écrite ou par une communication écrite dans laquelle le créancier réserve sans équivoque son droit à l'exécution.

2. La prescription des autres actions est interrompue par une sommation écrite, si elle est suivie dans les six mois par un acte d'interruption tel qu'il est décrit à l'article précédent.

Art. 318. (3.11.18) Erkenning van het recht tot welks bescherming een rechtsvordering dient, stuit de verjaring van de rechtsvordering tegen hem die het recht erkent.

Acknowledgment of the right whose protection is served by a right of action interrupts the prescription of the right of action as against the person who acknowledges the right.

La reconnaissance d'un droit que sert à protéger une action interrompt la prescription de l'action à l'égard de l'auteur de la reconnaissance.

Art. 319. (3.11.18a) - 1. Door stuiting van de verjaring van een rechtsvordering, anders dan door het instellen van een eis die door toewijzing wordt gevolgd, begint een nieuwe verjaringstermijn te lopen met de aanvang van de volgende dag. Is een bindend advies gevraagd en verkregen, dan begint de nieuwe verjaringstermijn te lopen met de aanvang van de dag, volgende op die waarop het bindend advies is uitgebracht.
- 2. De nieuwe verjaringstermijn is gelijk aan de oorspronkelijke, doch niet langer dan vijf jaren. Niettemin treedt de verjaring in geen geval op een eerder tijdstip in dan waarop ook de oorspronkelijke termijn zonder stuiting zou zijn verstreken.

---

[1] Cette institution, qui vient de la pratique et est acceptée par les tribunaux, vise à soumettre un différend sur l'interprétation du contrat à l'avis d'un tiers, à l'avis duquel les parties se soumettent d'avance. L'institution est moins formelle que l'arbitrage et en diffère notamment en ce qu'en cas d'inexécution de l'avis un litige sur le fond peut s'engager devant les tribunaux, alors que, dans le cas de l'arbitrage, les tribunaux doivent homologuer la décision arbitrale pour qu'elle devienne exécutoire.

1. The interruption of prescription of a right of action otherwise than by the institution of an action which is upheld starts a new prescription period as of the beginning of the following day. Where a binding opinion has been requested and obtained, the new prescription period begins to run at the beginning of the day following the one on which the binding opinion has been rendered.
2. The new prescription period is equal to the original one but may not exceed five years. Nevertheless, the prescription is in no event completed until the time when the original period without interruption would have expired.

1. L'interruption de la prescription d'une action, autrement que par l'exercice d'une action en justice qui est ultérieurement accueillie, fait courir une nouvelle prescription à compter du lendemain. Dans le cas d'une demande et de l'obtention d'un avis liant les parties, cette nouvelle prescription court à compter du lendemain du jour où l'avis a été donné.

2. Le délai de la prescription nouvelle est identique à celui de l'ancienne, mais en aucun cas ne dépasse cinq ans. Néanmoins, la prescription n'est en aucun cas acquise avant que, à défaut d'interruption, le délai original ne soit également écoulé.

Art. 320. (3.11.19) Wanneer een verjaringstermijn zou aflopen tijdens het bestaan van een verlengingsgrond of binnen zes maanden na het verdwijnen van een zodanige grond, loopt de termijn voort totdat zes maanden na het verdwijnen van die grond zijn verstreken.

Where a prescription period would otherwise expire during the existence of a cause of extension or within six months after the disappearance of such a cause, the period continues to run for six months from the disappearance of this cause.

Dans le cas où la prescription s'écoulerait alors qu'il existe une cause de prolongation ou dans les six mois de sa disparition, le délai est prolongé jusqu'au moment où se sont écoulés six mois à compter de la disparition de cette cause de prolongation.

Art. 321. (3.11.20) - 1. Een grond voor verlenging van de verjaring bestaat:
a. tussen niet van tafel en bed gescheiden echtgenoten;
b. tussen een wettelijke vertegenwoordiger en de onbekwame die hij vertegenwoordigt;
c. tussen een bewindvoerder en de rechthebbende voor wie hij het bewind voert, ter zake van vorderingen die dit bewind betreffen;
d. tussen rechtspersonen en haar bestuurders;
e. tussen een beneficiair aanvaarde nalatenschap en een erfgenaam;
f. tussen de schuldeiser en zijn schuldenaar die opzettelijk het bestaan van de schuld of de opeisbaarheid daarvan verborgen houdt.
- 2. De onder b en c genoemde gronden voor verlenging duren voort totdat de eindrekening van de wettelijke vertegenwoordiger of de bewindvoerder is gesloten.

1. There is cause for extension of prescription:
a. between spouses not separated from bed and board;
b. between a legal representative and the incapable person whom he represents;

1. Il y a cause de prolongation de prescription:
a. Entre des époux non séparés de corps;
b. Entre le représentant légal et l'incapable qu'il représente;

c. between an administrator and the beneficiary for whom he administers with respect to claims concerning the administration;
d. between legal persons and their directors;
e. between a succession accepted under the benefit of inventory and an heir;
f. between the creditor and a debtor who deliberately hides the existence of the debt or its exigibility.
2. The causes of extension referred to *sub* b and c continue until the final account of the legal representative or administrator has been closed.

c. Entre l'administrateur et le bénéficiaire de l'administration, relativement aux créances touchant celle-ci;
d. Entre la personne morale et ses dirigeants;
e. Entre la succession acceptée sous bénéfice d'inventaire et un héritier;
f. Entre le créancier et son débiteur qui délibérément cache l'existence de la dette ou son exigibilité.
2. Les causes de prolongation mentionnées aux points b. et c. continuent à exister jusqu'à la fermeture du compte que rend le représentant légal ou l'administrateur.

Art. 322. (3.11.20a) - 1. De rechter mag niet ambtshalve het middel van verjaring toepassen.
- 2. Afstand van verjaring geschiedt door een verklaring van hem die de verjaring kan inroepen.
- 3. Voordat de verjaring voltooid is, kan geen afstand van verjaring worden gedaan.

1. The judge may not *ex officio* apply the defence resulting from prescription.
2. Prescription may be renounced by a declaration of the person who can invoke it.
3. There can be no renunciation of prescription until its completion.

1. Le juge ne peut appliquer d'office le moyen de la prescription.
2. Celui qui peut se prévaloir d'une prescription acquise l'abandonne par une déclaration à cet effet.
3. On ne peut abandonner une prescription avant qu'elle ne soit acquise.

Art. 323. (3.11.20b) - 1. Door voltooiing van de verjaring van de rechtsvordering tot nakoming van een verbintenis gaan de pand- of hypotheekrechten die tot zekerheid daarvan strekken, teniet.
- 2. Nochtans verhindert de verjaring niet dat het pandrecht op het verbonden goed wordt uitgeoefend, indien dit bestaat in een roerende zaak of een recht aan toonder of order en deze zaak of het toonder- of orderpapier in de macht van de pandhouder of een derde is gebracht.
- 3. De rechtsvordering tot nakoming van een verbintenis tot zekerheid waarvan een hypotheek strekt, verjaart niet voordat twintig jaren zijn verstreken na de aanvang van de dag volgend op die waarop de hypotheek aan de verbintenis is verbonden.

1. The completion of the prescription period of the right of action to claim performance of an obligation extinguishes the rights of pledge and hypothec securing it.
2. Nevertheless, the prescription does not prevent the right of pledge from being exercised against the encumbered

1. La prescription d'une action en exécution d'une obligation met fin aux droits de gage et d'hypothèque qui la garantissent.
2. Néanmoins, la prescription n'empêche pas l'exercice du droit de gage sur le bien grevé qui consiste en une chose mobilière ou

property if the property consists of a moveable thing or a right payable to bearer or order, and if this thing or the document payable to bearer or order has been brought under the control of the pledgee or a third party.

en un droit au porteur ou à ordre et que la chose ou le titre au porteur ou à ordre a été placé en la puissance du créancier gagiste ou d'un tiers.

3. The right of action to claim performance of an obligation secured by hypothec is not prescribed until twenty years from the beginning of the day following the one on which the hypothec has been attached to the obligation.

3. L'action en exécution d'une obligation garantie par hypothèque ne se prescrit pas avant vingt ans à compter du lendemain du jour où l'hypothèque est venue s'attacher à l'obligation.

Art. 324. (3.11.20c) - 1. De bevoegdheid tot tenuitvoerlegging van een rechterlijke of arbitrale uitspraak verjaart door verloop van twintig jaren na de aanvang van de dag, volgende op die van de uitspraak, of, indien voor tenuitvoerlegging daarvan vereisten zijn gesteld waarvan de vervulling niet afhankelijk is van de wil van degene die de uitspraak heeft verkregen, na de aanvang van de dag, volgende op die waarop deze vereisten zijn vervuld.
- 2. Wordt vóórdat de verjaring is voltooid, door een der partijen ter aantasting van de ten uitvoer te leggen veroordeling een rechtsmiddel of een eis ingesteld, dan begint de termijn eerst met de aanvang van de dag, volgende op die waarop het geding daarover is geëindigd.
- 3. De verjaringstermijn bedraagt vijf jaren voor wat betreft hetgeen ingevolge de uitspraak bij het jaar of kortere termijn moet worden betaald.
- 4. Voor wat betreft renten, boeten, dwangsommen en andere bijkomende veroordelingen, treedt de verjaring, behoudens stuiting of verlenging, niet later in dan de verjaring van de bevoegdheid tot tenuitvoerlegging van de hoofdveroordeling.

1. The power to execute forceably a judicial or arbitral decision is prescribed by twenty years from the beginning of the day following the decision or, if conditions have been attached to execution, the fulfilment of which does not depend on the will of the person who has obtained the decision, from the beginning of the day following the one on which these conditions have been fulfilled.

1. Le droit d'obtenir l'exécution forcée d'une décision judiciaire ou arbitrale se prescrit par vingt ans à compter du lendemain du jour de la décision, ou, si l'exécution a été soumise à des conditions dont l'accomplissement ne dépend pas de la volonté de celui qui a obtenu la décision, à compter du lendemain du jour où ces conditions sont accomplies.

2. Where, before the completion of the prescription period, a legal recourse or action is instituted by one of the parties to attack the decision to be executed, the period does not begin to run until the beginning of the day following the one on which the proceedings relating thereto have been terminated.

2. Lorsque, avant que la prescription ne soit acquise, l'une des parties attaque la condamnation au moyen d'une action en justice ou d'une voie de recours, la prescription ne court qu'à compter du lendemain du jour de la fin du litige.

3. Payments to be made annually or more frequently pursuant to the decision are prescribed by five years.

3. La prescription est de cinq ans pour les sommes que la décision déclare payables annuellement ou par période plus courte.

4. Except for interruption or extension, the prescription of judicial orders for interest, penalties, forfeitures[1] and other accessory judicial orders takes place no later than the prescription of the power to execute forceably the principal judicial order.

4. Les intérêts, peines, astreintes et autres condamnations accessoires se prescrivent, sauf interruption ou prolongation, dans un délai ne pouvant dépasser celui qui s'applique au droit d'obtenir l'exécution forcée de la condamnation principale.

Art. 325. (3.11.20d) - 1. Op de verjaring van het vorige artikel zijn de artikelen 319-323 van overeenkomstige toepassing.
- 2. De verjaring van het vorige artikel wordt gestuit door:
a. betekening van de uitspraak of schriftelijke aanmaning;
b. erkenning van de in de uitspraak vastgestelde verplichting;
c. iedere daad van tenuitvoerlegging, mits daarvan binnen de door de wet voorgeschreven tijd of, bij gebreke van zodanig voorschrift, met bekwame spoed mededeling aan de wederpartij wordt gedaan.

1. Articles 319 - 323 apply *mutatis mutandis* to the prescription of the preceding article.
2. The prescription of the preceding article is interrupted by:
a. service of the decision or written warning;
b. acknowledgment of the obligation determined in the decision;
c. any act of execution, provided that the other party is notified of it within the period provided for by law or, in the absence of such a provision, expeditiously.

1. Les articles 319 à 323 s'appliquent par analogie à la prescription prévue à l'article précédent.
2. La prescription prévue à l'article précédent est interrompue:
a. Par la signification de la décision ou par une sommation écrite;
b. Par la reconnaissance de l'obligation établie par la décision;
c. Par tout acte d'exécution forcée, pourvu que communication en soit faite à l'autre partie dans le délai prévu par la loi ou, à défaut, promptement.

Art. 326. (3.11.21) Buiten het vermogensrecht vinden de voorafgaande artikelen overeenkomstige toepassing, voor zover de aard van de betrokken rechtsverhouding zich daartegen niet verzet.

The preceding articles apply *mutatis mutandis* to areas of the law other than patrimonial law to the extent that they are not incompatible with the nature of the juridical relationship involved.

Les articles précédents s'appliquent par analogie au droit autre que patrimonial, dans la mesure où la nature du rapport juridique ne s'y oppose pas.

[1] "Forfeiture" is a somewhat awkward translation of the Dutch term "dwangsom" or the French term "astreinte"; it is a judicially imposed penalty to enforce indirectly an obligation to do or not to do; the sum "forfeited" for non-compliance with the order is payable to the creditor of the obligation.

BOEK 5
ZAKELIJKE RECHTEN

BOOK 5
REAL RIGHTS

LIVRE CINQIÈME
DES DROITS RÉELS

TITEL 1 EIGENDOM IN HET ALGEMEEN

TITLE 1 OWNERSHIP IN GENERAL

TITRE PREMIER DE LA PROPRIÉTÉ EN GÉNÉRAL

Art. 1. (5.1.1) - 1. Eigendom is het meest omvattende recht dat een persoon op een zaak kan hebben.
- 2. Het staat de eigenaar met uitsluiting van een ieder vrij van de zaak gebruik te maken, mits dit gebruik niet strijdt met rechten van anderen en de op wettelijke voorschriften en regels van ongeschreven recht gegronde beperkingen daarbij in acht worden genomen.
- 3. De eigenaar van de zaak wordt, behoudens rechten van anderen, eigenaar van de afgescheiden vruchten.

1. Ownership is the most comprehensive right which a person can have in a thing.
2. To the exclusion of everybody else, the owner is free to use the thing provided that this use not be in violation of the rights of others and that it respect the limitations based upon statutory rules and rules of unwritten law.
3. Without prejudice to the rights of others, the owner of the thing becomes owner of the fruits once separated.

1. La propriété est le droit le plus étendu qu'une personne puisse avoir sur une chose.
2. Le propriétaire a la liberté, à l'exclusion de tous, d'utiliser la chose, pourvu que cet usage ne soit pas contraire aux droits d'autres personnes et que soient respectées les restrictions découlant de la loi ou des règles non écrites.
3. Sous réserve des droits d'autrui, les fruits une fois séparés appartiennent au propriétaire de la chose.

Art. 2. (5.1.4.) De eigenaar van een zaak is bevoegd haar van een ieder die haar zonder recht houdt, op te eisen.

The owner of a thing is entitled to revendicate it from any person who detains it without right.

Le propriétaire d'une chose peut la revendiquer contre toute personne qui la détient sans droit.

Art. 3. (5.1.5) Voor zover de wet niet anders bepaalt, is de eigenaar van een zaak eigenaar van al haar bestanddelen.

To the extent that the law does not provide otherwise, the owner of a thing is owner of all its component parts.

Dans la mesure où la loi ne dispose pas autrement, toutes les composantes appartiennent au propriétaire d'une chose.

TITEL 2 EIGENDOM VAN ROERENDE ZAKEN

TITLE 2 OWNERSHIP OF MOVEABLE THINGS

TITRE DEUXIÈME DE LA PROPRIÉTÉ DES CHOSES MOBILIÈRES

Art. 4. (5.2.1) Hij die een aan niemand toebehorende roerende zaak in bezit neemt, verkrijgt daarvan de eigendom.

A person who takes possession of a moveable thing which does not belong to anybody acquires ownership thereof.

Celui qui prend possession d'une chose mobilière n'appartenant à personne en acquiert la propriété.

Art. 5. (5.2.3) - 1. Hij die een onbeheerde zaak vindt en onder zich neemt, is verplicht:

a. met bekwame spoed overeenkomstig lid 2, eerste zin, van de vondst aangifte te doen, tenzij hij terstond na de vondst daarvan mededeling heeft gedaan aan degene die hij als eigenaar of als tot ontvangst bevoegd mocht beschouwen;

b. met bekwame spoed tevens overeenkomstig lid 2, tweede zin, mededeling van de vondst te doen, indien deze is gedaan in een woning, een gebouw of een vervoermiddel, tenzij hij krachtens het bepaalde onder a, slot ook niet tot aangifte verplicht was;

c. de zaak in bewaring te geven aan de gemeente die dit vordert.

- 2. De in lid 1 onder a bedoelde aangifte kan in iedere gemeente worden gedaan bij de daartoe aangewezen ambtenaar. De in lid 1 onder b bedoelde mededeling geschiedt bij degene die de woning bewoont of het gebouw of vervoermiddel in gebruik of exploitatie heeft, dan wel bij degene die daar voor hem toezicht houdt.

- 3. De vinder is te allen tijde bevoegd de zaak aan enige gemeente in bewaring te geven. Zolang hij dit niet doet, is hij verplicht zelf voor bewaring en onderhoud zorg te dragen.

- 4. De vinder kan van de in lid 2, eerste zin, bedoelde ambtenaar een bewijs van aangifte of van inbewaringgeving verlangen.

1. The person who finds and takes control of a vacant thing must:

a. promptly declare the discovery in accordance with the first sentence of paragraph 2, unless he has forthwith after the discovery given notice of it to the person whom he could consider as owner or as entitled to receive the thing;

b. also communicate the discovery promptly in accordance with the second sentence of paragraph 2, if it has been made in a dwelling, building or means of transportation, unless he was not obliged to declare the discovery according to the preceding paragraph *in fine*;

1. Celui qui trouve une chose vacante et qui la prend sous son contrôle est tenu:

a. De déclarer la découverte promptement, en se conformant à la première phrase du paragraphe 2, à moins que, immédiatement après sa découverte, il n'en ait avisé celui qu'il pouvait considérer comme propriétaire ou comme autorisé à la recevoir;

b. En outre, de communiquer la découverte promptement, en se conformant à la deuxième phrase du paragraphe 2, si celle-ci a été faite dans une demeure, un édifice ou un moyen de transport, à moins que, en vertu de ce qui est disposé à la fin du paragraphe précédent, il ne soit pas non plus tenu de dénoncer sa découverte;

c. deposit the thing with the Commune demanding it.

2. In every Commune the declaration referred to in paragraph 1 *sub* a may be made to the civil servant so designated. The communication referred to in paragraph 1 *sub* b is made to the person inhabiting the dwelling or the person using or exploiting the building or means of transportation, or to the person who, on the latter's behalf, supervises it.

3. At all times the finder is entitled to deposit the thing with any Commune. As long as he does not do so, he is obliged to ensure the conservation and the maintenance of the thing.

4. The finder may demand a document in proof of the declaration or of the deposit from the civil servant referred to in paragraph 2, first sentence.

c. De déposer la chose auprès de la commune qui le demande.

2. La déclaration visée au point a. du paragraphe premier peut être faite dans chaque commune auprès de l'officier désigné à cette fin. La communication visée au point b. du paragraphe 1er a lieu auprès de celui qui habite la demeure ou qui utilise ou exploite l'édifice ou le moyen de transport ou de la personne qui, au nom de ce dernier, en a la surveillance.

3. Celui qui a trouvé une chose peut en tout temps la déposer à une commune. Tant qu'il ne l'a pas fait, il est tenu de veiller lui-même à sa conservation et à son entretien.

4. Celui qui a trouvé une chose et l'a déposée peut exiger de l'officier visé à la première phrase du paragraphe 2 une pièce justificative de la déclaration ou du dépôt.

Art. 6. (5.2.4) - 1. De vinder die aan de hem in artikel 5 lid 1 gestelde eisen heeft voldaan, verkrijgt de eigendom van de zaak één jaar na de in artikel 5 lid 1 onder a bedoelde aangifte of mededeling, mits de zaak zich op dat tijdstip nog bevindt in de macht van de vinder of van de gemeente.

- 2. Is de zaak anders dan op haar vordering aan de gemeente in bewaring gegeven en valt zij onder de niet-kostbare zaken, aangewezen bij of krachtens een algemene maatregel van bestuur als bedoeld in artikel 12 onder b, dan is lid 1 niet van toepassing en is de burgemeester drie maanden na de inbewaringgeving bevoegd de zaak voor rekening van de gemeente te verkopen of haar om niet aan een derde over te dragen of te vernietigen.

- 3. Is de zaak in bewaring gegeven aan de gemeente en is noch lid 1, noch lid 2 van toepassing, dan is de burgemeester één jaar na de inbewaringgeving bevoegd de zaak voor rekening van de gemeente te verkopen of haar om niet aan een derde over te dragen of te vernietigen.

- 4. De vorige leden gelden niet, wanneer de eigenaar of een ander die tot ontvangst van de zaak bevoegd is, zich daartoe heeft aangemeld bij degene die de zaak in bewaring heeft vóórdat de toepasselijke termijn is verstreken of, in de gevallen van de leden 2 en 3, op een tijdstip na het verstrijken van de termijn, waarop de gemeente de zaak redelijkerwijs nog te zijner beschikking kan stellen.

1. A finder who has complied with the requirements imposed upon him in article 5 paragraph 1 acquires ownership of the thing one year after the declaration or communication referred to in article 5 paragraph 1 *sub* a, provided that at that time the thing is still under the control of the finder or of the Commune.

1. Celui qui, ayant trouvé une chose, a satisfait aux exigences qui lui sont imposées au paragraphe premier de l'article 5 en acquiert la propriété un an après la déclaration ou de la communication visées au point a. du paragraphe 1er de l'article 5, pourvu que la chose se trouve encore à cette date en sa puissance ou en celle de la commune.

2. Where the thing has been deposited with a Commune otherwise than upon its demand, and where it is one of the non-valuable things designated by or pursuant to a regulation as referred to in article 12 *sub* b, the first paragraph does not apply and the burgomaster may, three months after the deposit, sell the thing on account of the Commune, transfer it to a third person by gratuitous title or destroy it.
3. Where the thing has been deposited with the Commune and neither paragraphs 1 or 2 apply, the burgomaster may, one year after the deposit, sell the thing on account of the Commune, transfer it to a third person by gratuitous title or destroy it.
4. The preceding paragraphs do not apply where the owner or another person entitled to receive the thing has presented himself for that purpose to the depositary before the expiry of the applicable term or, in the cases provided for in paragraphs 2 and 3, on a date thereafter when the Commune can still reasonably put the thing at his disposal.

2. Lorsque la chose a été déposée auprès de la commune autrement qu'à la demande de celle-ci et qu'elle fait partie des choses non précieuses désignées par décret visé au point b. de l'article 12 ou en vertu d'un tel décret, le paragraphe premier ne s'applique pas et le maire peut, après trois mois suivant le dépôt, vendre la chose pour le compte de la commune, la transférer à un tiers à titre gratuit ou la détruire.
3. Lorsque la chose a été déposée auprès de la commune et que ni le paragraphe premier ni le deuxième ne s'appliquent, le maire peut, après un an suivant le dépôt, vendre la chose pour le compte de la commune, la transférer à un tiers à titre gratuit ou la détruire.
4. Les paragraphes précédents ne s'appliquent pas lorsque le propriétaire, ou une autre personne qui a le droit de recevoir la chose s'est présenté à cette fin chez le dépositaire avant l'expiration du délai applicable ou, dans les cas prévus aux paragraphes 2 et 3, à une date ultérieure où la commune peut encore raisonnablement mettre la chose à sa disposition.

Art. 7. (5.2.5) De vinder kan, door de zaak onverwijld af te geven aan de bewoner van de woning of de gebruiker of exploitant van de ruimte waar de vondst is gedaan, dan wel aan degene die daar voor hem toezicht houdt, zijn rechtspositie met alle daaraan verbonden verplichtingen doen overgaan op die bewoner, gebruiker of exploitant met dien verstande dat geen recht op beloning bestaat.

By giving the thing without delay to the inhabitant of the dwelling, to the person using or exploiting the space where the discovery has been made or to the person who on the latter's behalf supervises such space, the finder can transmit his juridical position to such inhabitant, user or person exploiting, including all obligations attached thereto, but there is no right to a reward.

Celui qui a trouvé la chose peut, en remettant la chose sans délai à l'occupant de la demeure ou à l'usager ou l'exploitant de l'espace où elle a été trouvée, ou à la personne qui, au nom de ce dernier, en a la surveillance, transmettre sa situation juridique, avec toutes les obligations y afférentes, à cet occupant, cet usager ou cet exploitant, étant entendu qu'il n'existe pas de droit à récompense.

Art. 8. (5.2.6) - 1. Indien een aan de gemeente in bewaring gegeven zaak aan snel tenietgaan of achteruitgang onderhevig is of wegens de onevenredig hoge kosten of ander nadeel de bewaring daarvan niet langer van de gemeente kan worden gevergd, is de burgemeester bevoegd haar te verkopen.
- 2. Indien de zaak zich niet voor verkoop leent, is de burgemeester bevoegd haar om niet aan een derde in eigendom over te dragen of te vernietigen.
- 3. Indien de gevonden zaak een dier is, is de burgemeester na verloop van twee weken, nadat het dier door de gemeente in bewaring is genomen,

bevoegd het zo mogelijk tegen betaling van een koopprijs, en anders om niet, aan een derde in eigendom over te dragen. Mocht ook dit laatste zijn uitgesloten, dan is de burgemeester bevoegd het dier te doen afmaken. De termijn van twee weken behoeft niet te worden in acht genomen, indien het dier slechts met onevenredig hoge kosten gedurende dat tijdvak kan worden bewaard, of afmaking om geneeskundige redenen vereist is.
- 4. De opbrengst treedt in de plaats van de zaak.

1. If a thing which, deposited with a Commune, is susceptible of loss or rapid deterioration, or if the Commune can no longer be required to keep it because of disproportionately high costs or other prejudice, the burgomaster is entitled to sell it.
2. If the thing does not lend itself to being sold, the burgomaster is entitled to transfer its ownership to a third person by gratuitous title or to destroy it.
3. If the thing found is an animal, the burgomaster is entitled, two weeks after it has been taken into custody, to transfer its ownership to a third person, if possible against the payment of a purchase price or otherwise by gratuitous title. Where even this last possibility is excluded, the burgomaster is entitled to have the animal destroyed. The period of two weeks need not be observed if the costs of keeping the animal during that time are disproportionately high or if destruction is required for medical reasons.
4. The proceeds take the place of the thing.

1. Si la chose déposée auprès de la commune est sujette à perte ou détérioration rapides ou que, en raison des frais disproportionnés ou d'un autre préjudice, sa conservation ne peut plus être exigée de la commune, le maire peut la vendre.

2. Si la chose ne se prête pas à la vente, le maire peut en transférer la propriété à un tiers à titre gratuit ou la détruire.

3. Si la chose trouvée est un animal, le maire peut, après un délai de deux semaines à compter de l'acceptation en dépôt à la commune, en transférer la propriété à un tiers, si possible contre paiement d'un prix d'achat, sinon à titre gratuit. Lorsque même cette dernière possibilité est exclue, le maire peut le faire abattre. Il n'est pas tenu de respecter ce délai si la garde de l'animal risque d'entraîner des frais disproportionnés ou que l'abattage est requis pour des raisons médicales.

4. Le produit se substitue à la chose.

Art. 9. (5.2.6a) Bestaat de aan de gemeente in bewaring gegeven zaak in geld, dan is de gemeente slechts verplicht aan degene die haar kan opeisen, een gelijk bedrag uit te keren, en vervalt deze verplichting zodra de burgemeester tot verkoop voor rekening van de gemeente bevoegd zou zijn geweest.

Where the thing deposited with the Commune consists of a sum of money, the Commune is only obliged to pay an equal amount to the person who can claim it; this obligation ceases once the burgomaster would have been entitled to sell it on account of the Commune.

Lorsque la chose déposée auprès de la commune consiste en une somme d'argent, la commune est tenue seulement de verser, à la personne qui peut la réclamer, une somme égale, et cette obligation s'éteint dès que le maire aurait pu vendre pour le compte de la commune.

Art. 10. (5.2.7) - 1. Hij die de zaak opeist van de gemeente of van de vinder die aan de hem in artikel 5 lid 1 gestelde eisen heeft voldaan, is verplicht de kosten van bewaring en onderhoud en tot opsporing van de eigenaar of een andere tot ontvangst bevoegde te vergoeden. De gemeente of de vinder is bevoegd de afgifte op te schorten totdat deze verplichting is

nagekomen. Indien degene die de zaak opeist, de verschuldigde kosten niet binnen een maand nadat ze hem zijn opgegeven, heeft voldaan, wordt hij geacht zijn recht op de zaak te hebben prijsgegeven.
- 2. De vinder die aan de op hem rustende verplichtingen heeft voldaan, heeft naar omstandigheden recht op een redelijke beloning.

1. A person who claims the thing from the Commune, or from the finder who has complied with the requirements imposed upon him by article 5 paragraph 1, must reimburse the costs of keeping and maintenance, and of locating the owner or other person entitled to receive the thing. The Commune or finder is entitled to suspend the return of the thing until this obligation has been performed. If the person who revendicates the thing has not paid the costs owed within the month from the time they have been indicated to him, he is deemed to have abandoned his right to the thing.

2. A finder who has complied with the obligations incumbent upon him is entitled, according to the circumstances, to a reasonable reward.

1. Celui qui réclame la chose à la commune ou à la personne qui, l'ayant trouvée, a satisfait aux conditions qui lui sont imposées au paragraphe premier de l'article 5 est tenu de rembourser les frais de conservation et d'entretien, ainsi que ceux qui ont été engagés pour la recherche du propriétaire ou d'une autre personne autorisée à la recevoir. La commune ou la personne qui a trouvé la chose peut différer la remise jusqu'à l'exécution de cette obligation. Si la personne qui revendique la chose n'a pas réglé, dans le mois suivant la date où elle en a été avisée, les frais engagés, elle est censée avoir renoncé à son droit sur la chose.

2. Celui qui, ayant trouvé une chose, a rempli les obligations lui en résultant a droit, selon les circonstances, à une récompense normale.

Art. 11. (5.2.8) Indien een vinder die op grond van artikel 6 lid 1 eigenaar is geworden van een aan de gemeente in bewaring gegeven zaak, zich niet binnen één maand na zijn verkrijging bij de gemeente heeft aangemeld om de zaak in ontvangst te nemen, is de burgemeester bevoegd de zaak voor rekening van de gemeente te verkopen, om niet aan een derde over te dragen of te vernietigen.

If a finder who, by virtue of article 6 paragraph 1, has become owner of a thing deposited with a Commune does not, within one month from his acquisition, apply to the Commune to take delivery of the thing, the burgomaster is entitled to sell the thing on account of the Commune, to transfer it to a third person by gratuitous title or to destroy it.

Si la personne qui, par application du paragraphe 1er de l'article 6, est devenue propriétaire d'une chose trouvée par elle et déposée auprès de la commune ne s'y est pas présentée, dans le mois suivant cette acquisition, pour en prendre livraison, le maire peut la vendre pour le compte de la commune, la transférer à un tiers à titre gratuit ou la détruire.

Art. 12. (5.2.8a) Bij of krachtens algemene maatregel van bestuur kunnen:
- **a. nadere regels worden gesteld omtrent de uitoefening van de uit de artikelen 5-11 voor de gemeenten voortvloeiende bevoegdheden;**
- **b. groepen van niet-kostbare zaken worden aangewezen, waarvoor artikel 6 lid 2 geldt;**
- **c. nadere regels worden gesteld omtrent de aanwijzing van bepaalde soorten personen en instellingen, waarbij deze, geheel of gedeeltelijk en al dan niet onder nadere voorwaarden, worden vrijgesteld van de aangifteplicht van artikel 5 lid 1 onder a of voor de afwikkeling van vondsten worden gelijkgesteld met een gemeente;**

d. voor de afwikkeling van vondsten door personen of instellingen als bedoeld onder c groepen van niet afgehaalde zaken met gevonden zaken worden gelijkgesteld.

By or pursuant to regulation:

a. more detailed rules may be issued regarding the exercise of the rights of Communes flowing from articles 5 - 11;

b. groups of non-valuable things may be designated to which article 6 paragraph 2 applies;

c. more detailed rules may be issued designating certain categories of persons and institutions and exempting them, in whole or in part, and possibly subject to conditions, from the duty to declare, referred to in article 5 paragraph 1 *sub* a, or assimilating them to a Commune for the purpose of processing discoveries;

d. groups of things which have not been retrieved may be assimilated to things found for the purpose of processing discoveries by persons or institutions referred to *sub* c.

Par décret ou en vertu d'un décret

a. Peuvent être prises des dispositions précises concernant l'exercice des pouvoirs découlant pour les communes des articles 5 à 11;

b. Peuvent être désignés des groupes de choses non précieuses, auxquelles s'applique le deuxième paragraphe de l'article 6;

c. Peuvent être prises des dispositions précises concernant la désignation de certaines catégories de personnes ou d'institutions, par lesquelles celles-ci, en tout ou partie et éventuellement sous des conditions à préciser, sont exemptées de l'obligation de déclaration visée au point a. du paragraphe 1er de l'article 5 ou qui, aux fins de la liquidation des objets trouvés, sont assimilées aux communes;

d. Peuvent, en vue de la disposition des objets trouvés par des personnes ou institutions visées au point c., être assimilées à des choses trouvées des groupes de choses non retirées.

Art. 13. (5.2.9) - 1. Een schat komt voor gelijke delen toe aan degene die hem ontdekt, en aan de eigenaar van de onroerende of roerende zaak, waarin de schat wordt aangetroffen.
- 2. Een schat is een zaak van waarde, die zolang verborgen is geweest dat daardoor de eigenaar niet meer kan worden opgespoord.
- 3. De ontdekker is verplicht van zijn vondst aangifte te doen overeenkomstig artikel 5 lid 1 onder a. Indien geen aangifte is gedaan of onzeker is aan wie de zaak toekomt, kan de gemeente overeenkomstig artikel 5 lid 1 onder c vorderen dat deze aan haar in bewaring wordt gegeven, totdat vaststaat wie rechthebbende is.

1. A treasure belongs, in equal shares, to the person discovering it and to the owner of the immoveable or moveable thing in which it is found.
2. A treasure is a thing of value which has remained hidden for such a long time that, as a consequence, the owner can no longer be located.

1. Le trésor revient, par parts égales, à celui qui l'a découvert et au propriétaire de la chose immobilière ou mobilière dans laquelle il a été trouvé.
2. Un trésor est une chose de valeur qui est restée cachée si longtemps que le propriétaire ne peut plus en être retrouvé.

3. The discoverer of the treasure must declare his discovery according to article 5 paragraph 1 *sub* a. If no declaration has been made or if it is uncertain to whom the thing belongs, the Commune may demand, according to article 5 paragraph 1 *sub* c, that the thing be deposited with it until such time as it has been determined who the person entitled to the thing is.

3. Le découvreur est tenu de déclarer sa découverte conformément au point a. du paragraphe 1er de l'article 5. À défaut d'une telle déclaration ou dans l'incertitude sur la personne à qui revient la chose, la commune peut demander, conformément au point c. du paragraphe 1er de l'article 5, que la chose soit déposée auprès d'elle, jusqu'à ce qu'il soit établi qui en est titulaire.

Art. 14. (5.2.10) - 1. De eigendom van een roerende zaak die een bestanddeel wordt van een andere roerende zaak die als hoofdzaak is aan te merken, gaat over aan de eigenaar van deze hoofdzaak.
- 2. Indien geen der zaken als hoofdzaak is aan te merken en zij toebehoren aan verschillende eigenaars, worden dezen mede-eigenaars van de nieuwe zaak, ieder voor een aandeel evenredig aan de waarde van de zaak.
- 3. Als hoofdzaak is aan te merken de zaak waarvan de waarde die van de andere zaak aanmerkelijk overtreft of die volgens verkeersopvatting als zodanig wordt beschouwd.

1. The ownership of a moveable thing which becomes a component part of another moveable thing, which itself is to be regarded as the principal thing, passes to the owner of the principal thing.
2. If none of the things can be regarded as the principal thing, and if they belong to different owners, these owners become co-owners of the new thing, each for a share proportionate to the value of the thing.
3. A thing is deemed to be a principal thing where its value considerably exceeds that of the other thing, or where according to common opinion it is considered as such.

1. La propriété d'une chose mobilière qui devient composante d'une autre chose mobilière devant être considérée comme la chose principale passe au propriétaire de celle-ci.
2. Si aucune des choses ne peut être considérée comme la chose principale et qu'elles appartiennent à des propriétaires différents, ceux-ci deviennent copropriétaires de la nouvelle chose, chacun pour une part proportionnelle à la valeur de la chose.
3. Est réputée principale la chose dont la valeur dépasse considérablement celle de l'autre ou qui est considérée comme telle d'après l'opinion généralement admise.

Art. 15. (5.2.11) Worden roerende zaken die aan verschillende eigenaars toebehoren door vermenging tot één zaak verenigd, dan is het vorige artikel van overeenkomstige toepassing.

The preceding article applies *mutatis mutandis* where moveable things belonging to different owners are amalgamated so as to form a single thing.

L'article précédent s'applique par analogie à la chose mobilière formée par le mélange de choses mobilières appartenant à différents propriétaires.

Art. 16. (5.2.12) - 1. Indien iemand uit een of meer roerende zaken een nieuwe zaak vormt, wordt deze eigendom van de eigenaar van de oorspronkelijke zaken. Behoorden deze toe aan verschillende eigenaars, dan zijn de vorige twee artikelen van overeenkomstige toepassing.
- 2. Indien iemand voor zichzelf een zaak vormt of doet vormen uit of mede uit een of meer hem niet toebehorende roerende zaken, wordt hij

eigenaar van de nieuwe zaak, tenzij de kosten van de vorming dit wegens hun geringe omvang niet rechtvaardigen.
- 3. Bij het verwerken van stoffen tot een nieuwe stof of het kweken van planten zijn de vorige leden van overeenkomstige toepassing.

1. If a person creates a new thing out of one or more moveable things, this thing is owned by the owner of the original things. The two preceding articles apply *mutatis mutandis* where these things belonged to different owners.
2. If a person creates a thing for himself, or has such a thing so created in whole or in part out of one or more moveable things not belonging to him, he becomes owner of the new thing, unless the costs of creation are so low as not to justify this result.
3. The preceding paragraphs apply *mutatis mutandis* to the transformation of materials into a new material or to the cultivation of plants.

1. La chose nouvelle formée d'une ou de plusieurs choses mobilières primitives appartient au propriétaire de celles-ci. Les deux articles précédents s'appliquent par analogie lorsqu'elles appartenaient à différents propriétaires.
2. Celui qui forme ou fait former pour lui-même une chose, en employant, en tout ou en partie, une ou plusieurs choses mobilières ne lui appartenant pas devient propriétaire de cette chose, à moins que les frais de formation, en raison de leur faible importance, ne le justifient pas.
3. Les paragraphes précédents s'appliquent par analogie à la transformation de matières en une matière nouvelle et à la culture des plantes.

Art. 17. (5.2.15) Degene die krachtens zijn genotsrecht op een zaak gerechtigd is tot de vruchten daarvan, verkrijgt de eigendom der vruchten door haar afscheiding.

The person who, pursuant to his right of enjoyment of a thing, is entitled to its fruits acquires the ownership thereof upon their separation.

Celui qui, en vertu de son droit de jouissance sur une chose, est titulaire des fruits en acquiert la propriété par leur séparation.

Art. 18. (5.2.16) De eigendom van een roerende zaak wordt verloren, wanneer de eigenaar het bezit prijsgeeft met het oogmerk om zich van de eigendom te ontdoen.

The owner who abandons possession of a moveable thing, with the intent of divesting himself of ownership, loses ownership of it.

La propriété d'une chose mobilière se perd lorsque le propriétaire renonce à sa possession en vue de se départir de la propriété.

Art. 19. (5.2.17) - 1. De eigenaar van tamme dieren verliest daarvan de eigendom, wanneer zij, nadat zij uit zijn macht zijn gekomen, zijn verwilderd.
- 2. De eigenaar van andere dieren verliest daarvan de eigendom, wanneer zij de vrijheid verkrijgen en de eigenaar niet terstond beproeft ze weder te vangen of zijn pogingen daartoe staakt.

1. The owner of domesticated animals loses ownership of them where they have become wild after having escaped from his custody.

1. Le propriétaire d'animaux apprivoisés en perd la propriété lorsqu'ils sont devenus sauvages après avoir échappé à son contrôle.

2. The owner of other animals loses ownership of them where they gain freedom and the owner does not forthwith attempt to recapture them or stops his attempts to do so.

2. Le propriétaire d'autres animaux en perd la propriété lorsqu'ils s'échappent et qu'il n'essaie pas immédiatement de les reprendre ou qu'il arrête ses efforts à cette fin.

TITEL 3 EIGENDOM VAN ONROERENDE ZAKEN

TITLE 3 OWNERSHIP OF IMMOVEABLE THINGS

TITRE TROISIÈME DE LA PROPRIÉTÉ DES CHOSES IMMOBILIÈRES

Art. 20. (5.3.1) De eigendom van de grond omvat, voor zover de wet niet anders bepaalt:
a. de bovengrond;
b. de daaronder zich bevindende aardlagen;
c. het grondwater dat door een bron, put of pomp aan de oppervlakte is gekomen;
d. het water dat zich op de grond bevindt en niet in open gemeenschap met water op eens anders erf staat;
e. gebouwen en werken die duurzaam met de grond zijn verenigd, hetzij rechtstreeks, hetzij door vereniging met andere gebouwen en werken, voor zover ze geen bestanddeel zijn van eens anders onroerende zaak;
f. met de grond verenigde beplantingen.

To the extent not otherwise provided for by law, ownership of land[1] comprises:
a. the surface;
b. the layers of soil under the surface;
c. subsoil water which has surfaced by means of a spring, well or pump;
d. water which is on the land and not in direct connection with water on the land of another person;
e. buildings and works durably united with the land, either directly or through incorporation with other buildings or works, to the extent that they are not component parts of an immoveable thing of another person;
f. plants united with the land.

Dans la mesure où la loi ne dispose pas autrement, la propriété du fonds comporte:
a. La surface;
b. Les couches de terre au dessous;
c. L'eau souterraine portée à la surface par une source, un puits ou une pompe;
d. L'eau qui se trouve sur le fonds et qui ne communique pas librement avec l'eau du fonds d'autrui;
e. Les constructions et ouvrages unis de façon durable au fonds, soit directement, soit par incorporation à d'autres constructions ou ouvrages, dans la mesure où ils ne sont pas composantes d'un immeuble appartenant à autrui;
f. Les plantations unies au fonds.

Art. 21. (5.3.2) - 1. De bevoegdheid van de eigenaar van de grond om deze te gebruiken, omvat de bevoegdheid tot gebruik van de ruimte boven en onder de oppervlakte.

[1] In this title the English term "land" is either the translation of the Dutch term "grond" (more or less "soil" in English) or the translation of the Dutch term "erf" (more or less "piece of property" in English). Where this title speaks of "land" in the combination of "land and water", the English "land" is the literal translation of the identical Dutch term "land".

- 2. Het gebruik van de ruimte boven en onder de oppervlakte is aan anderen toegestaan, indien dit zo hoog boven of zo diep onder de oppervlakte plaats vindt, dat de eigenaar geen belang heeft zich daartegen te verzetten.
- 3. De vorige leden zijn niet van toepassing op de bevoegdheid tot vliegen.

1. The right of the owner of land to use it includes the right to use what is above and below the surface.
2. Other persons may use what is above and below the surface if this takes place so high above or so deep below the surface that the owner has no interest to object thereto.

3. The preceding paragraphs do not apply to the right of overflight.

1. Le droit du propriétaire d'utiliser le fonds s'étend à l'usage de l'espace au-dessus et au-dessous de la surface.
2. Il est permis à d'autres personnes d'utiliser l'espace au-dessus et au-dessous de la surface si cet usage a lieu, par rapport à la surface, à une hauteur ou à une profondeur telle que le propriétaire n'a pas l'intérêt requis pour s'y opposer.
3. Les paragraphes précédents ne s'appliquent pas au droit de survol.

Art. 22. (5.3.3) Wanneer een erf niet is afgesloten, mag ieder er zich op begeven, tenzij de eigenaar schade of hinder hiervan kan ondervinden of op duidelijke wijze kenbaar heeft gemaakt, dat het verboden is zonder zijn toestemming zich op het erf te bevinden, een en ander onverminderd hetgeen omtrent openbare wegen is bepaald.

Where land has not been enclosed, any person may enter it, except if damage or nuisance is thereby caused to the owner or except if the owner has clearly indicated that it is forbidden to be on the land without his permission. The foregoing is without prejudice to the provisions regarding public roads.

Lorsque un fonds n'est pas clos, chacun peut y pénétrer, à moins que le propriétaire puisse en subir un préjudice ou un trouble ou qu'il n'ait indiqué de façon claire qu'il est interdit de s'y trouver sans sa permission, le tout sous réserve des dispositions relatives au chemin public.

Art. 23. (5.3.4) - 1. Is een voorwerp of een dier anders dan door opzet of grove nalatigheid van de eigenaar op de grond van een ander terecht gekomen, dan moet de eigenaar van de grond hem op zijn verzoek toestaan het voorwerp of het dier op te sporen en weg te voeren.
- 2. De bij de opsporing en wegvoering aangerichte schade moet door de eigenaar van het voorwerp of het dier aan de eigenaar van de grond worden vergoed. Voor deze vordering heeft laatstgenoemde een retentierecht op het voorwerp of het dier.

1. Where an object or animal finds itself on the land of another person otherwise than through the intentional fault or gross negligence of its owner, the owner of the land must, upon request, permit the owner of the object or the animal to search for and remove it.

1. Lorsqu'un objet ou un animal se trouve, autrement que par le dol ou la négligence grossière du propriétaire, sur le fonds d'autrui, celui-ci doit permettre au propriétaire, à sa requête, d'aller chercher l'objet ou l'animal et de l'enlever.

2. The owner of the object or animal must compensate the owner of the land for the damage done by the search and the removal. The owner of the land has a right of retention on the object or animal with respect to this claim.

2. Le propriétaire de l'objet ou de l'animal doit indemniser le propriétaire du fonds du préjudice causé lors de la recherche ou de l'enlèvement. Ce dernier a pour cette créance un droit de rétention sur l'objet ou sur l'animal.

Art. 24. (5.3.5) Aan de Staat behoren onroerende zaken die geen andere eigenaar hebben.

Immoveable things which have no other owner belong to the State.

Les choses immobilières qui n'ont pas d'autre propriétaire appartiennent à l'État.

Art. 25. (5.3.6) De bodem van de territoriale zee en van de Waddenzee is eigendom van de Staat.

The State is owner of the seabed of the territorial sea and of the "Waddenzee".

Le fond de la mer territoriale et de la *Waddenzee* est propriété de l'État.

Art. 26. (5.3.7) De stranden der zee tot aan de duinvoet worden vermoed eigendom van de Staat te zijn.

The State is presumed to be the owner of seashore beaches up to the foot of the dunes.

Les plages de la mer jusqu'au pied des dunes sont présumées être propriété de l'État.

Art. 27. (5.3.7a) - 1. De grond waarop zich openbare vaarwateren bevinden, wordt vermoed eigendom van de Staat te zijn.
- 2. Dit vermoeden werkt niet tegenover een openbaar lichaam:
a. dat die wateren onderhoudt en het onderhoud niet van de Staat heeft overgenomen;
b. dat die wateren onderhield en waarvan dit onderhoud door de Staat of door een ander openbaar lichaam is overgenomen.

1. The State is presumed to be the owner of the land on which there are public waterways.
2. This presumption does not operate against:
a. a public body which maintains those waters and has not taken over the maintenance from the State;
b. a public body which maintained those waters where this maintenance has been taken over by the State or another public body.

1. Les fonds sur lesquels se trouvent des eaux navigables publiques sont présumés être propriété de l'État.
2. Cette présomption n'a pas d'effet à l'égard de la collectivité publique:
a. Qui entretient ces eaux et n'a pas repris la charge d'entretien à l'État;
b. Qui entretenait ces eaux et dont la charge d'entretien a été reprise par l'État ou par une autre collectivité publique.

Art. 28. (5.3.8) - 1. Onroerende zaken die openbaar zijn, met uitzondering van de stranden der zee, worden, wanneer zij door een openbaar lichaam worden onderhouden, vermoed eigendom van dat openbare lichaam te zijn.
- 2. Dit vermoeden werkt niet tegenover hem van wie het onderhoud is overgenomen.

1. Except for seashore beaches, a public body is presumed to be the owner of immoveable things which are public and are maintained by it.
2. This presumption does not operate against the person from whom the maintenance has been taken over.

1. À l'exception des plages de la mer, les immeubles publics qui sont entretenus par une collectivité publique sont présumés être propriété de celle-ci.
2. Cette présomption n'a pas d'effet à l'égard de celui à qui l'entretien a été repris.

Art. 29. (5.3.9) De grens van een langs een water liggend erf verplaatst zich met de oeverlijn, behalve in geval van opzettelijke drooglegging of tijdelijke overstroming. Een overstroming is niet tijdelijk, indien tien jaren na de overstroming het land nog door het water wordt overspoeld en de drooglegging niet is begonnen.

The boundary of riparian land moves with the shoreline except in the event of intentional reclamation or temporary inundation of land. An inundation is not temporary if, ten years after it occurred, the land is still flooded and reclamation has not begun.

La limite d'un fonds riverain se déplace suivant la rive, sauf dans le cas d'assèchement délibéré ou d'inondation temporaire. Une inondation n'est pas temporaire si, dix ans après sa survenance, la terre est toujours inondée et que l'assèchement n'a pas été amorcé.

Art. 30. (5.3.10) - 1. Een verplaatsing van de oeverlijn wijzigt de grens niet meer, nadat deze is vastgelegd, hetzij door de eigenaars van land en water overeenkomstig artikel 31, hetzij door de rechter op vordering van een hunner tegen de ander overeenkomstig artikel 32. De vastlegging geldt jegens een ieder.
- 2. Indien bij de vastlegging in plaats van de werkelijke eigenaar van een erf iemand die als zodanig in de openbare registers was ingeschreven, partij is geweest, is niettemin het vorige lid van toepassing, tenzij de werkelijke eigenaar tegen inschrijving van de akte of het vonnis verzet heeft gedaan voordat zij is geschied.

1. A movement of the shoreline no longer changes the boundary, where it has been settled either by the owners of land and water according to article 31, or by the judge upon the demand of one of them against the other according to article 32. The settlement of the boundary has force against everybody.
2. The preceding paragraph even applies if a person, who appears in the public registers as owner, has been party to the settlement instead of the true owner of the land, unless the true owner, before registration, opposed the registration of the deed or judgment.

1. Le déplacement de la rive ne modifie plus la limite après que les propriétaires de la terre et de l'eau l'ont fixée conformément à l'article 31 ou que, à la demande de l'un contre l'autre, le juge l'a fait conformément à l'article 32. La limite fixée vaut à l'égard de tous.
2. Le paragraphe précédent s'applique même si, au lieu du propriétaire véritable, une personne inscrite comme tel sur les registres publics a été partie à la fixation, à moins que le propriétaire véritable n'ait fait opposition à l'inscription de l'acte ou du jugement avant qu'elle n'ait eu lieu.

Art. 31. (5.3.10a) - 1. De vastlegging van de grens door de eigenaars van land en water geschiedt bij een daartoe bestemde notariële akte, binnen veertien dagen gevolgd door de inschrijving daarvan in de openbare registers.

- 2. De bewaarder der registers is bevoegd van de inschrijving kennis te geven aan ieder die als rechthebbende of beslaglegger op een der erven staat ingeschreven.
- 3. Voor zover de in de akte beschreven grens van de toenmalige oeverlijn afwijkt, kan een derde die op het ogenblik van de inschrijving een recht op een der erven heeft, daarvan huurder of pachter is of daarop een beslag heeft doen inschrijven, de toenmalige oeverlijn als vastgelegde grens aanmerken.

1. The settlement of the boundary by the owners of land and water is done by a notarial deed intended for that purpose, followed within fourteen days by its entry in the public registers.
2. The registrar is entitled to give notice of the registration to every person who is registered as title-holder or seizor of one of the properties[1].
3. To the extent that the boundary described in the deed deviates from the then current shoreline, a third person who, at the time of registration, has a right to one of the properties, is the lessee of it or has registered a seizure against it, may regard such current shoreline as the settled boundary.

1. La fixation de la limite par les propriétaires de la terre et de l'eau a lieu par acte notarié à cet effet, suivi dans les quatorze jours de son inscription sur les registres publics.
2. Le conservateur des registres peut informer de l'inscription toute personne inscrite comme titulaire ou saisissant d'un des fonds.
3. Dans la mesure où la limite décrite dans l'acte s'écarte de la rive formée à l'époque, le tiers qui, au moment de l'inscription, a un droit sur l'un des fonds, en est le preneur ou y a fait inscrire une saisie peut considérer comme la limite fixée la rive formée à l'époque.

Art. 32. (5.3.10b) - 1. Een vordering tot vastlegging van de grens wordt slechts toegewezen, indien de instelling ervan in de openbare registers is ingeschreven en allen die toen als rechthebbende of beslaglegger op een der erven stonden ingeschreven, tijdig in het geding zijn geroepen.
- 2. De rechter bepaalt de grens overeenkomstig de oeverlijn op het tijdstip van de inschrijving van de vordering. Alvorens de eis toe te wijzen, kan hij de maatregelen bevelen en de bewijsopdrachten doen, die hij in het belang van niet-verschenen belanghebbenden nuttig oordeelt.
- 3. De kosten van de vordering komen ten laste van de eiser.
- 4. Verzet, hoger beroep en cassatie moeten op straffe van niet-ontvankelijkheid binnen acht dagen na het instellen van het rechtsmiddel worden ingeschreven in de registers, bedoeld in de artikelen 85 en 433 van het Wetboek van Burgerlijke Rechtsvordering. In afwijking van artikel 81 van dat wetboek begint de verzettermijn te lopen vanaf de betekening van het vonnis aan de ingeschrevene, ook als de betekening niet aan hem in persoon geschiedt, tenzij de rechter hiertoe nadere maatregelen heeft bevolen en aan dat bevel niet is voldaan.
- 5. De vastlegging treedt in op het tijdstip dat het vonnis waarbij de vordering is toegewezen, in de openbare registers wordt ingeschreven. Deze inschrijving geschiedt niet voordat het vonnis in kracht van gewijsde is gegaan.

[1] In this and the following articles the word "properties" ("erven" in the Dutch text) is not used in any technical, juridical sense, but rather in the generic sense of several parcels of land.

1. An action to settle the boundary will only be granted if the institution of the action has been entered in the public registers and all persons who were then registered as title-holders or seizors of one of the properties have been timely joined in the action.
2. The judge settles the boundary according to the shoreline at the time of the registration of the action. Before upholding the action, he can order such measures and the submission of such evidence as he deems to be useful for interested parties who have not appeared.
3. The costs of the action are borne by the plaintiff.
4. On pain of disallowance and within eight days from the time that they are initiated, opposition, appeal and cassation must be entered in the registers referred to in articles 85 and 443 of the Code of Civil Procedure. Contrary to article 81 of that Code, the opposition period begins to run from the time the judgment has been served upon the person registered, even if service to him does not take place in person, unless the judge has ordered further measures in this respect and such order has not been complied with.
5. The settlement takes effect at the time of entry in the public registers of the judgment upholding the action. Registration may not take place before the judgment has become final.

1. L'action en fixation de limite n'est accueillie que si elle a été inscrite sur les registres publics et si tous ceux qui y étaient alors inscrits comme titulaire ou saisissant de l'un des fonds ont été appelés en cause en temps utile.

2. Le juge fixe la limite conformément à la rive formée au moment où l'action est inscrite. Avant d'accueillir la demande, il peut ordonner les mesures et l'administration des preuves qu'il juge utiles dans l'intérêt des personnes intéressées qui n'ont pas comparu.
3. Les dépens de la demande sont à la charge du demandeur.
4. L'opposition, l'appel et le pourvoi en cassation doivent, à peine d'irrecevabilité, être inscrits dans les huit jours de leur formation sur les registres visés aux articles 85 et 433 du Code de procédure civile. Par dérogation à l'article 81 de ce code, le délai d'opposition court à compter de la signification du jugement à la personne inscrite, même si la signification n'est pas faite à personne, à moins que le juge n'ait ordonné des mesures précises à ce sujet et que cet ordre n'ait pas été suivi.

5. La fixation prend effet au moment de l'inscription sur les registres du jugement accueillant la demande. L'inscription n'a pas lieu avant que celui-ci n'ait acquis force de chose jugée.

Art. 33. (5.3.11) - 1. Verplaatst zich, nadat de grens is vastgelegd, de oeverlijn van een openbaar water landinwaarts, dan moet de eigenaar van het overspoelde erf het gebruik van het water overeenkomstig de bestemming dulden.
- 2. Verplaatst zich, nadat de grens is vastgelegd, de oeverlijn van een water dat de eigenaar van het aanliggende erf voor enig doel mag gebruiken, in de richting van het water, dan kan de eigenaar van dat erf vorderen dat hem op de drooggekomen grond een of meer erfdienstbaarheden worden verleend, waardoor hij zijn bevoegdheden ten aanzien van het water kan blijven uitoefenen.
- 3. Het vorige lid is van overeenkomstige toepassing ten behoeve van hem die het water voor enig doel mag gebruiken en daartoe een erfdienstbaarheid op het aan het water liggende erf heeft.
- 4. In geval van grensvastlegging overeenkomstig artikel 32 zijn de vorige leden reeds van toepassing, wanneer de oeverlijn zich na de inschrijving van de vordering verplaatst.

1. Where, after the settlement of the boundary, the shoreline of public water moves inland, the owner of the flooded land must allow others to use the water according to its destination.
2. Where, after the settlement of the boundary, the shoreline of water which the riparian owner is entitled to use for a certain purpose moves outward, he may demand that he be granted one or more servitudes upon the reclaimed land so as to allow him to continue to exercise his rights with respect to the water.
3. The preceding paragraph applies *mutatis mutandis* to the person who is entitled to use the water for a certain purpose and has a servitude upon the riparian land for that purpose.
4. In the event of settlement of the boundary pursuant to article 32, the preceding paragraphs apply as of the time that the shoreline moves after the registration of the action.

1. Lorsque, après la fixation de la limite, la rive d'une eau publique se déplace vers la terre, le propriétaire du fonds inondé doit tolérer l'usage de l'eau conformément à sa destination.
2. Lorsque, après la fixation de la limite, la rive d'un cours d'eau que le propriétaire riverain a le droit d'utiliser à une fin précise se retire de la terre, celui-ci peut demander que lui soient accordées sur les fonds asséchés une ou plusieurs servitudes lui permettant de continuer à exercer ses droits sur l'eau.
3. Le paragraphe précédent s'applique par analogie à celui qui a le droit d'utiliser l'eau à une fin précise et qui a sur le fonds riverain une servitude à cet effet.
4. Dans le cas de fixation d'une limite conformément à l'article 32, les paragraphes précédents s'appliquent dès le moment où la rive se déplace après l'inscription de l'action.

Art. 34. (5.3.12) De oeverlijn in de zin van de vorige vijf artikelen wordt bepaald door de normale waterstand, of, bij wateren waarvan het peil periodiek wisselt, door de normale hoogwaterstand. Grond, met andere dan gewoonlijk in het water levende planten begroeid, wordt echter gerekend aan de landzijde van de oeverlijn te liggen, ook al wordt die grond bij hoogwater overstroomd.

The shoreline referred to in the five preceding articles is determined by the ordinary water level or, in the case of periodically changing water levels, by the ordinary high water mark. Land overgrown with plants, other than those which usually live in water is, however, deemed to be on the land side of the shoreline even if that land is flooded at high tide.

La rive au sens des cinq articles précédents est déterminée d'après le niveau normal de l'eau ou, dans le cas d'eaux dont le niveau varie de façon périodique, d'après la crue normale. Le sol qui porte des plantes autres que celles vivant normalement dans l'eau est réputé cependant être du côté du fonds par rapport à la rive, même s'il est inondé lors des crues.

Art. 35. (5.3.13) - 1. Nieuw duin dat zich op het strand vormt, behoort aan de eigenaar van het aan het strand grenzende duin, wanneer beide duinen een geheel zijn geworden, zodanig dat zij niet meer van elkander kunnen worden onderscheiden.
- 2. Daarentegen verliest deze eigenaar de grond welke door afneming van het duin deel van het strand wordt.
- 3. Uitbreiding of afneming van een duin als bedoeld in de leden 1 en 2 brengt geen wijziging meer in de eigendom nadat de grens is vastgesteld, hetzij door de eigenaars van strand en duin, hetzij door de rechter op vordering van een hunner tegen de ander. De artikelen 30-32 zijn van overeenkomstige toepassing.
- 4. Buiten het geval van de leden 1 en 2 brengt uitbreiding of afneming van een duin geen wijziging in de eigendom.

1. A new dune formed on a beach belongs to the owner of the dune adjoining the beach, when both dunes have become one whole so that they can no longer be distinguished from each other.
2. This owner, however, loses the land which becomes part of the beach by erosion of the dune.
3. Expansion or erosion of a dune as referred to in paragraphs 1 and 2 no longer modify ownership, once the boundary has been settled either by the owners of the beach and the dune, or by the judge upon the demand of one of them against the other. Articles 30 - 32 apply *mutatis mutandis*.
4. Apart from the cases referred to in paragraphs 1 and 2, expansion or erosion of a dune do not modify ownership.

1. La dune nouvelle qui se forme sur la plage appartient au propriétaire de la dune contiguë à cette plage, lorsque les deux dunes forment un tout au point que l'on ne peut plus les distinguer.

2. En revanche, ce propriétaire perd le fonds qui, par le rétrécissement de la dune, devient partie de la plage.
3. L'augmentation ou le rétrécissement d'une dune visée aux paragraphes 1er et 2 ne modifie plus la propriété une fois que la limite a été fixée par les propriétaires de la plage et de la dune, ou par le juge à la demande de l'un d'eux contre l'autre. Les articles 30 à 32 s'appliquent par analogie.

4. Hormis les cas prévus aux paragraphes 1er et 2, l'augmentation ou le rétrécissement d'une dune ne modifie pas la propriété.

Art. 36. (5.3.14) Dient een muur, hek, heg of greppel, dan wel een niet bevaarbaar stromend water, een sloot, gracht of dergelijke watergang als afscheiding van twee erven, dan wordt het midden van deze afscheiding vermoed de grens tussen deze erven te zijn. Dit vermoeden geldt niet, indien een muur slechts aan één zijde een gebouw of werk steunt.

Where a wall, fence, hedge, trench, or non-navigable running water, ditch, canal or similar waterway serves as separation between two properties, the middle of this separation is presumed to be the boundary between these properties. This presumption is set aside if a wall supports a building or work only on one side.

Lorsqu'un mur, une clôture, une haie ou une rigole, ou encore un cours d'eau non navigable, un fossé, un canal ou une autre voie d'eau semblable sépare deux fonds, la limite des fonds est présumée se trouver au milieu de la séparation. Cette présomption est écartée si le mur sert d'appui à un ouvrage ou construction d'un seul côté.

TITEL 4 BEVOEGDHEDEN EN VERPLICHTINGEN VAN EIGENAARS VAN NABURIGE ERVEN

TITLE 4 RIGHTS AND OBLIGATIONS OF OWNERS OF NEIGHBOURING PROPERTIES

TITRE QUATRIÈME DES DROITS ET OBLIGATIONS DES PROPRIÉTAIRES DE FONDS VOISINS

Art. 37. (5.4.0) De eigenaar van een erf mag niet in een mate of op een wijze die volgens artikel 162 van Boek 6 onrechtmatig is, aan eigenaars van andere erven hinder toebrengen zoals door het verspreiden van rumoer,

trillingen, stank, rook of gassen, door het onthouden van licht of lucht of door het ontnemen van steun.

An owner of land[1] may not cause nuisance to owners of other properties to a degree or in a fashion which is unlawful according to article 162 of Book 6, for example by the emanation of noise, vibrations, foul odours, smoke or gas, or by depriving other owners of light, air or support.

Le propriétaire d'un fonds ne doit, dans une mesure ou d'une manière illicite suivant l'article 162 du Livre sixième, troubler la jouissance des propriétaires d'autres fonds, par exemple en créant du bruit, des vibrations, en répandant des mauvaises odeurs, de la fumée ou des gaz, en les privant de lumière ou d'air ou en enlevant des supports.

Art. 38. (5.4.1) Lagere erven moeten het water ontvangen dat van hoger gelegen erven van nature afloopt.

Lower land must receive the water which flows naturally from higher land.

Les fonds inférieurs doivent recevoir l'eau qui coule naturellement des fonds supérieurs.

Art. 39. (5.4.2) De eigenaar van een erf mag niet in een mate of op een wijze die volgens artikel 162 van Boek 6 onrechtmatig is, aan eigenaars van andere erven hinder toebrengen door wijziging te brengen in de loop, hoeveelheid of hoedanigheid van over zijn erf stromend water of van het grondwater, dan wel door gebruik van water dat zich op zijn erf bevindt en in open gemeenschap staat met het water op eens anders erf.

An owner of land may not cause nuisance to owners of other properties to a degree or in a fashion which is unlawful according to article 162 of Book 6, by modifying the course, quantity or quality of water flowing over his land or of ground water, or by the use of water which is on his land and in direct connection with the water on the land of another person.

Le propriétaire d'un fonds ne doit, dans une mesure ou d'une manière illicite suivant l'article 162 du Livre sixième, troubler la jouissance des propriétaires d'autres fonds en modifiant le cours, le débit ou la qualité des eaux qui coulent sur son fonds ou des eaux souterraines, ou encore en se servant des eaux qui se trouvent sur son fonds et qui communiquent librement avec celles du fonds d'autrui.

Art. 40. (5.4.3) - 1. De eigenaar van een erf dat aan een openbaar of stromend water grenst, mag van het water gebruik maken tot bespoeling, tot drenking van vee of tot andere dergelijke doeleinden, mits hij daardoor aan eigenaars van andere erven geen hinder toebrengt in een mate of op een wijze die volgens artikel 162 van Boek 6 onrechtmatig is.
- 2. Betreft het een openbaar water, dan is het vorige lid slechts van toepassing voor zover de bestemming van het water zich er niet tegen verzet.

[1] In this title "land" ("erf" in the Dutch text) means one piece of property. Sometimes, when the context so requires, "property" is used as synonym of "land" in this sense. Usually, the plural has been rendered in English as "properties" ("erven" in the Dutch text). Sometimes, when the context so requires, "lands" is used as synonym of "properties". Cf. also footnotes in Articles 20 and 31.

1. The owner of land adjoining public or running water may use the water for irrigation, watering cattle or other similar purposes, provided that in doing so he does not cause nuisance to owners of other properties to a degree or in a fashion which is unlawful according to article 162 of Book 6.
2. Where public water is concerned, the preceding paragraph only applies to the extent that the destination of the water so permits.

1. Le propriétaire d'un fonds riverain d'un cours d'eau ou d'une eau publique peut s'en servir pour l'irrigation, pour l'abreuvage des bêtes et à d'autres fins semblables, pourvu qu'il ne trouble pas par cela la jouissance des propriétaires d'autres fonds dans une mesure ou d'une manière illicite suivant l'article 162 du Livre sixième.
2. Dans le cas des eaux publiques, le paragraphe précédent ne s'applique que dans la mesure où leur destination ne s'y oppose pas.

Art. 41. (5.4.3a) Van de artikelen 38, 39 en 40 lid 1 kan bij verordening worden afgeweken.

Articles 38, 39 and 40 paragraph 1 may be varied by ordinance.

On peut déroger par règlement aux articles 38, 39 et 40, paragraphe 1er.

Art. 42. (5.4.4) - 1. Het is niet geoorloofd binnen de in lid 2 bepaalde afstand van de grenslijn van eens anders erf bomen, heesters of heggen te hebben, tenzij de eigenaar daartoe toestemming heeft gegeven of dat erf een openbare weg of een openbaar water is.
- 2. De in lid 1 bedoelde afstand bedraagt voor bomen twee meter te rekenen vanaf het midden van de voet van de boom en voor de heesters en heggen een halve meter, tenzij ingevolge een verordening of een plaatselijke gewoonte een kleinere afstand is toegelaten.
- 3. De nabuur kan zich niet verzetten tegen de aanwezigheid van bomen, heesters of heggen die niet hoger reiken dan de scheidsmuur tussen de erven.
- 4. Ter zake van een volgens dit artikel ongeoorloofde toestand is slechts vergoeding verschuldigd van de schade, ontstaan na het tijdstip waartegen tot opheffing van die toestand is aangemaand.

1. Unless the owner has consented, or the adjacent land is a public road or public water, trees, shrubs or hedges must not be within such distance from the boundary of the property of another person as determined in paragraph 2.
2. Unless a shorter distance is permitted pursuant to an ordinance or local usage, the distance referred to in paragraph 1, for trees, is two metres from the middle of the base of the tree, and half a metre for shrubs and hedges.
3. A neighbour cannot object to the presence of trees, shrubs or hedges which are not higher than the dividing wall between the properties.
4. A situation prohibited by this article gives rise to compensation for damage suffered only from the time by which a warning has been given to terminate the situation.

1. Il est interdit d'avoir des arbres, des arbustes ou des haies dans la distance fixée au paragraphe 2 de la limite du fonds d'autrui, à moins que le propriétaire n'y ait consenti ou que le fonds ne soit une voie ou une eau publique.
2. La distance visée au paragraphe 1er est de deux mètres à compter du milieu du pied de l'arbre et d'un demi-mètre pour les arbustes et les haies, à moins qu'une distance inférieure ne soit permise en vertu d'un règlement ou suivant l'usage local.
3. Le voisin ne peut s'opposer à la présence d'arbres, d'arbustes ou de haies dont la hauteur ne dépasse pas le mur séparatif des deux fonds.
4. Une situation non permise selon le présent article ne donne lieu à réparation que pour le préjudice survenu après la date à laquelle la sommation visait à la faire cesser.

Art. 43. (5.4.5) Onder muur wordt in deze en de volgende titel verstaan iedere van steen, hout of andere daartoe geschikte stof vervaardigde, ondoorzichtige afsluiting.

In this and the following title a wall means every opaque partition made of stone, wood or another appropriate material.

Par mur on entend, au présent titre et au titre suivant, toute clôture non transparente de pierre, de bois ou de toute autre matière appropriée.

Art. 44. (5.4.6) - 1. Indien een nabuur wiens beplantingen over eens anders erf heenhangen, ondanks aanmaning van de eigenaar van dit erf, nalaat het overhangende te verwijderen, kan laatstgenoemde eigenaar eigenmachtig het overhangende wegsnijden en zich toeëigenen.
- 2. Degene op wiens erf wortels van een ander erf doorschieten, mag deze voor zover ze doorgeschoten zijn weghakken en zich toeëigenen.

1. An owner of land may, in his own right, cut and appropriate plants which hang over his property and belong to a neighbour if the latter, despite a warning from the aforementioned owner of the land, fails to remove the overhanging plants.
2. A person may cut and appropriate roots to the extent that they extend upon his land from another property.

1. Le propriétaire d'un fonds, après avoir sommé son voisin d'enlever les parties des plantations appartenant à ce dernier qui avancent sur son fonds, peut, si ce dernier ne s'exécute pas, de sa propre autorité les couper et se les approprier.

2. Celui sur le fonds duquel avancent des racines provenant d'un autre fonds peut couper celles-ci dans la mesure où elles y avancent et se les approprier.

Art. 45. (5.4.7) Vruchten die van de bomen van een erf op een naburig erf vallen, behoren aan hem wie de vruchten van dit laatste erf toekomen.

Fruits which fall from the trees of one property onto a neighbouring property belong to the person who is entitled to the fruits of the neighbouring property.

Les fruits tombant des arbres d'un fonds sur un fonds voisin appartiennent à celui auquel reviennent les fruits de ce dernier fonds.

Art. 46. (5.4.8) De eigenaar van een erf kan te allen tijde van de eigenaar van het aangrenzende erf vorderen dat op de grens van hun erven behoorlijk waarneembare afpalingstekens gesteld of de bestaande zo nodig vernieuwd worden. De eigenaars dragen in de kosten hiervan voor gelijke delen bij.

At all times, the owner of land may demand from the owner of the adjacent property that reasonably visible marks be put on the boundary of their properties or that, if need be, existing ones be replaced. The owners share equally in the expenses.

Le propriétaire d'un fonds peut demander en tout temps à celui du fonds voisin que soient placées, à la limite des fonds, des bornes suffisamment visibles ou que celles qui existent soient remplacées, si nécessaire. Les propriétaires contribuent également aux frais.

Art. 47. (5.4.9) - 1. Indien de loop van de grens tussen twee erven onzeker is, kan ieder der eigenaars te allen tijde vorderen dat de rechter de grens bepaalt.
- 2. In geval van onzekerheid waar de grens tussen twee erven ligt, geldt niet het wettelijk vermoeden dat de bezitter eigenaar is.

- 3. Bij het bepalen van de grens kan de rechter naar gelang van de omstandigheden het gebied waarover onzekerheid bestaat, in gelijkwaardige of ongelijkwaardige delen verdelen dan wel het in zijn geheel aan een der partijen toewijzen, al dan niet met toekenning van een schadevergoeding aan een der partijen.

1. If the boundary between two properties is uncertain, each of the owners may at all times demand that the judge settle it.
2. In the event of uncertainty about the boundary between two properties, the legal presumption that the possessor is owner does not apply.
3. In settling the boundary the judge may, according to the circumstances, divide the area to which the uncertainty applies into parts of equal or unequal value, or he may assign the whole of it to one of the parties, in each case with or without compensation to either of them.

1. Si le tracé de la limite séparant deux fonds est incertain, chacun des propriétaires peut demander en tout temps que le juge la fixe.
2. Lorsqu'il y a incertitude relative à la limite séparant deux fonds, la présomption légale que le possesseur est propriétaire n'a pas lieu.
3. Lorsqu'il détermine la limite, le juge peut, suivant les circonstances, diviser le terrain sur lequel porte l'incertitude en parts de valeur égale ou inégale, ou l'attribuer en entier à l'une des parties, dans tous les cas avec ou sans indemnité à l'une des parties.

Art. 48. (5.4.10) De eigenaar van een erf is bevoegd dit af te sluiten.

The owner of land is entitled to enclose it.

Le propriétaire peut enclore son fonds.

Art. 49. (5.4.11) - 1. Ieder der eigenaars van aangrenzende erven in een aaneengebouwd gedeelte van een gemeente kan te allen tijde vorderen dat de andere eigenaar ertoe meewerkt, dat op de grens van de erven een scheidsmuur van twee meter hoogte wordt opgericht, voor zover een verordening of een plaatselijke gewoonte de wijze of de hoogte der afscheiding niet anders regelt. De eigenaars dragen in de kosten van de afscheiding voor gelijke delen bij.
- 2. Het vorige lid is niet toepasselijk, indien een der erven een openbare weg of een openbaar water is.

1. At all times, each owner of neigbouring properties in a built-up part of a Commune may demand that the other owner cooperate in erecting a dividing wall of a height of two metres on the boundary of the properties, to the extent that an ordinance or local usage does not provide otherwise for the manner or the height of the separation. The owners share equally in the costs of the separation.
2. The preceding paragraph does not apply if one of the properties is a public road or public water.

1. Chacun des propriétaires de fonds contigus situés dans la zone bâtie d'une commune peut demander en tout temps que l'autre prête son concours à l'érection, à la limite des fonds, d'un mur séparatif haut de deux mètres, dans la mesure où un règlement ou l'usage local ne fixent pas autrement le mode ou la hauteur de la séparation. Les propriétaires contribuent également aux frais de la séparation.
2. Le paragraphe précédent ne s'applique pas si l'un des fonds est une voie ou une eau publique.

Art. 50. (5.4.12) - 1. Tenzij de eigenaar van het naburige erf daartoe toestemming heeft gegeven, is het niet geoorloofd binnen twee meter van de

grenslijn van dit erf vensters of andere muuropeningen, dan wel balkons of soortgelijke werken te hebben, voor zover deze op dit erf uitzicht geven.
- 2. De nabuur kan zich niet verzetten tegen de aanwezigheid van zodanige openingen of werken, indien zijn erf een openbare weg of een openbaar water is, indien zich tussen de erven openbare wegen of openbare wateren bevinden of indien het uitzicht niet verder reikt dan tot een binnen twee meter van de opening of het werk zich bevindende muur. Uit dezen hoofde geoorloofde openingen of werken blijven geoorloofd, ook nadat de erven hun openbare bestemming hebben verloren of de muur is gesloopt.
- 3. De in dit artikel bedoelde afstand wordt gemeten rechthoekig uit de buitenkant van de muur daar, waar de opening is gemaakt, of uit de buitenste naar het naburige erf gekeerde rand van het vooruitspringende werk tot aan de grenslijn der erven of de muur.
- 4. Wanneer de nabuur als gevolg van verjaring geen wegneming van een opening of werk meer kan vorderen, is hij verplicht binnen een afstand van twee meter daarvan geen gebouwen of werken aan te brengen die de eigenaar van het andere erf onredelijk zouden hinderen, behoudens voor zover zulk een gebouw of werk zich daar reeds op het tijdstip van de voltooiing van de verjaring bevond.
- 5. Ter zake van een volgens dit artikel ongeoorloofde toestand is slechts vergoeding verschuldigd van schade, ontstaan na het tijdstip waartegen opheffing van die toestand is aangemaand.

1. Unless the owner of the neighbouring property has consented, windows or other openings in the wall, balconies or similar works must not be within two metres from the boundary of this property, to the extent that they have a view thereof.
2. A neighbour cannot object to the presence of such openings or works if his property is a public road or public water, if there are public roads or public waters between the properties or if the view does not extend beyond a wall situated within two metres from the opening or work. Openings or works which are permitted pursuant to this provision continue to be permitted even after the properties have lost their public destination or the wall has been demolished.
3. The distance referred to in this article is measured rectangularly from the outside of the wall where the opening has been made or from the ledge of the work facing the neighbouring property, to the boundary of the properties or to the wall.
4. Where as a result of prescription the neighbour can no longer demand the removal of an opening or work, he may not put up buildings or works within a distance of two metres from them which

1. À moins que le propriétaire du fonds voisin n'y ait consenti, il est interdit de pratiquer, dans les deux mètres de la limite, des fenêtres ou autres ouvertures dans un mur ou encore des balcons ou des ouvrages semblables, dans la mesure où ceux-ci donnent vue sur ce fonds.
2. Le voisin ne peut s'opposer à la présence de semblables ouvertures ou ouvrages si son fonds est une voie ou une eau publique, si des voies ou des eaux publiques se trouvent entre les deux fonds ou encore si la vue ne s'étend pas au-delà d'un mur qui se trouve dans les deux mètres de l'ouverture ou de l'ouvrage. Les ouvertures ou ouvrages permis à ce titre le demeurent, même après que les fonds ont perdu leur destination publique ou que le mur a été démoli.
3. La distance visée au présent article se mesure à l'angle droit à partir de l'extérieur du mur où l'ouverture a été faite ou du bord extrême tourné vers le fonds voisin de l'ouvrage avancé, jusqu'à la limite des fonds ou jusqu'au mur.
4. Lorsque le voisin, par suite de la prescription, ne peut plus demander l'enlèvement d'une ouverture ou d'un ouvrage, il est tenu de ne pas ériger, dans les deux mètres de ceux-ci, des constructions ou

would cause unreasonable nuisance to the owner of the other property, except to the extent that such building or work was already there at the time of the completion of the prescription period.
5. A situation which according to this article is unlawful gives rise to compensation for damage suffered only from the time by which a warning has been given to terminate the situation.

ouvrages qui gêneraient de manière anormale le propriétaire de l'autre fonds, sauf dans la mesure où la construction ou l'ouvrage s'y trouvait déjà au moment où la prescription s'est accomplie.
5. Une situation contraire au présent article ne donne lieu à réparation que pour le préjudice survenu après la date à laquelle la sommation visait à la faire cesser.

Art. 51. (5.4.13) In muren, staande binnen de in het vorige artikel aangegeven afstand, mogen steeds lichtopeningen worden gemaakt, mits zij van vaststaande en ondoorzichtige vensters worden voorzien.

Openings within the distance referred to in the preceding article may always be made in walls to allow the passage of light, provided that these openings have been fitted with opaque fixed windows.

On peut toujours pratiquer des jours dans les murs qui se trouvent à l'intérieur de la distance prévue à l'article précédent, pourvu qu'ils soient munis de fenêtres dormantes à verre non dépoli.

Art. 52. (5.4.14) - 1. Een eigenaar is verplicht de afdekking van zijn gebouwen en werken zodanig in te richten, dat daarvan het water niet op eens anders erf afloopt.
- 2. Afwatering op de openbare weg is geoorloofd, indien zij niet bij de wet of verordening verboden is.

1. An owner must install the roofing of his buildings and works in such a fashion that water will not flow from it onto the land of another person.
2. Unless forbidden by law or ordinance, drainage onto a public road is permitted.

1. Le propriétaire est tenu de poser la couverture de ses constructions et ouvrages de telle manière que l'eau ne s'en écoule pas sur le fonds d'autrui.
2. L'écoulement des eaux sur la voie publique est permis, s'il n'est pas interdit par la loi ou par règlement.

Art. 53. (5.4.15) Een eigenaar is verplicht er voor te zorgen dat geen water of vuilnis van zijn erf in de goot van eens anders erf komt.

An owner must ensure that no water or refuse from his land finds itself in the gutter of the property of another person.

Le propriétaire est tenu de veiller à ce que l'eau ou les ordures provenant de son fonds ne se retrouvent pas dans l'égout du fonds d'autrui.

Art. 54. (5.4.16) - 1. Is een gebouw of werk ten dele op, boven of onder het erf van een ander gebouwd en zou de eigenaar van het gebouw of werk door wegneming van het uitstekende gedeelte onevenredig veel zwaarder benadeeld worden dan de eigenaar van het erf door handhaving daarvan, dan kan de eigenaar van het gebouw of werk te allen tijde vorderen dat hem tegen schadeloosstelling een erfdienstbaarheid tot het handhaven van de bestaande toestand wordt verleend of, ter keuze van de eigenaar van het erf, een daartoe benodigd gedeelte van het erf wordt overgedragen.
- 2. Het vorige lid is van overeenkomstige toepassing, wanneer een gebouw of werk na verloop van tijd over andermans erf is gaan overhellen.
- 3. De vorige leden zijn niet van toepassing, indien dit voortvloeit uit een op de wet of rechtshandeling gegronde verplichting tot het dulden van

de bestaande toestand of indien de eigenaar van het gebouw of werk ter zake van de bouw of zijn verkrijging kwade trouw of grove schuld verweten kan worden.

1. Where part of a building or work has been constructed on, over or under the land of another person and where removal of the protruding part would be disproportionately more prejudicial to the owner of the building or work than its preservation would be to the owner of the land, the owner of the building or work may at all times demand that, against compensation, a servitude be granted to him in order to preserve the existing situation or that, at the option of the owner of the land, the required part of the land be transferred to him.

2. The preceding paragraph applies *mutatis mutandis* to a building or work which over the years has begun to lean over the land of another person.

3. The preceding paragraphs do not apply if this is the result of an obligation, arising from the law or a juridical act, to tolerate the existing situation or if the owner of the building or work can be held to have been in bad faith or grossly negligent with respect to the construction or his acquisition of the building or work.

1. Lorsqu'une construction ou un ouvrage a été érigé en partie sur le fonds d'autrui ou au-dessus ou au-dessous de celui-ci et que l'enlèvement de la partie qui dépasse causerait au propriétaire de la construction ou de l'ouvrage un préjudice disproportionnellement plus grave que celui que le maintien causerait au propriétaire de ce fonds, le propriétaire de la construction ou de l'ouvrage peut demander en tout temps que lui soit accordée, contre indemnité, une servitude visant le maintien de la situation existante; il peut également demander que, au choix du propriétaire du fonds, une partie du fonds nécessaire à cette fin lui soit transférée.

2. Le paragraphe précédent s'applique par analogie lorsqu'une construction ou un ouvrage, avec le temps, penche sur le fonds d'autrui.

3. Les deux paragraphes précédents ne s'appliquent pas si cela résulte d'une obligation découlant de la loi ou d'un acte juridique de tolérer une situation existante ou si l'on peut faire reproche au propriétaire de la construction ou de l'ouvrage de mauvaise foi ou de négligence grossière relativement à la construction ou à son acquisition.

Art. 55. (5.4.16a) Indien door een dreigende instorting van een gebouw of werk een naburig erf in gevaar wordt gebracht, kan de eigenaar van dat erf te allen tijde vorderen dat maatregelen worden genomen teneinde het gevaar op te heffen.

The owner of land which becomes endangered by the threat of collapse of a building or work on a neighbouring property, may at all times demand that measures be taken to remove the danger.

Si la menace de ruine d'une construction ou d'un ouvrage crée un danger pour le fonds voisin, le propriétaire de celui-ci peut demander en tout temps que soient prises des mesures afin d'enrayer le danger.

Art. 56. (5.4.17) Wanneer het voor het verrichten van werkzaamheden ten behoeve van een onroerende zaak noodzakelijk is van een andere onroerende zaak tijdelijk gebruik te maken, is de eigenaar van deze zaak gehouden dit na behoorlijke kennisgeving en tegen schadeloosstelling toe te staan, tenzij er voor deze eigenaar gewichtige redenen bestaan dit gebruik te weigeren of tot een later tijdstip te doen uitstellen.

Where, in order to perform work on an immoveable thing, it is necessary to use temporarily another immoveable thing, the owner of this thing must allow this to be done after reasonable notice and against compensation, unless he has serious reasons to refuse this use or to have it postponed until a later date.

Lorsqu'il est nécessaire, pour effectuer des travaux qui concernent un immeuble, de faire temporairement usage d'un autre immeuble, le propriétaire de celui-ci est tenu, sur avis convenable et contre indemnisation, de le permettre, à moins qu'il n'ait des motifs graves de refuser cet usage ou de le faire différer à une date ultérieure.

Art. 57. (5.4.18) - 1. De eigenaar van een erf dat geen behoorlijke toegang heeft tot een openbare weg of een openbaar vaarwater, kan van de eigenaars van de naburige erven te allen tijde aanwijzing van een noodweg ten dienste van zijn erf vorderen tegen vooraf te betalen of te verzekeren vergoeding van de schade welke hun door die noodweg wordt berokkend.
- 2. Indien zich na de aanwijzing van de noodweg onvoorziene omstandigheden voordoen, waardoor die weg een grotere last aan de eigenaar van het erf veroorzaakt dan waarmee bij het bepalen van de in lid 1 bedoelde vergoeding was gerekend, kan de rechter het bedrag van de vergoeding verhogen.
- 3. Bij de aanwijzing van de noodweg wordt rekening gehouden met het belang van het ingesloten erf, dat langs die weg de openbare weg of het openbare water zo snel mogelijk kan worden bereikt, en met het belang van de bezwaarde erven om zo weinig mogelijk overlast van die weg te ondervinden. Is een erf van de openbare weg afgesloten geraakt, doordat het ten gevolge van een rechtshandeling een andere eigenaar heeft gekregen dan een vroeger daarmee verenigd gedeelte dat aan de openbare weg grenst of een behoorlijke toegang daartoe heeft, dan komt dit afgescheiden gedeelte het eerst voor de belasting met een noodweg in aanmerking.
- 4. Wanneer een wijziging in de plaatselijke omstandigheden dat wenselijk maakt, kan een noodweg op vordering van een onmiddellijk belanghebbende eigenaar worden verlegd.
- 5. Een noodweg vervalt, hoelang hij ook heeft bestaan, zodra hij niet meer nodig is.

1. The owner of land which has no reasonable access to a public road or public waterway may at all times demand that the owners of the neighbouring properties designate an emergency road to his land against compensation for the damage which the emergency road causes them. The compensation must be paid in advance or security for payment must be furnished.
2. The judge may increase the amount of compensation if, after the designation of the emergency road, unforeseen circumstances arise which result in the road causing greater inconvenience to the owner of the property than was envisaged in the calculation of the compensation referred to in paragraph 1.

1. Le propriétaire d'un fonds qui n'a pas d'accès convenable à la voie ou à l'eau publique peut demander en tout temps aux propriétaires des fonds voisins de lui désigner un passage d'urgence desservant son fonds, moyennant une indemnité payée ou garantie d'avance pour le préjudice qui leur est ainsi causé.

2. Si, après la désignation du passage d'urgence, des circonstances imprévues en rendent l'usage plus onéreux pour le propriétaire du fonds concerné que ce qui avait été envisagé lors de l'établissement de l'indemnité visée au paragraphe 1er, le juge peut augmenter la somme de l'indemnité.

3. In designating the emergency road, account is taken of the interest which the enclosed land has to reach as quickly as possible, via that road, the public road or public waterway, and the interest which the servient lands have to suffer as little inconvenience as possible from that road. Where land having become enclosed as a result of a juridical act has an owner other than the owner of part of the land which used to be united to it and which borders the public road or has reasonable access to it, the part which has been separated from the rest is considered first for the purpose of an emergency road.

4. Where a change in local circumstances makes it desirable, the course of an emergency road can be changed upon the demand of a directly interested owner.

5. An emergency road, no matter how long it has existed, ceases to exist once it is no longer needed.

3. Dans la désignation du passage d'urgence, l'on tient compte de l'intérêt, pour le fonds enclavé, d'un accès le plus rapide possible à la voie publique ou aux eaux publiques, ainsi que de l'intérêt, pour les fonds grevés, de subir le moins d'inconvénients possible de ce passage. Lorsqu'un fonds devient enclavé par suite d'un acte juridique qui en fait passer la propriété à une personne autre que le propriétaire d'un fonds précédemment uni avec lui et qui borde la voie publique ou y a un accès convenable, ce dernier fonds est considéré en premier pour la charge du passage d'urgence.

4. Lorsqu'un changement des conditions locales le rend souhaitable, le passage d'urgence peut être déplacé à la demande d'un propriétaire directement intéressé.

5. Le passage d'urgence, quel que soit le temps pendant lequel il a existé, disparaît lorsqu'il n'est plus nécessaire.

Art. 58. (5.4.19) De eigenaar van een erf die water dat elders te zijner beschikking staat, door een leiding wil aanvoeren, kan tegen vooraf te betalen of te verzekeren schadevergoeding van de eigenaars der naburige erven vorderen te gedogen dat deze leiding door of over hun erven gaat.
- 2. De laatste vier leden van het vorige artikel vinden daarbij overeenkomstige toepassing.

1. The owner of land who, via a pipeline, wants to transport to his land water which is at his disposal elsewhere can, against compensation, demand that the owners of the neighbouring properties allow this pipeline to pass over or below their lands. The compensation must be paid in advance or security for payment must be furnished.

2. The last four paragraphs of the preceding article apply *mutatis mutandis*.

1. Le propriétaire d'un fonds qui veut y amener par un tuyau de l'eau dont il peut disposer ailleurs peut demander, contre indemnité payée ou garantie d'avance, que les propriétaires des fonds voisins tolèrent le passage du tuyau par leurs fonds ou sur ceux-ci.

2. Les quatre derniers paragraphes de l'article précédent s'appliquent par analogie.

Art. 59. (5.4.20) - 1. Wanneer de grens van twee erven in de lengterichting onder een niet bevaarbaar stromend water, een sloot, gracht of dergelijke watergang doorloopt, heeft de eigenaar van elk dier erven met betrekking tot die watergang in zijn gehele breedte dezelfde bevoegdheden en verplichtingen als een mede-eigenaar. Iedere eigenaar is verplicht de op zijn erf gelegen kant van het water, de sloot, de gracht of de watergang te onderhouden.
- 2. Iedere eigenaar is gerechtigd en verplicht hetgeen tot onderhoud daaruit wordt verwijderd, voor zijn deel op zijn erf te ontvangen.
- 3. Een door de eigenaars overeengekomen afwijkende regeling is ook bindend voor hun rechtverkrijgenden.

1. Where the boundary of two properties runs along the length under non-navigable running water, a ditch, canal or similar waterway, the owner of each property has the same rights and obligations as a co-owner with respect to this waterway over the full width. Each owner must maintain the side of the water, ditch, canal or waterway which is on his land.
2. Each owner has the right and obligation to receive on his land his share of what is removed from the waterway for maintenance.
3. Different arrangements made by the owners also bind their successors.

1. Lorsque la limite de deux fonds passe dans le sens de la longueur au-dessous d'un cours d'eau non navigable, d'un fossé, d'un canal ou d'une voie d'eau semblable, le propriétaire de chacun des fonds a, à l'égard de cette voie d'eau et sur toute sa largeur, les mêmes droits et obligations qu'un copropriétaire. Chaque propriétaire est tenu d'entretenir le bord de l'eau, du fossé, du canal ou de la voie d'eau situé sur son fonds.
2. Chaque propriétaire a le droit et l'obligation de recevoir sur son fonds sa part de ce qui est enlevé de l'eau aux fins d'entretien.
3. Les arrangements dérogatoires convenus entre propriétaires lient également leurs ayants cause.

TITEL 5 MANDELIGHEID

TITLE 5 COMMON OWNERSHIP[1]

TITRE CINQUIÈME DE LA MITOYENNETÉ

Art. 60. (5.5.1) Mandeligheid ontstaat, wanneer een onroerende zaak gemeenschappelijk eigendom is van de eigenaars van twee of meer erven en door hen tot gemeenschappelijk nut van die erven wordt bestemd bij een tussen hun opgemaakte notariële akte, gevolgd door inschrijving daarvan in de openbare registers.

Common ownership arises where an immoveable thing is owned in common by the owners of two or more properties[2] and where it is designated by them for the common benefit of those properties by a notarial deed between them, followed by its entry in the public registers.

La mitoyenneté naît lorsqu'une chose immobilière est la copropriété des propriétaires de plusieurs fonds qui la destinent à l'utilité commune de ces fonds par la passation d'un acte notarié entre eux suivi de son inscription dans les registres publics.

Art. 61. (5.5.1a) - 1. Mandeligheid die is ontstaan ingevolge het vorige artikel, eindigt:
- **a. wanneer de gemeenschap eindigt;**
- **b. wanneer de bestemming van de zaak tot gemeenschappelijk nut van de erven wordt opgeheven bij een tussen de mede-eigenaars opgemaakte notariële akte, gevolgd door inschrijving daarvan in de openbare registers;**
- **c. zodra het nut van de zaak voor elk van de erven is geëindigd.**

1 The Dutch term "mandeligheid" is hard to translate. Although "mitoyennety" is sometimes used in English, the term "common ownership" has been chosen, thereby following the example of the Draft Civil Code of Quebec (1977).

2 In this title the Dutch term "erven" has been translated as "properties". On the rare occasions when this title uses the Dutch singular "erf", it has been translated as "property". Cf. also the footnotes in Articles 20, 31 and 37.

- 2. Het feit dat het nut van de zaak voor elk van de erven is geëindigd, kan in de openbare registers worden ingeschreven.

1. Common ownership which has arisen by virtue of the preceding paragraph is terminated:
a. when the community ends;
b. when the designation of the thing for the common benefit of the properties is terminated by a notarial deed between the co-owners, followed by its entry in the public registers;
c. once the benefit of the thing has been terminated for each of the properties.
2. The fact that the benefit of the thing has been terminated for each of the properties can be entered in the public registers.

1. La mitoyenneté née en vertu de l'article précédent se termine:
a. Lorsque prend fin la communauté;
b. Lorsque est levée la destination de la chose à l'utilité commune des fonds par un acte notarié entre les copropriétaires suivi de son inscription dans les registres publics;
c. Dès que l'utilité de la chose a cessé pour chacun des fonds.
2. On peut inscrire dans les registres le fait que l'utilité de la chose a cessé pour chacun des fonds.

Art. 62. (5.5.2) - 1. Een vrijstaande scheidsmuur, een hek of een heg is gemeenschappelijk eigendom en mandelig, indien de grens van twee erven die aan verschillende eigenaars toebehoren, er in de lengterichting onderdoor loopt.
- 2. De scheidsmuur die twee gebouwen of werken, welke aan verschillende eigenaars toebehoren, gemeen hebben, is eveneens gemeenschappelijk eigendom en mandelig.

1. A free standing dividing wall, a fence or a hedge is held in common ownership if the boundary between two properties belonging to different owners runs along the length under this wall, fence or hedge.
2. The dividing wall common to two buildings and works belonging to different owners is also held in common ownership.

1. Un mur séparatif détaché, une clôture ou une haie est mitoyen et propriété commune, si la limite de deux fonds appartenant à des propriétaires différents y passe au-dessous dans le sens de la longueur.
2. Le mur séparatif commun à deux constructions ou ouvrages appartenant à des propriétaires différents est également mitoyen et propriété commune.

Art. 63. (5.5.3) - 1. Het recht op een mandelige zaak kan niet worden gescheiden van de eigendom der erven.
- 2. Een vordering tot verdeling van een mandelige zaak is uitgesloten.

1. The right to a thing which is held in common ownership cannot be severed from the ownership of the properties.
2. No action lies for the partition of a thing held in common ownership.

1. Le droit sur une chose mitoyenne ne peut être séparé de la propriété des fonds.
2. L'action en partage d'une chose mitoyenne est exclue.

Art. 64. (5.5.4) Mandeligheid brengt mede dat iedere mede-eigenaar aan de overige mede-eigenaars toegang tot de mandelige zaak moet geven.

Common ownership entails the obligation of each co-owner to give to the other co-owners access to the thing held in common ownership.

La mitoyenneté comporte l'obligation pour chaque copropriétaire de donner aux autres accès à la chose mitoyenne.

Art. 65. (5.5.5) Mandelige zaken moeten op kosten van alle mede-eigenaars worden onderhouden, gereinigd en, indien nodig, vernieuwd.

Things which are held in common ownership must be maintained, cleaned and, if necessary, renewed at the expense of all co-owners.

Les choses mitoyennes sont entretenues, nettoyées et, si nécessaire, renouvelées aux frais de tous les copropriétaires.

Art. 66. (5.5.6) - 1. Een mede-eigenaar van een mandelige zaak kan zijn aandeel in die zaak ook afzonderlijk van zijn erf aan de overige mede-eigenaars overdragen.
- 2. Indien een mede-eigenaar hiertoe op zijn kosten wil overgaan uit hoofde van de lasten van onderhoud, reiniging en vernieuwing in de toekomst, zijn de overige mede-eigenaars gehouden tot die overdracht mede te werken, mits hij hun zo nodig een recht van opstal of erfdienstbaarheid verleent, waardoor zij met betrekking tot de zaak hun rechten kunnen blijven uitoefenen.
- 3. De vorige leden zijn niet van toepassing op een muur die twee gebouwen of werken gemeen hebben, noch op een muur, hek of heg waardoor twee erven in een aaneengebouwd gedeelte van een gemeente van elkaar worden gescheiden.

1. A co-owner of a thing which is held in common ownership can, even separately from his property, transfer his share in the thing to the other co-owners.
2. If a co-owner, at his own expense, wants to do so because of future charges for maintenance, cleaning and renewal, the other co-owners must cooperate in the transfer, provided that, if necessary, he grants them a right of superficies or a servitude so as to allow them to continue to exercise their rights with respect to the thing.
3. The preceding paragraphs do not apply to a common wall of two buildings or works nor to a wall, fence or hedge separating two properties in a built-up part of a Commune.

1. Le copropriétaire d'une chose mitoyenne peut transférer aux autres sa part dans cette chose, même séparément du fonds.
2. Si un copropriétaire veut, à ses frais, effectuer ce transfert en raison des charges d'entretien, de nettoyage et de rénovation à venir, les autres copropriétaires sont tenus d'y prêter leur concours, pourvu qu'il leur accorde, si nécessaire, un droit de superficie ou de servitude leur permettant de continuer à exercer leurs droits sur la chose.
3. Les paragraphes précédents ne s'appliquent pas au mur commun à deux ouvrages ou constructions, ni au mur, à la clôture ou à la haie qui sépare deux fonds dans la zone bâtie d'une commune.

Art. 67. (5.5.7) - 1. Iedere mede-eigenaar mag tegen de mandelige scheidsmuur aanbouwen en daarin tot op de helft der dikte balken, ribben, ankers en andere werken aanbrengen, mits hij aan de muur en aan de door de buur bevoegdelijk daarmee verbonden werken geen nadeel toebrengt.
- 2. Behalve in noodgevallen kan een mede-eigenaar vorderen dat, vóór de andere mede-eigenaar begint met aanbrengen van het werk, deskundigen zullen vaststellen op welke wijze dit kan geschieden zonder nadeel voor de muur of voor bevoegd aangebrachte werken van de eerst vermelde eigenaar.

1. Each co-owner may build against a dividing wall which is held in common ownership and may install, up to half its thickness, beams, ribs, ancres and other works, provided that he cause no damage to the wall or to the works which the neighbour has rightfully connected to it.
2. Except in cases of emergency a co-owner may demand that, before the other co-owner proceeds to install the work, experts determine in which fashion this can take place without damage to the wall or the works which the former co-owner has rightfully installed.

1. Chaque copropriétaire peut construire contre le mur mitoyen séparatif et y installer, jusqu'au milieu de son épaisseur, poutres, chevrons, ancres et autres ouvrages, pourvu qu'il n'endommage pas le mur ni les ouvrages légalement y rattachés par le voisin.
2. Sauf cas d'urgence, le copropriétaire peut demander qu'avant que l'autre copropriétaire ne commence l'installation de l'ouvrage, des experts déterminent de quelle façon cela peut s'effectuer sans endommager le mur ou les ouvrages posés légalement par le premier copropriétaire.

Art. 68. (5.5.8) Iedere mede-eigenaar mag op de mandelige scheidsmuur tot op de helft der dikte een goot aanleggen, mits het water niet op het erf van de andere mede-eigenaar uitloost.

Each co-owner may construct a gutter on the dividing wall held in common ownership up to half of its thickness, provided that the water not discharge itself onto the property of the other co-owner.

Chaque copropriétaire peut poser sur le mur séparatif mitoyen une gouttière jusqu'au milieu de son épaisseur, pourvu que l'eau ne s'écoule pas sur le fonds de l'autre.

Art. 69. (5.5.8a) De artikelen 64, 65, 66 lid 2, 67 en 68 vinden geen toepassing voor zover een overeenkomstig artikel 168 van Boek 3 getroffen regeling anders bepaalt.

Articles 64, 65, 66 paragraph 2, 67 and 68 do not apply to the extent that rules made pursuant to article 168 of Book 3 provide otherwise.

Les articles 64, 65, 66, paragraphe 2, 67 et 68 ne s'appliquent pas dans la mesure où il y a des règles contraires établies conformément à l'article 168 du Livre troisième.

TITEL 6 ERFDIENSTBAARHEDEN

TITLE 6 SERVITUDES

TITRE SIXIÈME DES SERVITUDES

Art. 70. (5.6.1) - 1. Een erfdienstbaarheid is een last, waarmede een onroerende zaak - het dienende erf - ten behoeve van een andere onroerende zaak - het heersende erf - is bezwaard.
- 2. In de akte van vestiging van een erfdienstbaarheid kan aan de eigenaar van het heersende erf de verplichting worden opgelegd aan de eigenaar van het dienende erf op al dan niet regelmatig terugkerende tijdstippen een geldsom - de retributie - te betalen.

1. A servitude is a charge imposed upon an immoveable thing, the servient land, in favour of another immoveable thing, the dominant land.

1. La servitude est une charge imposée sur un immeuble, le fonds servant, en faveur d'un autre immeuble, le fonds dominant.

2. The deed establishing a servitude may impose an obligation upon the owner of the dominant land to pay to the owner of the servient land a sum of money -called the retribution-, payable at regular or at irregular intervals.

2. Il peut être stipulé dans l'acte constituant une servitude l'obligation pour le propriétaire du fonds dominant de payer au propriétaire du fonds servant une redevance payable par versements qui peuvent être périodiques ou non.

Art. 71. (5.6.2) - 1. De last die een erfdienstbaarheid op het dienende erf legt, bestaat in een verplichting om op, boven of onder een der beide erven iets te dulden of niet te doen. In de akte van vestiging kan worden bepaald dat de last bovendien een verplichting inhoudt tot het aanbrengen van gebouwen, werken of beplantingen die voor de uitoefening van die erfdienstbaarheid nodig zijn, mits deze gebouwen, werken en beplantingen zich geheel of gedeeltelijk op het dienende erf zullen bevinden.
- 2. De last die een erfdienstbaarheid op het dienende erf legt, kan ook bestaan in een verplichting tot onderhoud van het dienende erf of van gebouwen, werken of beplantingen die zich geheel of gedeeltelijk op het dienende erf bevinden of zullen bevinden.

1. The charge which a servitude imposes upon the servient land consists of an obligation to tolerate something or not to do something on, above or under one of the properties[1]. The deed of establishment may stipulate that the charge also include an obligation to construct buildings or works or to install plantations which are necessary for the exercise of the servitude, provided that these buildings, works or plantations will be wholly or partially situated on the servient land.
2. The charge which a servitude imposes upon the servient land may also consist of an obligation to maintain the servient land or the buildings, works or plantations which are or will be wholly or partially situated on the servient land.

1. La charge imposée par la servitude sur le fonds servant consiste en l'obligation de tolérer ou de ne pas faire quelque chose sur l'un des deux fonds ou au-dessus ou au-dessous de ce fonds. Il peut être prévu dans l'acte constitutif que la charge comporte, en outre, l'obligation d'ériger des constructions, ouvrages ou plantations nécessaires à l'exercice de la servitude, pourvu que ces constructions, ouvrages ou plantations se trouvent en tout ou en partie sur le fonds servant.

2. La charge imposée par la servitude au fonds servant peut également consister en l'obligation d'entretien du fonds servant ou de constructions, ouvrages ou plantations qui s'y trouvent ou s'y trouveront en tout ou en partie.

Art. 72. (5.6.3) Erfdienstbaarheden kunnen ontstaan door vestiging en door verjaring.

Servitudes are created by establishment and by prescription.

Les servitudes naissent par établissement et par prescription.

Art. 73. (5.6.4) - 1. De inhoud van de erfdienstbaarheid en de wijze van uitoefening worden bepaald door de akte van vestiging en, voor zover in die akte regelen daaromtrent ontbreken, door de plaatselijke gewoonte. Is een erfdienstbaarheid te goeder trouw geruime tijd zonder tegenspraak op

1 In this title the Dutch term "erf" has been translated as "land"; on the rare occasions when this title uses the Dutch plural "erven", it has been translated as "properties". In article 84 (5.6.10) of this title, the Dutch term "opstal" (the object of the right of superficies: *infra* title 8) has been translated as "property". Cf. also the footnotes in Articles 20, 31, 37 and 60.

een bepaalde wijze uitgeoefend, dan is in geval van twijfel deze wijze van uitoefening beslissend.
- 2. Niettemin kan de eigenaar van het dienende erf voor de uitoefening van de erfdienstbaarheid een ander gedeelte van het erf aanwijzen dan waarop de erfdienstbaarheid ingevolge het vorige lid dient te worden uitgeoefend, mits deze verplaatsing zonder vermindering van genot voor de eigenaar van het heersende erf mogelijk is. Kosten, noodzakelijk voor zodanige verandering, komen ten laste van de eigenaar van het dienende erf.

1. The contents and the manner of exercising the servitude are determined by the deed of establishment and, to the extent that the deed lacks rules in this respect, by local usage. The exercise of a servitude in a certain manner, in good faith, for a rather long period and unopposed, is decisive in case of doubt.

2. Nevertheless, for the exercise of the servitude the owner of the servient land may designate a part of the land other than that on which the servitude is to be exercised pursuant to the preceding paragraph, provided that this move is possible without diminishing the enjoyment of the owner of the dominant land. Expenses which are necessary for this change are borne by the owner of the servient land.

1. Le contenu de la servitude et le mode d'exercice sont déterminés par l'acte constitutif et, dans la mesure où des règles à ce sujet font défaut dans l'acte, par l'usage local. Lorsqu'une servitude a été exercée d'une manière déterminée et de bonne foi pendant un temps assez long sans contestation, ce mode d'exercice est déterminant en cas de doute.

2. Le propriétaire du fonds servant peut néanmoins fixer, pour l'exercice de la servitude, une autre partie du fonds que celle où elle doit s'exercer en vertu du paragraphe précédent, pourvu que ce déplacement puisse se réaliser sans perte de jouissance pour le propriétaire du fonds dominant. Les frais occasionnés par ce changement sont à la charge du propriétaire du fonds servant.

Art. 74. (5.6.5) De uitoefening der erfdienstbaarheid moet op de voor het dienende erf minst bezwarende wijze geschieden.

The servitude must be exercised in the manner which causes the least inconvenience to the servient land.

La servitude s'exerce de la façon la moins gênante pour le fonds servant.

Art. 75. (5.6.6) - 1. De eigenaar van het heersende erf is bevoegd om op zijn kosten op het dienende erf alles te verrichten wat voor de uitoefening van de erfdienstbaarheid noodzakelijk is.
- 2. Hij is eveneens bevoegd om op zijn kosten op het dienende erf gebouwen, werken en beplantingen aan te brengen, die voor de uitoefening van de erfdienstbaarheid noodzakelijk zijn.
- 3. Hij is verplicht het door hem op het dienende erf aangebrachte te onderhouden, voor zover dit in het belang van het dienende erf nodig is; hij is bevoegd het weg te nemen, mits hij het erf in de oude toestand terugbrengt.
- 4. De eigenaar van het dienende erf heeft geen recht van gebruik van de gebouwen, werken en beplantingen, die daarop door de eigenaar van het heersende erf rechtmatig zijn aangebracht.
- 5. In de akte van vestiging kan van de vorige leden worden afgeweken.
- 6. In geval van mandeligheid zijn in plaats van de leden 3 en 4 de uit dien hoofde geldende regels van toepassing.

1. The owner of the dominant land is entitled to do on the servient land, at his expense, all that is necessary for the exercise of the servitude.
2. He is also entitled to construct on the servient land, at his expense, buildings or works, or to install plantations which are necessary for the exercise of the servitude.
3. He has the obligation to maintain what he has constructed or installed on the servient land to the extent that this is necessary in the interest of the servient land; he is entitled to remove it provided that he restore the land to its original state.
4. The owner of the servient land does not have the right to use the buildings, works or plantations which the owner of the dominant land has lawfully constructed or installed on the servient land.
5. The deed of establishment may derogate from the preceding paragraphs.
6. In case of common ownership in the sense of title 5, the rules pertaining to that type of ownership apply instead of paragraphs 3 and 4.

1. Le propriétaire du fonds dominant peut faire, sur le fonds servant et à ses frais, tout ce qui est nécessaire pour l'exercice de la servitude.
2. Il peut également ériger, sur le fonds servant et à ses frais, des ouvrages, constructions et plantations nécessaires pour l'exercice de la servitude.
3. Il a l'obligation d'entretenir ce qu'il a érigé sur le fonds servant, dans la mesure où cela est nécessaire dans l'intérêt de ce fonds; il peut l'enlever, pourvu qu'il remette le fonds en l'état d'origine.
4. Le propriétaire du fonds servant ne peut utiliser les ouvrages, constructions et plantations que le propriétaire du fonds dominant y a légalement érigés.
5. On peut déroger aux paragraphes précédents dans l'acte constitutif.
6. En cas de mitoyenneté, les règles applicables de ce chef remplacent les paragraphes 3 et 4.

Art. 76. (5.6.7) - 1. Wanneer het heersende erf wordt verdeeld, blijft de erfdienstbaarheid bestaan ten behoeve van ieder gedeelte, ten voordele waarvan zij kan strekken.
- 2. Wanneer het dienende erf wordt verdeeld, blijft de last rusten op ieder gedeelte, ten aanzien waarvan naar de akte van vestiging en de aard der erfdienstbaarheid de uitoefening mogelijk is.
- 3. In de akte van vestiging kan van de vorige leden worden afgeweken.

1. Where the dominant land is divided, the servitude continues to exist in favour of each part to which it can be beneficial.
2. Where the servient land is divided, the charge continues to encumber each part, in respect of which the exercise of the servitude is possible, according to the deed of establishment and the nature of the servitude.
3. The deed of establishment may derogate from the preceding paragraphs.

1. Lorsque le fonds dominant est divisé, la servitude subsiste en faveur de chaque partie à laquelle elle peut profiter.
2. Lorsque le fonds servant est divisé, la charge continue de grever chaque partie sur laquelle, d'après l'acte constitutif et la nature de la servitude, l'exercice est possible.
3. On peut déroger aux paragraphes précédents dans l'acte constitutif.

Art. 77. (5.6.7a) - 1. Behoort het heersende of het dienende erf toe aan twee of meer personen, hetzij als deelgenoten, hetzij als eigenaars van verschillende gedeelten daarvan, dan zijn zij hoofdelijk verbonden tot nakoming van de uit de erfdienstbaarheid voortvloeiende geldelijke verplichtingen die tijdens hun recht opeisbaar worden, voor zover deze niet over hun rechten zijn verdeeld.

- 2. Na overdracht of toedeling van het heersende of het dienende erf of van een gedeelte daarvan of een aandeel daarin zijn de verkrijger en zijn rechtsvoorganger hoofdelijk verbonden voor de in lid 1 bedoelde geldelijke verplichtingen die in de voorafgaande twee jaren opeisbaar zijn geworden.
- 3. In de akte van vestiging kan van de vorige leden worden afgeweken, doch van het tweede lid niet ten nadele van de verkrijger.

1. Where the dominant or the servient land belongs to two or more persons, either as partners or as owners of different parts, they are solidarily liable for the performance of the pecuniary obligations which result from the servitude and become exigible during the existence of their right, to the extent that these obligations have not been divided over their rights.
2. After transfer or attribution[1] of the dominant or the servient land, or of a part or a share of it, the acquirer and his predecessor are solidarily liable for the pecuniary obligations, referred to in paragraph 1, which have become exigible in the two preceding years.

3. The deed of establishment may derogate from the preceding paragraphs but not from paragraph 2 where this would be detrimental to the acquirer.

1. Lorsque le fonds dominant ou le fonds servant appartient à plusieurs personnes, à titre de partenaires ou de propriétaires de différentes parties, ces personnes sont solidairement responsables de l'exécution des obligations pécuniaires qui résultent de la servitude et qui deviennent exigibles pendant l'existence de leur droit, dans la mesure où ces obligations n'ont pas été réparties sur leurs droits.
2. Après le transfert ou l'attribution[2] du fonds dominant ou du fonds servant, ou d'une partie de ceux-ci ou d'une part dans ceux-ci, l'acquéreur et son auteur sont solidairement responsables des obligations pécuniaires visées au paragraphe premier, qui sont devenues exigibles au cours des deux années précédentes.
3. Dans l'acte constitutif, on peut déroger aux paragraphes précédents, mais non au paragraphe 2 s'il y a préjudice à l'acquéreur.

Art. 78. (5.6.8) De rechter kan op vordering van de eigenaar van het dienende erf een erfdienstbaarheid wijzigen of opheffen:
a. op grond van onvoorziene omstandigheden welke van dien aard zijn dat naar maatstaven van redelijkheid en billijkheid ongewijzigde instandhouding van de erfdienstbaarheid niet van de eigenaar van het dienende erf kan worden gevergd;
b. indien ten minste twintig jaren na het ontstaan van de erfdienstbaarheid zijn verlopen en het ongewijzigd voortbestaan van de erfdienstbaarheid in strijd is met het algemeen belang.

Upon the demand of the owner of the servient land, the judge may modify or cancel a servitude:
a. on the ground of unforeseen circumstances which are of such a nature that, according to criteria of reasonableness and equity, one cannot require from the owner of the servient land that the servitude remain unchanged;

Le juge peut, à la demande du propriétaire du fonds servant, modifier ou supprimer une servitude:
a. En raison de circonstances imprévues d'une nature telle que, d'après des critères de la raison et de l'équité, le maintien intégral de la servitude ne puisse être imposé au propriétaire du fonds servant;

1 By "attribution" is meant an attribution in a partition.
2 À savoir, lors d'un partage.

b. if at least twenty years have passed since the time of creation of the servitude, and it is contrary to the general interest that the servitude remain unchanged.

b. Si se sont écoulés au moins vingt ans depuis la création de la servitude et que son existence continue sans changement soit contraire à l'intérêt général.

Art. 79. (5.6.8a) De rechter kan op vordering van de eigenaar van het dienende erf een erfdienstbaarheid opheffen, indien de uitoefening daarvan onmogelijk is geworden of de eigenaar van het heersende erf geen redelijk belang bij de uitoefening meer heeft, en het niet aannemelijk is dat de mogelijkheid van uitoefening of het redelijk belang daarbij zal terugkeren.

Upon the demand of the owner of the servient land, the judge may cancel a servitude if it has become impossible to exercise it or if the owner of the dominant land no longer has a reasonable interest to exercise it, and if it is unlikely that the possibility of exercise or the reasonable interest will return.

Le juge peut, à la demande du propriétaire du fonds servant, supprimer une servitude, si son exercice est devenu impossible ou si le propriétaire du fonds dominant n'y a plus d'intérêt suffisant et qu'il soit improbable que la possibilité d'exercice ou l'intérêt suffisant renaisse.

Art. 80. (5.6.8b) De rechter kan op vordering van de eigenaar van het heersende erf de inhoud van een erfdienstbaarheid, wanneer door onvoorziene omstandigheden de uitoefening blijvend of tijdelijk onmogelijk is geworden of het belang van de eigenaar van het heersende erf aanzienlijk is verminderd, zodanig wijzigen dat de mogelijkheid van uitoefening of het oorspronkelijke belang wordt hersteld, mits deze wijziging naar maatstaven van redelijkheid en billijkheid van de eigenaar van het dienende erf kan worden gevergd.

Where, by reason of unforeseen circumstances, it has become permanently or temporarily impossible to exercise the servitude or where the interest of the owner of the dominant land has been considerably diminished, the judge, upon the demand of the owner of the dominant land, may modify the contents of a servitude in such a manner that the possibility of exercise or the original interest be restored, provided that this change can be imposed upon the owner of the servient land according to criteria of reasonableness and equity.

Lorsque des circonstances imprévues ont rendu impossible, de façon permanente ou temporaire, l'exercice d'une servitude ou que l'intérêt du propriétaire du fonds dominant a diminué de façon appréciable, le juge peut, à la demande de ce dernier, modifier le contenu de la servitude de manière à rétablir la possibilité d'exercice ou l'intérêt initial, pourvu que, d'après des critères de la raison et de l'équité, l'on puisse imposer cette modification au propriétaire du fonds servant.

Art. 81. (5.6.8ba) - 1. De rechter kan een vordering als bedoeld in de artikelen 78-80 toewijzen onder door hem te stellen voorwaarden.
- 2. Rust op een der erven beperkt recht, dan is de vordering slechts toewijsbaar, indien de beperkt gerechtigde in het geding is geroepen. Bij het oordeel of aan de maatstaven van de artikelen 78 onder a, 79 en 80 is voldaan, dient mede met zijn belangen rekening te worden gehouden.

1. The judge may grant a demand pursuant to articles 78 - 80, subject to conditions to be determined by him.

1. Le juge peut accueillir une demande visée aux articles 78 à 80 aux conditions qu'il fixe.

2. Where one of the properties is encumbered with a dismembered right, the demand will not be granted, unless the holder of the dismembered right has been joined in the action. His interest must also be taken into account in judging whether the criteria of articles 78 *sub* a, 79 and 80 have been complied with.

2. Lorsqu'un des fonds est grevé d'un droit démembré, la demande ne peut être accueillie que si le titulaire de ce droit a été appelé en cause. En jugeant si les conditions de l'article 78, point a., et des articles 79 et 80 sont remplies, il doit être tenu compte également des intérêts de ce dernier.

Art. 82. (5.6.8c) - 1. Indien de eigenaar van het heersende erf uit hoofde van de aan de erfdienstbaarheid verbonden lasten en verplichtingen op zijn kosten afstand van zijn recht wil doen, is de eigenaar van het dienende erf gehouden hieraan mede te werken.
- 2. In de akte van vestiging kan voor de eerste twintig jaren anders worden bepaald.

1. If the owner of the dominant land wants to abandon his right, at his own expense, because of the charges and obligations attached to the servitude, the owner of the servient land must cooperate herein.
2. The deed of establishment may contain, for the first twenty years of the servitude, a stipulation to the contrary.

1. Si le propriétaire du fonds dominant veut, à ses frais, abandonner son droit en raison des charges et obligations afférentes à la servitude, le propriétaire du fonds servant est tenu d'y prêter son concours.

2. L'acte constitutif peut comporter une stipulation contraire pour les vingt premières années.

Art. 83. (5.6.9a) Indien op het tijdstip waarop het heersende en het dienende erf één eigenaar verkrijgen, een derde een der erven in huur of pacht of uit hoofde van een ander persoonlijk recht in gebruik heeft, gaat de erfdienstbaarheid pas door vermenging teniet bij het einde van dit gebruiksrecht.

If, at the time when one and the same person becomes owner of both the dominant and servient land, a third person leases one of the properties or has another personal right of use in it, the servitude is only extinguished by confusion at the extinction of this right.

Si, au moment où les fonds dominant et servant deviennent la propriété d'une seule personne, un tiers loue un des fonds ou y a un autre droit d'usage personnel, la servitude s'éteint par confusion seulement à l'extinction de ce droit.

Art. 84. (5.6.10) - 1. Hij die een recht van erfpacht, opstal of vruchtgebruik op een onroerende zaak heeft, kan een erfdienstbaarheid ten behoeve van deze zaak bedingen. Hij kan haar ook met een erfdienstbaarheid belasten.
- 2. Erfdienstbaarheden, bedongen door een beperkt gerechtigde ten behoeve van de zaak waarop zijn recht rust of door een opstaller ten behoeve van de opstal, gaan bij het einde van het beperkte recht slechts teniet, indien dit in de akte van vestiging van de erfdienstbaarheid is bepaald. Blijft de erfdienstbaarheid voortbestaan, dan staat een beding als bedoeld in artikel 82 lid 2 niet langer aan afstand van de erfdienstbaarheid in de weg.
- 3. Erfdienstbaarheden, gevestigd door een beperkt gerechtigde ten laste van de zaak waarop zijn recht rust of door een opstaller ten laste van de opstal, gaan teniet bij het einde van het beperkte recht, tenzij dit eindigt

door vermenging of afstand of de eigenaar van de zaak waarop het beperkte recht rustte bij een in de openbare registers ingeschreven akte heeft verklaard met de vestiging van de erfdienstbaarheid in te stemmen.
- 4. De erfpachter, opstaller of vruchtgebruiker wordt voor de toepassing van de overige artikelen van deze titel aangemerkt als eigenaar van het heersende, onderscheidenlijk het dienende erf.

1. A person who has a right of emphyteusis or superficies on an immoveable thing or has the usufruct of it may stipulate a servitude in favour of this thing. He may also encumber it with a servitude.
2. Servitudes, stipulated by the holder of a dismembered right in favour of the thing which is the object of his right, or by a superficiary in favour of the property of which he is the owner pursuant to his right, are not extinguished by the termination of the dismembered right, unless the deed of establishment of the servitude provides otherwise. Where the servitude continues to exist, a stipulation pursuant to article 82 paragraph 2 is no longer a bar to abandonment of the servitude.
3. Servitudes established by the holder of a dismembered right which impose charges upon the thing which is the object of his right, and servitudes established by a superficiary which impose charges upon the property of which he is the owner pursuant to his right, are extinguished by the termination of the dismembered right, unless the termination is by way of confusion or abandonment, or the owner of the thing which was the object of the dismembered right has declared by a deed entered in the public registers that he consents to the establishment of the servitude.
4. For the application of the other articles of this title, the emphyteutic holder, superficiary or usufructuary is deemed owner of the dominant, respectively the servient land.

1. Celui qui a sur un immeuble un droit d'emphytéose, de superficie ou d'usufruit peut stipuler une servitude en faveur de cet immeuble. Il peut également le grever d'une servitude.

2. Les servitudes stipulées par le titulaire d'un droit démembré en faveur de la chose grevée ou par le superficiaire en faveur des biens dont il a la propriété en vertu de son droit s'éteignent à l'expiration du droit démembré seulement s'il est ainsi stipulé dans l'acte constitutif. Lorsque la servitude continue d'exister, la stipulation visée à l'article 82, paragraphe 2 ne peut empêcher l'abandon de cette servitude.

3. Les servitudes établies par le titulaire d'un droit démembré à la charge de la chose grevée de son droit ou par le superficiaire à la charge des choses dont il a la propriété en vertu de son droit s'éteignent à l'expiration du droit démembré, à moins que cette fin ne résulte de la confusion ou de l'abandon ou que le propriétaire de la chose grevée ne déclare, par acte inscrit sur les registres publics, qu'il consent à l'établissement de la servitude.

4. Pour l'application des autres articles du présent titre, l'emphytéote, le superficiaire ou l'usufruitier est réputé propriétaire du fonds dominant ou du fonds servant, selon le cas.

TITEL 7 ERFPACHT

TITLE 7 EMPHYTEUSIS

TITRE SEPTIÈME DE L'EMPHYTÉOSE

Art. 85. (5.7.1.1) - 1. Erfpacht is een zakelijk recht dat de erfpachter de bevoegdheid geeft eens anders onroerende zaak te houden en te gebruiken.
- 2. In de akte van vestiging kan aan de erfpachter de verplichting worden opgelegd aan de eigenaar op al dan niet regelmatig terugkerende tijdstippen een geldsom - de canon - te betalen.

1. Emphyteusis is a real right which gives the emphyteutic holder the power to detain and to use the immoveable thing of another person.
2. The deed of establishment may impose an obligation upon the emphyteutic holder to pay a sum of money -called the canon- to the owner, payable at regular or at irregular intervals.

1. L'emphytéose est le droit réel qui confère à l'emphytéote la faculté de détenir et d'utiliser la chose immobilière d'autrui.

2. Il peut être stipulé, dans l'acte constitutif, l'obligation pour l'emphytéote de payer au propriétaire une redevance, le canon, payable par versements qui peuvent être périodiques ou non.

Art. 86. (5.7.1.2) Partijen kunnen in de akte van vestiging de duur van de erfpacht regelen.

The parties may provide, in the deed of establishment, for the duration of the emphyteusis.

Les parties peuvent fixer dans l'acte constitutif la durée de l'emphytéose.

Art. 87. (5.7.1.2a.) - 1. Een erfpacht kan door de erfpachter worden opgezegd, tenzij in de akte van vestiging anders is bepaald.
- 2. Een erfpacht kan door de eigenaar worden opgezegd, indien de erfpachter in verzuim is de canon over twee achtereenvolgende jaren te betalen of in ernstige mate tekortschiet in de nakoming van zijn andere verplichtingen. Deze opzegging moet op straffe van nietigheid binnen acht dagen worden betekend aan degenen die als beperkt gerechtigde of beslaglegger op de erfpacht in de openbare registers staan ingeschreven. Na het einde van de erfpacht is de eigenaar verplicht de waarde die de erfpacht dan heeft aan de erfpachter te vergoeden, na aftrek van hetgeen hij uit hoofde van de erfpacht van de erfpachter te vorderen heeft, de kosten daaronder begrepen.
- 3. Een beding dat ten nadele van de erfpachter van het vorige lid afwijkt is nietig. In de akte van vestiging kan aan de eigenaar de bevoegdheid worden toegekend tot opzegging, behoudens op grond van tekortschieten van de erfpachter in de nakoming van zijn verplichtingen.

1. Unless the deed of establishment provides otherwise, the emphyteutic holder may resiliate the emphyteusis.

1. L'emphytéote peut résilier l'emphytéose, sauf disposition contraire dans l'acte constitutif.

2. The owner may resiliate the emphyteusis if the emphyteutic holder is in default of paying the canon during two consecutive years, or if he fails seriously in the performance of his other obligations. On pain of nullity, the resiliation must be notified, within eight days, to the persons who appear in the public registers as holder of a dismembered right or as seizor of the emphyteusis. After the termination of the emphyteusis, the owner must reimburse the emphyteutic holder for the value which the emphyteusis then has, after deduction of what he can claim from the emphyteutic holder, including costs.
3. A stipulation which, to the detriment of the emphyteutic holder, derogates from the preceding paragraph is null. The deed of establishment may grant the owner the power to resiliate, except for failure of the emphyteutic holder to perform his obligations.

2. Le propriétaire peut résilier l'emphytéose, si l'emphytéote est en demeure de payer le canon pendant deux années consécutives ou qu'il manque de façon sérieuse à l'exécution de ses autres obligations. La résiliation doit, à peine de nullité, être signifiée dans les huit jours à ceux qui sont inscrits dans les registres publics en tant que titulaire de droit démembré ou saisissant de l'emphytéose. Après la fin de l'emphytéose, le propriétaire est tenu de rembourser à l'emphytéote la valeur qu'a alors l'emphytéose, déduction faite de qu'il peut lui réclamer au titre de l'emphytéose, dépens compris.

3. Est nulle la clause dérogeant au paragraphe précédent au détriment de l'emphytéote. Dans l'acte constitutif, la faculté de résiliation peut être accordée au propriétaire, sauf pour cause d'un manquement de l'emphytéote à l'exécution de ses obligations.

Art. 88. (5.7.1.2b) - 1. Iedere opzegging geschiedt bij exploit. Zij geschiedt tenminste een jaar voor het tijdstip waartegen wordt opgezegd, doch in het geval van artikel 87 lid 2 tenminste een maand voor dat tijdstip.
- 2. In het geval van artikel 87 lid 2 weigert de bewaarder de inschrijving van de opzegging als niet tevens wordt overgelegd de betekening daarvan aan degenen die in de openbare registers als beperkt gerechtigde of beslaglegger op de erfpacht stonden ingeschreven.

1. Resiliation takes place by summons. It takes place at least one year prior to the date on which it is to take effect, but in the case of article 87, paragraph 2 at least one month before that date.
2. In the case of article 87, paragraph 2 the registrar shall refuse to enter the resiliation, unless the notification, given to persons who appear in the public registers as holder of a dismembered right or as seizor of the emphyteusis, also be deposited.

1. La résiliation a lieu par exploit. Elle a lieu au moins un an avant la date où la résiliation prend effet, mais dans le cas prévu au paragraphe 2 de l'article 87, au moins un mois avant cette date.
2. Dans le cas prévu au paragraphe 2 de l'article 87, le conservateur refuse l'inscription de la résiliation s'il n'est pas présenté en même temps la signification de celle-ci à ceux qui sont inscrits dans les registres publics en tant que titulaires d'un droit démembré ou saisissants de l'emphytéose.

Art. 89. (5.7.1.3) - 1. Voor zover niet in de akte van vestiging anders is bepaald, heeft de erfpachter hetzelfde genot van de zaak als een eigenaar.
- 2. Hij mag echter zonder toestemming van de eigenaar niet een andere bestemming aan de zaak geven of een handeling in strijd met de bestemming van de zaak verrichten.
- 3. Voor zover niet in de akte van vestiging anders is bepaald, heeft de erfpachter, zowel tijdens de duur van de erfpacht als bij het einde daarvan, de bevoegdheid gebouwen, werken en beplantingen, die door hemzelf of een rechtsvoorganger onverplicht zijn aangebracht of van de eigenaar tegen

vergoeding der waarde zijn overgenomen, weg te nemen, mits hij de in erfpacht gegeven zaak in de oude toestand terugbrengt.

1. To the extent that the deed of establishment does not provide otherwise, the emphyteutic holder has the same enjoyment of the thing as an owner.
2. Without the permission of the owner, however, he may not change the destination of the thing nor perform an act contrary to its destination.
3. Provided that he restores the thing subject to the emphyteusis to its original condition and to the extent that the deed of establishment does not provide otherwise, the emphyteutic holder is entitled, during the emphyteusis as well as upon its termination, to remove buildings, works and plantations which he or a predecessor have constructed or installed, without being obliged to do so, or which they have taken over from the owner against reimbursement of the value.

1. Dans la mesure où l'acte constitutif n'y a pas été autrement prévu, l'emphytéote jouit de la chose comme un propriétaire.

2. Il ne peut cependant, sans le consentement du propriétaire, donner à la chose une autre destination ni faire un acte contraire à celle-ci.
3. Dans la mesure où l'acte constitutif n'y a pas été autrement prévu, l'emphytéote peut, tant au cours de l'emphytéose qu'à la fin de celle-ci, enlever les constructions, ouvrages et plantations que lui ou un de ses auteurs a érigés sans y être tenus, ou qu'il a repris au propriétaire contre remboursement de la valeur, pourvu qu'il remette la chose donnée en emphytéose en l'état d'origine.

Art. 90. (5.7.1.4) - 1. Voor zover niet in de akte van vestiging anders is bepaald, behoren vruchten die tijdens de duur der erfpacht zijn afgescheiden of opeisbaar geworden, en voordelen van roerende aard, die de zaak oplevert, aan de erfpachter.
- 2. Voordelen van onroerende aard behoren aan de eigenaar toe. Zij zijn eveneens aan de erfpacht onderworpen, tenzij in de akte van vestiging anders is bepaald.

1. To the extent that the deed of establishment does not privide otherwise, the fruits which have become separated or exigible during the emphyteusis, as well as the benefits of a moveable nature which the thing yields, belong to the emphyteutic holder.
2. Benefits of an immoveable nature belong to the owner. Unless the deed of establishment provides otherwise, they are also subject to the emphyteusis.

1. Dans la mesure où l'acte constitutif n'y a pas été autrement prévu, appartiennent à l'emphytéote les fruits séparés ou devenus exigibles au cours de l'emphytéose et les avantages mobiliers que procure la chose.

2. Les avantages immobiliers appartiennent au propriétaire. Ils sont soumis à l'emphytéose, sauf stipulation contraire dans l'acte constitutif.

Art. 91. (5.7.1.5) - 1. In de akte van vestiging kan worden bepaald dat de erfpacht niet zonder toestemming van de eigenaar kan worden overgedragen of toebedeeld. Een zodanige bepaling staat aan executie door schuldeisers niet in de weg.
- 2. In de akte van vestiging kan ook worden bepaald, dat de erfpachter zijn recht niet zonder toestemming van de eigenaar kan splitsen door overdracht of toedeling van de erfpacht op een gedeelte van de zaak.
- 3. Een beding als in de vorige leden bedoeld kan ook worden gemaakt ten aanzien van de appartementsrechten, waarin een gebouw door de erfpachter wordt gesplitst. Het kan slechts aan een verkrijger onder

bijzondere titel van een recht op het appartementsrecht worden tegengeworpen, indien het in de akte van splitsing is omschreven.
- 4. Indien de eigenaar de vereiste toestemming zonder redelijke gronden weigert of zich niet verklaart, kan zijn toestemming op verzoek van degene die haar behoeft, worden vervangen door een machtiging van de kantonrechter binnen wiens rechtsgebied de zaak of het grootste gedeelte daarvan is gelegen.

1. The deed of establishment may provide that the emphyteusis cannot be transferred or attributed[1] without the consent of the owner. Such a stipulation does not prevent execution by creditors.

2. The deed of establishment may also provide that the emphyteutic holder cannot divide his right, without the consent of the owner, by transfering or attributing the emphyteusis upon a part of the thing.

3. A stipulation referred to in the preceding paragraphs may also be made with respect to the apartment rights into which a building is divided by the emphyteutic holder. The stipulation may only be invoked against an acquirer by particular title of a right to the apartment right, if it has been described in the deed of division.

4. If the owner refuses to give the required consent without reasonable grounds, or if he remains silent, his consent may, upon the request of the person who needs it, be replaced by the authorization of the judge of the subdistrict court in whose jurisdiction the thing, or the larger part of it, is located.

1. Il peut être stipulé dans l'acte constitutif qu'une emphytéose ne peut être transférée ou attribuée, lors d'un partage, sans le consentement du propriétaire. Une telle stipulation n'empêche pas l'exécution forcée par les créanciers.

2. Il peut également être stipulé dans l'acte constitutif que l'emphytéote ne peut, sans le consentement du propriétaire, diviser son droit par le transfert ou par l'attribution de l'emphytéose sur une partie de la chose.

3. La clause visée aux paragraphes précédents peut également être stipulée à propos des droits d'appartement en lesquels l'édifice est divisé par l'emphytéote. Elle ne peut être opposée à l'acquéreur à titre particulier d'un droit sur le droit d'appartement que si elle a été expressément stipulée dans l'acte de division.

4. Si le propriétaire refuse le consentement requis sans motif valable ou ne se déclare pas, son consentement peut, à la requête de celui qui en a besoin, être remplacé par l'autorisation du juge d'instance dans le ressort duquel se situe la chose ou la plus grande partie de celle-ci.

Art. 92. (5.7.1.5a) - 1. Behoort de erfpacht toe aan twee of meer personen, hetzij als deelgenoten hetzij als erfpachter van verschillende gedeelten van de zaak, dan zijn zij hoofdelijk verbonden voor de gehele canon die tijdens hun recht opeisbaar wordt, voor zover deze niet over hun rechten verdeeld is.
- 2. Na overdracht of toedeling van de erfpacht op de zaak of een gedeelte daarvan of van een aandeel in de erfpacht zijn de verkrijger en zijn rechtsvoorganger hoofdelijk verbonden voor de door laatstgenoemde verschuldigde canon die in de voorafgaande vijf jaren opeisbaar is geworden.
- 3. In de akte van vestiging kan van de vorige leden worden afgeweken, doch van het tweede lid niet ten nadele van de verkrijger.

[1] "Attributed" refers to an attribution in partition.

1. Where two or more persons are entitled to the emphyteusis, either as partners or as emphyteutic holders of different parts of the thing, they are solidarily liable for the entire canon which becomes exigible during the existence of their right, to the extent that the canon has not been divided over their rights.
2. After transfer or attribution of the emphyteusis upon the thing or upon part of it, or a share in it, the acquirer and his predecessor are solidarily liable for the canon which is owed by the latter and which has become exigible during the five preceding years.
3. The deed of establishment may derogate from the preceding paragraphs, but not from paragraph 2 where this would be detrimental to the acquirer.

1. Lorsqu'une emphytéose appartient à plursieurs personnes, soit comme partenaires, soit comme emphytéotes de différentes parties d'une chose, elles sont solidairement responsables de l'ensemble du canon qui devient exigible pendant l'existence de leur droit, dans la mesure où cette obligation n'a pas été répartie sur ces droits.
2. Après le transfert ou l'attribution[1] de l'emphytéose sur l'ensemble ou une partie d'une chose, ou d'une part de l'emphytéose, l'acquéreur et son auteur sont solidairement responsables du canon dû par ce dernier, qui est devenu exigible au cours des cinq dernières années.
3. Dans l'acte constitutif, on peut déroger aux paragraphes précédents, mais non au paragraphe 2 au préjudice de l'acquéreur.

Art. 93. (5.7.1.5b) - 1. De erfpachter is bevoegd de zaak waarop het recht van erfpacht rust, geheel of ten dele in ondererfpacht te geven, voor zover in de akte van vestiging niet anders is bepaald. Aan de ondererfpachter komen ten aanzien van de zaak niet meer bevoegdheden toe dan de erfpachter jegens de eigenaar heeft.
- 2. De ondererfpacht gaat bij het einde van de erfpacht teniet, tenzij deze eindigt door vermenging of afstand. De eigenaar kan voor de ter zake van de erfpacht verschuldigde canon het recht van erfpacht vrij van ondererfpacht uitwinnen. Het in de vorige zinnen van dit lid bepaalde geldt niet, indien de eigenaar bij een in de openbare registers ingeschreven notariële akte heeft verklaard met de vestiging van de ondererfpacht in te stemmen.
- 3. Voor de toepassing van de overige artikelen van deze titel wordt de erfpachter in zijn verhouding tot de ondererfpachter als eigenaar aangemerkt.

1. To the extent that the deed of establishment does not provide otherwise, the emphyteutic holder is entitled to create a sub-emphyteusis on the whole or part of the thing which is the object of his right. The sub-emphyteutic holder does not have more rights in the thing than the emphyteutic holder has vis-à-vis the owner.
2. Unless the emphyteusis is terminated by confusion or abandonment, the sub-emphyteusis is extinguished upon the termination of the emphyteusis. For the canon owed pursuant to the emphyteusis, the owner may seize and execute against

1. L'emphytéote peut donner en sous-emphytéose tout ou partie de la chose grevée de son droit, dans la mesure où l'acte constitutif n'y a pas été autrement prévu. Le sous-emphytéote n'a pas plus de pouvoirs sur la chose qu'en a l'emphytéote envers le propriétaire.
2. La sous-emphytéose s'éteint à la fin de l'emphytéose, à moins que celle-ci ne se termine par confusion ou abandon. Le propriétaire peut saisir et exécuter, pour le canon dû au titre de l'emphytéose, le droit d'emphytéose libre de la sous-emphytéose.

[1] lors d'un partage.

the right of emphyteusis free of the sub-emphyteusis. The provisions of the preceding sentences do not apply if the owner has declared by notarial deed, entered in the public registers, that he consents to the establishment of the sub-emphyteusis.

Les dispositions des phrases précédentes ne s'appliquent pas si le propriétaire déclare, par acte notarié inscrit sur les registres publics, consentir à l'établissement de la sous-emphytéose.

3. In applying the other articles of this section, the emphyteutic holder is deemed to be the owner for the purpose of his relationship with the sub-emphyteutic holder.

3. Aux fins des autres articles de la présente section, l'emphytéote, dans son rapport avec le sous-emphytéote, est réputé être propriétaire.

Art. 94. (5.7.1.6) - 1. De erfpachter is bevoegd de zaak waarop het recht van erfpacht rust, te verhuren of te verpachten, voor zover in de akte van vestiging niet anders is bepaald.
- 2. Na het einde van de erfpacht is de eigenaar verplicht een bevoegdelijk aangegane verhuur of verpachting gestand te doen. Hij kan nochtans gestanddoening weigeren, voor zover zonder zijn toestemming hetzij de overeengekomen tijdsduur van de huur langer is dan met het plaatselijk gebruik overeenstemt of bedrijfsruimte in de zin van artikel 1624 is verhuurd voor een langere tijd dan vijf jaren, hetzij de verpachting is geschied voor een langere duur dan twaalf jaren voor hoeven en zes jaren voor los land, hetzij de verhuring of verpachting is geschied op ongewone voor hem bezwarende voorwaarden.
- 3. Hij verliest de bevoegdheid gestanddoening te weigeren, wanneer de huurder of pachter hem een redelijke termijn heeft gesteld om zich omtrent de gestanddoening te verklaren en hij zich niet binnen deze termijn heeft uitgesproken.
- 4. Indien de eigenaar volgens de vorige leden niet verplicht is tot gestanddoening van een door de erfpachter aangegane verhuring van woonruimte waarin de huurder bij het eindigen van de erfpacht zijn hoofdverblijf heeft en waarop de artikelen 1623a-1623f van toepassing zijn, moet hij de huurovereenkomst niettemin met de huurder voortzetten met dien verstande dat artikel 1623k, tweede lid, van overeenkomstige toepassing is.

1. To the extent that the deed of establishment does not provide otherwise, the emphyteutic holder is entitled to lease the thing which is the object of the emphyteusis.

1. Dans la mesure où l'acte constitutif n'y a pas été autrement prévu, l'emphytéote peut donner à bail la chose grevée de son droit.

2. After the termination of the emphyteusis, the owner must respect a lease which has been duly entered into. Nevertheless, he can refuse to do so to the extent that, without his consent, the agreed duration of the lease is longer than what is in accordance with local usage. The same applies where commercial space in the sense of article 1624 has been leased for a period exceeding five years; where the lease has been made for

2. Le propriétaire est tenu, après la fin de l'emphytéose, de respecter le bail conclu régulièrement. Toutefois, il peut s'y refuser dans la mesure où, sans son consentement, la durée convenue du bail dépasse ce que prévoit l'usage local; il en est de même lorsque, conformément à l'article 1624, de l'espace commercial a été donné à bail pour plus de cinq ans ou lorsque le bail portant sur une ferme a été conclu pour plus de douze ans ou le bail portant sur des terres

a period exceeding twelve years for farmsteads or six years for farm land; or where the lease contains unusual conditions onerous for the owner.
3. The owner loses the right to refuse to respect the lease where the lessee has given him a reasonable period to pronounce himself on the matter and he has not done so within that period.
4. If, pursuant to the preceding paragraphs, the owner is not obliged to respect the lease of a dwelling entered into by the emphyteutic holder, and if, upon the termination of the emphyteusis, the lessee has his principal place of residence in this dwelling to which articles 1623a - 1623f apply, he must nevertheless continue the contract of lease and hire with the lessee, in which case article 1623k, paragraph 2 applies *mutatis mutandis*.

agricoles pour plus de six ans, ou encore, lorsque le bail a été conclu à des conditions inhabituelles et onéreuses pour lui.

3. Il perd le droit de refus lorsque le preneur lui a fixé un délai raisonnable pour déclarer s'il entend respecter le bail et qu'il ne s'est pas prononcé dans ce délai.

4. Le propriétaire qui, conformément aux paragraphes précédents, n'est pas tenu de respecter le bail d'espace d'habitation conclu par l'emphytéote, dans lequel le locataire, au moment de la fin de l'emphytéose, a sa résidence principale et auquel s'appliquent les articles 1623a à 1623f, doit néanmoins continuer le bail avec ce dernier, étant entendu que le paragraphe 2 de l'article 1623k s'applique par analogie.

Art. 95. (5.7.1.7) Tot het instellen van rechtsvorderingen en het indienen van verzoekschriften ter verkrijging van een rechterlijke uitspraak die zowel het recht van de eigenaar als dat van de erfpachter betreft, is ieder van hen bevoegd, mits hij zorg draagt dat de ander tijdig in het geding wordt geroepen.

The owner as well as the emphyteutic holder are entitled to institute actions and to submit requests to obtain a judgment concerning the rights of each of them, provided that each ensure that the other is timely joined in the action.

Le propriétaire, aussi bien que l'emphytéote, peut intenter des actions et présenter des requêtes en vue d'obtenir un jugement qui concerne les droits de chacun d'eux, pourvu qu'il s'assure que l'autre soit appelé en cause en temps utile.

Art. 96. (5.7.1.8) - 1. Gewone lasten en herstellingen worden door de erfpachter gedragen en verricht. De erfpachter is verplicht, wanneer buitengewone herstellingen nodig zijn, aan de eigenaar van deze noodzakelijkheid kennis te geven en hem gelegenheid te verschaffen tot het doen van deze herstellingen. De eigenaar is niet tot het doen van enige herstelling verplicht.
- 2. De erfpachter is verplicht de buitengewone lasten die op de zaak drukken te voldoen.
- 3. In de akte van vestiging kan van de vorige leden worden afgeweken.

1. The emphyteutic holder bears the ordinary charges and makes the ordinary repairs. Where extraordinary repairs are necessary, the emphyteutic holder must notify the owner and give him the opportunity to make these repairs. The owner is not obliged to make any repairs.
2. The emphyteutic holder must pay for the extraordinary charges encumbering the thing.

1. L'emphytéote assume les charges et les réparations ordinaires. Lorsque des réparations extraordinaires sont nécessaires, l'emphytéote est tenu d'en aviser le propriétaire et de lui laisser la possibilité de les effectuer. Le propriétaire n'est tenu à aucune réparation.
2. L'emphytéote est tenu d'acquitter les charges extraordinaires grevant la chose.

3. The deed of establishment may derogate from the preceding paragraphs.

3. On peut déroger aux deux paragraphes précédents dans l'acte constitutif.

Art. 97. (5.7.1.8a) - 1. Indien vijf en twintig jaren na de vestiging van de erfpacht zijn verlopen, kan de rechter op vordering van de eigenaar of de erfpachter de erfpacht wijzigen of opheffen op grond van onvoorziene omstandigheden, welke van dien aard zijn dat naar maatstaven van redelijkheid en billijkheid ongewijzigde instandhouding van de akte van vestiging niet van de eigenaar of de erfpachter kan worden gevergd.
- 2. De rechter kan de vordering onder door hem vast te stellen voorwaarden toewijzen.
- 3. Rust op de erfpacht of op de zaak een beperkt recht, dan is de vordering slechts toewijsbaar, indien de beperkt gerechtigde in het geding is geroepen en ook te zijnen aanzien aan de maatstaf van lid 1 is voldaan.

1. Twenty-five years after the establishment of the emphyteusis and upon the demand of the owner or the emphyteutic holder, the judge may modify or cancel the emphyteusis on the ground of unforeseen circumstances which are of such a nature that according to criteria of reasonableness and equity, it cannot be required from the owner or the emphyteutic holder that the deed of establishment remain unchanged.
2. The judge may grant the demand subject to conditions to be determined by him.
3. Where the emphyteusis or the thing is encumbered with a dismembered right, the demand cannot be granted, unless the holder of the dismembered right has been joined in the action and the standard referred to in paragraph 1 has been satisfied, also in respect of him.

1. Si vingt-cinq ans se sont écoulés depuis l'établissement de l'emphytéose, le juge peut, à la demande du propriétaire ou de l'emphytéote, modifier ou supprimer l'emphytéose pour cause de circonstances imprévues telles que, d'après des critères de la raison et de l'équité, le maintien sans changement de la servitude ne puisse être imposé au propriétaire ou à l'emphytéote.

2. Le juge peut accueillir la demande aux conditions qu'il fixe.

3. Lorsque l'emphytéose ou la chose est grevée d'un droit démembré, la demande ne peut être accueillie que si l'emphytéote est appelé en cause et si la solution est conforme, à son égard également, à la condition énoncée au paragraphe premier.

Art. 98. (5.7.1.9a) - 1. Wanneer de tijd waarvoor de erfpacht is gevestigd, is verstreken en de erfpachter de zaak niet op dat tijdstip heeft ontruimd, blijft de erfpacht doorlopen, tenzij de eigenaar uiterlijk zes maanden na dat tijdstip doet blijken dat hij haar als geëindigd beschouwt. De eigenaar en de erfpachter kunnen de verlengde erfpacht opzeggen op de wijze en met inachtneming van de termijn vermeld in artikel 88.
- 2. Ieder beding dat ten nadele van de erfpachter van dit artikel afwijkt, is nietig.

1. When the term for which the emphyteusis has been established has expired, and the emphyteutic holder has not vacated the thing at that time, the emphyteusis continues to exist, unless, at the latest six months after that time, the owner makes it known that he considers it as terminated. The owner and the

1. Lorsque, à l'expiration du temps pour lequel l'emphytéose a été établie, l'emphytéote n'a pas délaissé la chose, l'emphytéose continue d'exister, à moins que le propriétaire ne fasse savoir, au plus tard six mois après cette date, qu'il la considère comme terminée. Le propriétaire et l'emphytéote peuvent résilier l'emphytéose

emphyteutic holder can resiliate the extended emphyteusis in the manner mentioned in article 88, observing the period mentioned therein.

prolongée de la façon indiquée à l'article 88 et en respectant le terme qui y est énoncé.

2. Every stipulation which, to the detriment of the emphyteutic holder, derogates from this article is null.

2. Est nulle toute stipulation qui, au préjudice de l'emphytéote, déroge au présent article.

Art. 99. (5.7.1.11) - 1. Na het einde van de erfpacht heeft de voormalige erfpachter recht op vergoeding van de waarde van nog aanwezige gebouwen, werken en beplantingen, die door hemzelf of een rechtsvoorganger zijn aangebracht of van de eigenaar tegen vergoeding der waarde zijn overgenomen.

- 2. In de akte van vestiging kan worden bepaald dat de erfpachter geen recht heeft op de in het eerste lid bedoelde vergoeding:

a. indien de in erfpacht gegeven grond een andere bestemming had dan die van woningbouw;

b. indien de erfpachter de gebouwen, werken en beplantingen niet zelf heeft bekostigd;

c. indien de erfpacht geëindigd is door opzegging door de erfpachter;

d. voor zover de gebouwen, werken en beplantingen onverplicht waren aangebracht en hij ze bij het einde van de erfpacht mocht wegnemen.

- 3. De eigenaar is bevoegd van de door hem ingevolge dit artikel verschuldigde vergoeding af te houden hetgeen hij uit hoofde van de erfpacht van de erfpachter te vorderen heeft.

1. After the termination of the emphyteusis, the former emphyteutic holder is entitled to be reimbursed for the value of the still remaining buildings, works and plantations which he or a predecessor have constructed or installed, or have taken over from the owner against reimbursement of the value.

2. The deed of establishment may provide that the emphyteutic holder is not entitled to the reimbursement referred to in the first paragraph:

a. if the land subject to the emphyteusis had a destination other than the construction of dwellings;

b. if the emphyteutic holder has not himself borne the costs of the buildings, works and plants;

c. if the emhyteusis has been terminated by resiliation by the emphyteutic holder;

d. to the extent that the emphyteutic holder has constructed or installed buildings, works and plantations without being obliged to do so and that he could remove them upon the termination of the emphyteusis.

1. Après la fin de l'emphytéose, l'emphytéote a droit au remboursement de la valeur des constructions, ouvrages et plantations encore existants que lui ou un de ses auteurs a érigés ou a repris au propriétaire contre remboursement de la valeur.

2. Il peut être stipulé dans l'acte constitutif que l'emphytéote n'a pas droit au remboursement visé au paragraphe premier:

a. Si le fonds donné en emphytéose avait une destination autre que la construction d'habitations;

b. Si l'emphytéote n'a pas supporté lui-même le coût des constructions, ouvrages et plantations;

c. Si l'emphytéose a été terminée par suite de la résiliation par l'emphytéote;

d. Dans la mesure où l'emphytéote a érigé sans y être tenu des constructions, ouvrages et plantations et qu'il pouvait les enlever à la fin de l'emphytéose.

3. The owner is entitled to deduct from the reimbursement which he owes pursuant to this article, the claims which he has against the emphyteutic holder pursuant to the emphyteusis.

3. Le propriétaire peut déduire du remboursement auquel il est tenu en vertu du présent article ce qu'il peut exiger de l'emphytéote au titre de l'emphytéose.

Art. 100. (5.7.1.12) - 1. De erfpachter heeft een retentierecht op de in erfpacht uitgegeven zaak totdat hem de verschuldigde vergoeding is betaald.
- 2. Ieder van het vorige lid afwijkend beding is nietig.
- 3. De eigenaar heeft een retentierecht op hetgeen de erfpachter mocht hebben afgebroken, totdat hem hetgeen hij uit hoofde van de erfpacht heeft te vorderen is voldaan.

1. The emphyteutic holder has a right of retention on the thing subject to the emphyteusis until he has been reimbursed for what is owing to him.
2. Every stipulation which derogates from the preceding paragraph is null.
3. The owner has a right of retention on that which the emphyteutic holder might have demolished until such time as he has been paid for the claims which he has pursuant to the emphyteusis.

1. L'emphytéote a un droit de rétention sur la chose donnée en emphytéose jusqu'au paiement du remboursement qui lui est dû.

2. Toute stipulation contraire au paragraphe précédent est nulle.
3. Le propriétaire a un droit de rétention sur ce qu'a pu démolir l'emphytéote jusqu'au paiement de ce qu'il peut exiger au titre de l'emphytéose.

TITEL 8 OPSTAL

TITLE 8 THE RIGHT OF SUPERFICIES

TITRE HUITIÈME DU DROIT DE SUPERFICIE

Art. 101. (5.8.1) - 1. Het recht van opstal is een zakelijk recht om in, op of boven een onroerende zaak van een ander gebouwen, werken of beplantingen in eigendom te hebben of te verkrijgen.
- 2. Het recht van opstal kan zelfstandig dan wel afhankelijk van een ander zakelijk recht of van een recht van huur of pacht op de onroerende zaak worden verleend.
- 3. In de akte van vestiging kan de opstaller de verplichting worden opgelegd aan de eigenaar op al dan niet regelmatig terugkerende tijdstippen een geldsom - de retributie - te betalen.

1. The right of superficies is a real right to own or to acquire buildings, works or plantations in, on or above an immoveable thing belonging to another.

2. The right of superficies can be granted independently of another real right, or it may depend upon such a right or upon a lease of the immoveable thing.

1. Le droit de superficie est le droit réel d'avoir ou d'acquérir la propriété de constructions, d'ouvrages et de plantations qui se trouvent dans l'immeuble d'autrui, sur celui-ci ou au-dessus de celui-ci.
2. Le droit de superficie peut être accordé de manière autonome ou dépendante d'un autre droit réel ou d'un droit de bail sur l'immeuble.

3. The deed of establishment may oblige the superficiary to pay a sum of money -the retribution- to the owner, payable at regular or irregular intervals.

3. Il peut être stipulé, dans l'acte constitutif, l'obligation pour le superficiaire de payer au propriétaire une redevance. La redevance peut être stipulée payable par versements qui peuvent être périodiques ou non.

Art. 102. (5.8.1a) De bevoegdheden van de opstaller tot het gebruiken, aanbrengen en wegnemen van de gebouwen, werken en beplantingen kunnen in de akte van vestiging worden beperkt.

The deed of establishment may limit the powers of the superficiary to use, install or remove buildings, works and plantations.

Les droits du superficiaire d'utiliser, d'ériger et d'enlever des ouvrages, constructions et plantations peuvent être limités dans l'acte constitutif.

Art. 103. (5.8.3) Bij gebreke van een regeling daaromtrent in de akte van vestiging heeft de opstaller ten aanzien van de zaak waarop zijn recht rust, de bevoegdheden die voor het volle genot van zijn recht nodig zijn.

In the absence of an arrangement to that effect in the deed of establishment, the superficiary has, in respect of the thing subject to his right, the powers which are necessary for the full enjoyment of his right.

À défaut de règles à ce sujet dans l'acte constitutif, le superficiaire a, sur la chose grevée de son droit, les pouvoirs nécessaires pour en tirer la pleine jouissance.

Art. 104. (5.8.4) - 1. De artikelen 92 en 95 zijn van overeenkomstige toepassing op het recht van opstal.
- 2. De artikelen 86, 87, 88, 91, 93, 94, 97 en 98 zijn van overeenkomstige toepassing op een zelfstandig recht van opstal.

1. Articles 92 and 95 apply *mutatis mutandis* to the right of superficies.
2. Articles 86, 87, 88, 91, 93, 94, 97 and 98 apply *mutatis mutandis* to an independent right of superficies.

1. Les articles 92 et 95 s'appliquent par analogie au droit de superficie.
2. Les articles 86, 87, 88, 91, 93, 94, 97 et 98 s'appliquent par analogie au droit autonome de superficie.

Art. 105. (5.8.6) - 1. Wanneer het recht van opstal tenietgaat, gaat de eigendom van de gebouwen, werken en beplantingen van rechtswege over op de eigenaar van de onroerende zaak waarop het rustte.
- 2. Voor zover niet in de akte van vestiging anders is bepaald, heeft de opstaller bij het einde van zijn recht de bevoegdheid gebouwen, werken en beplantingen die door hemzelf of een rechtsvoorganger onverplicht zijn aangebracht dan wel van de eigenaar tegen vergoeding der waarde zijn overgenomen weg te nemen, mits hij de onroerende zaak waarop het recht rustte in de oude toestand terugbrengt.
- 3. De artikelen 99 en 100 zijn van overeenkomstige toepassing, met dien verstande dat het aan de opstaller toekomende retentierecht slechts de gebouwen, werken en beplantingen omvat.

1. Upon the extinction of the right of superficies, the ownership of the buildings, works and plantations is transferred *de iure* to the owner of the immoveable thing which was subject to the superficies.
2. Provided that he restores the immoveable thing which was subject to his right to its original condition and to the extent that the deed of establishment does not provide otherwise, the superficiary is entitled, upon the termination of his right, to remove buildings, works and plantations which he or a predecessor has constructed or installed, without being obliged to do so, or which he has taken over from the owner against reimbursement of the value.
3. Articles 99 and 100 apply *mutatis mutandis*, but the right of retention of the superficiary only includes the buildings, works and plantations.

1. À l'extinction du droit de superficie, la propriété des constructions, ouvrages et plantations passe de plein droit au propriétaire de l'immeuble grevé.

2. Dans la mesure où il n'est pas stipulé autrement dans l'acte constitutif, le superficiaire a la faculté, à l'expiration de son droit, d'enlever les constructions, ouvrages et plantations que lui ou un de ses auteurs a érigés sans y être tenu ou qu'il a repris au propriétaire contre remboursement de la valeur, pourvu qu'il remette l'immeuble que grevait son droit en l'état d'origine.

3. Les articles 99 et 100 s'appliquent par analogie, étant entendu que le droit de rétention dont jouit le superficiaire ne s'étend qu'aux constructions, ouvrages et plantations.

TITEL 9 APPARTEMENTSRECHTEN

TITLE 9 APARTMENT RIGHTS

TITRE NEUVIÈME DES DROITS D'APPARTEMENT

AFDELING 1 Algemene bepalingen

Section 1 General provisions

Section première Dispositions générales

Art. 106. (5.10.1.1) - 1. Een eigenaar, erfpachter of opstaller is bevoegd zijn recht op een gebouw met toebehoren en op de daarbij behorende grond met toebehoren te splitsen in appartementsrechten.
- 2. Een appartementsrecht is op zijn beurt voor splitsing in appartementsrechten vatbaar. Een appartementseigenaar is hiertoe bevoegd, voor zover in de akte van splitsing niet anders is bepaald.
- 3. Onder appartementsrecht wordt verstaan een aandeel in de goederen die in de splitsing zijn betrokken, dat de bevoegdheid omvat tot het uitsluitend gebruik van bepaalde gedeelten van het gebouw die blijkens hun inrichting bestemd zijn of worden om als afzonderlijk geheel te worden gebruikt. Het aandeel kan mede omvatten de bevoegdheid tot het uitsluitend gebruik van bepaalde gedeelten van de bij het gebouw behorende grond.

- 4. Onder appartementseigenaar wordt verstaan de gerechtigde tot een appartementsrecht.
- 5. Onder gebouw wordt in deze titel mede verstaan een groep van gebouwen die in één splitsing zijn betrokken.
- 6. Een erfpachter of opstaller is tot een splitsing in appartementsrechten slechts bevoegd na verkregen toestemming van de grondeigenaar. Indien deze de vereiste toestemming kennelijk zonder redelijke grond weigert of zich niet verklaart, kan de toestemming op verzoek van degene die haar behoeft, worden vervangen door een machtiging van de kantonrechter binnen wiens rechtsgebied het gebouw of het grootste gedeelte daarvan is gelegen.

1. An owner, emphyteutic holder or superficiary is entitled to divide, into apartment rights, the right which he has in a building, the land belonging to it and their accessories.
2. In its turn, an apartment right is susceptible of being divided into apartment rights. An apartment owner is entitled to do so to the extent that the deed of division does not provide otherwise.
3. An apartment right means a share in the property which is involved in the division and includes the right to the exclusive use of certain portions of the building which, as indicated by their lay-out, are intended to be used as separate units. The share can also include the right to the exclusive use of certain portions of the land belonging to the building.
4. An apartment owner means the holder of an apartment right.
5. A building in this title also means a group of buildings which are involved in a single division.
6. An emphyteutic holder or superficiary is only entitled to divide his right into apartment rights after he has obtained permission from the owner of the land. If it is evident that the owner unreasonably refuses to give the required permission or if he remains silent, the permission can, upon the request of the person who needs it, be replaced by an authorization of the judge of the subdistrict court in whose jurisdiction the building, or the larger part of it, is situated.

1. Le propriétaire, l'emphytéote ou le superficiaire peut diviser en droits d'appartement son droit sur un édifice[1] et sur le fonds afférent ainsi que sur leurs accessoires.
2. Le droit d'appartement est à son tour divisible en droits d'appartement. Le propriétaire d'un appartement peut procéder à la division dans la mesure où il n'est pas stipulé autrement dans l'acte de division.
3. Par droit d'appartement, on entend une part des biens faisant l'objet de la division, part qui comprend le droit à l'usage exclusif de parties déterminées de l'édifice, lesquelles, d'après leur disposition, sont destinées à être utilisées comme entité distincte. La part peut également comporter le droit à l'usage exclusif de certaines parties du fonds afférent à l'édifice.
4. Par propriétaire d'appartement, on entend le titulaire du droit d'appartement.
5. Dans le présent titre, on entend par édifice également un groupe d'édifices faisant l'objet d'une seule division.
6. L'emphytéote ou superficiaire ne peut effectuer une division en droits d'appartement qu'après avoir obtenu le consentement du propriétaire du fonds. Si celui-ci refuse, manifestement sans motif raisonnable, le consentement requis ou qu'il ne se déclare pas, le consentement peut être remplacé, à la requête de celui qui en a besoin, par l'autorisation du juge d'instance dans le ressort duquel est situé l'édifice ou la plus grande partie de celui-ci.

[1] Le néerlandais emploie ici le mot *gebouw*, utilisé jusqu'ici en son sens général, traduit par le terme «construction». S'agissant d'appartements, *gebouw* prend un sens plus restreint que traduit mieux le terme français «édifice».

Art. 107. (5.10.1.1a) Een eigenaar, erfpachter of opstaller is ook bevoegd in verband met een door hem beoogde stichting of gewijzigde inrichting van een gebouw zijn recht op het gebouw met toebehoren en de daarbij behorende grond met toebehoren te splitsen in appartementsrechten. Ook in geval van zodanige splitsing ontstaan de appartementsrechten op het tijdstip van inschrijving van de akte van splitsing.

An owner, emphyteutic holder or superficiary is also entitled to divide, into apartment rights, the right he has in a building which he intends to construct or the lay-out of which he intends to change. The building includes the land belonging to it and accessories to both the land and building. Also in the event of such a division, the apartment rights are created at the time of registration of the deed of division.

Le propriétaire, l'emphytéote ou le superficiaire peut également, en prévision de l'érection ou de la disposition modifiée de l'édifice, diviser en droits d'appartement son droit sur l'édifice et ses accessoires, et sur le fonds afférent et ses accessoires. Dans le cas d'une telle division également, les droits d'appartement naissent au moment de l'inscription de l'acte de division.

Art. 108. (5.10.1.1b) - 1. De appartementseigenaars zijn jegens elkander verplicht de bouw en de inrichting van het gebouw en de daarbij behorende grond tot stand te brengen en in stand te houden in overeenstemming met het daaromtrent in de akte van splitsing bepaalde.
- 2. De rechter kan de uitspraak op een vordering, gegrond op het vorige lid, aanhouden wanneer een op artikel 144 lid 1 onder c, d of h gegrond verzoek aanhangig is.

1. Apartment owners have a reciprocal obligation to undertake and maintain the construction and the lay-out of the building and the land belonging to it, in accordance with the relevant provisions of the deed of division.
2. The judge may postpone his decision in an action based upon the preceding paragraph when a request based upon article 144, paragraph 1 *sub* c, d or h is pending.

1. Les propriétaires d'appartement ont l'obligation réciproque de réaliser et de conserver la construction et la disposition de l'édifice et du fonds afférent conformément à ce qui est prévu à ce sujet dans l'acte de division.
2. Le juge peut différer sa décision sur une demande fondée sur le paragraphe précédent, lorsqu'une requête présentée aux termes de l'article 144, paragraphe 1, points c., d. ou h. est pendante.

Art. 109. (5.10.1.2) - 1. De splitsing geschiedt door een daartoe bestemde notariële akte, gevolgd door inschrijving van die akte in de openbare registers.
- 2. Aan de minuut van de akte van splitsing wordt een tekening gehecht, aangevende de begrenzing van de onderscheidene gedeelten van het gebouw en de grond, die bestemd zijn als afzonderlijk geheel te worden gebruikt en waarvan volgens de akte het uitsluitend gebruik in een appartementsrecht zal zijn begrepen. De tekening dient te voldoen aan de eisen, krachtens de wet bedoeld in artikel 16 lid 2 van Boek 3 voor de inschrijving daarvan te stellen.
- 3. Waar in de bepalingen van deze titel wordt gesproken van de akte van splitsing, is hieronder de tekening begrepen, tenzij uit de bepaling het tegendeel blijkt.

1. The division takes place by notarial deed intended for that purpose, followed by its entry in the public registers.
2. A plan is attached to the minute of the deed of division which indicates the boundaries of the different portions of the building and land which are intended to be used as separate units and the exclusive use of which, according to the deed, is included in an apartment right. The plan must comply with the requirements of the law as referred to in article 16, paragraph 2 of Book 3 for the purposes of registration.
3. In the provisions of this title, the deed of division includes the plan, unless the contrary results from the provision.

1. La division a lieu par acte notarié à cet effet, suivi de son inscription sur les registres publics.
2. Est joint à la minute de l'acte de division un plan indiquant les limites des différentes parties de l'édifice et du fonds destinées à être utilisées comme entités distinctes et dont l'usage exclusif fera l'objet d'un droit d'appartement conformément à l'acte. Le plan doit satisfaire aux conditions prévues en application de la loi visée au paragraphe 2 de l'article 16 du Livre troisième pour l'inscription.

3. Lorsque, dans les dispositions du présent titre, il est question de l'acte de division, le plan y est inclus, à moins que le contraire ne résulte de la disposition.

Art. 110. (5.10.1.2a) - 1. Ondanks onbevoegdheid van degene die de splitsing heeft verricht, om over een daarin betrokken registergoed te beschikken, is de splitsing geldig, indien zij is gevolgd door een geldige overdracht van een appartementsrecht of vestiging van een beperkt recht op een appartementsrecht.
- 2. Een ongeldige splitsing wordt eveneens als geldig aangemerkt, wanneer een appartementsrecht is verkregen door verjaring.

1. Although the person who makes the division lacks the right to dispose of registered property involved in it, the division is valid if it is followed by a valid transfer of an apartment right or by the valid establishment of a dismembered right on an apartment right.
2. An invalid division is also deemed valid where an apartment right has been acquired by prescription.

1. Est valide la division effectuée par celui qui ne peut pas disposer du bien immatriculé qui en fait l'objet si elle est suivie d'un transfert valide d'un droit d'appartement ou par l'établissement valide d'un droit démembré sur un tel droit.

2. Une division invalide est également réputée valide lorsqu'un droit d'appartement a été acquis par prescription.

Art. 111. (5.10.1.4) De akte van splitsing moet inhouden:
a. de vermelding van de plaatselijke ligging van het gebouw;
b. een nauwkeurige omschrijving van de gedeelten van de onroerende zaken die bestemd zijn om als afzonderlijk geheel te worden gebruikt, welke omschrijving kan plaatsvinden door verwijzing naar de in artikel 109 lid 2 bedoelde tekening, alsmede de vermelding voor elk dier gedeelten, tot welk appartementsrecht de bevoegdheid tot gebruik daarvan behoort;
c. de kadastrale aanduiding van de appartementsrechten en de vermelding van de appartementseigenaar;
d. een reglement, waartoe geacht worden te behoren de bepalingen van een nauwkeurig aangeduid modelreglement dat is ingeschreven in de openbare registers ter plaatse waar de akte moet worden ingeschreven.

The deed of division must contain:

L'acte de division comporte:

a. mention of the geographical location of the building;
b. an accurate description of the portions of the immoveable things which are intended to be used as separate units as well as mention, for each of those portions, of the apartment right to which the right of use belongs. The above mentioned description can be made by reference to the plan mentioned in article 109 paragraph 2;
c. the cadastral designation of the apartment rights and mention of the apartment owner;
d. the by-laws which are deemed to include the provisions of accurately designated model by-laws which have been entered in the public registers of the place where the deed must be registered.

a. La mention de la situation géographique de l'édifice;
b. Une description précise des parties des immeubles destinées à être utilisées comme entités distinctes; cette description peut être faite par un renvoi au plan visé à l'article 109, paragraphe 2; la description indique également, pour chaque partie, le droit d'appartement dont relève la faculté de l'utiliser;
c. La désignation cadastrale des droits d'appartement et la mention du propriétaire d'appartement;
d. Un règlement, dont sont censées faire partie les dispositions du règlement-type désigné de façon précise et inscrit sur les registres publics du lieu où l'acte doit être inscrit.

Art. 112. (5.10.1.5) - 1. Het reglement moet inhouden:
a. welke schulden en kosten voor rekening van de gezamenlijke appartementseigenaars komen;
b. een regeling omtrent een jaarlijks op te stellen exploitatierekening, lopende over het voorafgaande jaar, en de door de appartementseigenaars te storten bijdragen;
c. een regeling omtrent het gebruik, het beheer en het onderhoud van de gedeelten die niet bestemd zijn om als afzonderlijk geheel te worden gebruikt;
d. door wiens zorg en tegen welke gevaren het gebouw ten behoeve van de gezamenlijke appartementseigenaars moet worden verzekerd;
e. de oprichting van een vereniging van eigenaars, die ten doel heeft het behartigen van gemeenschappelijke belangen van de appartementseigenaars, en de statuten van de vereniging.
- 2. De statuten van de vereniging van eigenaars moeten bevatten:
a. de naam van de vereniging en de gemeente waar zij haar zetel heeft. De naam van de vereniging moet aanvangen met de woorden: „Vereniging van Eigenaar'', hetzij voluit geschreven, hetzij afgekort tot „V. v. E.'', en voorts melding maken van de ligging van het gebouw;
b. het doel van de vereniging;
c. een regeling omtrent door de appartementseigenaars periodiek, tenminste jaarlijks, aan de vereniging verschuldigde bijdragen;
d. de wijze van bijeenroeping van de algemene vergadering en de bepaling van het aantal stemmen dat ieder der appartementseigenaars in de vergadering kan uitbrengen.
- 3. Het reglement kan een regeling inhouden, krachtens welke aan alle of bepaalde appartementsrechten mede verbonden is het lidmaatschap van een andere, nader in het reglement omschreven vereniging, voor zover dit lidmaatschap in overeenstemming is met de statuten van die vereniging.
- 4. Het reglement kan inhouden een regeling omtrent het gebruik, het beheer en het onderhoud van de gedeelten die bestemd zijn om als afzonderlijk geheel te worden gebruikt. Een zodanige regeling kan

inhouden dat de vergadering van eigenaars bevoegd is een appartementseigenaar of degene die zijn rechten uitoefent, om nader in het reglement aangegeven gewichtige redenen het gebruik van deze gedeelten te ontzeggen.

1. The by-laws must contain:
a. a provision indicating which debts and expenses are borne by the joint apartment owners;
b. provisions regarding the drafting of an annual revenue and expense account for the preceding year and the contributions to be made by the apartment owners;
c. provisions regarding the use, management and maintenance of the portions which are not intended to be used as separate units;
d. a provision indicating who must take out insurance on the building for the benefit of the joint apartment owners and against which risks;
e. the foundation of an association of owners the purpose of which it is to look after the common interests of the apartment owners, and the statutes of the association.
2. The statutes of the association of owners must contain:
a. the name of the association and of the Commune where it has its seat. The name of the association must begin with: "Vereniging van Eigenaars"[1], either in full or abbreviated as "V.v.E."[2], and must further make mention of the location of the building;
b. the purpose of the association;
c. provisions regarding amounts which the apartment owners owe to the association, and which are payable periodically but at least annually;
d. the manner of callting the general meeting and the determination of the number of votes which each of the apartment owners may cast in the meeting.

1. Le règlement comporte:
a. Des règles établissant les dettes et les frais incombant aux propriétaires d'appartement conjointement;
b. Des règles relatives au compte d'exploitation qui doit être établi annuellement sur l'exercice précédent, ainsi qu'aux cotisations que doivent verser les propriétaires d'appartement;
c. Des règles relatives à l'usage, à la gestion et à l'entretien des parties qui ne sont pas destinées à être utilisées comme entités distinctes;
d. Des règles prévoyant par les soins de qui et contre quels risques l'édifice doit être assuré au profit de l'ensemble des propriétaires d'appartement;
e. La création d'une association de propriétaires, ayant pour but d'agir dans l'intérêt commun des propriétaires d'appartement, et les statuts de cette association.
2. Les statuts de l'association des propriétaires contiennent:
a. Le nom de l'association et de la commune où elle a son siège. Le nom de l'association commence par les mots: «*Vereniging van Eigenaars*»[3], en toutes lettres ou en abrégé «V.v.E.», et fait mention de la situation de l'édifice;
b. Le but de l'association;
c. Des règles concernant les cotisations que versent périodiquement, au moins une fois par an, les propriétaires d'appartement à l'association;
d. Le mode de convocation de l'assemblée générale et la détermination du nombre de voix dont dispose chacun des propriétaires d'appartement à cette assemblée.

[1] Association of Owners.
[2] A.o.O.
[3] Association des propriétaires.

3. The by-laws may contain provisions pursuant to which the membership of another association, more fully described in the by-laws, is attached to all or certain apartment rights, to the extent that this membership is in conformity with the statutes of that association.

4. The by-laws may contain provisions regarding the use, management and maintenance of the portions which are intended to be used as separate units. Such provisions may determine that the association of owners has the power to deny the use of these portions to an apartment owner, or the person who exercises the latter's rights, for serious reasons, more fully set out in the by-laws.

3. Le règlement peut comporter des règles en vertu desquelles tous les droits d'appartement ou certains d'entre eux entraînent, en outre, la qualité de membre d'une autre association, décrite précisément dans le règlement, dans la mesure où cette qualité est conforme aux statuts de cette association.

4. Le règlement peut comporter des règles relatives à l'usage, à la gestion et à l'entretien des parties destinées à être utilisées comme entités distinctes. Ces règles peuvent prévoir que l'assemblée des propriétaires a le pouvoir d'interdire, pour des motifs graves prévus plus en détail au règlement, l'usage de ces parties à un propriétaire d'appartement ou à celui qui en exerce les droits.

Art. 113. (5.10.1.6) - 1. De aandelen die door de splitsing in appartementsrechten ontstaan, zijn gelijk, tenzij bij de akte van splitsing een andere verhouding is bepaald.
- 2. In de schulden en kosten die ingevolge de wet of het reglement voor rekening van de gezamenlijke appartementseigenaars komen, moeten zij onderling en jegens de vereniging van eigenaars voor elk appartementsrecht een gelijk deel bijdragen, tenzij daarvoor bij het reglement een andere verhouding is bepaald.
- 3. Indien de appartementseigenaars voor een in het vorige lid genoemde schuld jegens de schuldeisers gezamenlijk aansprakelijk zijn en de verschuldigde prestatie deelbaar is, zijn zij ieder verbonden voor een deel, in de verhouding bedoeld in het vorige lid.
- 4. Indien de appartementseigenaars voor een in lid 2 genoemde schuld gezamenlijk aansprakelijk zijn, is de vereniging voor die schuld hoofdelijk verbonden.
- 5. Voor de schulden der vereniging zijn zij die appartementseigenaar waren ten tijde van het ontstaan van de schuld, met de vereniging hoofdelijk verbonden, en wel, indien de prestatie deelbaar is, ieder voor een deel in de verhouding bedoeld in lid 2.

1. The shares which are created by the division into apartment rights are equal, unless the deed of division has provided for a different ratio.
2. The joint apartment owners must, amongst themselves and vis-à-vis the association of owners, contribute equally to the debts and expenses which they owe pursuant to the law or the by-laws with respect to each apartment right, unless a different ratio is provided for in the by-laws.

1. Les parts résultant d'une division en droits d'appartement sont égales, à moins qu'un autre rapport ne soit prévu dans l'acte de division.
2. À moins qu'un autre rapport ne soit prévu au règlement, les propriétaires d'appartement contribuent, entre eux et à l'égard de leur association, par parts égales pour chaque droit d'appartement aux dettes et aux frais qui leur incombent conjointement en vertu de la loi ou du règlement.

3. If the apartment owners are jointly liable to creditors for a debt mentioned in the preceding paragraph, and the prestation owed is divisible, they are each liable for a part according to the ratio referred to in the preceding paragraph.
4. If the apartment owners are jointly liable for a debt mentioned in paragraph 2, the association is solidarily liable with them.
5. Those persons, who were apartment owners at the time of the creation of a debt of the association, are solidarily liable for that debt with the association and if the prestation is divisible, each for a part according to the ratio referred to in paragraph 2.

3. Si les propriétaires d'appartement sont conjointement responsables à l'égard des créanciers d'une dette visée au paragraphe précédent et que la prestation due est divisible, chacun est tenu d'une part, selon le rapport visé au paragraphe précédent.
4. Si les propriétaires d'appartement sont conjointement responsables d'une dette visée au paragraphe 2, l'association en est tenue solidairement avec eux.
5. Ceux qui étaient propriétaires d'appartement au moment de la naissance d'une dette de l'association en sont solidairement tenus avec cette dernière, étant entendu que, si la prestation est divisible, chacun est tenu d'une part selon le rapport visé au paragraphe 2.

Art. 114. (5.10.1.7) - 1. Rust op het ogenblik van de inschrijving van de akte van splitsing een hypotheek, een beslag of een voorrecht op alle in de splitsing betrokken registergoederen, dan rust dit verband, beslag of voorrecht van dat ogenblik af op elk der appartementsrechten voor de gehele schuld.
- 2. Rust op het ogenblik van de inschrijving van de akte van splitsing een hypotheek, een beslag of een voorrecht op slechts een deel van de registergoederen, dan blijft de bevoegdheid tot uitwinning van dit deel ondanks de splitsing bestaan; door de uitwinning wordt met betrekking tot dat deel de splitsing beëindigd.
- 3. Een recht van erfdienstbaarheid, erfpacht, opstal of vruchtgebruik, dat op dat ogenblik van de inschrijving van de akte van splitsing rust op de registergoederen of een deel daarvan, bestaat daarna ongewijzigd voort.

1. Where, at the time of registration of the deed of division, all registered property involved in the division is encumbered with a hypothec, seized or subject to a privilege, this hypothec, seizure or privilege will, as of that time, attach itself to each apartment right for the entire debt.
2. Where, at the time of registration of the deed of division, only part of the registered property is encumbered with a hypothec, seized or subject to a privilege, the power to execute against this part continues to exist in spite of the division; execution terminates the division in respect of that part.
3. A servitude, emphyteusis, right of superficies or usufruct encumbering the registered property, or part of it, at the time of the registration of the deed of division, continues to exist without change after that time.

1. Lorsque, au moment de l'inscription de l'acte de division, une hypothèque, une saisie ou un privilège grève l'ensemble des biens immatriculés qui font l'objet de la division, cette sûreté, cette saisie ou ce privilège grève, à compter de ce moment, chacun des droits d'appartement pour la dette entière.
2. Lorsque, au moment de l'inscription de l'acte de division, une hypothèque, une saisie ou un privilège grève une partie seulement des biens immatriculés, le droit à l'exécution forcée sur cette partie continue d'exister nonobstant la division; l'exécution forcée met fin à la division pour ce qui concerne cette partie.
3. Le droit de servitude, d'emphytéose, de superficie ou d'usufruit qui grève les biens immatriculés ou une partie d'entre eux au moment de l'inscription de l'acte de division continue d'exister sans modification.

Art. 115. (5.10.1.8) - 1. Wanneer een recht van erfpacht of opstal in de splitsing wordt betrokken, wordt de canon of retributie die daarna opeisbaar wordt, over de appartementsrechten verdeeld in een verhouding als bedoeld in artikel 113 lid 2.
- 2. De vereniging van eigenaars is hoofdelijk verbonden voor de door een of meer appartementseigenaars verschuldigde canon of retributie.

1. Where a right of emphyteusis or of superficies is involved in the division, the *canon* or *retribution* which becomes exigible, after the division, is divided among the apartment rights according to the ratio referred to in article 113 paragraph 2.
2. The association of owners is solidarily liable with one or more apartment owners for the *canon* or *retribution* owed by the latter.

1. Lorsque la division porte sur un droit d'emphytéose ou de superficie, la redevance qui devient exigible subséquemment est répartie sur les droits d'appartement selon le rapport visé à l'article 113, paragraphe 2.
2. L'association des propriétaires est tenue solidairement avec le ou les propriétaires concernés de la redevance que doivent ceux-ci.

Art. 116. (5.10.1.8a) - 1. Wanneer een recht van erfpacht of opstal in de splitsing betrokken is, geldt ter aanvulling van de artikelen 87 leden 2 en 3 en 88 het in de volgende leden bepaalde.
- 2. Opzegging van het recht wegens verzuim in de betaling van de canon of retributie kan slechts geschieden, wanneer de gehele canon of retributie over twee achtereenvolgende jaren onbetaald is gebleven.
- 3. Rust op een of meer appartementsrechten een beperkt recht of een beslag dan zijn artikel 87 lid 2, tweede zin, en artikel 88 lid 2 mede van overeenkomstige toepassing met betrekking tot dit beperkte recht of dit beslag.
- 4. Is het voor een appartementsrecht verschuldigde deel van de canon of retributie over de twee achtereenvolgende jaren onbetaald gebleven, dan kan het appartementsrecht door de rechter op vordering van de grondeigenaar aan deze worden toegewezen. De dagvaarding moet op straffe van niet-ontvankelijkheid binnen acht dagen worden betekend aan hen die als beperkt gerechtigde of beslaglegger op het appartementsrecht in de openbare registers staan ingeschreven.
- 5. Door inschrijving in de openbare registers van het vonnis waarbij de toewijzing is uitgesproken, gaat het appartementsrecht op de grondeigenaar over en gaan de daarop rustende beperkte rechten en beslagen teniet. Deze inschrijving geschiedt niet, voordat het vonnis in kracht van gewijsde is gegaan. Na deze inschrijving is de grondeigenaar verplicht de waarde die het appartementsrecht heeft op het tijdstip van de inschrijving aan de gewezen appartementseigenaar te vergoeden, na aftrek van hetgeen hij uit hoofde van de erfpacht van de gewezen appartementseigenaar te vorderen heeft, de kosten daaronder begrepen.
- 6. In de akte van vestiging kan worden aangegeven op welke wijze de waarde als bedoeld in het vorige lid zal worden bepaald.
- 7. Ieder beding dat ten nadele van een appartementseigenaar van dit artikel afwijkt, is nietig.

1. Where a right of emphyteusis or of superficies is involved in the division, the provisions of the following paragraphs apply to supplement articles 87, paragraphs 2 and 3, and 88.

1. Lorsqu'un droit d'emphytéose ou de superficie fait l'objet d'une division, les dispositions contenues dans les paragraphes suivants s'appliquent pour compléter les articles 87, paragraphes 2 et 3, et 88.

2. Resiliation of this right for failure to pay the *canon* or *retribution* cannot be demanded, unless the whole *canon* or *retribution* has remained unpaid for two consecutive years.

3. Where one or more apartment rights have been seized or are encumbered with a dismembered right, article 87, paragraph 2, second sentence, and article 88, paragraph 2 also apply *mutatis mutandis* to this dismembered right or seizure.

4. Where the part of the *canon* or *retribution* owed for an apartment right has remained unpaid for two consecutive years, the judge may adjudge the apartment right to the owner of the land upon his demand. On pain of disallowance, the summons must be served, within eight days, on the persons who appear in the public registers as holder of a dismembered right or as seizor of the apartment right.

5. Entry in the public registers of the judgment which has pronounced the attribution transfers the apartment right to the owner of the land, and extinguishes the dismembered rights encumbering the apartment right and the seizures against it. Registration does not take place until the judgment has become final. After registration, the owner of the land must reimburse the former apartment owner for the value which the apartment right has at the time of registration minus his claims against the latter pursuant to the emphyteusis, including claims for expenses.

6. The deed of establishment may specify how the value referred to in the preceding paragraph will be determined.

7. Every stipulation which derogates from this article to the detriment of the apartment owner is null.

2. La résiliation de ce droit pour défaut de payer la redevance peut avoir lieu seulement lorsque celle-ci est restée entièrement impayée durant deux années consécutives.

3. Lorsqu'un ou plusieurs droits d'appartement sont grevés d'un droit démembré ou d'une saisie, la deuxième phrase du paragraphe 2 de l'article 87 et le paragraphe 2 de l'article 88 s'appliquent également, par analogie, à ce droit ou à cette saisie.

4. Lorsque la partie de la redevance qui est due sur un droit d'appartement est restée impayée durant deux années consécutives, le juge peut, à la demande du propriétaire du fonds, adjuger le droit d'appartement à ce dernier. L'assignation doit, à peine d'irrecevabilité, être signifiée dans les huit jours à ceux qui sont inscrits sur les registres publics comme titulaires de droit démembré sur le droit d'appartement ou comme saisissant de celui-ci.

5. L'inscription sur les registres publics du jugement prononçant l'attribution fait passer le droit d'appartement au propriétaire du fonds et éteint les droits démembrés et les saisies qui le grèvent. Cette inscription n'a pas lieu avant que le jugement n'ait acquis force de chose jugée. Après cette inscription, le propriétaire du fonds est tenu de rembourser à l'ancien propriétaire d'appartement la valeur du droit d'appartement au moment de l'inscription, déduction faite de ce qu'il peut lui réclamer en raison de l'emphytéose, dépens compris.

6. L'acte constitutif peut déterminer la façon dont sera établie la valeur visée au paragraphe précédent.

7. Est nulle toute stipulation dérogeant au présent article au détriment du propriétaire d'appartement.

Art. 117. (5.10.1.9) - 1. Een appartementsrecht kan als een zelfstandig registergoed worden overgedragen, toegedeeld, bezwaard en uitgewonnen.
- 2. Onverminderd het in artikel 114 lid 2 bepaalde kunnen goederen die in de splitsing betrokken zijn niet geheel of voor een deel worden overgedragen, verdeeld, bezwaard of uitgewonnen.
- 3. Beëindiging van de splitsing met betrekking tot een gedeelte van de in de splitsing betrokken registergoederen kan slechts geschieden door wijziging van de akte van splitsing.

- 4. In afwijking van lid 2 kunnen in de splitsing betrokken onroerende zaken door de gezamenlijke appartementseigenaars belast worden met een erfdienstbaarheid.

1. An apartment right can be transferred, attributed, encumbered and executed against as independent registered property.
2. Without prejudice to the provisions of article 114 paragraph 2, property which is involved in the division cannot be wholly or partially transferred, attributed, encumbered or executed.
3. Termination of the division in respect of a part of the registered property involved in the division cannot take place except by modification of the deed of division.
4. Contrary to paragraph 2, the joint apartment owners can encumber immoveable things involved in the division with a servitude.

1. Le droit d'appartement peut être transféré, attribué, grevé, ou saisi et exécuté comme un bien immatriculé autonome.

2. Sans préjudice des dispositions de l'article 114, paragraphe 2, les biens faisant l'objet d'une division ne peuvent être transférés, partagés, grevés ou saisis et exécutés en tout ou en partie.
3. Il ne peut être mis fin à la division relative à une partie des biens immatriculés en faisant l'objet que par la modification de l'acte de division.

4. Par dérogation au paragraphe 2, les propriétaires d'appartement peuvent conjointement grever d'une servitude des immeubles faisant l'objet de la division.

Art. 118. (5.10.1.9a) - 1. Een appartementseigenaar kan, voor zover in de akte van splitsing niet anders is bepaald, zonder medewerking van de overige appartementseigenaars op het gedeelte van de onroerende zaken dat bestemd is om als afzonderlijk geheel door hem te worden gebruikt, een erfdienstbaarheid vestigen ten behoeve van een ander gedeelte van die zaken of van een andere onroerende zaak.
- 2. Een appartementseigenaar kan, voor zover in de akte van splitsing niet anders is bepaald, zonder medewerking van de overige appartementseigenaars de vestiging van een erfdienstbaarheid die uitsluitend strekt ten behoeve van een gedeelte van de onroerende zaken dat bestemd is om als afzonderlijk geheel door hem te worden gebruikt, aannemen en van zodanige erfdienstbaarheid afstand doen.
- 3. De in dit artikel bedoelde erfdienstbaarheden gaan teniet, wanneer de bevoegdheid tot uitsluitend gebruik van het gedeelte dat met de erfdienstbaarheid is belast of ten behoeve waarvan de erfdienstbaarheid is bedongen eindigt.

1. To the extent that the deed of division does not provide otherwise, an apartment owner may, without the cooperation of the other apartment owners, establish a servitude on that portion of the immoveable things which is intended to be used by him as a separate unit, in favour of another portion of those things or of another immoveable thing.

1. Dans la mesure où il n'a pas été disposé autrement dans l'acte de division, le propriétaire d'appartement peut établir sur la partie des immeubles destinée à son usage comme entité distincte, sans le concours des autres propriétaires, une servitude au profit d'une autre partie de ces immeubles ou d'un autre immeuble.

2. To the extent that the deed of division does not provide otherwise, an apartment owner may, without the cooperation of the other apartment owners, accept the establishment of a servitude exclusively in favour of a portion of the immoveable things which is intended to be used by him as a separate unit. He may also, without their cooperation, abandon such a servitude.
3. The servitudes referred to in this article are extinguished when the right to exclusive use of the portion which is encumbered with the servitude, or in favour of which the servitude has been stipulated, is terminated.

2. Dans la mesure où il n'a pas été disposé autrement dans l'acte de division, le propriétaire d'appartement peut, sans le concours des autres propriétaires, accepter que soit établie une servitude au seul profit de la partie des immeubles destinée à son usage comme entité distincte; il peut également sans leur concours abandonner une telle servitude.

3. Les servitudes visées au présent article s'éteignent lorsque prend fin le droit à l'usage exclusif de la partie qui est grevée de la servitude ou au profit de laquelle elle a été stipulée.

Art. 119. (5.10.1.12) - 1. Een appartementseigenaar mag zonder toestemming van de overige appartementseigenaars in een gedeelte dat bestemd is om als afzonderlijk geheel door hem te worden gebruikt, veranderingen aanbrengen, mits deze geen nadeel aan een ander gedeelte toebrengen. Van hetgeen hij bij een geoorloofde verandering wegneemt wordt hij enig eigenaar.
- 2. Hij is verplicht de vereniging van eigenaars onverwijld van een verandering kennis te geven. Leidt de verandering tot een wijziging van de verzekeringspremie, dan komt het verschil voor rekening van hem en zijn rechtsopvolgers.
- 3. Blijkt ten gevolge van een verandering de waarde van de in de splitsing betrokken goederen bij de opheffing van de splitsing te zijn verminderd, dan wordt hiermede, ook al was de verandering geoorloofd, bij de verdeling van de gemeenschap rekening gehouden ten laste van hem die de verandering heeft aangebracht of zijn rechtsopvolger.
- 4. Bij het reglement kan van dit artikel worden afgeweken en kunnen voor de toepassing van lid 2 wijzigingen in de wijze van gebruik met veranderingen worden gelijkgesteld.

1. An apartment owner may, without the consent of the other apartment owners, alter a portion intended to be used by him as a separate unit, provided that the alterations do not cause harm to another portion. He becomes sole owner of anything removed on the occasion of a permissible alteration.
2. He must without delay notify the association of owners of any alteration. Where the alteration results in a modification of the insurance premium, he and his successors must bear the difference.
3. When the value of the property involved in the division proves, upon termination of the division, to have been diminished as a result of an alteration,

1. Le propriétaire d'appartement peut, sans le consentement des autres propriétaires, apporter des modifications à une partie destinée à son usage comme entité distincte, pourvu qu'il n'en résulte pas de préjudice pour une autre partie. Il devient seul propriétaire de ce qu'il enlève lors d'une modification permise.
2. Il est tenu de donner sans tarder à l'association des propriétaires avis d'une modification. Si la modification entraîne un changement de la prime d'assurance, la différence lui incombe ainsi qu'à ses ayants cause.
3. Lorsqu'il apparaît, au moment où il est mis fin à la division, que la valeur des biens qui en font l'objet a diminué par suite d'une modification, même permise, il en est tenu

even though permissible, this fact will be imputed in the division of the community to the person who has made the alteration or to his successor.
4. The by-laws may derogate from this article and may, for the application of paragraph 2, assimilate modifications in the way of use to alterations.

compte lors du partage de la communauté, en diminuant la part de celui qui a apporté la modification ou de son ayant cause.

4. Dans le règlement, on peut déroger à cet article et, aux fins du paragraphe 2, assimiler à des modifications les changements dans le mode d'usage.

Art. 120. (5.10.1.13) - 1. Onverminderd het in artikel 112 lid 4 bepaalde is een appartementseigenaar bevoegd het gedeelte dat bestemd is om als afzonderlijk geheel door hem te worden gebruikt, zelf te gebruiken of aan een ander in gebruik te geven, met inbegrip van het hem toekomende medegebruik van de gedeelten die niet bestemd zijn om als afzonderlijk geheel te worden gebruikt.
- 2. Voorschriften van het reglement omtrent gebruik, beheer en onderhoud zijn ook van toepassing op degeen die het gebruik verkrijgt. Andere bepalingen van het reglement kunnen in het reglement op de gebruiker van toepassing worden verklaard.
- 3. Ten aanzien van een huurder geldt een na het tot stand komen van de huurovereenkomst ingeschreven reglementsbepaling niet, tenzij hij daarin heeft toegestemd. Weigert hij zijn toestemming of verklaart hij zich niet, dan kan de kantonrechter binnen wiens rechtsgebied het gebouw of het grootste deel daarvan is gelegen, op verzoek van iedere appartementseigenaar beslissen dat de reglementsbepaling ten aanzien van de huurder komt te gelden.
- 4. Na opheffing van de splitsing zijn de gerechtigden tot de goederen die in de splitsing waren betrokken, verplicht een verhuur gestand te doen, mits de tijd van de verhuur in overeenstemming is met het plaatselijk gebruik en de verhuur niet op ongewone, voor hem bezwarende voorwaarden is geschied.

1. Without prejudice to the provisions of article 112 paragraph 4, an apartment owner is entitled to use himself, or to give to another person to use, the portion which is intended to be used by him as a separate unit, including the common use to which he is entitled in respect of the portions which are not intended to be used as separate units.
2. Provisions in the by-laws regarding use, management and maintenance also apply to the person who acquires the right of use. Other provisions in the by-laws may be declared applicable to him by those by-laws.
3. A provision in the by-laws, registered after a contract of lease and hire has been entered into, does not bind the lessee, unless he has consented to it. If he refuses to give his consent or remains silent, the judge of the subdistrict court in whose jurisdiction the building, or the larger part of it, is situated may,

1. Sans préjudice des dispositions de l'article 112, paragraphe 4, le propriétaire d'appartement peut utiliser lui-même ou permettre à un autre d'utiliser la partie destinée à son usage comme entité distincte; ce droit s'étend à l'usage commun qui lui revient des parties qui ne sont pas destinées à être utilisées comme entités distinctes.

2. Les dispositions du règlement relatives à l'usage, à la gestion et à l'entretien s'appliquent également à celui qui obtient le droit d'utilisation. Dans le règlement, on peut déclarer applicables à ce dernier d'autres dispositions du règlement.
3. Une disposition du règlement inscrite après la conclusion du bail ne produit pas effet à l'égard du locataire, à moins que celui-ci n'y ait consenti. S'il refuse son consentement ou ne se déclare pas, le juge d'instance dans le ressort duquel est situé l'édifice ou la plus grande partie de celui-ci peut décider, à la requête de tout propriétaire

upon the request of each apartment owner, decide that the provision in the by-laws will bind the lessee.

4. After termination of the division, those who are entitled to the property which was involved in the division must respect a lease, provided that its agreed duration is in accordance with local usage and that the lease does not contain unusual conditions onerous for them.

d'appartement, que la disposition produit effet à l'égard du locataire.

4. Après la levée de la division, les titulaires des biens qui en faisaient l'objet sont tenus de respecter le bail, pourvu que sa durée soit conforme à l'usage local et qu'il ne comporte pas de conditions inhabituelles et onéreuses pour eux.

Art. 121. (5.10.1.15) - 1. In alle gevallen waarin een appartementseigenaar voor het verrichten van een bepaalde handeling met betrekking tot de gedeelten die niet bestemd zijn als afzonderlijk geheel gebruikt te worden en, in het geval van een beding als bedoeld in artikel 112 lid 4, met betrekking tot gedeelten die bestemd zijn als afzonderlijk geheel gebruikt te worden, medewerking of toestemming behoeft van een of meer andere appartementseigenaars, van de vereniging van eigenaars of van haar organen, of waarin de vereniging of haar organen voor het verrichten van zodanige handeling toestemming behoeven van een of meer appartementseigenaars, kan die medewerking of toestemming op verzoek van degeen die haar behoeft, worden vervangen door een machtiging van de kantonrechter binnen wiens rechtsgebied het gebouw of het grootste gedeelte daarvan is gelegen. De machtiging kan worden verleend, indien de medewerking of toestemming zonder redelijke grond wordt geweigerd of degene die haar moet geven zich niet verklaart.
- 2. Gaat de handeling met kosten gepaard, dan kan de kantonrechter op verzoek van een appartementseigenaar of van de vereniging van eigenaars tevens bepalen in welke verhouding alle of bepaalde appartementseigenaars of de vereniging van eigenaars in de kosten moeten bijdragen.
- 3. Betreft het de aanbrenging van een nieuw werk of nieuwe installatie, dan kan de kantonrechter desverzocht ook een regeling vaststellen, bepalende dat en in welke verhouding de appartementseigenaars van alle of bepaalde appartementsrechten de kosten van onderhoud van het werk of de installatie in de toekomst zullen dragen.

1. In all cases where an apartment owner needs the cooperation or the consent of one or more other apartment owners, of the association of owners or of its organs in order to perform a certain act in respect of the portions which are not intended to be used as separate units and, in the event of a stipulation as referred to in article 112, paragraph 4, in respect of the portions which are intended to be used as separate units, that cooperation or consent can, upon the request of the person who needs it, be replaced by an authorization of the judge of the subdistrict court in whose jurisdiction the building, or the larger part of it, is situated. The foregoing also applies to cases where the association or

1. Dans tous les cas où le propriétaire d'appartement requiert, pour accomplir un acte déterminé relatif à des parties qui ne sont pas destinées à être utilisées comme entités distinctes ou, dans le cas de la stipulation visée à l'article 112, paragraphe 4, relatif à des parties destinées à être utilisées comme entités distinctes, le concours ou le consentement d'un ou de plusieurs propriétaires d'appartement, de l'association des propriétaires ou de ses organes, l'autorisation du juge d'instance dans le ressort duquel est situé l'édifice ou la plus grande partie de celui-ci, accordée à la requête de celui qui requiert le concours ou leconsentement, peut tenir lieu de ce concours ou de ce consentement. Il en est de même lorsque l'association ou ses organes

its organs need the consent of one or more apartment owners in order to perform such an act. The authorization may be granted if the cooperation or consent is refused without reasonable grounds, or the person who must give it remains silent.
2. Where the act involves expenses, the judge of the subdistrict court may also determine, upon the request of an apartment owner or the association of owners, the proportion in which all or certain apartment owners or the association of owners must contribute to the expenses.
3. Where the construction of a new work or a new installation is concerned, the judge of the subdistrict court may, upon request, also make rules providing that, and in which proportion the apartment owners of all or certain apartment rights will in the future bear the costs of maintenance of the work or installation.

requièrent pour un tel acte le consentement d'un ou de plusieurs propriétaires d'appartement. L'autorisation peut être accordée si celui qui doit le donner refuse sans motif valable ou ne se déclare pas.

2. Lorsque l'acte occasionne des frais, le juge d'instance peut décider, en outre, à la requête d'un propriétaire d'appartement ou de l'association des propriétaires, dans quelle proportion tous les propriétaires d'appartement ou certains d'entre eux, ou encore l'association des propriétaires, doivent contribuer à ces frais.
3. Lorsqu'il s'agit d'ériger un nouvel ouvrage ou de poser une nouvelle installation, le juge d'instance peut également, sur requête, établir des règles portant que les propriétaires de tous les droits d'appartement ou de certains de ceux-ci assumeront à l'avenir les frais d'entretien de cet ouvrage ou de cette installation et fixant leurs contributions respectives.

Art. 122. (5.10.1.15a) - 1. Overgang onder bijzondere titel of toedeling van een appartementsrecht omvat, voor zover niet anders is bepaald, mede de als appartementseigenaar verkregen rechten.
- 2. Na de overgang of toedeling moet de verkrijger onverwijld schriftelijk aan de vereniging van eigenaars mededeling doen van zijn verkrijging.
- 3. Voor de ter zake van het verkregene verschuldigde bijdragen die in het lopende of het voorafgaande boekjaar opeisbaar zijn geworden of nog zullen worden, zijn de verkrijger en de vroegere appartementseigenaar hoofdelijk aansprakelijk.
- 4. In het reglement kan worden bepaald in hoeverre voor bijdragen, genoemd in het vorige lid, alleen de vroegere eigenaar of alleen de verkrijger aansprakelijk zal zijn. In het reglement kan ook worden bepaald dat voor bepaalde bijdragen die later opeisbaar worden de vroegere appartementseigenaar in plaats van de verkrijger verbonden zal zijn.

1. To the extent not otherwise provided, transfer by particular title or attribution of an apartment right also includes the rights acquired as apartment owner.
2. After transfer or attribution, the acquirer must without delay give written notice to the association of owners of his acquisition.
3. The acquirer and the former apartment owner are solidarily liable for the contributions which are owed in respect of the acquired thing and which

1. La transmission à titre particulier et l'attribution d'un droit d'appartement s'étendent, dans la mesure où il n'est pas disposé autrement, aux droits acquis à titre de propriétaire d'appartement.
2. Après la transmission ou l'attribution, l'acquéreur doit, sans tarder et par écrit, aviser l'association des propriétaires de son acquisition.
3. L'acquéreur et l'ancien propriétaire d'appartement sont solidairement responsables des contributions qui sont dues sur ce qui a été acquis et qui sont échues ou

have become exigible, or will as yet become exigible in the current or preceding financial year.

4. The by-laws may provide for the extent to which either the former owner or the acquirer will be liable for contributions mentioned in the preceding paragraph. They may also provide that the former apartment owner instead of the acquirer will be bound for certain contributions which become exigible at a later date.

le seront durant l'exercice financier en cours ou le précédent.

4. Le règlement peut prévoir dans quelle mesure les contributions visées au paragraphe précédent sont à la seule charge de l'ancien propriétaire ou de l'acquéreur. Il peut également prévoir que l'ancien propriétaire sera tenu à la place de l'acquéreur de certaines contributions qui deviendront exigibles ultérieurement.

Art. 123. (5.10.1.15b) - 1. In geval van vruchtgebruik van een appartementsrecht treedt de vruchtgebruiker in de plaats van de appartementseigenaar ten aanzien van de aansprakelijkheid voor de gezamenlijke schulden en de aan de gezamenlijke appartementseigenaars en de vereniging van eigenaars verschuldigde bijdragen. De vruchtgebruiker is echter bevoegd de door hem betaalde bedragen, voor zover zij niet betrekking hebben op de gewone lasten en herstellingen, bij het einde van het vruchtgebruik van de appartementseigenaar terug te vorderen.

- 2. Wanneer de appartementseigenaar schulden of bijdragen als bedoeld in lid 1 heeft voldaan, kan hij van de vruchtgebruiker vorderen dat deze hem de betaalde bedragen, vermeerderd met de rente vanaf de dag der betaling, teruggeeft voor zover zij op gewone lasten en herstellingen betrekking hebben. Van de andere door de appartementseigenaar betaalde bedragen is de vruchtgebruiker slechts de rente van de dag der betaling tot het einde van het vruchtgebruik verschuldigd.

-3. Tenzij bij de instelling van het vruchtgebruik anders wordt bepaald wordt het aan een appartementsrecht verbonden stemrecht in de vergadering van eigenaars uitgeoefend door de vruchtgebruiker.

- 4. Artikel 122 is van overeenkomstige toepassing bij de vestiging, bij overdracht en bij het einde van het vruchtgebruik van een appartementsrecht.

1. The usufructuary of an apartment right, and not the apartment owner, is liable for the joint debts and the contributions owed to the joint apartment owners and the association of owners. Upon the termination of the usufruct, however, the usufructuary is entitled to reclaim from the apartment owner the amounts which he has paid, other than those for ordinary charges and repairs.

2. The apartment owner who has paid debts or contributions referred to in paragraph 1 can require the usufructuary to return to him the amounts paid plus interest as of the day of payment, to the extent that these amounts concern ordinary charges and repairs. The usufructary only owes interest from the

1. L'usufruitier d'un droit d'appartement prend la place du propriétaire pour ce qui est de la responsabilité des dettes conjointes et des contributions qui sont dues aux propriétaires d'appartement conjointement ou à leur association. L'usufruitier peut cependant demander au propriétaire d'appartement, à la fin de l'usufruit, le remboursement des sommes qu'il a payées, dans la mesure où elles ne concernent pas les charges et réparations ordinaires.

2. Le propriétaire d'appartement qui a payé les dettes ou contributions visées au paragraphe 1er peut demander à l'usufruitier de lui rembourser les sommes payées, majorées de l'intérêt à compter du jour du paiement, dans la mesure où elles concernent les charges et réparations ordinaires. Sur les autres sommes payées par le propriétaire

day of payment until the termination of the usufruct with respect to other amounts paid by the apartment owner.
3. Unless otherwise provided upon the establishment of the usufruct, the usufructuary exercises, in the association of owners, the right to vote which is attached to an apartment right.
4. Article 122 applies *mutatis mutandis* to the establishment, transfer and termination of the usufruct of an apartment right.

d'appartement, l'usufruitier ne doit que l'intérêt à compter du jour du paiement jusqu'à la fin de l'usufruit.
3. À moins qu'il ne soit disposé autrement lors de l'établissement de l'usufruit, l'usufruitier exerce le droit de vote dans l'assemblée des propriétaires afférent au droit d'appartement.
4. L'article 122 s'applique par analogie à l'établissement, au transfert et à la fin de l'usufruit d'un droit d'appartement.

AFDELING 2 De vereniging van eigenaars

Section 2
The association of owners

Section deuxième
De l'association de propriétaires

Art. 124. (5.10.2.0) - 1. De vereniging van eigenaars is een rechtspersoon.
- 2. Titel 1 van Boek 2 is slechts van toepassing behoudens de artikelen 4, 6, 13 lid 2, 17, 18, 19 leden 1-3, lid 5, tweede zin, en lid 6, 20, 21 en 22 en met inachtneming van de in de volgende artikelen van de onderhavige titel aangegeven afwijkingen.
- 3. Titel 2 van Boek 2 is slechts van toepassing voor zover de onderhavige afdeling daarnaar verwijst.

1. The association of owners is a legal person.
2. Title 1 of Book 2 applies except for articles 4, 6, 13, paragraph 2, 17, 18, 19. paragraphs 1 - 3, paragraph 5 second sentence, and paragraph 6, 20, 21 and 22, and in accordance with the following modifications contained in the following articles of this title.
3. Title 2 of Book 2 only applies to the extent that this title refers to it.

1. L'association des propriétaires constitue une personne morale.
2. Le titre premier du Livre deuxième ne s'applique que sous réserve des articles 4, 6, 13, paragraphe 2, 17, 18, 19, paragraphes 1er à 3, paragraphe 5, deuxième phrase, et paragraphe 6, 20, 21 et 22 et compte tenu des dérogations à ce titre indiquées aux articles qui suivent.
3. Le deuxième titre du Livre deuxième ne s'applique que dans la mesure où la présente section y renvoie.

Art. 125. (5.10.2.1) - 1. Aan de vergadering van eigenaars komen in de vereniging alle bevoegdheden toe, die niet door wet of statuten aan andere organen zijn opgedragen.
- 2. Iedere appartementseigenaar is van rechtswege lid van de vereniging van eigenaars. Wanneer een lid ophoudt appartementseigenaar te zijn, eindigt zijn lidmaatschap van rechtswege.
- 3. Behoren op het tijdstip van de inschrijving van de akte van splitsing alle appartementsrechten nog aan één persoon of dezelfde personen toe, dan ontstaat de vereniging eerst zodra de appartementsrechten aan verschillende personen toebehoren.
- 4. Artikel 40 lid 2 van Boek 2 is van toepassing.

1. The meeting of owners possesses all powers in the association except those which have been attributed to other organs by law or by the statutes.
2. *De iure* every apartment owner is a member of the association of onwers. Membership is terminated *de iure* where a member ceases to be an apartment owner.

3. Where, at the time of registration of the deed of division, all apartment rights still belong to a single person or to the same persons, the association does not come into existence until the apartment rights belong to different persons.
4. Article 40 paragraph 2 of Book 2 applies.

1. Tout pouvoir non confié à d'autres organes par la loi ou par les statuts revient dans l'association à l'assemblée des propriétaires.
2. Tout propriétaire d'appartement est de plein droit membre de l'association des propriétaires. Lorsqu'un membre cesse d'être propriétaire d'appartement, sa qualité de membre prend fin de plein droit.
3. Lorsque, à l'inscription de l'acte de division, une seule personne ou un seul groupe de personnes est titulaire de tous les droits d'appartement, l'association ne naît qu'au moment où les droits d'appartement appartiennent à des personnes distinctes.
4. L'article 40, paragraphe 2, du Livre deuxième s'applique.

Art. 126. (5.10.2.1a) - 1. De vereniging van eigenaars voert het beheer over de gemeenschap, met uitzondering van de gedeelten die bestemd zijn als afzonderlijk geheel te worden gebruikt.
- 2. De vereniging kan binnen de grenzen van haar bevoegdheid de gezamenlijke appartementseigenaars in en buiten rechte vertegenwoordigen.
- 3. De vereniging ziet toe op de nakoming van de verplichtingen die voor de appartementseigenaars uit het bij of krachtens de wet en het reglement bepaalde jegens elkander voortvloeien en kan te dien einde in rechte tegen hen optreden. Onder appartementseigenaars wordt hier begrepen hij die een gebruiksrecht aan een appartementseigenaar ontleent.

1. The association of owners manages the community except for the portions which are intended to be used as separate units.
2. Within the limits of its powers, the association can represent the joint apartment owners judicially and extra-judicially.
3. The association supervises the performance of the obligations which the apartment owners owe another as a result of the provisions of the law and the by-laws; for that purpose, it can act in justice against them. In this context an apartment owner includes the person who derives a right of use from an apartment owner.

1. L'association des propriétaires gère la communauté, à l'exception des parties destinées à être utilisées comme entités distinctes.
2. L'association peut, dans les limites de ses pouvoirs, représenter les propriétaires d'appartement conjoints dans les actes civils et en justice.
3. L'association surveille l'exécution des obligations réciproques incombant aux propriétaires en vertu des dispositions de la loi ou du règlement; à cette fin, elle peut agir en justice contre eux. Par propriétaire d'appartement, on entend à cette fin également celui qui tient d'un propriétaire d'appartement un droit d'utilisation.

Art. 127. (5.10.2.1b) - 1. Alle appartementseigenaars hebben toegang tot de vergadering van eigenaars. De besluiten worden genomen bij volstrekte meerderheid van de uitgebrachte stemmen, voor zover de statuten niet anders bepalen.
- 2. Tenzij de statuten anders bepalen, wordt de voorzitter van de vergadering van eigenaars door de vergadering uit de leden der vereniging benoemd. Zowel de voorzitter als het bestuur van de vereniging zijn bevoegd de vergadering bijeen te roepen.

1. All apartment owners have access to the meeting of owners. Unless otherwise provided by the statutes, decisions are taken by an absolute majority of the votes cast.
2. Unless otherwise provided by the statutes, the chairman of the meeting of owners is appointed from amongst the members of the association. Both the chairman and the board of directors of the association have the power to convene the meeting.

1. Tout propriétaire d'appartement a accès à l'assemblée des propriétaires. Dans la mesure où les statuts ne disposent pas autrement, les décisions sont prises à la majorité absolue des voix exprimées.
2. À moins de disposition contraire dans les statuts, le président de l'assemblée des propriétaires est nommé par celle-ci parmi les membres de l'association. Le président, comme le conseil d'administration de l'association, a le pouvoir de convoquer l'assemblée.

Art. 128. (5.10.2.1c) - 1. De vergadering van eigenaars is bevoegd regels te stellen betreffende het gebruik van de gedeelten die niet bestemd zijn als afzonderlijk geheel te worden gebruikt, voor zover het reglement daarover geen bepalingen bevat.
- 2. Iedere appartementseigenaar kan een gebruiker vragen te verklaren of hij bereid is een in het vorige lid bedoelde regel na te leven. Is de gebruiker daartoe niet bereid of verklaart hij zich niet, dan kan de kantonrechter binnen wiens rechtsgebied het gebouw of het grootste gedeelte daarvan is gelegen, op verzoek van iedere appartementseigenaar beslissen dat de regel ten aanzien van de gebruiker komt te gelden.

1. In the absence of provisions to that effect in the by-laws, the meeting of owners has the power to make rules for the use of the portions which are not intended to be used as separate units.

2. Every apartment owner can ask a user to declare whether he is willing to comply with a rule as mentioned in the preceding paragraph. Where the user is not willing to do so, or remains silent, the judge of the subdistrict court in whose jurisdiction the building, or the larger part of it, is situated may, upon the request of any apartment owner, decide that the rule will bind the user.

1. Dans la mesure où le règlement ne comporte pas de disposition à ce sujet, l'assemblée des propriétaires peut établir des règles relatives à l'usage des parties qui ne sont pas destinées à être utilisées comme entités distinctes.
2. Tout propriétaire d'appartement peut demander à un utilisateur de déclarer s'il consent à respecter une règle visée au paragraphe précédent. Lorsque l'utilisateur n'y consent pas ou ne se déclare pas, le juge d'instance dans le ressort duquel est situé l'édifice ou la plus grande partie de celui-ci, peut décider, à la requête de tout propriétaire d'appartement, que la règle produit effet à l'égard de l'utilisateur.

Art. 129. (5.10.2.1ca) - 1. Voor de toepassing van artikel 14 van Boek 2 wordt de akte van splitsing gelijkgesteld met de statuten.
- 2. Voor de toepassing van artikel 15 lid 1 onder c van Boek 2 geldt het reglement dat krachtens artikel 111 onder d deel van de akte van splitsing uitmaakt, niet als een reglement.

1. In applying article 14 of Book 2, the deed of division is assimilated to the statutes.

1. Pour l'application de l'article 14 du Livre deuxième, l'acte de division est assimilé aux statuts.

2. In applying article 15, paragraph 1 *sub* c of Book 2, the by-laws which, pursuant to article 111 *sub* d, form part of the deed of division, are not considered as such.

2. Pour l'application de l'article 15, paragraphe 1er, point c., du Livre deuxième, n'est pas réputé être un règlement celui qui, conformément à l'article 111, point d., fait partie de l'acte de division .

Art. 130. (5.10.2.1d) - 1. In afwijking van artikel 15 lid 3 van Boek 2 geschiedt de vernietiging van een besluit van een orgaan van de vereniging van eigenaars door een uitspraak van de kantonrechter binnen wiens rechtsgebied het gebouw of het grootste gedeelte daarvan is gelegen, op verzoek van degene die de vernietiging krachtens dit lid kan vorderen.
- 2. Het verzoek tot vernietiging moet worden gedaan binnen een maand na de dag waarop de verzoeker van het besluit heeft kennis genomen of heeft kunnen kennis nemen.
- 3. De verzoeker, alle andere stemgerechtigden en de vereniging van eigenaars worden bij name opgeroepen om op het verzoek te worden gehoord. Hoger beroep kan slechts worden ingesteld binnen een maand na de dagtekening der eindbeschikking.
- 4. De rechter voor wie het verzoek aanhangig is, is bevoegd het besluit te schorsen totdat op het verzoek onherroepelijk is beslist.

1. Contrary to article 15 paragraph 3 of Book 2, the annulment of a decision of an organ of the association of owners takes place by a decision of the judge of the subdistrict court in whose jurisdiction the building, or the larger part of it, is situated, upon the request of the person who can demand such annulment pursuant to that paragraph.
2. The request to annul must be made within one month following the day when the person so requesting has become aware of the decision or has been able to become aware of it.
3. The person who makes the request, all other persons entitled to vote and the association of owners are individually summoned in order to be heard. Any appeal must be taken within one month following the date of the final judicial decision.
4. The judge seized of the request may suspend the decision until the request has been irrevocably decided upon.

1. Par dérogation à l'article 15, paragraphe 3, du Livre deuxième, l'annulation d'une décision d'un organe de l'association des propriétaires est prononcée par jugement du juge d'instance dans le ressort duquel est situé l'édifice ou la plus grande partie de celui-ci, à la requête de celui qui peut demander l'annulation en application de ce paragraphe.
2. La requête en annulation est présentée dans le mois suivant le jour où le requérant a eu ou a pu avoir connaissance de la décision.
3. Le requérant, toutes autres personnes ayant droit de vote à l'assemblée des propriétaires et l'association des propriétaires sont nommément appelés en cause afin d'être entendus sur la requête. L'appel ne peut être formé que dans le délai d'un mois suivant la date de la décision judiciaire définitive.
4. Le juge saisi de la requête peut suspendre la décision de l'assemblée jusqu'à ce qu'une décision irrévocable ait été prise sur la requête.

Art. 131. (5.10.2.1e) - 1. Het bestuur van de vereniging wordt gevormd door één bestuurder, tenzij de statuten bepalen dat er twee of meer zullen zijn. In het laatste geval wordt de vereniging, voor zover in de statuten niet anders is bepaald, tegenover derden door ieder der bestuurders vertegenwoordigd.
- 2. Het bestuur wordt door de vergadering van eigenaars, al dan niet uit de leden, benoemd en kan te allen tijde door haar worden geschorst of

ontslagen. Een veroordeling tot herstel van de dienstbetrekking tussen de vereniging en een bestuurder kan door de rechter niet worden uitgesproken.
- 3. Voor zover de statuten niet anders bepalen, beheert het bestuur de middelen der vereniging en draagt het zorg voor de tenuitvoerlegging van de besluiten van de vergadering van eigenaars.
- 4. Bij besluit van de vergadering van eigenaars kan van het vorige lid worden afgeweken en kunnen aan het bestuur aanwijzingen met betrekking tot de uitoefening van zijn taak worden gegeven. Deze besluiten kunnen niet worden ingeroepen tegen de wederpartij, tenzij zij haar bekend waren of behoorden te zijn.

1. Unless the statutes provide that there shall be two or more directors, the board of directors of the association is composed of one director. Where there is more than one director, each director represents the association with respect to third parties, unless the statutes provide otherwise.
2. The meeting of owners appoints the board of directors, the members of which may or may not be members of the association; at all times the meeting can suspend or dismiss the board. The judge cannot pronounce judgment against the association to reinstate a director.
3. To the extent that the statutes do not provide otherwise, the board of directors administers the funds of the association and ensures the execution of the decisions of the meeting of owners.
4. A decision of the meeting of owners may derogate from the preceding paragraph and give directives to the board of directors for the performance of its duties. Such decisions cannot be invoked against the other party, unless he knew or should have known of them.

1. Le conseil d'administration de l'association se compose d'un syndic[1], à moins que les statuts n'en prévoient deux ou plus. Dans ce dernier cas, chacun des syndics représente l'association envers les tiers, dans la mesure où les statuts ne disposent pas autrement.

2. Le conseil est nommé par l'assemblée des propriétaires et choisi parmi ceux-ci ou à l'extérieur; l'assemblée peut en tout temps le suspendre ou le révoquer. Le juge ne peut condamner l'association à réintégrer le syndic.

3. Dans la mesure où les statuts ne disposent pas autrement , le conseil gère les fonds de l'association et exécute les décisions de l'assemblée des propriétaires.

4. Par décision de l'assemblée des propriétaires, on peut déroger au paragraphe précédent et donner au conseil d'administration des directives relatives à l'exécution de ses fonctions. Ces décisions ne peuvent être invoquées à l'encontre de l'autre partie, à moins qu'elles ne soient connues d'elle ou n'aient dû l'être.

Art. 132. (5.10.2.1f) De appartementseigenaars en de gebruikers van de voor het gebruik als afzonderlijk geheel bestemde gedeelten zijn verplicht een bestuurder en door hem aan te wijzen personen toegang tot die gedeelten te verschaffen, wanneer dit voor de vervulling van de taak van het bestuur noodzakelijk is.

The apartment owners and the users of the portions intended for use as separate units must give a director, or the persons to be designated by him, access to those portions where this is necessary for the fulfilment of the duties of the board of directors.

Les propriétaires d'appartement et les utilisateurs des parties destinées à être utilisées comme entités distinctes sont tenus de donner accès à ces parties au syndic et aux personnes par lui désignées, lorsque cela est nécessaire pour exécuter les fonctions du conseil d'administration.

1 Le néerlandais emploie le terme *bestuurder*, qui se traduit littéralement par dirigeant.

Art. 133. (5.10.2.1g) - 1. Bij belet of ontstentenis van het bestuur wordt dit vervangen door de voorzitter van de vergadering van eigenaars, tenzij in de statuten of door de vergadering een andere voorziening is getroffen.
- 2. In gevallen waarin de vereniging of de gezamenlijke appartementseigenaars een belang hebben, tegenstrijdig met dat van een bestuurder, treedt de voorzitter van de vergadering van eigenaars bij belet of ontstentenis van andere bestuurders eveneens in de plaats van het bestuur.

1. In the event of absence or impediment of the board of directors, it is replaced by the chairman of the meeting of owners, unless the statutes or the meeting have made other arrangements.
2. In cases where there is a conflict of interest between the association or the joint apartment owners on the one hand and a director on the other, the chairman of the meeting of owners also replaces the board of directors in the event of absence or impediment of other directors.

1. À défaut de dispositions autres prévues dans les statuts ou par l'assemblée, le conseil d'administration, au cas d'empêchement ou d'absence, est remplacé par le président de l'assemblée des propriétaires.
2. Le président de l'assemblée des propriétaires remplace également le conseil d'administration lorsque l'intérêt de l'association ou de l'ensemble des propriétaires d'appartement entre en conflit avec celui d'un syndic et qu'il y a empêchement ou absence d'autres syndics.

Art. 134. (5.10.2.1h) - 1. Exploiten en kennisgevingen, gericht tot de gezamenlijke appartementseigenaars, kunnen aan de persoon of de woonplaats van een bestuurder van de vereniging worden gedaan; zij behoeven dan niet de namen en de woonplaatsen van de appartementseigenaars te bevatten.
- 2. De bestuurder deelt de appartementseigenaars onverwijld de inhoud van het exploit of de kennisgeving mede.

1. Summons or notices addressed to the joint apartment owners may be delivered to a director of the association in person or to his domicile, in which case they need not contain the names and domiciles of the apartment owners.

2. The director must notify the apartment owners forthwith of the contents of the summons or notice.

1. Les exploits et avis adressés aux propriétaires d'appartement conjoints peuvent être remis à un syndic de l'association en personne ou à son domicile; il n'est pas alors nécessaire qu'ils contiennent les nom et domicile des propriétaires d'appartement.
2. Le syndic avise sans tarder les propriétaires d'appartement du contenu de l'exploit ou de l'avis.

Art. 135. (5.10.2.1i) De artikelen 45 lid 4, 47, 48 en 49 van Boek 2 zijn van toepassing.

Articles 45, paragraph 4, 47, 48 and 49 of Book 2 apply.

Les articles 45, paragraphe 4, 47, 48 et 49 du Livre deuxième s'appliquent.

AFDELING 3 Rechten uit verzekeringsovereenkomsten

Section 3
Rights resulting from insurance contracts

Section troisième
Des droits découlant des contrats d'assurance

Art. 136. (5.10.3.1) - 1. Hij, die krachtens het reglement verplicht is het gebouw te doen verzekeren, vertegenwoordigt de gezamenlijke appartementseigenaars bij de uitoefening van de rechten die uit de verzekeringsovereenkomst voortvloeien, en voert voor hen het beheer over de ontvangen verzekeringspenningen.
- 2. Zodra tot herstel is besloten, worden de verzekeringspenningen tot dit doel aangewend, met dien verstande dat de verhouding van de waarde van de appartementsrechten na het herstel dezelfde moet zijn als tevoren. Bij de berekening van die waarde mag echter geen rekening worden gehouden met hetgeen een appartementseigenaar in het gedeelte dat hij als afzonderlijk geheel gebruikt, heeft aangebracht, tenzij hij hiervan tijdig aan de vereniging van eigenaars had kennis gegeven.
- 3. Herstel van schade aan gedeelten die bestemd zijn om als afzonderlijk geheel te worden gebruikt, geschiedt zoveel mogelijk volgens de aanwijzingen van de appartementseigenaars die het aangaat.
- 4. Uitkering aan ieder der appartementseigenaars van het hem toekomende aandeel in de assurantiepenningen geschiedt slechts:
a. indien na het herstel van de schade een overschot aanwezig blijkt te zijn;
b. indien drie maanden zijn verlopen nadat de vergadering van eigenaars heeft besloten van herstel of verder herstel af te zien;
c. in geval van opheffing van de splitsing.
- 5. Van het bepaalde in dit artikel kan in het reglement worden afgeweken.

1. The person who, pursuant to the by-laws, must have the building insured represents the joint apartment owners in the exercise of the rights resulting from the insurance contract; he administers for them the insurance proceeds received.
2. As soon as a decision has been taken to make repairs, the insurance proceeds are used for this purpose, in which case the relationship between the values of the apartment rights must be the same after the repairs as before. In calculating that value, however, account may not be taken of the additions which an apartment owner has made to the portion which he uses as a separate unit, unless he had timely notified the association of owners of this fact.
3. Repairs of damage done to portions which are intended to be used as separate units are made, as much as possible, according to the directives of the apartment owners concerned.

1. Celui qui, en vertu du règlement, est tenu de faire assurer l'édifice représente les propriétaires d'appartement conjoints dans l'exercice des droits résultant du contrat d'assurance et gère pour eux l'indemnité d'assurance reçue.
2. Dès que la réparation a été décidée, l'indemnité d'assurance est employée à cette fin, étant entendu que le rapport de valeur des droits d'appartement après la réparation doit être le même qu'auparavant. Dans le calcul de la valeur, il n'est cependant pas tenu compte des ajouts que le propriétaire d'appartement a apportés à la partie qu'il utilise comme entité distincte, à moins qu'il n'en ait avisé l'association des propriétaires en temps utile.
3. La réparation du dommage subi par les parties destinées à être utilisées comme entités distinctes s'effectue autant que possible suivant les directives des propriétaires d'appartement concernés.

4. Payment to each apartment owner of his share in the insurance proceeds is only made:
a. if, after the damage has been repaired, there proves to be a surplus;
b. if three months have passed after a decision of the association of owners to abandon repairs or further repairs;
c. in the event of termination of the division.
5. The by-laws may derogate from the provisions of this article.

4. La remise, à chacun des propriétaires d'appartement, de la part lui revenant de l'indemnité d'assurance a lieu seulement:
a. Si, après la réparation du préjudice, il apparaît un solde positif;
b. Si trois mois se sont écoulés depuis que l'assemblée des propriétaires a décidé de renoncer à la réparation ou à la continuation de celle-ci;
c. Dans le cas de la levée de la division.
5. Le règlement peut déroger aux dispositions du présent article.

Art. 137. Gereserveerd.

Reserved.

Réservé.

Art. 138. (5.10.3.1b) Geschillen over herstel of de wijze van herstel beslist de kantonrechter binnen wiens rechtsgebied het gebouw of het grootste gedeelte daarvan is gelegen, op verzoek van de meest gerede partij. Hoger beroep kan slechts worden ingesteld binnen een maand na de dagtekening van de eindbeschikking.

Upon the request of a directly interested party, the judge of the subdistrict court in whose jurisdiction the building, or the larger part of it, is situated, decides upon disputes regarding repairs or the manner of effectuating them. Any appeal must be taken within one month from the date of the final decision.

Les conflits relatifs à la réparation ou à ses modalités relèvent du juge d'instance dans le ressort duquel est situé l'édifice ou la plus grande partie de celui-ci, saisi par requête de la partie la plus diligente. L'appel ne peut être formé que dans le délai d'un mois suivant la date de la décision définitive.

AFDELING 4 Wijziging van de akte van splitsing en opheffing van de splitsing

Section 4 Modification of the deed of division and termination of the division

Section quatrième Des manières de modifier l'acte de division et de lever la division

Art. 139. (5.10.4.1) - 1. Wijziging van de akte van splitsing kan slechts geschieden met medewerking van alle appartementseigenaars. Zij behoeft de toestemming van hen die een beperkt recht op een appartementsrecht hebben, alsmede van hen die daarop beslag hebben gelegd. Ook is toestemming nodig van de gerechtigden tot een erfdienstbaarheid, indien hun recht door de wijziging wordt verkort.
- 2. Indien de wijziging uitsluitend betrekking heeft op het reglement, is de toestemming van de beslagleggers niet nodig.
- 3. De wijziging geschiedt door een daartoe bestemde notariële akte, gevolgd door inschrijving van die akte in de openbare registers. Indien de wijziging betrekking heeft op de begrenzing van gedeelten van het gebouw

of de daarbij behorende grond die bestemd zijn als afzonderlijk geheel te worden gebruikt, is artikel 109 lid 2 van overeenkomstige toepassing.

1. A modification of the deed of division may only take place with the cooperation of all apartment owners. The permission of holders of a dismembered right to an apartment right as well as of seizors of that apartment right is required. The permission of persons entitled to a servitude is also necessary if their right is to be limited as a result of the modification.
2. The permission of seizors is unnecessary if the modification exclusively concerns the by-laws.
3. The modification is made by a notarial deed intended for that purpose, followed by its entry in the public registers. Article 109 paragraph 2 applies *mutatis mutandis* if the modification relates to the boundary of portions of the building or the land belonging to it which are intended to be used as separate units.

1. La modification de l'acte de division ne peut avoir lieu qu'avec le concours de tous les propriétaires d'appartement. Elle requiert le consentement des personnes qui ont un droit démembré sur un droit d'appartement ainsi que des personnes qui ont saisi celui-ci. Elle requiert également le consentement de ceux qui ont une servitude, si la modification a pour effet de restreindre leur droit.

2. La modification qui porte exclusivement sur le règlement ne requiert pas le consentement des saisissants.
3. La modification est effectuée par acte notarié à cette fin, suivi de l'inscription de celui-ci sur les registres publics. Si la modification porte sur les limites de parties de l'édifice ou du fonds afférent, qui sont destinées à être utilisées comme entités distinctes, l'article 109, paragraphe 2, s'applique par analogie.

Art. 140. (5.10.4.2) - 1. Indien een of meer der in het eerste lid van het vorige artikel genoemden zich niet verklaren of zonder redelijke grond weigeren hun medewerking of toestemming te verlenen, kan deze worden vervangen door een machtiging van de kantonrechter binnen wiens rechtsgebied het gebouw of het grootste gedeelte daarvan is gelegen.
- 2. De machtiging kan slechts worden verleend op verzoek van een of meer appartementseigenaars aan wie ten minste de helft van het aantal stemmen in de vergadering van eigenaars toekomt.
- 3. De machtiging kan ook op verzoek van twee appartementseigenaars, of op verzoek van een appartementseigenaar aan wie verschillende appartementsrechten toebehoren worden verleend, wanneer de wijziging uitsluitend strekt tot een verandering van de onderlinge begrenzing der gedeelten die bestemd zijn door hen als afzonderlijk geheel te worden gebruikt, al dan niet gepaard gaande met een verandering in de onderlinge verhouding van hun aandelen in de goederen die in de splitsing zijn betrokken, of van hun bijdragen in de schulden en kosten die ingevolge de wet of het reglement voor rekening van de gezamenlijke appartementseigenaars komen.
- 4. Alle personen wier medewerking of toestemming ingevolge artikel 139 is vereist, worden bij name opgeroepen om op een verzoek als in de vorige leden bedoeld te worden gehoord.

1. If one or more persons mentioned in the first paragraph of the preceding article remain silent or refuse to cooperate or consent without reasonable ground, this cooperation or permission may be replaced by an authorization of the judge of the subdistrict court in whose jurisdiction the building, or the larger part of it, is situated.
2. The authorization may only be granted upon the request of one or more apartment owners holding at least one half of the number of votes in the meeting of owners.
3. The authorization may also be granted upon the request of two apartment owners, or of one apartment owner with several apartment rights, where the modification is exclusively intended to change the mutual boundary of the portions which are intended to be used by them as separate units, whether or not accompanied by a change in the mutual relationship between their shares in the property involved in the division, or their contributions to the debts and expenses which the joint apartment owners bear by virtue of the law or the by-laws.
4. All persons whose cooperation or permission is required pursuant to article 139, are individually summoned to be heard upon a request as referred to in the preceding paragraphs.

1. Si une ou plusieurs personnes visées au premier paragraphe de l'article précédent ne se déclarent pas ou refusent sans motif valable[1] de prêter leur concours ou de donner leur consentement, ceux-ci peuvent être remplacés par l'autorisation du juge d'instance dans le ressort duquel est situé l'édifice ou la plus grande partie de celui-ci.

2. L'autorisation n'est accordée qu'à la requête d'un ou de plusieurs propriétaires d'appartement ayant au moins la moitié des voix à l'assemblée des propriétaires.

3. L'autorisation peut aussi être accordée à la requête de deux propriétaires d'appartement, ou d'un propriétaire d'appartement titulaire de plusieurs droits d'appartement, lorsque la modification vise exclusivement à changer la limite mutuelle des parties destinées à servir à leur usage comme entités distinctes, que cette modification comporte ou non un changement dans le rapport de leurs parts dans les biens qui font l'objet de la division ou de leurs contributions aux dettes et aux frais incombant, en vertu de la loi ou du règlement, aux propriétaires d'appartement conjointement.
4. Toutes les personnes dont le concours ou le consentement est requis en vertu de l'article 139 sont nommément appelées afin d'être entendues sur une requête visée aux paragraphes précédents.

Art. 141. (5.10.4.2a) - 1. Bij gebreke van de in de twee voorgaande artikelen bedoelde toestemming of daarvoor in de plaats tredende machtiging wordt de wijziging vernietigd bij rechterlijke uitspraak op vordering van degeen wiens toestemming achterwege is gebleven.
- 2. De bevoegdheid om vernietiging te vorderen verjaart door verloop van een jaar, welke termijn begint met de aanvang van de dag, volgende op die waarop degeen die de vernietiging kan vorderen kennis heeft genomen van de wijziging dan wel hem schriftelijk van die wijziging mededeling is gedaan.
- 3. De rechter kan de vordering afwijzen, wanneer de eiser geen schade lijdt of hem een redelijke schadeloosstelling wordt aangeboden en voor de betaling hiervan voldoende zekerheid is gesteld.

[1] Le terme néerlandais *redelijk* se rend difficilement en français. La traduction littérale «raisonnable» ne convient pas ici.

1. Failing the permission or the authorization which takes its place as referred to in the two preceding articles, the modification is annulled by judgment upon the demand of the person whose permission has not been given.
2. The right to claim an annulment is prescribed by one year from the day following the one on which the person who can claim the annulment has become aware of the modification or has been notified of it in writing.
3. The judge may reject the action where the plaintiff suffers no damage or where reasonable compensation is offered to him for the payment of which sufficient security has been furnished.

1. Faute du consentement ou de l'autorisation qui le remplace prévus aux deux articles précédents, la modification est annulée par jugement à la demande de celui dont le consentement a fait défaut.

2. Le droit de demander l'annulation se prescrit par un an à compter du lendemain du jour où la personne qui peut l'exercer a pris connaissance de la modification ou en a été avisée par écrit.

3. Le juge peut rejeter la demande lorsque le demandeur ne subit pas de préjudice ou qu'un dédommagement raisonnable lui est offert pour le paiement duquel sûreté suffisante est fournie.

Art. 142. (5.10.4.2b) - 1. Beperkte rechten en beslagen, waarmee de appartementsrechten zijn belast, rusten na de wijziging van de akte van splitsing op de gewijzigde appartementsrechten, tenzij de akte van wijziging anders bepaalt.
- 2. Voorrechten blijven na de wijziging bestaan.

1. After the modification of the deed of division, dismembered rights and seizures encumbering the apartment rights attach to the modified apartment rights, unless the deed of modification provides otherwise.
2. After modification, privileges continue to exist.

1. Après la modification de l'acte de division, les droits démembrés et les saisies grevant les droits d'appartement portent sur les droits ainsi modifiés, sauf disposition contraire dans l'acte de modification.

2. Les privilèges continuent d'exister après la modification.

Art. 143. (5.10.4.2c) - 1. De splitsing wordt van rechtswege opgeheven:
a. bij het eindigen van een in de splitsing betrokken recht van erfpacht of opstal, wanneer naast dit recht geen andere registergoederen in de splitsing betrokken zijn en de beëindiging niet gepaard gaat met de vestiging van een nieuw recht van erfpacht of opstal van de appartementseigenaars op dezelfde onroerende zaak;
b. door inschrijving in de openbare registers van het vonnis waarbij een in de splitsing betrokken kadastraal perceel in zijn geheel is onteigend, wanneer geen andere percelen in de splitsing betrokken zijn.
- 2. In alle andere gevallen geschiedt de opheffing van de splitsing door een daartoe bestemde notariële akte, gevolgd door inschrijving van die akte in de openbare registers. De artikelen 139 lid 1, 140 leden 1, 2 en 4 en 141 zijn van overeenkomstige toepassing.

1. The division is terminated *de iure*:
a. by the termination of a right of emphyteusis or of superficies involved in the division, unless, besides this right, other registered property is involved in the division,

1. La division est levée de plein droit:
a. À l'expiration d'un droit d'emphytéose ou de superficie faisant l'objet de la division, lorsque, en dehors de ce droit, aucun autre bien immatriculé n'a fait l'objet de la division et que l'expiration

or the termination is accompanied by the establishment of a new right of emphyteusis or of superficies of the apartment owners on the same immoveable thing;

b. by entry in the public registers of a judgment expropriating an entire cadastral lot involved in the division, unless other lots are also involved in it.

2. In all other cases, the termination of the division is made by a notarial deed intended for that purpose, followed by its entry in the public registers. Articles 139 paragraph 1, 140 paragraphs 1, 2 and 4, and 141 apply *mutatis mutandis.*

ne donne pas lieu à l'établissement d'un nouveau droit d'emphytéose ou de superficie des propriétaires d'appartement sur le même immeuble;

b. Par l'inscription sur les registres publics du jugement d'expropriation de l'ensemble d'une parcelle cadastrale faisant l'objet de la division, lorsqu'aucune autre parcelle n'en fait l'objet.

2. Dans tous les autres cas, la levée de la division a lieu par acte notarié à cette fin, suivi de l'inscription de celui-ci sur les registres publics. L'article 139, paragraphe 1er, l'article 140, paragraphes 1er, 2 et 4 et l'article 141 s'appliquent par analogie.

Art. 144. (5.10.4.2d) - 1. Op verzoek van een persoon wiens medewerking of toestemming tot de wijziging van de akte van splitsing of tot opheffing van de splitsing is vereist, kan de kantonrechter binnen wiens rechtsgebied het gebouw of het grootste gedeelte daarvan is gelegen, bevelen dat de akte van splitsing wordt gewijzigd dan wel de splitsing wordt opgeheven:

a. wanneer de akte van splitsing niet voldoet aan de in de artikelen 111 en 112 gestelde vereisten;

b. wanneer uit de inrichting van de gedeelten van het gebouw die bestemd zijn als afzonderlijk geheel te worden gebruikt, deze bestemming niet blijkt;

c. wanneer de bouw of inrichting van het gebouw dan wel de inrichting van de daarbij behorende grond niet of niet meer beantwoordt aan de omschrijving in de akte van splitsing;

d. in geval van splitsing met toepassing van artikel 107, wanneer de stichting of de gewijzigde inrichting van het gebouw niet binnen een termijn van drie jaren te rekenen vanaf de dag van de inschrijving is voltooid;

e. wanneer een recht van erfpacht of opstal dat naast een of meer andere registergoederen in de splitsing betrokken is, eindigt;

f. wanneer een deel der in de splitsing betrokken registergoederen is uitgewonnen, een gedeelte van de kadastrale percelen is onteigend, of degene die de splitsing verricht heeft onbevoegd was over een deel der in de splitsing betrokken registergoederen te beschikken;

g. wanneer het gebouw ernstig is beschadigd of geheel of gedeeltelijk is gesloopt, tenzij herstel binnen redelijke tijd is te verwachten;

h. wanneer alle appartementseigenaars zich bij een overeenkomst tot de wijziging of opheffing hebben verbonden.

- 2. Aan de toewijzing van het verzoek kan de rechter voorwaarden verbinden.

- 3. Artikel 140 lid 4 is van overeenkomstige toepassing.

1. Upon the request of a person whose cooperation or permission is required for the modification of the deed of division or for the termination of the division, the judge of the subdistrict court in whose jurisdiction the building, or the larger part

1. Le juge d'instance dans le ressort duquel est situé un édifice qui fait l'objet d'une division ou la plus grande partie de celui-ci, peut, à la requête d'une personne dont le concours ou le consentement est requis pour la modification de l'acte de

of it, is situated may order that the deed of division be modified or that the division be terminated:

a. where the deed of division does not conform to the requirements of articles 111 and 112;
b. where the lay-out of the portions of the building which are intended to be used as separate units does not show this destination;
c. where the construction or lay-out of the building or the lay-out of the land belonging to it does not or does no longer conform to the description in the deed of division;
d. in the event of division with application of article 107, where the construction or the modified lay-out of the building has not been completed within a period of three years from the day of registration;
e. upon the termination of a right of emphyteusis or of superficies which is involved in the division in addition to other registered property;
f. where part of the registered property involved in the division has been executed against; where part of the cadastral lots has been expropriated; or where the person who has made the division did not have the right to dispose of part of the registered property involved in the division;
g. where the building has been seriously damaged or wholly or partially demolished, unless it is to be expected that repairs will be made within a reasonable period;
h. where all apartment owners have entered into a contract to modify or to terminate the division.

2. The judge may grant the request subject to conditions.
3. Article 140 paragraph 4 applies *mutatis mutandis*.

division ou pour la levée de la division, ordonner que l'acte soit modifié ou la division, levée:

a. Lorsque l'acte de division n'est pas conforme aux conditions prévues aux articles 11 et 112;
b. Lorsque la disposition des parties de l'édifice destinées à être utilisées comme entités distinctes ne fait pas apparaître cette destination;
c. Lorsque la construction ou la disposition de l'édifice ou la disposition du fonds afférent ne correspond pas ou ne correspond plus à la description dans l'acte de division;
d. Dans le cas d'une division soumise à l'article 107, lorsque la construction ou la disposition modifiée de l'édifice n'a pas été achevée dans les trois ans à compter du jour de l'inscription;
e. Lorsque prend fin un droit d'emphytéose ou de superficie qui fait, avec d'autres biens immatriculés, l'objet de la division;
f. Lorsqu'une partie des biens faisant l'objet de la division a été saisie et exécutée, qu'une partie des parcelles cadastrales a été expropriée ou que celui qui a accompli la division n'avait pas le pouvoir de disposer d'une partie des biens immatriculés qui en font l'objet;
g. Lorsque l'édifice a été sérieusement endommagé ou a été démoli en tout ou en partie, à moins que l'on ne puisse prévoir la réparation dans un délai raisonnable;
h. Lorsque tous les propriétaires d'appartement se sont engagés par contrat à la modification ou à la levée de la division.

2. Le juge peut accueillir la requête sous conditions.
3. L'article 140, paragraphe 4, s'applique par analogie.

Art. 145. (5.10.4.2e) - 1. De appartementseigenaars zijn verplicht aan een bevel als bedoeld in het vorige artikel uitvoering te geven, zodra de beschikking in kracht van gewijsde is gegaan. De in de artikelen 139 lid 1 en 143 lid 2 bedoelde toestemming is in dit geval niet vereist.
- 2. Indien de kantonrechter met toepassing van artikel 300 van Boek 3 een vertegenwoordiger heeft aangewezen, stelt hij op verzoek van de meest gerede partij of ambtshalve diens salaris vast; het salaris komt ten laste van de vertegenwoordigde.

1. Once the decision has become final, the apartment owners must comply with an order as referred to in the preceding article. In this case the permission, referred to in articles 139 paragraph 1 and 143 paragraph 2, is not required.

2. If, in applying article 300 of Book 3, the judge of the subdistrict court has appointed a representative, he determines his salary at the request of a directly interested party or *ex officio*; the salary is paid by the person who is represented.

1. Les propriétaires d'appartement sont tenus d'exécuter une ordonnance visée à l'article précédent dès que la décision a acquis force de chose jugée. Le consentement visé à l'article 139, paragraphe 1er, et à l'article 143, paragraphe 2, n'est pas requis dans ce cas.

2. Le juge d'instance qui, par application de l'article 300 du Livre troisième, a désigné un représentant fixe, à la requête de la partie la plus diligente ou d'office, la rémunération de celui-ci; la rémunération est à la charge du représenté.

Art. 146. (5.10.4.2f) Beperkte rechten, beslagen en voorrechten op een appartementsrecht rusten na opheffing van de splitsing op het aandeel van de gewezen appartementseigenaar in de goederen die in de splitsing betrokken waren.

After termination of the division, dismembered rights to an apartment right, seizures against and privileges upon that right attach to the share of the former apartment owner in the property involved in the division.

Les droits démembrés, les saisies et les privilèges grevant un droit d'appartement portent, après la levée de la division, sur la part de l'ancien propriétaire d'appartement dans les biens qui faisaient l'objet de la division.

Art. 147. (5.10.4.2g) - 1. De vereniging van eigenaars wordt door opheffing van de splitsing van rechtswege ontbonden.
- 2. De vereffening geschiedt met inachtneming van de volgende afwijkingen van de artikelen 23-24 van Boek 2.
- 3. De vereffenaar draagt hetgeen na voldoening der schuldeisers van het vermogen van de ontbonden vereniging is overgebleven, over aan hen die bij de opheffing van de splitsing appartementseigenaar waren, ieder voor een aandeel als bedoeld in artikel 113 lid 1.
- 4. De artikelen 23 lid 2, eerste zin, en lid 4 en 23c lid 4 van Boek 2 zijn niet van toepassing. De in artikel 23b lid 4 van Boek 2 bedoelde nederlegging geschiedt binnen het kanton waar het gebouw of het grootste gedeelte daarvan is gelegen. In plaats van de in artikel 23c lid 2 en 24 lid 2 van Boek 2 aangewezen rechter geldt als bevoegd diezelfde rechter binnen wiens rechtsgebied het gebouw of het grootste gedeelte daarvan is gelegen.

1. *De iure*, termination of the division dissolves the association of owners.

2. Liquidation is done in accordance with the following derogations from articles 23 - 24 of Book 2.

3. After the payment of creditors, the person who effectuates the liquidation remits the balance of the patrimony of the dissolved association to the persons who were apartment owners at the termination of the division, each for a share as referred to in article 113 paragraph 1.

1. L'association des propriétaires est dissoute de plein droit par la levée de la division.

2. La liquidation a lieu compte tenu des dérogations suivantes aux articles 23 et 24 du Livre deuxième.

3. Le liquidateur remet le solde du patrimoine de l'association dissoute, après paiement des créanciers, à ceux qui étaient propriétaires d'appartement lors de la levée de la division, chacun pour une part telle que visée à l'article 113, paragraphe 1er.

4. Articles 23 paragraph 2 first sentence, and paragraph 4, and 23c paragraph 4 of Book 2 do not apply. The deposit referred to in article 23b paragraph 4 of Book 2 takes place in the subdistrict in which the building, or the larger part of it, is situated. Instead of the judge referred to in articles 23c paragraph 2 and 24 paragraph 2 of Book 2, the judge of the same level in whose jurisdiction the building, or the larger part of it, is situated, has jurisdiction.

4. Les article 23, paragraphe 2, première phrase, et paragraphe 4 ainsi que l'article 23c, paragraphe 4, du Livre deuxième ne s'appliquent pas. Le dépôt visé à l'article 23b, paragraphe 4, du Livre deuxième a lieu dans le canton où est situé l'édifice ou la plus grande partie de celui-ci. Au lieu du juge désigné aux articles 23c, paragraphe 2, et 24, paragraphe 2, du Livre deuxième, est compétent le juge de même degré dans le ressort duquel est situé l'édifice ou la plus grande partie de celui-ci.

BOEK 6
ALGEMEEN GEDEELTE VAN HET VERBINTENISSENRECHT

BOOK 6
GENERAL PART OF THE LAW OF OBLIGATIONS

LIVRE SIXIÈME
PARTIE GÉNÉRALE DU DROIT DES OBLIGATIONS

TITEL 1 VERBINTENISSEN IN HET ALGEMEEN

TITLE 1 OBLIGATIONS IN GENERAL

TITRE PREMIER DES OBLIGATIONS EN GÉNÉRAL

AFDELING 1 Algemene bepalingen

Section 1 General provisions

Section première Dispositions générales

Art. 1. (6.1.1.1) Verbintenissen kunnen slechts ontstaan, indien dit uit de wet voortvloeit.

Obligations can only arise if such results from the law.

Les obligations ne peuvent naître que si cela résulte de la loi.

Art. 2. (6.1.1.2) - 1. Schuldeiser en schuldenaar zijn verplicht zich jegens elkaar te gedragen overeenkomstig de eisen van redelijkheid en billijkheid.
- 2. Een tussen hen krachtens wet, gewoonte of rechtshandeling geldende regel is niet van toepassing, voor zover dit in de gegeven omstandigheden naar maatstaven van redelijkheid en billijkheid onaanvaardbaar zou zijn.

1. A creditor and debtor must, as between themselves, act in accordance with the requirements of reasonableness and equity.
2. A rule binding upon them by virtue of law, usage or a juridical act does not apply to the extent that, in the given circumstances, this would be unacceptable according to criteria of reasonableness and equity.

1. Le créancier et le débiteur sont tenus de se comporter l'un envers l'autre suivant les exigences de la raison et de l'équité.
2. La règle à laquelle leur rapport est soumis en vertu de la loi, de l'usage ou d'un acte juridique ne s'applique pas dans la mesure où, en la circonstance, cela serait inacceptable d'après des critères de la raison et de l'équité.

Art. 3. (6.1.1.3) - 1. Een natuurlijke verbintenis is een rechtens niet-afdwingbare verbintenis.
- 2. Een natuurlijke verbintenis bestaat:
a. wanneer de wet of een rechtshandeling aan een verbintenis de afdwingbaarheid onthoudt;
b. wanneer iemand jegens een ander een dringende morele verplichting heeft van zodanige aard dat naleving daarvan, ofschoon rechtens niet afdwingbaar, naar maatschappelijke opvattingen als voldoening van een aan die ander toekomende prestatie moet worden aangemerkt.

1. A natural obligation is one which cannot be enforced at law.
2. A natural obligation exists:
a. where the law or a juridical act deprives an obligation of its enforceability;

1. Est une obligation naturelle celle dont le droit ne permet pas de forcer l'exécution.
2. Il y a obligation naturelle:
a. Lorsque la loi ou un acte juridique prive l'obligation d'une action visant à forcer l'exécution;

b. where a person has toward another person an imperative moral duty of such a nature that its performance, although unenforceable at law, must according to societal views be considered as the performance of a prestation to which that other person is entitled.

b. Lorsqu'une personne a, envers une autre, un devoir moral impérieux d'une nature telle que l'exécution, bien que le droit ne permette pas qu'elle soit forcée, doive néanmoins être considérée, d'après l'opinion communément reçue, comme l'exécution d'une prestation qui revient à cette autre personne.

Art. 4. (6.1.1.4) Op natuurlijke verbintenissen zijn de wettelijke bepalingen betreffende verbintenissen van overeenkomstige toepassing, tenzij de wet of haar strekking meebrengt dat een bepaling geen toepassing mag vinden op een niet-afdwingbare verbintenis.

The provisions of the law respecting obligations apply *mutatis mutandis* to natural obligations, unless the law or its necessary implication entail that such a provision may not apply to an unenforceable obligation.

Les dispositions de la loi relatives aux obligations s'appliquent par analogie aux obligations naturelles, à moins qu'il ne découle de la loi ou de sa portée qu'une disposition ne peut être applicable dans le cas d'une obligation dont le droit ne permet pas de forcer l'exécution.

Art. 5. (6.1.1.5) - 1. Een natuurlijke verbintenis wordt omgezet in een rechtens afdwingbare door een overeenkomst van de schuldenaar met de schuldeiser.
- 2. Een door de schuldenaar tot de schuldeiser gericht aanbod tot een zodanige overeenkomst om niet, geldt als aanvaard, wanneer het aanbod ter kennis van de schuldeiser is gekomen en deze het niet onverwijld heeft afgewezen.
- 3. Op de overeenkomst zijn de bepalingen betreffende schenkingen en giften niet van toepassing.

1. A natural obligation is transformed into an obligation enforceable at law by contract between debtor and creditor.

2. An offer by the debtor to the creditor to enter into such a contract by gratuitous title is deemed to have been accepted, where it has come to the attention of the creditor and he has not rejected it without delay.

3. The provisions respecting gifts and other liberalities do not apply to such a contract.

1. L'obligation naturelle se transforme en une obligation dont le droit permet de forcer l'exécution[1] par l'effet d'un contrat entre le débiteur et le créancier.

2. L'offre adressée par le débiteur au créancier de conclure un tel contrat à titre gratuit est réputée acceptée lorsque le créancier qui en a eu connaissance ne l'a pas rejetée sans tarder.

3. Le contrat n'est pas régi par les dispositions relatives aux donations et autres libéralités.

---

[1] Le néerlandais n'emploie pas ici le terme habituel *burgerlijke verbintenis* qui correspond au terme français *obligation civile.*

AFDELING 2 Pluraliteit van schuldenaren en hoofdelijke verbondenheid

Section 2
Plurality of debtors and solidarity among debtors

Section deuxième
De la pluralité des débiteurs et de la solidarité entre débiteurs

Art. 6. (6.1.2.1) - 1. Is een prestatie door twee of meer schuldenaren verschuldigd, dan zijn zij ieder voor een gelijk deel verbonden, tenzij uit wet, gewoonte of rechtshandeling voortvloeit dat zij voor ongelijke delen of hoofdelijk verbonden zijn.
- 2. Is de prestatie ondeelbaar of vloeit uit wet, gewoonte of rechtshandeling voort dat de schuldenaren ten aanzien van een zelfde schuld ieder voor het geheel aansprakelijk zijn, dan zijn zij hoofdelijk verbonden.
- 3. Uit een overeenkomst van een schuldenaar met zijn schuldeiser kan voortvloeien dat, wanneer de schuld op twee of meer rechtsopvolgers overgaat, dezen voor ongelijke delen of hoofdelijk verbonden zullen zijn.

1. Where two or more debtors owe one and the same prestation, they are liable for equal shares, unless, as a result of the law, usage or a juridical act, they are liable for unequal shares or are solidarily liable.
2. Where the prestation is indivisible, or where as a result of the law, usage or a juridical act the debtors are each liable for the whole of the same debt, they are solidarily liable.
3. A contract between debtor and creditor may have as a result that, where a debt is transmitted to two or more successors, they will be liable for unequal shares or will be solidarily liable.

1. Lorsque plusieurs débiteurs sont obligés à une seule prestation, chacun d'eux est tenu pour une part égale, à moins qu'il ne résulte de la loi, de l'usage ou d'un acte juridique qu'ils sont tenus pour des parts inégales ou solidairement.
2. Lorsque la prestation est indivisible ou qu'il résulte de la loi, de l'usage ou d'un acte juridique que les débiteurs d'une même dette sont obligés pour le tout, ils sont solidaires.
3. Il peut résulter d'un contrat entre le débiteur et le créancier que, en cas de transmission à plusieurs ayants droit, ceux-ci sont obligés pour des parts inégales ou solidairement.

Art. 7. (6.1.2.2) - 1. Indien twee of meer schuldenaren hoofdelijk verbonden zijn, heeft de schuldeiser tegenover ieder van hen recht op nakoming voor het geheel.
- 2. Nakoming door een der schuldenaren bevrijdt ook zijn medeschuldenaren tegenover de schuldeiser. Hetzelfde geldt, wanneer de schuld wordt gedelgd door inbetalinggeving of verrekening, alsmede wanneer de rechter op vordering van een der schuldenaren artikel 60 toepast, tenzij hij daarbij anders bepaalt.

1. If two or more debtors are solidarily liable, the creditor has against each of them the right to full performance.
2. Performance by one of the debtors also discharges his co-debtors with respect to the creditor. The same applies where the debt is extinguished by giving in payment, by compensation or where the judge, upon the demand of one of the debtors, applies article 60, unless in doing so he determines otherwise.

1. Si plusieurs débiteurs sont engagés solidairement, le créancier a droit, envers chacun d'eux, à l'exécution intégrale.
2. L'exécution effectuée par l'un des débiteurs libère également les codébiteurs à l'égard du créancier. Il en est de même lorsque la dette est éteinte par dation en paiement ou compensation, ainsi que dans le cas où le juge, à la demande de l'un des débiteurs, applique l'article 60, à moins qu'il n'en décide autrement.

Art. 8. (6.1.2.2a) Op de rechtsbetrekkingen tussen de hoofdelijke schuldenaren onderling is artikel 2 van overeenkomstige toepassing.

Article 2 applies *mutatis mutandis* to the juridical relations between the solidary debtors.

L'article 2 s'applique par analogie aux rapports juridiques entre les débiteurs solidaires.

Art. 9. (6.1.2.3) - 1. Iedere hoofdelijke schuldenaar is bevoegd namens de overige schuldenaren een aanbod tot afstand om niet van het vorderingsrecht te aanvaarden, voor zover de afstand ook de andere schuldenaren betreft.
- 2. Uitstel van betaling, door de schuldeiser aan een der schuldenaren verleend, werkt ook ten aanzien van zijn medeschuldenaren, voor zover blijkt dat dit de bedoeling van de schuldeiser is.

1. On behalf of the other debtors, each solidary debtor is entitled to accept an offer by the creditor to renounce,[1] by gratuitous title, his right to claim the debt, to the extent that the renunciation also applies to the co-debtors.
2. An extension granted by the creditor for payment to one of the debtors also applies to his co-debtors, to the extent that this proves to be the creditor's intention.

1. Chaque débiteur solidaire peut accepter au nom des autres débiteurs une offre de renonciation[2] à la créance à titre gratuit, dans la mesure où la renonciation s'applique également à eux.

2. Le délai de paiement accordé par le créancier à l'un des débiteurs produit également effet à l'égard des codébiteurs, dans la mesure où il apparaît que telle est l'intention du créancier.

Art. 10. (6.1.2.4) - 1. Hoofdelijke schuldenaren zijn, ieder voor het gedeelte van de schuld dat hem in hun onderlinge verhouding aangaat, verplicht overeenkomstig de volgende leden in de schuld en in de kosten bij te dragen.
- 2. De verplichting tot bijdragen in de schuld die ten laste van een der hoofdelijke schuldenaren wordt gedelgd voor meer dan het gedeelte dat hem aangaat, komt op iedere medeschuldenaar te rusten voor het bedrag van dit meerdere, telkens tot ten hoogste het gedeelte van de schuld dat de medeschuldenaar aangaat.
- 3. In door een hoofdelijke schuldenaar in redelijkheid gemaakte kosten moet iedere medeschuldenaar bijdragen naar evenredigheid van het gedeelte van de schuld dat hem aangaat, tenzij de kosten slechts de schuldenaar persoonlijk betreffen.

1. Solidary debtors must contribute to the debt and the expenses, each for the share which concerns him according to their mutual relationship, and in accordance with the following paragraphs.

1. Les débiteurs solidaires sont obligés, chacun pour la part le concernant dans leurs rapports réciproques, de contribuer à la dette et aux frais conformément aux paragraphes suivants.

1 "To renounce" and "renunciation" have been used here to translate the Dutch "afstand" where debts are concerned. In Books 3 and 5, "abandonment" has been used for what is in Dutch law the same concept, applied to real rights. See footnote at art. III: 81.

2 S'agissant de créances, le terme «renonciation», pour traduire le terme néerlandais *afstand*, paraît mieux convenir en français que le terme «abandon», employé aux Livres troisième et cinquième à propos de droits réels. Dans le droit néerlandais, il s'agit du même concept juridique. Voir note à l'art. 81 du Livre troisième.

2. The obligation to contribute to a debt which is discharged at the expense of one of the solidary co-debtors for more than the share that concerns him, comes to rest upon each co-debtor for the amount of this surplus, each time up to the share of the debt which concerns him.
3. In proportion to the share of the debt which concerns him, each co-debtor must contribute to the reasonable expenses incurred by a solidary debtor, unless they are personal to the latter.

2. Lorsque la dette est acquittée à la charge d'un des débiteurs solidaires pour plus de la part le concernant, l'obligation de contribution passe pour ce surplus à chacun des codébiteurs, dans tous les cas jusqu'à concurrence maximale de la part de la dette le concernant.
3. Les codébiteurs solidaires contribuent, chacun en proportion de la part de la dette le concernant, aux frais raisonnables qu'a engagés l'un d'entre eux, à moins que ces frais ne soient que les siens propres.

Art. 11. (6.1.2.5) - 1. Een uit hoofde van het vorige artikel tot bijdragen aangesproken medeschuldenaar kan de verweermiddelen die hij op het tijdstip van het ontstaan van de verplichting tot bijdragen jegens de schuldeiser had, ook inroepen tegen de hoofdelijke schuldenaar die de bijdrage van hem verlangt.
- 2. Niettemin kan hij een zodanig verweermiddel niet tegen deze schuldenaar inroepen, indien het na hun beider verbintenis is ontstaan uit een rechtshandeling die de schuldeiser met of jegens de aangesprokene heeft verricht.
- 3. Een beroep op verjaring van de rechtsvordering van de schuldeiser komt de tot bijdragen aangesprokene slechts toe, indien op het tijdstip van het ontstaan van de verplichting tot bijdragen zowel hijzelf als degene die de bijdrage verlangt, jegens de schuldeiser de voltooiing van de verjaring had kunnen inroepen.
- 4. De vorige leden zijn slechts van toepassing, voor zover uit de rechtsverhouding tussen de schuldenaren niet anders voortvloeit.

1. A co-debtor who, pursuant to the preceding article, has been called upon to contribute to a debt can invoke, against the solidary debtor demanding such contribution, the defences which he had against the creditor at the time when the obligation to contribute arises.
2. Nevertheless, he cannot invoke such a defence against his solidary co-debtor where it has arisen after the creation of their obligation from a juridical act which the creditor has performed with or in respect of the person called upon to contribute.
3. The person who has been called upon to contribute cannot invoke the prescription of the right of action of the creditor, unless both he and the person who is formally asking for the contribution could have invoked the completion of the prescription against the creditor at the time when the obligation to contribute arises.

1. Le codébiteur sommé de payer sa contribution en vertu de l'article précédent peut invoquer contre le débiteur solidaire qui lui demande sa contribution les exceptions qu'il avait à l'encontre du créancier lors de la naissance de l'obligation de contribution.
2. Il ne peut cependant invoquer contre ce débiteur une telle exception si celle-ci résulte d'un acte juridique que le créancier, après la naissance de l'obligation commune, a accompli avec ou envers le débiteur sommé.
3. Le débiteur sommé de payer sa contribution ne peut se prévaloir de la prescription de l'action du créancier que si, lors de la naissance de l'obligation de contribution, lui-même aussi bien que la personne qui lui réclame la contribution avait pu opposer au créancier la prescription accomplie.

4. The preceding paragraphs only apply to the extent that the juridical relationship between the debtors does not produce a different result.

4. Les paragraphes précédents ne s'appliquent que dans la mesure où il n'en résulte pas autrement du rapport juridique entre les débiteurs.

Art. 12. (6.1.2.7) - 1. Wordt de schuld ten laste van een hoofdelijke schuldenaar gedelgd voor meer dan het gedeelte dat hem aangaat, dan gaan de rechten van de schuldeiser jegens de medeschuldenaren en jegens derden krachtens subrogatie voor dit meerdere op die schuldenaar over, telkens tot ten hoogste het gedeelte dat de medeschuldenaar of de derde aangaat in zijn verhouding tot die schuldenaar.
- 2. Door de subrogatie wordt de vordering, indien zij een andere prestatie dan geld betrof, omgezet in een geldvordering van gelijke waarde.

1. Where the debt is discharged at the expense of a solidary debtor for more than the share which concerns him, he is subrogated for the surplus in the rights of the creditor against the co-debtors and third parties, in each case up to the share of each co-debtor or third party according to his relationship with that debtor.
2. Where the debt consists of a prestation other than the payment of money, it is converted by the subrogation into a money debt of equal value.

1. Lorsque la dette est acquittée à la charge d'un des débiteurs solidaires pour plus de la part le concernant, celui-ci est subrogé pour le surplus dans les droits du créancier à l'égard des codébiteurs et des tiers, dans chaque cas jusqu'à concurrence maximale des parts qui les concernent dans leurs rapports avec lui.
2. La créance qui portait sur une prestation non pécuniaire se transforme par la subrogation en une créance pécuniaire de même valeur.

Art. 13. (6.1.2.7a) - 1. Blijkt verhaal op een hoofdelijke schuldenaar voor een vordering als bedoeld in de artikelen 10 en 12 geheel of gedeeltelijk onmogelijk, dan wordt het onverhaalbaar gebleken deel over al zijn medeschuldenaren omgeslagen naar evenredigheid van de gedeelten waarvoor de schuld ieder van hen in hun onderlinge verhouding aanging.
- 2. Werd de schuld geheel of gedeeltelijk gedelgd ten laste van een hoofdelijke schuldenaar wie de schuld zelf niet aanging en blijkt op geen van de medeschuldenaren wie de schuld wel aanging verhaal mogelijk, dan wordt het onverhaalbaar gebleken deel over alle medeschuldenaren wie de schuld niet aanging, omgeslagen naar evenredigheid van de bedragen waarvoor ieder op het tijdstip van de delging van de schuld jegens de schuldeiser aansprakelijk was.
- 3. Ieder der in een omslag betrokkenen blijft gerechtigd het bijgedragene alsnog van hem die geen verhaal bood, terug te vorderen.

1. Where it proves wholly or partially impossible to take recourse against a solidary debtor for a debt referred to in articles 10 and 12, the share which has proved to be irrecoverable is attributed to all his co- debtors in proportion to the share of the debt that concerns each of them according to their mutual relationship.

1. Lorsque le recouvrement d'une créance, telle que visée aux articles 10 et 12, contre un débiteur solidaire se révèle impossible en tout ou en partie, la part s'avérant irrécouvrable est répartie sur tous les codébiteurs en proportion des parts de la dette les concernant d'après leurs rapports réciproques.

2. Where the debt was wholly or partially discharged at the expense of a solidary debtor whom it did not concern, and where it proves impossible to take recourse against the co-debtors whom the debt does concern, the share which has proved to be irrecoverable is attributed to all the co-debtors whom it did not concern in proportion to the amounts for which each of them was liable toward the creditor at the time of discharge of the debt.

3. Each person involved in an attribution remains entitled to reclaim the amount which he has contributed from the person against whom it was impossible to take recourse.

2. Lorsque la dette est acquittée en tout ou en partie à la charge d'un débiteur solidaire qu'elle ne concerne pas personnellement et que le recouvrement ne se révèle possible d'aucun des codébiteurs qu'elle concerne, la part s'avérant irrécouvrable est alors répartie entre tous les codébiteurs que la dette ne concerne pas, en proportion de la somme que chacun devait au créancier lors de l'acquittement de la dette.

3. Chacun de ceux qui ont été parties à la répartition conserve la faculté de demander plus tard sa contribution à celui contre qui le recouvrement fut impossible.

Art. 14. (6.1.2.7b) Afstand door de schuldeiser van zijn vorderingsrecht jegens een hoofdelijke schuldenaar bevrijdt deze niet van zijn verplichting tot bijdragen. De schuldeiser kan hem niettemin van zijn verplichting tot bijdragen jegens een mede-schuldenaar bevrijden door zich jegens deze laatste te verbinden zijn vordering op hem te verminderen met het bedrag dat als bijdrage gevorderd had kunnen worden.

Renunciation by a creditor of his right to claim a debt from a solidary debtor does not release the latter from his obligations to make contributions. Nevertheless, the creditor can release him from his obligation to make contributions to a co-debtor by obliging himself towards the latter to reduce his claim by the amount which could have been claimed as contribution.

La renonciation par le créancier à sa créance envers un débiteur solidaire ne libère pas ce dernier de son obligation de contribution. Le créancier peut néanmoins le libérer de son obligation de contribution à l'égard d'un codébiteur, en s'engageant envers ce dernier à réduire sa créance sur lui du montant qui aurait pu être demandé à titre de contribution.

AFDELING 3 Pluraliteit van schuldeisers

Section 3
Plurality of creditors

Section troisième
De la pluralité de créanciers

Art. 15. (6.1.3.1) - 1. Is een prestatie aan twee of meer schuldeisers verschuldigd, dan heeft ieder van hen een vorderingsrecht voor een gelijk deel, tenzij uit wet, gewoonte of rechtshandeling voortvloeit dat de prestatie hun voor ongelijke delen toekomt of dat zij gezamenlijk één vorderingsrecht hebben.

- 2. Is de prestatie ondeelbaar of valt het recht daarop in een gemeenschap, dan hebben zij gezamenlijk één vorderingsrecht.

- 3. Aan de schuldenaar kan niet worden tegengeworpen dat het vorderingsrecht in een gemeenschap valt, wanneer dit recht voortspruit uit een overeenkomst die hij met de deelgenoten heeft gesloten, maar hij niet wist noch behoefde te weten dat dit recht van die gemeenschap ging deel uitmaken.

1. Where a prestation is owed to two or more creditors, each of them has the right to claim an equal share, unless, as a result of the law, usage or a juridical act, they are entitled to unequal shares of the prestation or they have jointly a single claim.
2. Where the prestation is indivisible or the right to it is held in community, they have jointly a single claim.

3. The fact that the right to claim is held in community cannot be invoked against the debtor where this right results from a contract he has entered into with the partners, provided that he did not know nor ought to know that the right would be held in community.

1. La prestation due à plusieurs créanciers confère à chacun d'eux une créance pour une part égale, à moins qu'il ne résulte de la loi, de l'usage ou d'un acte juridique que la prestation leur revient pour des parts inégales ou qu'ils ont conjointement une seule créance.
2. Lorsque la prestation est indivisible ou que le droit dont elle est l'objet fait partie d'une communauté, les créanciers ont conjointement une seule créance.
3. Le débiteur ne peut se voir opposer qu'une créance fait partie d'une communauté, lorsque cette créance résulte d'un contrat qu'il a conclu avec les partenaires, mais qu'il ne savait ni ne devait savoir que cette créance allait faire partie de la communauté.

Art. 16. (6.1.3.2) Wanneer met de schuldenaar is overeengekomen dat twee of meer personen als schuldeiser de prestatie van hem voor het geheel kunnen vorderen, des dat de voldoening aan de een hem ook jegens de anderen bevrijdt, doch in de onderlinge verhouding van die personen de prestatie niet aan hen allen gezamenlijk toekomt, zijn op hun rechtsverhouding jegens de schuldenaar de in geval van gemeenschap geldende regels van overeenkomstige toepassing.

Where it has been agreed with the debtor that two or more persons who, among themselves, are not all jointly entitled to the prestation, can each as creditor claim the whole prestation from him, and that payment to one releases him with respect to the others, the rules pertaining to community apply *mutatis mutandis* to their juridical relationship with the debtor.

Lorsqu'il a été convenu avec le débiteur que plusieurs personnes peuvent, en tant que créanciers, lui demander la prestation intégrale, étant entendu que le paiement fait à l'un d'eux le libère à l'égard des autres également, mais que dans le rapport entre ces personnes la prestation ne revient pas à tous conjointement, les règles relatives à la communauté s'appliquent par analogie au rapport juridique entre elles et le débiteur.

AFDELING 4 Alternatieve verbintenissen

Section 4
Alternative obligations

Section quatrième
Des obligations alternatives

Art. 17. (6.1.4.1) - 1. Een verbintenis is alternatief, wanneer de schuldenaar verplicht is tot één van twee of meer verschillende prestaties ter keuze van hemzelf, van de schuldeiser of van een derde.
- 2. De keuze komt toe aan de schuldenaar, tenzij uit wet, gewoonte of rechtshandeling anders voortvloeit.

1. An obligation is alternative where the debtor must perform one of two or more different prestations at his choice, at the choice of the creditor or at that of a third party.

1. L'obligation est alternative lorsque le débiteur est tenu d'accomplir une seule de plusieurs prestations différentes, à son choix ou à celui du créancier ou d'un tiers.

2. The choice belongs to the debtor, unless the law, usage or a juridical act produce a different result.

2. Le choix appartient au débiteur, à moins qu'il n'en résulte autrement de la loi, de l'usage ou d'un acte juridique contraire.

Art. 18. (6.1.4.2) Een alternatieve verbintenis wordt enkelvoudig door het uitbrengen van de keuze door de daartoe bevoegde.

An alternative obligation becomes a simple obligation through the choice made by the person who is entitled to do so.

L'obligation alternative devient simple par le choix de celui qui en a la faculté.

Art. 19. (6.1.4.3) - 1. Wanneer de keuze aan een der partijen toekomt, gaat de bevoegdheid om te kiezen op de andere partij over, indien deze haar wederpartij een redelijke termijn heeft gesteld tot bepaling van haar keuze en deze daarbinnen haar keuze niet heeft uitgebracht.
- 2. De bevoegdheid om te kiezen gaat echter niet over op de schuldeiser voordat deze het recht heeft om nakoming te vorderen, noch op de schuldenaar voordat deze het recht heeft om te voldoen.
- 3. Indien op de vordering een pandrecht of een beslag rust en de aangevangen executie bij gebreke van een keuze niet kan worden voortgezet, kan de pandhouder of de beslaglegger aan beide partijen een redelijke termijn stellen om overeenkomstig hun onderlinge rechtsverhouding een keuze uit te brengen. Indien de keuze niet binnen deze termijn geschiedt, gaat de bevoegdheid tot kiezen op de pandhouder of beslaglegger over. Zij zijn gehouden niet nodeloos van deze bevoegdheid gebruik te maken.

1. Where one of the parties is entitled to make the choice, the right to choose passes to the other party if it has given its counterpart a reasonable period in which to determine the choice and the latter has not chosen within this period.
2. The right to choose, however, does not pass to the creditor until he becomes entitled to claim performance, nor to the debtor until he has the right to perform.
3. If the claim has been pledged or seized and if the execution, once commenced, cannot continue failing a choice, the pledgee or the seizor can give both parties a reasonable period to make a choice in accordance with their mutual relationship. If the choice does not take place within this period, the right to choose passes to the pledgee or the seizor. They must not use this right needlessly.

1. Lorsque le choix revient à l'une des parties, la faculté de choisir passe à l'autre, si celle-ci a fixé à la première un délai raisonnable afin d'arrêter son choix et que celle-ci ne l'a pas fait dans le délai imparti.

2. La faculté de choisir ne passe pas cependant au créancier avant qu'il n'ait le droit de demander l'exécution, ni au débiteur avant que celui-ci n'ait le droit d'exécuter.
3. Si la créance est grevée d'un droit de gage ou d'une saisie et que l'exécution commencée ne peut être poursuivie faute de choix, le gagiste ou saisissant peut fixer aux deux parties un délai convenable pour effectuer le choix conformément à leur rapport juridique réciproque. Si le choix n'a pas lieu à l'intérieur de ce délai, la faculté de choisir passe au gagiste ou saisissant. Ils sont tenus de ne pas se servir inutilement de cette faculté.

Art. 20. (6.1.4.4) - 1. De onmogelijkheid om een of meer der prestaties te verrichten doet geen afbreuk aan de bevoegdheid om te kiezen.
- 2. Indien de keuze aan de schuldenaar toekomt, is deze echter niet bevoegd een onmogelijke prestatie te kiezen, tenzij de onmogelijkheid een

gevolg is van een aan de schuldeiser toe te rekenen oorzaak of deze met de keuze instemt.

1. Impossibility to perform one or more of the prestations does not affect the right to choose.
2. However, if the choice is the debtor's, he may not choose an impossible prestation, unless the impossibility results from a cause which is imputable to the creditor, or the latter consents to the choice.

1. L'impossibilité d'exécuter une ou plusieurs prestations ne touche pas la faculté de choisir.
2. Si le choix appartient au débiteur, celui-ci ne peut cependant choisir une prestation impossible, à moins que l'impossibilité ne résulte d'une cause imputable au créancier ou que celui-ci ne consente à l'option retenue.

AFDELING 5 Voorwaardelijke verbintenissen

Section 5 Conditional obligations

Section cinquième Des obligations conditionnelles

Art. 21. (6.1.5.1) Een verbintenis is voorwaardelijk, wanneer bij rechtshandeling haar werking van een toekomstige onzekere gebeurtenis afhankelijk is gesteld.

An obligation is conditional where, in virtue of a juridical act, its effect has been made dependent upon a future and uncertain event.

L'obligation est conditionnelle lorsque, par acte juridique, on a fait dépendre son effet d'un événement futur et incertain.

Art. 22. (6.1.5.2) Een opschortende voorwaarde doet de werking der verbintenis eerst met het plaatsvinden der gebeurtenis aanvangen; een ontbindende voorwaarde doet de verbintenis met het plaatsvinden der gebeurtenis vervallen.

A suspensive condition causes the obligation to take effect upon the occurrence of the event; a resolutory condition extinguishes the obligation upon the occurrence of the event.

La condition suspensive fait commencer l'effet de l'obligation à l'arrivée de l'événement; la condition résolutoire éteint l'obligation à l'arrivée de l'événement.

Art. 23. (6.1.5.3) - 1. Wanneer de partij die bij de niet-vervulling belang had, de vervulling heeft belet, geldt de voorwaarde als vervuld, indien redelijkheid en billijkheid dit verlangen.
- 2. Wanneer de partij die bij de vervulling belang had, deze heeft teweeggebracht, geldt de voorwaarde als niet vervuld, indien redelijkheid en billijkheid dit verlangen.

1. If reasonableness and equity so require, the condition is deemed fulfilled in the event that the party who has an interest in the non-fulfilment of the condition prevents its fulfilment.

1. La condition est réputée accomplie, si la raison et l'équité l'exigent, lorsque la partie qui y avait intérêt en a empêché l'accomplissement.

2. If reasonableness and equity so require, the condition is deemed not to be fulfilled in the event that the party who has an interest in the fulfilment of the condition brings about its fulfilment.

2. La condition est réputée défaillie, si la raison et l'équité l'exigent, lorsque la partie qui y avait intérêt en a provoqué l'accomplissement.

Art. 24. (6.1.5.4) - 1. Nadat een ontbindende voorwaarde is vervuld, is de schuldeiser verplicht de reeds verrichte prestaties ongedaan te maken, tenzij uit de inhoud of strekking van de rechtshandeling anders voortvloeit.
- 2. Strekt de verplichting tot ongedaanmaking tot teruggave van een goed, dan komen de na de vervulling van de voorwaarde afgescheiden natuurlijke of opeisbaar geworden burgerlijke vruchten aan de schuldenaar toe en zijn de artikelen 120-124 van Boek 3 van overeenkomstige toepassing met betrekking tot hetgeen daarin is bepaald omtrent de vergoeding van kosten en van schade, voor zover die kosten en die schade na de vervulling zijn ontstaan.

1. After fulfilment of a resolutory condition, the creditor must undo the prestations which have already been performed, unless the content or the necessary implication of the juridical act produce a different result.
2. Where the obligation to undo involves restitution of property, the natural fruits which have become separated and the civil fruits which have become exigible after the fulfilment of the condition belong to the debtor; articles 120 - 124 of Book 3 apply *mutatis mutandis* to the compensation for costs and damage to the extent that they have arisen after the fulfilment.

1. Après l'accomplissement d'une condition résolutoire, le créancier est tenu d'anéantir[1] les prestations déjà effectuées, à moins que il n'en résulte autrement du contenu ou de la portée de l'acte juridique.

2. Lorsque l'obligation d'anéantissement a pour objet la restitution d'un bien, les fruits naturels qui ont été séparés après l'accomplissement de la condition et les fruits civils devenus exigibles après cet événement reviennent au débiteur; dans ce cas, les articles 120 à 124 du Livre troisième s'appliquent par analogie, pour ce qui y est prévu au sujet du remboursement de frais et de la réparation du dommage, dans la mesure où ces frais et ce dommage ont pris naissance après l'accomplissement de la condition.

Art. 25. (6.1.5.4a) Is een krachtens een verbintenis onder opschortende voorwaarde verschuldigde prestatie vóór de vervulling van de voorwaarde verricht, dan kan overeenkomstig afdeling 2 van titel 4 ongedaanmaking van de prestatie worden gevorderd, zolang de voorwaarde niet in vervulling is gegaan.

Where a prestation owed pursuant to an obligation under a suspensive condition has been performed before the fulfilment of the condition, a demand may be made that the prestation be undone according to section 2 of title 4 as long as the condition has not been fulfilled.

Lorsqu'une prestation qui est due en vertu d'une obligation sous condition suspensive a été effectuée avant l'accomplissement de la condition, l'anéantissement peut en être demandé conformément à la section deuxième du titre quatrième, tant que la condition n'est pas accomplie.

[1] Ce terme traduit le nouveau mot néerlandais *ongedaanmaken*. Voir aussi les articles 311 du Livre troisième et 25, 210 et 211 du Livre sixième.

Art. 26. (6.1.5.5) Op voorwaardelijke verbintenissen zijn de bepalingen betreffende onvoorwaardelijke verbintenissen van toepassing, voor zover het voorwaardelijk karakter van de betrokken verbintenis zich daartegen niet verzet.

The provisions regarding unconditional obligations apply to conditional obligations to the extent that the conditional character of the obligation in question so permits.

Les obligations conditionnelles sont soumises aux dispositions relatives aux obligations simples, dans la mesure où leur caractère conditionnel ne s'y oppose pas.

AFDELING 6 Nakoming van verbintenissen

Section 6 Performance of obligations

Section sixième De l'exécution des obligations

Art. 27. (6.1.6.1) Hij die een individueel bepaalde zaak moet afleveren, is verplicht tot de aflevering voor deze zaak zorg te dragen op de wijze waarop een zorgvuldig schuldenaar dit in de gegeven omstandigheden zou doen.

A person who is obliged to deliver a thing certain and determinate must care for it until delivery, in the manner in which a prudent debtor would do so in the circumstances.

Celui qui est obligé de livrer une chose certaine et déterminée est tenu d'y apporter, jusqu'au moment de la livraison, les soins qu'y apporterait un débiteur prudent en la circonstance.

Art. 28. (6.1.6.2) Indien de verschuldigde zaak of zaken slechts zijn bepaald naar de soort en binnen de aangeduide soort verschil in kwaliteit bestaat, mag hetgeen de schuldenaar aflevert, niet beneden goede gemiddelde kwaliteit liggen.

If the thing or the things due are only determined as to kind, and if there exists a difference of quality within the kind as indicated, the debtor may not deliver a thing of less than average good quality.

Si la ou les choses dues ne sont déterminées que par leur espèce et que la qualité varie au sein de l'espèce indiquée, ce que livre le débiteur ne peut être de qualité inférieure à la bonne moyenne.

Art. 29. (6.1.6.3) De schuldenaar is zonder toestemming van de schuldeiser niet bevoegd het verschuldigde in gedeelten te voldoen.

The debtor is not entitled to make partial payments of his debt, without the permission of the creditor.

Le débiteur ne peut, sans le consentement du créancier, payer par parties ce qui est dû.

Art. 30. (6.1.6.4) - 1. Een verbintenis kan door een ander dan de schuldenaar worden nagekomen, tenzij haar inhoud of strekking zich daartegen verzet.
- 2. De schuldeiser komt niet in verzuim, indien hij een door een derde aangeboden voldoening weigert met goedvinden van de schuldenaar.

1. A person other than the debtor can perform an obligation, unless this is contrary to its content or necessary implication.
2. The creditor does not come into default if, with the consent of the debtor, he refuses performance offered by a third person.

1. L'obligation peut être exécutée par une personne autre que le débiteur, à moins que son contenu ou sa portée ne s'y oppose.

2. Le créancier ne se constitue pas en demeure s'il refuse, avec le consentement du débiteur, l'exécution qui lui est offerte par un tiers.

Art. 31. (6.1.6.5) Betaling aan een onbekwame schuldeiser bevrijdt de schuldenaar, voor zover het betaalde de onbekwame tot werkelijk voordeel heeft gestrekt of in de macht is gekomen van diens wettelijke vertegenwoordiger.

Payment to an incapable creditor releases the debtor to the extent that what has been been paid has actually benefitted the incapable person or has come under the control of his legal representative.

Le paiement fait au créancier incapable libère le débiteur dans la mesure où ce qui a été payé a réellement profité à l'incapable ou est venu en la puissance de son représentant légal.

Art. 32. (6.1.6.6) Betaling aan een ander dan de schuldeiser of dan degene die met hem of in zijn plaats bevoegd is haar te ontvangen, bevrijdt de schuldenaar, voor zover degene aan wie betaald moest worden de betaling heeft bekrachtigd of erdoor is gebaat.

Payment to a person other than the creditor or to a person who together with or on behalf of the creditor is entitled to receive payment, releases the debtor to the extent that the person to whom the payment had to be made has ratified it or has benefitted from it.

Le paiement fait à une personne autre que le créancier ou celui qui, avec lui ou à sa place, peut le recevoir libère le débiteur dans la mesure où celui auquel le paiement devait être fait l'a ratifié ou en a profité.

Art. 33. (6.1.6.6a) Is de betaling gedaan in weerwil van een beslag of terwijl de schuldeiser wegens een beperkt recht, een bewind of een soortgelijk beletsel onbevoegd was haar te ontvangen, en wordt de schuldenaar deswege genoodzaakt opnieuw te betalen, dan heeft hij verhaal op de schuldeiser.

Where payment has been made despite a seizure, or during a period in which the creditor was unable to receive payment because of a dismembered right, a regime of administration or a similar impediment, and where as a consequence the debtor is made to pay again, he has a recourse against the creditor.

Lorsque le paiement a été effectué en dépit d'une saisie ou pendant que le créancier, en raison d'un droit démembré, d'un régime d'administration ou d'un empêchement semblable, ne pouvait le recevoir, le débiteur qu'on oblige, de ce fait, de payer de nouveau, a un recours contre lui.

Art. 34. (6.1.6.7) - 1. De schuldenaar die heeft betaald aan iemand die niet bevoegd was de betaling te ontvangen, kan aan degene aan wie betaald moest worden, tegenwerpen dat hij bevrijdend heeft betaald, indien hij op redelijke gronden heeft aangenomen dat de ontvanger der betaling als schuldeiser tot de prestatie gerechtigd was of dat uit anderen hoofde aan hem moest worden betaald.

- 2. Indien iemand zijn recht om betaling te vorderen verliest, in dier voege dat het met terugwerkende kracht aan een ander toekomt, kan de schuldenaar een inmiddels gedane betaling aan die ander tegenwerpen, tenzij hetgeen hij omtrent dit verlies kon voorzien, hem van de betaling had behoren te weerhouden.

1. A debtor who has paid a person who was not entitled to receive payment, can invoke his release by payment against the person to whom the payment should have been made, if he had reasonable grounds to believe that the recipient of the payment was entitled to the prestation as creditor or that payment was to be made to him for another reason.
2. If a person loses his right to claim payment in the sense that the right belongs retroactively to another person, the debtor can invoke against that other person a payment made in the meantime, unless what he could foresee regarding this loss should have kept him from paying.

1. Le débiteur qui a payé à une personne ne pouvant recevoir le paiement peut opposer sa libération à celui qui devait recevoir le paiement, s'il a cru, pour des motifs raisonnables, que celui qui a reçu le paiement avait droit à la prestation en tant que créancier ou que, à un autre titre, paiement devait lui être fait.

2. Si une personne perd son droit de demander paiement, en ce sens que ce droit revient rétroactivement à une autre personne, le débiteur peut opposer à cette autre le paiement fait avant le moment de la perte du droit, sauf si ce qu'il pouvait prévoir au sujet de cette perte n'avait dû le retenir de payer.

Art. 35. (6.1.6.7a) - 1. Is in geval van betaling door een derde te zijnen aanzien aan de vereisten van één der leden van het vorige artikel voldaan, dan kan hij te zijnen behoeve de bevrijdende werking van die betaling inroepen.
- 2. De schuldenaar kan de bevrijdende werking van die betaling te zijnen behoeve inroepen, indien, bij betaling door hemzelf, ook wat hem betreft aan die vereisten zou zijn voldaan.

1. Where payment made by a third person fulfills, with respect to that person, the requirements of either of the paragraphs of the preceding article, the third person can invoke the releasing force of that payment in his favour.
2. The debtor can invoke the releasing force of that payment in his own favour if, through his own payment, he would also with respect to himself have complied with those requirements.

1. Lorsque, dans le cas du paiement fait par un tiers, les conditions prévues à l'un des paragraphes de l'article précédent sont remplies à l'égard de ce tiers, celui-ci peut invoquer en sa faveur l'effet libératoire du paiement.
2. Le débiteur peut invoquer en sa faveur l'effet libératoire de tel paiement dans le cas où, s'il avait lui-même payé, les conditions auraient également été remplies à son égard.

Art. 36. (6.1.6.7b) In de gevallen, bedoeld in de twee voorgaande artikelen, heeft de ware gerechtigde verhaal op degene die de betaling zonder recht heeft ontvangen.

In the cases referred to in the two preceding articles, the person who in reality is entitled to payment has recourse against a person who has received payment without having a right to it.

Dans les cas prévus aux deux articles précédents, le véritable titulaire du droit a un recours contre celui qui a reçu le paiement sans y avoir droit.

Art. 37. (6.1.6.7c) De schuldenaar is bevoegd de nakoming van zijn verbintenis op te schorten, indien hij op redelijke gronden twijfelt aan wie de betaling moet geschieden.

The debtor is entitled to suspend the performance of his obligation if he has reasonable doubts as to the person to whom the payment must be made.

Le débiteur peut suspendre l'exécution de l'obligation s'il a un doute raisonnable sur la personne à qui revient le paiement.

Art. 38. (6.1.6.9) Indien geen tijd voor de nakoming is bepaald, kan de verbintenis terstond worden nagekomen en kan terstond nakoming worden gevorderd.

If no term has been set for the performance of an obligation, it may be performed as well as claimed immediately.

Si aucun terme n'a été fixé, l'exécution de l'obligation peut avoir lieu et peut être demandée immédiatement.

Art. 39. (6.1.6.9a) - 1. Is wel een tijd voor de nakoming bepaald, dan wordt vermoed dat dit slechts belet dat eerdere nakoming wordt gevorderd.
- 2. Betaling vóór de vervaldag geldt niet als onverschuldigd.

1. Where a term for performance has been set, it is presumed only to prevent the obligation from being claimed earlier.

2. Payment before the due date is not considered undue.

1. Lorsqu'il a été fixé un terme pour l'exécution, il est présumé avoir pour seul effet d'empêcher une action en exécution avant cette date.

2. Le paiement avant l'échéance n'est pas réputé indu.

Art. 40. (6.1.6.10) De schuldenaar kan de tijdsbepaling niet meer inroepen:
a. wanneer hij in staat van faillissement is verklaard;
b. wanneer hij in gebreke blijft de door hem toegezegde zekerheid te verschaffen;
c. wanneer door een aan hem toe te rekenen oorzaak de voor de vordering gestelde zekerheid verminderd is, tenzij het overgeblevene nog een voldoende waarborg voor de voldoening oplevert.

A debtor loses the benefit of the term:

a. when he has been declared bankrupt;
b. when he is in default to furnish security promised by him;
c. where security which has been furnished for the debt has been diminished by a cause which can be imputed to him, unless the remaining security still constitutes a sufficient guarantee for the performance of the obligation.

Le débiteur ne peut plus invoquer le bénéfice du terme:

a. Lorsqu'il a fait faillite;
b. Lorsqu'il est en défaut de fournir les sûretés qu'il a promises;
c. Lorsque les sûretés garantissant la créance ont été diminuées par une cause qui lui est imputable, à moins que celles qui restent constituent encore une garantie suffisante pour l'exécution de l'obligation.

Art. 41. (6.1.6.11) Indien geen plaats voor de nakoming is bepaald, moet de aflevering van een verschuldigde zaak geschieden:
a. in geval van een individueel bepaalde zaak: ter plaatse waar zij zich bij het ontstaan van de verbintenis bevond;

b. in geval van een naar de soort bepaalde zaak: ter plaatse waar de schuldenaar zijn beroep of bedrijf uitoefent of, bij gebreke daarvan, zijn woonplaats heeft.

If no place has been determined for the performance of an obligation, delivery of a thing due must take place:
a. in the event of a thing certain and determinate, at the place where it was at the time when the obligation has arisen;
b. in the event of a thing determined as to kind, at the place where the debtor exercises his profession or business, or, in the absence thereof, at the place where he is domiciled.

Si le lieu de l'exécution n'a pas été fixé, la chose due doit être livrée:
a. Dans le cas d'une chose certaine et déterminée, à l'endroit où elle se trouvait lors de la naissance de l'obligation;
b. Dans le cas d'une chose déterminée par son espèce, à l'endroit où le débiteur exerce son activité professionnelle ou a établi son entreprise ou, à défaut, à son domicile.

Art. 42. (6.1.6.12) Hij die ter nakoming van een verbintenis een zaak heeft afgeleverd waarover hij niet bevoegd was te beschikken, kan vorderen dat deze wordt afgegeven aan degene aan wie zij toekomt, mits hij tegelijkertijd een andere, aan de verbintenis beantwoordende zaak aanbiedt en het belang van de schuldeiser zich niet tegen teruggave verzet.

A person who, in the performance of an obligation, has delivered to another a thing he had no right to dispose of, can require that the thing be given to the person to whom it belongs, provided that, at the same time, he offers to deliver another thing corresponding to the obligation, and that the interest of the creditor is not opposed to the thing being given back.

Celui qui a exécuté une obligation en livrant une chose dont il ne pouvait disposer peut demander que celle-ci soit remise à la personne à qui elle revient, pourvu qu'il offre en même temps une autre chose conforme à l'obligation et que l'intérêt du créancier ne s'oppose pas à la remise.

Art. 43. (6.1.6.13) - 1. Verricht de schuldenaar een betaling die zou kunnen worden toegerekend op twee of meer verbintenissen jegens een zelfde schuldeiser, dan geschiedt de toerekening op de verbintenis welke de schuldenaar bij de betaling aanwijst.
- 2. Bij gebreke van zodanige aanwijzing geschiedt de toerekening in de eerste plaats op de opeisbare verbintenissen. Zijn er ook dan nog meer verbintenissen waarop de toerekening zou kunnen plaatsvinden, dan geschiedt deze in de eerste plaats op de meest bezwarende en zijn de verbintenissen even bezwarend, op de oudste. Zijn de verbintenissen bovendien even oud, dan geschiedt de toerekening naar evenredigheid.

1. A payment by a debtor which can be imputed to two or more obligations towards the same creditor, is imputed to the obligation indicated by the debtor in his payment.
2. In the absence of such an indication, the payment is first imputed to the exigible obligations. If, even in that case, there are several such obligations, it is first imputed to the most onerous

1. Lorsque le paiement fait par un débiteur peut s'imputer à plusieurs obligations à l'égard du même créancier, l'imputation s'effectue sur celle qu'indique le débiteur lors du paiement.
2. À défaut d'indication, le paiement s'impute d'abord aux obligations exigibles. S'il existe toujours plusieurs obligations exigibles, l'imputation se fait d'abord sur la plus onéreuse et, si les obligations sont

obligation and where the obligations are equally onerous, to the oldest. Furthermore, where the obligations have arisen at the same time, the payment is imputed proportionally.

également onéreuses, sur la plus ancienne. Lorsque les obligations ont en plus la même ancienneté, l'imputation se fait proportionnellement.

Art. 44. (6.1.6.14) - 1. Betaling van een op een bepaalde verbintenis toe te rekenen geldsom strekt in de eerste plaats in mindering van de kosten, vervolgens in mindering van de verschenen rente en tenslotte in mindering van de hoofdsom en de lopende rente.
- 2. De schuldeiser kan, zonder daardoor in verzuim te komen, een aanbod tot betaling weigeren, indien de schuldenaar een andere volgorde voor de toerekening aanwijst.
- 3. De schuldeiser kan volledige aflossing van de hoofdsom weigeren, indien daarbij niet tevens de verschenen en lopende rente alsmede de kosten worden voldaan.

1. Payment of a sum of money, which is to be imputed to a specific obligation, is first applied against costs, then against interest past due, and finally against the capital sum and the current interest.
2. A creditor can, without coming into default, reject an offer to pay if the debtor indicates a different order of imputation.
3. A creditor can reject full repayment of the capital sum if the interest past due, the current interest and the costs are not also paid at the same time.

1. Le paiement d'une somme d'argent imputable sur une obligation déterminée a pour objet d'abord l'acquittement des frais, puis celui des intérêts échus et enfin celui du capital et l'intérêt courant.
2. Le créancier peut, sans se constituer en demeure, refuser l'offre de paiement si le débiteur indique un ordre d'imputation différent.
3. Le créancier peut refuser le remboursement intégral du capital s'il ne reçoit pas en même temps le paiement de l'intérêt échu et courant ainsi que des frais.

Art. 45. (6.1.6.15) Slechts met toestemming van de schuldeiser kan een schuldenaar zich van zijn verbintenis bevrijden door een andere prestatie dan de verschuldigde, al mocht zij van gelijke of zelfs hogere waarde zijn.

Only with the permission of the creditor can a debtor discharge his obligation by performing a prestation other than the one he owes, be that other prestation of equal or even higher value.

Le débiteur ne peut qu'avec le consentement du créancier se libérer d'une obligation par une prestation différente de celle qui est due, quoiqu'elle soit de valeur égale ou même supérieure.

Art. 46. (6.1.6.15a) - 1. Wanneer de schuldeiser een cheque, postcheque, overschrijvingsorder of een ander hem bij wijze van betaling aangeboden papier in ontvangst neemt, wordt vermoed dat dit geschiedt onder voorbehoud van goede afloop.
- 2. Is de schuldeiser bevoegd de nakoming van een op hem rustende verplichting tot het tijdstip van de betaling op te schorten, dan behoudt hij dit opschortingsrecht totdat zekerheid van goede afloop bestaat of door hem had kunnen worden verkregen.

1. Where the creditor takes delivery of a cheque, postal order, transfer order or another document tendered to him by

1. Le créancier qui prend livraison d'un chèque, d'un mandat-poste, d'un mandat de virement ou d'un autre titre qui lui est offert

way of payment, it is presumed to be subject to the existence of sufficient funds.

aux fins de paiement est présumé le faire sous réserve de provision suffisante.

2. Where the creditor is entitled to suspend performance of an obligation which he owes until the time of payment, he retains this right of suspension until he is certain or could have been certain of the sufficiency of funds.

2. Lorsque le créancier peut suspendre l'exécution d'une obligation qui lui incombe jusqu'au moment du paiement, il conserve le droit de suspension jusqu'au moment où il a ou aurait pu avoir la certitude d'une provision suffisante.

Art. 47. (6.1.6.16) - 1. De kosten van betaling komen ten laste van degene die de verbintenis nakomt.
- 2. De kosten van een kwitantie komen ten laste van degene ten behoeve van wie het stuk wordt afgegeven.

1. The costs of payment are borne by the person who performs the obligation.
2. The costs of a quittance are borne by the person in whose favour it is issued.

1. Les frais de paiement sont à la charge de celui qui exécute l'obligation.
2. Les frais de la quittance sont à la charge de celui au profit de qui elle est délivrée.

Art. 48. (6.1.6.17) - 1. De schuldeiser is verplicht voor iedere voldoening een kwitantie af te geven, tenzij uit overeenkomst, gewoonte of billijkheid anders voortvloeit.
- 2. Indien de schuldeiser een ter zake van de schuld afgegeven bewijsstuk heeft, kan de schuldenaar bij voldoening bovendien de afgifte van dat bewijsstuk vorderen, tenzij de schuldeiser een redelijk belang heeft bij het behoud van het stuk en daarop de nodige aantekening tot bewijs van de bevrijding van de schuldenaar stelt.
- 3. De schuldenaar kan de nakoming van zijn verbintenis opschorten, indien de schuldeiser niet voldoet aan het voorschrift van het eerste lid.

1. The creditor must issue a quittance for each payment, unless contract, usage or equity produce a different result.

1. Le créancier remet une quittance pour chaque paiement, à moins qu'il n'en résulte autrement du contrat, de l'usage ou de l'équité.

2. If the creditor has documentary evidence of the debt, the debtor can, upon payment, also claim that this documentary evidence be given to him, unless the creditor has a reasonable interest in keeping it and inscribes the necessary annotation on it as proof of the release of the debtor.

2. Si le créancier détient un titre constatant la dette, le débiteur qui a payé peut demander, en outre, la remise du titre, à moins que le créancier n'ait un intérêt raisonnable à le conserver et qu'il y porte la mention nécessaire pour établir la libération du débiteur.

3. If the creditor does not comply with the rule of paragraph 1, the debtor can suspend the performance of his obligation.

3. Le débiteur peut suspendre l'exécution de l'obligation, si le créancier ne respecte pas la disposition du paragraphe premier.

Art. 49. (6.1.6.17a) - 1. Bij voldoening van een vordering aan toonder of order kan de schuldenaar eisen dat een kwijting op het papier wordt gesteld en dat hem het papier wordt afgegeven.
- 2. Indien de voldoening niet de gehele vordering betreft of de schuldeiser het papier nog voor de uitoefening van andere rechten nodig heeft, kan hij het papier behouden, mits hij naast de kwijting die op het papier is gesteld, tevens een afzonderlijke kwijting afgeeft.

- 3. Hij kan, ongeacht of geheel of gedeeltelijk voldaan wordt, volstaan met de enkele afgifte van een kwijting, mits hij op verlangen van de wederpartij aantoont dat het papier vernietigd of waardeloos geworden is, of zekerheid stelt voor twintig jaren of een zoveel kortere tijdsduur als verwacht mag worden dat de wederpartij nog aan een vordering uit hoofde van het papier bloot zal kunnen staan.
- 4. De schuldenaar kan de nakoming van zijn verbintenis opschorten, indien de schuldeiser niet aan de vorige leden voldoet.

1. Upon the payment of a debt payable to bearer or to order, the debtor can require that a discharge be indicated on the document and that it be given to him.
2. If payment does not cover the entire debt or if the creditor still needs the document for the exercise of other rights, he can keep it, provided that, besides the discharge indicated on the document, he also issue a separate quittance.
3. Irrespective of whether payment is in part or in full, it is sufficient for the creditor merely to issue a quittance provided that, upon the demand of the other party, he show that the document has been destroyed or has become worthless, or that he furnish security for a period of twenty years or for such shorter period as the other party may be subject to a claim under the document.
4. If the creditor does not comply with the preceding paragraphs, the debtor can suspend the performance of his obligation.

1. Le débiteur qui paie une dette au porteur ou à ordre[1] peut demander qu'une décharge soit inscrite sur le titre et que celui-ci lui soit remis.
2. Si le paiement ne couvre pas l'ensemble de la créance ou que le créancier a encore besoin du titre pour l'exercice d'autres droits, il peut conserver celui-ci, pourvu que, en plus de la décharge inscrite sur le titre, il remette une quittance distincte.
3. Que le paiement soit intégral ou partiel, le créancier peut se contenter de la seule remise d'une quittance pourvu qu'il démontre, à la demande de l'autre partie, que le titre a été détruit ou est devenu caduc ou qu'il fournisse sûreté pour vingt ans ou pour une période moindre, pendant laquelle on peut s'attendre que l'autre partie pourra être exposée à une action fondée sur le titre.
4. Le débiteur peut suspendre l'exécution de l'obligation si le créancier ne respecte pas les dispositions énoncées aux paragraphes précédents.

Art. 50. (6.1.6.18) - 1. Moeten op achtereenvolgende tijdstippen gelijksoortige prestaties worden verricht, dan leveren de kwitanties van twee achtereenvolgende termijnen het vermoeden op dat ook de vroegere termijnen zijn voldaan.
- 2. Indien de schuldeiser een kwitantie afgeeft voor de hoofdsom, wordt vermoed dat ook de rente en de kosten zijn voldaan.

1. Where prestations of the same kind must be performed successively, the quittances for two successive prestations create the presumption that the previous ones have also been performed.
2. If the creditor issues a quittance for the principal sum, it is presumed that the interest and costs have also been paid.

1. Lorsque des prestations de même nature doivent être accomplies à des moments successifs, les quittances portant sur deux prestations successives font présumer que celles qui les précèdent ont également été accomplies.
2. La quittance remise par le créancier pour le principal fait présumer que les intérêts et les frais ont également été acquittés.

[1] Le terme «dette au porteur ou à ordre» est à rapprocher du terme «droit au porteur ou à ordre», qui apparaît à l'article 86 du Livre troisième.

Art. 51. (6.1.6.21) - 1. Wanneer uit de wet voortvloeit dat iemand verplicht is tot het stellen van zekerheid of dat het stellen van zekerheid voorwaarde is voor het intreden van enig rechtsgevolg, heeft hij die daartoe overgaat, de keuze tussen persoonlijke en zakelijke zekerheid.
- 2. De aangeboden zekerheid moet zodanig zijn, dat de vordering en, zo daartoe gronden zijn, de daarop vallende rente en kosten behoorlijk gedekt zijn en dat de schuldeiser daarop zonder moeite verhaal zal kunnen nemen.
- 3. Is de gestelde zekerheid door een niet aan de schuldeiser toe te rekenen oorzaak onvoldoende geworden, dan is de schuldenaar verplicht haar aan te vullen of te vervangen.

1. Where, as a result of the law, a person must furnish security, or where putting up security is a condition for a juridical effect to arise, the person furnishing security has the choice between personal and real security.
2. The security offered must be such that the debt and, if applicable, the interest on the debt and the costs are sufficiently covered and that the creditor will be able to realize it without difficulty.
3. Where the security furnished has become insufficient due to a cause which cannot be imputed to the creditor, the debtor must supplement or replace it.

1. Lorsqu'il résulte de la loi qu'une personne est obligée de donner des sûretés ou qu'un effet juridique se produise à la condition que sûreté soit donnée, celui qui la donne peut choisir entre la sûreté personnelle et la sûreté réelle.
2. La sûreté offerte doit couvrir adéquatement la créance et, s'il y a lieu, les intérêts et frais afférents et permettre au créancier de recouvrer sa créance sans difficulté.
3. Lorsque la sûreté donnée est devenue insuffisante pour des raisons non imputables au créancier, le débiteur est obligé d'y suppléer ou de la remplacer.

AFDELING 7 Opschortingsrechten

Section 7
Rights to suspend performance

Section septième
Des droits de suspension

Art. 52. (6.1.6A.1) - 1. Een schuldenaar die een opeisbare vordering heeft op zijn schuldeiser, is bevoegd de nakoming van zijn verbintenis op te schorten tot voldoening van zijn vordering plaatsvindt, indien tussen vordering en verbintenis voldoende samenhang bestaat om deze opschorting te rechtvaardigen.
- 2. Een zodanige samenhang kan onder meer worden aangenomen ingeval de verbintenissen over en weer voortvloeien uit dezelfde rechtsverhouding of uit zaken die partijen regelmatig met elkaar hebben gedaan.

1. A debtor who has an exigible claim against his creditor is entitled to suspend the performance of his obligation until his claim is paid, if there is a sufficent relationship between the claim and the obligation to justify this suspension.
2. Such a relationship may exist, amongst other things, in the event that the reciprocal obligations result from the same juridical relationship or from regular previous dealings between the parties.

1. Le débiteur qui a une créance exigible sur son créancier peut suspendre l'exécution de son obligation jusqu'au paiement de la créance, s'il existe entre la créance et l'obligation un lien suffisant pour justifier la suspension.
2. Un tel lien peut se présenter, entre autres, lorsque les obligations réciproques résultent d'un seul rapport juridique ou de relations d'affaires que les parties ont eues entre elles régulièrement.

Art. 53. (6.1.6A.2) Een opschortingsrecht kan ook worden ingeroepen tegen de schuldeisers van de wederpartij.

A right to suspend performance can also be invoked against the creditors of the other party.

Le droit de suspension peut être invoqué à l'encontre des créanciers de l'autre partie.

Art. 54. (6.1.6A.3) Geen bevoegdheid tot opschorting bestaat:
a. voor zover de nakoming van de verbintenis van de wederpartij wordt verhinderd door schuldeisersverzuim;
b. voor zover de nakoming van de verbintenis van de wederpartij blijvend onmogelijk is;
c. voor zover op de vordering van de wederpartij geen beslag is toegelaten.

No right of suspension exists:
a. to the extent that the performance of the obligation of the other party is prevented by the creditor's default;
b. to the extent that the performance of the obligation of the other party is permanently impossible;
c. to the extent that the claim of the other party is exempt from seizure.

La faculté de suspension n'existe pas:
a. Dans la mesure où l'exécution de l'obligation de l'autre partie est rendue impossible par la demeure du créancier;
b. Dans la mesure où l'exécution de l'obligation de l'autre partie est impossible de façon permanente;
c. Dans la mesure où la créance de l'autre partie est insaisissable.

Art. 55. (6.1.6A.4) Zodra zekerheid is gesteld voor de voldoening van de verbintenis van de wederpartij, vervalt de bevoegdheid tot opschorting, tenzij deze voldoening daardoor onredelijk zou worden vertraagd.

The right to suspend performance ceases as soon as security has been furnished for the performance of the obligation of the other party, unless this performance would thereby be unreasonably delayed.

La constitution de sûretés pour l'exécution de l'obligation qui incombe à l'autre partie éteint le droit de suspension sauf s'il en résultait un retard déraisonnable dans cette exécution.

Art. 56. (6.1.6A.5) Een bevoegdheid tot opschorting blijft ook na verjaring van de vordering op de wederpartij in stand.

A right to suspend performance continues to exist even after the prescription of the claim against the other party.

Le droit de suspension continue d'exister même après la prescription de la créance contre l'autre partie.

Art. 57. (6.1.6A.6) Indien een bevoegdheid tot opschorting voldoet aan de omschrijving van het retentierecht in artikel 290 van Boek 3, zijn de bepalingen van de onderhavige afdeling van toepassing, voor zover daarvan in afdeling 4 van titel 10 van Boek 3 niet is afgeweken.

If a right to suspend performance corresponds to the description of the right of retention of article 290 of Book 3, the provisions of this section apply to the extent that section 4 of title 10 of Book 3 does not derogate from them.

Si le droit de suspension correspond à la description du droit de rétention visé à l'article 290 du Livre troisième, on applique les dispositions de la présente section, dans la mesure où il n'y est pas dérogé à la section quatrième du titre dixième du Livre troisième.

AFDELING 8 Schuldeisersverzuim

Section 8
Creditor's default

Section huitième
La demeure[1] *du créancier*

Art. 58. (6.1.7.1) De schuldeiser komt in verzuim, wanneer nakoming van de verbintenis verhinderd wordt doordat hij de daartoe noodzakelijke medewerking niet verleent of doordat een ander beletsel van zijn zijde opkomt, tenzij de oorzaak van verhindering hem niet kan worden toegerekend.

Unless the cause of non-performance cannot be imputed to him, the creditor comes into default where the performance of the obligation is prevented because he does not provide the necessary cooperation therefore or because another impediment arises on his part.

À moins que la cause d'empêchement ne lui soit pas imputable, le créancier se constitue en demeure lorsque l'obligation ne peut être exécutée en raison de son défaut de prêter le concours requis à cette fin ou de la survenance d'un autre obstacle de son côté.

Art. 59. (6.1.7.2) De schuldeiser komt eveneens in verzuim, wanneer hij ten gevolge van hem toe te rekenen omstandigheden niet voldoet aan een verplichting zijnerzijds jegens de schuldenaar en deze op die grond bevoegdelijk de nakoming van zijn verbintenis jegens de schuldeiser opschort.

The creditor also comes into default where, for reasons imputable to him, he does not comply with a duty which he owes to the debtor, who, for that reason, rightfully suspends the performance of his obligation towards the creditor.

Le créancier se constitue également en demeure lorsque, en raison de circonstances qui lui sont imputables, il ne remplit pas son engagement envers le débiteur et que celui-ci, pour ce motif, suspend valablement l'exécution de son obligation envers lui.

Art. 60. (6.1.7.3) Is de schuldeiser in verzuim, dan kan de rechter op vordering van de schuldenaar bepalen dat deze van zijn verbintenis bevrijd zal zijn, al dan niet onder door de rechter te stellen voorwaarden.

Where the creditor is in default, the judge may discharge the debtor, upon his demand, from his obligation, with or without conditions to be determined by the judge.

Lorsque le créancier est en demeure, le juge, à la demande du débiteur, peut déterminer que celui-ci est libéré, s'il y a lieu aux conditions qu'il fixe.

Art. 61. (6.1.7.4) - 1. Verzuim van de schuldeiser maakt een einde aan verzuim van de schuldenaar.
- 2. Zolang de schuldeiser in verzuim is, kan de schuldenaar niet in verzuim geraken.

1. The creditor's default terminates the debtor's default.
2. The debtor cannot come into default as long as the creditor is in default.

1. La demeure du créancier met fin à celle du débiteur.
2. Tant que le créancier est en demeure, le débiteur ne peut l'être.

[1] Le Code civil néerlandais introduit ici un concept nouveau, rendu par le terme «demeure» (*mora*) habituellement réservé au comportement du débiteur.

Art. 62. (6.1.7.5) Gedurende het verzuim van de schuldeiser is deze niet bevoegd maatregelen tot executie te nemen.

The creditor is not entitled to take measures for the purpose of execution while he is himself in default.

Le créancier ne peut, pendant sa demeure, prendre des mesures d'exécution forcée.

Art. 63. (6.1.7.6) De schuldenaar heeft, binnen de grenzen der redelijkheid, recht op vergoeding van de kosten, gevallen op een aanbod of een inbewaringstelling als bedoeld in de artikelen 66-70 of op andere wijze als gevolg van het verzuim gemaakt.

Within the bounds of reasonableness, a debtor is entitled to compensation for costs incurred in tendering or in making a deposit pursuant to articles 66 - 70, or for costs otherwise attributable to the default.

Le débiteur a droit, dans les limites du raisonnable, au remboursement des frais résultant des offres ou de la consignation visée aux articles 66 à 70, ou autrement engagés à la suite de la demeure.

Art. 64. (6.1.7.7) Komt tijdens het verzuim van de schuldeiser een omstandigheid op, die behoorlijke nakoming geheel of gedeeltelijk onmogelijk maakt, dan wordt dit niet aan de schuldenaar toegerekend, tenzij deze door zijn schuld of die van een ondergeschikte is tekortgeschoten in de zorg die in de gegeven omstandigheden van hem mocht worden gevergd.

An event occurring during the default of the creditor making proper performance wholly or partially impossible, is not imputed to the debtor, unless by his fault or that of his servant he has failed to exercise the care which could have been expected from him in the circumstances.

L'événement qui survient pendant la demeure du créancier et qui rend en tout ou partie impossible l'exécution convenable de l'obligation n'est pas imputé au débiteur à moins que celui-ci, par sa faute ou celle de son préposé, n'ait manqué aux soins qu'on pouvait exiger de lui en la circonstance.

Art. 65. (6.1.7.8) Wanneer bij een verbintenis tot aflevering van soortzaken de schuldenaar bepaalde, aan de verbintenis beantwoordende zaken voor de aflevering heeft aangewezen en de schuldeiser daarvan heeft verwittigd, dan is hij in geval van verzuim van de schuldeiser nog slechts tot aflevering van deze zaken verplicht. Hij blijft echter bevoegd tot aflevering van andere zaken die aan de verbintenis beantwoorden.

Where, in an obligation to deliver things determined as to kind, the debtor has designated for delivery certain things corresponding to the obligation and has informed the creditor thereof, he is only obligated to deliver these things if the creditor is in default. He remains entitled, however, to deliver other things corresponding to the obligation.

Le débiteur d'une obligation de livrer des choses de genre, qui a désigné aux fins de livraison certaines choses conformes à l'obligation et qui en a informé le créancier, n'est tenu, au cas de demeure de celui-ci, qu'à la livraison de ces choses. Il peut cependant livrer d'autres choses conformes à l'obligation.

Art. 66. (6.1.7.9) Strekt de verbintenis tot betaling van een geldsom of tot aflevering van een zaak, dan is in geval van verzuim van de schuldeiser de schuldenaar bevoegd het verschuldigde ten behoeve van de schuldeiser in bewaring te stellen.

Where the obligation is to pay a sum of money or to deliver a thing and the creditor is in default, the debtor is entitled to deposit for the benefit of the creditor what is owed.

Le débiteur d'une obligation portant sur le paiement d'une somme d'argent ou sur la livraison d'une chose peut, au cas de demeure du créancier, consigner ce qui est dû au profit de celui-ci.

Art. 67. (6.1.7.10) De inbewaringstelling van een geldsom geschiedt door consignatie overeenkomstig de wet, die van een af te leveren zaak door deze in bewaring te geven aan iemand die zijn bedrijf maakt van het bewaren van zaken als de betrokkene ter plaatse waar de aflevering moet geschieden. Op deze bewaring zijn de regels betreffende gerechtelijke bewaring van toepassing, voor zover uit de artikelen 68-71 niet anders voortvloeit.

Deposit of a sum of money is made by tender and deposit according to the law; deposit of a thing to be delivered is made by depositing it with a person whose business it is to take custody of such things at the place where delivery must take place. The rules concerning judicial deposit apply to this custody to the extent that articles 68 - 71 do not produce a different result.

La consignation d'une somme d'argent s'effectue suivant les règles prévues par la loi; celle d'une chose à livrer s'effectue en la déposant auprès d'une personne qui fait le commerce de dépôt de choses comme la présente, à l'endroit où la livraison doit avoir lieu. À ce dépôt s'appliquent les règles relatives au dépôt judiciaire, dans la mesure où il ne découle pas autrement des articles 68 à 71.

Art. 68. (6.1.7.11) Gedurende de bewaring loopt over een in bewaring gestelde geldsom geen rente ten laste van de schuldenaar.

During the deposit, the debtor does not incur interest charges on a deposited sum of money.

Pendant le dépôt, les intérêts sur la somme consignée ne courent pas contre le débiteur.

Art. 69. (6.1.7.12) - 1. Gedurende de bewaring kan de schuldeiser zijn verzuim slechts zuiveren door het in bewaring gestelde te aanvaarden.
- 2. Zolang de schuldeiser het in bewaring gestelde niet heeft aanvaard, is de bewaargever bevoegd het uit de bewaring terug te nemen.

1. During the deposit, the creditor can only remedy his default by accepting what has been deposited.
2. As long as the creditor has not accepted what has been deposited, the depositor is entitled to remove it from custody.

1. Pendant le dépôt, le créancier ne peut purger sa demeure qu'en acceptant ce qui a été consigné.
2. Tant que le créancier n'a pas accepté ce qui a été consigné, le déposant peut le retirer de la consignation.

Art. 70. (6.1.7.13) De bewaarder mag de zaak slechts aan de schuldeiser afgeven, indien deze hem alle kosten van de bewaring voldoet. Hij is na de afgifte verplicht aan de bewaargever terug te betalen, wat deze reeds had voldaan. Is de zaak afgegeven, vóórdat de schuldeiser alle kosten voldeed, dan gaan de rechten te dier zake door de betaling aan de bewaargever op de bewaarder over.

The depositary may only remit the thing to the creditor if the latter pays him all the costs of the custody. After remitting, he must reimburse to the depositor what the latter had already paid. Where the thing has been remitted before the creditor has paid all costs, the rights pertaining thereto are transferred to the depositary by the payment to the depositor.

Le dépositaire ne peut remettre la chose au créancier que si celui-ci acquitte tous les frais de la consignation. Après la remise, il est tenu de rembourser au déposant ce que celui-ci avait déjà acquitté. Lorsque la chose a été remise avant que le créancier n'ait acquitté tous les frais, les droits les concernant passent au dépositaire par le paiement au déposant.

Art. 71. (6.1.7.13a) De rechtsvordering tegen de schuldenaar verjaart niet later dan de rechtsvordering tot uitlevering van het in bewaring gestelde.

The right of action against the debtor is prescribed no later than the right of action to demand remittance of what has been deposited.

L'action contre le débiteur se prescrit au plus tard au moment où est prescrite l'action en livraison de ce qui a été consigné.

Art. 72. (6.1.7.14) In geval van hoofdelijke verbondenheid gelden de rechtsgevolgen van het verzuim van de schuldeiser jegens ieder van de schuldenaren.

In the event of solidarity, the legal effects of the default of the creditor apply to each of the debtors.

La demeure du créancier produit ses effets à l'égard de chacun des débiteurs d'une obligation solidaire.

Art. 73. (6.1.7.16) Weigert de schuldeiser een aanbod van een derde, dan zijn de artikelen 60, 62, 63 en 66-70 ten behoeve van de derde van overeenkomstige toepassing, mits het aanbod aan de verbintenis beantwoordt en de derde bij de voldoening een gerechtvaardigd belang heeft.

Where the creditor rejects tender by a third party, articles 60, 62, 63 and 66 - 70 apply *mutatis mutandis* to the benefit of the third party, provided that this tender corresponds to the obligation and that the third party has a legitimate interest in its performance.

Lorsque le créancier refuse l'offre de paiement faite par un tiers, on applique par analogie au profit du tiers les articles 60, 62, 63 et 66 à 70, pourvu que cette offre soit conforme à l'obligation et que le tiers ait un intérêt légitime à l'exécution.

AFDELING 9 De gevolgen van het niet nakomen van een verbintenis

Section 9 The effects of the non-performance of an obligation

Section neuvième Des effets de l'inexécution de l'obligation

§1. Algemene bepalingen

§1. General provisions

§1. Dispositions générales

Art. 74. (6.1.8.1) - 1. Iedere tekortkoming in de nakoming van een verbintenis verplicht de schuldenaar de schade die de schuldeiser daardoor lijdt te vergoeden, tenzij de tekortkoming de schuldenaar niet kan worden toegerekend.

- 2. Voor zover nakoming niet reeds blijvend onmogelijk is, vindt lid 1 slechts toepassing met inachtneming van hetgeen is bepaald in de tweede paragraaf betreffende het verzuim van de schuldenaar.

1. Every failure in the performance of an obligation obliges the debtor to repair the damage which the creditor suffers therefrom, unless the failure cannot be imputed to the debtor.
2. To the extent that performance is not already permanently impossible, paragraph 1 only applies subject to the provisions of 2 respecting the default of the debtor.

1. Tout manquement dans l'exécution oblige le débiteur à réparer le dommage qu'en subit le créancier, à moins que le défaut ne soit pas imputable au débiteur.

2. Dans la mesure où l'exécution n'est pas déjà impossible de façon permanente, le paragraphe 1er ne s'applique que compte tenu des dispositions du §2 relatives à la demeure du débiteur.

Art. 75. (6.1.8.2) Een tekortkoming kan de schuldenaar niet worden toegerekend, indien zij niet is te wijten aan zijn schuld, noch krachtens wet, rechtshandeling of in het verkeer geldende opvattingen voor zijn rekening komt.

A failure in the performance cannot be imputed to the debtor if it does not result from his fault, and if he cannot be held accountable for it by law, juridical act or common opinion either.

Le manquement n'est pas imputable au débiteur, s'il ne résulte pas de sa faute ni ne lui incombe en vertu de la loi ou d'un acte juridique, ou suivant l'opinion généralement admise.

Art. 76. (6.1.8.3) Maakt de schuldenaar bij de uitvoering van een verbintenis gebruik van de hulp van andere personen, dan is hij voor hun gedragingen op gelijke wijze als voor eigen gedragingen aansprakelijk.

Where, in the performance of an obligation, the debtor uses the services of other persons, he is responsible for their acts as if they were his own.

Le débiteur qui, dans l'exécution de l'obligation, emploie les services de tierces personnes répond de leurs actes de la même façon que des siens propres.

Art. 77. (6.1.8.3a) Wordt bij de uitvoering van een verbintenis gebruik gemaakt van een zaak die daartoe ongeschikt is, dan wordt de tekortkoming die daardoor ontstaat de schuldenaar toegerekend, tenzij dit, gelet op inhoud en strekking van de rechtshandeling waaruit de verbintenis voortspruit, de in het verkeer geldende opvattingen en de overige omstandigheden van het geval, onredelijk zou zijn.

Where, in the performance of an obligation, a thing is used which is unfit for the purpose, the resulting failure is imputed to the debtor, unless this would be unreasonable in view of the content and necessary implication of the juridical act from which the obligation arises, common opinion and other circumstances of the case.

Le manquement dans l'exécution de l'obligation qui résulte de l'emploi d'une chose impropre à cet usage est imputable au débiteur, à moins que ce soit déraisonnable, eu égard au contenu et à la portée de l'acte juridique dont résulte l'obligation, de l'opinion généralement admise et des autres circonstances de l'espèce.

Art. 78. (6.1.8.4) - 1. Indien een tekortkoming de schuldenaar niet kan worden toegerekend, maar hij in verband met die tekortkoming een voordeel geniet dat hij bij behoorlijke nakoming niet zou hebben gehad,

heeft de schuldeiser met toepassing van de regels betreffende ongerechtvaardigde verrijking recht op vergoeding van zijn schade tot ten hoogste het bedrag van dit voordeel.
- 2. Bestaat dit voordeel uit een vordering op een derde, dan kan de schuldenaar aan het vorige lid voldoen door overdracht van die vordering.

1. If a failure in the performance cannot be imputed to the debtor, but if the latter derives a benefit in connection with that failure which he would not have had in the case of proper performance, the creditor is entitled to compensation for his damage by application of the rules relating to unjustified enrichment up to the maximum of the amount of this benefit.
2. Where the benefit takes the form of a claim against a third person, the debtor may comply with the preceding paragraph by transferring the claim.

1. Si le manquement n'est pas imputable au débiteur, mais que celui-ci réalise, en rapport avec le défaut, un avantage qu'une exécution convenable ne lui aurait pas assuré, le créancier a droit, par application des règles relatives à l'enrichissement injustifié, à la réparation du dommage qu'il en subit, jusqu'à concurrence maximale de cet avantage.

2. Lorsque l'avantage consiste en une créance contre un tiers, le débiteur peut se conformer au paragraphe précédent en transférant cette créance.

Art. 79. (6.1.8.4a) Is de schuldeiser wiens schuldenaar door een hem niet toe te rekenen oorzaak verhinderd is na te komen, desondanks in staat zelf zich door executie of verrekening het verschuldigde te verschaffen, dan is hij daartoe bevoegd.

Where the debtor is prevented from performing by a cause which cannot be imputed to him but the creditor is nevertheless in the position to procure for himself, by execution or by compensation, that what is owed to him, the creditor may do so.

Lorsqu'une cause qui ne lui est pas imputable vient empêcher le débiteur d'exécuter l'obligation et que le créancier est néanmoins en mesure, par l'exécution forcée ou par compensation, de se procurer lui-même ce qui est dû, il peut y procéder.

Art. 80. (6.1.8.5) - 1. De gevolgen van niet-nakoming treden reeds in voordat de vordering opeisbaar is:
a. indien vaststaat dat nakoming zonder tekortkoming onmogelijk zal zijn;
b. indien de schuldeiser uit een mededeling van de schuldenaar moet afleiden dat deze in de nakoming zal tekortschieten; of
c. indien de schuldeiser goede gronden heeft te vrezen dat de schuldenaar in de nakoming zal tekortschieten en deze niet voldoet aan een schriftelijke aanmaning met opgave van die gronden om zich binnen een bij die aanmaning gestelde redelijke termijn bereid te verklaren zijn verplichtingen na te komen.
- 2. Het oorspronkelijke tijdstip van opeisbaarheid blijft gelden voor de verschuldigdheid van schadevergoeding wegens vertraging en de toerekening aan de schuldenaar van onmogelijk worden van nakoming tijdens zijn verzuim.

1. The consequences of non-performance take effect even before the claim is exigible:
a. if it is certain that performance without failure will be impossible;

1. L'inexécution produit effet avant même que la créance soit exigible:

a. S'il est établi que l'exécution sans manquement sera impossible;

b. if the creditor must conclude from a communication by the debtor that the latter will fail in the performance; or

c. if the creditor has good reasons to fear that the debtor will fail in the performance and the debtor does not comply with a written warning indicating those reasons and requesting the debtor to confirm that he is willing to perform his obligations within a reasonable period specified in that warning.

2. The original moment of exigibility remains valid for the obligation to pay damages for delay and for the purpose of imputation to the debtor of the obligation becoming impossible to perform during his default.

b. Si une communication du débiteur doit porter le créancier à conclure que le débiteur manquera à l'exécution de l'obligation;

c. Si le créancier a de bonnes raisons de craindre que le débiteur manquera à l'exécution de l'obligation et si ce dernier n'obtempère pas à une sommation écrite énonçant ces raisons, qui l'enjoint de se déclarer prêt à exécuter ses obligations dans un délai raisonnable fixé dans la sommation.

2. S'apprécient toujours au moment où la créance devait initialement devenir exigible l'obligation de réparer le dommage résultant du retard et l'imputabilité au débiteur de l'impossibilité d'exécution survenue durant la demeure.

§2. Verzuim van de schuldenaar

§2. Debtor's default

§2. De la demeure du débiteur

Art. 81. (6.1.8.6) De schuldenaar is in verzuim gedurende de tijd dat de prestatie uitblijft nadat zij opeisbaar is geworden en aan de eisen van de artikelen 82 en 83 is voldaan, behalve voor zover de vertraging hem niet kan worden toegerekend of nakoming reeds blijvend onmogelijk is.

Except to the extent that the delay cannot be imputed to him or performance is already permanently impossible, the debtor is in default during the period that the prestation is not rendered, once it has become exigible and the requirements of articles 82 and 83 have been met.

Le débiteur est en demeure durant le temps où la prestation, après être devenue exigible, se fait attendre et que les conditions visées aux articles 82 et 83 sont remplies, sauf dans la mesure où le retard ne peut lui être imputé ou que l'exécution est déjà devenue impossible de façon permanente.

Art. 82. (6.1.8.7) - 1. Het verzuim treedt in, wanneer de schuldenaar in gebreke wordt gesteld bij een schriftelijke aanmaning waarbij hem een redelijke termijn voor de nakoming wordt gesteld, en nakoming binnen deze termijn uitblijft.

- 2. Indien de schuldenaar tijdelijk niet kan nakomen of uit zijn houding blijkt dat aanmaning nutteloos zou zijn, kan de ingebrekestelling plaatsvinden door een schriftelijke mededeling waaruit blijkt dat hij voor het uitblijven van de nakoming aansprakelijk wordt gesteld.

1. Default commences when the debtor is put into default by a written warning granting him a reasonable period for the performance and when there is no performance within this period.

2. If the debtor is in a temporary impossibility to perform or if it is evident from his attitude that a warning would serve no purpose, he may be put into

1. La demeure a lieu lorsque le débiteur est mis en demeure par une sommation écrite fixant un délai d'exécution adéquat et que l'obligation n'est pas exécutée dans ce délai.

2. Si le débiteur est temporairement dans l'impossibilité d'exécuter l'obligation ou que son attitude indique qu'une sommation serait inutile, la mise en demeure peut être faite par

default by a written declaration to the effect that he is held liable for his non-performance.

communication écrite faisant apparaître qu'il est tenu responsable du défaut d'exécution.

Art. 83. (6.1.8.8) Het verzuim treedt zonder ingebrekestelling in:
a. wanneer een voor de voldoening bepaalde termijn verstrijkt zonder dat de verbintenis is nagekomen, tenzij blijkt dat de termijn een andere strekking heeft;
b. wanneer de verbintenis voortvloeit uit onrechtmatige daad of strekt tot schadevergoeding als bedoeld in artikel 74 lid 1 en de verbintenis niet terstond wordt nagekomen;
c. wanneer de schuldeiser uit een mededeling van de schuldenaar moet afleiden dat deze in de nakoming van de verbintenis zal tekortschieten.

Default commences without the formality of putting into default:
a. where a term which has been set for payment lapses without the obligation having been performed, unless it appears that the term has another purpose;
b. where the obligation results from an unlawful act or relates to reparation of damage as referred to in article 74 paragraph 1 and the obligation is not immediately performed;
c. where the creditor must conclude from a communication by the debtor that the latter will fail in the performance of the obligation.

La demeure a lieu sans mise en demeure:
a. Lorsque le délai fixé pour le paiement s'écoule sans que l'obligation n'ait été exécutée, à moins qu'il n'apparaisse que le délai a une autre portée;
b. Lorsque l'obligation résulte d'un acte illicite ou a pour objet la réparation de dommage visée à l'article 74, paragraphe 1, et qu'elle n'est pas exécutée immédiatement;
c. Lorsque une communication du débiteur doit porter le créancier à conclure que le débiteur manquera à l'exécution de l'obligation.

Art. 84. (6.1.8.10) Elke onmogelijkheid van nakoming, ontstaan tijdens het verzuim van de schuldenaar en niet toe te rekenen aan de schuldeiser, wordt aan de schuldenaar toegerekend; deze moet de daardoor ontstane schade vergoeden, tenzij de schuldeiser de schade ook bij behoorlijke en tijdige nakoming zou hebben geleden.

Every impossibility to perform which has arisen during the default of the debtor and which cannot be imputed to the creditor, is imputed to the debtor; the latter must repair the damage resulting therefrom, unless the creditor would have suffered the damage even in the case of proper and prompt performance.

Toute impossibilité d'exécution survenue durant la demeure du débiteur et non imputable au créancier est imputée au débiteur; celui-ci est tenu de réparer le dommage qui en résulte, à moins que le créancier ne l'eût subi, même au cas d'exécution normale et non tardive de l'obligation.

Art. 85. (6.1.8.10a) Tot vergoeding van schade wegens vertraging in de nakoming is de schuldenaar slechts verplicht over de tijd waarin hij in verzuim is geweest.

The debtor must repair the damage for delay in performance only for the time that he has been in default.

Le débiteur n'est tenu de réparer le dommage résultant du retard dans l'exécution de son obligation que pour la durée de sa demeure.

Art. 86. (6.1.8.10b) De schuldeiser kan een na het intreden van het verzuim aangeboden nakoming weigeren, zolang niet tevens betaling wordt aangeboden van de inmiddels tevens verschuldigd geworden schadevergoeding en van de kosten.

The creditor may refuse performance offered after the beginning of the default, so long as the offer does not also comprise the payment of damages which have, in the meantime, become due, as well as of costs.

Le créancier peut refuser une exécution offerte après l'avènement de la demeure, tant que l'offre ne comporte pas également le paiement des dommages-intérêts qui en découlent et des frais.

Art. 87. (6.1.8.11) - 1. Voor zover nakoming niet reeds blijvend onmogelijk is, wordt de verbintenis omgezet in een tot vervangende schadevergoeding, wanneer de schuldenaar in verzuim is en de schuldeiser hem schriftelijk mededeelt dat hij schadevergoeding in plaats van nakoming vordert.
- 2. Geen omzetting vindt plaats, die door de tekortkoming, gezien haar ondergeschikte betekenis, niet wordt gerechtvaardigd.

1. To the extent that performance is not already permanently impossible, the obligation is converted into one to pay damages by equivalence where the debtor is in default and the creditor notifies him in writing that he claims damages instead of performance.
2. Conversion does not take place where the minor importance of the failure in the performance of the obligation does not justify it.

1. Dans la mesure où l'exécution n'est pas déjà impossible de façon permanente, l'obligation inexécutée se transforme en celle de fournir une réparation par équivalent, lorsque le créancier avise par écrit le débiteur en demeure qu'il demande la réparation du dommage au lieu de l'exécution.
2. La transformation n'a pas lieu lorsqu'elle est injustifiée en regard de l'importance mineure du manquement dans l'exécution.

§3. Verdere gevolgen van niet-nakoming

§3. Other effects of non-performance

§3. Des autres effets de l'inexécution

Art. 88. (6.1.8.13) - 1. De schuldenaar die in de nakoming van zijn verbintenis is tekort geschoten, kan aan de schuldeiser een redelijke termijn stellen, waarbinnen deze moet mededelen welke van de hem bij de aanvang van de termijn ten dienste staande middelen hij wenst uit te oefenen, op straffe van slechts aanspraak te kunnen maken:
a. op de schadevergoeding waarop de tekortkoming recht geeft en, zo de verbintenis strekt tot betaling van een geldsom, op die geldsom;
b. op ontbinding van de overeenkomst waaruit de verbintenis voortspruit, indien de schuldenaar zich erop beroept dat de tekortkoming hem niet kan worden toegerekend.
- 2. Heeft de schuldeiser nakoming verlangd, doch wordt daaraan niet binnen een redelijke termijn voldaan, dan kan hij al zijn rechten wederom doen gelden; het vorige lid is van overeenkomstige toepassing.

1. The debtor who has failed in the performance of his obligation may grant a reasonable period to the creditor within which the latter must notify him of the remedies he wishes to exercise and which are at his disposal at the beginning of this period; in case of non-compliance by the creditor, he may only claim:

a. the reparation of damage to which the failure entitles him and, if the obligation is one for the payment of a sum of money, that sum;
b. the setting aside of the contract from which the obligation arises, if the debtor invokes the fact that the non-performance cannot be imputed to him.

2. Where the creditor has demanded performance, and the demand is not complied with within a reasonable period, all his rights are newly revived; the preceding paragraph applies *mutatis mutandis*.

1. Le débiteur qui a manqué à l'exécution de son obligation peut fixer au créancier un délai raisonnable pour faire savoir lequel des moyens à sa disposition au début de ce délai il entend exercer; à défaut de se déclarer dans le délai imparti, le créancier peut prétendre seulement

a. À la réparation du dommage à laquelle donne droit le manquement et, si l'obligation porte sur le paiement d'une somme d'argent, à cette somme;
b. À la résiliation du contrat dont résulte l'obligation, si le débiteur fait valoir que le manquement ne lui est pas imputable.

2. Lorsque le créancier a demandé l'exécution, mais que celle-ci n'a pas lieu dans un délai raisonnable, il peut à nouveau faire valoir tous ses droits; le paragraphe précédent s'applique par analogie.

Art. 89. (6.1.8.14) De schuldeiser kan op een gebrek in de prestatie geen beroep meer doen, indien hij niet binnen bekwame tijd nadat hij het gebrek heeft ontdekt of redelijkerwijze had moeten ontdekken, bij de schuldenaar terzake heeft geprotesteerd.

The creditor may no longer invoke a defect in the prestation if he has not complained to the debtor promptly after he has discovered or should reasonably have discovered the defect.

Le défaut dans la prestation ne peut plus être invoqué par le créancier qui n'a pas promptement protesté à cet effet auprès du débiteur après qu'il a découvert ou aurait normalement dû découvrir le défaut.

Art. 90. (6.1.8.14a) - 1. Bij een verhindering tot aflevering van een zaak die aan snel tenietgaan of achteruitgaan onderhevig is of waarvan om een andere reden de verdere bewaring zo bezwaarlijk is dat zij in de gegeven omstandigheden niet van de schuldenaar kan worden gevergd, is deze bevoegd de zaak op een geschikte wijze te doen verkopen. De schuldenaar is jegens de schuldeiser tot een zodanige verkoop gehouden, wanneer diens belangen deze verkoop onmiskenbaar eisen of de schuldeiser te kennen geeft de verkoop te verlangen.
- 2. De netto-opbrengst treedt voor de zaak in de plaats, onverminderd de rechten van de schuldeiser wegens tekortkomingen in de nakoming van de verbintenis.

1. In the event of an impediment to deliver a thing which may perish or deteriorate rapidly, or to deliver a thing the further custody of which, for some other reason, is so onerous that, in the given circumstances, it cannot be

1. En cas d'empêchement de livrer une chose sujette à perte ou détérioration rapides ou dont la conservation pour une autre raison est si onéreuse qu'elle ne peut être requise du débiteur en la circonstance, celui-ci peut faire vendre la chose d'une manière

required from the debtor, the latter is entitled to have the thing sold in a proper manner. The debtor is held towards the creditor to such a sale where the latter's interests unmistakingly require it, or where the creditor makes it known that he demands the sale.
2. The net proceeds take the place of the thing, without prejudice to the rights of the creditor for failure in the performance of the obligation.

convenable. Le débiteur est tenu à l'égard du créancier à une telle vente lorsque les intérêts de celui-ci l'exigent indéniablement ou que celui-ci a fait savoir qu'il demande la vente.

2. Le produit net de la vente se substitue à la chose, sans préjudice des droits du créancier en raison de manquements dans l'exécution de l'obligation.

§4. Boetebeding

§4. Penal clause

§4. De la clause pénale

Art. 91. (6.1.8.16) Als boetebeding wordt aangemerkt ieder beding waarbij is bepaald dat de schuldenaar, indien hij in de nakoming van zijn verbintenis tekortschiet, gehouden is een geldsom of een andere prestatie te voldoen, ongeacht of zulks strekt tot vergoeding van schade of enkel tot aansporing om tot nakoming over te gaan.

Any stipulation which provides that a debtor, should he fail in the performance of his obligation, must pay a sum of money or perform another prestation, is considered to be a penal clause, irrespective of whether this is to repair damage or only to induce performance.

Est réputée clause pénale toute stipulation portant que le débiteur qui manque à l'exécution de son obligation est tenu de payer une somme d'argent ou de fournir une autre prestation, que cela serve de réparation de dommage ou seulement d'incitation à exécuter l'obligation.

Art. 92. (6.1.8.17) - 1. De schuldeiser kan geen nakoming vorderen zowel van het boetebeding als van de verbintenis waaraan het boetebeding verbonden is.
- 2. Hetgeen ingevolge een boetebeding verschuldigd is treedt in de plaats van de schadevergoeding op grond van de wet.
- 3. De schuldeiser kan geen nakoming vorderen van het boetebeding, indien de tekortkoming niet aan de schuldenaar kan worden toegerekend.

1. The creditor may not demand performance of both the penal clause and the obligation to which the penal clause attaches.
2. That which is owed pursuant to a penal clause takes the place of reparation of damage due by law.
3. The creditor may not demand performance of the penal clause where the failure in the performance cannot be imputed to the debtor.

1. Le créancier ne peut demander à la fois l'exécution de la clause pénale et celle de l'obligation à laquelle elle se rapporte.
2. La peine découlant d'une clause pénale se substitue à la réparation légale du dommage.
3. Le créancier ne peut demander l'exécution d'une clause pénale, si le manquement dans l'exécution de l'obligation n'est pas imputable au débiteur.

Art. 93. (6.1.8.17a) Voor het vorderen van nakoming van het boetebeding is een aanmaning of een andere voorafgaande verklaring nodig in dezelfde gevallen als deze is vereist voor het vorderen van schadevergoeding op grond van de wet.

A warning or other previous declaration is required in order to demand performance of the penal clause in the same cases as this is required to claim reparation of damage due by law.

La demande d'exécution d'une clause pénale doit être précédée d'une sommation ou autre déclaration préalable dans les mêmes cas où celle-ci est requise pour la demande de réparation légale du dommage.

Art. 94. (6.1.8.18) - 1. Op verlangen van de schuldenaar kan de rechter, indien de billijkheid dit klaarblijkelijk eist, de bedongen boete matigen, met dien verstande dat hij de schuldeiser ter zake van de tekortkoming niet minder kan toekennen dan de schadevergoeding op grond van de wet.
- 2. Op verlangen van de schuldeiser kan de rechter, indien de billijkheid dit klaarblijkelijk eist, naast een bedongen boete die bestemd is in de plaats te treden van de schadevergoeding op grond van de wet, aanvullende schadevergoeding toekennen.
- 3. Van lid 1 afwijkende bedingen zijn nietig.

1. The judge may reduce the stipulated penalty upon the demand of the debtor if it is evident that equity so requires; the judge, however, may not award the creditor less than the reparation of damage due by law for failure in the performance of the obligation.
2. The judge may award supplementary compensation upon the demand of the creditor if it is evident that equity so requires; this compensation is in addition to the stipulated penalty intended to replace reparation due by law.
3. Stipulations derogating from paragraph 1 are null.

1. À la demande du débiteur, le juge peut, si l'équité l'exige manifestement, modérer la peine stipulée, étant entendu qu'il ne peut accorder au créancier, relativement à un manquement dans l'exécution, moins que la réparation légale du dommage.

2. Outre la peine stipulée qui est destinée à se substituer à la réparation légale du dommage, le juge peut, à la demande du créancier et si l'équité l'exige manifestement, accorder une réparation supplémentaire.
3. La stipulation dérogeant au paragraphe 1 est nulle.

AFDELING 10 Wettelijke verplichtingen tot schadevergoeding

Section 10
Legal obligations to repair damage

Section dixième
Des obligations légales de réparation de dommage

Art. 95. (6.1.9.1) De schade die op grond van een wettelijke verplichting tot schadevergoeding moet worden vergoed, bestaat in vermogensschade en ander nadeel, dit laatste voor zover de wet op vergoeding hiervan recht geeft.

The damage which must be repaired pursuant to a legal obligation to make reparation consists of patrimonial damage and other harm, the latter to the extent that the law grants a right to reparation thereof.

Le dommage sur lequel porte l'obligation légale de réparation englobe le dommage patrimonial et d'autres pertes, celles-ci dans la mesure où la loi donne droit à leur réparation.

Art. 96. (6.1.9.2) - 1. Vermogensschade omvat zowel geleden verlies als gederfde winst.
- 2. Als vermogensschade komen mede voor vergoeding in aanmerking:

a. redelijke kosten ter voorkoming of beperking van schade die als gevolg van de gebeurtenis waarop de aansprakelijkheid berust, mocht worden verwacht;
b. redelijke kosten ter vaststelling van schade en aansprakelijkheid;
c. redelijke kosten ter verkrijging van voldoening buiten rechte,
wat de kosten onder b en c betreft, behoudens voor zover in het gegeven geval krachtens artikel 57 lid 6 van het Wetboek van Burgerlijke Rechtsvordering de regels betreffende proceskosten van toepassing zijn.

1. Patrimonial damage comprises both the loss sustained by the creditor and the profit of which he has been deprived.
2. Furthermore, the following costs may be claimed as patrimonial damage:
a. reasonable costs to prevent or mitigate damage which could be expected as a result of the event giving rise to liability;
b. reasonable costs incurred in assessing damage and liability;
c. reasonable costs incurred in obtaining extrajudicial payment;

except, concerning the costs *sub* b and c, to the extent that, in the given case, the rules regarding judicial costs apply pursuant to article 57 paragraph 6 of the Code of Civil Procedure.

1. Le dommage patrimonial comprend la perte subie et le gain manqué.
2. Sont, en outre, sujets à réparation, au titre de dommage patrimonial:
a. Les frais raisonnables engagés en vue de prévenir ou de réduire le dommage prévisible à la suite de l'événement sur lequel se fonde la responsabilité;
b. Les frais raisonnables engagés en vue de déterminer le dommage et la responsabilité;
c. Les frais raisonnables engagés en vue d'obtenir paiement par voie extra-judiciaire,

sauf, pour ce qui est des frais évoqués aux points b. et c., dans la mesure où, en l'espèce, les règles relatives aux frais de procès s'appliquent en vertu de l'article 57, paragraphe 6 du Code de procédure civile.

Art. 97. (6.1.9.3) De rechter begroot de schade op de wijze die het meest met de aard ervan in overeenstemming is. Kan de omvang van de schade niet nauwkeurig worden vastgesteld, dan wordt zij geschat.

The judge evaluates the damage in the manner best corresponding to its nature. Where the extent of the damage cannot be determined precisely, it is estimated.

Le juge évalue le dommage de la manière qui correspond le mieux à la nature de celui-ci. Lorsque l'étendue du dommage ne peut être établie avec précision, elle est estimée.

Art. 98. (6.1.9.4) Voor vergoeding komt slechts in aanmerking schade die in zodanig verband staat met de gebeurtenis waarop de aansprakelijkheid van de schuldenaar berust, dat zij hem, mede gezien de aard van de aansprakelijkheid en van de schade, als een gevolg van deze gebeurtenis kan worden toegerekend.

Reparation can only be claimed for damage which is related to the event giving rise to the liability of the debtor in such a fashion that the damage, also taking into account its nature and that of the liability, can be imputed to the debtor as a result of this event.

La réparation ne s'étend qu'au dommage dont le rapport avec l'événement sur lequel se fonde la responsabilité du débiteur est tel que, compte également tenu de la nature de la responsabilité et du dommage, il peut être imputé au débiteur comme étant la conséquence de cet événement.

Art. 99. (6.1.9.4a) Kan de schade een gevolg zijn van twee of meer gebeurtenissen voor elk waarvan een andere persoon aansprakelijk is, en

staat vast dat de schade door ten minste één van deze gebeurtenissen is ontstaan, dan rust de verplichting om de schade te vergoeden op ieder van deze personen, tenzij hij bewijst dat deze niet het gevolg is van een gebeurtenis waarvoor hijzelf aansprakelijk is.

Where the damage may have resulted from two or more events for each of which a different person is liable, and where it has been determined that the damage has arisen from at least one of these events, the obligation to repair the damage rests upon each of these persons, unless he proves that the damage is not the result of the event for which he himself is liable.

Lorsque le dommage peut être la conséquence de plusieurs événements, chacun étant la responsabilité d'une personne différente, et qu'il est établi que le dommage résulte d'au moins un de ces événements, l'obligation de réparation incombe à chacune de ces personnes, à moins qu'elle ne justifie que le dommage n'est pas la conséquence d'un événement dont elle-même est responsable.

Art. 100. (6.1.9.5) Heeft een zelfde gebeurtenis voor de benadeelde naast schade tevens voordeel opgeleverd, dan moet, voor zover dit redelijk is, dit voordeel bij de vaststelling van de te vergoeden schade in rekening worden gebracht.

Where one and the same event has created both damage and benefit for the victim, the benefit must, to the extent that this is reasonable, be computed in determining the damage to be repaired.

Lorsqu'un seul événement crée à la fois un dommage et un avantage pour la personne lésée, cet avantage doit être comptabilisé dans la détermination du dommage à réparer, dans la mesure où cela est raisonnable.

Art. 101. (6.1.9.6) - 1. Wanneer de schade mede een gevolg is van een omstandigheid die aan de benadeelde kan worden toegerekend, wordt de vergoedingsplicht verminderd door de schade over de benadeelde en de vergoedingsplichtige te verdelen in evenredigheid met de mate waarin de aan ieder toe te rekenen omstandigheden tot de schade hebben bijgedragen, met dien verstande dat een andere verdeling plaatsvindt of de vergoedingsplicht geheel vervalt of in stand blijft, indien de billijkheid dit wegens de uiteenlopende ernst van de gemaakte fouten of andere omstandigheden van het geval eist.

- 2. Betreft de vergoedingsplicht schade, toegebracht aan een zaak die een derde voor de benadeelde in zijn macht had, dan worden bij toepassing van het vorige lid omstandigheden die aan de derde toegerekend kunnen worden, toegerekend aan de benadeelde.

1. Where circumstances which can be imputed to the victim have contributed to the damage, the obligation to repair is diminished by apportioning the damage between the victim and the person who has the obligation to repair, in proportion to the degree in which the circumstances which can be imputed to each of them, have contributed to the damage. The apportionment may vary or the obligation

1. Lorsqu'une circonstance imputable à la personne lésée contribue au dommage, l'obligation de réparation est réduite par la répartition du dommage entre la personne lésée et celui qui est tenu à réparation, selon le degré auquel les circonstances imputables à chacun d'eux y ont contribué; il peut y avoir répartition différente, suppression intégrale ou maintien intégral de l'obligation de réparation, si l'équité l'exige en raison de

to repair can either be completely extinguished or not apportioned at all, if equity so requires due to the different degree of gravity of the faults committed or any other circumstances of the case.

la différence de gravité des fautes commises ou d'autres circonstances de l'espèce.

2. Where the obligation to repair pertains to damage done to a thing which was under the control of a third person on behalf of the victim, circumstances which can be imputed to the third person are, for the purpose of the application of the preceding paragraph, imputed to the victim.

2. Lorsque l'obligation de réparation porte sur un dommage causé à une chose qu'un tiers a en sa puissance pour le compte la personne lésée, les circonstances imputables au tiers, pour l'application du paragraphe précédent, sont imputées à cette dernière.

Art. 102. (6.1.9.8) - 1. Rust op ieder van twee of meer personen een verplichting tot vergoeding van dezelfde schade, dan zijn zij hoofdelijk verbonden. Voor de bepaling van hetgeen zij krachtens artikel 10 in hun onderlinge verhouding jegens elkaar moeten bijdragen, wordt de schade over hen verdeeld met overeenkomstige toepassing van artikel 101, tenzij uit wet of rechtshandeling een andere verdeling voortvloeit.
- 2. Wanneer de schade mede een gevolg is van een omstandigheid die aan de benadeelde kan worden toegerekend, vindt artikel 101 toepassing op de vergoedingsplicht van ieder van de in het vorige lid bedoelde personen afzonderlijk, met dien verstande dat de benadeelde in totaal van hen niet meer kan vorderen dan hem zou zijn toegekomen, indien voor de omstandigheden waarop hun vergoedingsplichten berusten, slechts één persoon aansprakelijk zou zijn geweest. Indien verhaal op een der tot bijdragen verplichte personen niet ten volle mogelijk blijkt, kan de rechter op verlangen van een hunner bepalen dat bij toepassing van artikel 13 het onvoldaan gebleven deel mede over de benadeelde omgeslagen wordt.

1. Two or more persons who are each obliged to repair the same damage, are solidarily liable. In order to determine their contribution as amongst themselves according to article 10, the damage is apportioned amongst them by applying article 101 *mutatis mutandis*, unless another division results from law or a juridical act.
2. Where circumstances which can be imputed to the victim have contributed to the damage, article 101 applies to the obligation to repair of each individual person mentioned in the preceding paragraph. In total, however, the victim cannot claim more from them than he could have if only one person had been liable for the circumstances giving rise to the obligation to repair. If it proves impossible to recover the full amount from one of the persons obliged to contribute, the judge may, upon the demand of one of them, determine that, for the application of article 13, that

1. Lorsque plusieurs personnes sont obligées de réparer le même dommage, elles y sont solidairement tenues. Afin de déterminer leur contribution en vertu de l'article 10 dans leurs rapports réciproques, le dommage est réparti entre elles par application analogique de l'article 101, à moins qu'une autre répartition ne résulte de la loi ou d'un acte juridique.
2. Lorsqu'une circonstance imputable à la personne lésée contribue au dommage, l'article 101 s'applique à l'obligation de réparation de chacune des personnes visées au paragraphe précédent prises isolément, étant entendu que la personne lésée ne peut leur réclamer, en totalité, plus qu'il ne lui serait revenu si une seule personne avait été responsable des circonstances sur lesquelles se fondent leurs obligations de réparation. S'il se révèle impossible de recouvrer la part entière d'une des personnes tenues à contribution, le juge, à la demande d'une d'entre elles, peut déterminer que, en vue de l'application de l'article 13, la personne

which has remained unpaid will also be attributed to the victim.

lésée sera également mise à contribution pour la somme non recouvrée.

Art. 103. (6.1.9.9) Schadevergoeding wordt voldaan in geld. Nochtans kan de rechter op vordering van de benadeelde schadevergoeding in andere vorm dan betaling van een geldsom toekennen. Wordt niet binnen redelijke termijn aan een zodanige uitspraak voldaan, dan herkrijgt de benadeelde zijn bevoegdheid om schadevergoeding in geld te verlangen.

Reparation of damage is paid in money. Nevertheless, upon the demand of the victim, the judge may award reparation in a form other than the payment of a sum of money. Where such a judgment is not executed within a reasonable period, the victim regains the right to demand reparation in money.

La réparation du dommage s'effectue en argent. Le juge peut néanmoins, à la demande de la personne lésée, accorder la réparation sous une forme autre que le paiement d'une somme d'argent. Lorsque suite n'est pas donnée à un tel jugement dans un délai raisonnable, la personne lésée recouvre la faculté de demander réparation en argent.

Art. 104. (6.1.9.9a) Indien iemand die op grond van onrechtmatige daad of een tekortkoming in de nakoming van een verbintenis jegens een ander aansprakelijk is, door die daad of tekortkoming winst heeft genoten, kan de rechter op vordering van die ander de schade begroten op het bedrag van die winst of op een gedeelte daarvan.

If a person who is liable towards another on the basis of an unlawful act or a failure in the performance of an obligation, has derived profit from that act or failure, the judge may evaluate the damage, upon the demand of this other person, according to the amount of that profit or a part thereof.

Si une personne qui est responsable envers une autre par suite d'un acte illicite ou d'un manquement dans l'exécution d'une obligation a tiré profit de cet acte ou de ce défaut, le juge peut, à la demande de cette autre, évaluer le dommage à la totalité ou à une partie de ce profit.

Art. 105. (6.1.9.10) - 1. De begroting van nog niet ingetreden schade kan door de rechter geheel of gedeeltelijk worden uitgesteld of na afweging van goede en kwade kansen bij voorbaat geschieden. In het laatste geval kan de rechter de schuldenaar veroordelen, hetzij tot betaling van een bedrag ineens, hetzij tot betaling van periodiek uit te keren bedragen, al of niet met verplichting tot zekerheidstelling; deze veroordeling kan geschieden onder door de rechter te stellen voorwaarden.
- 2. Voor zover de rechter de schuldenaar veroordeelt tot betaling van periodiek uit te keren bedragen, kan hij in zijn uitspraak bepalen dat deze op verzoek van elk van de partijen door de rechter die in eerste aanleg van de vordering tot schadevergoeding heeft kennis genomen, kan worden gewijzigd, indien zich na de uitspraak omstandigheden voordoen, die voor de omvang van de vergoedingsplicht van belang zijn en met de mogelijkheid van het intreden waarvan bij de vaststelling der bedragen geen rekening is gehouden.

1. The judge may wholly or partially postpone the evaluation of damage which has not yet occurred; he may also immediately evaluate future damage after an assessment of the probabilities. In the

1. Le juge peut différer en tout ou en partie l'évaluation d'un dommage non encore réalisé; il peut aussi, sur appréciation des chances favorables et défavorables, la faire par anticipation. Dans ce dernier cas,

latter case, the judge may order the debtor either to pay a lump sum or to make instalment payments, accompanied or not by an obligation to furnish security; this order may be subject to conditions determined by the judge.

2. To the extent that the judge orders the debtor to make periodic instalment payments, he may determine in his judgment that these instalments can be modified at the request of each of the parties by the judge who was seized of the demand for reparation in the first instance, if, after judgment, circumstances arise which affect the extent of the obligation to repair, the possibility of which has not been taken into account in determining the instalments.

le juge peut condamner le débiteur au paiement d'une somme globale ou à des versements périodiques, assortis ou non d'une obligation de fournir sûreté; il peut assortir cette condamnation de conditions.

2. Dans la mesure où le juge condamne le débiteur à effectuer des versements périodiques, il peut prévoir que ceux-ci sont modifiables, sur la requête de chacune des parties, par le juge qui a connu de la demande de réparation en première instance, si se produisent, après la décision, des circonstances touchant l'étendue de l'obligation de réparation et si cette possibilité n'a pas été prise en considération lors de la détermination des montants.

Art. 106. (6.1.9.11) - 1. Voor nadeel dat niet in vermogensschade bestaat, heeft de benadeelde recht op een naar billijkheid vast te stellen schadevergoeding:

a. indien de aansprakelijke persoon het oogmerk had zodanig nadeel toe te brengen;

b. indien de benadeelde lichamelijk letsel heeft opgelopen, in zijn eer of goede naam is geschaad of op andere wijze in zijn persoon is aangetast;

c. indien het nadeel gelegen is in aantasting van de nagedachtenis van een overledene en toegebracht is aan de niet van tafel en bed gescheiden echtgenoot of een bloedverwant tot in de tweede graad van de overledene, mits de aantasting plaatsvond op een wijze die de overledene, ware hij nog in leven geweest, recht zou hebben gegeven op schadevergoeding wegens het schaden van zijn eer of goede naam.

- 2. Het recht op een vergoeding, als in het vorige lid bedoeld, is niet vatbaar voor overgang en beslag, tenzij het bij overeenkomst is vastgelegd of ter zake een vordering in rechte is ingesteld. Voor overgang onder algemene titel is voldoende dat de gerechtigde aan de wederpartij heeft medegedeeld op de vergoeding aanspraak te maken.

1. The victim has the right to an equitably determined reparation of harm other than patrimonial damage:

a. if the person liable had the intention to inflict such harm;

b. if the victim has suffered physical injury, injury to honour or reputation or if his person has been otherwise afflicted;

c. if the harm consists of injury to the memory of a deceased person inflicted upon the non-separated spouse or upon a blood relative up to the second degree, provided that the

1. Celui qui subit un préjudice autre que patrimonial a droit à une réparation déterminée suivant l'équité:

a. Si la personne responsable avait l'intention de causer un tel préjudice;

b. Si la victime a subi une lésion corporelle, a été atteinte dans son honneur ou sa réputation ou, d'une manière autre, dans sa personne;

c. Si le préjudice consiste en l'atteinte à la mémoire d'un défunt et a été causé à l'époux non séparé de corps ou à un parent jusqu'au deuxième degré du défunt, pourvu que l'atteinte soit portée

injury took place in a fashion which would have given the deceased, had he still been alive, the right to reparation of injury to honour or reputation.

2. The right to reparation referred to in the preceding paragraph cannot be transferred or seized, unless agreed upon by contract or unless an action for such reparation has been instituted. For transfer by general title, it is sufficient that the title-holder has notified the other party that he claims reparation.

d'une manière qui, du vivant du défunt, lui aurait donné droit à réparation pour atteinte à son honneur ou à sa réputation.

2. Le droit à réparation visé au paragraphe précédent est intransmissible et insaisissable, à moins qu'il n'ait été établi par contrat ou qu'il ne fasse l'objet d'une action en justice. Pour le transfert à titre universel, il suffit que le titulaire du droit ait communiqué à l'autre partie qu'il lui réclame réparation.

Art. 107. (6.1.9.11a) - 1. Indien iemand ten gevolge van een gebeurtenis waarvoor een ander aansprakelijk is, lichamelijk of geestelijk letsel oploopt, is die ander behalve tot vergoeding van de schade van de gekwetste zelf, ook verplicht tot vergoeding van de kosten die een derde anders dan krachtens een verzekering ten behoeve van de gekwetste heeft gemaakt en die deze laatste, zo hij ze zelf zou hebben gemaakt, van die ander had kunnen vorderen.

- 2. Hij die krachtens het vorige lid door de derde tot schadevergoeding wordt aangesproken kan hetzelfde verweer voeren dat hem jegens de gekwetste ten dienste zou hebben gestaan.

1. If a person suffers physical or mental injury as a result of an event for which another person is liable, that other person must not only repair the damage of the injured person himself, but also defray the costs which a third person, otherwise than pursuant to insurance, has incurred for the benefit of the injured, and which the latter, had he incurred them himself, would have been able to claim from that other person.

2. He who has been asked by the third person for reparation pursuant to the preceding paragraph, has the same defences as he would have had against the injured person.

1. Si une personne subit une lésion corporelle ou mentale à la suite d'un événement dont une autre personne est responsable, celle-ci est tenue, outre la réparation du dommage causé à la personne lésée elle-même, au remboursement des frais qu'a engagés un tiers au profit de la personne lésée, autrement qu'en exécution d'une assurance, et que celle-ci, si elle les avait engagés elle-même, aurait pu demander à cette autre.

2. Celui qui, par application du paragraphe précédent, est sommé par le tiers de réparer le dommage peut faire valoir les mêmes moyens de défense dont il aurait disposé à l'égard de la personne lésée.

Art. 108. (6.1.9.12) - 1. Indien iemand ten gevolge van een gebeurtenis waarvoor een ander jegens hem aansprakelijk is overlijdt, is die ander verplicht tot vergoeding van schade door het derven van levensonderhoud:

a. aan de niet van tafel en bed gescheiden echtgenoot en de minderjarige wettige of onwettige kinderen van de overledene, tot ten minste het bedrag van het hun krachtens de wet verschuldigde levensonderhoud;

b. aan andere bloed- of aanverwanten van de overledene, mits deze reeds ten tijde van het overlijden geheel of ten dele in hun levensonderhoud voorzag of daartoe krachtens rechterlijke uitspraak verplicht was;

c. aan degenen die reeds vóór de gebeurtenis waarop de aansprakelijkheid berust, met de overledene in gezinsverband samenwoonden en in wier levensonderhoud hij geheel of voor een

groot deel voorzag, voor zover aannemelijk is dat een en ander zonder het overlijden zou zijn voortgezet en zij redelijkerwijze niet voldoende in hun levensonderhoud kunnen voorzien;

d. aan degene die met de overledene in gezinsverband samenwoonde en in wiens levensonderhoud de overledene bijdroeg door het doen van de gemeenschappelijke huishouding, voor zover hij schade lijdt doordat na het overlijden op andere wijze in de gang van deze huishouding moet worden voorzien.

- 2. Bovendien is de aansprakelijke verplicht aan degene te wiens laste de kosten van lijkbezorging zijn gekomen, deze kosten te vergoeden, voor zover zij in overeenstemming zijn met de omstandigheden van de overledene.

- 3. Hij die krachtens de vorige leden tot schadevergoeding wordt aangesproken, kan hetzelfde verweer voeren, dat hem tegenover de overledene zou hebben ten dienste gestaan.

1. If a person dies as a result of an event for which another person is liable toward him, that other person must repair damage for loss of support suffered by:

a. the non-separated spouse and the minor legitimate or illegitimate children of the deceased, at least up to the amount of the support to which they are entitled by law;

b. other relatives by blood or marriage of the deceased, provided that, at the time of his death, the deceased already wholly or partially supported them or was obliged to do so by judicial decision;

c. the persons who, already before the event giving rise to liability, lived with the deceased as his family and were wholly or largely supported by the deceased, to the extent that it can be assumed that this situation would have continued, had the death not occurred, and that these persons cannot reasonably provide sufficiently for their own support;

d. the person who lived together with the deceased as family and to whose support the latter contributed by looking after the common household, to the extent that this person suffers damage because, after the death, other arrangements must be made to provide for this household.

2. In addition, the person liable must compensate the person who has borne the costs of the funeral expenses, to the extent that they are in conformity with the status of the deceased.

1. Si une personne décède à la suite d'un événement dont une autre personne est responsable, celle-ci doit réparation du dommage résultant de la perte d'aliments:

a. Au conjoint non séparé de corps et aux enfants mineurs légitimes ou illégitimes du défunt, au moins jusqu'à concurrence du montant des aliments qui leur sont accordés par la loi;

b. Aux autres parents et alliés du défunt, si, au moment de son décès, il pourvoyait déjà en tout ou en partie à leur entretien ou s'il y était tenu par décision judiciaire;

c. À ceux qui, avant l'événement qui fonde la responsabilité, habitaient en famille avec le défunt et à l'entretien desquels il pourvoyait en tout ou en grande partie, dans la mesure où il est vraisemblable que, n'eût été le décès, cette situation se serait poursuivie et qu'ils ne peuvent de manière adéquate pourvoir à leur entretien;

d. À la personne qui habitait en famille avec le défunt et à l'entretien duquel contribuait ce dernier en s'occupant du ménage commun, dans la mesure où elle subit un dommage du fait qu'après le décès la bonne marche du ménage doit être assurée d'une façon autre.

2. La personne responsable est, en outre, obligée de rembourser les frais funéraires à celui qui les a payés, dans la mesure où ils correspondent à la situation du défunt.

3. The person who has been asked for reparation of damage pursuant to the preceding paragraphs, has the same defences as he would have had against the deceased person.

3. Celui qui est sommé de réparer le dommage par application des paragraphes précédents peut faire valoir les mêmes moyens de défense dont il aurait disposé à l'égard du défunt.

Art. 109. (6.1.9.12a) - 1. Indien toekenning van volledige schadevergoeding in de gegeven omstandigheden waaronder de aard van de aansprakelijkheid, de tussen partijen bestaande rechtsverhouding en hun beider draagkracht, tot kennelijk onaanvaardbare gevolgen zou leiden, kan de rechter een wettelijke verplichting tot schadevergoeding matigen.
- 2. De matiging mag niet geschieden tot een lager bedrag dan waarvoor de schuldenaar zijn aansprakelijkheid door verzekering heeft gedekt of verplicht was te dekken.
- 3. Ieder beding in strijd met lid 1 is nietig.

1. The judge may reduce a legal obligation to repair damage if awarding full reparation would lead to clearly unacceptable results in the given circumstances, including the nature of the liability, the juridical relationship between the parties and their financial capacity.
2. The reduction may not exceed the amount for which the debtor has covered his liability by insurance or was obliged to do so.
3. Any stipulation derogating from paragraph 1 is null.

1. Le juge peut réduire l'obligation légale de réparation, si l'octroi d'une réparation intégrale entraînait des conséquences manifestement inacceptables dans les circonstances, qui englobent la nature de la responsabilité, le rapport juridique entre les parties et leurs moyens respectifs.
2. La réduction ne peut porter la réparation à une somme inférieure à celle pour laquelle le débiteur a assuré ou était tenu d'assurer sa responsabilité.
3. Toute stipulation contraire au paragraphe 1 est nulle.

Art. 110. (6.1.9.12b) Opdat de aansprakelijkheid die ter zake van schade kan ontstaan niet hetgeen redelijkerwijs door verzekering kan worden gedekt, te boven gaat, kunnen bij algemene maatregel van bestuur bedragen worden vastgesteld, waarboven de aansprakelijkheid zich niet uitstrekt. Afzonderlijke bedragen kunnen worden bepaald naar gelang van onder meer de aard van de gebeurtenis, de aard van de schade en de grond van de aansprakelijkheid.

Maximum liability amounts can be set by regulation, so that the liability which may arise from damage does not exceed that which can reasonably be covered by insurance. Separate amounts can be fixed according to, amongst others, the nature of the event and of the damage, and the ground for the liability.

Pour éviter que la responsabilité pouvant être engagée à propos d'un dommage ne dépasse ce qui peut raisonnablement être assuré, peuvent être fixées par décret des sommes au delà desquelles la responsabilité ne s'étend pas. Des sommes distinctes peuvent être fixées selon, entre autres, la nature de l'événement et du dommage, ainsi que la cause de responsabilité.

AFDELING 11 Verbintenissen tot betaling van een geldsom

Section 11
Obligations to pay a sum of money

Section onzième
Des obligations portant sur le paiement d'une somme d'argent

Art. 111. (6.1.9A.1) Een verbintenis tot betaling van een geldsom moet naar haar nominale bedrag worden voldaan, tenzij uit wet, gewoonte of rechtshandeling anders voortvloeit.

An obligation to pay a sum of money must be performed at its nominal value, unless law, usage or a juridical act produce a different result.

L'obligation portant sur le paiement d'une somme d'argent est acquittée à sa valeur nominale, à moins qu'il n'en résulte différemment de la loi, l'usage ou l'acte juridique.

Art. 112. (6.1.9A.2) Het geld dat ter voldoening van de verbintenis wordt betaald, moet op het tijdstip van de betaling gangbaar zijn in het land in welks geld de betaling geschiedt.

Money paid to perform the obligation must, at the time of payment, be current money in the country in whose currency the payment is made.

L'obligation est acquittée en argent qui, au moment du paiement, est couramment utilisé au pays en la monnaie duquel s'effectue le paiement.

Art. 113. (6.1.9A.2a) Bij betaling in Nederlands wettig betaalmiddel wordt de verschuldigde geldsom, indien deze niet vijf cent of een veelvoud daarvan beloopt, afgerond op het meest nabij gelegen bedrag dat deelbaar is door vijf en tenminste vijf cent bedraagt.

For payment in Netherlands legal currency, if the sum of money owed is five cents or a multiple thereof, it is rounded off to the closest amount divisible by five, with a minimum of five cents.

Lors d'un paiement en monnaie légale néerlandaise, la somme due, si elle n'est pas de cinq cents ou d'un multiple, est arrondie à la somme la plus proche divisible par cinq et d'au moins cinq cents.

Art. 114. (6.1.9A.3) - 1. Bestaat in een land waar de betaling moet of mag geschieden ten name van de schuldeiser een rekening, bestemd voor girale betalingen, dan kan de schuldenaar de verbintenis voldoen door het verschuldigde bedrag op die rekening te doen bijschrijven, tenzij de schuldeiser betaling op die rekening geldig heeft uitgesloten.
- 2. In het geval van het vorige lid geschiedt de betaling op het tijdstip waarop de rekening van de schuldeiser wordt gecrediteerd.

1. Where the creditor has a postal account in a country where the payment must or may be made, the debtor can perform the obligation by having that account credited with the amount due, unless the creditor has validly excluded payment into that account.

1. Lorsque le créancier a un compte destiné aux virements scripturaux dans un pays où doit ou peut avoir lieu le paiement, le débiteur peut acquitter l'obligation en faisant créditer ce compte de la somme due, à moins que le créancier n'ait valablement exclu paiement à ce compte.

2. In the case referred to in the preceding paragraph, payment is made at the time when the account of the creditor is credited.

2. Dans le cas prévu au paragraphe précédent, le paiement a lieu au moment où le compte du créancier est crédité.

Art. 115. (6.1.9A.4) De plaats waar de betaling moet geschieden wordt bepaald door de artikelen 116-118, tenzij uit wet, gewoonte of rechtshandeling voortvloeit dat op een andere plaats moet of mag worden betaald.

The place of payment is determined by articles 116 - 118, unless as a result of law, usage or a juridical act payment must or may be made at another place.

Le lieu de paiement est prévu par les articles 116 à 118, à moins qu'il ne résulte de la loi, de l'usage ou d'un acte juridique que le paiement doit ou peut avoir lieu à un autre endroit.

Art. 116. (6.1.9A.5) - 1. De betaling moet worden gedaan aan de woonplaats van de schuldeiser op het tijdstip van de betaling.
- 2. De schuldeiser is bevoegd een andere plaats voor de betaling aan te wijzen in het land van de woonplaats van de schuldeiser op het tijdstip van de betaling of op het tijdstip van het ontstaan van de verbintenis.

1. Payment must be made at the creditor's domicile at the time of payment.
2. The creditor is entitled to designate another place for payment in the country where he has his domicile at the time of payment or at the time when the obligation arises.

1. Le paiement s'effectue au domicile du créancier à la date du paiement.

2. Le créancier peut désigner pour le paiement un autre endroit dans le pays où il a son domicile à la date du paiement ou de la naissance de l'obligation.

Art. 117. (6.1.9A.6) Indien de betaling overeenkomstig artikel 116 moet geschieden op een andere plaats dan de woonplaats van de schuldeiser op het tijdstip van het ontstaan van de verbintenis en het voldoen aan de verbintenis daardoor voor de schuldenaar aanmerkelijk bezwaarlijker zou worden, is deze bevoegd de betaling op te schorten, totdat de schuldeiser in een der in artikel 116 lid 2 bedoelde landen een andere plaats voor de betaling heeft aangewezen, waaraan een zodanig bezwaar niet is verbonden.

If, according to article 116, payment must be made at a place other than the domicile of the creditor at the time when the obligation arises, and if, as a consequence thereof, the performance of the obligation would become considerably more onerous for the debtor, he is entitled to suspend payment until the creditor has designated another place for payment in one of the countries referred to in article 116 paragraph 2 to which such an inconvenience does not apply.

Si le paiement, conformément à l'article 116, doit s'effectuer à un endroit autre que le domicile du créancier à la date de la naissance de l'obligation et qu'il soit de ce fait nettement plus onéreux pour le débiteur, celui-ci peut suspendre le paiement jusqu'à ce que le créancier ait désigné dans l'un des pays visés à l'article 116, paragraphe 2 un endroit qui ne présente pas un tel inconvénient.

Art. 118. (6.1.9A.7) Indien de verbintenis is ontstaan bij de uitoefening van bedrijfs- of beroepsbezigheden van de schuldeiser, geldt in de artikelen

116 en 117 de plaats van vestiging waar die bezigheden worden uitgeoefend, als woonplaats van de schuldeiser.

If the obligation has arisen in carrying out the creditor's business or professional activities, the place of business where those activities are carried out is considered to be the domicile of the creditor for the purposes of articles 116 and 117.

Si l'obligation est née dans le cadre de l'entreprise ou des activités professionnelles du créancier, le domicile de celui-ci, aux fins des articles 116 et 117, est réputé être l'endroit où cette entreprise ou ces activités sont exercées.

Art. 119. (6.1.9A.8) - 1. De schadevergoeding, verschuldigd wegens vertraging in de voldoening van een geldsom, bestaat in de wettelijke rente van die som over de tijd dat de schuldenaar met de voldoening daarvan in verzuim is geweest.
- 2. Telkens na afloop van een jaar wordt het bedrag waarover de wettelijke rente wordt berekend, vermeerderd met de over dat jaar verschuldigde rente.
- 3. Een bedongen rente die hoger is dan die welke krachtens de vorige leden verschuldigd zou zijn, loopt in plaats daarvan door nadat de schuldenaar in verzuim is gekomen.

1. Reparation owed for delay in the payment of a sum of money consists of legal interest on that sum over the period that the debtor has been in default of payment.
2. At the end of every year, the amount on which legal interest is calculated is increased by the interest owed over that year.
3. Stipulated interest which is higher than that which would be owed pursuant to the preceding paragraphs applies instead of legal interest, after the debtor has come into default.

1. La réparation due pour retard dans le paiement d'une somme d'argent consiste en les intérêts légaux que porte cette somme pour la période pendant laquelle le débiteur a été en demeure de payer.
2. À la fin de chaque année, les intérêts de l'année s'ajoutent à la somme sur laquelle ils sont calculés.
3. Les intérêts conventionnels supérieurs à ceux qui seraient dus en vertu des paragraphes précédents courent au lieu des intérêts légaux à compter de la demeure du débiteur.

Art. 120. (6.1.9A.9) De wettelijke rente wordt bij algemene maatregel van bestuur vastgesteld. Wettelijke rente die loopt op het tijdstip van inwerkingtreding van een nieuwe bij algemene maatregel van bestuur vastgestelde rentevoet, wordt met ingang van dat tijdstip volgens de nieuwe rentevoet berekend.

Legal interest rates are fixed by regulation. Legal interest accumulating at the time of the coming into force of a new interest rate fixed by regulation is, as of that time, calculated according to the new rate.

Le taux des intérêts légaux est fixé par décret. Les intérêts légaux qui courent au moment de l'entrée en vigueur du nouveau taux fixé par décret sont calculés selon ce taux à compter de cette date.

Art. 121. (6.1.9A.10) - 1. Strekt een verbintenis tot betaling van ander geld dan dat van het land waar de betaling moet geschieden, dan is de schuldenaar bevoegd de verbintenis in het geld van de plaats van betaling te voldoen.

- 2. Het vorige lid geldt niet, indien uit wet, gewoonte of rechtshandeling voortvloeit dat de schuldenaar verplicht is tot betaling effectief in het geld tot betaling waarvan de verbintenis strekt.

1. Where, pursuant to an obligation, payment must be made in a currency other than that of the country where payment must be made, the debtor is entitled to pay in the currency of the place of payment.
2. The preceding paragraph does not apply if, as a result of law, usage or juridical act, the debtor is obliged to effective payment in the currency which is the object of the obligation.

1. Lorsque l'obligation porte sur le paiement d'une somme d'argent libellée en monnaie différente de celle du pays où doit avoir lieu le paiement, le débiteur peut acquitter la dette dans la monnaie du lieu de paiement.
2. Le paragraphe précédent ne s'applique pas s'il résulte de la loi, de l'usage ou de l'acte juridique que le débiteur est tenu au paiement effectif dans la monnaie sur laquelle porte l'obligation.

Art. 122. (6.1.9A.11) - 1. Strekt een verbintenis tot betaling van ander geld dan dat van het land waar de betaling moet geschieden en is de schuldenaar niet in staat of beweert hij niet in staat te zijn in dit geld te voldoen, dan kan de schuldeiser voldoening in het geld van de plaats van betaling vorderen.
- 2. Het vorige lid geldt mede, indien de schuldenaar verplicht is tot betaling effectief in het geld tot betaling waarvan de verbintenis strekt.

1. Where, pursuant to an obligation, payment must be made in a currency other than that of the country where payment must be made and the debtor is unable or claims to be unable to pay in this currency, the creditor can demand payment in the currency of the place of payment.
2. The preceding paragraph also applies if the debtor is obliged to effective payment in the currency which is the object of the obligation.

1. Lorsque l'obligation porte sur le paiement d'une somme d'argent libellée en monnaie différente de celle du pays où doit avoir lieu le paiement et que le débiteur est ou se prétend hors d'état de l'acquitter en cette monnaie, le créancier peut demander l'acquittement dans la monnaie du lieu du paiement.
2. Le paragraphe précédent s'applique également si le débiteur est tenu au paiement effectif dans la monnaie sur le paiement de laquelle porte l'obligation.

Art. 123. (6.1.9A.12) - 1. Ingeval in Nederland een rechtsvordering wordt ingesteld ter verkrijging van een geldsom, uitgedrukt in buitenlands geld, kan de schuldeiser veroordeling vorderen tot betaling te zijner keuze in dat buitenlandse geld of in Nederlands geld.
- 2. De schuldeiser die een in buitenlands geld luidende executoriale titel in Nederland kan executeren, kan het hem verschuldigde bij deze executie opeisen in Nederlands geld.
- 3. De vorige leden gelden mede, indien de schuldenaar verplicht is tot betaling effectief in het geld tot betaling waarvan de verbintenis strekt.

1. Where an action is brought in the Netherlands to obtain a sum of money expressed in foreign currency, the creditor can, at his option, ask for judgment in the foreign currency or in Dutch currency.

1. Lorsqu'une action est intentée aux Pays-Bas en vue d'obtenir une somme d'argent libellée en monnaie étrangère, le créancier peut demander la condamnation, à son choix, en monnaie étrangère ou en monnaie néerlandaise.

2. A creditor who can execute in the Netherlands an executory title expressed in foreign currency may, upon execution, claim the amount due in Dutch currency.

3. The preceding paragraphs also apply if the debtor is obliged to effective payment in the currency which is the object of the obligation.

2. Le créancier qui a le droit d'exécuter aux Pays-Bas un titre exécutoire libellé en monnaie étrangère peut demander ce qui lui est dû, lors de l'exécution forcée, en monnaie néerlandaise.

3. Les paragraphes précédents s'appliquent également si le débiteur est tenu au paiement effectif dans la monnaie sur le paiement de laquelle porte l'obligation.

Art. 124. (6.1.9A.13) Wordt de verbintenis als gevolg van toepassing van de artikelen 121, 122 of 123 of van omzetting in een vordering tot schadevergoeding overeenkomstig het bepaalde in afdeling 9 van titel 1 voldaan in ander geld dan tot betaling waarvan zij strekt, dan geschiedt de omrekening naar de koers van de dag waarop de betaling plaatsvindt.

Where, as a result of the application of articles 121, 122 or 123 or of conversion into a claim for reparation of damage according to section 9 of title 1, the obligation is performed in a currency other than that which is the object of the obligation, the currency exchange rate is that of the day of payment.

Lorsqu'une obligation, par suite de l'application des articles 121, 122 ou 123, ou de sa transformation en action en réparation conformément aux dispositions de la section neuvième du titre premier, est acquittée dans une monnaie différente de celle sur le paiement de laquelle porte l'obligation, la conversion s'effectue suivant le cours du change au jour de paiement.

Art. 125. (6.1.9A.14) - 1. Artikel 119 laat onverlet het recht van de schuldeiser op vergoeding van de schade die hij heeft geleden, doordat na het intreden van het verzuim de koers van het geld tot betaling waarvan de verbintenis strekt, zich ten opzichte van die van het geld van een of meer andere landen heeft gewijzigd.
- 2. Het vorige lid is niet van toepassing, indien de verbintenis strekt tot betaling van Nederlands geld, de betaling in Nederland moet geschieden en de schuldeiser op het tijdstip van het ontstaan van de verbintenis zijn woonplaats in Nederland had.

1. Article 119 does not affect the right of the creditor to claim reparation for damage suffered as a result of the exchange rate of the currency, which is the object of the obligation, having changed in relation to that of the currency of one or more other countries, after the date of default.
2. The preceding paragraph does not apply if, pursuant to the obligation, payment must be made in the Netherlands, in Dutch currency and the creditor had his domicile in the Netherlands at the time when the obligation has arisen.

1. L'article 119 laisse intact le droit du créancier à la réparation du dommage qu'il a subi du fait que, depuis la demeure, s'est modifié le taux de change de la monnaie sur le paiement de laquelle porte l'obligation par rapport à celles d'autres pays.

2. Le paragraphe précédent ne s'applique pas si l'obligation doit s'acquitter en monnaie néerlandaise, si le paiement doit avoir lieu aux Pays-Bas et si le créancier avait son domicile aux Pays-Bas à la date de naissance de l'obligation.

Art. 126. (6.1.9A.15) Voor de toepassing van deze afdeling geldt als koers de koers tegen welke de schuldeiser zich onverwijld het geld kan

verschaffen, zulks met inachtneming van hetgeen uit wet, gewoonte en inhoud of strekking van de verbintenis mocht voortvloeien.

For the purposes of this section, exchange rate means the rate at which the creditor can, without delay, procure the required currency, having due regard to the effects of law, usage, the content or the necessary implication of the obligation.

Aux fins de la présente section, on entend par taux de change celui auquel le créancier peut sans délai se procurer l'argent, en tenant compte de ce qui peut découler de la loi, de l'usage ou encore du contenu ou de la portée de l'obligation.

AFDELING 12 Verrekening

Section 12 Compensation[1]

Section douzième De la compensation

Art. 127. (6.1.10.4) - 1. Wanneer een schuldenaar die de bevoegdheid tot verrekening heeft, aan zijn schuldeiser verklaart dat hij zijn schuld met een vordering verrekent, gaan beide verbintenissen tot hun gemeenschappelijk beloop teniet.
- 2. Een schuldenaar heeft de bevoegdheid tot verrekening, wanneer hij een prestatie te vorderen heeft die beantwoordt aan zijn schuld jegens dezelfde wederpartij en hij bevoegd is zowel tot betaling van de schuld als tot het afdwingen van de betaling van de vordering.
- 3. De bevoegdheid tot verrekening bestaat niet ten aanzien van een vordering en een schuld die in van elkaar gescheiden vermogens vallen.

1. Where a debtor who is entitled to compensation, makes a declaration to his creditor that his debt be compensated by a claim, both obligations are extinguished up to the amount which they have in common.
2. A debtor is entitled to compensation where he can claim from a party a prestation which corresponds to his debt to the same party, and where he has both the right to pay the debt and the right to enforce payment of the claim.
3. There is no right to compensation for a claim and a debt which form part of separate patrimonies.

1. Lorsque un débiteur qui peut compenser déclare au créancier qu'il y a compensation entre sa dette et une créance, les deux obligations s'éteignent jusqu'à concurrence de leur montant commun.
2. Le débiteur peut compenser lorsqu'il peut demander une prestation correspondant à sa dette envers la même personne et qu'il a le droit de payer la dette, aussi bien que de forcer le paiement de la créance.
3. Le pouvoir de compensation n'existe pas à l'égard d'une créance et d'une dette faisant partie de patrimoines séparés.

Art. 128. (6.1.10.5) - 1. De schuldeiser van een vordering aan toonder of order brengt deze in verrekening door zijn verrekeningsverklaring op het papier te stellen en dit aan de wederpartij af te geven.
- 2. Indien de verrekening niet zijn gehele vordering betreft of hij het papier nog voor de uitoefening van andere rechten nodig heeft, kan hij het papier behouden, mits hij de verklaring niet alleen op het papier stelt, maar haar ook schriftelijk tot de wederpartij richt.

[1] Unlike in some other places in this translation, in section 12 the word "compensation" does not relate to compensation of damage, but to a mode of extinguishing obligations.

- 3. Hij kan, ongeacht of de verrekening de gehele vordering betreft, bij enkele, niet op het papier gestelde schriftelijke verklaring verrekenen, mits hij op verlangen van de wederpartij aantoont dat het papier vernietigd of waardeloos geworden is, of zekerheid stelt voor twintig jaren of voor een zoveel kortere tijdsduur als verwacht mag worden dat de wederpartij nog aan een vordering uit hoofde van het papier bloot zal kunnen staan.

1. The creditor of a claim payable to bearer or order effects compensation by inscribing his declaration of compensation on the document and by remitting it to the other party.
2. If the compensation does not cover the creditor's entire claim or where he still needs the document to exercise other rights, the creditor may retain the document, provided that he does not only inscribe the declaration on the document but also addresses it in writing to the other party.
3. Irrespective of whether the compensation covers the entire claim, the creditor may effect compensation by means of a mere written declaration which has not been inscribed on the document provided that, upon the demand of the other party, he can show that the document has been destroyed or become worthless, or provided that he furnish security for twenty years or such shorter period as the other party can still be expected to be subject to a claim pursuant to the document.

1. Le titulaire d'une créance au porteur ou à ordre[1] effectue la compensation en inscrivant sur le titre une déclaration à cet effet et en le remettant à l'autre partie.

2. Si la compensation ne porte pas sur la créance entière ou que le créancier a besoin du titre pour exercer d'autres droits, il peut le conserver, pourvu non seulement qu'il inscrive la déclaration sur le titre, mais adresse également celle-ci par écrit à l'autre partie.

3. La compensation, qu'elle porte ou non sur la créance entière, peut s'effectuer par une simple déclaration écrite qui n'est pas inscrite sur le titre, pourvu que le créancier, à la demande de l'autre partie, démontre que le titre a été détruit ou est devenu caduc, ou qu'il fournisse sûreté pour vingt ans ou pour une période moindre pendant laquelle on peut s'attendre que l'autre partie soit encore exposée à une action fondée sur le titre.

Art. 129. (6.1.10.6) - 1. De verrekening werkt terug tot het tijdstip, waarop de bevoegdheid tot verrekening is ontstaan.
- 2. Is over één der vorderingen of over beide reeds opeisbare rente betaald, dan werkt de verrekening niet verder terug dan tot het einde van de laatste termijn waarover rente is voldaan.
- 3. Indien voor de bepaling van de werking van een verrekening bij geldschulden een koersberekening nodig is, geschiedt deze volgens dezelfde maatstaven als wanneer op de dag der verrekening wederzijdse betaling had plaatsgevonden.

1. Compensation is retroactive to the time that the right to compensation has arisen.
2. Where exigible interest has already been paid on one or on both claims, the compensation is retroactive no further than to the end of the last term for which interest has been paid.

1. La compensation rétroagit à la date où est née la faculté de compensation.

2. Lorsque sur l'une des créances ou sur les deux ont déjà été payés des intérêts exigibles, la compensation ne rétroagit pas au delà du terme de la dernière période sur laquelle des intérêts ont été payés.

[1] Le terme «créance au porteur ou à ordre» est à rapprocher du terme «droit au porteur ou à ordre», qui apparaît à l'article 86 du Livre troisième.

3. The rate of exchange necessary to determine the effect of a compensation of money debts, is calculated according to the same criteria as in the case where mutual payment would have taken place on the day of compensation.

3. Si, pour apprécier l'effet d'une compensation portant sur des sommes d'argent, il est nécessaire de déterminer le taux de change, on l'établit suivant les mêmes critères que dans le cas où paiement réciproque avait eu lieu au jour de la compensation.

Art. 130. (6.1.10.7) - 1. Is een vordering onder bijzondere titel overgegaan, dan is de schuldenaar bevoegd ondanks de overgang ook een tegenvordering op de oorspronkelijke schuldeiser in verrekening te brengen, mits deze tegenvordering uit dezelfde rechtsverhouding als de overgegane vordering voortvloeit of reeds vóór de overgang aan hem is opgekomen en opeisbaar geworden.
- 2. Het vorige lid is van overeenkomstige toepassing, wanneer op een vordering beslag is gelegd of een beperkt recht is gevestigd waarvan mededeling aan de schuldenaar is gedaan.
- 3. De vorige leden zijn niet van toepassing, indien de overgang of de vestiging van het beperkte recht een vordering aan toonder of order betrof en is geschied overeenkomstig artikel 93 van Boek 3.

1. Where a claim has been transferred by particular title, the debtor is nevertheless entitled to compensate a counter claim against the original creditor, provided that this counter claim results from the same juridical relationship as the transferred claim or that it had already become part of the patrimony of the debtor before the transfer, and had become exigible.
2. The preceding paragraph applies *mutatis mutandis* to a claim which has been seized or upon which a dismembered right has been established, notice of which has been given to the debtor.
3. The preceding paragraphs do not apply if the transfer or establishment of the dismembered right involves a claim payable to bearer or order, and if this has been done according to article 93 of Book 3.

1. Lorsqu'une créance a été transmise à titre particulier, le débiteur peut, malgré la transmission, la compenser avec sa créance contre le créancier initial, pourvu que cette créance résulte du même rapport juridique que celle qui a été transmise ou que, avant la transmission, elle soit entrée dans le patrimoine du débiteur et qu'elle soit devenue exigible.

2. Le paragraphe précédent s'applique par analogie au cas de la saisie d'une créance ou de la constitution d'un droit démembré sur celle-ci, dont le débiteur a reçu communication.

3. Les paragraphes précédents ne s'appliquent pas si la transmission ou constitution du droit démembré porte sur une créance au porteur ou à ordre et qu'elle a eu lieu conformément à l'article 93 du Livre troisième.

Art. 131. (6.1.10.8) - 1. De bevoegdheid tot verrekening eindigt niet door verjaring van de rechtsvordering.
- 2. Uitstel van betaling of van executie, bij wijze van gunst door de schuldeiser verleend, staat aan verrekening door de schuldeiser niet in de weg.

1. The right to compensation is not terminated by the prescription of the right of action.

1. La faculté de compensation ne prend pas fin par la prescription de l'action.

2. A period of grace which the creditor has granted for payment or execution does not prevent him from compensating.

2. Le délai de grâce pour le paiement ou pour l'exécution forcée accordé par le créancier ne l'empêche pas de compenser.

Art. 132. (6.1.10.9) Wordt een verrekeningsverklaring uitgebracht door een daartoe bevoegde, dan kan niettemin de wederpartij die grond had om nakoming van haar verbintenis te weigeren, aan de verrekeningsverklaring haar werking ontnemen door op de weigeringsgrond een beroep te doen, onverwijld nadat die verklaring werd uitgebracht en zij tot dit beroep in staat was.

Where a declaration of compensation has been issued by a person who is entitled to do so, the other party who had grounds to refuse to perform his obligation can remove the effect of the declaration, as soon as it was issued and he was able to do so, by invoking the grounds for refusal without delay.

Lorsqu'une personne qui en a la faculté fait une déclaration de compensation, l'autre partie qui était fondée à refuser l'exécution de l'obligation peut priver cette déclaration d'effet en invoquant le motif de refus dès que la déclaration a été faite et qu'elle était en mesure de l'invoquer.

Art. 133. (6.1.10.10) Nadat de ene partij een verrekeningsverklaring heeft uitgebracht, kan de andere partij, mits onverwijld, aan die verklaring haar werking ontnemen door alsnog gebruik te maken van een eigen bevoegdheid tot verrekening, doch alleen indien deze laatste verrekening verder terugwerkt.

After such time as one party has issued a declaration of compensation, the other party can remove the effect of this declaration by using his own right to compensation without delay, but only if this latter compensation exceeds the retroactive effect of the former.

Après qu'une partie a fait une déclaration de compensation, l'autre partie, à la condition d'agir sans tarder, peut priver cette déclaration d'effet en exerçant sa propre faculté de compensation, mais seulement si cette dernière compensation rétroagit à une date antérieure à celle qui découle de la première.

Art. 134. (6.1.10.11) De schuldenaar uit een wederkerige overeenkomst, die tot verrekening bevoegd is, kan aan de verklaring van zijn wederpartij, strekkende tot ontbinding van de overeenkomst wegens niet-nakoming, haar werking ontnemen door onverwijld van zijn bevoegdheid tot verrekening gebruik te maken.

A debtor in a synallagmatic contract who is entitled to compensation can remove the effect of the other party's declaration which would set aside the contract for non-performance, by using his right to compensation without delay.

Le débiteur dans un contrat synallagmatique qui a la faculté de compensation peut priver d'effet la déclaration de l'autre partie portant résiliation du contrat pour cause d'inexécution, en exerçant sans tarder cette faculté.

Art. 135. (6.1.10.12) Een schuldenaar is niet bevoegd tot verrekening:
a. voor zover beslag op de vordering van de wederpartij niet geldig zou zijn;
b. indien zijn verplichting strekt tot vergoeding van schade die hij opzettelijk heeft toegebracht.

A debtor is not entitled to compensation:

Le débiteur ne peut compenser:

a. to the extent that seizure of the claim of the other party would not be valid;
b. if the object of his obligation is to make reparation for damage which he has intentionally inflicted.

a. Dans la mesure où la saisie de la créance de l'autre partie serait invalide;
b. Si son obligation porte sur la réparation du dommage qu'il a causé intentionnellement.

Art. 136. (6.1.10.13) De rechter kan een vordering ondanks een beroep van de gedaagde op verrekening toewijzen, indien de gegrondheid van dit verweer niet op eenvoudige wijze is vast te stellen en de vordering overigens voor toewijzing vatbaar is.

The judge may grant judgment in favour of the plaintiff notwithstanding the fact that the defendant invokes compensation, if the validity of this defence cannot easily be ascertained and the action would otherwise succeed.

Le juge peut accueillir une demande à laquelle le défendeur oppose la compensation, si le bien-fondé de cette défense ne peut être déterminé de façon simple et si les autres conditions pour l'accueillir sont réunies.

Art. 137. (6.1.10.15) - 1. Voor zover een verrekeningsverklaring onvoldoende aangeeft welke verbintenissen in de verrekening zijn betrokken, geldt de volgorde van toerekening, aangegeven in de artikelen 43 lid 2 en 44 lid 1.
- 2. De wederpartij van degene die heeft verklaard te verrekenen, kan door een onverwijld protest aan die verklaring haar werking ontnemen, indien de toerekening op de haar verschuldigde hoofdsom, kosten en met inachtneming van artikel 129 te berekenen rente in deze verklaring in een andere volgorde is geschied dan die van artikel 44 lid 1.

1. To the extent that a declaration of compensation does not sufficiently specify the obligations involved in the compensation, the order of imputation referred to in articles 43 paragraph 2 and 44 paragraph 1 applies.
2. The counterpart of the person who has declared to compensate can remove the effect of that declaration by protesting, without delay, if the imputation to capital sum owed, costs and interest to be calculated in accordance with article 129, has been done in this declaration in an order other than the one provided for in article 44 paragraph 1.

1. Dans la mesure où la déclaration de compensation indique insuffisamment les obligations qui en font l'objet, l'ordre d'imputation est établi suivant les articles 43, paragraphe 2 et 44, paragraphe 1er.

2. Celui à qui l'autre partie fait une déclaration de compensation peut priver cette déclaration d'effet par un protêt immédiat, si la déclaration effectue l'imputation sur la somme principale qui lui est due, sur les frais et sur les intérêts à calculer, compte tenu de l'article 129, selon un ordre différent de celui qui est prévu à l'article 44, paragraphe 1er.

Art. 138. (6.1.10.16) - 1. De omstandigheid dat de plaats van voldoening der verbintenissen niet dezelfde is, sluit verrekening niet uit. Hij die verrekent, is in dit geval verplicht zijn wederpartij de schade te vergoeden die deze lijdt, doordat niet wederzijds te bestemder plaatse voldoening geschiedt.
- 2. De wederpartij van degene die ondanks een verschil in de plaats van nakoming heeft verrekend, kan door een onverwijld protest aan de verklaring tot verrekening haar werking ontnemen, als zij er een gerechtvaardigd belang bij heeft dat geen verrekening, maar nakoming plaatsvindt.

1. The fact that the obligations must be paid in different places does not prevent compensation. In this event, the person who compensates must make reparation for the damage which the other party suffers because mutual payment is not made at the place due.
2. The counterpart of the person who has compensated notwithstanding a difference in the place of payment can remove the effect of the declaration of compensation by protesting without delay, if he has a justified interest that there be no compensation, but rather performance of the obligation.

1. Le fait que des obligations doivent être payées à des lieux différents ne fait pas obstacle à la compensation. Celui qui compense est tenu d'indemniser l'autre partie du dommage que celui-ci subit du fait que les paiements réciproques n'ont pas lieu à l'endroit prévu.
2. Celui contre qui l'autre partie a compensé malgré la différence des lieux peut priver la déclaration de compensation d'effet par un protêt immédiat, s'il a un intérêt légitime à ce qu'il y ait exécution et non compensation.

Art. 139. (6.1.10.17) - 1. De borg en degene wiens goed voor de schuld van een ander verbonden is, kunnen de opschorting van hun aansprakelijkheid inroepen, voor zover de schuldeiser bevoegd is zijn vordering met een opeisbare schuld aan de schuldenaar te verrekenen.
- 2. Zij kunnen de bevrijding van hun aansprakelijkheid inroepen, voor zover de schuldeiser een bevoegdheid tot verrekening met een schuld aan de schuldenaar heeft doen verloren gaan, tenzij hij daartoe een redelijke grond had of hem geen schuld treft.

1. A surety and a person whose property is liable for the debt of another can invoke the suspension of their liability, to the extent that the creditor is entitled to compensate his claim with an exigible debt to the debtor.
2. Unless the creditor acted reasonably or was not at fault, they can invoke the extinction of their liability to the extent that the creditor has caused the loss of a right to compensation with respect to the debtor.

1. La caution et celui dont le bien sert de sûreté pour la dette d'autrui peuvent invoquer la suspension de leur responsabilité, dans la mesure où le créancier peut compenser sa créance avec une dette exigible envers le débiteur.
2. Ils peuvent invoquer l'extinction de leur responsabilité, dans la mesure où le créancier a fait perdre une faculté de compenser sa créance avec une dette envers le débiteur, à moins que le créancier n'ait un motif raisonnable ou qu'il ne soit pas fautif.

Art. 140. (6.1.10.18) - 1. Moeten tussen twee partijen krachtens wet, gewoonte of rechtshandeling geldvorderingen en geldschulden in één rekening worden opgenomen, dan worden zij in de volgorde waarin partijen volgens de voorgaande artikelen van deze afdeling of krachtens hun onderlinge rechtsverhouding tot verrekening bevoegd worden, dadelijk van rechtswege verrekend en is op ieder tijdstip alleen het saldo verschuldigd. Artikel 137 is niet van toepassing.
- 2. De partij die de rekening bijhoudt, sluit deze jaarlijks af en deelt het op dat tijdstip verschuldigde saldo mede aan de wederpartij met opgave van de aan deze nog niet eerder medegedeelde posten waaruit het is samengesteld.
- 3. Indien de wederpartij niet binnen redelijke tijd tegen het ingevolge het vorige lid medegedeelde saldo protesteert, geldt dit als tussen partijen vastgesteld.
- 4. Na vaststelling van het saldo kan ten aanzien van de afzonderlijke posten geen beroep meer worden gedaan op het intreden van verjaring of op het verstrijken van een vervaltermijn. De rechtsvordering tot betaling van

het saldo verjaart door verloop van vijf jaren na de dag, volgende op die waarop de rekening is geëindigd en het saldo opeisbaar is geworden.
- 5. Uit de tussen partijen bestaande rechtsverhouding kan anders voortvloeien dan in de vorige leden is bepaald.

1. Where pursuant to law, usage or a juridical act, money claims and money debts must be included into one account between two parties, compensation operates immediately and *de iure*, in the order in which the parties become entitled to compensation according to the preceding articles of this section, or pursuant to their mutual juridical relationship. At all times, only the balance is owed. Article 137 does not apply.
2. The party administering the account closes it annually and communicates to the other party what the outstanding balance is at that time, with mention of those items composing the account which have not as yet been communicated to the other party.
3. If the other party does not, within a reasonable period, contest the balance as communicated pursuant to the preceding paragraph, this balance is deemed to be the one determined by the parties.
4. After the determination of the balance, the completion of a prescription period or of a term of forfeiture can no longer be invoked with regard to the individual items. The right of action to claim payment of the balance is prescribed by five years from the day following the one on which the account has been closed and the balance has become exigible.
5. Rules other than the ones provided for in the preceding paragraphs may result from the juridical relationship between the parties.

1. Lorsque, entre deux parties, des créances et des dettes en argent doivent, en vertu de la loi, de l'usage ou d'un acte juridique, être portées à un seul compte, elles se compensent immédiatement de plein droit dans l'ordre où, suivant les articles précédents de la présente section ou en vertu de leur rapport réciproque, les parties acquièrent la faculté de compensation. À tout moment, seul le solde est dû. L'article 137 ne s'applique pas.
2. La partie qui tient la comptabilité clôt les comptes annuellement et communique à l'autre partie le solde dû à cette date, en en indiquant les postes dont cette dernière n'avait pas encore reçu communication.
3. Si l'autre partie ne proteste pas dans un délai raisonnable contre le solde qui lui est communiqué par application du paragraphe précédent, ce solde est réputé établi entre les parties.
4. Le solde une fois établi, on ne peut invoquer, à l'égard des postes séparés, la prescription acquise ou la déchéance d'un terme. L'action en paiement du solde se prescrit par cinq ans à compter du jour suivant celui où le compte se termine et où le solde est devenu exigible.
5. Il peut résulter du rapport juridique des parties une dérogation aux dispositions des paragraphes prédécents.

Art. 141. (6.1.10.19) Indien een verbintenis geheel of gedeeltelijk door verrekening tenietgaat, zijn de leden 1 en 2 van artikel 48 van overeenkomstige toepassing.

Paragraphs 1 and 2 of article 48 apply *mutatis mutandis* to an obligation which is wholly or partially extinguished by compensation.

Si une obligation s'éteint en tout ou en partie par compensation, les paragraphes 1er et 2 de l'article 48 s'appliquent par analogie.

TITEL 2 OVERGANG VAN VORDERINGEN EN SCHULDEN EN AFSTAND VAN VORDERINGEN

TITLE 2 TRANSFER OF CLAIMS AND DEBTS AND RENUNCIATION[1] OF CLAIMS

TITRE DEUXIÈME DE LA TRANSMISSION DES CRÉANCES ET DES DETTES ET DE LA RENONCIATION[2] AUX CRÉANCES

AFDELING 1 Gevolgen van overgang van vorderingen

Section 1 Consequences of transfer of claims

Section première Des effets de la transmission des créances

Art. 142. (6.2.1.1) - 1. Bij overgang van een vordering op een nieuwe schuldeiser verkrijgt deze de daarbij behorende nevenrechten, zoals rechten van pand en hypotheek en uit borgtocht, voorrechten en de bevoegdheid om de ter zake van de vordering en de nevenrechten bestaande executoriale titels ten uitvoer te leggen.
- 2. Onder de nevenrechten zijn tevens begrepen het recht van de vorige schuldeiser op bedongen rente of boete of op een dwangsom, behalve voor zover de rente opeisbaar of de boete of dwangsom reeds verbeurd was op het tijdstip van de overgang.

1. The new creditor to whom a claim is transferred acquires the rights which are accessory to the claim, such as rights resulting from pledge, hypothec, suretyship, privileges, and the power to enforce executory titles relating to the claim and the accessory rights.

2. The accessory rights also include the right of the previous creditor to stipulated interest, to a stipulated penalty or to a forfeiture, except to the extent that the interest, the penalty or the forfeiture were already exigible at the time of the transfer of the claim.

1. Lors de la transmission d'une créance, le nouveau créancier en acquiert les droits accessoires, tels les droits de gage et d'hypothèque ainsi que ceux résultant du cautionnement, les privilèges et la faculté de procéder à l'exécution forcée des titres exécutoires relatifs à la créance ou aux droits accessoires.

2. Les droits accessoires s'étendent également au droit du créancier précédent aux intérêts ou à une peine conventionnels ou à une astreinte, sauf dans la mesure où les intérêts étaient déjà exigibles et la peine ou l'astreinte, déjà encourue lors de la transmission.

Art. 143. (6.2.1.2) - 1. In geval van overgang van een vordering is de vorige schuldeiser verplicht de op de vordering en op de nevenrechten betrekking hebbende bewijsstukken af te geven aan de nieuwe schuldeiser. Behoudt hij zelf belang bij een bewijsstuk, dan is hij slechts verplicht om aan de nieuwe schuldeiser op diens verlangen en op diens kosten een afschrift of uittreksel af te geven, waaruit met overeenkomstige bewijskracht als uit het oorspronkelijke stuk van de vordering blijkt.

[1] Renunciation vs abandonment; see note at article 9.

[2] Sur le choix du terme «renonciation» de préférence à «abandon», voir la note à l'article 9.

- 2. De vorige schuldeiser is tevens verplicht tot afgifte van de in het vorige artikel bedoelde executoriale titels of, indien hijzelf belang bij deze titels behoudt, om de nieuwe schuldeiser tot tenuitvoerlegging daarvan in de gelegenheid te stellen.
- 3. In geval van overgang van de gehele vordering is de vorige schuldeiser verplicht de zich in zijn handen bevindende panden af te geven aan de nieuwe schuldeiser.
- 4. In geval van overgang van een vordering waaraan hypotheek is verbonden, is de vorige schuldeiser verplicht desverlangd ertoe mede te werken dat uit de openbare registers van deze overgang blijkt.

1. Where a claim is transferred, the previous creditor must give to the new creditor the documentary evidence pertaining to the claim and the accessory rights. If such evidence remains of importance to the previous creditor, the new creditor is only entitled, upon his demand and at his expense, to a copy or extract which must witness the claim with comparable evidentiary force.

2. The previous creditor must also give to the new creditor the executory titles referred to in the preceding article or, if they remain important to him, the opportunity to use them for the purpose of execution.
3. Where an entire claim is transferred, the previous creditor must give to the new creditor any pledged property which is under his control.
4. Where a claim guaranteed by hypothec is transferred, the previous creditor must, upon demand, give his cooperation so that the public registers will reflect this transfer.

1. Le créancier dont la créance est transmise à un autre remet à celui-ci les instruments de preuve se rapportant à la créance ou aux droits accessoires. Si un instrument de preuve continue à présenter un intérêt pour lui, il est seulement tenu d'en remettre au nouveau créancier, à la demande et aux frais de celui-ci, une copie ou un extrait, attestant la créance avec une force probante comparable à celle de l'instrument original.
2. L'ancien créancier remet également les titres exécutoires visés à l'article précédent, ou, si un titre continue à présenter un intérêt pour lui, il permet au nouveau créancier de s'en servir aux fins d'une exécution forcée.

3. Dans le cas de la transmission de l'ensemble de la créance, l'ancien créancier remet au nouveau les gages qu'il détient.

4. Dans le cas de la transmission d'une créance garantie par hypothèque, l'ancien créancier est tenu, sur demande, de prêter son concours pour que la transmission apparaisse dans les registres publics.

Art. 144. (6.2.1.3) - 1. Brengt de overdracht van een vordering mee dat verplichtingen die uit het schuldeiserschap of uit nevenrechten voortvloeien, overgaan op de nieuwe schuldeiser, dan staat de vorige schuldeiser in voor de nakoming van deze verplichtingen.
- 2. Lid 1 is niet van toepassing in geval van overdracht van een vordering aan toonder of order overeenkomstig artikel 93 van Boek 3.

1. Where as the result of the transfer of a claim, obligations of the creditor or obligations flowing from accessory rights are transferred to the new creditor, the previous creditor must warrant the performance of these obligations.

1. Lorsque la transmission d'une créance entraîne le passage des obligations découlant de la position du créancier ou des droits accessoires au nouveau créancier, le créancier précédent est garant de l'exécution de ces obligations.

2. Paragraph 1 does not apply to the transfer of a claim payable to bearer or order according to article 93 of Book 3.

2. Le paragraphe premier ne s'applique pas dans le cas de la transmission des créances au porteur ou à ordre, conformément à l'article 93 du Livre troisième.

Art. 145. (6.2.1.4) Overgang van een vordering laat de verweermiddelen van de schuldenaar onverlet.

The transfer of a claim does not affect the debtor's defences.

La transmission d'une créance laisse intacts les moyens de défense du débiteur.

Art. 146. (6.2.1.4a) - 1. Na een overdracht overeenkomstig artikel 93 van Boek 3 van een vordering aan toonder of aan order kan de schuldenaar een verweermiddel, gegrond op zijn verhouding tot een vorige schuldeiser, niet tegenwerpen aan de verkrijger en diens rechtsopvolgers, tenzij op het tijdstip van de overdracht het verweermiddel bekend was aan de verkrijger of voor hem kenbaar was uit het papier.
- 2. Een beroep op onbekwaamheid of onbevoegdheid kan ook jegens een daarmee niet bekende verkrijger worden gedaan, indien zij ten tijde van zijn verkrijging kenbaar was uit een in een openbaar register opgenomen inschrijving, bij of krachtens de wet voorgeschreven teneinde kennisneming mogelijk te maken van de feiten waarop de onbevoegdheid of onbekwaamheid berust.

1. After transfer of a claim payable to bearer or order according to article 93 of Book 3, the debtor cannot invoke against the acquirer of the claim or his successors a defence which is based upon his relationship with a previous creditor, unless, at the time of the transfer, the acquirer knew the defence or could have known of it from the document.
2. Incapacity[1] can even be invoked against an acquirer who was unaware of it, if it could be known at the time of acquisition from an entry in a public register provided for by, or pursuant to the law in order to make it possible to take cognizance of the facts on which the incapacity is based.

1. Le débiteur d'une créance au porteur ou à ordre ne peut, après la transmission de celle-ci conformément à l'article 93 du Livre troisième, opposer à l'acquéreur ou à ses ayants cause un moyen de défense fondé sur son rapport avec le créancier précédent, à moins que, au moment de la transmission, l'acquéreur ait connu le moyen ou eût pu le connaître par le titre.
2. L'incapacité[2] est opposable même à l'acquéreur qui n'en a pas connaissance, si, au moment de l'acquisition, elle apparaissait d'une inscription sur un registre public, telle que prescrite par la loi ou en vertu d'elle, afin de permettre aux tiers de prendre connaissance des faits sur lesquels se fonde l'incapacité.

Art. 147. (6.2.1.5) In geval van overdracht van een papier aan toonder of aan order verliest degene die volgens dat papier schuldenaar is, en aan wie is toe te rekenen dat het papier tegen zijn wil in omloop is of dat zijn handtekening vals of het papier vervalst is, de bevoegdheid zich daarop te beroepen tegenover de verkrijger te goeder trouw en diens rechtsopvolgers.

---

[1] The Dutch text uses distinct terms for general incapacity (*onbekwaamheid*) and special incapacity (*onbevoegdheid*).

[2] Le néerlandais emploie des termes distincts pour l'incapacité générale (*onbekwaamheid*) et l'incapacité spéciale (*onbevoegdheid*).

In the case of transfer of a document payable to bearer or order, the debtor who appears on the face of the document, and to whom it can be imputed that the document is in circulation against his will, that his signature is false or that the document has been falsified, loses his right to invoke these facts against an acquirer in good faith and his successors.

La transmission d'un titre au porteur ou à ordre fait perdre, à celui qui y apparaît comme débiteur et à qui est imputable la mise en circulation contre sa volonté ou la contrefaçon de sa signature ou du titre, la faculté de faire valoir ces faits à l'encontre de l'acquéreur de bonne foi de cette créance et de ses ayants cause.

Art. 148. (6.2.1.6) De artikelen 146 en 147 zijn van overeenkomstige toepassing in geval van vestiging van een beperkt recht op een vordering aan toonder of aan order.

Articles 146 and 147 apply *mutatis mutandis* to the establishment of a dismembered right upon a claim payable to bearer or order.

Les articles 146 et 147 s'appliquent par analogie à la constitution d'un droit démembré sur une créance au porteur ou à ordre.

Art. 149. (6.2.1.6a) - 1. Oefent de schuldenaar na overgang van de vordering onder bijzondere titel jegens de oorspronkelijke schuldeiser een bevoegdheid uit tot vernietiging of ontbinding van de rechtshandeling waaruit de vordering voortspruit, dan is hij verplicht om de nieuwe schuldeiser zo spoedig mogelijk daarvan mededeling te doen, tenzij de vernietiging of ontbinding niet aan deze kan worden tegengeworpen.
- 2. Na verjaring van de rechtsvordering tot vernietiging of ontbinding wordt een beroep op de vernietigings- of ontbindingsgrond ter afwering van een op de rechtshandeling steunende rechtsvordering of andere rechtsmaatregel gericht tot de nieuwe schuldeiser en is de schuldenaar verplicht zo spoedig mogelijk nadien mededeling daarvan aan de oorspronkelijke schuldeiser te doen.
- 3. De vorige leden zijn van overeenkomstige toepassing ter zake van de uitoefening van een bevoegdheid van de schuldenaar tot vernietiging of ontbinding, nadat op de vordering met mededeling aan hem een beperkt recht is gevestigd.

1. A debtor who, after the transfer of a claim by particular title, exercises against the original creditor a right to annul or to set aside the juridical act from which the claim arises, must notify the new creditor thereof as soon as possible, unless the annulment or the setting aside of the act cannot be invoked against the latter.
2. Where the ground for annulment or for the setting aside of the act is invoked after prescription of the right of action to annul or to set aside, in defence against a right of action or other legal measure based upon the juridical act, it is invoked against the new creditor and the debtor must, as soon as possible thereafter, notify the original creditor thereof.

1. Le débiteur qui, après la transmission à titre particulier de la créance, exerce envers le créancier d'origine un pouvoir d'annuler ou de résilier l'acte juridique dont résulte la créance est tenu d'en aviser le plus tôt possible le nouveau créancier, à moins que l'annulation ou la résiliation ne soit inopposable à ce dernier.
2. Après la prescription de l'action en annulation ou résiliation, le motif d'annulation ou de résiliation que l'on veut faire valoir à l'encontre d'une action ou autre voie de droit fondée sur l'acte juridique est invoqué contre le nouveau créancier et le débiteur est tenu, aussitôt que possible après l'avoir fait valoir, d'en aviser le créancier d'origine.

3. The preceding paragraphs apply *mutatis mutandis* to the exercise by the debtor of a right to annul or to set aside an act, after the establishment of a dismembered right on the claim and notification thereof to him.

3. Les paragraphes précédents s'appliquent par analogie en matière de l'exercice par le débiteur de la faculté d'annulation ou résiliation, après que, avec communication au débiteur, un droit démembré a été établi sur la créance.

AFDELING 2 Subrogatie

Section Subrogation

Section deuxième De la subrogation

Art. 150. (6.2.2.7) Een vordering gaat bij wijze van subrogatie over op een derde:

a. indien een hem toebehorend goed voor de vordering wordt uitgewonnen;

b. indien hij de vordering voldoet omdat een hem toebehorend goed voor de vordering verbonden is;

c. indien hij de vordering voldoet om uitwinning te voorkomen van een hem niet toebehorend goed, mits door de uitwinning een recht dat hij op het goed heeft, verloren zou gaan of de voldoening van een hem toekomend vorderingsrecht in gevaar zou worden gebracht;

d. krachtens overeenkomst tussen de derde die de vordering voldoet en de schuldenaar, mits de schuldeiser op het tijdstip van de voldoening deze overeenkomst kende of hem daarvan kennis was gegeven.

A claim is transferred to a third party by way of subrogation:

a. if property belonging to the third party is seized and executed against in satisfaction of the claim;

b. if the third party pays a claim because property belonging to him constitutes security for the claim;

c. if the third party pays a claim in order to prevent seizure and execution of property not belonging to him, provided that seizure and execution would make him lose a right which he has in the property or that the payment of a claim to which he is entitled would be endangered;

d. pursuant to a contract between the third party paying the claim and the debtor, provided that the creditor was aware of this contract at the time of payment or had been notified of it.

Une créance se transmet par subrogation à un tiers:

a. Si le bien lui appartenant a fait l'objet d'une exécution forcée pour le recouvrement de la créance;

b. S'il paie la créance parce qu'un bien lui appartenant en est garant;

c. S'il paie la créance afin d'éviter l'exécution forcée d'un bien ne lui appartenant pas, pourvu que cette exécution lui fasse perdre un droit qu'il a sur ce bien ou mette en danger le paiement d'une créance lui revenant;

d. Par contrat conclu entre le tiers qui paie la créance et le débiteur, pourvu que le créancier, au moment du paiement, ait eu connaissance de cette entente ou en ait été informé.

Art. 151. (6.2.2.8) - 1. Subrogatie overeenkomstig artikel 150 vindt niet plaats voor zover de schuld de derde aangaat in zijn verhouding tot de schuldenaar.

- 2. De rechten van de schuldeiser jegens borgen en personen die geen schuldenaar zijn, gaan slechts op de derde over tot ten hoogste de

bedragen, waarvoor de schuld ieder van hen aangaat in hun verhouding tot de schuldenaar.

1. There is no subrogation according to article 150 to the extent that the debt concerns the third party in his relationship with the debtor.
2. The rights of the creditor against sureties and persons other than debtors are transferred to the third party up to the maximum amount for which the debt concerns each of them in their relationship with the debtor.

1. La subrogation conforme à l'article 150 n'a pas lieu dans la mesure où la dette concerne le tiers dans son rapport avec le débiteur.
2. Les droits du créancier à l'égard des cautions et des personnes qui ne sont pas débitrices ne se transmettent que jusqu'à concurrence maximale des sommes pour lesquelles la dette concerne chacune d'elles dans leur rapport avec le débiteur.

Art. 152. (6.2.2.9) - 1. Blijkt verhaal krachtens subrogatie overeenkomstig artikel 150 geheel of gedeeltelijk onmogelijk, dan wordt het onvoldaan gebleven deel over de gesubrogeerde en andere in lid 2 van het vorige artikel genoemde derden omgeslagen naar evenredigheid van de bedragen waarvoor ieder op het tijdstip van de voldoening jegens de schuldeiser aansprakelijk was.
- 2. De gesubrogeerde kan van geen der andere bij de omslag betrokken derden een groter bedrag vorderen dan de oorspronkelijke schuldeiser op het tijdstip van de voldoening op deze had kunnen verhalen.
- 3. Ieder der in de omslag betrokkenen blijft gerechtigd het bijgedragene alsnog van hem die geen verhaal bood, terug te vorderen.

1. Where recourse pursuant to subrogation according to article 150 proves to be wholly or partially impossible, the part which has remained unpaid is apportioned among the subrogated party and the other third parties referred to in paragraph 2 of the preceding article in proportion to the amounts for which each party was liable toward the creditor at the time of payment.
2. The subrogated party cannot claim more from any of the other third parties involved in the apportionment than the original creditor could have claimed from them at the time of payment.
3. Each party involved in the apportionment remains entitled to reclaim as yet his contribution from the party against whom recovery was impossible.

1. Lorsque le recouvrement en vertu d'une subrogation qui a lieu conformément à l'article 150 se révèle impossible en tout ou en partie, la somme non recouvrée est répartie entre le tiers subrogé et les autres tiers mentionnés au paragraphe 2 de l'article précédent en proportion des sommes dont chacun était tenu à l'égard du créancier au moment du paiement.
2. Le subrogé ne peut demander aux autres tiers qui sont parties à la répartition une somme supérieure à celle dont le créancier d'origine aurait pu chercher le recouvrement au moment du paiement.
3. Chacune des parties à la répartition conserve son recours pour demander plus tard sa contribution à celui contre qui le recouvrement fut impossible.

Art. 153. (6.2.2.9a) In het geval van subrogatie in de hoofdvordering verkrijgt de gesubrogeerde het recht op bedongen rente slechts voor zover deze betrekking heeft op het tijdvak na de overgang.

In the case of subrogation of the principal claim, the subrogated party only acquires the right to stipulated interest to the extent

Le subrogé dans une créance principale n'acquiert le droit aux intérêts conventionnels que dans la mesure où ils se rapportent

that it pertains to the period following the transfer.

à la période écoulée depuis la transmission.

Art. 154. (6.2.2.9b) De schuldeiser is jegens degene die, zo hij de vordering voldoet, zal worden gesubrogeerd, verplicht zich te onthouden van elke gedraging die ten koste van deze afbreuk doet aan de rechten waarin hij mag verwachten krachtens de subrogatie te zullen treden.

The creditor must abstain from any act that would prejudice the rights which a person may expect to receive pursuant to subrogation, if by his payment he would be subrogated.

Le créancier est tenu envers celui qui, en payant la créance, y sera subrogé de s'abstenir de tout acte qui peut nuire à ce dernier en portant atteinte aux droits dont celui-ci peut s'attendre à devenir titulaire en vertu de la subrogation.

AFDELING 3 Schuld- en contractsoverneming

Section 3 Take-over of debts and contracts

Section troisième De la reprise de dette et de la cession de contrat

Art. 155. (6.2.3.10) Een schuld gaat van de schuldenaar over op een derde, indien deze haar van de schuldenaar overneemt. De schuldoverneming heeft pas werking jegens de schuldeiser, indien deze zijn toestemming geeft nadat partijen hem van de overneming kennis hebben gegeven.

A debt is transferred from the debtor to a third party, if the latter takes it over from the debtor. The take-over only has effect against the creditor if he gives his consent, after the parties have notified him of the take-over.

Une dette se transmet du débiteur à un tiers si celui-ci la lui reprend[1]. La reprise ne produit effet à l'égard du créancier que si ce dernier y consent après que les parties l'en ont informé.

Art. 156. (6.2.3.11) - 1. Heeft de schuldeiser bij voorbaat zijn toestemming tot een schuldoverneming gegeven, dan vindt de overgang plaats, zodra de schuldenaar tot overeenstemming is gekomen met de derde en partijen de schuldeiser schriftelijk van de overneming kennis hebben gegeven.
- 2. De schuldeiser kan een bij voorbaat gegeven toestemming niet herroepen, tenzij hij zich de bevoegdheid daartoe bij de toestemming heeft voorbehouden.

1. Where the creditor has consented in advance to the take-over of a debt, the transfer takes place as soon as the debtor and the third party have reached an agreement and they have notified the creditor of the take-over in writing.

1. Lorsque le créancier a consenti à l'avance à la reprise de dette, la transmission a lieu dès que le débiteur s'est entendu avec le tiers et que les parties en ont informé par écrit le créancier.

[1] Le néerlandais emploie l'expression «reprise de dette» pour l'institution que le français désigne habituellement «cession de dette».

2. The creditor may not revoke consent given in advance, unless he has reserved this right at the time of consent.

2. Le créancier ne peut révoquer le consentement donné à l'avance, à moins qu'il ne se soit réservé cette faculté en le donnant.

Art. 157. (6.2.3.12) - 1. De bij de vordering behorende nevenrechten worden na het tijdstip van de overgang tegen de nieuwe in plaats van tegen de oude schuldenaar uitgeoefend.
- 2. Tot zekerheid van de overgegane schuld strekkende rechten van pand en hypotheek op een aan een der partijen toebehorend goed blijven bestaan; die op een niet aan partijen toebehorend goed en rechten uit borgtocht gaan door de overgang teniet, tenzij de pand- of hypotheekgever of borg tevoren in handhaving heeft toegestemd.
- 3. Voorrechten op bepaalde goederen waarop de schuldeiser niet tevens een verhaalsrecht jegens derden heeft, gaan door de overgang teniet, tenzij de schuldoverneming plaatsvindt ter uitvoering van de overdracht van een onderneming waartoe ook het goed waarop het voorrecht rust, behoort. Voorrechten op het vermogen van de schuldenaar gelden na de overgang als voorrechten op het vermogen van de nieuwe schuldenaar.
- 4. Bedongen renten en boeten, alsmede dwangsommen die vóór de overgang aan de schuldenaar werden opgelegd, worden door de nieuwe in plaats van door de oude schuldenaar verschuldigd, voor zover zij na het tijdstip van de overgang zijn opeisbaar geworden of verbeurd.

1. After the time of transfer, rights which are accessory to the claim are exercised against the new rather than the former debtor.
2. Rights of pledge and hypothec on property belonging to one of the parties, and serving as security for the transferred debt continue to exist; such rights on property not belonging to the parties and rights of suretyship are extinguished by the transfer, unless the grantor of the pledge or hypothec or the surety has previously consented to the continuance of these rights.

3. Privileges on certain specific property on which the creditor does not also have a right of recourse with respect to third parties, are extinguished by the transfer, unless the take-over of the debt takes place to execute the transfer of an undertaking which also includes the property subject to the privilege. After the transfer, privileges attaching to the patrimony of the debtor are deemed to be attached to the patrimony of the new debtor.
4. The new rather than the former debtor is responsible for stipulated interest and penalties, as well as for

1. Les droits accessoires afférents à la créance s'exercent après la transmission contre le nouveau débiteur, et non contre l'ancien.
2. Les droits de gage et d'hypothèque garantissant la dette transmise, qui grèvent les biens appartenant à l'une des parties, continuent d'exister; ceux qui grèvent un bien n'appartenant pas aux parties, ainsi que les droits résultant d'un cautionnement s'éteignent par la transmission, à moins que celui qui a constitué le gage ou l'hypothèque, ou que la caution n'ait consenti auparavant à ce qu'ils soient maintenus.
3. Les privilèges grevant certains biens sur lesquels le créancier n'a pas également un droit de recouvrement à l'égard de tiers s'éteignent par la transmission, à moins que la reprise de dette n'ait lieu en exécution du transfert d'une entreprise dont fait également partie le bien grevé du privilège. Les privilèges portant sur le patrimoine du débiteur sont réputés, après la transmission, grever le patrimoine du nouveau débiteur.

4. Les intérêts et peines conventionnels, de même que les astreintes imposées au débiteur avant la transmission sont dus par

forfeitures imposed upon the debtor before the transfer, to the extent that they have become exigible or forfeited after the time of transfer.

le nouveau débiteur, et non par l'ancien, dans la mesure où ils sont devenus exigibles ou ont été encourus après le moment de la transmission.

Art. 158. (6.2.3.13) Indien de rechtsverhouding tussen de vorige en de nieuwe schuldenaar op grond waarvan de schuld is overgenomen, nietig, vernietigd of ontbonden is, kan de schuldeiser de schuld weer op de vorige schuldenaar doen overgaan door daartoe strekkende kennisgevingen aan de beide betrokken partijen; elk van hen kan de schuldeiser daartoe een redelijke termijn stellen.

If the juridical relationship between the former and the new debtor pursuant to which the debt has been taken over, is null, has been annulled, or has been set aside, the creditor may have the debt transferred back to the former debtor by notices to that effect addressed to both parties involved; each of them can give the creditor a reasonable period to that effect.

Si le rapport juridique entre le précédent et le nouveau débiteur en vertu duquel la dette a été reprise est nul, annulé ou résilié, le créancier peut de nouveau faire passer la dette au débiteur précédent par des avis à cet effet aux deux parties concernées; chacune d'elles peut fixer au créancier un délai raisonnable à cette fin.

Art. 159. (6.2.3.14) - 1. Een partij bij een overeenkomst kan haar rechtsverhouding tot de wederpartij met medewerking van deze laatste overdragen aan een derde bij een tussen haar en de derde opgemaakte akte.
- 2. Hierdoor gaan alle rechten en verplichtingen over op de derde, voor zover niet ten aanzien van bijkomstige of reeds opeisbaar geworden rechten of verplichtingen anders is bepaald.
- 3. Artikel 156 en de leden 1-3 van artikel 157 zijn van overeenkomstige toepassing.

1. A contracting party can, with the cooperation of his co-contracting party, transfer his juridical relationship with this co-contracting party to a third party by a deed drawn up between himself and the third party.
2. The foregoing has the effect of transferring all rights and obligations to the third party, to the extent not otherwise provided for with respect to rights and obligations which are secondary or have already become exigible.
3. Article 156 and paragraphs 1 - 3 of article 157 apply *mutatis mutandis*.

1. Une partie à un contrat peut, avec le concours de l'autre partie, transmettre son rapport juridique avec cette dernière à un tiers, par un acte dressé entre elle et le tiers.

2. La transmission fait passer tous les droits et obligations au tiers, dans la mesure où il n'a pas été disposé autrement au sujet de droits ou obligations secondaires ou de ceux qui sont déjà devenus exigibles.

3. L'article 156 et les paragraphes 1er à 3 de l'article 157 s'appliquent par analogie.

AFDELING 4 Afstand en vermenging

Section 4
Renunciation and confusion

Section quatrième
De la renonciation et de la confusion

Art. 160. (6.2.4.14a) - 1. Een verbintenis gaat teniet door een overeenkomst van de schuldeiser met de schuldenaar, waarbij hij van zijn vorderingsrecht afstand doet.
- 2. Een door de schuldeiser tot de schuldenaar gericht aanbod tot afstand om niet geldt als aanvaard, wanneer de schuldenaar van het aanbod heeft kennisgenomen en het niet onverwijld heeft afgewezen.
- 3. De artikelen 48 leden 1 en 2 en 49 leden 1-3 zijn van overeenkomstige toepassing.

1. An obligation is extinguished by a contract between creditor and debtor whereby the creditor renounces his claim.
2. An offer to renunciate by gratuitous title, addressed by the creditor to the debtor, is deemed accepted when it has come to the attention of the debtor and he has not rejected it without delay.
3. Articles 48, paragraphs 1 and 2, and 49, paragraphs 1-3 apply *mutatis mutandis*.

1. L'obligation s'éteint par contrat entre le créancier et le débiteur, par lequel le premier renonce à sa créance.
2. L'offre de renonciation à titre gratuit adressée par le créancier au débiteur est réputée acceptée lorsque le débiteur en a pris connaissance et ne l'a pas rejetée sans tarder.
3. Les paragraphes 1er et 2 de l'article 48 et les paragraphes 1er à 3 de l'art. 49 s'appliquent par analogie.

Art. 161. (6.2.4.14b) - 1. Een verbintenis gaat teniet door vermenging, wanneer door overgang van de vordering of de schuld de hoedanigheid van schuldeiser en die van schuldenaar zich in één persoon verenigen.
- 2. Het vorige lid is niet van toepassing:
a. zolang de vordering en de schuld in van elkaar gescheiden vermogens vallen;
b. in geval van overdracht overeenkomstig artikel 93 van Boek 3 van een vordering aan toonder of order;
c. indien de voormelde vereniging van hoedanigheden het gevolg is van een rechtshandeling onder ontbindende voorwaarde, zolang niet vaststaat dat de voorwaarde niet meer in vervulling kan gaan.
- 3. Tenietgaan van een verbintenis door vermenging laat de op de vordering rustende rechten van derden onverlet.

1. An obligation is extinguished by confusion when, by the transfer of a claim or debt, the qualities of creditor and debtor are combined in one and the same person.
2. The preceding paragraph does not apply:
a. as long as the claim and the debt form part of separate patrimonies;
b. in case of transfer, according to article 93 of Book 3, of a claim payable to bearer or order;

1. L'obligation s'éteint par confusion, lorsque la transmission de la créance ou de la dette réunit en une seule personne les qualités de créancier et de débiteur.
2. Le paragraphe précédent ne s'applique pas:
a. Tant que la créance et la dette font partie de patrimoines distincts;
b. Au cas de transmission, conformément à l'article 93 du Livre troisième, d'une créance au porteur ou à ordre;

c. if the aforementioned combination of the qualities of creditor and debtor is the result of a juridical act under a resolutory condition, as long as it has not been determined that the condition can no longer be fulfilled.
3. The extinction of an obligation by confusion does not affect the rights of third persons encumbering the claim.

c. Si la susdite réunion des qualités résulte d'un acte juridique sous condition résolutoire, tant qu'il n'est pas établi que la condition ne peut plus être remplie;

3. L'extinction de l'obligation par confusion laisse intacts les droits des tiers grevant la créance.

TITEL 3 ONRECHTMATIGE DAAD

TITLE 3 UNLAWFUL ACT[1]

TITRE TROISIÈME DE L'ACTE ILLICITE

AFDELING 1 Algemene bepalingen

Section 1 General provisions

Section première Dispositions générales

Art. 162. (6.3.1.1) - 1. Hij die jegens een ander een onrechtmatige daad pleegt, welke hem kan worden toegerekend, is verplicht de schade die de ander dientengevolge lijdt, te vergoeden.
- 2. Als onrechtmatige daad worden aangemerkt een inbreuk op een recht en een doen of nalaten in strijd met een wettelijke plicht of met hetgeen volgens ongeschreven recht in het maatschappelijk verkeer betaamt, een en ander behoudens de aanwezigheid van een rechtvaardigingsgrond.
- 3. Een onrechtmatige daad kan aan de dader worden toegerekend, indien zij te wijten is aan zijn schuld of aan een oorzaak welke krachtens de wet of de in het verkeer geldende opvattingen voor zijn rekening komt.

1. A person who commits an unlawful act toward another which can be imputed to him, must repair the damage which the other person suffers as a consequence thereof.
2. Except where there is a ground of justification, the following acts are deemed to be unlawful: the violation of a right, an act or omission violating a statutory duty or a rule of unwritten law pertaining to proper social conduct.
3. An unlawful act can be imputed to its author if it results from his fault or from a cause for which he is answerable according to law or common opinion.

1. Celui qui commet envers autrui un acte illicite pouvant lui être imputé est tenu de réparer le dommage que ce dernier en subit.

2. Sont réputés illicites, sauf fait justificatif, l'atteinte à un droit ainsi que l'acte ou l'omission contraire à un devoir légal ou à une règle non écrite qui énonce ce qui est convenable dans le commerce social.

3. L'acte illicite est imputable à l'auteur s'il résulte de sa faute ou d'une cause dont il doit répondre en vertu de la loi ou suivant l'opinion généralement admise.

---

[1] The term "unlawful act" was chosen to avoid (a) using the word "delict" with its criminal law connotations, (b) a choice between the outdated civilian terms "delict" and "quasi-delict", and "offence" and "quasi-offence", and (c) the common law connotations of the term "tort".

Art. 163. (6.3.1.2) Geen verplichting tot schadevergoeding bestaat, wanneer de geschonden norm niet strekt tot bescherming tegen de schade zoals de benadeelde die heeft geleden.

There is no obligation to repair damage when the violated norm does not have as its purpose the protection from damage such as that suffered by the victim.

L'obligation de réparation n'existe pas lorsque la norme transgressée n'a pas pour objet la protection contre le dommage tel que la personne lésée l'a subi.

Art. 164. (6.3.1.2a) Een gedraging van een kind dat de leeftijd van veertien jaren nog niet heeft bereikt, kan aan hem niet als een onrechtmatige daad worden toegerekend.

Conduct of a child under fourteen years of age cannot be imputed to him as an unlawful act.

La conduite d'un enfant qui n'a pas encore atteint l'âge de quatorze ans ne peut lui être imputée comme acte illicite.

Art. 165. (6.3.1.2b) - 1. De omstandigheid dat een als een doen te beschouwen gedraging van een persoon van veertien jaren of ouder verricht is onder invloed van een geestelijke of lichamelijke tekortkoming, is geen beletsel haar als een onrechtmatige daad aan de dader toe te rekenen.
- 2. Is jegens de benadeelde tevens een derde wegens onvoldoende toezicht aansprakelijk, dan is deze derde jegens de dader verplicht tot bijdragen in de schadevergoeding voor het gehele bedrag van zijn aansprakelijkheid jegens de benadeelde.

1. The fact that a person of fourteen years of age or older has adopted a conduct, which must be considered as an act, under the influence of a mental or physical handicap, does not prevent it from being imputed to him as an unlawful act.
2. Where a third person is also liable to the victim for insufficient supervision, that third person is obliged toward the wrongdoer to contribute to the reparation of the damage for the full amount of his liability to the victim.

1. Le fait qu'une personne de quatorze ans ou plus a adopté une conduite, qu'il faut considérer comme un acte, sous l'effet d'une incapacité mentale ou physique n'empêche pas que cette conduite lui soit imputée comme acte illicite.

2. Le tiers qui, en raison d'une surveillance insuffisante, est coresponsable envers la personne lésée est tenu, à l'égard de l'auteur du dommage, de contribuer à la réparation jusqu'à concurrence de la somme intégrale de sa responsabilité envers la personne lésée.

Art. 166. (6.3.1.5) - 1. Indien één van tot een groep behorende personen onrechtmatig schade toebrengt en de kans op het aldus toebrengen van schade deze personen had behoren te weerhouden van hun gedragingen in groepsverband, zijn zij hoofdelijk aansprakelijk indien deze gedragingen hun kunnen worden toegerekend.
- 2. Zij moeten onderling voor gelijke delen in de schadevergoeding bijdragen, tenzij in de omstandigheden van het geval de billijkheid een andere verdeling vordert.

1. If a member of a group of persons unlawfully causes damage and if the risk of causing this damage should have prevented these persons from their collective conduct, they are solidarily liable if the conduct can be imputed to them.
2. Among themselves, they must contribute to the reparation of the damage in equal parts, unless in the circumstances of the case equity requires a different apportionment.

1. Si une personne faisant partie d'un groupe cause un dommage de manière illicite et si le risque de causer ainsi un dommage avait dû retenir les membres du groupe d'adopter ùne telle conduite collective, ceux-ci sont solidairement responsables si cette conduite leur est imputable.
2. Ils contribuent, entre eux, à la réparation du dommage par parts égales, à moins que, en la circonstance, l'équité exige une répartition différente.

Art. 167. (6.3.1.5a) - 1. Wanneer iemand krachtens deze titel jegens een ander aansprakelijk is ter zake van een onjuiste of door onvolledigheid misleidende publicatie van gegevens van feitelijke aard, kan de rechter hem op vordering van die ander veroordelen tot openbaarmaking van een rectificatie op een door de rechter aan te geven wijze.
- 2. Hetzelfde geldt, indien aansprakelijkheid ontbreekt, omdat de publicatie aan de dader wegens diens onbekendheid met de onjuistheid of onvolledigheid niet als een onrechtmatige daad is toe te rekenen.
- 3. In het geval van lid 2 kan de rechter die de vordering toewijst bepalen dat de kosten van het geding en van de openbaarmaking van de rectificatie geheel of gedeeltelijk moeten worden gedragen door degene die de vordering heeft ingesteld. Elk der partijen heeft voor het gedeelte van de kosten van het geding en van de openbaarmaking van de rectificatie dat ingevolge de uitspraak door haar moet worden gedragen, verhaal op ieder die voor de door de publicatie ontstane schade aansprakelijk is.

1. Where, pursuant to this title, a person is liable to another for inaccurate publication or, because of incompleteness, misleading publication of data of a factual nature, the judge may, upon the demand of that other person, order him to publish a rectification in a manner to be determined by the judge.
2. The same applies if there is no liability as a result of the fact that the publication cannot be imputed to the author as an unlawful act because of his unawareness of the inaccuracy or incompleteness.
3. In the event that paragraph 2 applies, the judge who grants the action may determine that the costs of the action and of the publication of the rectification must be wholly or partially borne by the person who has instituted the action. Each of the parties may take recourse against any person who is liable for the damage resulting from the publication,

1. Lorsqu'une personne, par application du présent titre, est responsable à l'égard d'une autre personne en raison d'une publication de données factuelles qui est inexacte ou, par son caractère incomplet, trompeuse, le juge peut, à la demande de cette dernière, la condamner à publier une rectification de la manière qu'il détermine.
2. Il en est de même dans le cas d'absence de responsabilité du fait que la publication n'est pas imputable comme acte illicite à l'auteur qui en ignorait le caractère inexact ou incomplet.
3. Dans le cas visé au paragraphe 2, le juge, en accueillant la demande, peut déterminer que les frais du procès et de la publication de la rectification sont assumés en tout ou en partie par celui qui a intenté la demande. Chacune des parties a, pour la partie des frais du procès et de la publication de la rectification, qui lui incombe par l'effet du jugement, recours contre toute personne

for that part of the costs of the action and of the publication of the rectification that must be borne by him pursuant to the judgment.

responsable du dommage résultant de la publication.

Art. 168. (6.3.1.5b) - 1. De rechter kan een vordering, strekkende tot verbod van een onrechtmatige gedraging, afwijzen op de grond dat deze gedraging op grond van zwaarwegende maatschappelijke belangen behoort te worden geduld. De benadeelde behoudt zijn recht op vergoeding van de schade overeenkomstig de onderhavige titel.
- 2. In het geval van artikel 170 is de ondergeschikte voor deze schade niet aansprakelijk.
- 3. Wordt aan een veroordeling tot schadevergoeding of tot het stellen van zekerheid daarvoor niet voldaan, dan kan de rechter alsnog een verbod van de gedraging opleggen.

1. The judge may reject an action to obtain an order prohibiting unlawful conduct on the ground that such conduct should be tolerated for reasons of important societal interests. The victim retains his right to reparation of damage according to this title.
2. In the case referred to in article 170, the servant is not liable for this damage.

3. The judge may as yet issue an order prohibiting the conduct where a condemnation to pay damages or to furnish security is not complied with.

1. Le juge peut rejeter la demande visant à faire interdire une conduite illicite, au motif que cette conduite doit être tolérée en raison d'intérêts pressants de la société. La personne lésée conserve son droit à la réparation du dommage conformément au présent titre.
2. Dans le cas visé à l'article 170, le préposé n'est pas responsable de ce dommage.
3. Lorsque la condamnation à réparation ou à fournir des sûretés n'est pas respectée, le juge peut alors prononcer l'interdiction de la conduite en question.

AFDELING 2 Aansprakelijkheid voor personen en zaken

Section 2
Liability for persons and things

Section deuxième
De la responsabilité du fait d'autrui et du fait des choses

Art. 169. (6.3.2.1) - 1. Voor schade aan een derde toegebracht door een als een doen te beschouwen gedraging van een kind dat nog niet de leeftijd van veertien jaren heeft bereikt en aan wie deze gedraging als een onrechtmatige daad zou kunnen worden toegerekend als zijn leeftijd daaraan niet in de weg zou staan, is degene die de ouderlijke macht of de voogdij over het kind uitoefent, aansprakelijk.
- 2. Voor schade, aan een derde toegebracht door een fout van een kind dat de leeftijd van veertien jaren al wel maar die van zestien jaren nog niet heeft bereikt, is degene die de ouderlijke macht of de voogdij over het kind uitoefent, aansprakelijk, tenzij hem niet kan worden verweten dat hij de gedraging van het kind niet heeft belet.

1. A person who exercises parental authority or guardianship over a child of under fourteen years of age is liable for damage done to another by such conduct

1. Celui qui exerce l'autorité parentale ou la tutelle sur un enfant qui n'a pas encore atteint l'âge de quatorze ans est responsable du dommage causé à un tiers par une

of that child which must be considered as an act, where this act, but for the child's age, could be imputed to him as an unlawful act.
2. A person who exercises parental authority or guardianship over a child between fourten and sixteen years of age is liable for damage done to another by the fault of that child, unless one cannot reproach that person for not preventing the conduct of the child.

conduite de l'enfant, qu'il faut considérer comme un acte, et qui lui serait imputé comme un acte illicite si son âge n'y faisait obstacle.
2. Celui qui exerce l'autorité parentale ou la tutelle sur un enfant qui a atteint l'âge de quatorze ans, mais non celui de seize ans, est responsable du dommage causé à un tiers par la faute de l'enfant, à moins qu'aucun reproche ne puisse lui être fait de n'avoir pas empêché la conduite de ce dernier.

Art. 170. (6.3.2.2) - 1. Voor schade, aan een derde toegebracht door een fout van een ondergeschikte, is degene in wiens dienst de ondergeschikte zijn taak vervult aansprakelijk, indien de kans op de fout door de opdracht tot het verrichten van deze taak is vergroot en degene in wiens dienst hij stond, uit hoofde van hun desbetreffende rechtsbetrekking zeggenschap had over de gedragingen waarin de fout was gelegen.
- 2. Stond de ondergeschikte in dienst van een natuurlijke persoon en was hij niet werkzaam voor een beroep of bedrijf van deze persoon, dan is deze slechts aansprakelijk, indien de ondergeschikte bij het begaan van de fout handelde ter vervulling van de hem opgedragen taak.
- 3. Zijn de ondergeschikte en degene in wiens dienst hij stond, beiden voor de schade aansprakelijk, dan behoeft de ondergeschikte in hun onderlinge verhouding niet in de schadevergoeding bij te dragen, tenzij de schade een gevolg is van zijn opzet of bewuste roekeloosheid. Uit de omstandigheden van het geval, mede gelet op de aard van hun verhouding, kan anders voortvloeien dan in de vorige zin is bepaald.

1. The master in whose service a servant fulfills his duties is liable for damage done to another by the fault of the servant, if the likelihood that a fault would be committed has been increased by the order to perform the duties of the servant, and if the master, pursuant to his juridical relationship with the servant, had control over the conduct constituting the fault.
2. Where the servant did not work in the framework of the master's profession or business, a master who is a natural person is only liable if the servant, in committing the fault, acted in the performance of the duty which he had been ordered to carry out.

3. Where both the master and the servant are liable for the damage, the servant, in his mutual relationship with the master, does not have to contribute to the reparation of the damage, unless the damage results from the servant's malice,

1. Lorsqu'un préposé cause par sa faute un dommage à un tiers, le commettant au service duquel il remplit ses fonctions en est responsable si l'ordre d'exécuter les fonctions du préposé a augmenté la probabilité de la faute et si le commettant, en vertu de son rapport juridique avec le préposé, avait autorité sur les actes constitutifs de la faute.

2. Lorsque le préposé est au service d'une personne physique et qu'il ne travaille pas dans le cadre des activités professionnelles ou de l'entreprise de celle-ci, le commettant est responsable seulement si le préposé, au moment de commettre la faute, agissait dans l'exécution de la fonction qui lui a été confiée.
3. Lorsque le préposé et le commettant sont tous deux responsables du dommage, le préposé, dans leur rapport réciproque, ne contribue pas à la réparation, à moins que le dommage ne résulte de son dol ou d'une insouciance délibérée. Il peut découler des

or from his conscious recklessness. The circumstances of the case, also taking into account the nature of their relationship, may produce a result which is different from the one determined in the previous sentence.

circonstances de l'espèce, compte tenu également de la nature du rapport, une solution différente de celle prévue à la phrase précédente.

Art. 171. (6.3.2.3) Indien een niet ondergeschikte die in opdracht van een ander werkzaamheden ter uitoefening van diens bedrijf verricht, jegens een derde aansprakelijk is voor een bij die werkzaamheden begane fout, is ook die ander jegens de derde aansprakelijk.

If a non-servant who performs activities to carry on the business of another person at the latter's orders, is liable toward a third person for a fault committed in the course of those activities, that other person is also liable to the third person.

Si une personne qui exerce des activités dans le cadre de l'entreprise d'une autre et sur les instructions de celle-ci, sans être son préposé, est responsable envers un tiers par suite d'une faute commise dans le cours de ces activités, l'autre personne est, elle aussi, responsable envers le tiers.

Art. 172. (6.3.2.4) Indien een gedraging van een vertegenwoordiger ter uitoefening van de hem als zodanig toekomende bevoegdheden een fout jegens een derde inhoudt, is ook de vertegenwoordigde jegens de derde aansprakelijk.

If the conduct of a representative in the exercise of the powers resulting from the representation constitutes a fault towards another, the person who is represented is also liable toward that other person.

Si la conduite du représentant dans l'exercice des pouvoirs lui revenant en cette qualité constitue une faute envers un tiers, le représenté est, lui aussi, responsable envers ce tiers.

Art. 173. (6.3.2.5) - 1. De bezitter van een roerende zaak waarvan bekend is dat zij, zo zij niet voldoet aan de eisen die men in de gegeven omstandigheden aan de zaak mag stellen, een bijzonder gevaar voor personen of zaken oplevert, is, wanneer dit gevaar zich verwezenlijkt, aansprakelijk, tenzij aansprakelijkheid op grond van de vorige afdeling zou hebben ontbroken indien hij dit gevaar op het tijdstip van ontstaan daarvan zou hebben gekend.

- 2. Indien de zaak niet aan de in het vorige lid bedoelde eisen voldoet wegens een gebrek als bedoeld in afdeling 3 van titel 3, bestaat geen aansprakelijkheid op grond van het vorige lid voor schade als in die afdeling bedoeld, tenzij

a. alle omstandigheden in aanmerking genomen, aannemelijk is dat het gebrek niet bestond op het tijdstip waarop het produkt in het verkeer is gebracht of dat het gebrek op een later tijdstip is ontstaan; of

b. het betreft zaakschade ter zake waarvan krachtens afdeling 3 van titel 3 geen recht op vergoeding bestaat op grond van de in die afdeling geregelde franchise.

- 3. De vorige leden zijn niet van toepassing op dieren, motorrijtuigen, schepen en luchtvaartuigen.

1. The possessor of a moveable thing which is known to constitute a special danger for persons or things if it does not meet the standards which, in the given

1. Le possesseur d'une chose mobilière qui, de commune renommée, constitue un danger particulier pour les personnes ou les choses si elle ne remplit pas les conditions

circumstances, may be set for such a thing, is liable when this danger materializes, unless, pursuant to the preceding section, there would have been no liability if the possessor would have known the danger at the time it has arisen.

2. If the thing does not meet the standards referred to in the preceding paragraph because of a defect as referred to in section 3 of title 3, there is no liability on the basis of the preceding paragraph for damage as referred to in that section, unless

a. taking into consideration all the circumstances, it is likely that the defect did not exist at the time when the product was put into circulation, or that the defect has arisen at a later date; or

b. damage to things is concerned for which, pursuant to section 3 of title 3, there is no right to reparation because of the franchise provided for in that section.

3. The preceding paragraphs do not apply to animals, motor vehicles, vessels and aircraft.

habituellement requises pour une telle chose en la circonstance, est responsable lorsque le danger se réalise, à moins que la responsabilité, en vertu de la section précédente, n'eût pas été engagée s'il avait eu connaissance du danger au moment où celui-ci s'est déclaré.

2. Si la chose ne répond pas aux conditions visées au paragraphe précédent en raison d'un vice visé à la section troisième du titre troisième, la responsabilité en vertu du paragraphe précédent pour le dommage visé à cette section n'est pas engagée, à moins

a. Que, toutes circonstances prises en compte, il soit plausible que le vice n'existait pas au moment où le produit a été mis en circulation ou que le vice soit né à une date subséquente;

b. Qu'il s'agisse de dommage aux choses, qui, en vertu de la section troisième du titre troisième, ne donne pas droit à réparation en raison de la franchise prévue à cette section.

3. Les paragraphes précédents ne s'appliquent pas aux animaux, aux véhicules à moteur, aux navires et aux aéronefs.

Art. 174. (6.3.2.7) - 1. De bezitter van een opstal die niet voldoet aan de eisen die men daaraan in de gegeven omstandigheden mag stellen, en daardoor gevaar voor personen of zaken oplevert, is, wanneer dit gevaar zich verwezenlijkt, aansprakelijk, tenzij aansprakelijkheid op grond van de vorige afdeling zou hebben ontbroken indien hij dit gevaar op het tijdstip van het ontstaan ervan zou hebben gekend.

- 2. Bij erfpacht rust de aansprakelijkheid op de bezitter van het erfpachtsrecht. Bij openbare wegen rust zij op het overheidslichaam dat moet zorgen dat de weg in goede staat verkeert, bij leidingen op de leidingbeheerder, behalve voor zover de leiding zich bevindt in een gebouw of werk en strekt tot toevoer of afvoer ten behoeve van dat gebouw of werk.

- 3. Onder opstal in dit artikel worden verstaan gebouwen en werken, die duurzaam met de grond zijn verenigd, hetzij rechtstreeks, hetzij door vereniging met andere gebouwen of werken.

- 4. Degene die in de openbare registers als eigenaar van de opstal of van de grond staat ingeschreven, wordt vermoed de bezitter van de opstal te zijn.

- 5. Voor de toepassing van dit artikel wordt onder openbare weg mede begrepen het weglichaam, alsmede de weguitrusting.

1. The possessor of a construction which does not meet the standards which, in the given circumstances, may be set for it and thereby constitutes a danger for persons or things, is liable

1. Le possesseur d'une construction qui ne remplit pas les conditions qu'on peut exiger en l'espèce et qui, de ce fait, constitue un danger pour les personnes ou les choses est responsable lorsque le danger se réalise,

when this danger materializes, unless, pursuant to the preceding section, there would have been no liability if the possessor would have known the danger at the time it has arisen.
2. In the case of emphyteusis, the liability rests upon the possessor of the right of emphyteusis. In the case of public roads, it rests upon the public authority in charge of the proper maintenance of the roads; in the case of conduits, it rests upon the person managing them, except to the extent that the conduit is located in a building or work and serves to supply or drain that building or work.
3. In this article, construction means buildings and works, durably united with land, either directly or through incorporation with other buildings or works.
4. The person who is entered in the public registers as owner of the construction or the land, is presumed to be the possessor of the construction.
5. For the purposes of this article, a public road includes the foundation and surface of the road, and their accessories.

à moins que la responsabilité, en vertu de la section précédente, n'eût pas été engagée s'il avait eu connaissance du danger au moment où celui-ci s'est déclaré.
2. Dans le cas d'une emphytéose, la responsabilité incombe au possesseur du droit emphytéotique. Dans le cas des chemins publics, elle incombe à l'autorité publique chargée d'assurer leur bon état; dans le cas des conduites, elle incombe à la personne chargée de l'administration, sauf dans la mesure où il s'agit des conduites d'adduction et d'écoulement desservant une construction ou un ouvrage, qui se trouvent à l'intérieur de ceux-ci.
3. Par construction, on entend au présent article la construction et l'ouvrage qui sont unis au fonds de façon durable soit directement, soit par incorporation à d'autres constructions ou ouvrages.
4. Celui qui est inscrit dans les registres publics comme le propriétaire de la construction ou du fonds est présumé être le possesseur de la construction.
5. Pour l'application du présent article, le chemin public englobe les fondations, la chaussée et les accessoires.

Art. 175-178. Gereserveerd.

Reserved (for provisions on dangerous substances).

Réservés (pour des dispositions relatives aux matières dangereuses).

Art. 179. (6.3.2.8) De bezitter van een dier is aansprakelijk voor de door het dier aangerichte schade, tenzij aansprakelijkheid op grond van de vorige afdeling zou hebben ontbroken indien hij de gedraging van het dier waardoor de schade werd toegebracht, in zijn macht zou hebben gehad.

The possessor of an animal is liable for the damage done by the animal, unless, pursuant to the preceding section, there would have been no liability if the possessor would have had control over the behaviour of the animal by which the damage was done.

Le possesseur d'un animal est responsable du dommage causé par celui-ci, à moins que la responsabilité, en vertu de la section précédente, n'eût pas été engagée s'il avait eu le contrôle du comportement de l'animal par lequel le dommage a été causé.

Art. 180. (6.3.2.9) - 1. In de gevallen van de artikelen 173, 174 en 179 zijn medebezitters hoofdelijk aansprakelijk.
- 2. In geval van overdracht van een zaak onder opschortende voorwaarde van voldoening van een tegenprestatie rust de aansprakelijkheid uit de artikelen 173, 174 en 179 vanaf het tijdstip van deze overdracht op de verkrijger.

1. In the cases referred to in articles 173, 174 and 179, co-possessors are solidarily liable.
2. In the event of transfer of a thing under the suspensive condition that a counterprestation be performed, the liability resulting from articles 173, 174 and 179 rests upon the acquirer as of the time of this transfer.

1. Dans les cas visés aux articles 173, 174 et 179, les co-possesseurs sont solidairement responsables.
2. Dans le cas de transfert d'une chose sous condition suspensive du paiement d'une contre-prestation, la responsabilité visée aux articles 173, 174 et 179 incombe à l'acquéreur à compter du transfert.

Art. 181. (6.3.2.10) - 1. Worden de in de artikelen 173, 174 en 179 bedoelde zaken, opstallen of dieren gebruikt in de uitoefening van een bedrijf, dan rust de aansprakelijkheid uit de artikelen 173, 174 lid 1 en lid 2, eerste zin, en 179 op degene die het bedrijf uitoefent, tenzij het een opstal betreft en het ontstaan van de schade niet met de uitoefening van het bedrijf in verband staat.
- 2. Worden de zaken, opstallen of dieren in de uitoefening van een bedrijf gebruikt door ze ter beschikking te stellen voor gebruik in het bedrijf van een ander, dan wordt die ander als de uit hoofde van het vorige lid aansprakelijke persoon aangemerkt.

1. Where the things, constructions or animals referred to in articles 173, 174 and 179 are used to carry on a business, the liability referred to in articles 173, 174 paragraphs 1 and 2 first sentence, and 179 rests upon the person carrying on the business, unless a construction is involved and the origin of the damage is not related to the carrying on of the business.
2. Where things, constructions or animals are used in carrying on a business by putting them at the disposal of another person carrying on a business, that other person is deemed to be the person who is liable pursuant to the preceding paragraph.

1. Lorsque les choses, constructions ou animaux visés aux articles 173, 174 et 179 sont employés dans le cadre d'une entreprise, la responsabilité visée à l'article 173, 174, paragraphes 1er et 2, première phrase, et 179 incombe à celui qui exerce cette entreprise, à moins qu'il ne s'agisse d'une construction et que la réalisation du dommage ne soit sans rapport avec l'entreprise.
2. Lorsque l'emploi des choses, constructions ou animaux dans le cadre d'une entreprise consiste à les mettre à la disposition d'une autre personne pour usage dans le cadre de l'entreprise de celle-ci, cette dernière est réputée être la personne responsable pour l'application du paragraphe précédent.

Art. 182. Gereserveerd.

Reserved.

Réservé.

Art. 183. (6.3.2.11) - 1. Ter zake van aansprakelijkheid op grond van deze afdeling kan de aangesprokene geen beroep doen op zijn jeugdige leeftijd of geestelijke of lichamelijke tekortkomingen.
- 2. Degene die de ouderlijke macht of de voogdij uitoefent over een kind dat nog niet de leeftijd van veertien jaren heeft bereikt, is in zijn plaats uit de artikelen 173 en 179 voor de daar bedoelde zaken en dieren aansprakelijk, tenzij deze worden gebruikt in de uitoefening van een bedrijf.

1. For liability pursuant to this section, the defendant may not invoke his young age or a mental or physical handicap.

2. The person who exercises parental authority or guardianship over a child under fourteen years of age, is liable in his place for the things and animals referred to in articles 173 and 179, unless they are used to carry on a business.

1. Celui qui est poursuivi en responsabilité en vertu de la présente section ne peut invoquer son jeune âge ou une incapacité mentale ou physique.

2. Celui qui exerce l'autorité parentale ou la tutelle sur un enfant qui n'a pas encore atteint l'âge de quatorze ans est, par application des articles 173 et 179, responsable, à la place de ce dernier, des choses et animaux qui y sont visés, à moins qu'ils ne soient employés dans le cadre d'une entreprise.

Art. 184. Gereserveerd.

Reserved.

Réservé.

AFDELING 3 Produktenaansprakelijkheid

Section 3 Products liability[1]

Section troisième De la responsabilité du fait des produits[2]

Art. 185. (1407a B.W.) - 1. De producent is aansprakelijk voor schade veroorzaakt door een gebrek in zijn produkt, tenzij:

a. hij het produkt niet in het verkeer heeft gebracht;

b. het, gelet op de omstandigheden, aannemelijk is dat het gebrek dat de schade heeft veroorzaakt, niet bestond op het tijdstip waarop hij het

1 (1) This section contains articles 1407a - 1407i of the existing Civil Code as enacted in order to implement the EEC Council Directive of 25 July 1985 (OJEC No. L 210) on the approximation of the laws, regulations and administrative provisions of the Member States concerning liability for defective products; (2) At the coming into force of the New Civil Code, these articles will be transferred to this section 6.3.3 and will be numbered 185 through 193; (3) At the time of printing the text of this translation, final Parliamentary approval had not yet been given to articles 1407a - 1407i; (4) At the coming into force of the New Civil Code, article 193a (the old art. 1407i) will not be transferred to this section, it being superfluous next to the new article 197 of Book 6 which will contain a reference to article 185 (old article 1407a); (5) The Dutch text of articles 1407a - 1407i was intended to be a fairly literal translation of the text of the EEC Council Directive; where this retranslation from Dutch into English deviates from the English text of the Directive, this is often the consequence of the overall system and terminology of this translation of the New Civil Code.

2 La présente section comporte les articles 1407a à 1407i du Code civil actuel, que le gouvernement néerlandais a adoptés pour se conformer à la directive du Conseil de la Communauté européenne du 25 juillet 1985 (JO CE N° L 210) sur l'harmonisation des législations des États membres en matière de responsabilité pour produits défectueux. Au moment de l'impression de la présente traduction, les articles 1407a à 1497i n'avaient pas encore été adoptés en dernière lecture au Parlement néerlandais. Au moment de la mise en vigueur des parties du nouveau Code civil réunies dans la présente traduction - prévue pour le 1er janvier 1992 - ces articles, à l'exception de l'article 1407i, seront transférés tels quels à la section troisième du titre troisième du Livre sixième du nouveau Code et seront numérotés 185 à 193. L'article 193a (l'ancien art.1407i) ne sera pas transféré au nouveau Code car il sera superflu au regard de l'article 197 du Livre sixième, qui renverra à l'article 185 (l'ancien 1407a) du même Livre. Le texte néerlandais des articles 1407a à 1407i se veut une transposition assez littérale de la directive du Conseil de la CE; dans la retraduction du texte néerlandais vers le français, la terminologie de la directive a été généralement suivie, sauf dans les cas où un terme différent s'imposait en raison du système conceptuel du nouveau Code néerlandais ou de la terminologie adoptée ailleurs dans la traduction. Par exemple, s'agissant de celui qui subit un préjudice en raison du vice caché, le terme «personne lésée» a été préférée à «victime», que l'on trouve dans la directive.

produkt in het verkeer heeft gebracht, dan wel dat gebrek later is ontstaan;

c. het produkt noch voor de verkoop of voor enige andere vorm van verspreiding met een economisch doel van de producent is vervaardigd, noch is vervaardigd of verspreid in het kader van de uitoefening van zijn beroep of bedrijf;

d. het gebrek een gevolg is van het feit dat het produkt in overeenstemming is met dwingende wetsvoorschriften;

e. het op grond van de stand van de wetenschappelijke en technische kennis op het tijdstip waarop hij het produkt in het verkeer bracht, onmogelijk was het bestaan van het gebrek te ontdekken;

f. wat de producent van een grondstof of fabrikant van een onderdeel betreft, het gebrek is te wijten aan het ontwerp van het produkt waarvan de grondstof of het onderdeel een bestanddeel vormt, dan wel aan de instructies die door de fabrikant van het produkt zijn verstrekt.

- 2. De aansprakelijkheid van de producent wordt verminderd of opgeheven rekening houdende met alle omstandigheden, indien de schade is veroorzaakt zowel door een gebrek in het produkt als door schuld van de benadeelde of een persoon voor wie de benadeelde aansprakelijk is.

- 3. De aansprakelijkheid van de producent wordt niet verminderd, indien de schade is veroorzaakt zowel door een gebrek in het produkt als door een gedraging van een derde.

1. The producer shall be liable for the damage caused by a defect in his product:

a. unless he has not put the product into circulation;

b. unless, taking into account the circumstances, it is probable that the defect, which has caused the damage, did not exist at the time when he has put the product into circulation, or that this defect has arisen at a later date;

c. unless the product has not been manufactured for the purpose of sale by the producer or for any other form of distribution by him with an economic objective; or unless it has not been manufactured or distributed in the framework of the course of his profession or business;

d. unless the defect is a result of the fact that the product conforms with mandatory rules issued by the public authorities;

e. unless it was impossible to discover the existence of the defect on the basis of the state of scientific and technical knowledge, at the time when he has put the product into circulation;

1. Le producteur est responsable du dommage causé par le vice de son produit, à moins

a. Qu'il n'ait pas mis en circulation le produit;

b. Que, compte tenu des circonstances, il y ait lieu d'estimer que le vice ayant causé le dommage n'existait pas au moment de la mise en circulation du produit, ou est né postérieurement;

c. Que le produit n'ait été ni fabriqué pour la vente ou une autre forme de distribution dans un but économique du producteur, ni fabriqué ou distribué dans le cadre d'une entreprise ou activité professionnelle;

d. Que le vice soit dû à la conformité du produit aux règles impératives émanant des pouvoirs publics;

e. Que l'état des connaissances scientifiques et techniques au moment de la mise en circulation du produit n'ait pas permis de déceler le vice;

f. unless, as far as the producer of raw material or the manufacturer of a component part is concerned, the defect is due to the design of the product of which the raw material or the component part forms a component; or unless it is due to the instructions which have been given by the manufacturer of the product.

2. The liability of the producer is reduced or eliminated if, taking into account all the circumstances, the damage has been caused both by a defect in the product and by the fault of the victim or of a person for whom the victim is responsible.

3. The liability of the producer is not reduced if the damage has been caused both by a defect in the product and by the conduct of a third person.

f. S'agissant du producteur d'une matière première ou du fabricant d'une partie composante, que le vice soit imputable à la conception du produit dans lequel la matière première ou la partie composante a été incorporée ou aux instructions données par le fabricant du produit.

2. La responsabilité du producteur est réduite ou supprimée, compte tenu des circonstances, si le dommage est causé tant par le vice du produit que par la faute de la personne lésée ou d'une personne dont elle est responsable.

3. La responsabilité du producteur n'est pas réduite si le dommage est causé conjointement par le vice du produit et par la conduite d'un tiers.

Art. 186. (1407b B.W.) - 1. Een produkt is gebrekkig, indien het niet de veiligheid biedt die men daarvan mag verwachten, alle omstandigheden in aanmerking genomen en in het bijzonder

a. de presentatie van het produkt;

b. het redelijkerwijs te verwachten gebruik van het produkt;

c. het tijdstip waarop het produkt in het verkeer wordt gebracht.

- 2. Een produkt mag niet als gebrekkig worden beschouwd uitsluitend omdat nadien een beter produkt in het verkeer is gebracht.

1. A product is defective if it does not provide the safety which one could expect thereof, taking into account all the circumstances and in particular

a. the presentation of the product;

b. the reasonably anticipated use of the product;

c. the time when the product was put into circulation.

2. A product may not be considered defective for the sole reason that a better product has subsequently been put into circulation.

1. Un produit est défectueux, s'il n'offre pas la sécurité qu'on peut en attendre, compte tenu de toutes les circonstances et en particulier

a. De la présentation du produit;

b. De l'usage du produit auquel on peut raisonnablement s'attendre;

c. Du moment de la mise en circulation du produit.

2. Le produit ne peut être considéré comme défectueux par le seul fait qu'un produit plus perfectionné a été mis en circulation postérieurement à lui.

Art. 187. (1407c B.W.) - 1. Onder „produkt" wordt voor de toepassing van artikel 185 tot en met 193a verstaan een roerende zaak, ook nadat deze een bestanddeel is gaan vormen van een andere roerende of onroerende zaak, alsmede electriciteit, zulks met uitzondering van landbouwprodukten en produkten van de jacht. Onder „landbouwprodukten" worden verstaan produkten van de bodem, van de feefokkerij en van de visserij, met uitzondering van produkten die een eerste bewerking of verwerking hebben ondergaan.

- 2. Onder „producent" wordt voor de toepassing van artikel 185 tot en met 193a verstaan de fabrikant van een eindprodukt, de producent van een grondstof of de fabrikant van een onderdeel, alsmede een ieder die zich als

producent presenteert door zijn naam, zijn merk of een ander onderscheidingsteken op het produkt aan te brengen.
- 3. Onverminderd de aansprakelijkheid van de producent, wordt een ieder die een produkt in de Europese Gemeenschap invoert om dit te verkopen, te verhuren, te leasen of anderszins te verstrekken in het kader van zijn commerciële activiteiten, beschouwd als de producent; zijn aansprakelijkheid is dezelfde als die van de producent.
- 4. Indien niet kan worden vastgesteld wie de producent van het produkt is, wordt elke leverancier als producent ervan beschouwd, tenzij hij de benadeelde binnen een redelijke termijn de identiteit meedeelt van de producent of van degene die hem het produkt heeft geleverd. Indien ten aanzien van een in de Europese Gemeenschap geïmporteerd produkt niet kan worden vastgesteld wie de importeur van dat produkt is, wordt eveneens elke leverancier als producent ervan beschouwd, tenzij hij de benadeelde binnen een redelijke termijn de identiteit meedeelt van de importeur in de Gemeenschap of van een leverancier binnen de Gemeenschap die hem het produkt heeft geleverd.

1. For the purposes of articles 185 - 193a inclusive, a <product> means a moveable thing, even after it has become a component of another moveable or immoveable thing, as well as electricity, but with the exception of agricultural and hunting products. <Agricultural products> mean products of the soil, of stock-farming and of fisheries, with the exception of products which have undergone a first treatment or processing.
2. For the purposes of articles 185 - 193a inclusive, a <producer> means the manufacturer of a finished product, the producer of raw material, or the manufacturer of a component part, as well as any person who presents himself as producer by putting his name, trade mark or other distinctive sign on the product.
3. Without prejudice to the liability of the producer, any person who imports a product into the European Community for the purpose of selling, renting, or leasing[1] it, or of making it available in any other fashion in the framework of his commercial activities, is considered as a producer; his liability is identical to that of the producer.
4. If it cannot be ascertained who the producer of a product is, each of its suppliers is considered as producer, unless, within a reasonable period, he communicates to the victim the identity of

1. Par «produit», on entend, aux fins de l'application des articles 185 à 193a compris, une chose mobilière, même après qu'elle a été incorporée à une autre chose mobilière ou immobilière, ainsi que l'électricité, mais à l'exception des produits agricoles et des produits de la chasse. Par «produits agricoles», on entend les produits du sol, de l'élevage et de la pêche, à l'exception des produits qui ont subi une première transformation.
2. Par «producteur», on entend, aux fins de l'application des articles 185 à 193a compris, le fabricant d'un produit fini, le producteur d'une matière première ou le fabricant d'une partie composante, de même que toute personne qui se présente comme producteur en apposant sur le produit son nom, sa marque ou un autre signe distinctif.
3. Sans préjudice de la responsabilité du producteur, est considérée comme producteur toute personne qui importe un produit dans la Communauté économique européenne en vue de vente, de louage, de crédit-bail ou d'une autre forme de distribution dans le cadre de ses activités commerciales; sa responsabilité est identique à celle du producteur.
4. Si le producteur du produit ne peut être identifié, tout fournisseur en sera considéré comme producteur, à moins qu'il ne communique à la personne lésée, dans un délai raisonnable, l'identité du producteur ou

[1] In this article "renting" refers to the traditional contract of lease and hire, whereas "leasing" refers to the more recent procurement and financing technique of precisely that name.

the producer or of the person who has supplied him with the product. If, with respect to a product imported into the European Community, it cannot be ascertained who its importer is, each of the product's suppliers is likewise considered as producer, unless, within a reasonable period, he communicates to the victim the identity of the importer into the Community or of a supplier within the Community who has supplied the product to him.

de la personne qui lui a fourni le produit. Si, en ce qui concerne un produit importé dans la Communauté économique européenne, le producteur ne peut être identifié, tout fournisseur en sera de même considéré comme producteur, à moins qu'il ne communique à la personne lésée, dans un délai raisonnable, l'identité de l'importateur dans la Communauté économique européenne ou du fournisseur à l'intérieur de la Communauté qui lui a fourni le produit.

Art. 188. (1407ca B.W.) De benadeelde moet de schade, het gebrek en het oorzakelijk verband tussen het gebrek en de schade bewijzen.

The victim must prove the damage, the defect and the causal link between the defect and the damage.

La personne lésée est obligée de prouver le dommage, le vice et le lien de causalité entre le vice et le dommage.

Art. 189. (1407d B.W.) Indien verschillende personen op grond van artikel 185, eerste lid, aansprakelijk zijn voor dezelfde schade, is elk hunner voor het geheel aansprakelijk.

If, on the basis of article 185, paragraph 1, several persons are liable for the same damage, each of them shall be liable for the whole.

Si, en application de l'article 185, paragraphe premier, plusieurs personnes sont responsables du même dommage, chacune d'elles est responsable pour le tout.

Art. 190. (1407e B.W.) - 1. De aansprakelijkheid, bedoeld in artikel 185, eerste lid, bestaat voor
a. schade door dood of lichamelijk letsel;
b. schade door het produkt toegebracht aan een andere zaak die gewoonlijk voor gebruik of verbruik in de privésfeer is bestemd en door de benadeelde ook hoofdzakelijk in de privésfeer is gebruikt of verbruikt, met toepassing van een franchise ten belope van f1263,85.
- 2. Het bedrag genoemd in het eerste lid wordt bij algemene maatregel van bestuur aangepast, indien op grond van artikel 18, tweede lid, van de EEG-richtlijn van 25 juli 1985 (*Pb EG* nr. L 210) de in die richtlijn genoemde bedragen worden herzien.

1. The liability referred to in article 185, paragraph 1, covers
a. damage by death or bodily injury;
b. damage done by the product to another thing, which is usually intended for use or consumption in a private capacity, and which has indeed been used or consumed by the victim, principally in a private capacity, under application of a franchise in the amount of DFL. 1,263.85.

1. La responsabilité visée à l'article 185, paragraphe premier, est engagée pour
a. Le dommage résultant de la mort ou de la lésion corporelle
b. Le dommage causé par le produit à une autre chose normalement destinée à l'usage ou à la consommation privés et principalement utilisée ou consommée ainsi par la personne lésée, sous déduction d'une franchise de Hfl. 1 263,85.

2. The amount referred to in paragraph 1 is adjusted by regulation if, on the basis of article 18, paragraph 2, of the EEC Directive of July 25, 1985 (OJEC No. L 210), the amounts mentioned in that Directive are revised.

2. Le montant mentionné au paragraphe premier est rectifiée par décret, si en vertu de l'article 18, paragraphe deuxième, de la directive de la Communauté économique européenne du 25 juillet 1985 (JO CE n° L 210) les montants mentionnés à cette directive sont révisés.

Art. 191. (1407f B.W.) - 1. De rechtsvordering tot schadevergoeding van de benadeelde tegen de producent ingevolge artikel 185, eerste lid, verjaart door verloop van drie jaren na de aanvang van de dag, volgende op die waarop de benadeelde met de schade, het gebrek en de identiteit van de producent bekend is geworden of had moeten worden.
- 2. Het recht op schadevergoeding van de benadeelde jegens de producent ingevolge artikel 185, eerste lid, vervalt door verloop van tien jaren na de aanvang van de dag, volgende die op waarop de producent de zaak die de schade heeft veroorzaakt, in het verkeer heeft gebracht. Hetzelfde geldt voor het recht van een derde die mede voor de schade aansprakelijk is, terzake van regres jegens de producent.

1. The action of the victim against the producer for reparation of damage pursuant to article 185, paragraph 1, is prescribed by the lapse of three years from the beginning of the day following the one on which the victim has become or should have become aware of the damage, the defect and the identity of the producer.
2. The right of the victim against the producer for reparation of damage pursuant to article 185, paragraph 1, is extinguished by the lapse of ten years from the beginning of the day following the one on which the producer has put into circulation the thing which has caused the damage. The same applies to the right of a third person who is also liable for the damage, with respect to his recursory action against the producer.

1. L'action en réparation du dommage intentée par la personne lésée contre le producteur en application de l'article 185, paragraphe premier, se prescrit par trois ans à compter du début du jour suivant celui où la personne lésée a eu ou aurait dû avoir connaissance du dommage, du vice et de l'identité du producteur.

2. Le droit à la réparation du dommage qu'a la personne lésée à l'encontre du producteur en application de l'article 185, paragraphe premier, s'éteint à l'expiration d'un délai de dix ans à compter du début du jour suivant celui où le producteur a mis en circulation le produit qui a causé le dommage. Il en est de même du droit de recours du tiers coresponsable du dommage contre le producteur.

Art. 192. (1407g B.W.) - 1. De aansprakelijkheid van de producent uit hoofde van deze afdeling kan jegens de benadeelde niet worden uitgesloten of beperkt.
- 2. Is jegens de benadeelde tevens een derde aansprakelijk die het produkt niet gebruikt in de uitoefening van een beroep of bedrijf, dan kan niet ten nadele van die derde worden afgeweken van de regels inzake het regres.

1. The liability of the producer pursuant to articles 185 - 193a inclusive may not be excluded or reduced with respect to the victim.

1. La responsabilité du producteur en vertu des articles 185 à 193a compris ne peut être limitée ou exclue à l'égard de la personne lésée.

2. Where a third person, who does not use the product in the course of a profession or business, is also liable toward the victim, no derogation is allowed to the detriment of that third person from the rules regarding the recursory action.

2. Lorsqu'un tiers qui ne se sert pas du produit dans l'exercice d'une activité professionnelle ou d'une entreprise est également responsable à l'égard de la personne lésée, il ne peut être dérogé, au détriment du tiers, aux règles concernant le droit de recours.

Art. 193. (1407h B.W.) Het recht op schadevergoeding jegens de producent uit hoofde van deze afdeling komt de benadeelde toe, onverminderd alle andere rechten of vorderingen.

The right of the victim against the producer for reparation of damage pursuant to articles 185 - 193a inclusive, is without prejudice to all other rights or actions.

Le droit à la réparation du dommage à l'encontre du producteur en application des articles 185 à 193a compris revient à la personne lésée sans préjudice de tous autres droits ou actions.

Art. 193a. (1407i B.W.) - 1. Artikel 185, eerste lid, blijft buiten toepassing

a. bij de vaststelling van het totale bedrag waarvoor aansprakelijkheid naar burgerlijk recht zou bestaan, vereist voor de berekening van het bedrag waarvoor verhaal bestaat krachtens de artikelen 90, eerste lid, van de Wet op de Arbeidsongeschiktheidsverzekering, 52a van de Ziektewet, 83b, eerste lid, van de Ziekenfondswet en 8 van de Wet Arbeidsongeschiktheidsvoorziening Militairen;

b. bij de vaststelling van het bedrag, bedoeld in artikel 3 van de Verhaalswet ongevallen ambtenaren, waarboven de gehoudenheid krachtens die wet of krachtens artikel N 11 van de Algemene Burgerlijke Pensioenwet zich niet uitstrekt.

- 2. Het recht op schadevergoeding jegens de producent uit hoofde van artikel 185 tot en met 193a is niet vatbaar voor subrogatie krachtens artikel 284 van het Wetboek van Koophandel, behoudens voor zover de uitkering door de verzekeraar de aansprakelijkheid van de verzekerde betreft en een ander krachtens deze artikelen mede aansprakelijk is.

- 3. Degene wiens verhaal of subrogatie door het eerste en tweede lid wordt uitgesloten, kan de in het tweede lid bedoelde rechten evenmin krachtens overeenkomst verkrijgen of te zijnen behoeve door de gerechtigde op diens naam doen uitoefenen.

Article 185, paragraph 1 does not apply:

a. in the determination of the total amount for which there would be liability according to private law, this determination being required for the calculation of the amount for which there is recourse pursuant to article 90, paragraph 1 of the *Wet op de Arbeidsongeschiktheids-verzekering*[1], article 52a of the

L'article 185, paragraphe premier, ne s'applique pas

a. Aux fins de la détermination du montant global qu'engagerait la responsabilité selon le droit civil, cette détermination étant nécessaire pour calculer le montant pour lequel un recours existe en vertu des articles 90, paragraphe premier, de la *Wet op de Arbeidsongeschiktheidsverzekering*, 52a de la *Ziektewet*, 83b, paragraphe

1 Act on Insurance of Incapacity to Work.

Ziektewet[1], article 83b, paragraph 1 of the *Ziekenfondswet*[2], and article 8 of the *Wet Arbeidsongeschiktheidsvoorziening Militairen*[3];

b. in the determination of the amount referred to in article 3 of the *Verhaalswet ongevallen ambtenaren*[5] and above which there is no responsibility pursuant to that Act or pursuant to article N 11 of the *Algemene Burgerlijke Pensioenwet*[6].

2. The right to reparation of damage against the producer pursuant to articles 185 - 193a inclusive, is not susceptible of subrogation pursuant to article 284 of the Code of Commerce, except to the extent that the insurance benefit concerns the liability of the insured person and that another person was also liable pursuant to these articles.

3. The person whose recourse or subrogation has been excluded by paragraphs 1 and 2, cannot acquire the rights referred to in the second paragraph by contract either, nor can he have them exercised in his favour by the title-holder in the latter's name.

premier, de la *Ziekenfondswet* et 8 de la *Wet Arbeidsongeschiktheidsvoorziening Militairen*[4];

b. Aux fins de la détermination du montant visé à l'article 3 de la *Verhaalswet ongevallen ambtenaren*[7] constituant le maximum de la responsabilité en vertu de cette loi ou de l'article N 11 de la *Algemene Burgerlijke Pensioenwet*[8].

2. Le droit à la réparation du dommage à l'encontre du producteur en vertu des articles 185 à 193a compris est insusceptible de subrogation par l'application de l'article 284 du Code de commerce, sauf dans la mesure où la prestation de l'assureur concerne la responsabilité de l'assuré et qu'une autre personne était coresponsable en vertu de ces dispositions.

3. Celui dont le recours ou la subrogation est exclu par l'effet des paragraphes premier et deuxième ne peut non plus obtenir les droits visés au paragraphe deuxième par contrat ni les faire exercer à son profit par le titulaire au nom de celui-ci.

AFDELING 4 Misleidende reclame

Section 4 Misleading publicity

Section quatrième De la publicité trompeuse

Art. 194. (6.3.4.1) Hij die omtrent goederen of diensten die door hem of degene ten behoeve van wie hij handelt in de uitoefening van een beroep of bedrijf worden aangeboden, een mededeling openbaar maakt of laat openbaar maken, handelt onrechtmatig, indien deze mededeling in een of meer opzichten misleidend is, zoals ten aanzien van:

a. de aard, samenstelling, hoeveelheid, hoedanigheid, eigenschappen of gebruiksmogelijkheden;

b. de herkomst, de wijze of het tijdstip van vervaardigen;

c. de omvang van de voorraad;

1 Illness Act.

2 Illness Insurance Act.

3 Act on Incapacity of Military Personnel to Work.

4 *Wet op de Arbeidsongeschiktheidsverzekering* - Loi sur l'assurance pour inaptitude au travail; *Ziektewet* - Loi sur les maladies et l'invalidité; *Ziekenfondswet* - Loi sur l'assurance-maladie; *Wet Arbeidsongeschiktheidsvoorziening Militairen* - Loi portant des dispositions relatives à l'inaptitude au travail des militaires.

5 Act on Recourse for Accidents of Civil Servants.

6 General Civil Pension Act.

7 *Verhaalswet ongevallen ambtenaren* - Loi concernant les recours en matière d'accidents des fonctionnaires.

8 *Algemene Burgerlijke Pensioenwet* - Loi générale concernant le régime de retraite civil.

d. de prijs of de wijze van berekenen daarvan;
e. de aanleiding of het doel van de aanbieding;
f. de toegekende onderscheidingen, getuigschriften of andere door derden uitgebrachte beoordelingen of gedane verklaringen, of de gebezigde wetenschappelijke of vaktermen, technische bevindingen of statistische gegevens;
g. de voorwaarden, waaronder goederen worden geleverd of diensten worden verricht of de betaling plaatsvindt;
h. de omvang, inhoud of tijdsduur van de garantie;
i. de identiteit, hoedanigheden, bekwaamheid of bevoegdheid van degene door wie, onder wiens leiding of toezicht of met wiens medewerking de goederen zijn of worden vervaardigd of aangeboden of de diensten worden verricht;
j. vergelijking met andere goederen of diensten.

A person who makes public or causes to be made public information regarding goods or services which he, or the person for whom he acts, offers in the course of a profession or business, acts unlawfully if this information is misleading in one or more respects, such as with regard to:

a. the nature, composition, quantity, quality, characteristics or possibilities for use;
b. the origin, the manner and time of production;
c. the volume of the supply;
d. the price or its method of calculation;
e. the reason or purpose of the special offer;
f. the prizes awarded, the testimonials or other opinions or declarations which third persons have given, or the scientific or professional terms used, the technical results or statistical data;
g. the conditions under which goods are supplied, services are rendered or payment is made;
h. the extent, content or duration of the warranty;
i. the identity, qualities, skill or competence of the person by whom, or under whose guidance or supervision, or with whose cooperation the goods are or have been produced or the services are rendered;
j. comparison with other goods or services.

Celui qui rend ou fait rendre publique une communication au sujet de biens ou de services qu'il offre lui-même dans le cadre d'une activité professionnelle ou d'une entreprise, ou qu'offre celui pour qui il agit, commet un acte illicite, si cette communication est trompeuse à un ou à plusieurs égards, tels

a. La nature, composition, quantité, qualité, les propriétés ou les applications possibles;
b. L'origine, ou le mode ou la date de fabrication;
c. L'importance de son stock;
d. Le prix ou la façon de le calculer;
e. La raison ou le but de l'offre spéciale;
f. Les distinctions obtenues, les attestations ou autres appréciations produites par des tiers ou des déclarations faites par eux, les termes de science ou du métier employés, les constatations techniques ou les données statistiques;
g. Des conditions de livraison des biens, d'exécution des services ou de paiement;
h. L'ampleur, le contenu et la durée de la garantie;
i. L'identité, les qualités, la compétence ou les pouvoirs de celui qui fabrique ou a fabriqué les biens ou qui les offre ou qui effectue les services, ou de celui qui dirige, surveille ou prête son concours à ces activités;
j. La comparaison avec d'autres biens et services.

Art. 195. (6.3.4.2) - 1. Indien een vordering ingevolge artikel 194 wordt ingesteld tegen iemand die inhoud en inkleding van de mededeling geheel of ten dele zelf heeft bepaald of doen bepalen, rust op hem de bewijslast ter zake van de juistheid of volledigheid van de feiten die in de mededeling zijn vervat of daardoor worden gesuggereerd en waarop het beweerde misleidende karakter van de mededeling berust, behoudens voor zover deze bewijslastverdeling onredelijk is.
- 2. Indien volgens artikel 194 onrechtmatig is gehandeld door iemand die inhoud en inkleding van de mededeling geheel of ten dele zelf heeft bepaald of doen bepalen, is hij voor de dientengevolge ontstane schade aansprakelijk, tenzij hij bewijst dat zulks noch aan zijn schuld is te wijten noch op andere grond voor zijn rekening komt.

1. If, pursuant to article 194, an action is brought against a person who himself, in whole or in part, has determined or has caused to be determined the content and presentation of the information, this person carries the burden of proof with respect to the accuracy or completeness of the facts which are contained in the information or are suggested by it, and on which the alleged misleading nature of the information is based, except to the extent that this apportionment of the burden of proof is unreasonable.
2. If, according to article 194, there has been an unlawful act of a person who, in whole or in part, has himself determined or has caused to be determined the content and presentation of the information, this person is liable for the damage resulting therefrom, unless he proves that it is not his fault and that he should not be responsible for it for another reason.

1. Si l'action fondée sur l'article 194 est intentée contre une personne qui a en tout ou partie elle-même déterminé ou fait déterminer le contenu ou la présentation de la communication, il lui incombe le fardeau de la preuve du caractère exact ou complet des faits que comporte la communication ou qu'elle suggère et sur lequel repose son prétendu caractère trompeur, sauf dans la mesure où cette répartition du fardeau de la preuve est déraisonnable.

2. Si la personne qui a en tout ou partie elle-même déterminé ou fait déterminer le contenu ou la présentation de la communication a agi de manière illicite selon l'article 194, elle est reponsable du dommage en résultant, à moins qu'elle ne prouve que cela n'est pas dû à sa faute ni ne lui incombe pour une autre raison.

Art. 196. (6.3.4.3) - 1. Indien iemand door het openbaar maken of laten openbaar maken van een in artikel 194 omschreven mededeling aan een ander schade heeft toegebracht of dreigt toe te brengen, kan de rechter hem op vordering van die ander niet alleen het openbaar maken of laten openbaar maken van zodanige mededeling verbieden, maar ook hem veroordelen tot het op een door de rechter aangegeven wijze openbaar maken of laten openbaar maken van een rectificatie van die mededeling.
- 2. Vorderingen als in het vorige lid bedoeld komen mede toe aan:
a. rechtspersonen met volledige rechtsbevoegdheid, die ten doel hebben, de behartiging van belangen van personen die een beroep of een bedrijf uitoefenen of van eindgebruikers van niet voor een beroep of bedrijf bestemde goederen of diensten, indien deze belangen door het openbaar maken van de mededeling zijn of dreigen te worden aangetast;
b. andere rechtspersonen met volledige rechtsbevoegdheid, mits de mededeling redelijkerwijs geacht kan worden verband te houden met het door hen nagestreefde doel, en dit doel door het openbaar maken van de mededeling wordt of dreigt te worden aangetast.

- 3. Indien een vordering als in de vorige leden bedoeld wordt toegewezen jegens iemand die niet tevens aansprakelijk is voor de in artikel 195 lid 2 bedoelde schade, is artikel 167 lid 3 van overeenkomstige toepassing.

1. If a person has caused damage to another or is likely to do so by making information described in article 194 public or by causing it to be made public, the judge, upon the demand of that other person, may not only forbid the former person from making such information public and from causing it to be made public, but he may also condemn him to publish a rectification of that information or to have it published, in the manner indicated by the judge.

2. Actions as referred to in the preceding paragraph can also be taken by:

a. legal persons with full legal capacity whose purpose it is to take care of the interests of persons who exercise a profession or business, or of final users of goods or services not destined for a profession or business, if these interests are or are likely to be affected by making the information public;

b. other legal persons with full legal capacity provided that the information can reasonably be considered to be connected with the purpose which they pursue, and that this purpose is or is likely to be affected by making the information public.

3. Article 167, paragraph 3 applies *mutatis mutandis* if an action as referred to in the preceding paragraphs is granted against a person who is not also liable for the damage referred to in article 195, paragraph 2.

1. Si une personne, en rendant publique ou en faisant rendre publique une communication prévue à l'article 194 cause un dommage à une autre ou risque de lui en causer, le juge peut, à la demande de cette autre, non seulement lui interdire le fait de rendre publique ou de faire rendre publique la communication, mais aussi la condamner à rendre publique ou à faire rendre publique, de la manière qu'il détermine, une rectification de cette communication.

2. La demande visée au paragraphe précédent revient aussi

a. Aux personnes morales ayant la pleine capacité juridique qui ont pour but de veiller aux intérêts de personnes exerçant une activité professionnelle ou entreprise ou encore d'utilisateurs finals de biens ou de services non destinés à l'exercice d'une activité professionnelle ou d'une entreprise, si la publication de la communication porte atteinte à ces intérêts ou risque de le faire.

b. À d'autres personnes morales ayant la pleine capacité juridique, pourvu que l'on puisse normalement estimer que la communication a un rapport avec le but qu'elles poursuivent et que la publication de la communication porte atteinte à ce but ou risque de le faire

3. Si la demande visée aux paragraphes précédents est accueillie à l'encontre d'une personne qui n'est pas en même temps responsable du dommage visé à l'article 195, paragraphe 2, l'article 167, paragraphe 3, s'applique par analogie.

AFDELING 5 Tijdelijke regeling verhaalsrechten

Section 5 Temporary rules regarding rights of recourse

Section cinquième Régime temporaire des droits de recouvrement

Art. 197. (6.3.5.1) - 1. De artikelen 165, 166, 169, 171, 173 en 174 blijven buiten toepassing:

a. bij de vaststelling van het totale bedrag waarvoor aansprakelijkheid naar burgerlijk recht zou bestaan, vereist voor de berekening van het bedrag waarvoor verhaal bestaat krachtens de artikelen 90, eerste lid, van de Wet op de Arbeidsongeschiktheidsverzekering, 52a van de Ziektewet, 83b, eerste lid, van de Ziekenfondswet en 8 van de Wet Arbeidsongeschiktheidsvoorziening Militairen;

b. bij de vaststelling van het bedrag, bedoeld in artikel 3 van de Verhaalswet ongevallen ambtenaren waarboven de gehoudenheid krachtens die wet of krachtens artikel N 11 van de Algemene Burgerlijke Pensioenwet zich niet uitstrekt.

- 2. Rechten uit de artikelen 165, 166, 169, 171, 173 en 174 zijn niet vatbaar voor subrogatie:

a. krachtens artikel 284 van het Wetboek van Koophandel, behoudens voor zover de uitkering door de verzekeraar de aansprakelijkheid van de verzekerde betreft en een ander krachtens deze artikelen mede aansprakelijk was;

b. krachtens artikel 6, derde lid, van de Wet voorlopige regeling schadefonds geweldsmisdrijven.

- 3. Degene wiens verhaal of subrogatie door de vorige leden wordt uitgesloten, kan de in het tweede lid bedoelde rechten evenmin krachtens overeenkomst verkrijgen of te zijnen behoeve door de gerechtigde op diens naam doen uitoefenen.

1. Articles 165, 166, 169, 171, 173 and 174 do not apply:

a. in the determination of the total amount for which there would be liability according to private law, this determination being required for the calculation of the amount for which there is recourse pursuant to article 90, paragraph 1 of the *Wet op de Arbeidsongeschiktheids-verzekering*[1], article 52a of the *Ziektewet*, article 83b, paragraph 1 of the *Ziekenfondswet*, and article 8 of the *Wet Arbeidsongeschiktheids-voorziening Militairen*;

b. in the determination of the amount referred to in article 3 of the *Verhaalswet ongevallen ambtenaren*[3] and above which there is no responsibility pursuant to that Act or pursuant to article N 11 of the *Algemene Burgerlijke Pensioenwet*.

2. Rights resulting from articles 165, 166, 169, 171, 173 and 174 are not susceptible of subrogation:

1. Les articles 165, 166, 169, 171, 173 et 174 ne s'appliquent pas:

a. Aux fins de la détermination du montant global qu'engagerait la responsabilité selon le droit civil, cette détermination étant nécessaire pour calculer le montant pour lequel un recours existe en vertu des articles 90, paragraphe premier, de la *Wet op de Arbeidsongeschiktheidsverzekering*, 52a de la *Ziektewet*, 83b, paragraphe premier, de la *Ziekenfondswet* et 8 de la *Wet Arbeidsongeschiktheidsvoorziening Militairen*[2];

b. Aux fins de la détermination du montant visé à l'article 3 de la *Verhaalswet ongevallen ambtenaren*[4] constituant le maximum de la responsabilité en vertu de cette loi ou de l'article N 11 de la *Algemene Burgerlijke Pensioenwet*.

2. Les droits résultant des articles 165, 166, 169, 171, 173 et 174 sont insusceptibles de subrogation:

1 See translation of the Acts at footnote relating to art. 193.

2 Voir traduction dans la note relative à l'article 193.

3 Act on Recourse for Accidents of Civil Servants.

4 *Verhaalswet ongevallen ambtenaren* - Loi concernant les recours en matière d'accidents des fonctionnaires.

a. pursuant to article 284 of the Code of Commerce, except to the extent that the insurance benefit concerns the liability of the insured person and that another person was also liable pursuant to these articles;

b. pursuant to article 6, paragraph 3 of the *Wet voorlopige regeling schadefonds geweldsmisdrijven.*

3. The person whose recourse or subrogation is excluded by the preceding paragraphs can not acquire the rights referred to in the second paragraph by contract either, nor can he have them exercised in his favour by the title-holder in the latter's name.

a. Par l'application de l'article 284 du Code de commerce, sauf dans la mesure où la prestation de l'assureur concerne la responsabilité de l'assuré et qu'une autre personne était coresponsable en vertu de ces dispositions.

b. Par l'application de l'article 6, paragraphe troisième de la *Wet voorlopige regeling schadefonds geweldsmisdrijven.*

3. Celui dont le recours ou la subrogation est exclu par l'effet des paragraphes précédents ne peut non plus obtenir les droits visés au paragraphe deuxième par contrat ni les faire exercer à son profit par le titulaire au nom de celui-ci.

TITEL 4 VERBINTENISSEN UIT ANDERE BRON DAN ONRECHTMATIGE DAAD OF OVEREENKOMST

TITLE 4 OBLIGATIONS ARISING FROM SOURCES OTHER THAN UNLAWFUL ACT OR CONTRACT

TITRE QUATRIÈME DES OBLIGATIONS RÉSULTANT DE SOURCES AUTRES QUE L'ACTE ILLICITE OU LE CONTRAT

AFDELING 1 Zaakwaarneming

Section 1 Management of the affairs of another

Section première De la gestion d'affaires

Art. 198. (6.4.1.1) Zaakwaarneming is het zich willens en wetens en op redelijke grond inlaten met de behartiging van eens anders belang, zonder de bevoegdheid daartoe aan een rechtshandeling of een elders in de wet geregelde rechtsverhouding te ontlenen.

Management of another's affairs occurs where a person consciously and with good reason undertakes to look after the interest of another without having the power to do so pursuant to a juridical act or another juridical relationship provided for elsewhere by law.

Par gestion d'affaires, on entend le fait pour une personne d'intervenir sciemment et pour un motif raisonnable dans l'administration des intérêts d'une autre personne, sans en avoir le pouvoir en vertu d'un acte juridique ou d'un rapport juridique prévu ailleurs par la loi.

Art. 199. (6.4.1.2) - 1. De zaakwaarnemer is verplicht bij de waarneming de nodige zorg te betrachten en, voor zover dit redelijkerwijze van hem kan worden verlangd, de begonnen waarneming voort te zetten.

- 2. De zaakwaarnemer doet, zodra dit redelijkerwijze mogelijk is, aan de belanghebbende verantwoording van hetgeen hij heeft verricht. Heeft hij voor de belanghebbende gelden uitgegeven of ontvangen, dan doet hij daarvan rekening.

1. The manager must exercise the necessary care in his management and, to the extent that this can reasonably be required of him, he must continue the management which he has begun.
2. As soon as reasonably possible, the manager reports to the interested party on what he has done. He must render an account of the funds which he has spent or received on behalf of the interested party.

1. Le gérant est tenu d'apporter à la gestion les soins appropriés et, dans la mesure où il est convenable de le lui imposer, de continuer la gestion entreprise.

2. Dès que cela lui est normalement possible, le gérant rend compte au géré de ce qu'il a accompli. S'il a perçu ou dépensé des sommes d'argent au profit de ce dernier, il en établit le compte.

Art. 200. (6.4.1.3) - 1. De belanghebbende is, voor zover zijn belang naar behoren is behartigd, gehouden de zaakwaarnemer de schade te vergoeden, die deze als gevolg van de waarneming heeft geleden.
- 2. Heeft de zaakwaarnemer in de uitoefening van een beroep of bedrijf gehandeld, dan heeft hij, voor zover dit redelijk is, bovendien recht op een vergoeding voor zijn verrichtingen, met inachtneming van de prijzen die daarvoor ten tijde van de zaakwaarneming gewoonlijk werden berekend.

1. The interested party must compensate the manager for damage which he has suffered as a result of the management, to the extent that his interest has been properly looked after.
2. Where the manager has acted in the course of a business or profession, he has, to the extent that this is reasonable, the further right to be paid for his activities in accordance with the prices usually charged for such activities at the time of the management.

1. Le géré, dans la mesure où ses intérêts ont été convenablement administrés, est tenu d'indemniser le gérant du dommage que celui-ci a subi par suite de la gestion.

2. Le gérant qui a agi dans l'exercice d'une activité professionnelle ou entreprise a droit, en outre, dans la mesure où cela convient, à une rémunération, conformément aux prix habituels de ces services au moment de la gestion.

Art. 201. (6.4.1.4) Een zaakwaarnemer is bevoegd rechtshandelingen te verrichten in naam van de belanghebbende, voor zover diens belang daardoor naar behoren wordt behartigd.

A manager is entitled to perform juridical acts in the name of the interested party, to the extent that the latter's interest is properly looked after.

Le gérant peut accomplir des actes juridiques au nom du géré dans la mesure où cela sert convenablement les intérêts de ce dernier.

Art. 202. (6.4.1.5) Heeft iemand die is opgetreden ter behartiging van eens anders belang, zich zonder redelijke grond daarmede ingelaten of dit belang niet naar behoren behartigd, dan kan de belanghebbende door goedkeuring van het optreden zijn bevoegdheid prijsgeven jegens hem het gebrek in te roepen. Aan de belanghebbende kan door hem een redelijke termijn voor de goedkeuring worden gesteld.

Where a person who has acted with a view to looking after the interest of another, has done so without good reason or has not properly done so, the interested party may, by approving the acts, renunciate the right to invoke the defect against the manager. The interested party can be given a reasonable period for the approval.

Lorsqu'une personne a agi dans l'intérêt d'une autre sans motif raisonnable ou qu'elle n'a pas covenablement administré cet intérêt, le géré peut, en approuvant ces actes, renoncer à la faculté d'invoquer ce défaut envers le gérant. Celui-ci peut lui fixer un délai adéquat pour l'approbation.

AFDELING 2 Onverschuldigde betaling

Section 2 Undue payment

Section deuxième Du paiement de l'indu

Art. 203. (6.4.2.1) - 1. Degene die een ander zonder rechtsgrond een goed heeft gegeven, is gerechtigd dit van de ontvanger als onverschuldigd betaald terug te vorderen.
- 2. Betreft de onverschuldigde betaling een geldsom, dan strekt de vordering tot teruggave van een gelijk bedrag.
- 3. Degene die zonder rechtsgrond een prestatie van andere aard heeft verricht, heeft eveneens jegens de ontvanger recht op ongedaanmaking daarvan.

1. A person who has given property to another without legal ground is entitled to reclaim it from the recipient as having been paid unduly.
2. Where the undue payment consists of a sum of money, the claim is for the same amount.
3. The person who, without legal ground, has performed a prestation other than those mentioned above also has the right to demand from the recipient that this prestation be undone.

1. Celui qui, sans fondement juridique, a donné un bien à un autre peut en demander la restitution à celui qui l'a reçu, comme paiement de l'indu.
2. Lorsque le paiement de l'indu porte sur une somme d'argent, la créance a pour objet la restitution d'une somme égale.
3. Celui qui a accompli sans fondement juridique une prestation d'autre nature peut en demander l'anéantissement à celui qui l'a reçue.

Art. 204. (6.4.2.3) - 1. Heeft de ontvanger in een periode waarin hij redelijkerwijze met een verplichting tot teruggave van het goed geen rekening behoefde te houden, niet als een zorgvuldig schuldenaar voor het goed zorg gedragen, dan wordt hem dit niet toegerekend.
- 2. Degene die namens een ander, maar onbevoegd een niet aan die ander verschuldigde geldsom heeft ontvangen, is van zijn verplichting tot teruggave bevrijd, voor zover hij die geldsom aan die ander heeft doorbetaald in een periode waarin hij redelijkerwijze met die verplichting geen rekening behoefde te houden.

1. Where the recipient has not taken care of the property as a prudent debtor would do, during a period in which he did not reasonably have to foresee the possibility of the existence of an obligation to give the property back, this lack of care will not be imputed to him.

1. N'est pas imputé à celui qui a reçu un bien le fait de n'en avoir pas pris soin comme un débiteur prudent pendant la période où il ne devait pas normalement s'attendre à devoir le restituer.

2. The person who, on behalf of another but without being entitled to do so, has received a sum of money which was not owed to that other person, is liberated from his obligation to give it back, to the extent that he has turned it over to that other person during a period in which he did not reasonably have to foresee the existence of that obligation.

2. Celui qui a reçu au nom d'une autre personne, mais sans en avoir le pouvoir, une somme d'argent qui n'était pas due à cette dernière est libéré de l'obligation de restitution dans la mesure où il l'a versée à cette autre personne pendant une période où il ne devait pas normalement s'attendre à devoir la restituer.

Art. 205. (6.4.2.4) Heeft de ontvanger het goed te kwader trouw aangenomen, dan is hij zonder ingebrekestelling in verzuim.

The recipient who has accepted property in bad faith, is in default *de iure*.

Celui qui a reçu un bien de mauvaise foi est en demeure de plein droit.

Art. 206. (6.4.2.5) De artikelen 120, 121, 123 en 124 van Boek 3 zijn van overeenkomstige toepassing met betrekking tot hetgeen daarin is bepaald omtrent de afgifte van vruchten en de vergoeding van kosten en schade.

Articles 120, 121, 123 and 124 of Book 3 apply *mutatis mutandis* with respect to what is provided for in those articles regarding the remittance of fruits and the compensation for costs and damage.

Les articles 120, 121, 123 et 124 du Livre troisième s'appliquent par analogie, pour ce qui y est disposé au sujet de la remise des fruits, du remboursement des dépenses et de la réparation du dommage.

Art. 207. (6.4.2.6) De ontvanger heeft, tenzij hij het goed te kwader trouw heeft aangenomen, binnen de grenzen van de redelijkheid ook recht op vergoeding van de kosten van het ontvangen en teruggeven van het goed, alsmede van uitgaven in de in artikel 204 bedoelde periode die zouden zijn uitgebleven als hij het goed niet had ontvangen.

Unless the recipient has accepted property in bad faith, he also has, within the bounds of reasonableness, the right to reimbursement of the costs incurred in accepting and returning the property, as well as of the expenditures which he has made during the period referred to in article 204, and which would not have been made had he not received the property.

À moins de l'avoir accepté de mauvaise foi, celui qui a reçu un bien a, en outre, droit, dans des limites normales, au remboursement des frais engagés pour la réception et la restitution du bien, de même que des dépenses effectuées pendant la période visée à l'article 204, qui n'auraient pas été faites s'il n'avait pas reçu le bien.

Art. 208. (6.4.2.6a) De ontvanger verliest zijn recht op de in de beide vorige artikelen bedoelde vergoedingen, indien de wederpartij afstand doet van haar recht op terugvordering en, voor zover nodig, het onverschuldigd betaalde ter bevrijding van deze vergoedingen op haar kosten aan de ontvanger overdraagt. De ontvanger is verplicht aan een zodanige overdracht mede te werken.

The recipient loses the right to the indemnities referred to in the two preceding articles if the other party renounces his right to reclaim the

Celui qui a reçu un bien perd son droit aux indemnités prévues aux deux articles précédents si l'autre partie renonce à son droit à la restitution et, dans la mesure où

property and, to the extent necessary and at his own expense, transfers what has been unduly paid to the recipient in order to be relieved of these indemnities. The recipient must cooperate in such a transfer.

cela est nécessaire, lui transfère, en acquittement des indemnités et à ses frais, ce qui a été payé indûment. Celui qui a reçu le bien est tenu de prêter son concours à un tel transfert.

Art. 209. (6.4.2.7) Op de onbekwame die een onverschuldigde betaling heeft ontvangen, rusten de in deze afdeling omschreven verplichtingen slechts, voor zover het ontvangene hem tot werkelijk voordeel heeft gestrekt of in de macht van zijn wettelijke vertegenwoordiger is gekomen.

The obligations of this section apply to an incapable person who has received an undue payment only to the extent that what he has received has actually benefitted him or has come under the control of his legal representative.

L'incapable qui a reçu un paiement indu est soumis aux obligations décrites dans la présente section dans la seule mesure où le bien reçu lui a réellement profité ou est venu en la puissance de son représentant légal.

Art. 210. (6.4.2.8) - 1. Op de ongedaanmaking van prestaties die niet in het geven van een goed hebben bestaan, zijn de artikelen 204-209 van overeenkomstige toepassing.
- 2. Sluit de aard van de prestatie uit dat zij ongedaan wordt gemaakt, dan treedt, voor zover dit redelijk is, vergoeding van de waarde van de prestatie op het ogenblik van ontvangst daarvoor in de plaats, indien de ontvanger door de prestatie is verrijkt, indien het aan hem is toe te rekenen dat de prestatie is verricht, of indien hij erin had toegestemd een tegenprestatie te verrichten.

1. Articles 204 - 209 apply *mutatis mutandis* to the undoing of prestations which do not consist of the giving of property.
2. Where the nature of the prestation is such that it cannot be undone, reimbursement of the value of the prestation at the time of receipt will take its place to the extent that this is reasonable, if the recipient has been enriched by the prestation, if it can be imputed to him that the prestation has been performed or if he had consented to perform a counterprestation.

1. S'appliquent par analogie à l'anéantissement des prestations autres que celles de donner un bien les articles 204 à 209.
2. La prestation dont la nature exclut l'anéantissement est remplacée, dans la mesure où cela est convenable, par le remboursement de sa valeur au moment de la réception, si la prestation a enrichi celui qui l'a reçue, s'il lui est imputable qu'elle a été rendue, ou s'il avait consenti à fournir une contre-prestation.

Art. 211. (6.4.2.9) - 1. Kan een prestatie die op grond van een nietige overeenkomst is verricht, naar haar aard niet ongedaan worden gemaakt en behoort zij ook niet in rechte op geld te worden gewaardeerd, dan is een tot ongedaanmaking van een tegenprestatie of tot vergoeding van de waarde daarvan strekkende vordering, voor zover deze deswege in strijd met redelijkheid en billijkheid zou zijn, eveneens uitgesloten.
- 2. Is ingevolge het vorige lid terugvordering van een overgedragen goed uitgesloten, dan brengt de nietigheid van de overeenkomst niet de nietigheid van de overdracht mede.

1. Where a prestation, performed pursuant to a contract which is null, cannot by its nature be undone and where this prestation should not be judicially evaluated in monetary terms either, an action to undo a counterprestation or to be reimbursed for the value thereof is also excluded to the extent that this action would therefore be contrary to reasonableness and equity.
2. Where pursuant to the preceding paragraph transferred property cannot be reclaimed, the nullity of the contract does not entail nullity of the transfer.

1. Lorsqu'une prestation effectuée en vertu d'un contrat nul exclut, par sa nature, l'anéantissement et qu'il ne convient pas non plus de l'évaluer en argent par voie judiciaire, la demande de faire anéantir la contre-prestation ou d'en faire rembourser la valeur est également exclue dans la mesure où cette demande serait de ce fait contraire à la raison et à l'équité.

2. Lorsque la répétition d'un bien transféré est exclue en vertu de l'article précédent, la nullité du contrat n'entraîne pas celle du transfert.

AFDELING 3 Ongerechtvaardigde verrijking

Section 3 Unjustified enrichment

Section troisième De l'enrichissement injustifié

Art. 212. (6.4.3.1) - 1. Hij die ongerechtvaardigd is verrijkt ten koste van een ander, is verplicht, voor zover dit redelijk is, diens schade te vergoeden tot het bedrag van zijn verrijking.
- 2. Voor zover de verrijking is verminderd als gevolg van een omstandigheid die niet aan de verrijkte kan worden toegerekend, blijft zij buiten beschouwing.
- 3. Is de verrijking verminderd in de periode waarin de verrijkte redelijkerwijze met een verplichting tot vergoeding van de schade geen rekening behoefde te houden, dan wordt hem dit niet toegerekend. Bij de vaststelling van deze vermindering wordt mede rekening gehouden met uitgaven die zonder de verrijking zouden zijn uitgebleven.

1. A person who has been unjustifiably enriched at the expense of another must, to the extent this is reasonable, make reparation for the damage suffered by that other person up to the amount of his enrichment.
2. A decrease in the enrichment is not taken into consideration to the extent that it results from a cause which cannot be imputed to the enriched person.
3. A decrease in the enrichment during the period in which the enriched person did not reasonably have to foresee the existence of an obligation to make reparation for damage, is not imputed to him. In determining this decrease, the expenses which would not have been made had there been no enrichment, are also taken into account.

1. Celui qui a été enrichi injustement aux dépens d'autrui doit, dans la mesure où cela est convenable, réparer le dommage de celui-ci jusqu'à concurrence de son enrichissement.

2. L'enrichissement n'est pas considéré dans la mesure où il a diminué par suite de circonstances non imputables à l'enrichi.

3. Lorsque l'enrichissement a diminué au cours de la période pendant laquelle l'enrichi ne devait pas normalement s'attendre à devoir réparer le dommage, cette diminution ne lui est pas imputable. Lors de l'évaluation de cette diminution, il est également tenu compte des dépenses qui n'auraient pas été effectuées, n'eût été l'enrichissement.

TITEL 5 OVEREENKOMSTEN IN HET ALGEMEEN

TITLE 5 CONTRACTS IN GENERAL

TITRE CINQUIÈME DES CONTRATS EN GÉNÉRAL

AFDELING 1 Algemene bepalingen

Section 1 General provisions

Section première Dispositions générales

Art. 213. (6.5.1.1) - 1. Een overeenkomst in de zin van deze titel is een meerzijdige rechtshandeling, waarbij een of meer partijen jegens een of meer andere een verbintenis aangaan.
- 2. Op overeenkomsten tussen meer dan twee partijen zijn de wettelijke bepalingen betreffende overeenkomsten niet toepasselijk, voor zover de strekking van de betrokken bepalingen in verband met de aard van de overeenkomst zich daartegen verzet.

1. A contract in the sense of this title is a multilateral juridical act whereby one or more parties assume an obligation towards one or more other parties.
2. The provisions of the law pertaining to contracts do not apply to contracts between more than two parties, to the extent that the necessary implication of the relevant provisions, taking into consideration the nature of the contract, leads to incompatibility.

1. Le contrat s'entend au présent titre comme l'acte juridique multilatéral par lequel une ou plusieurs parties s'obligent envers une ou plusieurs autres.
2. Les dispositions de la loi relatives aux contrats ne s'appliquent pas à ceux qui sont conclus entre plus de deux parties, dans la mesure où l'objet des dispositions, en regard de la nature du contrat, s'y oppose.

Art. 214. (6.5.1.2) - 1. Een overeenkomst door een der partijen gesloten in de uitoefening van haar bedrijf of beroep, is behalve aan de wettelijke bepalingen ook onderworpen aan een standaardregeling, wanneer voor de bedrijfstak waartoe het bedrijf behoort, of voor het beroep ten aanzien van zodanige overeenkomst een standaardregeling geldt. De bijzondere soorten van overeenkomsten waarvoor standaardregelingen kunnen worden vastgesteld en de bedrijfstak of het beroep, waarvoor elk dezer regelingen bestemd is te gelden, worden bij algemene maatregel van bestuur aangewezen.
- 2. Een standaardregeling wordt vastgesteld, gewijzigd en ingetrokken door een daartoe door Onze Minister van Justitie te benoemen commissie. Bij de wet worden nadere regelen gesteld omtrent de wijze van samenstelling en de werkwijze van de commissies.
- 3. De vaststelling, wijziging of intrekking van een standaardregeling wordt niet van kracht voordat zij door Ons is goedgekeurd en met Ons goedkeuringsbesluit in de Nederlandse Staatscourant is afgekondigd.
- 4. Bij een standaardregeling kan worden afgeweken van wettelijke bepalingen, voor zover daarvan ook afwijking bij overeenkomst, al of niet met inachtneming van een bepaalde vorm, is toegelaten. De vorige zin lijdt uitzondering, wanneer uit een wettelijke bepaling iets anders voortvloeit.

- 5. Partijen kunnen in hun overeenkomst van een standaardregeling afwijken. Een standaardregeling kan echter voor afwijking een bepaalde vorm voorschrijven.

1. A contract entered into by a party in the course of his business or profession is not only subject to the provisions of the law, but also to standard terms if such standard terms exist for the trade of which the business forms part, or for the profession in respect of the contract in question. The particular kinds of contracts for which standard terms may be made and the trade or profession to which each set of these standard terms is intended to apply, are designated by regulation.
2. Standard terms are made, modified and repealed by a commission to be appointed by Our[1] Minister of Justice. Rules regarding the composition and functioning of commissions are made by law.
3. The making, modification or repeal of standard terms does not come into force until approved by Us and published in the "Nederlandse Staatscourant"[2] together with Our decision to approve.

4. Standard terms may derogate from provisions of the law to the extent that such derogation, whether or not in observing a certain formality, is allowed by contract. The preceding sentence applies, unless a provision of the law leads to a different result.
5. Parties may derogate from standard terms by contract. Standard terms, however, may prescribe a certain formality for derogations.

1. Le contrat conclu par l'une des parties dans l'exercice de son entreprise ou de son activité professionnelle est régi non seulement par la loi, mais également par le règlement-type, lorsque, pour le secteur dont fait partie cette entreprise ou activité professionnelle, un tel règlement a été établi pour le contrat concerné. Les espèces particulières de contrats pour lesquels peuvent être établis des règlements-cadre et le secteur d'entreprise ou d'activité professionnelle auquel s'adresse chacun de ces règlements sont désignés par décret.
2. Le règlement-type est établi, modifié et abrogé par une commission nommée à cette fin par Notre ministre de la Justice. La loi prévoit des règles précises concernant la composition et le mode de fonctionnement des commissions.
3. L'établissement, la modification ou l'abrogation d'un règlement-type ne prend pas effet avant que Nous l'ayons approuvé et que ce règlement, ainsi que Notre décision à cette fin, aient été publiés dans la *Nederlandse Staatscourant*[3].
4. Le règlement-type peut déroger aux dispositions de la loi, dans la mesure où il est permis d'y déroger par contrat, que ce soit en observant des formes déterminées ou non. La phrase précédente souffre exception lorsqu'il résulte autrement d'une disposition de la loi.
5. Les parties peuvent déroger par contrat au règlement-type. Le règlement peut cependant prescrire une forme déterminée pour la dérogation.

Art. 215. (6.5.1.4) Voldoet een overeenkomst aan de omschrijving van twee of meer door de wet geregelde bijzondere soorten van overeenkomsten, dan zijn de voor elk van die soorten gegeven bepalingen naast elkaar op de overeenkomst van toepassing, behoudens voor zover deze bepalingen niet wel verenigbaar zijn of de strekking daarvan in verband met de aard van de overeenkomst zich tegen toepassing verzet.

---

1 "Our" or "Us" refers to the Crown.
2 Dutch Official Gazette.
3 *Nederlandse Staatscourant* - Gazette officielle des Pays-Bas.

Where a contract meets the description of two or more particular kinds of contracts provided for by law, the rules applicable to each of them apply to this contract concurrently, except to the extent that these provisions are not easily compatible or that their necessary implication, in relation to the nature of the contract, results in incompatibility.

Lorsqu'un contrat se conforme à la description de plusieurs espèces particulières de contrats prévues par la loi, les dispositions relatives à chacune d'elles lui sont concurremment applicables, sauf dans la mesure où ces dispositions ne sont pas facilement conciliables ou que leur portée, en rapport avec la nature du contrat, s'oppose à l'application.

Art. 216. (6.5.1.6) Hetgeen in deze en de volgende drie afdelingen is bepaald, vindt overeenkomstige toepassing op andere meerzijdige vermogensrechtelijke rechtshandelingen, voor zover de strekking van de betrokken bepalingen in verband met de aard van de rechtshandeling zich daartegen niet verzet.

The provisions of this section and of the next three sections apply *mutatis mutandis* to other multilateral patrimonial juridical acts, to the extent that the necessary implication of the relevant provisions, taking into consideration the nature of the juridical act, does not result in incompatibility.

Les dispositions de la présente section et des trois suivantes s'appliquent par analogie à d'autres actes juridiques multilatéraux d'ordre patrimonial dans la mesure où l'objet des dispositions concernées, en regard de la nature de l'acte juridique, ne s'y oppose pas.

AFDELING 2 Het tot stand komen van overeenkomsten

Section 2
The formation of contracts

Section deuxième
De la formation des contrats

Art. 217. (6.5.2.1) - 1. Een overeenkomst komt tot stand door een aanbod en de aanvaarding daarvan.
- 2. De artikelen 219-225 zijn van toepassing, tenzij iets anders voortvloeit uit het aanbod, uit een andere rechtshandeling of uit een gewoonte.

1. A contract is formed by an offer and its acceptance.
2. Articles 219 - 225 apply unless the offer, another juridical act or usage produce a different result.

1. Le contrat se forme par une offre et son acceptation.
2. Les articles 219 à 225 s'appliquent, à moins qu'il n'en résulte autrement de l'offre, d'un autre acte juridique ou d'un usage.

Art. 218. (6.5.2.1a) Een aanbod is geldig, nietig of vernietigbaar overeenkomstig de regels voor meerzijdige rechtshandelingen.

An offer is valid, null or subject to annulment according to the rules applicable to multilateral juridical acts.

L'offre est valide, nulle ou annulable, selon les règles applicables aux actes juridiques multilatéraux.

Art. 219. (6.5.2.2) - 1. Een aanbod kan worden herroepen, tenzij het een termijn voor de aanvaarding inhoudt of de onherroepelijkheid ervan op andere wijze uit het aanbod volgt.

- 2. De herroeping kan slechts geschieden, zolang het aanbod niet is aanvaard en evenmin een mededeling, houdende de aanvaarding is verzonden. Bevat het aanbod de mededeling dat het vrijblijvend wordt gedaan, dan kan de herroeping nog onverwijld na de aanvaarding geschieden.
- 3. Een beding waarbij één der partijen zich verbindt om, indien de wederpartij dit wenst, met haar een bepaalde overeenkomst te sluiten, geldt als een onherroepelijk aanbod.

1. An offer may be revoked, unless it includes a term for acceptance, or irrevocability results otherwise from the offer.
2. Revocation may only take place as long as the offer has not been accepted and a communication accepting the offer has not been expedited. Where the offer states that it is without commitment, revocation can take place even after acceptance, if it is done without delay.
3. A stipulation whereby one party binds himself to enter into a certain contract with another party at the latter's option is deemed to be an irrevocable offer.

1. L'offre est révocable, à moins qu'elle ne comporte un délai pour l'acceptation ou que l'irrévocabilité n'en résulte autrement.

2. La révocation peut avoir lieu seulement tant que l'offre n'a pas été acceptée et qu'une communication portant acceptation n'a pas été expédiée. Lorsque l'offre porte la mention qu'elle est faite sans engagement, la révocation peut même avoir lieu sans délai après l'acceptation.
3. La stipulation par laquelle l'une des parties s'engage à conclure un contrat déterminé avec l'autre, si celle-ci le désire, est réputée offre irrévocable.

Art. 220. (6.5.2.3) - 1. Een bij wijze van uitloving voor een bepaalde tijd gedaan aanbod kan wegens gewichtige redenen worden herroepen of gewijzigd.
- 2. In geval van herroeping of wijziging van een uitloving kan de rechter aan iemand die op grond van de uitloving met de voorbereiding van een gevraagde prestatie is begonnen, een billijke schadeloosstelling toekennen.

1. An offer of reward made for a specific period can be revoked or modified for serious reasons.
2. In the event of revocation or modification of an offer of reward, the judge may grant equitable compensation to a person who, on the basis of the offer, has begun to prepare the requested prestation.

1. L'offre de récompense faite pour un temps déterminé peut être révoquée ou modifée pour des motifs sérieux.
2. En cas de révocation ou de modification d'une offre de récompense, le juge peut accorder une indemnité équitable à celui qui, sur la foi de cette offre, a commencé la préparation de la prestation demandée.

Art. 221. (6.5.2.4) - 1. Een mondeling aanbod vervalt, wanneer het niet onmiddellijk wordt aanvaard, een schriftelijk aanbod, wanneer het niet binnen een redelijke tijd wordt aanvaard.
- 2. Een aanbod vervalt, doordat het wordt verworpen.

1. A verbal offer lapses when it is not immediately accepted; a written offer lapses when it has not been accepted within a reasonable period.

2. An offer lapses when it is rejected.

1. L'offre verbale devient caduque lorsqu'elle n'est pas acceptée immédiatement; l'offre écrite devient caduque lorsqu'elle n'est pas acceptée dans un délai normal.
2. L'offre devient caduque par le rejet.

Art. 222. (6.5.2.5) Een aanbod vervalt niet door de dood of het verlies van handelingsbekwaamheid van een der partijen, noch doordat een der partijen de bevoegdheid tot het sluiten van de overeenkomst verliest als gevolg van een bewind.

An offer does not lapse upon the death or the loss of legal capacity of one of the parties, nor upon the loss by one of the parties of the power to enter into the contract as the result of a regime of administration.

L'offre ne devient pas caduque par la mort ou par la survenance de l'incapacité de l'une des parties, ni par le fait, pour l'une des parties, de perdre la faculté de conclure le contrat par l'effet d'un régime d'administration.

Art. 223. (6.5.2.5a) - 1. De aanbieder kan een te late aanvaarding toch als tijdig gedaan laten gelden, mits hij dit onverwijld aan de wederpartij mededeelt.
- 2. Indien een aanvaarding te laat plaatsvindt, maar de aanbieder begrijpt of behoort te begrijpen dat dit voor de wederpartij niet duidelijk was, geldt de aanvaarding als tijdig gedaan, tenzij hij onverwijld aan de wederpartij mededeelt dat hij het aanbod als vervallen beschouwt.

1. An offeror can treat a late acceptance as a timely one provided that he communicates this decision to the other party without delay.
2. Unless, without delay, he communicates to the other party that he considers the offer to have lapsed, a late acceptance is deemed to have been made on time where the offeror understands or ought to understand that the lateness was not apparent to the other party.

1. L'offrant peut traiter l'acceptation tardive comme faite à temps, pourvu qu'il en informe sans tarder l'autre partie.

2. L'acceptation tardive dont l'offrant comprenait ou devait comprendre que l'acceptant ignorait le caractère tardif est réputée avoir été faite à temps, à moins que l'offrant n'informe sans tarder l'autre partie de sa décision de considérer l'offre comme caduque.

Art. 224. (6.5.2.7) Indien een aanvaarding de aanbieder niet of niet tijdig bereikt door een omstandigheid op grond waarvan zij krachtens artikel 37 lid 3, tweede zin, van Boek 3 niettemin haar werking heeft, wordt de overeenkomst geacht tot stand te zijn gekomen op het tijdstip waarop zonder de storende omstandigheid de verklaring zou zijn ontvangen.

If acceptance does not, or does not timely, reach the offeror because of a fact on the basis of which the acceptance nevertheless produces effect pursuant to article 37 paragraph 3, second sentence of Book 3, the contract is deemed to have been entered into at the time when, without the intervening fact, the declaration would have been received.

Si l'acceptation ne parvient pas ou pas à temps à l'offrant par suite d'une circonstance qui néanmoins, en vertu de l'article 37, paragraphe 3, deuxième phrase, du Livre troisième, ne le prive pas d'effet, le contrat est réputé s'être formé au moment où, n'eût été cette circonstance intervenante, la déclaration aurait été reçue.

Art. 225. (6.5.2.8) - 1. Een aanvaarding die van het aanbod afwijkt, geldt als een nieuw aanbod en als een verwerping van het oorspronkelijke.
- 2. Wijkt een tot aanvaarding strekkend antwoord op een aanbod daarvan slechts op ondergeschikte punten af, dan geldt dit antwoord als aanvaarding en komt de overeenkomst overeenkomstig deze aanvaarding tot stand, tenzij de aanbieder onverwijld bezwaar maakt tegen de verschillen.

- 3. Verwijzen aanbod en aanvaarding naar verschillende algemene voorwaarden, dan komt aan de tweede verwijzing geen werking toe, wanneer daarbij niet tevens de toepasselijkheid van de in de eerste verwijzing aangegeven algemene voorwaarden uitdrukkelijk van de hand wordt gewezen.

1. An acceptance which deviates from the offer is considered to be a new offer and a rejection of the original offer.
2. Unless the offeror objects to the differences without delay, where a reply intended to accept an offer only deviates from the offer on points of minor importance, the reply is considered to be an acceptance and the contract is formed according to the latter.
3. Where offer and acceptance refer to different general conditions, the second reference is without effect, unless it explicitly rejects the applicability of the general conditions as indicated in the first reference.

1. L'acceptation qui s'écarte de l'offre équivaut à une nouvelle offre et entraîne le rejet de l'offre initiale.
2. Lorsqu'une réponse qui a pour but l'acceptation d'une offre y déroge seulement sur des points mineurs, elle équivaut à une acceptation et le contrat se forme selon celle-ci, à moins que l'offrant ne présente sans tarder des objections aux différences.

3. Lorsque l'offre et l'acceptation renvoient à des conditions générales différentes, le deuxième renvoi ne produit pas effet s'il ne comporte pas également le rejet exprès de l'application des conditions qui font l'objet du premier renvoi.

Art. 226. (6.5.2.9) Stelt de wet voor de totstandkoming van een overeenkomst een vormvereiste, dan is dit voorschrift van overeenkomstige toepassing op een overeenkomst waarbij een partij in wier belang het strekt, zich tot het aangaan van een zodanige overeenkomst verbindt, tenzij uit de strekking van het voorschrift anders voortvloeit.

Unless the necessary implication of the rule produces a different result, where the law requires a formality in order to enter into a contract, this rule applies *mutatis mutandis* to a contract whereby a party in whose interest the formality has been given binds himself to enter into such a contract.

Lorsque la loi soumet la formation du contrat à l'accomplissement d'une formalité, cette disposition s'applique par analogie à la convention par laquelle une partie dont l'intérêt est protégé par la formalité s'engage à conclure un tel contrat, à moins qu'il n'en résulte autrement de l'objet de la disposition concernée.

Art. 227. (6.5.2.10) De verbintenissen die partijen op zich nemen, moeten bepaalbaar zijn.

The obligations which parties assume must be determinable.

Les obligations auxquelles s'engagent les parties doivent être déterminables.

Art. 228. (6.5.2.11) - 1. Een overeenkomst die is tot stand gekomen onder invloed van dwaling en bij een juiste voorstelling van zaken niet zou zijn gesloten, is vernietigbaar:

a. indien de dwaling te wijten is aan een inlichting van de wederpartij, tenzij deze mocht aannemen dat de overeenkomst ook zonder deze inlichting zou worden gesloten;

b. indien de wederpartij in verband met hetgeen zij omtrent de dwaling wist of behoorde te weten, de dwalende had behoren in te lichten;

c. indien de wederpartij bij het sluiten van de overeenkomst van dezelfde onjuiste veronderstelling als de dwalende is uitgegaan, tenzij zij ook bij een juiste voorstelling van zaken niet had behoeven

te begrijpen dat de dwalende daardoor van het sluiten van de overeenkomst zou worden afgehouden.
- 2. De vernietiging kan niet worden gegrond op een dwaling die een uitsluitend toekomstige omstandigheid betreft of die in verband met de aard van de overeenkomst, de in het verkeer geldende opvattingen of de omstandigheden van het geval voor rekening van de dwalende behoort te blijven.

1. A contract which has been entered into under the influence of error and which would not have been entered into had there been a correct assessment of the facts, can be annulled:
a. if the error is imputable to information given by the other party, unless the other party could assume that the contract would have been entered into even without this information;
b. if the other party, in view of what he knew or ought to know regarding the error, should have informed the party in error;
c. if the other party in entering into the contract has based himself on the same incorrect assumption as the party in error, unless the other party, even if there had been a correct assessment of the facts, would not have had to understand that the party in error would therefore be prevented from entering into the contract.
2. The annulment cannot be based on an error as to an exclusively future fact or an error for which, given the nature of the contract, common opinion or the circumstances of the case, the party in error should remain accountable.

1. Le contrat formé sous l'influence d'une erreur, qui n'aurait pas été conclu s'il y avait eu une vue juste des choses, est annulable:
a. Si l'erreur est attribuable à un renseignement fourni par l'autre partie, à moins que cette dernière pût présumer que le contrat aurait été conclu même en l'absence de ce renseignement;
b. Si l'autre partie, eu égard à ce qu'elle savait ou devait savoir au sujet de l'erreur, aurait dû renseigner la partie qui a commis l'erreur;
c. Si l'autre partie, en concluant le contrat, s'est fondée sur la même croyance inexacte que la partie qui a commis l'erreur, sauf le cas où même une vue juste des choses n'avait pas dû lui faire comprendre que celle-ci aurait retenu la partie dans l'erreur de conclure le contrat.
2. L'annulation ne peut être fondée sur l'erreur qui porte uniquement sur une circonstance future ou qui, eu égard à la nature du contrat, à l'opinion généralement admise ou aux circonstances de l'espèce, doit incomber à la partie qui a commis l'erreur.

Art. 229. (6.5.2.12) Een overeenkomst die de strekking heeft voort te bouwen op een reeds tussen partijen bestaande rechtsverhouding, is vernietigbaar, indien deze rechtsverhouding ontbreekt, tenzij dit in verband met de aard van de overeenkomst, de in het verkeer geldende opvattingen of de omstandigheden van het geval voor rekening van degene die zich op dit ontbreken beroept, behoort te blijven.

A contract in furtherance of an already existing juridical relationship between the parties can be annulled if this relationship does not exist, unless the person who invokes the defect should be accountable

Le contrat conclu pour donner suite à un rapport juridique déjà existant entre les parties est annulable si ce rapport fait défaut, à moins que ce défaut, eu égard à la nature du contrat, à l'opinion généralement admise

for it in view of the nature of the contract, common opinion or the circumstances of the case.

ou aux circonstances de l'espèce, doive incomber à celui qui l'invoque.

Art. 230. (6.5.2.12a) - 1. De bevoegdheid tot vernietiging op grond van de artikelen 228 en 229 vervalt, wanneer de wederpartij tijdig een wijziging van de gevolgen van de overeenkomst voorstelt, die het nadeel dat de tot vernietiging bevoegde bij instandhouding van de overeenkomst lijdt, op afdoende wijze opheft.
- 2. Bovendien kan de rechter op verlangen van een der partijen, in plaats van de vernietiging uit te spreken, de gevolgen van de overeenkomst ter opheffing van dit nadeel wijzigen.

1. The power to annul a contract on the basis of articles 228 and 229 lapses when the other party timely proposes a modification to the effects of the contract which adequately removes the prejudice which the person entitled to the annulment suffers by the continuance of the contract.
2. Furthermore, instead of pronouncing the annulment the judge may, upon the demand of one of the parties, modify the effects of the contract to remove this prejudice.

1. La faculté d'annulation par application des articles 228 et 229 s'éteint lorsque l'autre partie propose en temps utile une modification des effets du contrat, mettant fin de façon adéquate au préjudice que le maintien du contrat cause au titulaire de cette faculté.
2. Le juge peut, en outre, à la demande de l'une des parties, au lieu de prononcer l'annulation du contrat, en modifier les effets afin de supprimer le préjudice.

AFDELING 3 Algemene voorwaarden

Section 3
General conditions

Section troisième
Des conditions générales

Art. 231. (6.5.2A.1) In deze afdeling wordt verstaan onder:
a. algemene voorwaarden: een of meer schriftelijke bedingen die zijn opgesteld teneinde in een aantal overeenkomsten te worden opgenomen, met uitzondering van bedingen die de kern van de prestaties aangeven;
b. gebruiker: degene die algemene voorwaarden in een overeenkomst gebruikt;
c. wederpartij: degene die door ondertekening van een geschrift of op andere wijze de gelding van algemene voorwaarden heeft aanvaard.

In this section:
a. general conditions mean one or more written stipulations which have been drafted to be included into a number of contracts, with the exception of stipulations going to the essence of the prestations;
b. the user means the person who uses general conditions in a contract;

Dans la présente section, on entend par:
a. «Conditions générales»: une ou plusieurs stipulations écrites formulées en vue de leur inclusion dans un certain nombre de contrats, à l'exception de celles qui décrivent les prestations essentielles;
b. «Utilisateur»: celui qui emploie des conditions générales dans un contrat;

c. the other party means the person who, in writing or in any other way, has accepted the applicability of general conditions.

c. «L'autre partie»: celui qui, en signant un écrit ou autrement, a accepté l'application des conditions générales.

Art. 232. (6.5.2A.2) Een wederpartij is ook dan aan de algemene voorwaarden gebonden als bij het sluiten van de overeenkomst de gebruiker begreep of moest begrijpen dat zij de inhoud daarvan niet kende.

The other party is bound by general conditions even if, at the time of entering into the contract, the user understood or ought to understand that the other party did not know the content of the conditions.

L'autre partie est soumise aux conditions générales, même si, lors de la conclusion du contrat, l'utilisateur comprenait ou devait comprendre qu'elle n'en connaissait pas le contenu.

Art. 233. (6.5.2A.2a) Een beding in algemene voorwaarden is vernietigbaar
a. indien het, gelet op de aard en de overige inhoud van de overeenkomst, de wijze waarop de voorwaarden zijn tot stand gekomen, de wederzijds kenbare belangen van partijen en de overige omstandigheden van het geval, onredelijk bezwarend is voor de wederpartij; of
b. indien de gebruiker aan de wederpartij niet een redelijke mogelijkheid heeft geboden om van de algemene voorwaarden kennis te nemen.

A stipulation in general conditions may be annulled:
a. if it is unreasonably onerous to the other party, taking into consideration the nature and the further content of the contract, the manner in which the conditions have arisen, the mutually apparent interests of the parties and the other circumstances of the case;
b. if the user has not afforded the other party a reasonable opportunity to take cognizance of the general conditions.

Une stipulation faisant partie de conditions générales est annulable:
a. Si elle est anormalement onéreuse pour l'autre partie, compte tenu de la nature du contrat et de son contenu, de la manière dont les conditions sont nées et des intérêts réciproquement évidents des parties et des autres circonstances de l'espèce;
b. Si l'utilisateur n'a pas offert à l'autre partie une possibilité suffisante de prendre connaissance des conditions générales.

Art. 234. (6.5.2A.2b) - 1. De gebruiker heeft aan de wederpartij de in artikel 233 onder b bedoelde mogelijkheid geboden, indien hij
a. hetzij de algemene voorwaarden voor of bij het sluiten van de overeenkomst aan de wederpartij ter hand heeft gesteld,
b. hetzij, indien dit redelijkerwijs niet mogelijk is, voor de totstandkoming van de overeenkomst aan de wederpartij heeft bekend gemaakt dat de voorwaarden bij hem ter inzage liggen of bij een door hem opgegeven Kamer van Koophandel en Fabrieken of een griffie van een gerecht zijn gedeponeerd, alsmede dat zij op verzoek zullen worden toegezonden.
- 2. Indien de voorwaarden niet voor of bij het sluiten van de overeenkomst aan de wederpartij zijn ter hand gesteld, zijn de bedingen tevens vernietigbaar indien de gebruiker de voorwaarden niet op verzoek van de wederpartij onverwijld op zijn kosten aan haar toezendt.

- 3. Het in de leden 1 onder b en 2 omtrent de verplichting tot toezending bepaalde is niet van toepassing, voor zover deze toezending redelijkerwijze niet van de gebruiker kan worden gevergd.

1. The user has afforded the other party an opportunity as referred to in article 233 *sub* b, if:
a. he has given a copy of the general conditions to the other party before or at the time of entering into the contract,
b. or, if this is not reasonably possible, he has informed the other party, before the formation of the contract, that he has the conditions available for inspection, or that they have been deposited with a Chamber of Commerce and Industry indicated by him, or with the registrar of a court, as well as that they will be sent to the other party upon request.
2. Furthermore, if a copy of the conditions has not been given to the other party before or at the time of entering into the contract, the stipulations may be annulled if the user does not, without delay and at his costs, send the conditions to the other party upon his request.
3. The provisions of paragraphs 1 *sub* b and 2 regarding the obligation to send the conditions do not apply to the extent that sending them cannot reasonably be required from the user.

1. L'utilisateur a offert à l'autre partie la possibilité visée au point b. de l'article 233, s'il a:
a. Soit remis un exemplaire des conditions générales à l'autre partie avant la conclusion du contrat ou lors de celle-ci;
b. Soit, si cela n'est pas normalement possible, informé l'autre partie, avant la formation du contrat, que les conditions générales sont disponibles pour consultation chez lui ou ont été déposées auprès d'une Chambre de commerce et de l'industrie, qu'il indique, ou d'un greffe d'un tribunal, et que, sur requête de l'autre, elles lui seront envoyées.
2. Si les conditions n'ont pas été remises à l'autre partie avant la conclusion du contrat ou lors de celle-ci, les stipulations sont également annulables si, sur requête de l'autre partie, l'utilisateur ne lui envoie pas les conditions sans tarder et à ses frais.
3. Les dispositions des paragraphes 1er, point b., et 2 relatives à l'envoi ne s'appliquent pas dans la mesure où l'on ne peut raisonnablement imposer l'envoi à l'utilisateur.

Art. 235. (6.5.2A.2c) - 1. Op de vernietigingsgronden bedoeld in de artikelen 233 en 234, kan geen beroep worden gedaan door
a. een rechtspersoon bedoeld in artikel 360 van Boek 2, die ten tijde van het sluiten van de overeenkomst laatstelijk haar jaarrekening openbaar heeft gemaakt, of ten aanzien waarvan op dat tijdstip laatstelijk artikel 403 lid 1 van Boek 2 is toegepast;
b. een partij op wie het onder a bepaalde niet van toepassing is, indien op voormeld tijdstip bij haar vijftig of meer personen werkzaam zijn of op dat tijdstip uit een opgave op grond van artikel 17a van de Handelsregisterwet volgt dat bij haar vijftig of meer personen werkzaam zijn.
- 2. Op de vernietigingsgrond bedoeld in artikel 233 onder a, kan mede een beroep worden gedaan door een partij voor wie de algemene voorwaarden door een gevolmachtigde zijn gebruikt, mits de wederpartij meermalen overeenkomsten sluit waarop dezelfde of nagenoeg dezelfde algemene voorwaarden van toepassing zijn.
- 3. Op de vernietigingsgronden bedoeld in de artikelen 233 en 234, kan geen beroep worden gedaan door een partij die meermalen dezelfde of nagenoeg dezelfde algemene voorwaarden in haar overeenkomsten gebruikt.

- 4. De termijn bedoeld in artikel 52 lid 1 onder d van Boek 3, begint met de aanvang van de dag, volgende op die waarop een beroep op het beding is gedaan.

1. The grounds of annulment referred to in articles 233 and 234 cannot be invoked by:
a. a legal person as referred to in article 360 of Book 2 who, at the time of entering into the contract, has lastly made public its annual account, or a legal person in respect of whom, at that time, article 403 paragraph 1 of Book 2 has lastly been applied;
b. a party to whom the provision of sub-paragraph a does not apply, if, at the aforementioned time, fifty or more persons work there or if, at that time, a declaration pursuant to article 17a of the *Handelsregisterwet*[1] shows that fifty or more persons work there.
2. The ground of annulment referred to in article 233 *sub* a can also be invoked by a party for whom the general conditions have been used by a procurator, provided that the other party enter repeatedly into contracts to which the same or almost the same general conditions apply.
3. The grounds of annulment referred to in articles 233 and 234 cannot be invoked by a party who uses the same or almost the same general conditions in its contracts repeatedly.
4. The period referred to in article 52 paragraph 1 *sub* d of Book 3 commences upon the beginning of the day following the one on which the stipulation has been invoked.

1. Ne peut invoquer les causes d'annulation visées aux articles 233 et 234:
a. La personne morale visée à l'article 360 du Livre deuxième, qui, à la date de la conclusion du contrat, a déjà publié dans un passé récent ses comptes annuels ou à l'égard de laquelle à cette date l'article 403, paragraphe 1, du Livre deuxième, a été appliqué dans un passé récent.
b. La personne à laquelle ne s'applique pas le sous-paragraphe a., si à la date sus-visée elle emploie cinquante personnes ou plus, ou si, à cette date, il découle d'une déclaration en application de l'article 17a de la *Handelsregisterwet*[2] qu'elle emploie cinquante personnes ou plus.
2. Peut également invoquer la cause d'annulation visée au point a. de l'article 233 la personne pour qui le procureur a employé les conditions générales, pourvu que l'autre partie conclue de façon répétée des contrats auxquels s'appliquent des conditions générales identiques ou presque identiques.
3. Ne peut invoquer les causes d'annulation visées aux articles 233 et 234 la personne qui emploie de façon répétée des conditions générales identiques ou presque identiques dans ses contrats.
4. Le terme visé au point d. du paragraphe 1er de l'article 52 du Livre troisième commence au lendemain du jour où la stipulation a été invoquée.

Art. 236. (6.5.2A.3) Bij een overeenkomst tussen een gebruiker en een wederpartij, natuurlijk persoon, die niet handelt in de uitoefening van een beroep of bedrijf, wordt als onredelijk bezwarend aangemerkt een in de algemene voorwaarden voorkomend beding
a. dat de wederpartij geheel en onvoorwaardelijk het recht ontneemt de door de gebruiker toegezegde prestatie op te eisen;
b. dat de aan de wederpartij toekomende bevoegdheid tot ontbinding, zoals deze in afdeling 5 van titel 5 is geregeld, uitsluit of beperkt;
c. dat een de wederpartij volgens de wet toekomende bevoegdheid tot opschorting van de nakoming uitsluit of beperkt of de gebruiker een

1 Act on the Register of Commerce.
2 *Handelsregisterwet* - Loi relative au registre de commerce.

verdergaande bevoegdheid tot opschorting verleent dan hem volgens de wet toekomt;

d. dat de beoordeling van de vraag of de gebruiker in de nakoming van een of meer van zijn verbintenissen is te kort geschoten aan hem zelf overlaat, of dat de uitoefening van de rechten die de wederpartij ter zake van een zodanige tekortkoming volgens de wet toekomen, afhankelijk stelt van de voorwaarde dat deze eerst een derde in rechte heeft aangesproken;

e. krachtens hetwelk de wederpartij aan de gebruiker bij voorbaat toestemming verleent zijn uit de overeenkomst voortvloeiende verplichtingen op een der in afdeling 3 van titel 2 bedoelde wijzen op een derde te doen overgaan, tenzij de wederpartij te allen tijde de bevoegdheid heeft de overeenkomst te ontbinden, of de gebruiker jegens de wederpartij aansprakelijk is voor de nakoming door de derde, of de overgang plaatsvindt in verband met de overdracht van een onderneming waartoe zowel die verplichtingen als de daartegenover bedongen rechten behoren;

f. dat voor het geval uit de overeenkomst voor de gebruiker voortvloeiende rechten op een derde overgaan, ertoe strekt bevoegdheden of verweermiddelen die de wederpartij volgens de wet jegens die derde zou kunnen doen gelden, uit te sluiten of te beperken;

g. dat een wettelijke verjarings- of vervaltermijn waarbinnen de wederpartij enig recht moet geldend maken, tot een verjarings- onderscheidenlijk vervaltermijn van minder dan een jaar verkort;

h. dat voor het geval bij de uitvoering van de overeenkomst schade aan een derde wordt toegebracht door de gebruiker of door een persoon of zaak waarvoor deze aansprakelijk is, de wederpartij verplicht deze schade hetzij aan de derde te vergoeden, hetzij in haar verhouding tot de gebruiker voor een groter deel te dragen dan waartoe zij volgens de wet verplicht zou zijn;

i. dat de gebruiker de bevoegdheid geeft de door hem bedongen prijs binnen drie maanden na het sluiten van de overeenkomst te verhogen, tenzij de wederpartij bevoegd is in dat geval de overeenkomst te ontbinden;

j. dat in geval van een overeenkomst tot het geregeld afleveren van zaken, elektriciteit daaronder begrepen, of tot het geregeld doen van verrichtingen, leidt tot stilzwijgende verlenging of vernieuwing van meer dan een jaar;

k. dat de bevoegdheid van de wederpartij om bewijs te leveren uitsluit of beperkt, of dat de uit de wet voortvloeiende verdeling van de bewijslast ten nadele van de wederpartij wijzigt, hetzij doordat het een verklaring van haar bevat omtrent de deugdelijkheid van de haar verschuldigde prestatie, hetzij doordat het haar belast met het bewijs dat een tekortkoming van de gebruiker aan hem kan worden toegerekend;

l. dat ten nadele van de wederpartij afwijkt van artikel 37 van Boek 3, tenzij het betrekking heeft op de vorm van door de wederpartij af te leggen verklaringen of bepaalt dat de gebruiker het hem door de wederpartij opgegeven adres als zodanig mag blijven beschouwen totdat hem een nieuw adres is meegedeeld;

m. waarbij een wederpartij die bij het aangaan van de overeenkomst werkelijke woonplaats in een gemeente in Nederland heeft, woonplaats kiest anders dan voor het geval zij te eniger tijd geen bekende werkelijke woonplaats in die gemeente zal hebben, tenzij de

overeenkomst betrekking heeft op een registergoed en woonplaats ten kantore van een notaris wordt gekozen;

n. dat voorziet in de beslechting van een geschil door een ander dan hetzij de rechter die volgens de wet bevoegd zou zijn, hetzij een of meer arbiters, tenzij het de wederpartij een termijn gunt van tenminste een maand nadat de gebruiker zich schriftelijk jegens haar op het beding heeft beroepen, om voor beslechting van het geschil door de volgens de wet bevoegde rechter te kiezen.

In a contract between a user and the other party, where the latter is a natural person not acting in the course of a business or profession, the following stipulations contained in general conditions are deemed to be unreasonably onerous:

a. a stipulation which totally and unconditionally takes away the other party's right to claim the prestation promised by the user;
b. a stipulation limiting or excluding the other party's right to set aside the contract, as provided for by section 5 of title 5;
c. a stipulation limiting or excluding the right which, pursuant to the law, the other party has to suspend performance, or one giving the user a more extensive power of suspension than he is entitled to pursuant to the law;
d. a stipulation permitting the user himself to determine the question whether he has failed in the performance of one or more of his obligations, or one making the exercise of the rights which, pursuant to the law, the other party has with respect to such failure, dependent upon the condition that the other party must first have taken judicial action against a third person;
e. a stipulation pursuant to which the other party grants advance permission to the user to have his obligations flowing from the contract transferred to a third person in one of the manners referred to in section 3 of title 2, unless the other party is at all times entitled to set aside the contract, the user is liable toward the other party for performance by the third person, or the transfer takes place in connection with the transfer of a business to which both those

Dans un contrat conclu entre un utilisateur et une autre partie, personne naturelle, qui n'agit pas dans le cadre d'une activité professionnelle ou d'une entreprise, est réputée anormalement onéreuse la stipulation faisant partie des conditions générales:

a. Enlevant à l'autre partie intégralement et inconditionnellement le droit de demander la prestation promise par l'utilisateur;
b. Excluant ou restreignant le pouvoir de résiliation revenant à l'autre partie, tel qu'il est prévu à la section cinquième du titre cinquième;
c. Excluant ou restreignant le pouvoir de suspension d'exécution qui revient à l'autre partie de par la loi, ou accordant à l'utilisateur un pouvoir de suspension plus étendu que celui qui lui revient de par la loi;
d. Laissant à l'utilisateur lui-même la faculté de juger s'il a manqué à l'exécution de ses obligations, ou faisant dépendre l'exercice de droits revenant de par la loi à l'autre partie relativement à un tel manquement de la condition d'avoir d'abord poursuivi un tiers en justice.
e. Comportant l'autorisation par avance, de la part de l'autre partie, à l'utilisateur de transmettre à un tiers d'une des façons visées à la section troisième du titre deuxième les obligations qui lui viennent du contrat, à moins que l'autre partie n'ait en tout temps le pouvoir de résilier le contrat, ou que l'utilisateur soit responsable à l'égard de l'autre partie de l'exécution par le tiers, ou enfin que la transmission ait lieu dans le cadre du transfert de l'entreprise à laquelle appartiennent ces obligations

obligations and the rights stipulated in exchange therefor belong;

f. a stipulation intended to exclude or limit rights or defences which the other party could use, pursuant to the law, against a third person in the event that rights of the user flowing from the contract are transferred to that third person;

g. a stipulation shortening a prescription period or a term of forfeiture within which the other party must use any right, to a period or term of less than one year;

h. a stipulation which, in the event that in the performance of the contract damage is done to a third person by the user or by a person or thing for which he is liable, obliges the other party either to compensate that third person or to contribute to the compensation, in his relationship with the user, for a larger share than he would have to pursuant to the law;

i. a stipulation which gives the user the right to increase, within three months from entering into the contract, the price which he has stipulated, unless in that case the other party is entitled to set aside the contract;

j. a stipulation leading to the tacit prolongation or renewal for more than one year of a contract for the regular delivery of things, including electricity, or for the regular performance of services;

k. a stipulation excluding or limiting the right of the other party to furnish evidence, or modifying the apportionment of the burden of proof flowing from the law to the detriment of the other party, either because it contains a declaration of the other party regarding the quality of the prestation which is owed to him, or because it charges him with the proof that a failure of the user can be imputed to the latter;

l. a stipulation derogating from article 37 of Book 3 to the detriment of the other party, unless it pertains to the form of the declarations to be made

aussi bien que les droits convenus corrélativement;

f. Visant à exclure ou à restreindre, pour le cas de la transmission à un tiers des droits résultant du contrat pour l'utilisateur, les pouvoirs ou les moyens de défense que l'autre partie de par la loi pourrait faire valoir à l'encontre du tiers;

g. Réduisant à moins d'un an un délai légal de prescription ou de déchéance dans lequel l'autre partie doit faire valoir un droit;

h. Obligeant l'autre partie, pour le cas où l'utilisateur ou une personne ou une chose dont il est responsable cause un dommage à un tiers dans l'exécution du contrat, soit à dédommager le tiers, soit à assumer le dommage, dans son rapport avec l'utilisateur, pour une part plus grande que celle dont elle serait tenue de par la loi;

i. Accordant à l'utilisateur le pouvoir d'augmenter, dans les trois mois de la conclusion du contrat, le prix qu'il a stipulé, à moins que l'autre partie puisse alors résilier le contrat;

j. Conduisant à la prolongation ou au renouvellement tacite de plus d'un an du contrat prévoyant la livraison régulière de choses, l'électricité comprise, ou la prestation régulière de services;

k. Excluant ou restreignant le pouvoir de l'autre partie de rapporter des preuves, ou modifiant le fardeau de la preuve découlant de la loi au détriment de celle-ci, soit du fait qu'elle comporte une déclaration de sa part au sujet de la bonne qualité de la prestation qui lui est due, soit du fait qu'elle lui impose la preuve qu'un manquement de l'utilisateur soit imputable à ce dernier;

l. Dérogeant, au détriment de l'autre partie, à l'article 37 du Livre troisième, à moins que la stipulation ne se rapporte à la forme des déclarations que

by the other party, or provides that the user may continue to consider the address given to him by the other party as such until a new address has been communicated to him;

m. a stipulation whereby the other party who, at the time of entering into the contract, has his real domicile in a Commune in The Netherlands, elects domicile for a purpose other than not having at any time a known, real domicile in that Commune, unless the contract pertains to registered property and domicile is elected at the office of a notary;

n. a stipulation providing for dispute settlement by a person other than the judge who would have jurisdiction according to the law or one or more arbitrators, unless it gives to the other party a period of at least one month from the date when the user has invoked the stipulation in writing against the other party, to choose for dispute settlement by the judge who has jurisdiction according to the law.

doit faire celle-ci, ou qu'elle ne dispose que l'utilisateur puisse continuer à considérer l'adresse fournie par l'autre partie comme telle jusqu'à ce qu'une nouvelle adresse ne lui ait été communiquée;

m. Comportant choix de domicile par l'autre partie qui, lors de la formation du contrat, a domicile réel dans une commune aux Pays-Bas, autrement que pour le cas où elle n'aurait plus de domicile réel connu dans cette commune, à moins que le contrat ne porte sur un bien immatriculé et que domicile ne soit élu à l'étude d'un notaire;

n. Portant un mode de règlement de différends par une personne autre que soit le juge qui serait compétent de par la loi, soit un ou plusieurs arbitres, à moins que la stipulation n'accorde à l'autre partie le délai d'au moins un mois après que l'utilisateur l'ait invoquée par écrit à son égard, afin d'opter pour le règlement du différend par le juge compétent de par la loi.

Art. 237. (6.5.2A.4) Bij een overeenkomst tussen een gebruiker en een wederpartij, natuurlijk persoon, die niet handelt in de uitoefening van een beroep of bedrijf, wordt vermoed onredelijk bezwarend te zijn een in de algemene voorwaarden voorkomend beding

a. dat de gebruiker een, gelet op de omstandigheden van het geval, ongebruikelijk lange of onvoldoende bepaalde termijn geeft om op een aanbod of een andere verklaring van de wederpartij te reageren;

b. dat de inhoud van de verplichtingen van de gebruiker wezenlijk beperkt ten opzichte van hetgeen de wederpartij, mede gelet op de wettelijke regels die op de overeenkomst betrekking hebben, zonder dat beding redelijkerwijs mocht verwachten;

c. dat de gebruiker de bevoegdheid verleent een prestatie te verschaffen die wezenlijk van de toegezegde prestatie afwijkt, tenzij de wederpartij bevoegd is in dat geval de overeenkomst te ontbinden;

d. dat de gebruiker van zijn gebondenheid aan de overeenkomst bevrijdt of hem de bevoegdheid daartoe geeft anders dan op in de overeenkomst vermelde gronden welke van dien aard zijn dat deze gebondenheid niet meer van hem kan worden gevergd;

e. dat de gebruiker een ongebruikelijk lange of onvoldoende bepaalde termijn voor de nakoming geeft;

f. dat de gebruiker of een derde geheel of ten dele bevrijdt van een wettelijke verplichting tot schadevergoeding;

g. dat een de wederpartij volgens de wet toekomende bevoegdheid tot verrekening uitsluit of beperkt of de gebruiker een verdergaande bevoegdheid tot verrekening verleent dan hem volgens de wet toekomt;

h. dat als sanctie op bepaalde gedragingen van de wederpartij, nalaten daaronder begrepen, verval stelt van haar toekomende rechten of van de bevoegdheid bepaalde verweren te voeren, behoudens voor zover deze gedragingen het verval van die rechten of verweren rechtvaardigen;

i. dat voor het geval de overeenkomst wordt beëindigd anders dan op grond van het feit dat de wederpartij in de nakoming van haar verbintenis is tekort geschoten, de wederpartij verplicht een geldsom te betalen, behoudens voor zover het betreft een redelijke vergoeding voor door de gebruiker geleden verlies of gederfde winst;

j. dat de wederpartij verplicht tot het sluiten van een overeenkomst met de gebruiker of met een derde, tenzij dit, mede gelet op het verband van die overeenkomst met de in dit artikel bedoelde overeenkomst, redelijkerwijze van de wederpartij kan worden gevergd;

k. dat voor een overeenkomst als bedoeld in artikel 236 onder j een duur bepaalt van meer dan een jaar, tenzij de wederpartij de bevoegdheid heeft de overeenkomst telkens na een jaar op te zeggen;

l. dat de wederpartij aan een opzegtermijn bindt die langer is dan drie maanden of langer dan de termijn waarop de gebruiker de overeenkomst kan opzeggen;

m. dat voor de geldigheid van een door de wederpartij te verrichten verklaring een strengere vorm dan het vereiste van een onderhandse akte stelt;

n. dat bepaalt dat een door de wederpartij verleende volmacht onherroepelijk is of niet eindigt door haar dood of ondercuratelestelling, tenzij de volmacht strekt tot levering van een registergoed.

In a contract between a user and the other party, where the latter is a natural person not acting in the course of a business or profession, the following stipulations contained in general conditions are presumed to be unreasonably onerous:

a. a stipulation which, taking into account the circumstances of the case, gives the user an unusually long or an insufficiently determined period to react to an offer or another declaration of the other party;

b. a stipulation which materially limits the content of the obligations of the user with respect to what the other party could reasonably expect without such stipulation, also taking into account the rules of law which pertain to the contract;

c. a stipulation giving the user the right to render a prestation materially deviating from the promised prestation, unless the other party has the power to set the contract aside in that case;

Dans un contrat conclu entre un utilisateur et une autre partie, personne naturelle, qui n'agit pas dans le cadre d'une activité professionnelle ou d'une entreprise, est présumée anormalement onéreuse la stipulation faisant partie des conditions générales:

a. Donnant à l'utilisateur un délai inhabituellement long ou insuffisamment déterminé, compte tenu des circonstances de l'espèce, pour réagir à une offre ou à une autre communication de l'autre partie;

b. Restreignant de façon essentielle le contenu des obligations de l'utilisateur en regard de ce à quoi l'autre partie, compte tenu également des dispositions de la loi relatives au contrat en question, pouvait normalement s'attendre en l'absence de la stipulation;

c. Accordant à l'utilisateur le pouvoir de fournir une prestation qui déroge essentiellement à celle convenue, à moins que l'autre partie ne puisse alors résilier le contrat;

d. a stipulation which frees the user from being bound to the contract, or which gives him the right to free himself on grounds other than those mentioned in the contract and of such a nature that he cannot be required to remain bound;
e. a stipulation giving the user an unusually long or an insufficiently determined period for performance;
f. a stipulation which frees the user or a third person in whole or in part from a legal obligation to repair damage;
g. a stipulation limiting or excluding a right of compensation that the other party has pursuant to the law, or one giving the user a more extensive right to compensation than he has according the law;
h. a stipulation providing for the forfeiture of rights of the other party or of his power to bring forward certain defences as a sanction for a certain conduct of his, including omissions, except to the extent that this conduct justifies the forfeiture of those rights or defences;
i. a stipulation obliging the other party to pay a sum of money in the event that the contract is terminated for a reason other than the fact that he has failed in the performance of his obligation, except to the extent that it concerns a reasonable compensation for loss suffered by the user or for profit of which he has been deprived;
j. a stipulation obliging the other party to enter into a contract with the user or with a third person, unless this can reasonably be required from the other party, also taking into account the relationship of that contract with the contract referred to in this article;
k. a stipulation fixing a duration of more than one year for a contract as referred to in article 236 *sub* j, unless the other party has the right to resiliate the contract after each year;
l. a stipulation binding the other party to a resiliation period of more than three months, or for longer than the period according to which the user can cancel the contract;

d. Déchargeant l'utilisateur de ses obligations en vertu du contrat ou lui accordant le pouvoir de s'en libérer autrement qu'aux motifs prévus au contrat qui sont de nature telle que le respect des obligations ne peut plus lui être imposé;
e. Accordant à l'utilisateur un délai d'exécution inhabituellement long ou insuffisamment déterminé;
f. Déchargeant l'utilisateur ou un tiers en tout ou en partie de l'obligation légale de réparer le dommage;
g. Excluant ou restreignant le pouvoir de compensation revenant à l'autre partie de par la loi ou accordant à l'utilisateur un pouvoir de compensation plus étendu que celui qui lui revient de par la loi;
h. Portant, comme sanction d'une conduite déterminée de l'autre partie, omissions comprises, déchéance de droits lui revenant ou du pouvoir de faire valoir des moyens déterminés de défense, sauf dans la mesure où la conduite justifie cette déchéance;
i. Portant que, pour le cas où le contrat prend fin autrement que par un manquement de l'autre partie dans l'exécution de son obligation, elle soit obligée à payer une somme d'argent, sauf dans la mesure où il s'agit d'une indemnité normale pour la perte subie ou le profit manqué par l'utilisateur;
j. Obligeant l'autre partie à conclure un contrat avec l'utilisateur ou avec un tiers, à moins que, compte tenu également du rapport entre ce contrat et celui qui est visé au présent article, il convienne de l'imposer à l'autre partie;
k. Prévoyant, pour le contrat visé au point j. de l'article 236, une durée de plus d'un an, à moins que l'autre partie n'ait le pouvoir de résilier le contrat à la fin de chaque année;
l. Obligeant l'autre partie à respecter un délai de résiliation dépassant les trois mois ou le délai de résiliation pour l'utilisateur;

m. a stipulation requiring a more stringent form than that of a deed under private signature for the validity of a declaration to be made by the other party;
n. a stipulation which provides that procuration given by the other party be irrevocable or that it not be terminated by his death or his placement under curatorship, unless the procuration is intended for delivery of registered property.

m. Posant, pour la validité d'une déclaration que doit faire l'autre partie, une condition de forme plus sévère que celle de l'acte sous seing privé;
n. Disposant que la procuration fournie par l'autre partie est irrévocable ou qu'elle ne prend pas fin par la mort ou par la mise en curatelle, à moins que la procuration ne vise le transfert d'un bien immatriculé.

Art. 238. (6.5.2A.4a) Bij een overeenkomst als bedoeld in de artikelen 236 en 237, kan jegens de wederpartij geen beroep worden gedaan
a. op het feit dat de overeenkomst in naam van een derde is gesloten, indien dit beroep berust op het enkele feit dat een beding van deze strekking in de algemene voorwaarden voorkomt;
b. op het feit dat de algemene voorwaarden beperkingen bevatten van de bevoegdheid van een gevolmachtigde van de gebruiker, die zo ongebruikelijk zijn dat de wederpartij ze zonder het beding niet behoefde te verwachten, tenzij zij ze kende.

In a contract as referred to in articles 236 and 237, one cannot invoke against the other party:
a. the fact that the contract has been entered into in the name of a third person, if this is based on the sole fact that a stipulation to that effect appears in the general conditions;
b. the fact that the general conditions contain limitations upon the power of a procurator of the user which are so unusual that the other party, in the absence of the stipulation, did not have to expect them, unless he knew of them.

Dans le contrat visé aux article 236 et 237, ne peut être invoqué à l'encontre de l'autre partie:
a. Le fait que le contrat a été conclu au nom d'un tiers, si l'argument a pour seul fondement qu'une stipulation à cet effet figure aux conditions générales;
b. Le fait que les conditions générales comportent des restrictions au pouvoir du procureur de l'utilisateur, qui sont si inusitées que, en l'absence de la stipulation, l'autre partie ne devait pas s'y attendre, à moins qu'elle ne les ait connu.

Art. 239. (6.5.2A.5) - 1. Bij algemene maatregel van bestuur kunnen de onderdelen a–n van artikel 237 worden gewijzigd en kan hun toepassingsgebied worden beperkt.
- 2. Alvorens een voordracht tot vaststelling, wijziging of intrekking van een maatregel als bedoeld in het eerste lid te doen, hoort Onze Minister van Justitie de naar zijn oordeel representatieve organisaties van hen die bij het sluiten van de overeenkomsten waarop de maatregel betrekking heeft, algemene voorwaarden plegen te gebruiken en van hen die bij die overeenkomsten als hun wederpartij plegen op te treden.
- 3. Een besluit als in het eerste lid bedoeld wordt zodra het is vastgesteld toegezonden aan de voorzitters van de beide Kamers van de Staten-Generaal. Een dergelijk besluit treedt niet in werking dan nadat twee maanden zijn verstreken sinds de datum van uitgifte van het Staatsblad waarin het is geplaatst.

1. Paragraphs a - n of article 237 can be modified and their scope of application can be limited by regulation.
2. Before proposing the making, modification or repeal of a regulation as referred to in paragraph 1, Our Minister of Justice shall hear organizations which, in his opinion, are representative of those who, in entering into contracts to which the regulation applies, habitually use general conditions, and of those who habitually act as the other party in those contracts.
3. As soon as it has been issued, a regulation as referred to in paragraph 1 shall be sent to the chairpersons of both Chambers of the States General. Such a regulation does not enter into force until after the lapse of two months from the date of issue of the *Staatsblad*[1] in which it appears.

1. Un décret peut modifier les alinéas a à n de l'article 237 et restreindre leur domaine d'application.
2. Avant de faire une proposition visant à prendre, modifier ou abroger un décret tel que visé au paragraphe 1er, Notre ministre de la Justice entend les organisations qu'il estime représentatives de ceux qui ont l'habitude d'utiliser des conditions générales lors de la conclusion des contrats sur lesquels porte le décret, et de ceux qui ont l'habitude de se porter cocontractants à ces contrats.
3. Dès qu'est pris un décret tel que visé au paragraphe 1er, il est envoyé aux présidents des deux Chambres des États-Généraux. Un tel décret n'entre en vigueur que deux mois après la date de publication de la livraison du *Staatsblad*[2] dans laquelle il paraît.

Art. 240. (6.5.2A.6) - 1. Op vordering van een rechtspersoon als bedoeld in lid 3 kunnen bepaalde bedingen in bepaalde algemene voorwaarden onredelijk bezwarend worden verklaard; de artikelen 233 onder a, 236 en 237 zijn van overeenkomstige toepassing. Voor de toepassing van de vorige zin wordt een beding in algemene voorwaarden dat in strijd is met een dwingende wetsbepaling, als onredelijk bezwarend aangemerkt.
- 2. De vordering kan worden ingesteld tegen de gebruiker, alsmede tegen een rechtspersoon met volledige rechtsbevoegdheid die ten doel heeft de behartiging van belangen van personen die een beroep of bedrijf uitoefenen, indien hij het gebruik van de algemene voorwaarden door die personen bevordert.
- 3. De vordering komt toe aan rechtspersonen met volledige rechtsbevoegdheid die ten doel hebben de behartiging van belangen van personen die een beroep of bedrijf uitoefenen of van eindgebruikers van niet voor een beroep of bedrijf bestemde goederen of diensten. Zij kan slechts betrekking hebben op algemene voorwaarden die worden gebruikt of bestemd zijn te worden gebruikt in overeenkomsten met personen wier belangen door de rechtspersoon worden behartigd.
- 4. De eiser is niet ontvankelijk indien niet blijkt dat hij, alvorens de vordering in te stellen, de gebruiker of, in het geval bedoeld in artikel 1003 van het Wetboek van Burgerlijke Rechtsvordering, de aldaar bedoelde vereniging, de gelegenheid heeft geboden om in onderling overleg de algemene voorwaarden zodanig te wijzigen dat de bezwaren die grond voor de vordering zouden opleveren, zijn weggenomen. Een termijn van zes maanden na schriftelijke kennisgeving van de bezwaren is daartoe in elk geval voldoende.
- 5. Voor zover een rechtspersoon met het gebruik van bedingen in algemene voorwaarden heeft ingestemd, komt hem geen vordering als bedoeld in lid 1 toe.

1 State Gazette.
2 *Staatsblad* - Journal officiel des Pays-Bas.

1. Upon the demand of a legal person as referred to in paragraph 3, certain stipulations in certain general conditions may be declared to be unreasonably onerous; articles 233 *sub* a, 236 and 237 apply *mutatis mutandis*. For the purposes of the preceding sentence, a stipulation in general conditions which is contrary to an imperative provision of law is deemed to be unreasonably onerous.

2. The action may be instituted against the user, as well as against a legal person with full legal capacity whose purpose it is to take care of the interests of persons who exercise a profession or business, if the legal person promotes the use of the general conditions by those persons.

3. The action may be instituted by legal persons with full legal capacity whose purpose it is to take care of the interests of persons who exercise a profession or business or of final users of goods or services not destined for a profession or business. The action can only pertain to general conditions which are used or are destined to be used in contracts with persons whose interests are taken care of by the legal person.

4. The plaintiff's action is only admissible if there is evidence that, before the action was brought, he has given the user or, in the case referred to in article 1003 of the Code of Civil Procedure, the association referred to in that article, the opportunity to modify the general conditions in mutual consultation in such a fashion that the objections which would be the ground for the action, are removed. A period of six months after written notification of the objections suffices for that purpose in any case.

5. A legal person may not make the demand referred to in paragraph 1, to the extent that he has agreed to the use of stipulations in general conditions.

1. Sur une action intentée par une personne morale telle que visée au paragraphe 3, peuvent être déclarées anormalement onéreuses des stipulations précises faisant partie de conditions générales déterminées; les articles 233, au point a., 236 et 237 s'appliquent par analogie. Pour l'application de la phrase précédente, une stipulation dans des conditions générales contraire à une disposition impérative de la loi est réputée anormalement onéreuse.

2. L'action peut être intentée à un utilisateur, de même qu'à une personne morale ayant pleine capacité juridique qui a pour but de veiller aux intérêts de personnes exerçant une activité professionnelle ou une entreprise, si elle promeut l'emploi des conditions générales par celles-ci.

3. L'action revient à des personnes morales ayant la pleine capacité juridique, qui ont pour but de veiller aux intérêts de personnes exerçant un métier ou une entreprise ou encore d'utilisateurs finals de biens ou de services non destinés à l'exercice d'un métier ou d'une entreprise. Elle ne peut porter que sur les conditions générales qui sont employées ou qui sont destinées à l'être dans des contrats avec des personnes aux intérêts desquelles veille la personne morale.

4. Le demandeur n'est pas recevable s'il ne justifie pas que, avant d'intenter la poursuite, il a offert, à l'utilisateur ou, dans le cas de l'article 1003 du Code de procédure civile, à l'association visée, la possibilité de modifier les conditions générales d'un commun accord de manière à lever les objections pouvant fonder l'action. Un délai de six mois après avis écrit des objections est de toute façon suffisant.

5. Dans la mesure où une personne morale a consenti à l'utilisation de stipulations faisant partie de conditions générales, l'action visée au paragraphe 1er ne lui revient pas.

Art. 241. (6.5.2A.7) - 1. Het Gerechtshof te 's-Gravenhage is bij uitsluiting bevoegd tot kennisneming van vorderingen als in het vorige artikel bedoeld.

- 2. De in het vorige artikel bedoelde rechtspersonen hebben de bevoegdheden, geregeld in de artikelen 285 en 376 van het Wetboek van Burgerlijke Rechtsvordering; artikel 379 van dat wetboek is niet van toepassing.
- 3. Op vordering van de eiser kan aan de uitspraak worden verbonden
a. een verbod van het gebruik van de door de uitspraak getroffen bedingen of van het bevorderen daarvan;
b. een gebod om een aanbeveling tot het gebruik van deze bedingen te herroepen;
c. een veroordeling tot het openbaar maken of laten openbaar maken van de uitspraak, zulks op door de rechter te bepalen wijze en op kosten van de door de rechter aan te geven partij of partijen.
- 4. De rechter kan in zijn uitspraak aangeven op welke wijze het onredelijk bezwarend karakter van de bedingen waarop de uitspraak betrekking heeft, kan worden weggenomen.
- 5. Geschillen terzake van de tenuitvoerlegging van de in lid 3 bedoelde veroordelingen, alsmede van de veroordeling tot betaling van een dwangsom, zo deze is opgelegd, worden bij uitsluiting door het Gerechtshof te 's-Gravenhage beslist.

1. The Court of Appeal at The Hague has exclusive jurisdiction to hear actions as referred to in the preceding article.
2. The legal persons referred to in the preceding article have the rights provided for by articles 285 and 376 of the Code of Civil Procedure; article 379 of that Code does not apply.
3. Upon the demand of the plaintiff the decision may be accompanied by:
a. a prohibition to use or to promote stipulations affected by the decision;
b. an order to revoke a recommendation to use these stipulations;
c. a condemnation to publish the decision or to have it published, in a manner determined by the judge and at the expense of the party or parties indicated by the judge.
4. The judge may indicate in his decision in which manner the unreasonable onerous character of the stipulations to which the decision pertains can be removed.
5. Disputes regarding the execution of the condemnations referred to in paragraph 3, as well as of the condemnation to pay a forfeiture, if imposed, are exclusively decided upon by the Court of Appeal at The Hague.

1. La Cour d'appel de La Haye a compétence exclusive pour connaître des actions visées à l'article précédent.
2. Les personnes morales visées à l'article précédent ont les pouvoirs prévus aux articles 285 et 376 du Code de procédure civile; l'article 379 de ce code ne s'applique pas.
3. À la demande du demandeur, peut être joint au jugement:
a. L'interdiction d'utiliser les stipulations frappées du jugement ou d'en promouvoir l'utilisation;
b. L'ordre de révoquer la recommandation d'utiliser ces stipulations;
c. La condamnation à publier ou à faire publier le jugement, de la manière déterminée par le juge et aux frais de la ou des parties qu'il désigne.
4. Le juge peut indiquer dans le jugement la façon d'enlever le caractère anormalement onéreux des stipulations qui en sont frappées.
5. Les litiges relatifs à l'exécution des condamnations visées au paragraphe 3, de même qu'à la condamnation au paiement d'une astreinte, le cas échéant, relèvent de la compétence exclusive de la Cour d'appel de La Haye.

Art. 242. (6.5.2A.8) - 1. Op vordering van een of meer van degenen tegen wie de in artikel 240 lid 1 bedoelde uitspraak is gedaan, kan de rechter die uitspraak wijzigen of opheffen op grond dat zij tengevolge van een

wijziging in de omstandigheden niet langer gerechtvaardigd is. De vordering wordt ingesteld tegen de rechtspersoon op wiens vordering de uitspraak was gedaan.
- 2. Indien de rechtspersoon op wiens vordering de uitspraak was gedaan, is ontbonden, wordt de zaak met een verzoekschrift ingeleid. Voor de toepassing van artikel 429f lid 1 van het Wetboek van Burgerlijke Rechtsvordering worden rechtspersonen als bedoeld in artikel 240 lid 3 als belanghebbenden aangemerkt.
- 3. Artikel 241 leden 1, 2, 3 onder c en 5 is van overeenkomstige toepassing.
- 4. De vorige leden zijn niet van toepassing voor zover de uitspraak betrekking had op een beding dat door de wet als onredelijk bezwarend wordt aangemerkt.

1. Upon the demand of one or more persons against whom the decision referred to in article 240 paragraph 1 has been rendered, the judge may modify or repeal the decision upon the ground that it is no longer justified as a result of a change in the circumstances. The action is instituted against the legal person upon whose demand the decision was rendered.
2. If the legal person upon whose demand the decision was rendered has been dissolved, the case is initiated by a petition. For the application of article 429f paragraph 1 of the Code of Civil Procedure, legal persons as referred to in article 240 paragraph 3 are considered as interested persons.
3. Article 241 paragraphs 1, 2, 3 *sub* c and 5 applies *mutatis mutandis*.

4. The preceding paragraphs do not apply to the extent that the decision pertained to a stipulation that the law deems to be unreasonably onerous.

1. Sur une action intentée par une ou plusieurs personnes à l'encontre desquelles a été prononcé le jugement visé au paragraphe 1er de l'article 240, le juge peut modifier ou révoquer le jugement au motif que, en raison des circonstances modifiées, il n'est plus justifié. L'action est intentée à la personne morale à la demande de laquelle le jugement a été prononcé.

2. Si la personne morale sur l'action de laquelle avait été rendu le jugement a été dissoute, l'affaire est introduite par requête. Pour l'application de l'article 429f, paragraphe 1er du Code de procédure civile, sont réputées intéressées les personnes visées à l'article 240, paragraphe 3.

3. Les paragraphes 1er, 2, 3, au point c., et 5 de l'article 241 s'appliquent par analogie.
4. Les paragraphes précédents ne s'appliquent pas dans la mesure où le jugement portait sur une stipulation réputée anormalement onéreuse de par la loi.

Art. 243. (6.5.2A.9) Een beding in algemene voorwaarden dat door degene jegens wie een verbod tot gebruik ervan is uitgesproken, in strijd met het verbod in een overeenkomst wordt opgenomen, is vernietigbaar. Artikel 235 is van overeenkomstige toepassing.

A stipulation in general conditions which a person, against whom a prohibition to use such stipulation has been issued, includes in a contract in violation of the prohibition may be annulled. Article 235 applies *mutatis mutandis*.

Est annulable la stipulation faisant partie de conditions générales introduite dans un contrat, en violation d'une interdiction, par celui contre qui a été prononcée l'interdiction de l'utiliser. L'article 235 s'applique par analogie.

Art. 244. (6.5.2A.10) - 1. Een persoon die handelt in de uitoefening van een beroep of bedrijf, kan geen beroep doen op een beding in een overeenkomst met een partij die terzake van de goederen of diensten waarop

die overeenkomst betrekking heeft, met gebruikmaking van algemene voorwaarden overeenkomsten met haar afnemers heeft gesloten, voor zover een beroep op dat beding onredelijk zou zijn wegens zijn nauwe samenhang met een in de algemene voorwaarden voorkomend beding dat krachtens deze afdeling is vernietigd of door een uitspraak als bedoeld in artikel 240 lid 1 is getroffen.
- 2. Is tegen de gebruiker een vordering als bedoeld in artikel 240 lid 1 ingesteld, dan is hij bevoegd die persoon in het geding te roepen teneinde voor recht te horen verklaren dat een beroep als bedoeld in het vorige lid onredelijk zou zijn. Artikel 241 leden 2, 3 onder c, 4 en 5 alsmede de artikelen 68, 69 en 73 van het Wetboek van Burgerlijke Rechtsvordering zijn van overeenkomstige toepassing.
- 3. Op de uitspraak is artikel 242 van overeenkomstige toepassing.
- 4. Op eerdere overeenkomsten met betrekking tot de voormelde goederen en diensten zijn de leden 1-3 van overeenkomstige toepassing.

1. A person acting in the course of a profession or business may not invoke a stipulation in a contract with a party who, using general conditions, has entered into contracts with its clients concerning the goods or services to which that contract applies, to the extent that invoking that stipulation would be unreasonable because of its close connection with a stipulation contained in the general conditions which, pursuant to this section, has been annulled or has been affected by a decision as referred to in article 240 paragraph 1.
2. Where an action as referred to in article 240 paragraph 1 has been instituted against the user, he is entitled to implead that person in order to have it judicially declared that invoking a stipulation as referred to in the preceding paragraph would be unreasonable. Article 241 paragraphs 2, 3 *sub* c, 4 and 5, as well as articles 68, 69 and 73 of the Code of Civil Procedure apply *mutatis mutandis*.
3. Article 242 applies *mutatis mutandis* to the decision.
4. Paragraphs 1 - 3 apply *mutatis mutandis* to earlier contracts pertaining to the aforementioned goods and services.

1. Une personne qui agit dans le cadre d'une activité professionnelle ou d'une entreprise ne peut, dans un contrat avec un cocontractant qui, au sujet de biens ou des services sur lesquels porte ce contrat, a conclu des contrats avec ses clients en utilisant des conditions générales, invoquer une stipulation, dans la mesure où il serait déraisonnable de l'invoquer en raison de son rapport étroit avec une stipulation faisant partie des conditions générales, qui a été annulée en application de la présente section ou qui a été frappée d'un jugement visé à l'article 240, paragraphe 1er.
2. L'utilisateur contre qui a été intentée une action visée à l'article 240, paragraphe 1er peut appeler en cause cette personne pour faire déclarer en justice qu'il serait déraisonnable d'invoquer la stipulation visée au paragraphe précédent. Les paragraphes 2, 3, au point c., 4 et 5, de l'article 241, de même que les articles 68, 69 et 73 du Code de procédure civile s'appliquent par analogie.
3. L'article 242 s'applique par analogie au jugement.
4. Les paragraphes 1er à 3 s'appliquent par analogie aux contrats antérieurs relatifs aux biens et services susvisés.

Art. 245. (6.5.2A.11) Deze afdeling is noch van toepassing op arbeidsovereenkomsten, noch op collectieve arbeidsovereenkomsten.

This section does not apply to contracts of employment or to collective contracts of employment.

La présente section ne s'applique ni aux contrats de travail ni aux conventions collectives de travail.

Art. 246. (6.5.2A.12) Noch van de artikelen 231-244, noch van de bepalingen van de in artikel 239 lid 1 bedoelde algemene maatregelen van bestuur kan worden afgeweken. De bevoegdheid om een beding krachtens deze afdeling door een buitengerechtelijke verklaring te vernietigen, kan niet worden uitgesloten.

No derogations from articles 231 - 244 are allowed, nor from the provisions of regulations referred to in article 239 paragraph 1. The right to annul a stipulation pursuant to this section by extrajudicial declaration may not be excluded.

On ne peut déroger ni aux articles 231 à 244 ni aux dispositions des décrets visés à l'article 239, paragraphe 1er. Ne peut être exclu le pouvoir d'annuler une stipulation en application de la présente section par une déclaration extrajudiciaire.

Art. 247. (6.5.2A.13) - 1. Op overeenkomsten tussen partijen die handelen in de uitoefening van een beroep of bedrijf en die beide in Nederland gevestigd zijn, is deze afdeling van toepassing, ongeacht het recht dat de overeenkomst beheerst.
- 2. Op overeenkomsten tussen partijen die handelen in de uitoefening van een beroep of bedrijf en die niet beide in Nederland gevestigd zijn, is deze afdeling niet van toepassing, ongeacht het recht dat de overeenkomst beheerst.
- 3. Een partij is in de zin van de leden 1 en 2 in Nederland gevestigd, indien haar hoofdvestiging, of, zo de prestatie volgens de overeenkomst door een andere vestiging dan de hoofdvestiging moet worden verricht, deze andere vestiging zich in Nederland bevindt.
- 4. Op overeenkomsten tussen een gebruiker en een wederpartij, natuurlijk persoon, die niet handelt in de uitoefening van een beroep of bedrijf, is, indien de wederpartij haar gewone verblijfplaats in Nederland heeft, deze afdeling van toepassing, ongeacht het recht dat de overeenkomst beheerst.

1. This section applies to contracts between parties who act in the course of a profession or business and who are both domiciled in The Netherlands, irrespective of the law applicable to the contract.
2. This section does not apply to contracts between parties who act in the course of a profession or business and who are not both domiciled in The Netherlands, irrespective of the law applicable to the contract.
3. For the purposes of paragraphs 1 and 2 a party is domiciled in The Netherlands, if its principal establishment is in The Netherlands, or where, according to the contract, the prestation must be performed by an establishment other than the principal one, if that other establishment is in The Netherlands.
4. This section applies to contracts between a user and the other party, where the latter is a natural person not acting in

1. Les contrats entre parties agissant dans le cadre d'une activité professionnelle ou d'une entreprise et toutes deux établies aux Pays-Bas sont soumis à la présente section, quel que soit le droit régissant le contrat.

2. Les contrats entre parties agissant dans le cadre d'une activité professionnelle ou d'une entreprise mais non toutes deux établies aux Pays-Bas ne sont pas soumis à la présente section, quel que soit le droit régissant le contrat.
3. Une partie est établie aux Pays-Bas au sens des paragraphes 1er et 2 si son établissement principal s'y trouve ou l'établissement autre que principal qui doit fournir la prestation en vertu du contrat.

4. Les contrats entre un utilisateur et une autre partie, personne naturelle, qui n'agit pas dans le cadre d'une activité

the course of a business or profession, if the other party has his habitual place of residence in the Netherlands, irrespective of the law applicable to the contract.

professionnelle ou d'une entreprise, sont soumis à la présente section, si celle-ci a sa résidence ordinaire aux Pays-Bas, quel que soit le droit régissant le contrat.

AFDELING 4 Rechtsgevolgen van overeenkomsten

Section 4 *Juridical effects of contracts*

Section quatrième *Des effets des contrats*

Art. 248. (6.5.3.1) - 1. Een overeenkomst heeft niet alleen de door partijen overeengekomen rechtsgevolgen, maar ook die welke, naar de aard van de overeenkomst, uit de wet, de gewoonte of de eisen van redelijkheid en billijkheid voortvloeien.
- 2. Een tussen partijen als gevolg van de overeenkomst geldende regel is niet van toepassing, voor zover dit in de gegeven omstandigheden naar maatstaven van redelijkheid en billijkheid onaanvaardbaar zou zijn.

1. A contract has not only the juridical effects agreed to by the parties, but also those which, according to the nature of the contract, result from the law, usage or the requirements of reasonableness and equity.
2. A rule binding upon the parties as a result of the contract does not apply to the extent that, in the given circumstances, this would be unacceptable according to criteria of reasonableness and equity.

1. Le contrat ne produit pas seulement les effets juridiques convenus entre les parties, mais également ceux qui, suivant la nature du contrat, découlent de la loi, de l'usage ou des exigences de la raison et de l'équité.

2. La règle à laquelle leur rapport est soumis par l'effet du contrat ne s'applique pas dans la mesure où, en la circonstance, cela serait inacceptable d'après des critères de la raison et de l'équité.

Art. 249. (6.5.3.2) De rechtsgevolgen van een overeenkomst gelden mede voor de rechtverkrijgenden onder algemene titel, tenzij uit de overeenkomst iets anders voortvloeit.

Unless the contract produces a different result, its juridical effects also bind successors by general title.

Les effets juridiques du contrat s'étendent également aux ayants cause à titre universel, à moins qu'il n'en résulte autrement du contrat.

Art. 250. (6.5.3.2a) Bij overeenkomst kan worden afgeweken van de volgende artikelen van deze afdeling, met uitzondering van de artikelen 251 lid 3, 252 lid 2 voor zover het de eis van een notariële akte betreft, en lid 3, 253 lid 1, 257, 258, 259 en 260.

A contract may derogate from the following articles of this section with the exception of articles 251, paragraph 3, 252, paragraph 2, inasmuch as the requirement of a notarial deed is concerned, and paragraph 3, 253, paragraph 1, 257, 258, 259 and 260.

Il peut être dérogé par contrat aux articles suivants de la présente section, à l'exception de l'article 251, paragraphe 3, de l'article 252, paragraphe 2, dans la mesure où cela touche la condition d'un acte notarié, et paragraphe 3, de l'article 253, paragraphe 1er, et des articles 257, 258, 259 et 260.

Art. 251. (6.5.3.3) - 1. Staat een uit een overeenkomst voortvloeiend, voor overgang vatbaar recht in een zodanig verband met een aan de schuldeiser

toebehorend goed, dat hij bij dat recht slechts belang heeft, zolang hij het goed behoudt, dan gaat dat recht over op degene die dat goed onder bijzondere titel verkrijgt.
- 2. Is voor het recht een tegenprestatie overeengekomen, dan gaat de verplichting tot het verrichten van die tegenprestatie mede over, voor zover deze betrekking heeft op de periode na de overgang. De vervreemder blijft naast de verkrijger jegens de wederpartij aansprakelijk, behoudens voor zover deze zich na de overgang in geval van uitblijven van de tegenprestatie van haar verbintenis kan bevrijden door ontbinding of beëindiging van de overeenkomst.
- 3. Het in de vorige leden bepaalde geldt niet, indien de verkrijger van het goed tot de wederpartij bij de overeenkomst een verklaring richt dat hij de overgang van het recht niet aanvaardt.
- 4. Uit de rechtshandeling waarbij het goed wordt overgedragen, kan voortvloeien dat geen overgang plaatsvindt.

1. Where a right susceptible of transfer and resulting from a contract relates to property belonging to the creditor in such a fashion that he only retains an interest in that right as long as he retains the property, the right is transferred to the person who acquires the property by particular title.
2. Where in exchange for the right a counterprestation has been agreed to, the obligation to perform that counterprestation is also transferred to the extent that it pertains to the period following the transfer. The alienator remains liable, with the acquirer, to the other party except to the extent that the other party can, after the transfer, release himself of his obligation by setting the contract aside or by terminating it in the event of non-performance of the counterprestation.
3. The provisions of the preceding paragraphs do not apply if the acquirer of the property addresses a declaration to the other party to the contract indicating that he does not accept the transfer of the right.
4. The juridical act by which the property is transferred may have as its result that no transfer of the right will take place.

1. Lorsqu'il résulte d'un contrat un droit susceptible de transmission qui a un lien tel avec un bien appartenant au créancier que celui-ci n'a d'intérêt dans ce droit que tant qu'il conserve le bien, le droit se transmet à l'acquéreur à titre particulier du bien.
2. Lorsque le droit fait l'objet d'une contre-prestation convenue, l'obligation d'effectuer cette contre-prestation se transmet avec ce droit dans la mesure où elle porte sur la période postérieure à la transmission. L'aliénateur reste tenu envers l'autre partie, à côté de l'acquéreur, sauf dans la mesure où celle-ci, après la transmission, peut se libérer de son obligation par la résiliation du contrat, ou en y mettant fin, au cas d'inexécution de la contre-prestation.
3. Les dispositions des paragraphes précédents sont sans effet si l'acquéreur du bien adresse à l'autre partie au contrat une déclaration indiquant qu'il n'accepte pas la transmission du droit.
4. Il peut découler de l'acte juridique par lequel est transmis le bien que le droit ne se transmet pas.

Art. 252. (6.5.3.4) - 1. Bij een overeenkomst kan worden bedongen dat de verplichting van een der partijen om iets te dulden of niet te doen ten aanzien van een haar toebehorend registergoed, zal overgaan op degenen die het goed onder bijzondere titel zullen verkrijgen, en dat mede gebonden zullen zijn degenen die van de rechthebbende een recht tot gebruik van het goed zullen verkrijgen.
- 2. Voor de werking van het in lid 1 bedoelde beding is vereist dat van de overeenkomst tussen partijen een notariële akte wordt opgemaakt,

gevolgd door inschrijving daarvan in de openbare registers. Degene jegens wie de verplichting bestaat, waarop het beding betrekking heeft, moet in de akte ter zake van de inschrijving woonplaats kiezen in Nederland.
- 3. Ook na inschrijving heeft het beding geen werking:
a. jegens hen die voor de inschrijving onder bijzondere titel een recht op het goed of tot gebruik van het goed hebben verkregen;
b. jegens een beslaglegger op het goed of een recht daarop, indien de inschrijving op het tijdstip van de inschrijving van het proces-verbaal van inbeslagneming nog niet had plaats gevonden;
c. jegens hen die hun recht hebben verkregen van iemand die ingevolge het onder a of b bepaalde niet aan de bedongen verplichting gebonden was.
- 4. Is voor de verplichting een tegenprestatie overeengekomen, dan gaat bij de overgang van de verplichting het recht op de tegenprestatie mee over, voor zover deze betrekking heeft op de periode na de overgang en ook het beding omtrent deze tegenprestatie in de registers ingeschreven is.
- 5. Dit artikel is niet van toepassing op verplichtingen die een rechthebbende beperken in zijn bevoegdheid het goed te vervreemden of te bezwaren.

1. A contract may stipulate that the obligation of one of the parties to tolerate or not to do something in respect of his registered property, will be transferred to the persons who will acquire the property by particular title, and that the stipulation may also bind those who will acquire a right to use the property from the title-holder.
2. For the stipulation referred to in paragraph 1 to have effect, a notarial deed must be drawn up of the contract between the parties, followed by its entry in the public registers. The creditor of the obligation to which the stipulation relates must, in the deed, elect domicile in The Netherlands for the purpose of registration.
3. Even after registration, the stipulation has no effect against:
a. the persons who, prior to registration, have acquired by particular title a right to the property or a right to use it;
b. the seizor of the property or of a right encumbering it, if the registration had not yet taken place at the time of registration of the minutes of seizure;
c. the persons who have acquired their right from a person who by virtue of the provisions of *sub* a or b was not bound by the stipulated obligation.

1. Il peut être stipulé au contrat que l'obligation de l'une des parties de tolérer ou d'omettre quelque chose à l'égard d'un bien immatriculé lui appartenant se transmettra aux acquéreurs éventuels à titre particulier du bien et qu'elle s'étendra en outre à ceux qui obtiendront de la part du titulaire un droit d'utiliser le bien.

2. La stipulation visée au paragraphe premier ne produit effet qu'à la condition que le contrat soit constaté par un acte notarié, suivi de son inscription sur les registres publics. Le créancier de l'obligation sur laquelle porte la stipulation doit, dans l'acte, élire domicile aux Pays-Bas aux fins de l'inscription.

3. Même après l'inscription, la stipulation ne produit pas d'effet:
a. À l'égard de ceux qui, avant l'inscription, ont acquis à titre particulier un droit sur le bien ou un droit d'utilisation de celui-ci;
b. À l'égard du saisissant du bien ou d'un droit le grevant, si l'inscription n'avait pas encore eu lieu au moment de l'inscription du procès-verbal de la saisie;
c. À l'égard de ceux qui tiennent leur droit d'une personne qui, par l'effet des dispositions du point a. ou b., n'était pas liée par l'obligation stipulée.

4. Where, in exchange for the obligation, a counterprestation has been agreed to, the right to that counterprestation is also transferred upon the transfer of the obligation to the extent that it pertains to the period following the transfer and that the stipulation with respect to this counterprestation has also been entered in the public registers.
5. This article does not apply to obligations which limit a title-holder in his power to alienate or encumber the property.

4. Lorsque l'obligation fait l'objet d'une contre-prestation convenue, le droit à cette contre-prestation se transmet avec elle, dans la mesure où il porte sur la période postérieure à la transmission et que la stipulation portant sur cette contre-prestation a également été inscrite sur les registres.

5. Le présent article ne s'applique pas aux obligations qui restreignent le pouvoir du titulaire d'aliéner ou de grever son bien.

Art. 253. (6.5.3.5) - 1. Een overeenkomst schept voor een derde het recht een prestatie van een der partijen te vorderen of op andere wijze jegens een van hen een beroep op de overeenkomst te doen, indien de overeenkomst een beding van die strekking inhoudt en de derde dit beding aanvaardt.
- 2. Tot de aanvaarding kan het beding door degene die het heeft gemaakt, worden herroepen.
- 3. Een aanvaarding of herroeping van het beding geschiedt door een verklaring, gericht tot een van de beide andere betrokkenen.
- 4. Is het beding onherroepelijk en jegens de derde om niet gemaakt, dan geldt het als aanvaard, indien het ter kennis van de derde is gekomen en door deze niet onverwijld is afgewezen.

1. A contract creates the right for a third person to claim a prestation from one of the parties or to invoke the contract in another manner against one of them, if the contract contains a stipulation to that effect and if the third person accepts it.
2. Until its acceptance, the stipulation can be revoked by the stipulator.
3. Acceptance or revocation of the stipulation takes place by a declaration addressed to one of the two other persons involved.
4. An irrevocable stipulation which, with respect to the third person, has been made by gratuitous title, is deemed accepted if it has come to the attention of the third person and he has not rejected it without delay.

1. Le contrat fait naître pour un tiers le droit de demander une prestation à l'une des parties ou autrement d'invoquer le contrat à son égard, s'il contient une stipulation à cet effet et que le tiers l'ait acceptée.

2. Jusqu'à l'acceptation, la stipulation est révocable par le stipulant.
3. L'acceptation ou la révocation de la stipulation s'effectue par une déclaration adressée à l'une des deux autres parties concernées.
4. La stipulation irrévocable faite, envers le tiers, à titre gratuit est réputée acceptée si elle est venue à sa connaissance et s'il ne l'a pas rejetée sans tarder.

Art. 254. (6.5.3.5a) - 1. Nadat de derde het beding heeft aanvaard, geldt hij als partij bij de overeenkomst.
- 2. Hij kan, indien dit met de strekking van het beding in overeenstemming is, daaraan ook rechten ontlenen over de periode vóór de aanvaarding.

1. Once the third person has accepted the stipulation, he is deemed to be a party to the contract.

1. Le tiers qui a accepté la stipulation est réputé partie au contrat.

2. The third person can also derive rights from the stipulation during the period prior to acceptance if this is in conformity with the necessary implication of the stipulation.

2. Il peut, si cela est conforme à l'objet de la stipulation, en tirer des droits portant sur la période antérieure à l'acceptation.

Art. 255. (6.5.3.6) - 1. Heeft een beding ten behoeve van een derde ten opzichte van die derde geen gevolg, dan kan degene die het beding heeft gemaakt, hetzij zichzelf, hetzij een andere derde als rechthebbende aanwijzen.
- 2. Hij wordt geacht zichzelf als rechthebbende te hebben aangewezen, wanneer hem door degene van wie de prestatie is bedongen, een redelijke termijn voor de aanwijzing is gesteld en hij binnen deze termijn geen aanwijzing heeft uitgebracht.

1. Where a stipulation for the benefit of a third person is without effect with respect to that third person, the stipulator can designate either himself or another third person as beneficiary.
2. The stipulator is deemed to have designated himself as beneficiary when the person from whom the prestation has been stipulated has given him a reasonable period for the designation and he has not done so within such period.

1. Lorsqu'une stipulation faite au profit d'un tiers ne produit pas d'effet à son égard, le stipulant peut désigner comme bénéficiaire soit lui-même soit un tiers différent.
2. Le stipulant est réputé s'être désigné lui-même lorsque le promettant lui a fixé un délai convenable pour la désignation et qu'il ne l'a pas effectuée dans ce délai.

Art. 256. (6.5.3.7) De partij die een beding ten behoeve van een derde heeft gemaakt, kan nakoming jegens de derde vorderen, tenzij deze zich daartegen verzet.

The party who has made a stipulation in favour of a third person may claim performance toward that third person, unless the latter objects.

La personne qui a stipulé au profit d'un tiers peut demander l'exécution envers celui-ci, à moins qu'il ne s'y oppose.

Art. 257. (6.5.3.8a) Kan een partij bij een overeenkomst ter afwering van haar aansprakelijkheid voor een gedraging van een aan haar ondergeschikte aan de overeenkomst een verweermiddel jegens haar wederpartij ontlenen, dan kan ook de ondergeschikte, indien hij op grond van deze gedraging door de wederpartij wordt aangesproken, dit verweermiddel inroepen, als ware hijzelf bij de overeenkomst partij.

Where a contracting party can derive a defence from the contract against his cocontracting party to shield him from liability for conduct by his servant, the servant may also invoke this defence, as if he were a party to the contract, if he is sued by the cocontracting party on the basis of this conduct.

Lorsqu'une partie à un contrat peut en tirer un moyen de défense à l'encontre de sa responsabilité résultant d'une conduite de son préposé, ce dernier, poursuivi par l'autre partie en raison de cette conduite, peut également opposer ce moyen, comme s'il était lui-même partie au contrat.

Art. 258. (6.5.3.11) - 1. De rechter kan op verlangen van een der partijen de gevolgen van een overeenkomst wijzigen of deze geheel of gedeeltelijk ontbinden op grond van onvoorziene omstandigheden welke van dien aard

zijn dat de wederpartij naar maatstaven van redelijkheid en billijkheid ongewijzigde instandhouding van de overeenkomst niet mag verwachten. Aan de wijziging of ontbinding kan terugwerkende kracht worden verleend.
- 2. Een wijziging of ontbinding wordt niet uitgesproken, voor zover de omstandigheden krachtens de aard van de overeenkomst of de in het verkeer geldende opvattingen voor rekening komen van degene die zich erop beroept.
- 3. Voor de toepassing van dit artikel staat degene op wie een recht of een verplichting uit een overeenkomst is overgegaan, met een partij bij die overeenkomst gelijk.

1. Upon the demand of one of the parties, the judge may modify the effects of a contract, or he may set it aside in whole or in part on the basis of unforeseen circumstances which are of such a nature that the cocontracting party, according to criteria of reasonableness and equity, may not expect that the contract be maintained in an unmodified form. The modification or the setting aside of the contract may be given retroactive force.
2. The modification or the setting aside of the contract is not pronounced to the extent that the person invoking the circumstances should be accountable for them according to the nature of the contract or common opinion.
3. For the purposes of this article, a person to whom a contractual right or obligation has been transferred, is assimilated to a contracting party.

1. Le juge peut, à la demande de l'une des parties, modifier les effets du contrat ou le résilier en tout ou en partie en raison de circonstances imprévues d'une nature telle que, d'après des critères de la raison et de l'équité, l'autre partie ne peut s'attendre au maintien intégral du contrat. La modification ou la résiliation peut être accordée avec effet rétroactif.
2. La modification ou la résiliation n'est pas prononcée dans la mesure où les circonstances invoquées par le demandeur, de par la nature du contrat ou de l'opinion généralement admise, lui incombent.
3. Pour l'application du présent article, est assimilé à une partie au contrat celui à qui a été transmis un droit ou une obligation en résultant.

Art. 259. (6.5.3.12) - 1. Indien een overeenkomst ertoe strekt een rechthebbende op of een gebruiker van een registergoed als zodanig te verplichten tot een prestatie die niet bestaat in of gepaard gaat met het dulden van voortdurend houderschap, kan de rechter op zijn verlangen de gevolgen van de overeenkomst wijzigen of deze geheel of gedeeltelijk ontbinden:
a. indien ten minste tien jaren na het sluiten van de overeenkomst zijn verlopen en het ongewijzigd voortduren van de verplichting in strijd is met het algemeen belang;
b. indien de schuldeiser bij de nakoming van de verplichting geen redelijk belang meer heeft en het niet aannemelijk is dat dit belang zal terugkeren.
- 2. Voor de termijn vermeld in lid 1 onder a telt mee de gehele periode waarin rechthebbenden op of gebruikers van het goed aan een beding van dezelfde strekking gebonden zijn geweest. De termijn geldt niet, voor zover de strijd met het algemeen belang hierin bestaat dat het beding een beletsel vormt voor verwerkelijking van een geldend bestemmingsplan.

1. If a contract is intended to oblige a person, in the capacity of title-holder or

1. Si un contrat a pour objet d'obliger le titulaire ou l'usager d'un bien immatriculé,

user of registered property, to a prestation which does not consist of or is not accompanied by the toleration of continuous detention, the judge may, upon the demand of this person, modify the effects of the contract, or he may set it aside in whole or in part:

a. if at least ten years have lapsed since the contract was entered into and if the unmodified continuation of the obligation is contrary to the general interest;
b. if the creditor no longer has a reasonable interest in the performance of the obligation and if it is unlikely that this interest will revive.

2. The period referred to in paragraph 1 *sub* a, encompasses the entire period during which title-holders or users of the property have been bound by a stipulation to the same effect. The period is not required to the extent that the contravention of the general interest consists of the stipulation being a bar to the realization of an existing destination plan.

en tant que tel, à une prestation qui neconsiste pas à tolérer une détention continue ni ne l'implique, le juge peut, à la demande de la personne obligée, modifier les effets du contrat ou le résilier en tout ou en partie:

a. Si se sont écoulés au moins dix ans depuis la conclusion du contrat et que la continuation intégrale de l'obligation soit contraire à l'intérêt général;
b. Si le créancier n'a plus d'intérêt suffisant à l'exécution de l'obligation et qu'il soit improbable que cet intérêt renaisse.

2. Le délai prévu au paragraphe 1er au point a. englobe toute la période pendant laquelle les titulaires ou usagers du bien ont été liés par une stipulation à l'effet identique. Le délai n'est pas requis dans la mesure où la stipulation est contraire à l'intérêt général en ce qu'elle empêche la réalisation d'un plan d'aménagement du territoire en vigueur.

Art. 260. (6.5.3.12a) - 1. Een wijziging of ontbinding als bedoeld in de artikelen 258 en 259 kan worden uitgesproken onder door de rechter te stellen voorwaarden.
- 2. Indien hij op grond van die artikelen de overeenkomst wijzigt of gedeeltelijk ontbindt, kan hij bepalen dat een of meer der partijen de overeenkomst binnen een bij de uitspraak vast te stellen termijn door een schriftelijke verklaring geheel zal kunnen ontbinden. De wijziging of gedeeltelijke ontbinding treedt niet in, voordat deze termijn is verstreken.
- 3. Is de overeenkomst die op grond van de artikelen 258 en 259 wordt gewijzigd of geheel of gedeeltelijk ontbonden, ingeschreven in de openbare registers, dan kan ook de uitspraak waarbij de wijziging of ontbinding plaatsvond, daarin worden ingeschreven, mits deze uitspraak in kracht van gewijsde is gegaan of uitvoerbaar bij voorraad is.
- 4. Wordt iemand te dier zake gedagvaard aan zijn overeenkomstig artikel 252 lid 2, eerste zin, gekozen woonplaats, dan zijn daarmee tevens gedagvaard al zijn rechtverkrijgenden die geen nieuwe inschrijving hebben genomen. Artikel 29 lid 2 en lid 3, tweede-vijfde zin, van Boek 3 zijn van overeenkomstige toepassing.
- 5. Andere rechtsfeiten die een ingeschreven overeenkomst wijzigen of beëindigen, zijn eveneens inschrijfbaar, voor zover het rechterlijke uitspraken betreft mits zij in kracht van gewijsde zijn gegaan of uitvoerbaar bij voorraad zijn.

1. The judge may pronounce a modification of the contract or set it

1. La modification ou la résiliation visée aux articles 258 et 259 peut être prononcée

aside, as referred to in articles 258 and 259, subject to conditions to be determined by him.

2. If, pursuant to these articles, the judge modifies, or partially sets the contract aside, he may determine that one or more of the contracting parties may totally set aside the contract by a written declaration within a period specified in the decision. The modification or partial setting aside of the contract does not take effect before this period has expired.

3. Where the contract which is modified, or wholly or partially set aside pursuant to articles 258 and 259, is entered in the public registers, the decision modifying or setting aside the contract can also be registered, provided that it has become final or is provisionally enforceable.

4. Where in this respect a person is summoned at the domicile which he has elected according to article 252 paragraph 2, first sentence, all his successors who have not made a new registration, have thereby also been summoned. Article 29 paragraph 2 and paragraph 3, second - fifth sentence of Book 3 apply *mutatis mutandis*.

5. Other juridical facts which modify or terminate a registered contract may also be registered; to the extent that judicial decisions are concerned, provided that they have become final or are provisionally enforceable.

aux conditions que le juge détermine.

2. Si, en application de ces articles, il modifie le contrat ou le résilie partiellement, il peut déterminer qu'une ou plusieurs parties peuvent, dans le délai qu'il fixe, le résilier totalement par une déclaration écrite. La modification ou la résiliation partielle ne prend pas effet avant l'expiration de ce délai.

3. Lorsque le contrat qui est modifié ou encore résilié en tout ou en partie, par application des articles 258 et 259, est inscrit sur les registres publics, le jugement de modification ou de résiliation peut également y être inscrit, pourvu qu'il ait acquis force de chose jugée ou qu'il soit exécutoire par provision.

4. La signification à cette fin d'une personne à son domicile élu conformément à la première phrase du paragraphe 2 de l'article 252 produit également effet à l'égard de tous ses ayants droit qui n'ont pas pris une nouvelle inscription. L'article 29, paragraphes 2 et 3, deuxième à cinquième phrases, du Livre troisième, s'applique par analogie.

5. Sont également susceptibles d'inscription les autres faits juridiques qui modifient un contrat inscrit ou y mettent fin, et, dans le cas de jugements, pourvu qu'ils aient acquis force de chose jugée ou qu'ils soient exécutoires par provision.

AFDELING 5 Wederkerige overeenkomsten

Section 5
Synallagmatic contracts

Section cinquième
Des contrats synallagmatiques

Art. 261. (6.5.4.1) - 1. Een overeenkomst is wederkerig, indien elk van beide partijen een verbintenis op zich neemt ter verkrijging van de prestatie waartoe de wederpartij zich daartegenover jegens haar verbindt.
- 2. De bepalingen omtrent wederkerige overeenkomsten zijn van overeenkomstige toepassing op andere rechtsbetrekkingen die strekken tot het wederzijds verrichten van prestaties, voor zover de aard van die rechtsbetrekkingen zich daartegen niet verzet.

1. A contract is synallagmatic if each of the parties assumes an obligation to obtain the prestation to which the other party, in exchange, obligates himself toward him.

1. Est synallagmatique le contrat par lequel chaque partie s'oblige en vue d'obtenir la prestation à laquelle l'autre s'engage envers elle en contrepartie.

2. The provisions respecting synallagmatic contracts apply *mutatis mutandis* to other juridical relationships intended for the reciprocal performance of prestations, to the extent that this is not incompatible with the nature of those juridical relationships.

2. Les dispositions relatives aux contrats synallagmatiques s'appliquent par analogie à d'autres rapports juridiques ayant pour objet des prestations réciproques, dans la mesure où la nature de ces rapports ne s'y oppose pas.

Art. 262. (6.5.4.2) - 1. Komt een der partijen haar verbintenis niet na, dan is de wederpartij bevoegd de nakoming van haar daartegenover staande verplichtingen op te schorten.
- 2. In geval van gedeeltelijke of niet behoorlijke nakoming is opschorting slechts toegelaten, voor zover de tekortkoming haar rechtvaardigt.

1. Where one of the parties does not perform his obligation, the other party is entitled to suspend performance of his correlative obligations.
2. In the event of partial or improper performance, suspension is only allowed to the extent justified by the failure to perform.

1. Lorsque l'une des parties n'exécute pas son obligation, l'autre partie peut suspendre l'exécution de ses obligations corrélatives.

2. En cas d'exécution partielle ou inadéquate, la suspension n'est permise que dans la mesure où le manquement la justifie.

Art. 263. (6.5.4.4) - 1. De partij die verplicht is het eerst te presteren, is niettemin bevoegd de nakoming van haar verbintenis op te schorten, indien na het sluiten van de overeenkomst te harer kennis gekomen omstandigheden haar goede grond geven te vrezen dat de wederpartij haar daartegenover staande verplichtingen niet zal nakomen.
- 2. In geval er goede grond bestaat te vrezen dat slechts gedeeltelijk of niet behoorlijk zal worden nagekomen, is de opschorting slechts toegelaten voor zover de tekortkoming haar rechtvaardigt.

1. The party who is obliged to perform first, is nevertheless entitled to suspend the performance of his obligation, if circumstances have come to his attention after the contract was entered into, giving him good reason to fear that the other party will not perform his correlative obligations.
2. In the event that there is good reason to fear that there will be partial or improper performance, suspension is only allowed to the extent justified by the failure to perform.

1. La partie qui est tenue d'exécuter sa prestation la première peut néanmoins en suspendre l'exécution si des circonstances dont elle a eu connaissance après la conclusion du contrat lui donnent de bonnes raisons de craindre que l'autre partie n'exécutera pas ses obligations corrélatives.

2. Lorsqu'il existe de bonnes raisons de craindre que l'exécution ne soit que partielle ou inadéquate, la suspension n'est permise que dans la mesure où le manquement la justifie.

Art. 264. (6.5.4.4a) In geval van opschorting op grond van de artikelen 262 en 263 zijn de artikelen 54 onder b en c en 55 niet van toepassing.

In the event of suspension on the basis of articles 262 and 263, articles 54 *sub* b and c and 55 do not apply.

En cas de suspension en application des articles 262 et 263, l'article 54, points b. et c., et l'article 55 ne s'appliquent pas.

Art. 265. (6.5.4.6) - 1. Iedere tekortkoming van een partij in de nakoming van een van haar verbintenissen geeft aan de wederpartij de bevoegdheid om de overeenkomst geheel of gedeeltelijk te ontbinden, tenzij de tekortkoming, gezien haar bijzondere aard of geringe betekenis, deze ontbinding met haar gevolgen niet rechtvaardigt.
- 2. Voor zover nakoming niet blijvend of tijdelijk onmogelijk is, ontstaat de bevoegdheid tot ontbinding pas, wanneer de schuldenaar in verzuim is.

1. Every failure of one party in the performance of one of his obligations gives the other party the right to set aside the contract in whole or in part, unless the failure, given its special nature or minor importance, does not justify the setting aside of the contract and the consequences flowing therefrom.
2. To the extent that performance is not permanently or temporarily impossible, the right to set the contract aside does not arise until the debtor is in default.

1. Tout manquement d'une partie dans l'exécution de l'une de ses obligations donne à l'autre le pouvoir de résilier[1] le contrat en tout ou en partie, à moins que le manquement, vu sa nature particulière ou son importance mineure, ne justifie pas cette résiliation avec ses effets.
2. Dans la mesure où l'exécution n'est pas impossible de façon temporaire ou permanente, le pouvoir de résiliation naît seulement lorsque le débiteur est en demeure.

Art. 266. (6.5.4.7) - 1. Geen ontbinding kan worden gegrond op een tekortkoming in de nakoming van een verbintenis ten aanzien waarvan de schuldeiser zelf in verzuim is.
- 2. Wordt echter tijdens het verzuim van de schuldeiser behoorlijke nakoming geheel of gedeeltelijk onmogelijk, dan kan de overeenkomst ontbonden worden, indien door schuld van de schuldenaar of zijn ondergeschikte is tekortgeschoten in de zorg die in de gegeven omstandigheden van hem mocht worden gevergd.

1. Setting aside a contract cannot be based upon a failure in the performance of an obligation in respect of which the creditor is himself in default.
2. Where, however, proper performance becomes wholly or partially impossible during the default of the creditor, the contract can be set aside if the debtor or his servant have, through their fault, failed to exercise the care which, in the given circumstances, could have been expected from them.

1. La résiliation ne peut être fondée sur un manquement dans l'exécution d'une obligation à l'égard de laquelle le créancier lui-même est en demeure.
2. Si cependant l'exécution adéquate devient impossible en tout ou en partie durant la demeure du créancier, le contrat peut être résilié si le débiteur ou son préposé a, par sa faute, manqué aux soins qu'on pouvait exiger de lui en la circonstance.

Art. 267. (6.5.4.8) - 1. De ontbinding vindt plaats door een schriftelijke verklaring van de daartoe gerechtigde.
- 2. Zij kan ook op zijn vordering door de rechter worden uitgesproken.

1. The contract is set aside by a written declaration of the person entitled to do so.

1. La résiliation s'effectue par une déclaration écrite de celui qui peut l'invoquer.

[1] Les termes «résilier» et «résiliation» ont été préférés à «résoudre» et «résolution», parce que le nouveau Code civil néerlandais permet à la partie qui y a droit de provoquer la résiliation par déclaration unilatérale (art. 267) et n'accorde pas à la résiliation d'effet rétroactif (art. 269).

2. It may also be pronounced by the judge upon the demand of such person.

2. Elle peut également, à la demande de celui-ci, être prononcée par le juge.

Art. 268. (6.5.4.8a) De bevoegdheid tot buitengerechtelijke ontbinding vervalt door verjaring van de rechtsvordering tot ontbinding. De verjaring staat niet in de weg aan gerechtelijke of buitengerechtelijke ontbinding ter afwering van een op de overeenkomst steunende rechtsvordering of andere rechtsmaatregel.

The right to set aside a contract by extrajudicial declaration lapses by the prescription of the right of action to set the contract aside. The prescription does not prevent the judicial or extrajudicial setting aside of the contract as a defence against a right of action or other legal measure based upon the contract.

Le pouvoir de résiliation extra-judiciaire disparaît par la prescription de l'action au même effet. La prescription n'empêche pas la résiliation judiciaire ou extra-judiciaire à l'encontre d'une action en justice ou autre mesure de droit fondée sur le contrat.

Art. 269. (6.5.4.9) De ontbinding heeft geen terugwerkende kracht, behoudens dat een aanbod tot nakoming, gedaan nadat de ontbinding is gevorderd, geen werking heeft, indien de ontbinding wordt uitgesproken.

The setting aside of a contract has no retroactive force, except that an offer to perform made after the demand to set the contract aside, has no effect if the setting aside is pronounced.

La résiliation ne rétroagit pas, sauf que l'offre d'exécution, faite après la demande de résiliation, ne produit pas d'effet si la résiliation est prononcée.

Art. 270. (6.5.4.10) Een gedeeltelijke ontbinding houdt een evenredige vermindering in van de wederzijdse prestaties in hoeveelheid of hoedanigheid.

Partial setting aside of a contract results in a qualitative or quantitive proportional reduction of the reciprocal obligations.

La résiliation partielle entraîne une réduction proportionnelle des prestations réciproques en quantité ou en qualité.

Art. 271. (6.5.4.14) Een ontbinding bevrijdt de partijen van de daardoor getroffen verbintenissen. Voor zover deze reeds zijn nagekomen, blijft de rechtsgrond voor deze nakoming in stand, maar ontstaat voor partijen een verbintenis tot ongedaanmaking van de reeds door hen ontvangen prestaties.

The setting aside of a contract liberates the parties from the obligations affected by it. To the extent that these obligations have already been performed, the legal ground for this performance remains intact, but an obligation arises for the parties to undo the prestations which they have already received.

La résiliation libère les parties des obligations qui en sont frappées. Dans la mesure où ces obligations ont déjà été exécutées, la cause fondant cette exécution subsiste, mais il naît pour les parties une obligation d'anéantir les prestations qu'elles ont déjà reçues.

Art. 272. (6.5.4.15) - 1. Sluit de aard van de prestatie uit dat zij ongedaan wordt gemaakt, dan treedt daarvoor een vergoeding in de plaats ten belope van haar waarde op het tijdstip van de ontvangst.

- 2. Heeft de prestatie niet aan de verbintenis beantwoord, dan wordt deze vergoeding beperkt tot het bedrag van de waarde die de prestatie voor de ontvanger op dit tijdstip in de gegeven omstandigheden werkelijk heeft gehad.

1. Where the prestation, by its nature, cannot be undone, compensation up to its value at the time of receipt takes its place.

2. Where the prestation did not conform to the obligation, this compensation is limited to the amount of the value which the prestation has actually had for the recipient at that time and in the given circumstances.

1. La prestation dont la nature exclut l'anéantissement est remplacée par une indemnité égale au montant de sa valeur au moment de la réception.

2. Lorsque la prestation n'était pas conforme à l'obligation, l'indemnité se limite au montant de la valeur réelle qu'en l'espèce la prestation a eue à cette date pour celui qui l'a reçue.

Art. 273. (6.5.4.16) Een partij die een prestatie heeft ontvangen, is vanaf het tijdstip dat zij redelijkerwijze met een ontbinding rekening moet houden, verplicht er als een zorgvuldig schuldenaar zorg voor te dragen dat de ingevolge die ontbinding verschuldigde ongedaanmaking van de prestatie mogelijk zal zijn. Artikel 78 is van overeenkomstige toepassing.

As of the time that a party, who has received a prestation, must reasonably foresee the possibility that the contract will be set aside, he is obliged to ensure, as a prudent debtor, that the undoing of the prestation, owed as a result of the setting aside of the contract, will be possible. Article 78 applies *mutatis mutandis*.

La partie qui a reçu une prestation veille, à compter du moment où elle devait normalement tenir compte de la possibilité d'une résiliation, comme un prudent débiteur à ce que l'anéantissement nécessaire à la suite de cette résiliation soit possible. L'article 78 s'applique par analogie.

Art. 274. (6.5.4.17) Heeft een partij in weerwil van een dreigende ontbinding te kwader trouw een prestatie ontvangen, dan wordt zij na de ontbinding geacht vanaf de ontvangst van de prestatie in verzuim geweest te zijn.

A party who, notwithstanding the impending setting aside of a contract, has received a prestation while in bad faith, is, after the setting aside, deemed to have been in default as of the time of the receipt of the prestation.

Après la résiliation, la partie qui, malgré l'imminence de celle-ci, a, de mauvaise foi, reçu une prestation est réputée avoir été en demeure à compter de la réception.

Art. 275. (6.5.4.18) De artikelen 120-124 van Boek 3 zijn van overeenkomstige toepassing met betrekking tot hetgeen daarin is bepaald omtrent de afgifte van vruchten en de vergoeding van kosten en schade.

The provisions of articles 120 - 124 of Book 3 regarding the restitution of fruits and the compensation for costs and damage apply *mutatis mutandis*.

Les articles 120 à 124 du Livre troisième s'appliquent par analogie, pour ce qui y est prévu au sujet de la remise des fruits, du remboursement des dépenses et de la réparation du dommage.

Art. 276. (6.5.4.19) Op de onbekwame die een prestatie heeft ontvangen, rusten de in deze afdeling omschreven verplichtingen slechts, voor zover het ontvangene hem tot werkelijk voordeel heeft gestrekt of in de macht van zijn wettelijke vertegenwoordiger is gekomen.

The obligations described in this section bind an incapable person who has received a prestation only to the extent that what he has received has actually benefitted him or has come under the control of his legal representative.

L'incapable qui a reçu une prestation est soumis aux obligations décrites dans la présente section dans la seule mesure où la prestation reçue lui a réellement profité ou est venue en la puissance de son représentant légal.

Art. 277. (6.5.4.20) - 1. Wordt een overeenkomst geheel of gedeeltelijk ontbonden, dan is de partij wier tekortkoming een grond voor ontbinding heeft opgeleverd, verplicht haar wederpartij de schade te vergoeden die deze lijdt, doordat geen wederzijdse nakoming doch ontbinding van de overeenkomst plaatsvindt.
- 2. Indien de tekortkoming niet aan de schuldenaar kan worden toegerekend, is het vorige lid slechts van toepassing binnen de grenzen van het in artikel 78 bepaalde.

1. Where a contract is set aside in whole or in part, the party whose failure in performing the obligation has been the cause of the setting aside, must make reparation for the damage which the other party suffers as there is no reciprocal performance, but rather the setting aside of the contract.
2. If the failure in the performance cannot be imputed to the debtor, the preceding paragraph only applies within the limits of the provisions of article 78.

1. Lorsqu'un contrat est en tout ou partie résilié, la partie dont le manquement dans l'exécution en constitue la cause est tenu d'indemniser l'autre du dommage que celle-ci subit du fait qu'il y a résiliation du contrat, et non exécution réciproque.
2. Si le manquement d'exécution n'est pas imputable au débiteur, le paragraphe précédent s'applique seulement dans les limites des dispositions de l'article 78.

Art. 278. (6.5.4.21) - 1. De partij die ontbinding kiest van een reeds uitgevoerde overeenkomst, nadat de verhouding in waarde tussen hetgeen wederzijds bij ongedaanmaking zou moeten worden verricht, zich te haren gunste heeft gewijzigd, is verplicht door bijbetaling de oorspronkelijke waardeverhouding te herstellen, indien aannemelijk is dat zij zonder deze wijziging geen ontbinding zou hebben gekozen.
- 2. Het vorige lid is van overeenkomstige toepassing ingeval de partij te wier gunste de wijziging is ingetreden, op andere grond dan ontbinding de stoot tot ongedaanmaking geeft en aannemelijk is dat zij daartoe zonder deze wijziging niet zou zijn overgegaan.

1. A party who elects to set aside a contract which has already been performed, after a change in his favour of the relative values of the prestations which would have to be undone reciprocally, must reestablish the original relative values by a supplementary payment if it is likely that he would not have chosen to set aside the contract without this change.

1. La partie qui opte pour la résiliation d'un contrat déjà exécuté, après que s'est modifié en sa faveur le rapport de valeur des prestations que se devraient les parties en cas d'anéantissement, est tenue de rétablir le rapport de valeur initial en versant une soulte, s'il est probable que, n'eût été la modification, elle n'aurait pas opté de la sorte.

2. The preceding paragraph applies *mutatis mutandis* in the event that the party in whose favour the change has taken place, provokes the undoing of the prestations in any other way than by setting aside the contract, and if it is likely that he would not have proceeded to do so without this change.

2. Le paragraphe précédent s'applique par analogie lorsque la partie en faveur de laquelle s'est modifié le rapport de valeur provoque l'anéantissement autrement que par la résiliation et qu'il est probable que, n'eût été la modification, elle ne l'aurait pas provoqué.

Art. 279. (6.5.4.22) - 1. Op overeenkomsten waaruit tussen meer dan twee partijen verbintenissen voortvloeien, vinden de bepalingen betreffende wederkerige overeenkomsten met inachtneming van de volgende leden overeenkomstige toepassing, voor zover de aard van de overeenkomst zich daartegen niet verzet.
- 2. De partij die een verbintenis op zich heeft genomen ter verkrijging van een daartegenover van een of meer der andere partijen bedongen prestatie, kan haar recht op ontbinding gronden op een tekortkoming in de nakoming van de verbintenis jegens haarzelf.
- 3. Schiet een partij met samenhangende rechten en verplichtingen zelf tekort in de nakoming van haar verbintenis, dan kunnen in ieder geval de overige partijen gezamenlijk de overeenkomst ontbinden.

1. The provisions respecting synallagmatic contracts apply *mutatis mutandis* to contracts resulting in obligations between more than two parties, with due observance of the provisions of the following paragraphs, and to the extent that this is not incompatible with the nature of the contract.
2. The party who has assumed an obligation in order to obtain a counterprestation stipulated from one or more of the other parties, can base his right to set aside the contract upon a failure in the performance of the obligations toward himself.
3. Where a party with interdependent rights and obligations himself fails in the performance of his obligation, the other parties may, in any event together, set aside the contract.

1. Les contrats dont résultent des obligations pour plus de deux parties sont soumis, par analogie et en tenant compte des paragraphes suivants, aux dispositions relatives aux contrats synallagmatiques, dans la mesure où la nature du contrat ne s'y oppose pas.

2. La partie qui s'est obligée en vue d'obtenir une prestation corrélative d'une ou de plusieurs autres parties peut fonder son droit à la résiliation sur un manquement dans l'exécution de l'obligation à son propre égard.

3. Lorsque une partie qui a des droits et des obligations interdépendants manque elle-même à l'exécution de son obligation, le contrat peut être résilié de toute façon par les autres parties de concert.

BOEK 7
BIJZONDERE OVEREENKOMSTEN

BOOK 7
SPECIAL CONTRACTS

LIVRE SEPTIÈME
DES CONTRATS PARTICULIERS

TITEL 1 KOOP EN RUIL

TITLE 1 SALE AND EXCHANGE

TITRE PREMIER DE LA VENTE ET DE L'ÉCHANGE

AFDELING 1 Koop: Algemene bepalingen

Section 1 Sale: General provisions

Section première De la vente: Dispositions générales

Art. 1. (7.1.1.1) Koop is de overeenkomst waarbij de een zich verbindt een zaak te geven en de ander om daarvoor een prijs in geld te betalen.

Sale is a contract whereby one person binds himself to give a thing, and the other to pay a price therefor in money.

La vente est le contrat par lequel une personne s'engage à donner une chose et l'autre, à en payer le prix en argent.

Art. 2-3. Gereserveerd.
Reserved.

Réservés.

Art. 4. (7.1.1.2) Wanneer de koop is gesloten zonder dat de prijs is bepaald, is de koper een redelijke prijs verschuldigd; bij de bepaling van die prijs wordt rekening gehouden met de door de verkoper ten tijde van het sluiten van de overeenkomst gewoonlijk bedongen prijzen.

Where a sale has been entered into without a determination of the price, the buyer owes a reasonable price; in determining that price, one takes account of the prices usually stipulated by the seller at the time of entering into the contract.

Lorsque la vente a été conclue sans qu'un prix n'ait été déterminé, l'acheteur doit un prix convenable; dans la détermination de ce prix, il est tenu compte des prix habituellement stipulés par le vendeur au moment de la conclusion du contrat.

Art. 5. (7.1.1.4) - 1. In deze titel wordt verstaan onder „consumentenkoop": de koop met betrekking tot een roerende zaak, die wordt gesloten door een verkoper die handelt in de uitoefening van een beroep of bedrijf, en een koper, natuurlijk persoon, die niet handelt in de uitoefening van een beroep of bedrijf.
- 2. Wordt de zaak verkocht door een gevolmachtigde die handelt in de uitoefening van een beroep of bedrijf, dan wordt de koop aangemerkt als een consumentenkoop, tenzij de koper ten tijde van het sluiten van de overeenkomst weet dat de volmachtgever niet handelt in de uitoefening van een beroep of bedrijf.
- 3. De vorige leden zijn niet van toepassing indien de overeenkomst een registergoed of door leidingen naar de verbruiker aangevoerd water of gas betreft.

1. In this title, a 'consumer sale' means the sale of a moveable thing entered into by a seller acting in the course of a business or profession, and by a buyer who is a natural person not acting in the course of a business or profession.

2. Where the thing is sold by a procurator acting in the course of a profession or business, the sale is considered to be a consumer sale, unless, at the time of entering into the contract, the buyer knows that the principal does not act in the course of a profession or business.

3. The preceding paragraphs do not apply if the contract pertains to registered property, or to water and gas supplied to the user by pipelines.

1. Au présent titre, on entend par «achat de consommation» celui qui porte sur une chose mobilière et qui est conclu entre un vendeur agissant dans le cadre d'une entreprise ou d'une activité professionnelle et un acheteur, personne naturelle, n'agissant pas dans un tel cadre.

2. Lorsque la chose est vendue par un procureur agissant dans le cadre d'une entreprise ou d'une profession, l'achat est réputé achat de consommation, sauf si, au moment de la conclusion du contrat, l'acheteur sait que l'auteur de la procuration n'agit pas dans le cadre d'une activité professionnelle ou d'une entreprise.

3. Les paragraphes précédents ne s'appliquent pas si le contrat porte sur un bien immatriculé ou sur l'eau ou le gaz acheminés par conduite à l'utilisateur.

Art. 6. (7.1.1.4a) - 1. Bij een consumentenkoop kan van de afdelingen 1-7 van deze titel niet ten nadele van de koper worden afgeweken en kunnen de rechten en vorderingen die de wet aan de koper ter zake van een tekortkoming in de nakoming van de verplichtingen van de verkoper toekent, niet worden beperkt of uitgesloten, behoudens bij een standaardregeling als bedoeld in artikel 214 van Boek 6.
- 2. Lid 1 is niet van toepassing op de artikelen 11, 12, 13, 26 en 35, doch bedingen in algemene voorwaarden waarbij ten nadele van de koper wordt afgeweken van die artikelen, worden als onredelijk bezwarend aangemerkt.

1. In a consumer sale, there may be no derogations, which are to the detriment of the buyer, from sections 1 - 7 of this title, and in such sale there may be no limitations on or exclusions of the rights and actions which the law grants to the buyer for failure in the performance of the obligations of the seller, except by standard terms as referred to in article 214 of Book 6.

2. Paragraph 1 does not apply to articles 11, 12, 13, 26 and 35; however, stipulations in general conditions derogating from those articles to the detriment of the buyer, are considered to be unreasonably onerous.

1. Lors d'un achat de consommation, on ne peut déroger, au détriment de l'acheteur, aux sections 1 à 7 du présent type, ni limiter ou exclure les droits et actions que la loi lui accorde en cas de manquement dans l'exécution des obligations du vendeur, sauf par voie de règlement-cadre tel qu'il est prévu à l'article 214 du Livre sixième.

2. Le paragraphe 1er ne s'applique pas aux articles 11, 12, 13, 26 et 35, mais les stipulations faisant partie de conditions générales dérogeant à ces articles au détriment de l'acheteur sont réputées anormalement onéreuses.

Art. 7. (7.1.1.5) - 1. Degene aan wie een zaak is toegezonden en die redelijkerwijze mag aannemen dat deze toezending is geschied ten einde hem tot een koop te bewegen, is ongeacht enige andersluidende mededeling van de verzender jegens deze bevoegd de zaak om niet te behouden, tenzij het hem is toe te rekenen dat de toezending is geschied.
- 2. Indien de ontvanger de zaak terugzendt, komen de kosten hiervan voor rekening van de verzender.

1. The person to whom a thing has been sent and who may reasonably assume that this has been done in order to induce him to buy is, irrespective of any communication by the sender to a different effect, entitled, in his relationship with the sender, to keep the thing by gratuitous title, unless it can be imputed to the recipient that the sending has taken place.
2. If the recipient sends the thing back, the costs hereof are borne by the sender.

1. Celui à qui a été envoyée une chose et qui a des raisons de croire que l'envoi a eu lieu afin de l'inciter à acheter peut, dans son rapport avec l'expéditeur, conserver la chose à titre gratuit sans égard à toute communication contraire de celui-ci, à moins que l'envoi ne soit imputable au destinataire.

2. Si le destinataire renvoie la chose, les frais en incombent à l'expéditeur.

Art. 8. Gereserveerd.

Reserved.

Réservé.

AFDELING 2 Verplichtingen van de verkoper

Section 2
Obligations of the seller

Section deuxième
Des obligations du vendeur

Art. 9. (7.1.2.1) - 1. De verkoper is verplicht de verkochte zaak met toebehoren in eigendom over te dragen en af te leveren. Onder toebehoren zijn de aanwezige titelbewijzen en bescheiden begrepen; voor zover de verkoper zelf daarbij belang behoudt, is hij slechts verplicht om aan de koper op diens verlangen en op diens kosten een afschrift of uittreksel af te geven.
- 2. Onder aflevering wordt verstaan het stellen van de zaak in het bezit van de koper.
- 3. In geval van koop met eigendomsvoorbehoud wordt onder aflevering verstaan het stellen van de zaak in de macht van de koper.

1. The seller is obliged to transfer the ownership of the thing sold and to deliver it with its accessories. The accessories include the title deeds and other documents; to the extent that the seller retains an interest in those documents, he is only obliged to give a copy or extract thereof to the buyer at the latter's demand and costs.
2. Delivery means putting the buyer into possession of the thing.

3. In the case of sale with reservation of title of ownership, delivery means bringing the thing under the control of the buyer.

1. Le vendeur est tenu de transférer la propriété de la chose et des accessoires et de les livrer. Les accessoires englobent les titres et autres pièces disponibles; dans la mesure où ceux-ci continuent à présenter un intérêt pour le vendeur, il est seulement tenu d'en remettre à l'acheteur, à la demande et aux frais de celui-ci, une copie ou un extrait.
2. Par livraison, on entend le fait de mettre la chose en la possession de l'acheteur.
3. Dans le cas d'une vente avec réserve de propriété, on entend par livraison le fait de mettre la chose en la puissance de l'acheteur.

Art. 10. (7.1.2.2) - 1. De zaak is voor risico van de koper van de aflevering af, zelfs al is de eigendom nog niet overgedragen. Derhalve blijft

hij de koopprijs verschuldigd, ongeacht tenietgaan of achteruitgang van de zaak door een oorzaak die niet aan de verkoper kan worden toegerekend.
- 2. Hetzelfde geldt van het ogenblik af, waarop de koper in verzuim is met het verrichten van een handeling waarmede hij aan de aflevering moet medewerken. Ingeval naar de soort bepaalde zaken zijn verkocht, doet het verzuim van de koper het risico eerst op hem overgaan, wanneer de verkoper de voor de uitvoering van de overeenkomst bestemde zaken heeft aangewezen en de koper daarvan heeft verwittigd.
- 3. Indien de koper op goede gronden het recht op ontbinding van de koop of op vervanging van de zaak inroept, blijft deze voor risico van de verkoper.
- 4. Wanneer de zaak na de aflevering voor risico van de verkoper is gebleven, is het tenietgaan of de achteruitgang ervan door toedoen van de koper eveneens voor rekening van de verkoper. De koper moet echter van het ogenblik af dat hij redelijkerwijs rekening moet houden met het feit dat hij de zaak zal moeten teruggeven, als een zorgvuldig schuldenaar voor het behoud ervan zorgen; artikel 78 van Boek 6 is van overeenkomstige toepassing.

1. The thing is at the risk of the buyer as of the delivery, even if ownership has not been transferred. As a consequence, the purchase price remains owed irrespective of the loss or deterioration of the thing by a cause which cannot be imputed to the seller.
2. The same applies as of the time when the buyer is in default of performing an act by which he must cooperate in the delivery. In the case of sale of things determined as to kind, the default of the buyer does not transfer the risk to him until the seller has specified the things destined for the performance of the contract and has notified the buyer thereof.
3. The thing remains at the risk of the seller if, on good grounds, the buyer invokes the right to set aside the sale or the right to have the thing replaced.
4. Where, after delivery, the thing has remained at the risk of the seller, the seller is also responsible for the thing's loss or deterioration by the act of the buyer. However, as of the time when the buyer must reasonably foresee that he must give the thing back, he is obliged to look after the safekeeping of the thing as a prudent debtor; article 78 of Book 6 applies *mutatis mutandis*.

1. L'acheteur assume le risque de la chose à compter de la livraison, même si la propriété n'en a pas encore été transférée. Il doit donc le prix d'achat, sans égard à la perte ou détérioration de la chose pour une cause non imputable au vendeur.

2. Il en est de même à compter du moment où l'acheteur est en demeure d'accomplir un acte par lequel il doit prêter son concours à la livraison. Dans le cas de choses déterminées par leur espèce, la demeure de l'acheteur ne lui fait transmettre le risque que lorsque le vendeur a désigné les choses destinées à l'exécution du contrat et en a informé l'acheteur.

3. Si l'acheteur invoque à juste titre le droit de résiliation de la vente ou de remplacement de la chose, le risque de celle-ci demeure à la charge du vendeur.
4. Lorsque, après la livraison, le risque de la chose est demeuré à la charge du vendeur, la perte ou détérioration de la chose par le fait de l'acheteur incombe également au vendeur. Toutefois, à compter du moment où l'acheteur doit cependant normalement prévoir qu'il sera obligé de rendre la chose, il est tenu de prendre soin de sa conservation comme un débiteur prudent; l'article 78 du Livre sixième s'applique par analogie.

Art. 11. (7.1.2.2a) Indien bij een consumentenkoop de zaak bij de koper wordt bezorgd door de verkoper of een door deze aangewezen vervoerder, is de zaak pas voor risico van de koper van de bezorging af, zelfs al was zij reeds eerder afgeleverd in de zin van artikel 9.

If, in a consumer sale, the seller or a carrier designated by him delivers the thing at the buyer's, the thing is only at the risk of the buyer as of that time, even if it had already been delivered in the sense of article 9.

Si, lors d'un achat de consommation, la chose est livrée chez l'acheteur par le vendeur ou par un transporteur désigné par ce dernier, le risque de la chose n'est à la charge de l'acheteur qu'au moment où elle lui a été livrée, lors même qu'elle lui a déjà été livrée au sens de l'article 9.

Art. 12. (7.1.2.3) - 1. Kosten van aflevering, die van weging en telling daaronder begrepen, komen ten laste van de verkoper.
- 2. Kosten van afhalen en kosten van een koopakte en van de overdracht komen ten laste van de koper.

1. The seller bears the costs of delivery, including those of weighing and counting.
2. The buyer bears the costs of removal, of a deed of sale and of transfer.

1. Les frais de livraison, pesage et comptage compris, sont à la charge du vendeur.
2. Les frais d'enlèvement, ainsi que ceux de l'acte de vente et du transfert, sont à la charge de l'acheteur.

Art. 13. (7.1.2.3a) Indien bij een consumentenkoop de zaak bij de koper wordt bezorgd door de verkoper of een door deze aangewezen vervoerder, kunnen daarvoor slechts kosten worden gevorderd, voor zover zij bij het sluiten van de overeenkomst door de verkoper afzonderlijk zijn opgegeven of door de verkoper de gegevens zijn verschaft op grond waarvan zij door hem worden berekend. Hetzelfde geldt voor kosten, verschuldigd voor andere werkzaamheden die de verkoper in verband met de koop voor de koper verricht.

If, in a consumer sale, the seller or a carrier designated by him delivers the thing at the buyer's, costs can only be claimed to the extent that the seller, at the time of entering into the contract, has indicated them separately, or that he has provided data on the basis of which he calculates them. The same applies to costs owed for other acts performed by the seller in connection with the sale.

Si, lors d'un achat de consommation, la chose est livrée chez l'acheteur par le vendeur ou par un transporteur désigné par ce dernier, des frais ne peuvent être réclamés que dans la mesure où ils ont été spécifiés séparément par le vendeur lors de la conclusion du contrat ou que celui-ci a fourni les données qu'il emploie pour les calculer. Il en est de même de frais engagés pour d'autres travaux effectués par le vendeur au profit de l'acheteur en rapport avec la vente.

Art. 14. (7.1.2.4) Van de dag van aflevering af komen de vruchten toe aan de koper, met dien verstande dat burgerlijke vruchten van dag tot dag berekend worden.

The fruits belong to the buyer, as of the day of delivery, upon the understanding that civil fruits are calculated from day to day.

À compter du jour de la livraison, les fruits reviennent à l'acheteur, étant entendu que les fruits civils sont calculés au jour le jour.

Art. 15. (7.1.2.5) - 1. De verkoper is verplicht de verkochte zaak in eigendom over te dragen vrij van alle bijzondere lasten en beperkingen, met uitzondering van die welke de koper uitdrukkelijk heeft aanvaard.

- 2. Ongeacht enig andersluidend beding staat de verkoper in voor de afwezigheid van lasten en beperkingen die voortvloeien uit feiten die vatbaar zijn voor inschrijving in de openbare registers, doch daarin ten tijde van het sluiten van de overeenkomst niet waren ingeschreven.

1. The seller is obliged to transfer the ownership of the thing sold free of all special charges and encumbrances, except for those which the buyer has specifically accepted.
2. Irrespective of any stipulation to the contrary, the seller warrants the absence of charges and encumbrances resulting from facts which are susceptible of being entered in the public registers, but which were not entered therein at the time when the contract was concluded.

1. Le vendeur est tenu de transférer la propriété de la chose vendue, libre de toutes charges et restrictions particulières, à l'exception de celles que l'acheteur a expressément acceptées.
2. Sans égard à toute stipulation contraire, le vendeur est garant de l'absence de charges ou restrictions découlant de faits qui sont susceptibles d'inscription sur les registres publics, mais n'y étaient pas inscrits lors de la conclusion du contrat.

Art. 16. (7.1.2.6) Wanneer tegen de koper een vordering wordt ingesteld tot uitwinning of tot erkenning van een recht waarmede de zaak niet belast had mogen zijn, is de verkoper gehouden in het geding te komen ten einde de belangen van de koper te verdedigen.

Where an action is brought against the buyer for eviction or for the recognition of a right which should not have encumbered the thing, the seller must be joined in the action in order to defend the interests of the buyer.

Lorsqu'est intentée contre l'acheteur une action en éviction ou en reconnaissance d'un droit qui n'aurait pas dû grever la chose, le vendeur est tenu d'entrer en cause afin de défendre les intérêts de l'acheteur.

Art. 17. (7.1.2.7) - 1. De afgeleverde zaak moet aan de overeenkomst beantwoorden.
- 2. Een zaak beantwoordt niet aan de overeenkomst indien zij niet de eigenschappen bezit die de koper op grond van de overeenkomst mocht verwachten. De koper mag verwachten dat de zaak de eigenschappen bezit die voor een normaal gebruik daarvan nodig zijn en waarvan hij de aanwezigheid niet behoefde te betwijfelen, alsmede de eigenschappen die nodig zijn voor een bijzonder gebruik dat bij de overeenkomst is voorzien.
- 3. Een andere zaak dan is overeengekomen, of een zaak van een andere soort, beantwoordt evenmin aan de overeenkomst. Hetzelfde geldt indien het afgeleverde in getal, maat of gewicht van het overeengekomene afwijkt.
- 4. Is aan de koper een monster of model getoond of verstrekt, dan moet de zaak daarmede overeenstemmen, tenzij het slechts bij wijze van aanduiding werd verstrekt zonder dat de zaak daaraan behoefde te beantwoorden.
- 5. Bij koop van een onroerende zaak wordt vermelding van de oppervlakte vermoed slechts als aanduiding bedoeld te zijn, zonder dat de zaak daaraan behoeft te beantwoorden.

1. The thing delivered must conform to the contract.
2. A thing does not conform to the contract if it does not possess the qualities which the buyer was entitled to

1. La chose livrée doit être conforme au contrat.
2. Une chose n'est pas conforme au contrat si elle ne possède pas les propriétés auxquelles l'acheteur pouvait s'attendre en

expect on the basis of the contract. The buyer may expect that the thing possesses the qualities which are necessary for a normal use thereof and the presence of which he did not have to doubt, as well as the qualities which are necessary for a special use provided for in the contract.
3. A thing other than the one agreed to, or a thing of a different kind does not conform to the contract either. The same applies if that what has been delivered deviates in number, size or weight from what has been agreed to.
4. Where a sample or model has been shown or given to the buyer, the thing must conform thereto, unless it has only been given by way of indication, without the necessity of the thing conforming thereto.
5. In the sale of an immoveable thing, the mention of surface dimensions is presumed to be meant only as an indication, without the necessity of the thing conforming thereto.

vertu du contrat. L'acheteur peut s'attendre à ce que la chose possède les propriétés qui sont nécessaires pour l'usage normal et dont il ne devait pas douter de la présence, de même que celles nécessaires pour un usage particulier prévu au contrat.

3. Une chose autre que convenue, ou une chose d'une espèce différente, n'est pas non plus conforme au contrat. Il en est de même si ce qui est livré s'écarte en nombre, en mesure ou en poids de ce qui a été convenu.

4. Lorsque l'acheteur s'est fait montrer ou remettre un échantillon ou modèle, la chose doit y être conforme, à moins que celui-ci n'ait été remis qu'à titre indicatif, sans que la chose dût s'y conformer.

5. Lors de la vente d'une chose immobilière, la mention de surface est présumée faite à titre indicatif, sans que la chose doive s'y conformer.

Art. 18. (7.1.2.7a) Bij de beoordeling van de vraag of een op grond van een consumentenkoop afgeleverde zaak aan de overeenkomst beantwoordt, gelden mededelingen die door of ten behoeve van een vorige verkoper van die zaak, handelend in de uitoefening van een beroep of bedrijf, omtrent de zaak zijn openbaar gemaakt, als mededelingen van de verkoper, behoudens voor zover deze een bepaalde mededeling kende noch behoorde te kennen of duidelijk heeft weersproken.

In determining whether a thing delivered pursuant to a consumer sale conforms to the contract, information regarding the thing made public by or on behalf of a previous seller of that thing, acting in the course of a profession or business, is deemed to be information from the seller, except to the extent that the latter neither knew nor ought to know certain information, or that he has clearly contradicted it.

Dans l'appréciation de la question de savoir si une chose livrée en exécution d'un achat de consommation est conforme au contrat, les communications rendues publiques au sujet de cette chose par un vendeur antérieur agissant dans le cadre d'une activité professionnelle ou d'une entreprise, ou à son profit, sont réputées celles du vendeur, sauf dans la mesure où ce dernier ne connaissait ni ne devait connaître une communication particulière ou l'a clairement contredite.

Art. 19. (7.1.2.8) - 1. In geval van een executoriale verkoop kan de koper zich er niet op beroepen dat de zaak behept is met een last of een beperking die er niet op had mogen rusten, of dat deze niet aan de overeenkomst beantwoordt, tenzij de verkoper dat wist.
- 2. Hetzelfde geldt indien de verkoop bij wijze van parate executie plaatsvindt, mits de koper dit wist of had moeten weten.

1. In the case of a sale for the purpose of execution, the buyer may not invoke the fact that the thing is subject to a charge or encumbrance which should not have encumbered it, or that the thing does not conform to the contract, unless the seller knew of it.
2. The same applies if the sale takes place by way of private execution, provided that the buyer knew or should have known this.

1. Dans le cas d'une vente forcée l'acheteur ne peut faire valoir que la chose est encombrée d'une charge ou restriction qui n'aurait pas dû la grever, ou qu'elle n'est pas conforme au contrat, à moins que le vendeur ne l'ait su.

2. Il en est de même si la vente a lieu en exécution d'une clause de voie parée, pourvu que l'acheteur l'ait su ou ait dû le savoir.

AFDELING 3 Bijzondere gevolgen van niet-nakoming van de verplichtingen van de verkoper

Section 3
Special effects of non-performance of the obligations of the seller

Section troisième
Des effets particuliers de l'inexécution des obligations du vendeur

Art. 20. (7.1.3.1) Is de zaak behept met een last of een beperking die er niet op had mogen rusten, dan kan de koper eisen dat de last of de beperking wordt opgeheven, mits de verkoper hieraan redelijkerwijs kan voldoen.

Where the thing is subject to a charge or an encumbrance which should not have encumbered it, the buyer may demand that the charge or encumbrance be removed, provided that the seller can reasonably comply herewith.

Lorsque la chose est encombrée d'une charge ou restriction qui n'aurait pas dû la grever, l'acheteur peut demander que la charge ou la restriction soit enlevée, pourvu que le vendeur soit normalement en mesure d'y pourvoir.

Art. 21. (7.1.3.2) - 1. Beantwoordt het afgeleverde niet aan de overeenkomst, dan kan de koper eisen:
a. aflevering van het ontbrekende;
b. herstel van de afgeleverde zaak, mits de verkoper hieraan redelijkerwijs kan voldoen;
c. vervanging van de afgeleverde zaak, tenzij de afwijking van het overeengekomene te gering is om dit te rechtvaardigen, dan wel de zaak na het tijdstip dat de koper redelijkerwijze met ongedaanmaking rekening moet houden, teniet of achteruit is gegaan doordat hij niet als een zorgvuldig schuldenaar voor het behoud ervan heeft gezorgd.
- 2. Indien bij een consumentenkoop de koper van een voor vervanging vatbare zaak herstel of vervanging daarvan overeenkomstig lid 1 onder b of c vordert, is de verkoper bevoegd tussen vervanging of teruggave van de koopprijs te kiezen. De verkoper is gehouden deze keuze binnen korte tijd te doen en vervolgens zijn verplichtingen binnen redelijke tijd na te komen; bij gebreke hiervan kan de koper zijn rechten op herstel of vervanging doen gelden.
- 3. Indien bij een consumentenkoop de verkoper niet binnen een redelijke tijd nadat hij daartoe door de koper schriftelijk is aangemaand, aan zijn verplichting tot herstel van de afgeleverde zaak heeft voldaan, is de koper

bevoegd het herstel door een derde te doen plaatsvinden en de kosten daarvan op de verkoper te verhalen.

1. Where what has been delivered does not conform to the contract, the buyer may demand:
a. delivery of what is lacking;
b. repair of the thing delivered, provided that the seller can reasonably comply herewith;
c. replacement of the thing delivered, unless the deviation from what has been agreed to is too minor to justify this, or unless, after the time when the buyer must reasonably foresee the possibility of undoing, the thing has been lost or has deteriorated because the buyer has not looked after its safekeeping as a prudent debtor;
2. If, in a consumer sale, and according to paragraph 1 *sub* b or c, the buyer demands the repair or the replacement of a thing susceptible of replacement, the seller is entitled to choose between replacement or the reimbursement of the purchase price. The seller must make this choice within a short period, and, subsequently, he must perform his obligations within a reasonable period; in the absence thereof the buyer may enforce his rights to repair or replacement.
3. If, in a consumer sale, the seller has not performed his obligation to repair the thing delivered, within a reasonable period after a written notice to that effect from the buyer, the latter is entitled to have the repair done by a third person and to claim the costs thereof from the seller.

1. Lorsque ce qui est livré n'est pas conforme au contrat, l'acheteur peut demander:
a. Livraison de ce qui manque;
b. Réparation de la chose livrée, pourvu que le vendeur soit normalement en mesure d'y pourvoir;
c. Remplacement de la chose livrée, à moins que l'écart par rapport à ce qui a été convenu soit trop peu important pour le justifier ou que la chose, après le moment où l'acheteur doit normalement tenir compte de l'anéantissement, soit perdue ou détériorée du fait qu'il n'a pas pris soin de sa conservation comme un bon débiteur.
2. Si, dans un achat de consommation, l'acheteur d'une chose susceptible de remplacement en demande la réparation ou le remplacement conformément aux points b. ou c. du paragraphe 1er, le vendeur a le pouvoir de choisir entre remplacement et remboursement du prix d'achat. Le vendeur est tenu d'effectuer le choix dans un bref délai et ensuite d'exécuter ses obligations dans un délai raisonnable; à défaut, l'acheteur peut faire valoir ses droits à la réparation ou au remplacement.
3. Si, dans un achat de consommation, le vendeur n'a pas satisfait à son obligation de réparation de la chose livrée dans un délai raisonnable après que l'acheteur l'y a sommé par écrit, ce dernier a la faculté de faire effectuer la réparation par un tiers et d'en recouvrer les frais contre le vendeur.

Art. 22. (7.1.3.3) De rechten genoemd in de artikelen 20 en 21 komen de koper toe onverminderd alle andere rechten of vorderingen.

The rights mentioned in articles 20 and 21 may be exercised by the buyer, without prejudice to all other rights or actions.

Les droits énoncés aux articles 20 et 21 reviennent à l'acheteur, sans préjudice de tous autres droits et actions.

Art. 23. (7.1.3.5) - 1. De koper kan er geen beroep meer op doen dat hetgeen is afgeleverd niet aan de overeenkomst beantwoordt, indien hij de verkoper daarvan niet binnen bekwame tijd nadat hij dit heeft ontdekt of redelijkerwijs had behoren te ontdekken, kennis heeft gegeven. Blijkt echter aan de zaak een eigenschap te ontbreken die deze volgens de

verkoper bezat, of heeft de afwijking betrekking op feiten die hij kende of behoorde te kennen doch die hij niet heeft meegedeeld, dan moet de kennisgeving binnen bekwame tijd na de ontdekking geschieden.
- 2. Rechtsvorderingen en verweren, gegrond op feiten die de stelling zouden rechtvaardigen dat de afgeleverde zaak niet aan de overeenkomst beantwoordt, verjaren door verloop van twee jaren na de overeenkomstig het eerste lid gedane kennisgeving. Doch de koper behoudt de bevoegdheid om aan een vordering tot betaling van de prijs zijn recht op vermindering daarvan door gedeeltelijke ontbinding van de koop of op schadevergoeding tegen te werpen.
- 3. De termijn loopt niet zolang de koper zijn rechten niet kan uitoefenen als gevolg van opzet van de verkoper.

1. The buyer may no longer invoke the fact that what has been delivered does not conform to the contract, unless he has notified the seller thereof within a reasonable period after he has or reasonably should have discovered this. However, where the thing proves to lack a quality which according to the seller it possessed, or where the deviation pertains to facts which the seller knew or ought to know but has not communicated, the notification must take place within a reasonable period after the discovery.
2. Rights of action and defences based on facts which would justify the position that the thing delivered does not conform to the contract are prescribed by the lapse of two years from the notification given according to paragraph 1. However, the buyer retains, as a defence against an action for payment, the power to invoke his right to a reduction in the purchase price through a partial setting aside of the sale or his right to reparation of damage.
3. The prescription period does not run as long as the buyer cannot exercise his rights as a result of the fraud of the seller.

1. L'acheteur ne peut plus faire valoir que ce qui a été livré ne correspond pas au contrat, s'il n'en a pas avisé le vendeur dans un délai raisonnable après qu'il l'a découvert ou aurait dû le découvrir. Toutefois, lorsque fait défaut une propriété que la chose possédait d'après le vendeur, ou que l'écart a trait à des faits qu'il connaissait ou devait connaître, mais n'a pas communiqués, l'avis doit avoir lieu dans un délai raisonnable après la découverte.
2. Les actions et les défenses fondées sur des faits qui tendent à justifier la thèse selon laquelle la chose livrée ne correspond pas au contrat se prescrivent par deux ans à compter de l'avis donné conformément au paragraphe 1er. L'acheteur conserve cependant le pouvoir d'opposer à une action en paiement du prix son droit à la réduction de celui-ci par résiliation partielle de la vente, ou à la réparation du dommage.
3. Le délai de prescription ne court pas tant que l'acheteur, par suite du dol du vendeur, ne peut exercer ses droits.

Art. 24. (7.1.3.7) - 1. Indien op grond van een consumentenkoop een zaak is afgeleverd die niet de eigenschappen bezit die de koper op grond van de overeenkomst mocht verwachten, heeft de koper jegens de verkoper recht op schadevergoeding overeenkomstig de afdelingen 9 en 10 van titel 1 van Boek 6.
- 2. Bestaat de tekortkoming in een gebrek als bedoeld in afdeling 3 van titel 3 van Boek 6, dan is de verkoper niet aansprakelijk voor schade als in die afdeling bedoeld, tenzij
a. hij het gebrek kende of behoorde te kennen,
b. hij de afwezigheid van het gebrek heeft toegezegd of
c. het betreft zaakschade terzake waarvan krachtens afdeling 3 van titel 3 van Boek 6 geen recht op vergoeding bestaat op grond van de in

die afdeling geregelde franchise, onverminderd zijn verweren krachtens de afdelingen 9 en 10 van titel 1 van Boek 6.

- 3. Indien de verkoper de schade van de koper vergoedt krachtens lid 2 onder a of b, is de koper verplicht zijn rechten uit afdeling 3 van titel 3 van Boek 6 aan de verkoper over te dragen.

1. If, pursuant to a consumer sale, a thing has been delivered which does not possess the qualities which the buyer was entitled to expect on the basis of the contract, he has, against the seller, the right to reparation of damage according to sections 9 and 10 of title 1 of Book 6.

2. Where the failure consists of a defect as referred to in section 3 of title 3 of Book 6, the seller is not liable for the damage referred to in that section, unless:

a. he knew or ought to know the defect;
b. he has promised the absence of the defect; or
c. damage to things is concerned for which, pursuant to section 3 of title 3 of Book 6, there is no right to compensation on the basis of the franchise provided for in that section, without prejudice to his defences pursuant to section 9 and 10 of title 1 of Book 6.

3. If, pursuant to paragraph 2 *sub* a or b, the seller repairs the buyer's damage, the latter must transfer his rights flowing from section 3 of title 3 of Book 6 to the seller.

1. Si, dans le cadre d'un achat de consommation, une chose a été livrée qui ne possède pas les propriétés auxquelles l'acheteur pouvait s'attendre en vertu du contrat, l'acheteur a, contre le vendeur, droit à la réparation du dommage conformément aux sections 9 et 10 du titre 1er du Livre sixième.

2. Lorsque le manquement consiste en un vice visé à la section 3 du titre 3 du Livre sixième, le vendeur n'est pas responsable du dommage visé à cette section, à moins

a. Qu'il n'ait connu ou n'ait dû connaître le vice;
b. Qu'il n'ait promis l'absence du vice;
c. Qu'il s'agisse de dommage aux choses ne donnant, en vertu de la section 3 du titre 3 du Livre sixième, pas droit à réparation en raison de la franchise qui y est prévue, sans préjudice des défenses en vertu des sections 9 et 10 du titre 1 du Livre sixième.

3. Si le vendeur répare le dommage de l'acheteur par application des points a. et b. du paragraphe 2, l'acheteur est tenu de lui transférer les droits qui lui reviennent de la section 3 du titre 3 du Livre sixième.

Art. 25. (7.1.3.9) - 1. Heeft de koper, in geval van een tekortkoming als bedoeld in artikel 24, een of meer van zijn rechten ter zake van die tekortkoming tegen de verkoper uitgeoefend, dan heeft de verkoper recht op schadevergoeding jegens degene van wie hij de zaak heeft gekocht, mits ook deze bij die overeenkomst in de uitoefening van zijn beroep of bedrijf heeft gehandeld. Kosten ter zake van verweer worden slechts vergoed voor zover zij in redelijkheid door de verkoper zijn gemaakt.

- 2. Op een beding tot uitsluiting of beperking van de aansprakelijkheid, bedoeld in lid 1, kan slechts een beroep worden gedaan, voorzover dit, gelet op alle omstandigheden van het geval, jegens de verkoper redelijk is.

- 3. Het recht op schadevergoeding krachtens lid 1 komt de verkoper niet toe indien de afwijking betrekking heeft op feiten die hij kende of behoorde te kennen, dan wel haar oorzaak vindt in een omstandigheid die is voorgevallen nadat de zaak aan hem werd afgeleverd.

- 4. Indien aan de zaak een eigenschap ontbreekt die deze volgens de verkoper bezat, is het recht van de verkoper op schadevergoeding krachtens lid 1 beperkt tot het bedrag waarop hij aanspraak had kunnen maken indien hij de toezegging niet had gedaan.

- 5. Op het verhaal krachtens eerdere koopovereenkomsten zijn de vorige leden van overeenkomstige toepassing.
- 6. De vorige leden zijn niet van toepassing voor zover het betreft schade als bedoeld in artikel 24 lid 2.

1. Where, in the case of a failure as referred to in article 24, the buyer has exercised one or more of his rights concerning that failure against the seller, the latter is entitled to reparation of damage with respect to the person from whom he has bought the thing, provided that this person too has, in contracting, acted in the course of his profession or business. Costs of defence are only reimbursed to the extent that the seller has reasonably incurred them.
2. A stipulation excluding or limiting the liability referred to in paragraph 1, can only be invoked to the extent that, taking into consideration all the circumstances of the case, this is reasonable toward the seller.
3. The seller has no right to reparation of damage pursuant to paragraph 1, if the deviation pertains to facts which he knew or ought to know, or if it finds its cause in a circumstance which has occurred after the thing was delivered to him.
4. If the thing lacks a quality which, according to the seller, it possessed, the right of the seller to reparation of damage pursuant to paragraph 1 is limited to the amount to which he could have laid a claim if he had not made the promise.
5. The preceding paragraphs apply *mutatis mutandis* to recourse pursuant to earlier contracts of sale.

6. The preceding paragraphs do not apply to the extent that damage as referred to in article 24 paragraph 2 is concerned.

1. Lorsque l'acheteur, dans le cas d'un manquement visé à l'article 24, a exercé contre le vendeur un ou plusieurs droits s'y rapportant, le vendeur a droit à réparation à l'égard de celui à qui il a acheté la chose, pourvu que, dans ce contrat, ce dernier également ait agi dans le cadre de son activité professionnelle ou de son entreprise. Les frais de défense engagés par le vendeur ne lui sont remboursés que dans la mesure où ils sont raisonnables.

2. La stipulation visant à exclure ou à restreindre la responsabilité visée au paragraphe 1er ne peut être invoquée que dans la mesure où, compte tenu des circonstances du cas, cela est juste pour le vendeur.
3. Le droit à la réparation du dommage par application du paragraphe 1er ne revient pas au vendeur si l'écart a trait à des faits qu'il connaissait ou devait connaître, ou s'il résulte d'une circonstance qui s'est produite après que la chose lui eut été livrée.
4. Si fait défaut une propriété que la chose possédait d'après le vendeur, le droit du vendeur à la réparation du dommage en vertu du paragraphe 1er est limité à la somme à laquelle il aurait pu prétendre s'il n'avait pas fait la promesse.
5. Les paragraphes précédents s'appliquent par analogie au recouvrement en application de contrats de vente antérieurs.
6. Les paragraphes précédents ne s'appliquent pas dans la mesure où il s'agit d'un dommage visé au paragraphe 2 de l'article 24.

AFDELING 4 Verplichtingen van de koper

Section 4
Obligations of the buyer

Section quatrième
Des obligations de l'acheteur

Art. 26. (7.1.4.1) - 1. De koper is verplicht de prijs te betalen.
- 2. De betaling moet geschieden ten tijde en ter plaatse van de aflevering. Bij een consumentenkoop kan de koper tot vooruitbetaling van ten hoogste de helft van de koopprijs worden verplicht.

- 3. Is voor de eigendomsoverdracht een notariële akte vereist, gevolgd door inschrijving daarvan in de daartoe bestemde openbare registers, dan moet het verschuldigde ten tijde van de ondertekening van de akte tenminste uit de macht van de koper zijn gebracht en behoeft het pas na de inschrijving in de macht van de verkoper te worden gebracht.

1. The buyer is obliged to pay the price.
2. Payment must take place at the time and place of delivery. In a consumer sale the buyer cannot be obliged to prepay more than half the purchase price.

3. Where a notarial deed is required for the transfer of ownership, followed by its entry into the public registers destined for that purpose, that what is owed must at least have been removed from the control of the buyer at the time of the signature of the deed, and it has to be brought under the control of the seller only after the registration.

1. L'acheteur est tenu de payer le prix.

2. Le paiement s'effectue au temps et lieu de la livraison. Dans un achat de consommation, on peut imposer à l'acheteur le paiement par anticipation d'au plus la moitié du prix d'achat.
3. Lorsque le transfert de la propriété requiert un acte notarié, suivi de son inscription sur les registres publics prévus à cette fin, ce qui est dû doit, au moment de la signature de l'acte, être mis au moins hors de la puissance de l'acheteur, mais doit être mis en la puissance du vendeur seulement après l'inscription.

Art. 27. (7.1.4.2) Wanneer de koper gestoord wordt of goede grond heeft te vrezen dat hij gestoord zal worden door een vordering tot uitwinning of tot erkenning van een recht op de zaak dat daarop niet had mogen rusten, kan hij de betaling van de koopprijs opschorten, tenzij de verkoper voldoende zekerheid stelt om het nadeel te dekken dat de koper dreigt te lijden.

Where the buyer is disturbed, or has good reason to fear that he will be disturbed by an action for eviction or for the recognition of a right which should not have encumbered the thing, he may suspend the payment of the purchase price, unless the seller furnishes sufficient security to cover the loss which the buyer risks suffering.

Lorsque l'acheteur est troublé ou a raison de craindre qu'il le sera par une action en éviction ou en reconnaissance d'un droit sur la chose qui n'aurait pas dû la grever, il peut suspendre le paiement du prix d'achat, à moins que le vendeur fournisse sûreté suffisante pour couvrir le préjudice que l'acheteur risque de subir.

Art. 28. (7.1.4.2b) Bij een consumentenkoop verjaart de rechtsvordering tot betaling van de koopprijs door verloop van twee jaren.

In a consumer sale, the right of action for payment of the purchase price is prescribed by the lapse of two years.

Dans un achat de consommation, l'action en paiement du prix de vente se prescrit par deux ans.

Art. 29. (7.1.4.3) - 1. Heeft de koper de zaak ontvangen doch is hij voornemens deze te weigeren, dan moet hij als een zorgvuldig schuldenaar voor het behoud ervan zorgen; hij heeft op de zaak een retentierecht totdat hij door de verkoper voor de door hem in redelijkheid gemaakte kosten schadeloos is gesteld.
- 2. De koper die voornemens is een aan hem verzonden en op de plaats van bestemming te zijner beschikking gestelde zaak te weigeren, moet, zo dit geen betaling van de koopprijs en geen ernstige bezwaren of onredelijke

kosten meebrengt, deze in ontvangst nemen, tenzij de verkoper op de plaats van bestemming aanwezig is of iemand aldaar bevoegd is zich voor zijn rekening met de zorg voor de zaak te belasten.

1. Where the buyer has received the thing but intends to reject it, he must look after its safekeeping as a prudent debtor; he has a right of retention on the thing until the seller has indemnified him for the costs which he has reasonably incurred.
2. The buyer who intends to reject a thing sent to him and made available to him at the place of destination, must take delivery of this thing, unless this entails payment of the purchase price, serious inconveniences or unreasonable costs, or unless the seller is present at the place of destination or a person who is entitled, at that place and on his behalf, to charge himself with the care of the thing.

1. L'acheteur qui a reçu la chose, mais qui a l'intention de la refuser, est tenu de prendre soin de sa conservation comme un débiteur prudent; il a un droit de rétention sur la chose jusqu'à ce que le vendeur l'ait indemnisé des frais normaux qu'il a engagés.
2. L'acheteur qui a l'intention de refuser une chose qui lui a été envoyée et qui a été mise à sa disposition au lieu de destination doit, si cela n'entraîne pas le paiement du prix de vente ni des inconvénients sérieux ou des frais anormaux, en prendre livraison, à moins que le vendeur ne soit présent au lieu de destination ou que quelqu'un sur place n'ait le pouvoir de se charger pour son compte des soins de la chose.

Art. 30. (7.1.4.5) Wanneer in de gevallen, in artikel 29 voorzien, de zaak aan snel tenietgaan of achteruitgang onderhevig is of wanneer de bewaring daarvan ernstige bezwaren of onredelijke kosten zou meebrengen, is de koper verplicht de zaak op een geschikte wijze te doen verkopen.

When, in the cases provided for in article 29, the thing is subject to rapid loss or deterioriation or, when its safekeeping would entail serious inconveniences or unreasonable costs, the buyer must have the thing sold in an appropriate manner.

Lorsque, dans les cas prévus à l'article 29, la chose est sujette à perte ou détérioration rapides, ou que son dépôt entraînerait des inconvénients sérieux ou des frais anormaux, l'acheteur est tenu de faire vendre la chose d'une manière convenable.

AFDELING 5 Bijzondere gevolgen van verzuim van de koper

*Section 5
Special effects of the default of the buyer*

*Section cinquième
Des effets particuliers de la demeure de l'acheteur*

Art. 31. (7.1.5.1) Indien de overeenkomst aan de koper de bevoegdheid geeft door aanwijzing van maat of vorm of op andere wijze de zaak te specificeren en hij daarmede in verzuim is, kan de verkoper daartoe zelf overgaan, met inachtneming van de hem bekende behoeften van de koper.

If the contract gives the buyer the power to specify the thing by indicating its measure, its form or in any other way and where the buyer is in default of doing so, the seller may proceed to do so himself taking acccount of the needs of the buyer as they are known to him.

Si le contrat donne à l'acheteur le pouvoir de déterminer la chose, en en indiquant la mesure ou la forme, ou d'une autre façon, et qu'il soit en demeure de ce faire, le vendeur peut y procéder lui-même, en tenant compte des besoins de l'acheteur qui lui sont connus.

Art. 32. (7.1.5.2) Ingeval de koper met de inontvangstneming in verzuim is, vindt artikel 30 overeenkomstige toepassing.

In the event that the buyer is in default of taking delivery, article 30 applies *mutatis mutandis*.

Dans le cas où l'acheteur est en demeure de prendre livraison, l'article 30 s'applique par analogie.

AFDELING 6 Bijzondere gevallen van ontbinding

Section 6 Special cases of setting aside the contract

Section sixième Des cas particuliers de résiliation

Art. 33. (7.1.6.1) Indien de aflevering van een roerende zaak op een bepaalde dag essentieel is en op die dag de koper niet in ontvangst neemt, levert zulks een grond op tot ontbinding als bedoeld in artikel 265 van Boek 6.

If it is of the essence that a moveable thing be delivered on a certain day, and if the buyer does not take delivery on that day, this produces a ground to set the contract aside as provided for in article 265 of Book 6.

Si la livraison d'une chose mobilière à une date précise est essentielle et que, à cette date, l'acheteur ne prenne pas livraison, il y a cause de résiliation telle que visée à l'article 265 du Livre sixième.

Art. 34. (7.1.6.2) De verkoper kan de koop door een schriftelijke verklaring ontbinden, indien het achterwege blijven van inontvangstneming hem goede grond geeft te vrezen dat de prijs niet zal worden betaald.

The seller may set aside the sale by a written declaration, if the fact that no delivery is taken gives him good reason to fear that the price will not be paid.

Le vendeur peut résilier la vente par une déclaration écrite, si le défaut de prendre livraison lui donne de bons motifs de craindre que le prix ne sera pas payé.

Art. 35. (7.1.6.2a) - 1. Indien de verkoper bij een consumentenkoop krachtens een bij die overeenkomst gemaakt beding de koopprijs na het sluiten van de koop verhoogt, is de koper bevoegd de koop door een schriftelijke verklaring te ontbinden, tenzij bedongen is dat de aflevering langer dan drie maanden na de koop zal plaatsvinden.
- 2. Voor de toepassing van lid 1 wordt onder koopprijs begrepen het bedrag dat bij het sluiten van de overeenkomst onder voorbehoud van prijswijziging voorlopig als koopprijs is opgegeven.

1. If, in a consumer sale and pursuant to a stipulation made therein, the seller increases the price after the conclusion of the sale, the buyer is entitled to set the contract aside by a written declaration, unless it has been stipulated that the delivery will take place more than three months after the sale.

1. Si, dans un achat de consommation, le vendeur, par application d'une clause stipulée au contrat, augmente le prix après la conclusion de la vente, l'acheteur a le pouvoir de résilier le contrat par déclaration écrite, à moins qu'il n'ait été stipulé que la livraison aura lieu plus de trois mois après la vente.

2. For the application of paragraph 1, the purchase price may mean the amount that has been provisionally indicated as purchase price at the time the contract was entered into subject to price modifications.

2. Pour l'application du paragraphe 1er, le prix de vente peut s'entendre de la somme qui, lors de la conclusion du contrat et sous réserve de modifications du prix, a été spécifiée provisoirement comme prix de vente.

AFDELING 7 Schadevergoeding

Section 7 Damages

Section septième Des dommages-intérêts

Art. 36. (7.1.7.1) - 1. In geval van ontbinding van de koop is, wanneer de zaak een dagprijs heeft, de schadevergoeding gelijk aan het verschil tussen de in de overeenkomst bepaalde prijs en de dagprijs ten dage van de niet-nakoming.
- 2. Voor de berekening van deze schadevergoeding is de in aanmerking te nemen dagprijs die van de markt waar de koop plaatsvond, of, indien er geen dergelijke dagprijs is of deze bezwaarlijk zou kunnen worden toegepast, de prijs van de markt die deze redelijkerwijs kan vervangen; hierbij wordt rekening gehouden met verschillen in de kosten van vervoer van de zaak.

1. Where, in the event that a sale is set aside, the thing has a current price, damages equal the difference between the price provided for in the contract and the price of the day on the day of non-performance.
2. In order to calculate these damages, the current price to be taken into consideration is that of the market where the sale has taken place, or, if there is no such current price or if it would be difficult to apply it, the price of the market which can reasonably replace this one; in doing so, one takes account of differences in the costs of transportation of the thing.

1. Dans le cas de résiliation de la vente, les dommages-intérêts, pour une chose qui a un prix courant, s'élèvent à la différence entre le prix déterminé au contrat et le prix courant à la date de l'inexécution.

2. Pour l'évaluation de ces dommages-intérêts, le prix courant à considérer est celui du marché où a eu lieu la vente ou, s'il n'y a pas de prix courant ou que celui-ci s'appliquerait difficilement, le prix du marché qui peut convenablement remplacer celui-ci; on tient compte des différences dans les frais de transport de la chose.

Art. 37. (7.1.7.2) Heeft de koper of de verkoper een dekkingskoop gesloten en is hij daarbij redelijk te werk gegaan, dan komt hem het verschil toe tussen de overeengekomen prijs en die van de dekkingskoop.

Where the buyer or the seller has entered into a replacement sale and, in doing so, has acted reasonably, he is entitled to the difference between the agreed price and that of the replacement sale.

La différence entre le prix convenu et celui de la vente de remplacement revient à l'acheteur ou au vendeur, qui a conclu un achat de remplacement ou une vente compensatoire, et qui y a procédé de manière convenable.

Art. 38. (7.1.7.3) De bepalingen van de twee voorgaande artikelen sluiten het recht op een hogere schadevergoeding niet uit ingeval meer schade is geleden.

The provisions of the two preceding articles do not preclude a higher amount of damages in the event that the damage suffered is greater.

Les dispositions des deux articles précédents n'excluent pas le droit à des dommages-intérêts supérieurs si le dommage subi est plus élevé.

AFDELING 8 Recht van reclame

Section 8
The right of revendication

Section huitième
Du droit de revendication

Art. 39. (7.1.8.1) - 1. De verkoper van een roerende, aan de koper afgeleverde zaak die niet een registergoed is, kan, indien de prijs niet betaald is en in verband daarmee aan de vereisten voor een ontbinding als bedoeld in artikel 265 van Boek 6 is voldaan, de zaak door een tot de koper gerichte schriftelijke verklaring terugvorderen. Door deze verklaring wordt de koop ontbonden en eindigt het recht van de koper of zijn rechtsverkrijger; de artikelen 271, 273, 275 en 276 van Boek 6 zijn van overeenkomstige toepassing.
- 2. Is slechts de prijs van een bepaald deel van het afgeleverde niet betaald, dan kan de verkoper slechts dat deel terugvorderen. Is ten aanzien van het geheel een deel van de prijs niet betaald, dan kan de verkoper een daaraan evenredig deel van het afgeleverde terugvorderen indien het afgeleverde voor een zodanige verdeling vatbaar is. In beide gevallen wordt de koop slechts voor het teruggevorderde deel van het afgeleverde ontbonden.
- 3. In alle andere gevallen van gedeeltelijke betaling van de prijs kan de verkoper slechts het afgeleverde in zijn geheel terugvorderen tegen teruggave van het reeds betaalde.

1. The seller of a moveable thing, other than registered property, which has been delivered to the buyer can revendicate the thing by a written declaration addressed to the buyer, if the price has not been paid and if in connection therewith the requirements to set aside the contract as referred to in article 265 of Book 6 have been met. This declaration sets the sale aside and terminates the rights of the buyer or his successor; articles 271, 273, 275 and 276 of Book 6 apply *mutatis mutandis*.
2. Where only the price of a certain part of what has been delivered has not been paid, the seller can merely revendicate that part. Where, in respect of the whole, a part of the price has not been paid, the seller can revendicate a corresponding part of what has been delivered, if that what has been delivered is susceptible of such division. In both cases the sale is only set aside for the revendicated part of what has been delivered.

1. Le vendeur qui a livré à l'acheteur une chose mobilière qui n'est pas un bien immatriculé peut, si le prix n'a pas été payé et que, de ce fait, les conditions de résiliation telles que prévues à l'article 265 du Livre sixième sont remplies, revendiquer la chose par une déclaration écrite adressée à l'acheteur. Par cette déclaration, la vente est résiliée et le droit de l'acheteur ou de son ayant droit prend fin; les articles 271, 273, 275 et 276 du Livre sixième s'appliquent par analogie.

2. Si le prix d'une partie seulement de ce qui a été livré n'a pas été payé, le vendeur ne peut revendiquer que cette partie. Si, pour l'ensemble, une partie du prix n'a pas été payée, le vendeur peut, si ce qui a été livré est susceptible d'une telle division, en revendiquer une partie correspondante. Dans les deux cas, la vente n'est résiliée que pour la partie revendiquée de ce qui a été livré.

3. In all other cases of partial payment of the price the seller can only revendicate what has been delivered in its totality against reimbursement of what has already been paid.

3. Dans tous les autres cas de paiement partiel du prix, le vendeur ne peut que revendiquer en entier ce qui a été livré contre remboursement de ce qui a déjà été payé.

Art. 40. (7.1.8.2) Is de koper in staat van faillissement verklaard of is aan hem surséance van betaling verleend, dan heeft de terugvordering geen gevolg, indien door de curator, onderscheidenlijk door de koper en de bewindvoerder, binnen een hun daartoe door de verkoper bij diens verklaring te stellen redelijke termijn de koopprijs wordt betaald of voor deze betaling zekerheid wordt gesteld.

Where the buyer has been declared bankrupt or where he has been put into receivership, revendication has no effect if the curator in the case of bankruptcy, or in the case of receivership the buyer and the administrator pay the purchase price or furnish security for this payment within a reasonable period given to them by the seller in his declaration.

Lorsque l'acheteur est en faillite ou s'est vu accorder un sursis de paiement, la revendication n'a pas d'effet si le syndic, dans le cas de la faillite, ou l'acheteur et l'administrateur, dans le cas du sursis, paient le prix de vente ou fournissent sûreté pour le paiement dans un délai raisonnable précisé par le vendeur dans sa déclaration.

Art. 41. (7.1.8.3) De bevoegdheid tot terugvordering kan slechts worden uitgeoefend voor zover het afgeleverde zich nog in dezelfde staat bevindt als waarin het werd afgeleverd.

The right to revendicate can only be exercised to the extent that the thing delivered is still in the same state as that in which it was delivered.

Le pouvoir de revendication ne peut être exercée que dans la mesure où ce qui a été livré se trouve toujours dans l'état où elle était lors de la livraison.

Art. 42. (7.1.8.4) - 1. Tenzij de zaak in handen van de koper is gebleven, vervalt de bevoegdheid tot terugvordering wanneer de zaak overeenkomstig artikel 90 lid 1 of artikel 91 van Boek 3 anders dan om niet is overgedragen aan een derde die redelijkerwijs niet behoefde te verwachten dat het recht zou worden uitgeoefend.
- 2. Is de zaak na de aflevering anders dan om niet in vruchtgebruik gegeven of verpand, dan is lid 1 van overeenkomstige toepassing.

1. Unless the thing has remained in the hands of the buyer, the right to revendicate lapses when, according to article 90 paragraph 1 or 91 of Book 3, the thing has been transferred, otherwise than by gratuitous title, to a third person who did not reasonably have to expect that the right would be exercised.
2. Where, after the delivery, the thing has been given in usufruct otherwise than by gratuitous title or has been pledged, paragraph 1 applies *mutatis mutandis*.

1. À moins que la chose soit demeurée entre les mains de l'acheteur, le pouvoir de revendication prend fin lorsque la chose, conformément aux articles 90, paragraphe 1er, ou 91 du Livre troisième, a été transférée autrement qu'à titre gratuit à un tiers qui ne devait pas normalement s'attendre à ce que la faculté soit exercée.
2. Lorsque la chose, après la livraison, a été donnée en usufruit autrement qu'à titre gratuit ou a été mise en gage, le paragraphe 1er s'applique par analogie.

Art. 43. (7.1.8.6) De verkoper kan zijn in artikel 39 omschreven bevoegdheid niet uitoefenen, indien de koper voor de volle koopprijs

handelspapier heeft geaccepteerd. Bij acceptatie voor een gedeelte van de prijs kan de verkoper die bevoegdheid slechts uitoefenen, indien hij ten behoeve van de koper zekerheid stelt voor de vergoeding van hetgeen de koper uit hoofde van zijn acceptatie zou moeten betalen.

The seller cannot exercise his right as described in article 39, if the buyer has accepted a commercial effect for the full purchase price. Upon acceptance for part of the price, the seller can only exercise that right if he furnishes security in favour of the buyer in order to compensate him for that which he would have to pay as a consequence of his acceptance.

Le vendeur ne peut exercer le pouvoir énoncé à l'article 39 si l'acheteur a accepté un effet de commerce pour l'intégralité du prix de vente. L'acceptation pour une partie du prix ne permet au vendeur de l'exercer que s'il fournit sûreté au profit de l'acheteur pour le remboursement de ce que ce dernier devrait payer du fait de l'acceptation.

Art. 44. (7.1.8.7) De in artikel 39 omschreven bevoegdheid van de verkoper vervalt, wanneer zowel zes weken zijn verstreken nadat de vordering tot betaling van de koopprijs opeisbaar is geworden, als zestig dagen, te rekenen van de dag waarop de zaak onder de koper of onder iemand van zijnentwege is opgeslagen.

The seller's right described in article 39 lapses when, simultaneously, six weeks have passed since the right to payment of the purchase price has become exigible, and sixty days counted from the day on which the thing has been deposited with the buyer or with someone on his behalf.

Le pouvoir énoncé à l'article 39 prend fin lorsque se seront écoulées à la fois une période de six semaines à compter du moment où la créance en paiement du prix de vente est devenue exigible et une période de soixante jours à compter de la date où la chose a été déposée auprès de l'acheteur ou d'une personne agissant pour lui.

AFDELING 9 Koop op proef

Section 9 Sale upon trial

Section neuvième De la vente à l'essai

Art. 45. (7.1.9.1) - 1. Koop op proef wordt geacht te zijn gesloten onder de opschortende voorwaarde dat de zaak de koper voldoet.
- 2. Laat deze een termijn, voldoende om de zaak te beoordelen, voorbijgaan zonder de verkoper van zijn beslissing in kennis te stellen, dan kan hij de zaak niet meer weigeren.

1. A sale upon trial is considered to have been entered into upon the suspensive condition of the thing satisfying the buyer.
2. Where the buyer allows to pass a period sufficient to judge the thing without notifying the seller of his decision, he can no longer reject the thing.

1. La vente à l'essai est considérée conclue sous la condition suspensive que l'acheteur soit satisfait de la chose.
2. Lorsque celui-ci laisse passer un délai suffisant pour juger la chose sans informer le vendeur de sa décision, il ne peut plus la refuser.

Art. 46. (7.1.9.2) Zolang de koop niet definitief is, is de zaak voor risico van de verkoper.

As long as the sale is not definitive, the seller bears the risk of the thing.

Tant que la vente n'est pas définitive, le risque de la chose incombe au vendeur.

AFDELING 10 Koop van vermogensrechten

Section 10 Sale of patrimonial rights

Section dixième De la vente de droits patrimoniaux

Art. 47. (7.1.10.1) Een koop kan ook op een vermogensrecht betrekking hebben. In dat geval zijn de bepalingen van de vorige afdelingen van toepassing voor zover dit in overeenstemming is met de aard van het recht.

A sale can also pertain to a patrimonial right. In such a case, the provisions of the preceding sections apply to the extent that this is in conformity with the nature of the right.

La vente peut également porter sur un droit patrimonial. Dans ce cas, les dispositions des sections précédentes s'appliquent dans la mesure où cela correspond à la nature du droit.

Art. 48. (7.1.10.2) - 1. Hij die een nalatenschap verkoopt zonder de goederen daarvan stuk voor stuk op te geven, is slechts gehouden voor zijn hoedanigheid van erfgenaam in te staan.
- 2. Heeft de verkoper reeds vruchten genoten, een tot de nalatenschap behorende vordering geïnd of goederen uit de nalatenschap vervreemd, dan moet hij die aan de koper vergoeden.
- 3. De koper moet aan de verkoper vergoeden hetgeen deze wegens de schulden en lasten der nalatenschap heeft betaald en hem voldoen hetgeen hij als schuldeiser van de nalatenschap te vorderen had.

1. The person who sells a succession, without an indication of the individual items of property included therein, is only bound to warrant his quality of heir.
2. The seller must reimburse the buyer for fruits which he has already received, for claims belonging to the succession which he has realized, and for property of the succession which he has alienated.
3. The buyer must reimburse the seller for what the latter has paid on account of the debts and charges of the succession, and he must pay the seller that which the latter could claim from the succession as a creditor.

1. Celui qui vend une succession sans déclarer individuellement les biens qui la composent n'est tenu à garantir que sa qualité d'héritier.
2. Le vendeur qui a déjà joui des fruits, a perçu une créance appartenant à la succession ou a aliéné des biens en faisant partie doit en indemniser l'acheteur.
3. L'acheteur doit rembourser au vendeur ce que ce dernier a payé au titre des dettes et des charges de la succession et lui payer ce qu'il pouvait réclamer à la succession à titre de créancier.

AFDELING 12 Ruil

Section 12 Exchange

Section douzième De l'échange

Art. 49. (7.1.12.1) Ruil is de overeenkomst waarbij partijen zich verbinden elkaar over en weer een zaak in de plaats van een andere te geven.

Exchange is a contract whereby the parties bind themselves to give each other reciprocally one thing in exchange for another.

L'échange est le contrat par lequel les parties s'engagent à se donner réciproquement une chose pour une autre.

Art. 50. (7.1.12.2) De bepalingen betreffende koop vinden overeenkomstige toepassing, met dien verstande dat elke partij wordt beschouwd als verkoper voor de prestatie die zij verschuldigd is, en als koper voor die welke haar toekomt.

The provisions regarding sale apply *mutatis mutandis*, it being understood that each party is considered as seller for the prestation which he owes and as buyer for the prestation which is owed to him.

Les dispositions relatives à la vente s'appliquent par analogie, étant entendu que chaque partie est considérée comme vendeur pour la prestation qu'elle doit et comme acheteur pour celle qui lui revient.

Art. 51-399. Gereserveerd.

Reserved.

Réservés.

TITEL 7 LASTGEVING

TITLE 7 MANDATE

TITRE SEPTIÈME DU MANDAT

Art. 400. (7.7.1) - 1. Lastgeving is de overeenkomst waarbij de ene partij, de lasthebber, zich jegens de andere partij, de lastgever, verbindt buiten dienstbetrekking voor rekening van de lastgever een of meer rechtshandelingen te verrichten.
- 2. De overeenkomst kan de lasthebber verplichten te handelen in eigen naam; zij kan ook verplichten te handelen in naam van de lastgever.

1. Mandate is a contract whereby one party, the mandatary, binds himself toward the other party, the mandator, to perform one or more juridical acts on account of the mandator without there being a relationship of employment.
2. The contract may oblige the mandatary to act in his own name; it may also oblige him to act in the name of the mandator.

1. Le mandat est le contrat par lequel une partie, le mandataire, s'engage envers l'autre, le mandant, sans être employée par lui, à accomplir pour le compte de celui-ci des actes juridiques.

2. Le contrat peut obliger le mandataire à agir en son propre nom; il peut également l'obliger à agir au nom du mandant.

Art. 401. (7.7.1a) De lasthebber moet bij zijn werkzaamheden de zorg van een goed lasthebber in acht nemen.

In his activities the mandatary must exercise the care of a good mandatary.

Le mandataire apporte à ses activités les soins d'un bon mandataire.

Art. 402. (7.7.1ab) - 1. De lasthebber is gehouden gevolg te geven aan tijdig gegeven en verantwoorde aanwijzingen omtrent de uitvoering van de last.
- 2. De lasthebber die op redelijke grond niet bereid is de last volgens de hem gegeven aanwijzingen uit te voeren, kan, zo de lastgever hem niettemin aan die aanwijzingen houdt, de overeenkomst opzeggen wegens gewichtige redenen.

1. The mandatary must follow timely and justifiable instructions regarding the performance of the mandate.
2. The mandatary who, upon reasonable grounds, is not willing to perform the mandate according to the instructions given to him, may, where the mandator nevertheless holds him to those instructions, resiliate the contract for serious reasons.

1. Le mandataire est tenu de donner suite aux instructions transmises en temps utile et justifiées concernant l'exécution du mandat.
2. Le mandataire qui, pour un motif raisonnable, n'est pas prêt à exécuter le mandat suivant les instructions à lui transmises peut, lorsque le mandant maintient néanmoins ces instructions, résilier le contrat pour des raisons sérieuses.

Art. 403. (7.7.1b) - 1. De lasthebber moet de lastgever op de hoogte houden van zijn werkzaamheden ter uitvoering van de last en hem onverwijld in kennis stellen van de voltooiing van de last, indien de lastgever daarvan onkundig is.
- 2. De lasthebber doet aan de lastgever verantwoording van de wijze waarop hij zich van de last heeft gekweten. Heeft hij bij de uitvoering van de last ten laste van de lastgever gelden uitgegeven of te diens behoeve gelden ontvangen, dan doet hij daarvan rekening.

1. The mandatary must keep the mandator informed of his activities in performing the mandate, and he must notify him without delay of the completion of the mandate, if the mandator is unaware thereof.
2. The mandatary must render account to the mandator of the manner in which he has discharged his mandate. Where, in performing the mandate, he has disbursed moneys at the expense of the mandator, or has received moneys to the latter's benefit, he must render account thereof.

1. Le mandataire tient le mandant au courant de ses activités dans l'exécution du mandat et l'informe sans tarder de son achèvement, si le mandant n'en a pas connaissance.

2. Le mandataire rend compte au mandant de la façon dont il a accompli le mandat. Lorsque, dans l'exécution du mandat, il a dépensé des sommes à la charge du mandant ou en a perçu à son profit, il en rend compte.

Art. 404. (7.7.1c) Indien de last is verleend met het oog op een persoon die met de lasthebber of in zijn dienst een beroep of een bedrijf uitoefent, is die persoon gehouden de werkzaamheden, nodig voor de uitvoering van de last, zelf te verrichten, behoudens voor zover uit de last voortvloeit dat hij deze onder zijn verantwoordelijkheid door anderen mag laten uitvoeren; alles onverminderd de aansprakelijkheid van de lasthebber.

If the mandate has been granted with consideration to a person who exercises a profession or a business with the mandator or in his service, that person must himself carry out the activities

Si le mandat a été accordé en considération d'une personne qui exerce une activité professionnelle ou entreprise avec le mandant ou à son service, cette personne est tenue d'effectuer elle-même les activités

necessary for the performance of the mandate, except to the extent that it results from the mandate itself that he may have it performed by others under his responsibility; the foregoing is without prejudice to the liability of the mandatary.

nécessaires à l'exécution du mandat, sauf dans la mesure où il résulte du mandat qu'elle peut le faire exécuter par d'autres sous sa responsabilité; le tout sans préjudice de la responsabilité du mandataire.

Art. 405. (7.7.1d) - 1. Indien de overeenkomst door de lasthebber in de uitoefening van zijn beroep of bedrijf is aangegaan, is de lastgever hem loon verschuldigd.
- 2. Indien loon is verschuldigd doch de hoogte niet door partijen is bepaald, is de lastgever het op de gebruikelijke wijze berekende loon of, bij gebreke daarvan, een redelijk loon verschuldigd.

1. The mandator owes remuneration to the mandatary, if the latter has entered into the contract in the course of his profession or business.
2. If remuneration is owed but if the amount has not been fixed by the parties, the mandator owes remuneration as calculated in the habitual manner or, in the absence thereof, a reasonable remuneration.

1. Si le contrat a été conclu par le mandataire dans le cadre d'une activité professionnelle ou d'une entreprise, le mandant lui doit une rémunération.
2. Si une rémunération est due, mais que les parties n'en ont pas fixé la somme, le mandant doit la rémunération calculée de façon habituelle ou, à défaut, une rémunération normale.

Art. 406. (7.7.1e) De lastgever moet aan de lasthebber de onkosten verbonden aan de uitvoering van de last vergoeden, voor zover deze niet in het loon zijn begrepen.

To the extent that they are not included in the remuneration, the mandator must reimburse the mandatary for the expenses connected with the performance of the mandate.

Le mandant doit rembourser au mandataire les frais afférents à l'exécution du mandat, dans la mesure où ils ne sont pas compris dans la rémunération.

Art. 407. (7.7.1f) - 1. Indien twee of meer personen te zamen een last hebben gegeven, zijn zij hoofdelijk tegenover de lasthebber verbonden.
- 2. Indien twee of meer personen te zamen een last hebben ontvangen, is ieder van hen voor het geheel aansprakelijk ter zake van een tekortkoming in de nakoming, tenzij de tekortkoming niet aan hem kan worden toegerekend.

1. If two or more persons have given a mandate together, they are solidarily liable toward the mandatary.
2. If two or more persons have received a mandate together, each of them is liable for the whole with respect to a failure in the performance, unless the failure cannot be imputed to him.

1. Si plusieurs personnes ont conjointement donné un mandat, elles sont solidairement engagées envers le mandataire.
2. Si plusieurs personnes ont conjointement reçu un mandat, chacune d'elles est pour le tout responsable d'un manquement dans l'exécution, à moins que ce manquement ne lui soit pas imputable.

Art. 408. (7.7.2) Indien een lastgeving met twee of meer lasthebbers is aangegaan, is ieder van hen bevoegd zelfstandig te handelen.

If a mandate has been entered into with two or more mandataries, each of them is entitled to act independently.

Si le mandat a été conclu avec plusieurs mandataires, chacun d'eux peut agir de façon autonome.

Art. 409. (7.7.3) - 1. Een lasthebber kan slechts als wederpartij van de lastgever optreden, indien de inhoud van de rechtshandeling zo nauwkeurig vaststaat dat strijd tussen beider belangen is uitgesloten.
- 2. Een lasthebber die slechts in eigen naam mag handelen, kan niettemin als wederpartij van de lastgever optreden, indien de inhoud van de rechtshandeling zo nauwkeurig vaststaat dat strijd tussen beider belangen is uitgesloten.
- 3. Indien de lastgever een persoon is als bedoeld in artikel 414 lid 3, is voor een rechtshandeling waarbij de lasthebber als zijn wederpartij optreedt, op straffe van vernietigbaarheid zijn schriftelijke toestemming vereist.
- 4. De lasthebber die in overeenstemming met de vorige leden als wederpartij van de lastgever optreedt, behoudt zijn recht op loon.

1. A mandatary can only act as co-contracting party[1] of the mandator, if the content of the juridical act is so precisely determined that conflict of interests between them is excluded.
2. A mandatary who may only act in his own name can nevertheless act as co-contracting party of the mandator, if the content of the juridical act is so precisely determined that conflict of interests between them is excluded.
3. If the mandator is a person as referred to in article 414 paragraph 3, his written permission is required, upon pain of annulment, for a juridical act in which the mandatary acts as co-contracting party of the mandator.
4. The mandatary who acts as the co-contracting party of the mandator, in accordance with the preceding paragraphs, retains his right to remuneration.

1. Le mandataire ne peut se porter cocontractant[2] du mandant que si le contenu de l'acte juridique est fixé de façon si précise que le conflit de leurs intérêts est exclu.
2. Le mandataire qui ne doit agir qu'en son nom propre peut néanmoins se porter cocontractant du mandant si le contenu de l'acte juridique est fixé de façon si précise que le conflit de leurs intérêts est exclu.
3. Si le mandant est une personne visée au paragraphe troisième de l'article 414, l'acte juridique dans lequel le mandataire agit comme son cocontractant requiert, à peine d'annulabilité, son autorisation écrite.
4. Le mandataire qui, conformément aux paragraphes précédents, agit comme cocontractant du mandant conserve son droit à rémunération.

Art. 410. (7.7.4) - 1. Een lasthebber mag slechts tevens als lasthebber van de wederpartij optreden, indien de inhoud van de rechtshandeling zo nauwkeurig vaststaat dat strijd tussen de belangen van beide lastgevers is uitgesloten.
- 2. Indien de lastgever een persoon is als bedoeld in artikel 414 lid 3, is voor de geoorloofdheid van een rechtshandeling waarbij de lasthebber ook als lasthebber van de wederpartij optreedt, zijn schriftelijke toestemming vereist.
- 3. Een lasthebber heeft geen recht op loon jegens een lastgever ten opzichte van wie hij in strijd met het in de vorige leden bepaalde handelt,

1 The Dutch term "wederpartij" has been translated as "other party" in Book 3. In the present, narrower context the term "co-contracting party" seems preferable.

2 Le terme néerlandais *wederpartij* a été traduit par «autre partie» au Livre troisième. Dans le présent contexte, le terme plus restreint «cocontractant» semble plus convenable.

onverminderd zijn gehoudenheid tot vergoeding van de dientengevolge door die lastgever geleden schade. Van deze bepaling kan niet ten nadele van een lastgever worden afgeweken.

1. A mandatary may only act as mandatary of another mandator as well, if the content of the juridical act is so precisely determined that conflict of interests between both mandators is excluded.
2. If the mandator is a person as referred to in article 414 paragraph 3, his written permission is required for the legality of a juridical act in which the mandatary acts as mandatary of the other mandator as well.
3. A mandatary is not entitled to remuneration in his relationship with the mandator in respect of whom he acts in violation of the provisions of the preceding paragraphs, and this without prejudice to the mandatary's obligation to repair the damage suffered by that mandator as a consequence thereof. There may be no derogation from this provision to the detriment of a mandator.

1. Le mandataire ne peut se porter en même temps mandataire d'un autre mandant que si le contenu de l'acte juridique est fixé de façon si précise que le conflit d'intérêts entre les deux mandants est exclu.

2. Si le mandant est une personne visée au paragraphe troisième de l'article 414, la licéité de l'acte juridique dans lequel le mandataire se porte en même temps mandataire de l'autre mandant requiert son autorisation écrite.
3. Le mandataire n'a pas droit à rémunération dans son rapport avec le mandant à l'égard duquel il agit en violation des dispositions des paragraphes précédents, sans préjudice de son obligation de réparation du dommage en résultant pour le mandant. On ne peut déroger à la présente disposition au détriment du mandant.

Art. 411. (7.7.4a) Indien een lasthebber in eigen naam een overeenkomst heeft gesloten met een derde die in de nakoming van zijn verplichtingen tekortschiet, is de derde binnen de grenzen van hetgeen omtrent zijn verplichting tot schadevergoeding overigens uit de wet voortvloeit, jegens de lasthebber mede gehouden tot vergoeding van de schade die de lastgever door de tekortkoming heeft geleden.

If, in his own name, a mandatary has entered into a contract with a third person who fails in the performance of his obligations, the third person must, with respect to the mandatary and within the bounds of what otherwise results from the law with respect to his obligation to repair damage, also repair the damage which the mandator has suffered through the failure.

Si le mandataire a conclu en son propre nom un contrat avec un tiers qui manque à l'exécution de ses obligations, le tiers est tenu envers le mandataire, dans les limites de ce qui résulte autrement de la loi en ce qui a trait à son obligation de réparation du dommage, à reparer aussi le dommage qu'a subi le mandant par suite du manquement.

Art. 412. (7.7.4b) - 1. Indien een lasthebber die in eigen naam een overeenkomst heeft gesloten met een derde, zijn verplichtingen jegens de lastgever niet nakomt of in staat van faillissement geraakt, kan de lastgever de voor overgang vatbare rechten van de lasthebber jegens de derde door een schriftelijke verklaring aan hen beiden op zich doen overgaan, behoudens voor zover zij in de onderlinge verhouding tussen lastgever en lasthebber aan deze laatste toekomen.
- 2. Dezelfde bevoegdheid heeft de lastgever indien de derde zijn verplichtingen tegenover de lasthebber niet nakomt, tenzij deze de lastgever voldoet alsof de derde zijn verplichtingen was nagekomen.

- 3. De lasthebber is in de gevallen in dit artikel bedoeld gehouden de naam van de derde aan de lastgever op diens verzoek mede te delen.

1. If a mandatary who has entered into a contract with a third person in his own name, does not perform his obligations with respect to the mandator or goes bankrupt, the mandator can have those rights of the mandatary with respect to the third person which are susceptible of transfer, transferred to him by a written declaration to both of them, except to the extent that these rights belong to the mandatary in his mutual relationship with the mandator.
2. The mandator has the same power if the third person does not perform his obligations with respect to the mandatary, unless the latter satisfies the mandator as if the third person had performed his obligations.
3. In the cases referred to in this article, the mandatary must inform the mandator, upon his request, of the name of the third person.

1. Si le mandataire qui a conclu en son propre nom un contrat avec un tiers n'exécute pas ses obligations envers le mandant ou fait faillite, le mandant peut, par une déclaration écrite adressée au mandataire et au tiers, se faire transmettre les droits susceptibles de transmission de celui-là à l'égard de celui-ci, sauf dans la mesure où, dans le rapport entre mandant et mandataire, ils reviennent à ce dernier.
2. Le mandant a le même pouvoir si le tiers n'exécute pas ses obligations envers le mandataire, à moins que celui-ci donne satisfaction au mandant comme si le tiers avait rempli ses obligations.
3. Le mandataire est tenu, dans les cas prévus au présent article, de communiquer le nom du tiers au mandant qui le requiert.

Art. 413. (7.7.4c) - 1. Indien een lasthebber die in eigen naam een overeenkomst heeft gesloten met een derde, zijn verplichtingen jegens de derde niet nakomt of in staat van faillissement geraakt, kan de derde na schriftelijke mededeling aan de lasthebber en de lastgever zijn rechten uit de overeenkomst tegen de lastgever uitoefenen, voor zover deze op het tijdstip van de mededeling op overeenkomstige wijze jegens de lasthebber gehouden is.
- 2. De lasthebber is in het geval in dit artikel bedoeld gehouden de naam van de lastgever aan de derde op diens verzoek mede te delen.

1. If a mandatary who has entered into a contract with a third person in his own name, does not perform his obligations with respect to the third person or goes bankrupt, the third person can exercise against the mandator the rights resulting from the contract after written notification to the latter and the mandatary, to the extent that the mandator is correspondingly obliged toward the mandatary at the time of the notification.
2. In the case referred to in this article the mandatary must inform the third person, upon his request, of the name of the mandator.

1. Si le mandataire qui a conclu en son propre nom un contrat avec un tiers n'exécute pas ses obligations envers celui-ci ou fait faillite, le tiers peut, après avis écrit au mandataire et au mandant, exercer envers le mandant les droits qui lui reviennent du contrat, dans la mesure où celui-ci, au moment de l'avis, est obligé de manière correspondante envers le mandataire.
2. Le mandataire est tenu, dans le cas prévu au présent article, de communiquer le nom du mandant au tiers qui le requiert.

Art. 414. (7.7.4d) - 1. De lastgever kan te allen tijde de overeenkomst opzeggen.

- 2. De lasthebber die de overeenkomst is aangegaan in de uitoefening van een beroep of bedrijf, kan, behoudens gewichtige redenen, de overeenkomst slechts opzeggen, indien zij voor onbepaalde duur geldt en niet door volbrenging eindigt.
- 3. Een natuurlijk persoon die een last heeft verstrekt anders dan in de uitoefening van een beroep of bedrijf is, onverminderd artikel 406 ter zake van een opzegging geen schadevergoeding verschuldigd. Van deze bepaling kan niet worden afgeweken.

1. The mandator may resiliate the contract at any time.
2. The mandatary who has entered into the contract in the course of a profession or business, may only cancel the contract otherwise than for serious reasons, if it is valid for an indefinite duration and if it is not terminated by accomplishment.
3. Without prejudice to article 406, a natural person who has granted a mandate otherwise than in the course of a profession or business, owes no reparation of damage with respect to a cancellation. There may be no derogation from this provision.

1. Le mandant peut résilier le contrat en tout temps.
2. Le mandataire qui a conclu le contrat dans le cadre d'une activité professionnelle ou d'une entreprise ne peut, sauf pour des raisons sérieuses, le résilier que s'il est conclu pour une période indéterminée et ne prend pas fin par l'accomplissement.
3. Sans préjudice de la disposition de l'article 406, la personne physique qui a accordé le mandat autrement que dans le cadre d'une activité professionnelle ou d'une entreprise ne doit aucune réparation du dommage en rapport avec la résiliation. On ne peut déroger à cette disposition.

Art. 415. (7.7.5) - 1. Lastgeving eindigt, behalve door opzegging overeenkomstig artikel 414, door:
a. de dood, de ondercuratelestelling of het faillissement van de lastgever, met dien verstande dat de dood of de ondercuratelestelling de overeenkomst doet eindigen op het tijdstip waarop de lasthebber daarvan kennis krijgt;
b. de dood, de ondercuratelestelling of het faillissement van de lasthebber.
- 2. Van artikel 414 lid 1 en van lid 1 onder a kan niet worden afgeweken. Voor zover de overeenkomst strekt tot het verrichten van een rechtshandeling in het belang van de lasthebber of van een derde, kan echter worden bepaald dat zij niet door de lastgever kan worden opgezegd, of dat zij niet eindigt door de dood of de ondercuratelestelling van de lastgever. Artikel 74 leden 1, tweede zin, 2 en 4 van Boek 3 is van overeenkomstige toepassing.
- 3. Eindigt de lastgeving door de dood of de ondercuratelestelling van de lastgever, dan is de lasthebber niettemin verplicht al datgene te doen wat de omstandigheden in het belang van de wederpartij eisen.
- 4. Eindigt de lastgeving door de dood van de lasthebber, dan zijn zijn erfgenamen, indien zij kennis dragen van de erfopvolging en van de lastgeving, verplicht al datgene te doen wat de omstandigheden in het belang van de wederpartij eisen. Een overeenkomstige verplichting rust op degenen in wier dienst of met wie de lasthebber een beroep of bedrijf uitoefende.

1. In addition to cancellation pursuant to article 414, mandate is terminated by:

1. Outre la résiliation effectuée conformément à l'article 414, mettent fin au mandat:

a. the death, the placement under curatorship or the bankruptcy of the mandator, upon the proviso that the death or the placement under curatorship terminates the contract at the time when the mandatary becomes aware thereof;
b. the death, the placement under curatorship or the bankruptcy of the mandatary.
2. There may be no derogation from article 414 paragraph 1 and from parapraph 1 *sub* a. To the extent, however, that the contract involves the performance of a juridical act in the interest of the mandatary or of a third person, it may be provided that it cannot be cancelled by the mandator, or that it will not terminate upon his death or placement under curatorship. Article 74 paragraphs 1, second sentence, 2 and 4 of Book 3 apply *mutatis mutandis.*
3. Where the mandate is terminated by the death or the placement under curatorship of the mandator, the mandatary must nevertheless do all that is required by the circumstances in the interest of the other party.
4. Where the mandate is terminated by the death of the mandatary, the heirs must do all that is required by the circumstances in the interest of the other party, if they have knowledge of the succession and the mandate. Those in whose service or with whom the mandatary exercised a profession or business have an analogous obligation.

a. La mort, la mise en curatelle ou la faillite du mandant, étant entendu que la mort et la mise en curatelle n'y mettent fin qu'au moment où le mandataire en prend connaissance;
b. La mort, la mise en curatelle ou la faillite du mandataire.
2. On ne peut déroger au paragraphe 1er de l'article 414 et au paragraphe 1er, point a., du présent article. Dans la mesure où le contrat porte sur l'accomplissement d'un acte juridique au profit du mandataire ou d'un tiers, il peut cependant être stipulé qu'il ne peut être résilié par le mandant, ou qu'il ne prend pas fin par la mort ou par la mise en curatelle de celui-ci. L'article 74 du Livre troisième, paragraphes 1er, deuxième phrase, 2 et 4 s'appliquent par analogie.
3. Lorsque le mandat prend fin par la mort ou par la mise en curatelle du mandant, le mandataire est néanmoins tenu de faire tout ce qui, en la circonstance, est requis dans l'intérêt de l'autre partie.
4. Lorsque le mandat prend fin par la mort du mandataire, les héritiers qui ont connaissance de la succession et du mandat sont tenus de faire tout ce qui, en la circonstance, est requis dans l'intérêt de l'autre partie. Une obligation analogue incombe à ceux au service desquels ou avec lesquels le mandataire exerçait une activité professionnelle ou entreprise.

Art. 416. (7.7.5a) - 1. Indien de overeenkomst eindigt voordat de last is volbracht of de tijd waarvoor zij is verleend, is verstreken en de verschuldigdheid van loon afhankelijk is van de volbrenging of van het verstrijken van die tijd, heeft de lasthebber recht op een naar redelijkheid vast te stellen deel van het loon. Bij de bepaling hiervan wordt onder meer rekening gehouden met de reeds door de lasthebber verrichte werkzaamheden, het voordeel dat de lastgever daarvan heeft, en de grond waarop de overeenkomst is geëindigd.
- 2. In het in lid 1 bedoelde geval heeft de lasthebber slechts recht op het volle loon indien het einde van de overeenkomst aan de lastgever is toe te rekenen en de betaling van het volle loon, gelet op alle omstandigheden van het geval, redelijk is. Op het bedrag van het loon worden de besparingen die voor de lasthebber uit de voortijdige beëindiging voortvloeien, in mindering gebracht.
- 3. Van deze bepaling kan niet worden afgeweken ten nadele van een lastgever als bedoeld in artikel 414 lid 3.

1. If the contract is terminated before the mandate has been accomplished, or the time for which it has been granted has lapsed, and if the indebtedness for remuneration is dependent upon the accomplishment or upon the lapse of that time, the mandatary is entitled to part of the remuneration to be determined according to reasonableness. In this determination, one takes account of, amongst others, the activities already performed by the mandatary, the benefit which the mandator derives therefrom, and the ground upon which the contract has been terminated.
2. In the case referred to in paragraph 1, the mandatary is only entitled to full remuneration if the termination of the contract can be imputed to the mandator, and if full remuneration is reasonable taking into account all the circumstances of the case. The savings which result for the mandatary from the premature termination, are deducted from the amount of the remuneration.
3. There may be no derogation from this provision to the detriment of a mandator as referred to in article 414 paragraph 3.

1. Si le contrat prend fin avant l'accomplissement du mandat ou l'écoulement du temps pour lequel il a été accordé, et que la rémunération n'est due qu'en fonction de l'achèvement ou de l'écoulement du temps, le mandataire a droit à une partie de la rémunération, à fixer raisonnablement. Dans la fixation de la rémunération, on tient compte, entre autres, des activités déjà accomplies par le mandataire, du profit que le mandant en retire, et de la cause qui a mis fin au mandat.

2. Dans le cas visé au paragraphe premier, le mandataire n'a droit à la pleine rémunération que si la fin du mandat est imputable au mandant et que le paiement de la pleine rémunération, compte tenu de toutes les circonstances, est convenable. De la somme de la rémunération sont déduites les économies résultant pour le mandataire de la fin prématurée du mandat.

3. On ne peut déroger à la présente disposition au détriment du mandant visé à l'article 414, paragraphe 3.

Art. 417. (7.7.5b) Een rechtsvordering tegen de lasthebber tot afgifte van stukken die hij ter zake van de last onder zich heeft gekregen, verjaart door verloop van vijf jaren na de aanvang van de dag, volgende op die waarop zijn bemoeiingen zijn geëindigd.

A right of action against the mandatary to remit documents which he has obtained with respect to the mandate, is prescribed by the lapse of five years from the beginning of the day following the one on which his endeavours have terminated.

L'action contre le mandataire en remise des documents dont il a acquis la possession en rapport avec le mandat se prescrit par cinq ans à compter du lendemain du jour où son intervention a pris fin.

Art. 418. (7.7.6) - 1. De artikelen 408-413 en 415 zijn van overeenkomstige toepassing op andere overeenkomsten dan lastgeving krachtens welke de ene partij verplicht of bevoegd is voor rekening van de andere partij rechtshandelingen te verrichten, voor zover de strekking van de betrokken bepalingen in verband met de aard van de overeenkomst zich daartegen niet verzet.
- 2. Het vorige lid is niet van toepassing op overeenkomsten tot het vervoeren of doen vervoeren van personen of zaken.

1. Article 408 - 413 and 415 apply *mutatis mutandis* to contracts other than

1. Les articles 408 à 413 et 415 s'appliquent par analogie à des contrats

mandate and pursuant to which one party is obliged or entitled to perform juridical acts on account of the other party, to the extent that this is not contrary to the necessary implication of the provisions involved, in connection with the nature of the contract.
2. The preceding paragraph does not apply to contracts to transport persons or things, or to have them transported.

autres que le mandat par lesquels une partie a l'obligation ou le pouvoir d'accomplir des actes juridiques pour le compte de l'autre partie, dans la mesure où l'objet des dispositions concernées en rapport avec la nature du contrat ne s'y oppose pas.
2. Le paragraphe précédent ne s'applique pas aux contrats pour transporter ou faire transporter des personnes ou des choses.

Art. 419-599. Gereserveerd.

Reserved.

Réservés.

TITEL 9 BEWAARNEMING

TITLE 9 DEPOSIT

TITRE NEUVIÈME DU DÉPÔT

Art. 600. (7.9.1) Bewaarneming is de overeenkomst waarbij de ene partij, de bewaarnemer, zich tegenover de andere partij, de bewaargever, verbindt, een zaak die de bewaargever hem toevertrouwt of zal toevertrouwen, te bewaren en terug te geven.

Deposit is a contract whereby one party, the depositary, obliges himself toward the other party, the depositor, to safekeep and return a thing which the latter entrusts or will entrust to him.

Le dépôt est le contrat par lequel une partie, le dépositaire, s'engage envers l'autre, le déposant, à garder une chose que celui-ci lui confie ou lui confiera, et à la restituer.

Art. 601. (7.9.2) - 1. Indien de overeenkomst door de bewaarnemer in de uitoefening van zijn beroep of bedrijf is aangegaan, is de bewaargever hem loon verschuldigd.
- 2. Indien loon verschuldigd is, doch de hoogte niet door partijen is bepaald, is de bewaargever het op de gebruikelijke wijze berekende loon of, bij gebreke daarvan, een redelijk loon verschuldigd.
- 3. De bewaargever moet aan de bewaarnemer de aan de bewaring verbonden onkosten vergoeden, voor zover deze niet in het loon zijn begrepen, alsook de schade die de bewaarnemer als gevolg van de bewaring heeft geleden.

1. The depositor owes remuneration to the depositary, if the latter has entered into the contract in the course of his profession or business.
2. If remuneration is owed but if the amount has not been fixed by the parties, the depositor owes remuneration as calculated in the usual manner or, in the absence thereof, a reasonable remuneration.

1. Si le contrat a été conclu par le dépositaire dans le cadre de son activité professionnelle ou de son entreprise, le déposant lui doit une rémunération.
2. Si une rémunération est due, mais que les parties n'en ont pas fixé la somme, le déposant doit la rémunération calculée de la façon habituelle ou, à défaut, une rémunération convenable.

3. To the extent that they are not included in the remuneration, the depositor must reimburse the depositary for the expenses connected with the deposit, as well as for the damage which the depositary has suffered as a result of the deposit.

3. Le déposant rembourse au mandataire les frais afférents au dépôt, dans la mesure où ils ne sont pas compris dans la rémunération, et répare le dommage qu'a subi le dépositaire par suite du dépôt.

Art. 602. (7.9.3) De bewaarnemer moet bij de bewaring de zorg van een goed bewaarder in acht nemen.

In his activities, the depositary must exercise the care of a good depositary.

Le dépositaire apporte à ses activités les soins d'un bon dépositaire.

Art. 603. (7.9.4) - 1. De bewaarnemer mag de zaak slechts gebruiken voor zover de bewaargever daarvoor toestemming heeft gegeven, of het gebruik nodig is om de zaak in goede staat te houden of te brengen.
- 2. Zonder toestemming van de bewaargever mag de bewaarnemer de zaak niet aan een derde in bewaring geven, tenzij dit in het belang van de bewaargever noodzakelijk is.
- 3. Voor gedragingen van een onderbewaarnemer met betrekking tot de zaak is de bewaarnemer op gelijke wijze aansprakelijk als voor eigen gedragingen, tenzij de bewaarneming niet tegen bewaarloon geschiedt en de bewaarnemer tot het in onderbewaring geven genoodzaakt was ten gevolge van hem niet toe te rekenen omstandigheden.

1. The depositary may only use the thing to the extent that the depositor has given his permission thereto, or that use is necessary to keep the thing in or to put it in a good state.
2. The depositary may not deposit, without the permission of the depositor, the thing with a third person, unless this is necessary in the interest of the depositor.
3. The depositary is liable for the acts of a sub-depositary with respect to the thing as if they were his own. acts, unless the deposit is not for remuneration and the depositary was forced to sub-deposit as a result of circumstances not imputable to him.

1. Le dépositaire ne peut utiliser la chose que dans la mesure où le déposant a donné son autorisation ou que l'utilisation est nécessaire afin de garder ou de mettre la chose en bon état.
2. Le dépositaire ne peut, sans l'autorisation du déposant, mettre la chose en dépôt auprès d'un tiers, à moins que cela ne soit nécessaire dans l'intérêt du déposant.
3. Le dépositaire répond des actes du sous-dépositaire en rapport avec la chose de la même façon que des siens propres, à moins que le dépôt n'ait pas lieu contre rémunération et que le dépositaire soit contraint au sous-dépôt par suite de circonstances qui ne lui sont pas imputables.

Art. 604. (7.9.5) De vruchten die de zaak in het tijdvak tussen de ontvangst en de teruggave oplevert, moeten door de bewaarnemer aan de bewaargever worden afgedragen.

The depositary must remit to the depositor the fruits which the thing yields in the period between its receipt and its return.

Le dépositaire doit remettre au déposant les fruits produits par la chose dans le délai entre le dépot et la restitution.

Art. 605. (7.9.6) - 1. De bewaargever kan onverwijlde teruggave en de bewaarnemer onverwijlde terugneming van de zaak vorderen.

- 2. Wegens gewichtige redenen kan de kantonrechter binnen wiens rechtsgebied de zaak zich bevindt, op verzoek van een van de partijen een van het vorige lid of van de overeenkomst afwijkend tijdstip voor de teruggave of terugneming bepalen. Dit lid is niet van toepassing in geval van gerechtelijke bewaring.
- 3. De teruggave moet geschieden op de plaats waar de zaak volgens de overeenkomst moet worden bewaard, tenzij bij de overeenkomst een andere plaats voor de teruggave is aangewezen.
- 4. De bewaarnemer is gehouden de zaak terug te geven in de staat waarin hij haar heeft ontvangen.

1. The depositor may demand that the thing be returned without delay, and the depositary that it be taken back without delay.
2. The judge of the subdistrict court in whose jurisdiction the thing is located may, for serious reasons and upon the request of one of the parties, determine a date for returning or taking back which differs from the preceding paragraph or from the contract. This paragraph does not apply to cases of judicial deposit.
3. The return must take place at the place where, according to the contract, the thing must be kept, unless a different place has been indicated in the contract for the return.
4. The depositary must return the thing in the state in which he has received it.

1. Le déposant peut demander la restitution sans délai de la chose, et le dépositaire, sa reprise sans délai.
2. Pour des motifs sérieux, le juge d'instance dans le ressort duquel se trouve la chose peut, sur requête de l'une des parties, déterminer pour la restitution ou la reprise un moment différent de celui prévu au paragraphe précédent ou au contrat. Le présent paragraphe ne s'applique pas dans le cas du dépôt judiciaire.
3. La restitution a lieu à l'endroit où la chose doit être gardée conformément au contrat, à moins que, dans celui-ci, un endroit différent n'ait été désigné.
4. Le dépositaire restitue la chose dans l'état où il l'a reçue.

Art. 606. (7.9.7) Indien twee of meer personen te zamen een zaak in bewaring hebben genomen, zijn zij hoofdelijk verbonden tot teruggave daarvan en tot vergoeding van de schade die het gevolg is van een tekortschieten in de nakoming van die verplichting, tenzij de tekortkoming aan geen van hen kan worden toegerekend.

If two or more persons have taken a thing into deposit together, they are solidarily liable for its return and for the compensation of the damage which is the result of a failure in the performance of that obligation, unless the failure cannot be imputed to any one of them.

Si plusieurs personnes ont conjointement pris une chose en dépôt, elles sont solidairement tenues de sa restitution et de la réparation du dommage résultant d'un manquement dans l'exécution de cette obligation, à moins que le manquement ne soit imputable à aucune d'elles.

Art. 607. (7.9.7a) - 1. Indien ter zake van een bewaarneming een ceel of een ander stuk aan toonder of order is afgegeven, geldt levering daarvan vóór de aflevering van de daarin aangeduide zaken als levering van die zaken.
- 2. Het eerste lid is niet van toepassing op registergoederen.

1. If, with respect to a deposit, a warrant or another document to bearer or order has been issued, the delivery thereof, before the delivery of the things

1. Si, en rapport avec le dépôt, un récépissé ou autre document au porteur ou a ordre a été délivré, sa délivrance avant la remise des choses qui y sont désignées vaut

indicated therein, is considered as the delivery of those things.

2. Paragraph 1 does not apply to registered property.

délivrance de ces choses.

2. Le paragraphe premier ne s'applique pas aux biens immatriculés.

Art. 608. (7.9.8) - 1. Indien een onderbewaarnemer door een bewaargever buiten overeenkomst voor met betrekking tot de zaak geleden schade wordt aangesproken, is hij jegens deze niet verder aansprakelijk dan hij zou zijn als wederpartij bij de overeenkomst, waarbij de bewaargever de zaak in bewaring gegeven heeft.

- 2. Indien een bewaarnemer buiten overeenkomst voor met betrekking tot de zaak geleden schade wordt aangesproken door een derde die geen bewaargever is, is hij niet verder aansprakelijk dan hij als wederpartij van de bewaargever uit de met deze gesloten overeenkomst zou zijn.

- 3. Indien een onderbewaarnemer door een zodanige derde wordt aangesproken, is hij niet verder aansprakelijk dan hij als bewaarnemer op grond van het vorige lid zou zijn.

- 4. De vorige leden kunnen niet worden ingeroepen door een bewaarnemer of onderbewaarnemer die bij het sluiten van de overeenkomst uit hoofde waarvan hij de zaak ontving, wist of had behoren te weten dat zijn wederpartij jegens degene door wie hij werd aangesproken, niet bevoegd was de zaak aan hem in bewaring te geven.

1. If a sub-depositary is sued extra-contractually by a depositor for damage suffered with respect to the thing, the former is liable toward the latter no further than he would be as co-contracting party in the contract by which the depositor has deposited the thing.

2. If a depositary is sued extra-contractually for damage suffered with respect to the thing by a third person who is not a depositor, he is liable no further than he would be as co-contracting party of the depositor pursuant to the contract entered into with this person.

3. If a sub-depositary is sued by such a third person, he is liable no further than he would be as depositary pursuant to the preceding paragraph.

4. The preceding paragraphs cannot be invoked by a depositary or sub-depositary who, when entering into the contract on the basis of which he received the thing, knew or should have known that his co-contracting party was not entitled, with respect to the person by whom he was sued, to deposit the thing with him.

1. Le sous-dépositaire, poursuivi extra-contractuellement par un déposant pour des dommages subis en rapport avec la chose, n'est pas, à l'égard de ce dernier, responsable davantage qu'il ne le serait comme partie au contrat par lequel le déposant a mis la chose en dépôt.

2. Le dépositaire, poursuivi extra-contractuellement par un tiers qui n'est pas le déposant pour des dommages subis en rapport avec la chose, n'est pas responsable davantage qu'il ne le serait comme cocontractant du déposant par le contrat conclu avec celui-ci.

3. Le sous-dépositaire poursuivi par un tel tiers n'est pas responsable de plus qu'il ne le serait comme dépositaire conformément au paragraphe précédent.

4. Les paragraphes précédents ne peuvent être invoqués par le dépositaire ou sous-dépositaire qui, lors de la conclusion du contrat en application duquel il a reçu la chose, savait ou devait savoir que son cocontractant, dans son rapport avec la personne qui l'a poursuivi, n'avait pas le pouvoir de déposer la chose auprès de lui.

Art. 609. (7.9.9) - 1. De hotelhouder is als een bewaarnemer aansprakelijk voor beschadiging of verlies van zaken, die in het hotel zijn meegebracht door een gast die daar zijn intrek heeft genomen.

- 2. Hij is niet aansprakelijk voor gedragingen van personen die de gast zelf in het hotel heeft meegebracht of uitgenodigd, en voor schade door zaken die de gast zelf heeft meegebracht.
- 3. Hij heeft op de in lid 1 bedoelde zaken een retentierecht voor al hetgeen hij van de gast te vorderen heeft ter zake van logies, kost, consumpties en als hotelhouder verrichte diensten.

1. A hotel-keeper is liable as a depositary for damage to or loss of things which have been brought to the hotel by a guest who has moved into it.
2. He is not liable for acts of persons whom the guest himself has brought or has invited to the hotel, nor for damage by things which the guest himself has brought with him.
3. He has a right of retention on the things referred to in paragraph 1 for all that he can claim from the guest with respect to accomodation, food, drinks and services performed as hotel-keeper.

1. L'hôtelier est responsable comme un dépositaire de l'endommagement ou de la perte de choses apportées à l'hôtel par un client qui s'y est installé.
2. Il n'est pas responsable des actes de personnes que le client a lui-même amenées ou invitées à l'hôtel, ni du dommage causé par des choses qu'a apportées le client lui-même.
3. Il a, sur les choses visées au paragraphe 1er, un droit de rétention pour tout ce qu'il peut réclamer au client au titre du logement, de la nourriture, des consommations et des services rendus comme hôtelier.

Art. 610-849. Gereserveerd.

Reserved.

Réservés.

TITEL 14 BORGTOCHT

TITLE 14 SURETYSHIP

TITRE QUATORZIÈME DU CAUTIONNEMENT

AFDELING 1 Algemene bepalingen

Section 1 General provisions

Section première Dispositions générales

Art. 850. (7.14.1.1) - 1. Borgtocht is de overeenkomst waarbij de ene partij, de borg, zich tegenover de andere partij, de schuldeiser, verbindt tot nakoming van een verbintenis, die een derde, de hoofdschuldenaar, tegenover de schuldeiser heeft of zal verkrijgen.
- 2. Voor de geldigheid van een borgtocht is niet vereist dat de hoofdschuldenaar deze kent.
- 3. Op borgtocht zijn de bepalingen omtrent hoofdelijke verbintenissen van toepassing, voor zover daarvan in deze titel niet wordt afgeweken.

1. Suretyship is a contract whereby one party, the surety, obliges himself toward the other party, the creditor, to perform an obligation to which a third person, the

1. Le cautionnement est le contrat par lequel une partie, la caution, s'engage envers l'autre, le créancier, à l'exécution d'une obligation dont un tiers, le débiteur

principal debtor, is or will be bound toward the creditor.
2. The validity of suretyship does not require that the principal debtor be aware of it.
3. The provisions regarding solidary obligations apply to suretyship, to the extent that this title does not derogate therefrom.

principal, est tenu à l'égard de ce dernier ou le sera.
2. La validité du cautionnement ne requiert pas que le débiteur principal en ait connaissance.
3. S'appliquent au cautionnement les dispositions relatives aux obligations solidaires, dans la mesure où il n'y est pas dérogé au présent titre.

Art. 851. (7.14.1.2) - 1. De borgtocht is afhankelijk van de verbintenis van de hoofdschuldenaar, waarvoor zij is aangegaan.
- 2. Borgtocht kan slechts voor toekomstige verbintenissen van de hoofdschuldenaar worden aangegaan, voor zover zij voldoende bepaalbaar zijn.

1. Suretyship is dependent upon the obligation of the principal debtor for which it has been entered into.
2. Suretyship can be entered into for future obligations of the principal debtor, to the extent only that they are sufficiently determinable.

1. Le cautionnement dépend de l'obligation du débiteur principal, en vue de laquelle il a été contracté.
2. Le cautionnement ne peut être contracté pour des obligations futures du débiteur principal que dans la mesure où elles sont suffisamment déterminables.

Art. 852. (7.14.1.3) - 1. Verweermiddelen die de hoofdschuldenaar jegens de schuldeiser heeft, kunnen ook door de borg worden ingeroepen, indien zij het bestaan, de inhoud of het tijdstip van nakoming van de verbintenis van de hoofdschuldenaar betreffen.
- 2. Indien de hoofdschuldenaar bevoegd is om ter vernietiging van de rechtshandeling waaruit de verbintenis voortspruit, een beroep op een vernietigingsgrond te doen en hem door de borg of door de schuldeiser een redelijke termijn is gesteld ter uitoefening van die bevoegdheid, is de borg gedurende die termijn bevoegd de nakoming van zijn verbintenis op te schorten.
- 3. Zolang de hoofdschuldenaar bevoegdelijk de nakoming van zijn verbintenis jegens de schuldeiser opschort, is ook de borg bevoegd de nakoming van zijn verbintenis op te schorten.

1. Defences which the principal debtor has against the creditor, can also be invoked by the surety if they relate to the existence, the content or the time of performance of the obligation of the principal debtor.
2. If the principal debtor is entitled to invoke a ground of annulment in order to annul the juridical act from which the obligation arises, and if the surety or the creditor has given him a reasonable period to exercise that right, the surety is entitled to suspend the performance of his obligation during that period.
3. As long as the principal debtor rightfully suspends the performance of

1. Les moyens de défense du débiteur principal contre le créancier peuvent également être invoqués par la caution, s'ils portent sur l'existence, le contenu ou le moment de l'exécution de l'obligation du débiteur principal.
2. Si le débiteur principal peut, afin d'annuler l'acte juridique dont résulte l'obligation, invoquer une cause d'annulation et qu'un délai raisonnable lui a été fixé par la caution ou par le créancier pour exercer ce pouvoir, la caution a le pouvoir de suspendre l'exécution de son obligation pendant ce délai.
3. Tant que le débiteur principal suspend à bon droit l'exécution de son obligation

his obligation toward the creditor, the surety too is entitled to suspend the performance of his obligation.

envers le créancier, la caution peut en faire de même de la sienne.

Art. 853. (7.14.1.4) Door voltooiing van de verjaring van de rechtsvordering tot nakoming van de verbintenis van de hoofdschuldenaar, gaat de borgtocht teniet.

Suretyship is extinguished by the completion of the prescription of the right of action to claim performance of the obligation from the principal debtor.

Le cautionnement s'éteint par la prescription acquise de l'action en exécution de l'obligation du débiteur principal.

Art. 854. (7.14.1.5) Strekt de verbintenis van de hoofdschuldenaar tot iets anders dan tot betaling van een geldsom, dan geldt de borgtocht voor de vordering tot schadevergoeding in geld, verschuldigd op grond van niet-nakoming van die verbintenis, tenzij uitdrukkelijk anders is bedongen.

Unless explicitly stipulated otherwise, where the obligation of the principal debtor has an object other than the payment of a sum of money, the suretyship is for the claim for damages owed on the basis of non-performance of that obligation.

Lorsque l'obligation du débiteur principal a un objet autre que le paiement d'une somme d'argent, le cautionnement porte sur la créance en dommages-intérêts dus à raison de l'inexécution de cette obligation, sauf stipulation contraire expresse.

Art. 855. (7.14.1.6) - 1. De borg is niet gehouden tot nakoming voordat de hoofdschuldenaar in de nakoming van zijn verbintenis is tekort geschoten.
- 2. De schuldeiser die de hoofdschuldenaar overeenkomstig artikel 82 van Boek 6 in gebreke stelt, is verplicht hiervan tegelijkertijd de borg mededeling te doen.

1. The surety is not obliged to perform until such time as the principal debtor has failed in the performance of his obligation.

2. The creditor who puts the principal debtor into default according to article 82 of Book 6, must at the same time notify the surety thereof.

1. La caution n'est pas tenue à l'exécution avant que le débiteur principal n'ait manqué à l'exécution de son obligation.

2. Le créancier qui met en demeure le débiteur principal, conformément à l'article 82 du Livre sixième, est tenu d'en aviser en même temps la caution.

Art. 856. (7.14.1.7) - 1. De borg is slechts wettelijke rente verschuldigd over het tijdvak dat hijzelf in verzuim is, tenzij de hoofdschuldenaar in verzuim is krachtens artikel 83 onder b van Boek 6.
- 2. De borg is gehouden de kosten van rechtsvervolging van de hoofdschuldenaar te vergoeden, indien hij tijdig door mededeling van het voornemen tot rechtsvervolging in de gelegenheid is gesteld deze kosten te voorkomen.

1. The surety owes legal interest only over the period that he himself is in default, unless the principal debtor is in default pursuant to article 83 *sub* b of Book 6.

1. La caution ne doit l'intérêt légal que sur la période pendant laquelle elle est elle-même en demeure, à moins que le débiteur principal ne soit en demeure par application de l'article 83, au point b., du Livre sixième.

2. The surety must reimburse the costs of the law suit against the principal debtor if, by timely notification of the intention to bring action, he has been given the opportunity to prevent these costs.

2. La caution est tenue de rembourser les frais de la poursuite intentée au débiteur principal, si elle a eu l'occasion en temps opportun, à la suite de la communication de l'intention de poursuivre, de les prévenir.

AFDELING 2 Borgtocht, aangegaan buiten beroep of bedrijf

Section 2 Suretyship other than in a profession or business

Section deuxième Du cautionnement contracté hors du cadre de l'activité professionnelle ou de l'entreprise

Art. 857. (7.14.2.1) De bepalingen van deze afdeling zijn van toepassing op borgtochten die zijn aangegaan door een natuurlijk persoon die noch handelde in de uitoefening van zijn beroep of bedrijf, noch handelde ten behoeve van de normale uitoefening van het bedrijf van een naamloze vennootschap of besloten vennootschap met beperkte aansprakelijkheid, waarvan hij bestuurder is en alleen of met zijn medebestuurders de meerderheid der aandelen heeft.

The provisions of this section apply to suretyships entered into by a natural person not acting in the course of a profession or business, nor acting for the benefit of the normal exploitation of the business of a company limited by shares or a private company with limited liability of which he is an officer and in which, alone or with his co-officers, he holds the majority of the shares.

Les dispositions de la présente section s'appliquent au cautionnement qu'a contracté une personne physique n'agissant ni dans le cadre de son activité professionnelle ou de son entreprise ni aux fins de l'exercice normal de l'entreprise d'une société anonyme ou à responsabilité limitée, dont elle est un des dirigeants et possède, seule ou avec ses co-dirigeants, la majorité des actions.

Art. 858. (7.14.2.2) - 1. Indien het bedrag van de verbintenis van de hoofdschuldenaar op het tijdstip van het aangaan van de borgtocht niet vaststaat, is de borgtocht slechts geldig, voor zover een in geld uitgedrukt maximum-bedrag is overeengekomen.
- 2. Overeenkomstig artikel 856 verschuldigde rente en kosten kunnen ongeacht dit maximum worden gevorderd.

1. If, at the time the suretyship is entered into, the amount of the obligation of the principal debtor is not determined, the suretyship is only valid to the extent that a maximum amount, expressed in money, has been agreed to.
2. Interest and costs owed according to article 856 can be claimed irrespective of this maximum.

1. Si le montant de l'obligation du débiteur principal n'est pas fixé au moment de contracter le cautionnement, celui-ci ne vaut que dans la mesure où une somme maximale exprimée en argent a été convenue.
2. L'intérêt et les frais dus conformément à l'article 856 peuvent être demandés sans égard à ce maximum.

Art. 859. (7.14.2.3) - 1. Tegenover de borg wordt de borgtocht slechts door een door hem ondertekend geschrift bewezen.

- 2. De borgtocht kan door alle middelen worden bewezen, indien vaststaat dat de borg de verbintenis van de hoofdschuldenaar geheel of gedeeltelijk is nagekomen.
- 3. Voor het bewijs van de overeenkomst die tot het aangaan van de borgtocht verplicht, geldt dezelfde eis als gesteld in lid 1 en in het geval van lid 2 dezelfde vrijheid.

1. The suretyship can only be proven against the surety, by a writing signed by him.
2. The suretyship can be proven by all means if it has been established that the surety has performed the obligation of the principal debtor in whole or in part.
3. The same requirement as referred to in paragraph 1, and the same latitude as referred to in paragraph 2, apply to the proof of the contract which obliges to enter into the suretyship.

1. Le cautionnement ne se prouve, à l'encontre de la caution, que par un écrit signé de sa main.
2. Le cautionnement se prouve par tous les moyens s'il est établi que la caution a exécuté tout ou partie de l'obligation du débiteur principal.
3. La preuve du contrat obligeant à contracter le cautionnement est soumise à la même condition que celle posée au paragraphe 1er et donne lieu à la même latitude que celle énoncée au paragraphe 2.

Art. 860. (7.14.2.4) De borg is niet gebonden, voor zover voor zijn verbintenis meer bezwarende voorwaarden zouden gelden dan die waaronder de hoofdschuldenaar gebonden is, behoudens voor zover het betreft de wijze waarop tegenover de borg het bewijs van bestaan en omvang van de verbintenis van de hoofdschuldenaar geleverd kan worden.

The surety is not bound to the extent that more onerous conditions would apply to his obligation than those under which the principal debtor is bound, except to the extent that they concern the manner in which proof of the existence and extent of the obligation of the principal debtor can be made against the surety.

La caution n'est pas tenue dans la mesure où son obligation serait sujette à des conditions plus onéreuses que celles auxquelles est soumis le débiteur principal, sauf pour autant que cela regarde la façon dont peut être rapportée, à l'encontre de la caution, la preuve de l'existence et de l'étendue de l'obligation du débiteur principal.

Art. 861. (7.14.2.5) - 1. Een borgtocht die voor toekomstige verbintenissen is aangegaan, kan:
a. te allen tijde worden opgezegd, indien zij niet voor een bepaalde duur geldt;
b. na vijf jaren worden opgezegd, indien zij wel voor een bepaalde duur geldt.
- 2. Na de opzegging duurt de borgtocht voor de reeds ontstane verbintenissen voort.
- 3. Een borg is niet verbonden voor toekomstige verbintenissen tot vergoeding van schade, waarvoor de hoofdschuldenaar jegens de schuldeiser aansprakelijk is, voor zover de schuldeiser de schade had kunnen voorkomen door een toezicht als redelijkerwijs van hem gevergd kon worden.
- 4. Een borg is evenmin verbonden voor toekomstige verbintenissen uit een rechtshandeling die de schuldeiser onverplicht heeft verricht, nadat hij bekend was geworden met omstandigheden die de mogelijkheid van verhaal op de hoofdschuldenaar aanmerkelijk hebben verminderd, zulks tenzij de borg uitdrukkelijk met de rechtshandeling heeft ingestemd of deze handeling geen uitstel kon lijden.

1. A suretyship entered into for future obligations may:
a. be cancelled at all times, if it is not for a certain and determinate period;
b. be cancelled after five years, if it is for a certain and determinate period.
2. After cancellation, the suretyship continues for obligations which have already arisen.
3. A surety is not bound for future obligations to repair damage for which the principal debtor is liable toward the creditor, to the extent that the creditor could have prevented the damage by such supervision as could reasonably be expected from him.

4. A surety is not bound either for future obligations arising from a juridical act which the creditor has performed without being obliged to do so, after he had become aware of circumstances which have considerably diminished the possibility of recovering against the principal debtor, and this unless the surety has explicitly consented to the juridical act or unless this act could not be postponed.

1. Le cautionnement contracté pour des obligations futures
a. Peut être résilié en tout temps, si sa durée n'est pas déterminée;
b. Peut être résilié au bout de cinq ans, si sa durée est déterminée.
2. Après la résiliation, le cautionnement continue pour les obligations déjà nées.

3. La caution n'est pas tenue des obligations futures en réparation du dommage dont le débiteur principal est responsable envers le créancier, dans la mesure où le créancier aurait pu prévenir le dommage en exerçant la surveillance que l'on pouvait normalement attendre de sa part.
4. La caution n'est pas non plus tenue des obligations futures résultant d'un acte juridique que le créancier a accompli sans y être tenu, après qu'il a eu connaissance de circonstances qui ont considérablement réduit la possibilité de recouvrement auprès du débiteur principal, et ce à moins que la caution ait donné son assentiment exprès à l'acte juridique ou que celui-ci ne pût souffrir de délai.

Art. 862. (7.14.2.6) Niet kan ten nadele van de borg worden afgeweken:
a. van de artikelen 852-856 en 858-861;
b. van de verplichtingen die de schuldeiser krachtens artikel 154 van Boek 6 jegens de borg heeft met het oog op diens mogelijke subrogatie.

There may be no derogations to the detriment of the surety
a. from articles 852 - 856 and 858 - 861;
b. from the obligations which, pursuant to article 154 of Book 6, the creditor has toward the surety in view of the possible subrogation of the latter.

On ne peut déroger au détriment de la caution
a. Aux articles 852 à 856 et 858 à 861;
b. Aux obligations du créancier envers la caution par application de l'article 154 du Livre sixième, en vue de la subrogation éventuelle de celle-ci.

Art. 863. (7.14.2.7) De bepalingen van deze afdeling zijn van overeenkomstige toepassing op overeenkomsten, waarbij iemand als bedoeld in artikel 857 zich verbindt tot een bepaalde prestatie voor het geval een derde een bepaalde verbintenis met een andere inhoud jegens de schuldeiser niet nakomt.

The provisions of this section apply *mutatis mutandis* to contracts by which a person, as referred to in article 857, obliges himself to a certain specific prestation in the event that a third person

Les dispositions de la présente section s'appliquent par analogie au contrat par lequel une personne visée à l'article 857 s'engage à une prestation déterminée pour le cas où un tiers n'exécute pas une obligation

does not perform toward the creditor a certain specific obligation with a different content.

déterminée de contenu différent à l'égard du créancier.

Art. 864. (7.14.2.8) - 1. Indien in opdracht en voor rekening van iemand als bedoeld in artikel 857 ter zake van de verbintenis van een ander een borgtocht of een overeenkomst als bedoeld in artikel 863 wordt aangegaan, heeft de opdrachtnemer voor hetgeen hij aan de schuldeiser heeft voldaan, geen recht op vergoeding jegens de opdrachtgever voor zover de onderhavige afdeling aan diens aansprakelijkheid als borg in de weg gestaan zou hebben. Artikel 861 is tussen opdrachtgever en opdrachtnemer van overeenkomstige toepassing.
- 2. Van het eerste lid kan slechts worden afgeweken, indien dit geschiedt bij een door de opdrachtgever ondertekend geschrift waarin de aard van de afwijking wordt omschreven, en het een opdracht betreft aan een bank of andere instelling die haar bedrijf van het verstrekken van borgtochten maakt.

1. If, upon the order and for the account of a person as referred to in article 857, a suretyship or contract as referred to in article 863 is entered into with respect to the obligation of another, the person receiving the order is not entitled toward the person giving the order to reimbursement of what he has paid to the creditor, to the extent that the present section would have been a bar to the liability, as surety, of the person giving the order. Article 861 applies *mutatis mutandis* between them.
2. Paragraph 1 may only be derogated from if this is done by a writing signed by the person giving the order in which the nature of the derogation is described, and if it involves an order to a bank or another institution which is in the business of granting suretyships.

1. Si, par ordre et pour le compte d'une personne visée à l'article 857, est conclu, en rapport avec l'obligation d'un autre, un cautionnement ou un contrat visé à l'article 863, celui qui a reçu l'ordre n'a pas droit, envers celui qui l'a donné, au remboursement de ce qu'il a payé au créancier, dans la mesure où la présente section aurait fait obstacle à la responsabilité du donneur d'ordre à titre de caution. L'article 861 s'applique entre eux par analogie.

2. Une dérogation au paragraphe 1er ne peut avoir lieu que si elle est faite par un écrit, signé par celui qui a donné l'ordre, dans lequel est décrite la nature de la dérogation et qu'elle touche l'ordre donné à une banque ou autre établissement faisant le commerce d'accorder des cautionnements.

AFDELING 3 De gevolgen van de borgtocht tussen de hoofdschuldenaar en de borg en tussen borgen en voor de verbintenis aansprakelijke niet-schuldenaren onderling

Section 3
The effects of the suretyship between the principal debtor and the surety, and between sureties and non-debtors liable for the obligation amongst themselves

Section troisième
Des effets du cautionnement entre le débiteur principal et la caution, et entre les cautions et les non-débiteurs tenus de l'obligation entre eux

Art. 865. (7.14.3.1) Op de rechtsbetrekkingen tussen hoofdschuldenaar en borg en op die tussen borgen en voor de verbintenis aansprakelijke niet-

schuldenaren onderling is artikel 2 van Boek 6 van overeenkomstige toepassing.

Article 2 of Book 6 applies *mutatis mutandis* to the juridical relations between principal debtor and surety, and to those between sureties and non-debtors liable for the obligation amongst themselves.

L'article 2 du Livre sixième s'applique par analogie aux rapports juridiques entre le débiteur principal et la caution, de même qu'à ceux entre les cautions et des non-débiteurs tenus de l'obligation entre eux.

Art. 866. (7.14.3.2) - 1. De borg heeft voor het gehele bedrag dat hij aan hoofdsom, rente en kosten aan de schuldeiser heeft moeten voldoen, krachtens artikel 10 van Boek 6 een vordering op de hoofdschuldenaar.
- 2. De borg kan noch aan artikel 10 van Boek 6, noch aan artikel 12 van Boek 6 een vordering op de hoofdschuldenaar ontlenen voor wettelijke rente over de periode waarin hij door hem persoonlijk betreffende omstandigheden in verzuim is geweest of voor kosten die hem persoonlijk betreffen of door hem in redelijkheid niet behoefden te worden gemaakt.
- 3. Heeft iemand zich ter zake van dezelfde verbintenis borg gesteld voor twee of meer hoofdelijk verbonden hoofdschuldenaren, dan zijn deze in afwijking van artikel 10 lid 1 van Boek 6 en artikel 12 lid 1 van Boek 6, jegens de borg hoofdelijk verbonden voor hetgeen deze aan hoofdsom, rente en kosten op hen kan verhalen.
- 4. Uit de rechtsverhouding tussen de borg en een of meer hoofdschuldenaren kan iets anders voortvloeien dan de leden 1-3 meebrengen.

1. Pursuant to article 10 of Book 6, the surety has a claim against the principal debtor for the entire amount that he has had to pay to the creditor in principal sum, interest and costs.
2. The surety cannot derive a claim against the principal debtor from article 10 of Book 6, nor from article 12 of Book 6 for legal interest over the period in which he has been in default by circumstances personal to him, or for costs which are personal to him or which he did not reasonably have to make.

3. Where a person has granted suretyship in respect of one and the same obligation for two or more solidary principal debtors, the latter are, by derogation from article 10 paragraph 1 and article 12 paragraph 1 of Book 6, solidarily liable toward the surety for what the latter can recover from them in principal sum, interest and costs.

4. The juridical relationship between the surety and one or more principal

1. Par application de l'article 10 du Livre sixième, la caution a, pour la totalité de la somme principale, de l'intérêt et des frais qu'elle a dû payer au créancier une créance contre le débiteur principal.
2. La caution ne peut puiser ni à l'article 10, ni à l'article 12 du Livre sixième une créance contre le débiteur principal pour l'intérêt légal sur la période pendant laquelle elle a été en demeure en raison de circonstances la concernant personnellement, ou pour les frais qui la regardent personnellement ou qu'il n'était pas normalement nécessaire d'engager.
3. Lorsqu'une personne s'est portée caution, en rapport avec la même obligation, pour plusieurs débiteurs principaux solidaires, ceux-ci sont, par dérogation aux articles 10, paragraphe 1er, et 12, paragraphe 1er, du Livre sixième, solidairement responsables envers la caution pour ce que celle-ci peut recouvrer sur eux au titre de la somme principale, de l'intérêt et des frais.
4. Il peut résulter du rapport juridique entre la caution et un ou plusieurs débiteurs

debtors may produce a result other than that which would flow from paragraphs 1 - 3.

principaux autre chose que ce qui découle des paragraphes 1er à 3.

Art. 867. (7.14.3.3) Indien de borg de verbintenis is nagekomen zonder de hoofdschuldenaar daarvan mededeling te doen en deze daarna zijnerzijds de schuldeiser heeft betaald, kan de hoofdschuldenaar tegenover de borg volstaan met overdracht aan deze van zijn vordering wegens onverschuldigde betaling op de schuldeiser.

If the surety has performed the obligation without notifying the principal debtor thereof, and if thereafter the latter, in his turn, has paid the creditor, it will suffice for the principal debtor, as regards the surety, to transfer to the latter his claim against the creditor for undue payment.

Si la caution a exécuté l'obligation sans en aviser le débiteur principal et qu'ensuite ce dernier a, de son côté, payé le créancier, le débiteur principal peut se contenter, à l'égard de la caution, de lui transférer l'action en paiement de l'indu contre le créancier.

Art. 868. (7.14.3.4) Een krachtens artikel 10 van Boek 6 aangesproken hoofdschuldenaar kan de verweermiddelen die hij op het tijdstip van het ontstaan van de verhaalsvordering jegens de schuldeiser had, ook inroepen tegen de borg; de leden 2 en 4 van artikel 11 van Boek 6 zijn van overeenkomstige toepassing.

A principal debtor who has been sued pursuant to article 10 of Book 6, may also, against the surety, invoke the defences which he had against the creditor at the time the claim for recovery has arisen; paragraphs 2 and 4 of article 11 of Book 6 apply *mutatis mutandis*.

Le débiteur principal, poursuivi en vertu de l'article 10 du Livre sixième, peut faire valoir à l'encontre de la caution également les moyens de défense qu'il avait contre le créancier au moment de la naissance de la créance en recouvrement; les paragraphes 2 et 4 de l'article 11 du Livre sixième s'appliquent par analogie.

Art. 869. (7.14.3.6) De borg te wiens laste de schuld is gedelgd, kan met overeenkomstige toepassing van artikel 152 van Boek 6 het onverhaalbaar gebleken gedeelte omslaan over zich zelf, zijn medeborgen en de niet-schuldenaren die voor de verbintenis aansprakelijk waren.

Under analogous application of article 152 of Book 6, the surety upon whose expense the debt has been discharged can apportion the part which has proven to be unrecoverable over himself, his co-sureties and the non-debtors who were liable for the obligation.

La caution à la charge de laquelle la dette a été acquittée peut, par application analogique de l'article 152 du Livre sixième, répartir entre elle-même, ses cofidéjusseurs et les non-débiteurs tenus de l'obligation la partie de la dette qui s'est révélée irrécouvrable.

Art. 870. (7.14.3.7) De achterborg die de verbintenis van de borg is nagekomen, kan ten behoeve van zich zelf het verhaal uitoefenen dat de borg, indien hij zelf de verbintenis was nagekomen, zou hebben gehad jegens de hoofdschuldenaar of jegens medeborgen of niet-schuldenaren die voor de verbintenis aansprakelijk waren.

The sub-surety who has performed the obligation of the surety, can in his own interest exercise the recourse which the

L'arrière-caution qui a exécuté l'obligation de la caution peut exercer à son propre profit le recours que la caution, si elle avait elle-

surety, if he had performed the obligation himself, would have had against the principal debtor, against co-sureties, or against non-debtors who were liable for the obligation.

même exécuté l'obligation, aurait eu contre le débiteur principal, les cofidéjusseurs ou les non-débiteurs tenus de l'obligation.

SUBJECT INDEX

(The numbers refer to the articles of the Code)

A

Subject Index

F

G

H

I

J

L

N

Subject Index

O

P

Q

R

S

T

U

V

W

INDEX ALPHABÉTIQUE

(Les chiffres renvoient aux articles du Code)

A

F

G

H

I

N

O

S

T

TREFWOORDREGISTER

(De nummers verwijzen naar de artikelen van het wetboek)

A

Trefwoordregister

C

D

F

G

H

L

N

O